G. K. CHESTERTON ... West London, the s... at St Paul's School a... .... became a professional writer in his twenties. He worked in all literary genres, but he was essentially a reflective and provocative essayist, and many of his books are collections of reprinted periodical essays. His literary criticism, particularly *Charles Dickens* (1906) and *The Victorian Age in Literature* (1913), is still invaluable. Chesterton's most famous novels are *The Napoleon of Notting Hill* (1904) and *The Man Who Was Thursday* (1908), but he is best known as a fiction writer for his stories about the priest-detective Father Brown, the first collection of which, *The Innocence of Father Brown*, appeared in 1911.

After being an agnostic in his youth, Chesterton accepted the truth of Christianity, and argued for it in many of his books; implicitly in *Heretics* (1905) and explicitly in *Orthodoxy* (1908) and subsequent works. Although his position was very close to Roman Catholicism—in which he was influenced by his friend Hilaire Belloc—Chesterton remained an Anglican until 1922, when he finally entered the Catholic Church. Much of his best work was done before 1914, but such later books as *A Short History of England* (1917), *The Everlasting Man* (1925), *William Cobbett* (1926), *Robert Louis Stevenson* (1927), and *St Thomas Aquinas* (1933) are important expositions of his thought.

W. W. ROBSON completed his work on *Father Brown* shortly before his death on 31 July 1993. He was Fellow and Tutor of Lincoln College, Oxford, for 22 years and later was David Masson Professor of English Literature at Edinburgh University, and he wrote several volumes of criticism, of which the most recent, *Critical Enquiries* (1993), includes his seminal essay 'Father Brown and Others'. His editions of Arthur Conan Doyle's *The Hound of the Baskervilles* and *The Case-Book of Sherlock Holmes* are in the Oxford Sherlock Holmes and World's Classics.

THE WORLD'S CLASSICS

G. K. CHESTERTON

Father Brown: A Selection

Edited with an Introduction by
W. W. ROBSON

Oxford   New York
OXFORD UNIVERSITY PRESS
1995

Oxford University Press, Walton Street, Oxford OX2 6DP
Oxford New York
Athens Auckland Bangkok Bombay
Calcutta Cape Town Dar es Salaam Delhi
Florence Hong Kong Istanbul Karachi
Kuala Lumpur Madras Madrid Melbourne
Mexico City Nairobi Paris Singapore
Taipei Tokyo Toronto
and associated companies in
Berlin Ibadan

Oxford is a trade mark of Oxford University Press

Editorial matter © the Estate of W. W. Robson 1995
Chronology © D. J. Conlon 1987

First published as a World's Classics paperback 1995

British Library Cataloguing in Publication Data
Data available

Library of Congress Cataloging in Publication Data
Chesterton, G. K. (Gilbert Keith), 1874–1936.
Father Brown—a selection / edited with an introduction by
W. W. Robson.
p. cm.—(The World's classics)
A selection of 28 of the best stories.
Includes bibliographical references.
1. Brown, Father (Fictitious character)—Fiction. 2. Catholic
Church—England—Clergy—Fiction. 3. Detective and mystery stories,
English. I. Robson, W. W. (William Wallace), 1923- . II. Title.
III. Series.
PR4453.C4A6 1995 823'.912—dc20 94–17038
ISBN 0–19–282309–4

1 3 5 7 9 10 8 6 4 2

Typeset by Best-set Typesetter Ltd., Hong Kong
Printed in Great Britain by BPC Paperbacks Ltd.
Aylesbury, Bucks

CONTENTS

Acknowledgements   vii

Introduction   ix

Note on the Text   xxi

Select Bibliography   xxiii

A Chronology of G. K. Chesterton   xxvi

FATHER BROWN: A SELECTION

from *The Innocence of Father Brown*
The Blue Cross   3
The Secret Garden   22
The Queer Feet   42
The Flying Stars   61
The Invisible Man   75
The Honour of Israel Gow   92
The Wrong Shape   107
The Hammer of God   125
The Eye of Apollo   142
The Sign of the Broken Sword   158

from *The Wisdom of Father Brown*
The Duel of Dr Hirsch   175
The Man in the Passage   190
The God of the Gongs   207
The Strange Crime of John Boulnois   222
The Fairy Tale of Father Brown   238

from *The Incredulity of Father Brown*
The Oracle of the Dog   251
The Dagger with Wings   273
The Ghost of Gideon Wise   295

from *The Secret of Father Brown*
The Mirror of the Magistrate   314
The Actor and the Alibi   333

The Worst Crime in the World 351
The Chief Mourner of Marne 368

from *The Scandal of Father Brown*
The Quick One 389
The Blast of the Book 411
The Green Man 425
The Crime of the Communist 445
The Point of a Pin 463
The Insoluble Problem 484

Appendix 1: The Origins of Father Brown 503

Appendix 2: Textual Variants 508

Explanatory Notes 518

ACKNOWLEDGEMENTS

W. W. ROBSON died in Edinburgh on 31 July 1993. He had drafted and revised the Introduction and Bibliography for this work, and written the notes for the selection he had made from the corpus of forty-nine published Father Brown stories. His wife Anne, his son Hugh, and his friend Owen Dudley Edwards (AHO) have prepared the present matter for the press. WWR had indicated further lines of inquiry he wished made, suggested clues for pursuit, and communicated new critical conclusions. We have followed his wish to clear up the origin of the stories, whence we established texts of the first ten (from *The Innocence of Father Brown*) by collation of British and American magazine versions with book publication. This necessitated additional annotation, and we have also added some quotations to the notes from his essay 'Father Brown and Others' written twenty years ago, where individual stories would benefit by its specific citation. Any editorial matter not written by him for this volume has been initialled AHO. In the Introduction asterisks have been used to separate an addition by AHO from the work of WWR.

His thanks and ours are due to staffs of the National Library of Scotland, Edinburgh University Library, the Bodleian Library, Oxford, and the British Library; to the late Father Anthony Ross, to Father Ian Boyd and the *Chesterton Review*, to Professor K. J. Fielding, to Mrs Gloria Ketchin, to Bonnie Dudley Edwards, to Dr Sarah Cullis, to Michael Cox, to Leila and Leslie Macfarlane, to Philip French, to Bernard Bergonzi, to Jackie Pritchard, to Jenni Calder, to Ernest Mehew, and above all to Judith Luna and Susie Casement. We thank each other. And, most deeply and gratefully, we thank him.

AHO

INTRODUCTION

IT is a standard critical complaint against Chesterton that he wrote no central work. No single book represents him at his best. It seems to be a case of (to quote the title of Belloc's novel of 1929) *The Missing Masterpiece*. But I do not think this is true. Rejoicing to concur with the common reader, I believe that the Father Brown stories, taken together, are Chesterton's masterpiece. A glance at the notes to this volume will show how rooted they are in the rich heritage of English literature. They have all the good qualities of his work in other genres, without his typical defects. They have the wit of Oscar Wilde, about whom Chesterton wrote so judiciously, using against him Aristotle's doctrine of the Mean. But they exhibit a balance and spaciousness never found in Wilde's work. Written in terse, sharp prose, they are drenched in poetry. This is what lifts them above all the other detective stories ever written.

In outward appearance Father Brown cuts a comic figure, especially in films (Alec Guinness played the part very intelligently) and television series. It is piquant to see the absent-minded clerical bumpkin as he fumbles with his umbrella turning out to have keen wits and criminological expertise. But the thought, the promptness of mind, the inner attitude of Father Brown cannot be conveyed by films or television.

Father Brown was said by another priest, Ronald Knox, to have come into existence in this way. G. K. Chesterton had (improbably—he was always a busy hack) no literary work on hand. He wandered into his publisher's office to ask if anything was in request and was told: 'Nothing in your line, Mr Chesterton, but the *Saturday Evening Post* wants some short detective stories.' To which Chesterton responded, 'Oh well, I don't know,' and promptly sat down then and there and wrote 'The Blue Cross', the first of the Father Brown stories.

It is certain that Father Brown was based on Monsignor John O'Connor. Chesterton describes the genesis of the priest-detective in his posthumous *Autobiography* (1936):

The point [of Father Brown] was to appear pointless; and one might say that his conspicuous quality was not being conspicuous. His commonplace exterior was meant to contrast with his unsuspected vigilance and intelligence; and that being so, of course, I made his appearance shabby and shapeless, his face round and expressionless, his manners clumsy, and so on. At the same time I did take some of his inner intellectual qualities from my friend, Father John O'Connor of Bradford, who has not, as a matter of fact, any of these external qualities. He is not shabby, but rather neat; he is not clumsy, but very delicate and dexterous; he not only is but looks amusing and amused. He is a sensitive and quick-witted Irishman, with the profound irony and some of the potential irritability of his race. My Father Brown was deliberately described as a Suffolk dumpling from East Anglia. That, and the rest of his description, was a deliberate disguise for the purpose of detective fiction. But for all that, there is a very real sense in which Father O'Connor was the intellectual inspiration of these stories; and of much more important things as well.

. . . I had gone to give a lecture at Keighley on the high moors of the West Riding, and . . . [met] the curate of the Roman Catholic Church, a small man with a smooth face and a demure but elvish expression [cf. J. R. R. Tolkien, also a Catholic].

. . . It was in one of [my] visits [to the district] that the incident occurred, which led me to take the liberty of putting him, or rather part of him, into a string of sensational stories . . . He told certain facts he knew about perverted practices . . . it was a curious experience to find that this quiet and pleasant celibate had plumbed those abysses far deeper than I. I had not imagined that the world could hold such horrors . . . When we returned to the house we fell into special conversation with two hearty and healthy young Cambridge undergraduates . . . They were no narrow athletes, . . . but interested in various sports and, in a breezy way, in various arts; and they began to discuss music and landscape with my friend Father O'Connor . . . The talk soon deepened into a discussion on matters more philosophical and moral; and when the priest had left the room, the two young men broke out into generous expressions of admiration, saying truly that he was a remarkable man . . . Then there fell a curious reflective silence, at the end of which one of the undergraduates suddenly burst out: '. . . I don't believe his sort of life is the right one . . . I believe in a fellow coming out into the world and facing the evil that's in it, and knowing something about the dangers and all that. It's a very beautiful thing to be innocent and ignorant [cf. *The Innocence of Father Brown*]; but I think it's a much finer thing not to be afraid of knowledge.'

To me, still almost shivering with the appallingly practical facts of which the priest had warned me, this comment came with such a colossal and crushing irony, that I nearly burst into a loud harsh laugh in the drawing-room . . .[1]

For his Father Brown, Chesterton wanted a character who would be (1) saintly and (2) inward with the criminal underworld. But in the Father Brown stories his criminological expertise soon fades out. The only villain he deals with is Flambeau, and Flambeau is hardly a typical professional criminal. Father Brown soon becomes (1) Chesterton's *alter ego* and (2) a symbol of Christianity—not merely of Roman Catholicism. This means that there cannot be a convincing fictional biography, a *DNB* article, on Father Brown, of the kind which T. S. Blakeney and S. C. Roberts wrote for Sherlock Holmes and Dr Watson. Father Brown has no Christian name. (The solitary reference to him as 'Paul' in the magazine version of 'The Sign of the Broken Sword' is an aberration.) Otherwise he is simply 'Father Brown' or 'the Rev. J. Brown', rarely 'Brown'. We are given to understand that he began his priestly vocation by dealing with tough characters in Chicago, but later he arrives in the United States as a first-time visitor. We are not told how and when and why he went to Chicago, nor how and when or why he came back again. Apart from his niece (in 'The Worst Crime in the World') we learn nothing of his family history. At one point he seems to be stationed in Latin America and moving in influential political circles, but he is normally parish priest of

---

[1] Monsignor John O'Connor (1870/1–1952) was a more scholarly figure than his *Father Brown on Chesterton* (1937, 1938) indicates (that work was probably weakened by a confessor's circumspection in relating what he felt he could tell of his penitent's soul). He published his *Poems, Original and Derived* (1932) and translations of Paul Claudel, St John of the Cross, Jacques Maritain, and Richard Crashaw. He also published *A Month of Sundays: The Foolishness of Father Brown*, whose only surviving copy known to us is in the University of Illinois (Urbana), and this, together with *The Weld Sermon* (1913), suggests that the few instances where Father Brown is shown composing sermons or activating the conscience of penitents are among his strongest imprints on the Father Brown portrait. But the mixture of childlike and brilliant insights (as shown, for instance, in his *Jerome Savonarola* (1946)) indicates another possible point of derivation. AHO

Cobhole in Essex—a fixture. Yet he seems to be as often away from his parish as Dr Watson was away from his practice. He seems to have no flock about him, no curates under him, and no bishop over him (except when he is in Central America— see 'The Resurrection of Father Brown'). His sidekick, his Watson, is Hercule Flambeau. Chesterton evidently intended Aristide Valentin, head of the Paris police, to have this role, but after 'The Secret Garden' Flambeau takes his place. Flambeau is based on Vidocq, Balzac's friend, the Parisian master criminal who reformed and became chief of police under Napoleon. (Cf. Maurice Leblanc's Arsène Lupin, ad-mired by T. S. Eliot, though denounced as a fascist by J. P. Sartre. Lupin became Jim Barnett, a private detective.) In the early phase of the Flambeau–Father Brown relationship we are mainly concerned with Father Brown's struggle to save the soul of Flambeau (Duroc). Later, Flambeau plays only an ancillary part. He does not appear in the *Incredulity*, he had only a marginal part in the *Secret*, and he appears only at the end of the *Scandal* to round off the Father Brown series with a companion piece to its first story, 'The Blue Cross'.

All the same Flambeau can be given a consistent, if sketchy, biography: Father Brown cannot. He has no local habitation, no presbytery, no housekeeper, no base corresponding to Baker Street. He appears and disappears in the stories without explanation. He is a parish priest without a parish (like John Wesley). He is far ahead, not only of the conventional Thomism of his day but even of the Neo-Thomism of Jacques Maritain and Étienne Gilson in theirs. His only rival in twen-tieth-century thought is Ludwig Wittgenstein—who according to M. C. Drury detested Father Brown. Father Brown is steeped in Scholastic philosophy: we catch the Aristotelian ring of all his arguments—but he combines Aquinas's logic with creative imagination. This is what, according to Dorothy L. Sayers, makes Dante a greater philosopher than his master Aquinas, because of his poetic dimension. But we are not told how Father Brown acquired his knowledge of St Thomas. Did he get it direct from the *Summa theologiae* (of which he boasted in 'The Secret Garden' that he could paraphrase any page)? Or was he guided, perhaps, by the popular expositions of Thomism by a (hypothetical) Septimus O'Toole (1845–91), Professor of Metaphysics at the Portadown Seminary of the Sixteen Sighs? And finally, what sort of Catholic is Father Brown—'cradle' or 'convert'? We are simply not told.

Father Brown, in short, is merely what the plot of a particular story requires him to be. His fundamental character is fixed: he shows no sign of development or retrogression. He is a combination of Sherlock Holmes with Christ. Christ went about forgiving people's sins; Father Brown went about exposing their crimes. Apart from his plot function Father Brown is incoherent as a character. He was wheeled out whenever Chesterton needed a few pounds for *G. K.'s Weekly*, or decided to treat an idea for an essay as a Father Brown story (e.g. 'The Man in the Passage', which is really a meditation on the mysterious concept known as a Mirror). Chesterton continued all his other, very various, literary and propagandist activities during the twenty-five years in which he continued to write Father Brown stories. Other great characters of fiction—Iago, Heathcliff, Dostoevsky's Stavrogin—have gaps in their histories, but they make sense as a whole; Father Brown does not. Never was a great character of literature treated more cavalierly by his creator.

*   *   *   *   *   *   *   *   *   *   *

Chesterton was already a well-known author, and the first reviews of the collected Father Brown stories, *The Innocence of Father Brown*, in 1911, were serious and lengthy. In the *Manchester Guardian* (July 1911) the journalist Dixon Scott wrote approvingly, 'a farrago of magnificent nonsense ... fantasy heightened by the vivid realism of the figures and scenes. Mr. Chesterton has the poet's gift for seeing the most commonplace things—moons or men's faces, hills, street-lamps, and houses—with a startling freshness and suddenness, as though they had been but that instant made.'

A review in the *Eye-Witness* was anonymous but almost certainly by Maurice Baring (1874–1945), the eminent journalist, novelist, poet, and man of letters. He noted that Chesterton 'has always been on the side of the popular taste, on the side of sensation and colour and mystery', praised his

powers of invention—'a capital story-teller'—and 'of creating
that atmosphere of bewildering darkness and half-seen horror
which a detective story requires'. He praised Chesterton's
characterization: 'Too many writers of detective stories neglect this human element. Yet it is an essential one. We are
only interested in crimes because they are committed by and
upon human beings.' He commented: 'It need hardly be said
that Mr Chesterton's preoccupation with his wild adventures
does not prevent him from throwing in a large number of
reflections on politics, theology, and morals. We wonder how
the ordinary detective story reader will like them; probably
very much, for they are very good, and he is a much more
rational person than prigs imagine.'

An anonymous reviewer in the *Athenaeum* (2 Sept. 1911)
commented rather more tartly: 'discerning readers already
know that, whatever the subject of Mr Chesterton's books,
they are apt to be full of his own views.'

The *Eye-Witness* was a magazine founded by Hilaire Belloc
and later run by G. K. Chesterton's brother Cecil. It was
succeeded in November 1912 by the *New Witness* (also under
Cecil), where the 1914 collection *The Wisdom of Father
Brown* was reviewed by J. K. Prothero, the name used by
Cecil's future wife, the journalist Ada Jones (12 Nov. 1914).
Although written in a lively style, her review has the irritating
faults of giving away the secrets of the plot and naming the
murderer.

From the earliest reviews, Father Brown's adventures were
compared to those of Sherlock Holmes: 'in literary brilliance
and originality of thought they must rank above the ingenious
structures of Sir Conan Doyle' (*Nation*, Aug. 1911).

Contemporary reviewers, like later critics, discussed the personality and appearance of Father Brown—'the experience,
logical powers, and courage of that stumpy little priest' (*Times
Literary Supplement*, 3 Aug. 1911); and in the same journal,
reviewing on 1 July 1926 *The Incredulity of Father Brown*,
another anonymous critic wrote: 'Amid these folk and their
terrifying fancies Father Brown moves in his atmosphere of
sober sanity. Confronted with corpses which have become
such in circumstances which lead ordinary folk to suggest the

most erudite explanation in conformity with the dictates of science or superstition, Father Brown applies the touchstone of common sense.'

Also in the *Times Literary Supplement* (reviewing *The Secret of Father Brown* (24 Sept. 1927): '... the observant priest, who, as the reader will notice, is in turn both round and square in his carefully undistinguished appearance.'

The Father Brown stories were for the general public the most popular of Chesterton's works, and the major source of his income. According to his secretary Dorothy Collins, she would tell him there was less than £100 left in the bank. 'He would nod gravely and murmur that that meant Father Brown again.'[2]

*   *   *   *   *   *   *   *   *

What then *is* Father Brown? Since Poe invented the modern detective story there have been three categories of fictional sleuth:

1. The amateur (Poe's Dupin, or Dorothy L. Sayers's Lord Peter Wimsey). He is often, but by no means always, hand in glove with the police. He has flair and genius rather than expert knowledge. This type of character has figured in some excellent stories, but has now fallen out of fashion—probably because it is so incredible.

2. The professional private detective. The most famous of these is of course Sherlock Holmes. But Holmes is a special case: he calls himself a consulting detective (Conan Doyle, who was a doctor, was thinking of Edinburgh hospital consultants like Joseph Bell). Another specialist investigator is Agatha Christie's Hercule Poirot. But the most recent version of this type, more conspicuous for legwork, is the 'private eye' as imagined by Dashiell Hammett or Raymond Chandler.

3. The police detective, Dickens's Inspector Bucket, or Wilkie Collins's Sergeant Cuff in *The Moonstone*. This type has had innumerable successors (e.g. Inspector French).

---

[2] Dudley Barker, *G. K. Chesterton* (1973), 267. The preceding paragraphs, between the asterisks, were added by AHO.

Nowadays he or she often occurs in what are called police procedurals, stories that seem to offer an authoritative account of police routine. Hence stories about (3) differ from (1) and (2) in their greater verisimilitude.

The superiority of Father Brown over fictitious detectives, then and now, is that he combines the advantages of (1) and (2). He is a private citizen who just happens to be around when the murders take place. He has little to do with the police. Yet he too is a professional; but his profession is the priesthood: he is a fisher of men.

What then are the Father Brown stories? The best of them are in *The Innocence of Father Brown* (1911), where the inspiration is freshest. Later Chesterton became fatigued and repeated himself: there are too many stories about the murder of American millionaires. But some of the later stories, such as 'The Dagger with Wings', are as good as any he wrote. First and foremost the Father Brown stories are short detective tales which have never been surpassed for ingenuity. The stories never have probability. Usually this does not matter in the least, though in a few cases, such as 'The Sins of Prince Saradine', the sheer impossibility of the events forces itself on the reader. (How could the trial of Antonelli possibly be imagined?) But there is never any resort to so-called fantasy, i.e. artistic irresponsibility. The stories proceed rationally from their *données*, however improbable these may be. Supernatural or magical explanations of the mysteries are always refuted or ruled out. Father Brown has no special mystical insight, only common sense and the wisdom of tradition, sharpened by observation and deduction, like his forerunner Sherlock Holmes, another anti-supernaturalist. It is notable that a frequent motif in the stories is the exposure of bogus mages.

More importantly, the stories are moral or metaphysical fables. In 'The Invisible Man' the social 'invisibility' of the murderer is the point of the story. People who are normally taken for granted (except by Father Brown) turn out to be crucial. In 'The Blast of the Book' the great intellectual Professor Openshaw does not notice the waiter (or his own clerk)

any more than the Twelve True Fishermen in 'The Queer Feet'
noticed the feigned waiter. Some of the parables are of a
philosophical or jurisprudential character. Christ in the story
of the Good Samaritan asked, 'Who is my neighbour?'; Father
Brown in 'The Fairy Tale of Father Brown' asks, 'What is a
weapon?' The nature of identity is the theme, not only of the
melodramatic 'Duel of Dr Hirsch', but of the farcical story
(which might have appeared among the *Tales of the Long
Bow*) called 'The Absence of Mr Glass' (he was absent from
the Nature of Things). Eerie meditations on mirrors and
solipsism are another feature, as in 'The Mirror of the
Magistrate' and 'The Man in the Passage'. They recall the
odd story called 'The Crime of Gabriel Gale', in *The Poet
and the Lunatics* (1929), in which the poet Gale cures a
friend of solipsism (it would spoil the story to say how he
did it). Psychological interest is all-pervasive, not only in
the major characters but in bit parts like housekeepers and
cleaning ladies. Even the psychology of dogs is explored, in
'The Oracle of the Dog'.

But above all the stories are aesthetic objects, works of art,
like a misericord or a predella. We are constantly reminded
that Chesterton began as a visual artist. Effects of light and
colour are common in his work (a link with his admired
Robert Louis Stevenson). They are not decoration but part of
his meaning. The essence of 'The Blue Cross' is in the finely
evoked change from day to night which forms the background
of the conversation about Reason between Father Brown and
the pretended priest Flambeau while 'the glory of the heavens
deepened and darkened around the sublime vulgarity of man'.
This artistic quality is shown everywhere, not least in the
felicity of titles like 'The Song of the Flying Fish' or 'The Salad
of Colonel Cray', which both reveal and conceal. It is mainly
shown in Chesterton's power (in which he rivals Dickens) to
suggest, if only in a few lines, the feel and atmosphere of
different places: London in 'The Eye of Apollo' ('That singular
smoky sparkle, at once a confusion and a transparence, which
is the strange secret of the Thames'), Paris in 'The Duel of Dr
Hirsch', Italy in 'The Paradise of Thieves', Scotland in 'The

Honour of Israel Gow', Oxford in 'The Crime of the Communist'. These effects are part of his essential meaning. One example is the icy landscape in 'The Sign of the Broken Sword'. It seems at first irrelevant to the story, until Father Brown reminds us of the frozen world to which Dante consigned the traitors. Another is the weird sinister atmosphere that (until the radiant close) pervades 'The Insoluble Problem', a sort of 'answer' to 'The Blue Cross', in which Father Brown decoys Flambeau, as, in the later story, the criminal Tiger Tyrone decoys Father Brown.

The nearest parallel I can think of to the aesthetic qualities of these stories is Kipling's *Puck of Pook's Hill* and *Rewards and Fairies*, in which another sophisticated artist weaves into pleasant entertainments his complex hints and textures. Like Kipling, Chesterton is a story-teller enthralling those (of whatever age) who are capable of youthful imagination. His greatest character is a 'Father', dreamed up by the childless man at Beaconsfield who surrounded himself with children. We have a true picture of Chesterton when Father Brown plays absorbedly with them in 'The Flying Stars' and 'The Pursuit of Mr Blue'. This is the real answer to the question: who is Father Brown? He is not a realistic picture of a secular priest (he has no fixed parish). He is less a person than a symbol of Christianity. But in so far as he is human he is the epitome of what was best in Chesterton. Like the short stories of Anton Chekhov (which they otherwise do not resemble) the Father Brown stories maintain an astonishingly high standard. Of the forty-nine that have been published—forty-eight from the five collections, plus a singleton, 'The Vampire of the Village'—it is impossible to mention any story that is evidently inferior or a failure, or without merits of some kind, though naturally these differ in character and value. So a choice which will easily satisfy everyone cannot be made. Nor is it possible to disclose in advance the contents of the chosen stories without spoiling the reader's pleasure: they depend too much on surprise and on novelty of setting and situation and the unpredictable twists and turns of the plots. Furthermore there is an *embarras de richesse*; this edition has not been able to accommodate more than twenty-eight stories. Personal taste inevitably plays a great part in this selection, as in any other. But I will try briefly to indicate the principles by which I have been guided in making it.

Most of the stories which feature Flambeau have been chosen, including all those in which he is a protagonist: 'The Blue Cross', 'The Queer Feet', 'The Flying Stars', and also 'The Invisible Man', 'The Honour of Israel Gow', 'The Eye of Apollo', 'The Sign of the Broken Sword', 'The God of the Gongs', and 'The Fairy Tale of Father Brown'. Flambeau has an initiating role in 'The Sins of Prince Saradine', but he is hardly essential to the action, and the story did not seem so good as to require its inclusion.

The general criteria of selection I have applied are originality, ingenuity of plot, profundity of moral or religious or philosophical 'message', and (rarely but unforgettably) tragedy, as in 'The Chief Mourner of Marne'. I will leave to the reader the pleasure of sorting out which of these apply to the chosen stories.

I should like to end by saying that, whatever my reservations about particular stories, the series as a whole seems to me more than just good entertainment. It is a major classic of English literature. Despite critical indifference, or hostility, or changes of fashion, the common reader continues to read Father Brown. Mainly, I think, this is because Chesterton's hold over his readers was, and is, so personal. There is good reason to think that many who never knew him—including myself, only a boy when he died in 1936—felt his death as a personal blow, like the loss of a father. People have sometimes asked me whether I thought G. K. Chesterton would ever 'come back'. My unspoken answer was that he would come back when more and more people find they no longer agree with Belloc's Mr Lambkin (the Prize Poet who wrote on the Benefits of the Electric Light) that

> Life is a vale, its paths are dark and rough
> Only because we do not know enough;

> When Science has discovered something more
> We shall be happier than we were before.

The whole meaning of Chesterton's life and work stands or
falls by the untruth of that proposition.

W. W. Robson

NOTE ON THE TEXT

THE first twelve Father Brown stories were published in Philadelphia by the *Saturday Evening Post*, and in London by the *Story-Teller* and *Cassell's Magazine* consecutively from July 1910 to July 1911, and rearranged (with 'The Eye of Apollo' considerably rewritten) for publication as the book *The Innocence of Father Brown* in October 1911. *Pall Mall Magazine* were the British magazine publishers of a further eleven between March 1913 and September 1914 which with the promised but not published 'The Fairy Tale of Father Brown' then appeared, rearranged, as *The Wisdom of Father Brown* in October 1914. The same journal, now *Nash's—Pall Mall Magazine*, published six new stories between December 1923 and July 1925 which with two others (one, 'The Ghost of Gideon Wise', previously published in *Cassell's*) became *The Incredulity of Father Brown* (1926). Six more from *Cassell's* and two previously in the *Story-Teller*, all between April 1925 and April 1927, appeared as *The Secret of Father Brown* in 1927, overarched by a conversation-piece split into a beginning ('The Secret of Father Brown') and end ('The Secret of Flambeau'). Cassell, publisher of all four volumes, brought them out in an omnibus volume (including several errors) as *The Father Brown Stories* (1929: noted in *The Times Literary Supplement*, 21 Oct. 1929, in the article 'An Omnibus Company' as one of many such newly published collections).

The *Story-Teller* printed seven new stories between October 1932 and March 1935 and these, together with the hitherto unpublished 'The Green Man', were brought out as *The Scandal of Father Brown* in 1935. Chesterton's death on 14 June 1936 was followed by the appearance in the *Strand* magazine in August of another story. The *Scandal* was added to the omnibus volume in November 1947, and the *Strand* item in 1953. An unpublished Father Brown story, apparently written in the last weeks of Chesterton's life, remains among the Chesterton MSS in the British Library at Bloomsbury (or possibly St Pancras).

The text of this edition has been established by a collation of the British and American magazine publication of the first ten stories with their book text (*The Innocence of Father Brown*) and omnibus texts, and thereafter by British magazine, book, and omnibus texts. We have worked on the rule of reason. Where book texts clearly indicated author's wishes in revision, we have followed them (omnibus sometimes corrected earlier errors, sometimes as evidently created new ones), but where magazines (either or both British and American) contain matter excluded from later texts probably by editorial mistake or space dictates, we have restored it. 'The Secret Garden' British magazine text lost several sentences (present in the American) apparently for reasons of space; these are remedied here but American errors in the same story while noted are kept from our main text. We noted, without using, variants in other stories which throw light on alterations in C's intentions, notably in 'The Wrong Shape'. We include the great Gothic architecture paragraph added by C to the book texts of 'The Hammer of God'. We note the huge discrepancy in 'The Eye of Apollo' as between all magazine and all book versions, while employing the latter for our texts. G. K. Chesterton (intro.), *A Century of Detective Stories* (1935), includes 'The Secret Garden'. So does his Everyman *Stories, Essays, and Poems* (1935), together with 'The Blue Cross', and 'The Queer Feet'. These anthologies, theoretically incorporating, have been employed as indicated. Few textual problems are present after the first ten stories.

SELECT BIBLIOGRAPHY

ON general Chestertoniana, Maisie Ward's *G. K. Chesterton* (1944) and *Return to Chesterton* (1952) are badly arranged and digested but full of valuable information and shrewd judgements. Other helpful biographers include Dudley Barker, *G. K. Chesterton* (1973), Alzina Stone Dale, *The Outline of Sanity* (1982), and Michael Coren, *Gilbert* (1989). Of memoirs, John O'Connor's *Father Brown on Chesterton* (1937) is disappointing and unfairly weakens O'Connor's somewhat inflated claims as Brown's original. W. R. Titterton, *G. K. Chesterton* (1936), is a self-deprecating memoir of Chesterton's journalistic world, the most likeable and possibly the best. Ada Jones, a descendant of Sheridan and as such a candidate for the original of the eponymous 'Actor and the Alibi', wrote (as Mrs Cecil Chesterton) a poisonous recollection *The Chestertons* (1941): see Graham Greene's mordant review reprinted in his *Collected Essays*. John D. Coates, *Chesterton and the Edwardian Cultural Crisis* (1984), and Margaret Canovan, *G. K. Chesterton: Radical Populist* (1977), illuminate the thought and action forming the background, not simply the backcloth, to the Father Brown stories. D. J. Conlon has most helpfully assembled critical comment chiefly from reviewers in *G. K. Chesterton: The Critical Judgments* (1976), although we have had to augment his findings; he has followed it with a sequel anthologizing posthumous comment, *G. K. Chesterton: A Half Century of Views* (1987).

C wrote little about his most successful creation, but his posthumously published *Autobiography* (1936) throws instructive light on him, in a little more detail than space would permit WWR to quote in the Introduction. John Sullivan, *G. K. Chesterton: A Bibliography* (1958) and *Chesterton Continued* (1968), are invaluable on C's British publication, but American data are urgently needed and here we have only had time to supply details and collation of the US publication of the *Innocence*. John Sullivan (ed.), *G. K. Chesterton: A*

Centenary Appraisal (1974), contains the great seminal study 'Father Brown and Others' by WWR: all subsequent Father Brown scholarship walks in its footsteps and we have quoted extensively from some of its specific judgements in our notes. It is thanks to the work Robson inaugurated here, continued in himself, and inspired in others that the Father Brown stories have won full recognition as distinguished literature. But the Sullivan collection is invaluable in general with contributions from such creative artists as Auden and Amis, such biographers as P. N. Furbank and Dudley Barker, such memorialists as Dorothy Collins and G. C. Heseltine, and such scholars as Christiane d'Haussy and Ian Boyd. Revd Professor Boyd's *The Novels of G. K. Chesterton* (1975) makes a first-class contribution to the ideological background of C's art, while not specifically concerned with Father Brown; and his editing of the *Chesterton Review* has been the academic nucleus around which the advancement of Chesterton scholarship in the last twenty years has consolidated. Its totality should be combed by all students of C and allied figures. It can have a hard cutting edge: e.g. Martin Gardner's *The Annotated Innocence of Father Brown* (1987) was very severely handled in a two-part review article (13/2–3 (May, Aug. 1987)), essential in any use of it (Gardner has silently modified his text in his revised edition (1988) in response to the harshest criticisms). Subsequent scholarship has qualified some of that review article's findings and, where these conflict with our Explanatory Notes, the latter must prevail. (The reviewer in question is one of WWR's posthumous editors here.)

On the Father Brown stories in the general context of the detective story, Howard Haycraft gives a digest of some of Father Brown's more adverse critics in his *Murder for Pleasure* (1942). WWR singled out for particular respect the Revd Eric Routley, *The Puritan Pleasures of the Detective Story* (1972), for its establishment of the place of Father Brown among fictional detectives. Julian Symons, *Bloody Murder* (1972, 1985, 1992), is the standard modern history of the detective story and rises admirably to this critical occasion: 'A reading of Chesterton reinforces the truth that the best detective stories have been written by artists and not by artisans.' R. F.

Stewart, ... *And Always a Detective* (1980), has useful findings, somewhat obsessively argued. Colin Watson, *Snobbery with Violence* (1971), fails to recognize how very far (as Symons says) Chesterton's radicalism was from the defensive conservatism of the inter-war 'Golden Age' writers Watson attacks. T. J. Binyon, *Murder will Out* (1989), finds the Father Brown stories masterpieces but unsatisfactory: in a way, it rather sums up the problem—Chesterton, like Conan Doyle, turned the detective story into great literature, and how dared they?

Meanwhile, the future of the subject lies in the line of investigation mapped out for us by W. W. Robson.

AHO

A CHRONOLOGY OF
G. K. CHESTERTON

1874   (29 May) Born at 32 Sheffield Terrace, Campden Hill, London W8

1881   The Chesterton family moves to 11 Warwick Gardens, London W14

1887   Attends St Paul's School

1892   Publishes 'The Song of Labour' in *The Speaker*

1892–5   Attends the Slade School of Art and University College

1895–1901 Employed as a reader by the publishers Redway, and later by Fisher Unwin

1900   *Greybeards at Play* and *The Wild Knight*. First meeting with Hilaire Belloc. Member of the Pharos Club and the Christian Social Union

1901   Marries Frances Blogg and moves to Overstrand Mansions, Battersea, London SW11. Begins his association with the *Daily News*. *The Defendant*

1902   *Twelve Types*

1903   *Robert Browning*

1904   *G. F. Watts* and *The Napoleon of Notting Hill*

1905   *The Club of Queer Trades* and *Heretics*. Begins to write 'Our Note-book' in the *Illustrated London News*. First half of *The Ball and the Cross* in *Commonwealth*

1906   *Charles Dickens*

1908   *The Man Who Was Thursday*, *All Things Considered*, and *Orthodoxy*

1909   Moves to Overroads, Beaconsfield. *George Bernard Shaw* and *Tremendous Trifles*

1910   *The Ball and the Cross*, *What's Wrong with the World*, *Alarms and Discursions*, and *William Blake*

1911   Begins to contribute to the *Eye-Witness*, later the *New Witness*. *Appreciations and Criticisms of the Works of Charles Dickens*, *The Innocence of Father Brown*, and *The Ballad of the White Horse*

1912   *Manalive* and *A Miscellany of Men*

1913   *The Victorian Age in Literature* and *Magic*, a play. Helps to reveal the Marconi scandal and is embittered by its corruption

1914   *The Flying Inn*, *The Wisdom of Father Brown*, and *The Barbarism of Berlin*. First half of *The Return of*

Don Quixote. Taken seriously ill and loses consciousness for three months

1915 Recovers from his illness, which was a kind of dropsy. *Letters to an Old Garibaldian, Poems, The Crimes of England*

1916 (October) Replaces his brother Cecil as editor of the *New Witness*

1917 *A Short History of England*

1918 Visits Ireland. Death of Cecil Chesterton

1919 *Irish Impressions*. Visits Palestine

1920 Undertakes a lecture tour in the United States. *The Superstition of Divorce, The Uses of Diversity*, and *The New Jerusalem*

1922 *Eugenics and other Evils, What I Saw in America*, and *The Man Who Knew Too Much*. Received into the Roman Catholic Church

1923 *Fancies versus Fads* and *St Francis of Assisi*

1925 (21 March) Editor of *G. K.'s Weekly* until his death. *The Superstitions of the Sceptic, Tales of the Long Bow, The Everlasting Man*, and *William Cobbett*

1926 *The Incredulity of Father Brown, The Outline of Sanity*, and *The Queen of Seven Swords*. Start of the Distributist League

1927 Visits Poland. *The Catholic Church and Conversion, The Return of Don Quixote, Collected Poems, The Secret of Father Brown, The Judgement of Dr Johnson, Robert Louis Stevenson*

1928 *Generally Speaking*. A broadcast debate with Bernard Shaw published as *Do We Agree?*

1929 Visits Rome. *The Poet and the Lunatics* and *The Thing*

1930 *Four Faultless Felons, The Resurrection of Rome*, and *Come to Think of It*

1930–1 Undertakes a second lecture tou of the United States

1931 *All is Grist*

1932 *Chaucer, Sidelights on New London and Newer York*, and *Christendom in Dublin*. Begins to broadcast regularly on the BBC

1933 *All I Survey* and *St Thomas Aquinas*

1934 *Avowals and Denials*. Visits Rome and Sicily

1935 *The Scandal of Father Brown* and *The Well and the Shallows*

1936 *As I Was Saying*. (14 June) Dies at Beaconsfield. *Autobiography*

1937 *The Paradoxes of Mr Pond*

CHRONOLOGY

Blue Curtain: Taken authority ill and been unconscious for some making.

1917 Becomes a man for hire, which was a kind of subsidy. Clinics in CM. Demolished rooms. The Crime. An animal.

1918 Chances. Religion his master feel by reason of the New illness.

1917 A Scout further at England.

1918 Mess Ireland, West of Ded. Charwoman

1919 and indignation, Visor Bill and a.

1920 Undertakes a lecture tour in and Oxford Street. The Stone Rose. Autumn. Daughter of Coventry and a fashion campaign.

1930 Everything and other. My What I Saw in America, and The Man Who Knew Too Much. Flee, up the French Catholic Church.

1921 Protest personally and a. Friend of Keats.

1925 To a family father of letters. Weekly, until his death. The experiences of the begun. Tale of the. Time in the the Innocence New and Student Catholic.

1929 The beginning of Father Brown. The Outline of Sanity and The Queen of Seven Sword. End of the Distributist League.

1933 Saint Poland. The Catholic Church returns anyway. The Return of Dad's vote. Culture. Poems. The Superstition Living Reason. The Judgment of Dr Johnson. Robert Louis Stevenson.

1934 Chaucer. Savonarola. A biographical debate. Why I am not Shaw published and so We Were.

1926 Upon Rome. My Paris and the Daughter and The Thing. The Resurrection Rivies. The Everlasting of Rome and Costa.

1927 The Modern of Cris.

1935 Undertakes a special feature tour of the United States and at a Crisis.

1929 Chosen investigators. John London and Master New and Chances down in Dublin. Begins broadcasting regularly on the BBC.

1933 All I Survey and St Thomas Aquinas.

1934 Avowals and Domestic. West, Rome and Family.

1935 The Scandal of Father Brown and The Well and the Shallows.

1936 and a New Autobiography. Died. Dies in Beaconsfield. Poems posthumously.

1937 The Paradoxes of Mr Pond.

FATHER BROWN

A Selection

THE BLUE CROSS

BETWEEN the silver ribbon of morning and the green glittering ribbon of sea, the boat touched Harwich* and let loose a swarm of folk like flies, among whom the man we must follow was by no means conspicuous—nor wished to be. There was nothing notable about him, except a slight contrast between the holiday gaiety of his clothes and the official gravity of his face. His clothes included a slight, pale grey jacket, a white waistcoat, and a silver straw hat with a grey-blue ribbon. His lean face was dark by contrast, and ended in a curt black beard that looked Spanish and suggested an Elizabethan ruff. He was smoking a cigarette with the seriousness of an idler. There was nothing about him to indicate the fact that the grey jacket covered a loaded revolver, that the white waistcoat covered a police card, or that the straw hat covered one of the most powerful intellects in Europe. For this was Valentin himself, the head of the Paris police and the most famous investigator of the world; and he was coming from Brussels to London to make the greatest arrest of the century.

Flambeau* was in England. The police of three countries had tracked the great criminal at last from Ghent to Brussels, from Brussels to the Hook of Holland;* and it was conjectured that he would take some advantage of the unfamiliarity and confusion of the Eucharistic Congress,* then taking place in London. Probably he would travel as some minor clerk or secretary connected with it; but, of course, Valentin could not be certain; nobody could be certain about Flambeau.

It is many years now since this colossus of crime suddenly ceased keeping the world in a turmoil; and when he ceased, as they said after the death of Roland,* there was a great quiet upon the earth. But in his best days (I mean, of course, his worst) Flambeau was a figure as statuesque and international as the Kaiser. Almost every morning the daily paper announced that he had escaped the consequences of one extraordinary crime by committing another. He was a Gascon of gigantic stature and bodily daring; and the wildest tales were told of his outbursts of athletic humour; how he turned the *juge d'instruction** upside down and stood him on his head, 'to clear his mind'; how he ran down the Rue de Rivoli with a policeman under each arm. It is due to him to say that his fantastic physical strength was generally employed in such bloodless though undignified scenes; his real crimes were chiefly those of ingenious and wholesale robbery. But each of his thefts was almost a new sin and would make a story by itself. It was he who ran the great Tyrolean Dairy Company in London, with no dairies, no cows, no carts, no milk, but with some thousand subscribers. These he served by the simple operation of moving the little milk-cans outside people's doors to the doors of his own customers. It was he who had kept up an unaccountable and close correspondence with a young lady whose whole letter-bag was intercepted, by the extraordinary trick of photographing his messages infinitesimally small upon the slides of a microscope. A sweeping simplicity, however, marked many of his experiments. It is said he once repainted all the numbers in a street in the dead of night merely to divert one traveller into a trap. It is quite certain that he invented a portable pillar-box, which he put up at corners in quiet sub-urbs on the chance of strangers dropping postal orders into it. Lastly he was known to be a startling acrobat; despite his huge figure, he could leap like a grasshopper and melt into the tree-tops like a monkey. Hence the great Valentin, when he set out to find Flambeau, was perfectly well aware that his adventures would not end when he had found him.

But how was he to find him? On this the great Valentin's ideas were still in process of settlement.

There was one thing which Flambeau, with all his dexterity of disguise, could not cover, and that was his singular height.* If Valentin's quick eye had caught a tall apple-woman, a tall grenadier, or even a tolerably tall duchess, he might have arrested them on the spot. But all along his train there was nobody that could be a disguised Flambeau, any more than a cat could be a disguised giraffe. About the people on the boat he had already satisfied himself; and the people picked up at Harwich or on the journey limited themselves with certainty to six. There was a short railway official travelling up to the terminus, three fairly short market-gardeners picked up two stations afterwards, one very short widow lady going up from a small Essex town, and a very short Roman Catholic priest going up from a small Essex village. When it came to the last case, Valentin gave it up and almost laughed. The little priest was so much the essence of those Eastern flats: he had a face as round and dull as a Norfolk dumpling; he had eyes as empty as the North Sea; he had several brown-paper parcels which he was quite incapable of collecting. The Eucharistic Congress had doubtless sucked out of their local stagnation many such creatures, blind and helpless, like moles disinterred. Valentin was a sceptic in the severe style of France, and could have no love for priests. But he could have pity for them, and this one might have provoked pity in anybody. He had a large, shabby umbrella, which constantly fell on the floor. He did not seem to know which was the right end of his return ticket. He explained with a moon-calf simplicity to everybody in the carriage that he had to be careful, because he had something made of real silver 'with blue stones' in one of his brown-paper parcels. His quaint blending of Essex flatness with saintly simplicity continuously amused the Frenchman till the priest arrived (somehow) at Stratford with all his parcels, and came back for his umbrella. When he did the last, Valentin even had the good nature to warn him not to take care of the silver by telling everybody about it. But to whomever he talked, Valentin kept his eye open for someone else; he looked out steadily for anyone, rich or poor, male or female, who was well up to six feet; for Flambeau was four inches above it.

He alighted at Liverpool Street,* however, quite conscientiously secure that he had not missed the criminal so far. He then went to Scotland Yard* to regularize his position and arrange for help in case of need; he then lit another cigarette and went for a long stroll in the streets of London. As he was walking in the streets and squares beyond Victoria, he paused suddenly and stood. It was a quaint, quiet square, very typical of London, full of an accidental stillness. The tall, flat houses round looked at once prosperous and uninhabited; the square of shrubbery in the centre looked as deserted as a green Pacific islet. One of the four sides was much higher than the rest, like a dais; and the line of this side was broken by one of London's admirable accidents—a restaurant that looked as if it had strayed from Soho.* It was an unreasonably attractive object, with dwarf plants in pots and long, striped blinds of lemon yellow and white. It stood specially high above the street, and in the usual patchwork way of London, a flight of steps from the street ran up to meet the front door almost as a fire-escape might run up to a first-floor window. Valentin stood and smoked in front of the yellow-white blinds and considered them long.

The most incredible thing about miracles is that they happen. A few clouds in heaven do come together into the staring shape of one human eye. A tree does stand up in the landscape of a doubtful journey in the exact and elaborate shape of a note of interrogation. I have seen both these things myself within the last few days. Nelson does die in the instant of victory;* and a man named Williams does quite accidentally murder a man named Williamson; it sounds like a sort of infanticide. In short, there is in life an element of elfin coincidence* which people reckoning on the prosaic may perpetually miss. As it has been well expressed in the paradox of Poe,* wisdom should reckon on the unforeseen.

Aristide Valentin was unfathomably French; and the French intelligence is intelligence specially and solely. He was not 'a thinking machine';* for that is a brainless phrase of modern fatalism and materialism. A machine only *is* a machine because it cannot think. But he was a thinking man, and a plain man at the same time. All his wonderful successes, that looked like conjuring, had been gained by plodding logic, by clear and commonplace French thought. The French electrify the world not by starting any paradox, they electrify it by carrying out a truism. They carry a truism so far—as in the French Revolution. But exactly because Valentin understood reason, he understood the limits of reason. Only a man who knows nothing of motors talks of motoring without petrol; only a man who knows nothing of reason talks of reasoning without strong, undisputed first principles. Here he had no strong first principles. Flambeau had been missed at Harwich; and, if he was in London at all, he might be anything from a tall tramp on Wimbledon Common* to a tall toastmaster at the Hôtel Métropole. In such a naked state of nescience, Valentin had a view and a method of his own.

In such cases he reckoned on the unforeseen. In such cases, when he could not follow the train of the reasonable, he coldly and carefully followed the train of the unreasonable. Instead of going to the right places—banks, police-stations, rendezvous—he systematically went to the wrong places; knocked at every empty house, turned down every *cul de sac*, went up every lane blocked with rubbish, went round every crescent that led him uselessly out of the way. He defended this crazy course quite logically. He said that if one had a clue this was the worst way; but if one had no clue at all it was the best, because there was just the chance that any oddity that caught the eye of the pursuer might be the same that had caught the eye of the pursued. Somewhere a man must begin, and it had better be just where another man might stop. Something about that flight of steps up to the shop, something about the quietude and quaintness of the restaurant, roused all the detective's rare romantic fancy and made him resolve to strike at random. He went up the steps, and sitting down by the window, asked for a cup of black coffee.

It was half-way through the morning, and he had not breakfasted; the slight litter of other breakfasts stood about on the table to remind him of his hunger; and adding a poached egg to his order, he proceeded musingly to shake some white sugar into his coffee, thinking all the time about Flambeau. He remembered how Flambeau had escaped, once by a pair of nail scissors, and once by a house on fire; once by having to pay for an unstamped letter, and once by getting people to look through a telescope at a comet that might destroy the world. He thought his detective brain as good as the criminal's, which was true. But he fully realized the disadvantage. 'The criminal is the creative artist; the detective only the critic,' he said with a sour smile, and lifted his coffee cup to his lips slowly, and put it down very quickly. He had put salt in it.

He looked at the vessel from which the silvery powder had come; it was certainly a sugar-basin; as unmistakably meant for sugar as a champagne-bottle for champagne. He wondered why they should keep salt in it. He looked to see if there were any more orthodox vessels. Yes, there were two salt-cellars quite full. Perhaps there was some speciality in the condiment in the salt-cellars. He tasted it; it was sugar. Then he looked round at the restaurant with a refreshed air of interest, to see if there were any other traces of that singular artistic taste which puts the sugar in the salt-cellars and the salt in the sugar-basin. Except for an odd splash of some dark fluid on one of the white-papered walls, the whole place appeared neat, cheerful and ordinary. He rang the bell for the waiter.

When that official hurried up, fuzzy-haired and somewhat blear-eyed at that early hour, the detective (who was not without an appreciation of the simpler forms of humour) asked him to taste the sugar and see if it was up to the high reputation of the hotel. The result was that the waiter yawned suddenly and woke up.

'Do you play this delicate joke on your customers every morning?' inquired Valentin. 'Does changing the salt and sugar never pall on you as a jest?'

The waiter, when this irony grew clearer, stammeringly assured him that the establishment had certainly no such intention; it must be a most curious mistake. He picked up the sugar-basin and looked at it; he picked up the salt-cellar and looked at that, his face growing more and more bewildered. At last he abruptly excused himself, and hurrying away, returned in a few seconds with the proprietor. The proprietor also examined the sugar-basin and then the salt-cellar; the proprietor also looked bewildered.

Suddenly the waiter seemed to grow inarticulate with a rush of words.

'I zink,' he stuttered eagerly, 'I zink it is those two clergymen.'

'What two clergymen?'

'The two clergymen,' said the waiter, 'that threw soup at the wall.'

'Threw soup at the wall?' repeated Valentin, feeling sure this must be some Italian metaphor.

'Yes, yes,' said the attendant excitedly, and pointing at the dark splash on the white paper; 'threw it over there on the wall.'

Valentin looked his query at the proprietor, who came to his rescue with fuller reports.

'Yes, sir,' he said, 'it's quite true, though I don't suppose it has anything to do with the sugar and salt. Two clergymen came in and drank soup here very early, as soon as the shutters were taken down. They were both very quiet, respectable people; one of them paid the bill and went out; the other, who seemed a slower coach altogether, was some minutes longer getting his things together. But he went at last. Only, the instant before he stepped into the street he deliberately picked up his cup, which he had only half emptied, and threw the soup* slap on the wall. I was in the back room myself, and so was the waiter; so I could only rush out in time to find the wall splashed and the shop empty. It didn't do any particular damage, but it was confounded cheek; and I tried to catch the men in the street. They were too far off though; I only noticed they went round the corner into Carstairs Street.'

The detective was on his feet, hat settled and stick in hand. He had already decided that in the universal darkness of his mind he could only follow the first odd finger that pointed; and this finger was odd enough. Paying his bill and clashing the glass doors behind him, he was soon swinging round into the other street.

It was fortunate that even in such fevered moments his eye was cool and quick. Something in a shop-front went by him like a mere flash; yet he went back to look at it. The shop was a popular greengrocer and fruiterer's, an array of goods set out in the open air and plainly ticketed with their names and prices. In the two most prominent compartments were two heaps, of oranges and of nuts respectively. On the heap of nuts lay a scrap of cardboard, on which was written in bold, blue chalk, 'Best tangerine oranges, two a penny.' On the oranges was the equally clear and exact description, 'Finest Brazil nuts, 4d.* a lb.' M. Valentin looked at these two placards and fancied he had met this highly subtle form of humour before, and that somewhat recently. He drew the attention of the red-faced fruiterer, who was looking rather sullenly up and down the street, to this inaccuracy in his advertisements. The fruiterer said nothing, but sharply put each card into its proper place. The detective, leaning elegantly on his walking-cane, continued to scrutinize the shop. At last he said: 'Pray excuse my apparent irrelevance, my good sir, but I should like to ask you a question in experimental psychology and the association of ideas.'

The red-faced shopman regarded him with an eye of menace; but he continued gaily, swinging his cane. 'Why,' he pursued, 'why are two tickets wrongly placed in a green-grocer's shop like a shovel hat* that has come to London for a holiday? Or, in case I do not make myself clear, what is the mystical association which connects the idea of nuts marked as oranges with the idea of two clergymen, one tall and the other short?'

The eyes of the tradesman stood out of his head like a snail's; he really seemed for an instant likely to fling himself upon the stranger. At last he stammered angrily: 'I don't know what you 'ave to do with it, but if you're one of their friends, you can tell 'em from me that I'll knock their silly 'eads off, parsons or no parsons, if they upset my apples again.'

'Indeed?' asked the detective, with great sympathy. 'Did they upset your apples?'

'One of 'em did,' said the heated shopman; 'rolled 'em all over the street. I'd 'ave caught the fool but for havin' to pick 'em up.'

'Which way did these parsons go?' asked Valentin.

'Up that second road on the left-hand side, and then across the square,' said the other promptly.

'Thanks,' said Valentin, and vanished like a fairy. On the other side of the second square he found a policeman, and said: 'This is urgent, constable; have you seen two clergymen in shovel hats?'

The policeman began to chuckle heavily. 'I 'ave, sir; and if you arst me, one of 'em was drunk. He stood in the middle of the road that bewildered that——'

'Which way did they go?' snapped Valentin.

'They took one of them yellow buses over there,' answered the man; 'them that go to Hampstead.'*

Valentin produced his official card and said very rapidly: 'Call up two of your men to come with me in pursuit,' and crossed the road with such contagious energy that the ponderous policeman was moved to almost agile obedience. In a minute and a half the French detective was joined on the opposite pavement by an inspector and a man in plain clothes.

'Well, sir,' began the former, with smiling importance, 'and what may——?'

Valentin pointed suddenly with his cane. 'I'll tell you on the top of that omnibus,' he said, and was darting and dodging across the tangle of the traffic. When all three sank panting on the top seats of the yellow vehicle, the inspector said: 'We could go four times as quick in a taxi.'

'Quite true,' replied their leader placidly, 'if we only had an idea of where we were going.'

'Well, where *are* you going?' asked the other, staring.

Valentin smoked frowningly for a few seconds; then, removing his cigarette, he said: 'If you *know* what a man's doing, get in front of him; but if you want to guess what he's doing, keep behind him. Stray when he strays; stop when he stops; travel as slowly as he. Then you may see what he saw and may act as he acted. All we can do is to keep our eyes skinned for a queer thing.'

'What sort of a queer thing do you mean?' asked the inspector.

'Any sort of queer thing,' answered Valentin, and relapsed into obstinate silence.

The yellow omnibus crawled up the northern roads for what seemed like hours on end; the great detective would not explain further, and perhaps his assistants felt a silent and growing doubt of his errand. Perhaps, also, they felt a silent and growing desire for lunch, for the hours crept long past the normal luncheon hour, and the long roads of the North London suburbs seemed to shoot out into length after length like an infernal telescope. It was one of those journeys on which a man perpetually feels that now at last he must have come to the end of the universe, and then finds he has only

come to the beginning of Tufnell Park.* London died away in
draggled taverns and dreary scrubs, and then was unaccount-
ably born again in blazing high streets and blatant hotels. It
was like passing through thirteen separate vulgar cities all just
touching each other. But though the winter twilight was already threatening the road ahead of them, the Parisian detective still sat silent and watchful, eyeing the frontage of the
streets that slid by on either side. By the time they had left
Camden Town* behind, the policemen were nearly asleep; at
least, they gave something like a jump as Valentin leapt erect,
struck a hand on each man's shoulder, and shouted to the
driver to stop.

They tumbled down the steps into the road without realizing why they had been dislodged; when they looked round for
enlightenment they found Valentin triumphantly pointing his
finger towards a window on the left side of the road. It was a
large window, forming part of the long façade of a gilt and
palatial public-house; it was the part reserved for respectable
dining, and labelled 'Restaurant.' This window, like all the
rest along the frontage of the hotel, was of frosted and figured
glass, but in the middle of it was a big, black smash, like a star
in the ice.

'Our cue at last,' cried Valentin, waving his stick; 'the place
with the broken window.'

'What window? What cue?' asked his principal assistant.
'Why, what proof is there that this has anything to do with
them?'

Valentin almost broke his bamboo stick with rage.

'Proof!' he cried. 'Good God! the man is looking for proof!
Why, of course, the chances are twenty to one that it has
nothing to do with them. But what else can we do? Don't you
see we must either follow one wild possibility or else go home
to bed?' He banged his way into the restaurant, followed by
his companions, and they were soon seated at a late luncheon
at a little table, and looking at the star of smashed glass from
the inside. Not that it was very informative to them even then.

'Got your window broken, I see,' said Valentin to the
waiter, as he paid his bill.

'Yes, sir,' answered the attendant, bending busily over the
change, to which Valentin silently added an enormous tip. The

waiter straightened himself with mild but unmistakable animation.

'Ah, yes, sir,' he said. 'Very odd thing, that, sir.'

'Indeed? Tell us about it,' said the detective with careless curiosity.

'Well, two gents in black came in,' said the waiter; 'two of those foreign parsons that are running about. They had a cheap and quiet little lunch, and one of them paid for it and went out. The other was just going out to join him when I looked at my change again and found he'd paid me more than three times too much. "Here," I says to the chap who was nearly out of the door, "you've paid too much." "Oh," he says, very cool, "have we?" "Yes," I says, and picks up the bill to show him. Well, that was a knock-out.'

'What do you mean?' asked his interlocutor.

'Well, I'd have sworn on seven Bibles that I'd put 4s. on that bill. But now I saw I'd put 14s., as plain as paint.'

'Well?' cried Valentin, moving slowly, but with burning eyes, 'and then?'

'The parson at the door he says, all serene, "Sorry to confuse your accounts, but it'll pay for the window." "What window?" I says. "The one I'm going to break," he says, and smashed that blessed pane with his umbrella.'

All three inquirers made an exclamation; and the inspector said under his breath: 'Are we after escaped lunatics?' The waiter went on with some relish for the ridiculous story:

'I was so knocked silly for a second, I couldn't do anything. The man marched out of the place and joined his friend just round the corner. Then they went so quick up Bullock Street that I couldn't catch them, though I ran round the bars to do it.'

'Bullock Street,' said the detective, and shot up that thoroughfare as quickly as the strange couple he pursued.

Their journey now took them through bare brick ways like tunnels; streets with few lights and even with few windows; streets that seemed built out of the blank backs of everything and everywhere. Dusk was deepening, and it was not easy even for the London policemen to guess in what exact direction they were treading. The inspector, however, was pretty certain that they would eventually strike some part of

Hampstead Heath.* Abruptly one bulging and gas-lit window broke the blue twilight like a bull's-eye lantern;* and Valentin stopped an instant before a little garish sweetstuff shop. After an instant's hesitation he went in; he stood amid the gaudy colours of the confectionery with entire gravity and bought thirteen chocolate cigars with a certain care. He was clearly preparing an opening; but he did not need one.

An angular, elderly young woman in the shop had regarded his elegant appearance with a merely automatic inquiry; but when she saw the door behind him blocked with the blue uniform of the inspector, her eyes seemed to wake up.

'Oh,' she said, 'if you've come about that parcel, I've sent it off already.'

'Parcel!' repeated Valentin; and it was his turn to look inquiring.

'I mean the parcel the gentleman left—the clergyman gentleman.'

'For goodness' sake,' said Valentin, leaning forward with his first real confession of eagerness, 'for Heaven's sake tell us what happened exactly.'

'Well,' said the woman, a little doubtfully, 'the clergymen came in about half an hour ago and bought some peppermints and talked a bit, and then went off towards the Heath. But a second after, one of them runs back into the shop and says, "Have I left a parcel?" Well, I looked everywhere and couldn't see one; so he says, "Never mind; but if it should turn up, please post it to this address," and he left me the address and a shilling for my trouble. And sure enough, though I thought I'd looked everywhere, I found he'd left a brown-paper parcel, so I posted it to the place he said. I can't remember the address now; it was somewhere in Westminster. But as the thing seemed so important, I thought perhaps the police had come about it.'

'So they have,' said Valentin shortly. 'Is Hampstead Heath near here?'

'Straight on for fifteen minutes,' said the woman, 'and you'll come right out on the open.' Valentin sprang out of the shop and began to run. The other detectives followed him at a reluctant trot.

The street they threaded was so narrow and shut in by shadows that when they came out unexpectedly into the void common and vast sky they were startled to find the evening still so light and clear. A perfect dome of peacock-green sank into gold amid the blackening trees and the dark violet distances. The glowing green tint was just deep enough to pick out in points of crystal one or two stars. All that was left of the daylight lay in a golden glitter across the edge of Hampstead and that popular hollow which is called the Vale of Health. * The holiday makers who roam this region had not wholly dispersed: a few couples sat shapelessly on benches; and here and there a distant girl still shrieked in one of the swings. The glory of heaven deepened and darkened around the sublime vulgarity of man; and standing on the slope and looking across the valley, Valentin beheld the thing which he sought.

Among the black and breaking groups in that distance was one especially black which did not break—a group of two figures clerically clad. Though they seemed as small as insects, Valentin could see that one of them was much smaller than the other. Though the other had a student's stoop and an inconspicuous manner, he could see that the man was well over six feet high. He shut his teeth and went forward, whirling his stick impatiently. By the time he had substantially diminished the distance and magnified the two black figures as in a vast microscope, he had perceived something else; something which startled him, and yet which he had somehow expected. Whoever was the tall priest, there could be no doubt about the identity of the short one. It was his friend of the Harwich train, the stumpy little *curé* of Essex whom he had warned about his brown-paper parcels.

Now, so far as this went, everything fitted in finally and rationally enough. Valentin had learned by his inquiries that morning that a Father Brown from Essex was bringing up a silver cross with sapphires, a relic of considerable value, to show some of the foreign priests at the congress. This undoubtedly was the 'silver with blue stones'; and Father Brown undoubtedly was the little greenhorn in the train. Now there was nothing wonderful about the fact that what Valentin had

found out Flambeau had also found out; Flambeau found out
everything. Also there was nothing wonderful in the fact that
when Flambeau heard of a sapphire cross he should try to
steal it; that was the most natural thing in all natural history.
And most certainly there was nothing wonderful about the
fact that Flambeau should have it all his own way with such
a silly sheep as the man with the umbrella and the parcels. He
was the sort of man whom anybody could lead on a string to
the North Pole; it was not surprising that an actor like
Flambeau, dressed as another priest, could lead him to
Hampstead Heath. So far the crime seemed clear enough; and
while the detective pitied the priest for his helplessness, he
almost despised Flambeau for condescending to so gullible a
victim. But when Valentin thought of all that had happened in
between, of all that had led him to his triumph, he racked his
brains for the smallest rhyme or reason in it. What had the
stealing of a blue-and-silver cross from a priest from Essex to
do with chucking soup at wallpaper? What had it to do with
calling nuts oranges, or with paying for windows first and
breaking them afterwards? He had come to the end of his
chase; yet somehow he had missed the middle of it. When he
failed (which was seldom), he had usually grasped the clue,
but nevertheless missed the criminal. Here he had grasped the
criminal, but still he could not grasp the clue.

The two figures that they followed were crawling like black
flies across the huge green contour of a hill. They were evidently sunk in conversation, and perhaps did not notice
where they were going; but they were certainly going to
the wilder and more silent heights of the Heath. As their
pursuers gained on them, the latter had to use the undignified
attitudes of the deer-stalker, to crouch behind clumps of
trees and even to crawl prostrate in deep grass. By these
ungainly ingenuities the hunters even came close enough to
the quarry to hear the murmur of the discussion, but no word
could be distinguished except the word 'reason' recurring
frequently in a high and almost childish voice. Once, over an
abrupt dip of land and a dense tangle of thickets, the detectives actually lost the two figures they were following. They
did not find the trail again for an agonizing ten minutes,
and then it led round the brow of a great dome of hill over-

looking an amphitheatre of rich and desolate sunset scenery. Under a tree in this commanding yet neglected spot was an old ramshackle wooden seat. On this seat sat the two priests still in serious speech together. The gorgeous green and gold still clung to the darkening horizon; but the dome above was turning slowly from peacock-green to peacock-blue, and the stars detached themselves more and more like solid jewels. Mutely motioning to his followers, Valentin contrived to creep up behind the big branching tree, and, standing there in deathly silence, heard the words of the strange priests for the first time.

After he had listened for a minute and a half, he was gripped by a devilish doubt. Perhaps he had dragged the two English policemen to the wastes of a nocturnal heath on an errand no saner than seeking figs on its thistles. For the two priests were talking exactly like priests, piously, with learning and leisure, about the most aerial enigmas of theology. The little Essex priest spoke the more simply, with his round face turned to the strengthening stars; the other talked with his head bowed, as if he were not even worthy to look at them. But no more innocently clerical conversation could have been heard in any white Italian cloister or black Spanish cathedral.

The first he heard was the tail of one of Father Brown's sentences, which ended: '. . . what they really meant in the Middle Ages by the heavens being incorruptible.'

The taller priest nodded his bowed head and said:

'Ah, yes, these modern infidels appeal to their reason; but who can look at those millions of worlds and not feel that there may well be wonderful universes above us where reason is utterly unreasonable?'

'No,' said the other priest; 'reason is always reasonable, even in the last limbo, in the lost borderland of things. I know that people charge the Church with lowering reason, but it is just the other way. Alone on earth, the Church makes reason really supreme. Alone on earth, the Church affirms that God Himself is bound by reason.'

The other priest raised his austere face to the spangled sky and said:

'Yet who knows if in that infinite universe——?'

'Only infinite physically,' said the little priest, turning sharply in his seat, 'not infinite in the sense of escaping from the laws of truth.'

Valentin behind his tree was tearing his finger-nails with silent fury. He seemed almost to hear the sniggers of the English detectives whom he had brought so far on a fantastic guess only to listen to the metaphysical gossip of two mild old parsons. In his impatience he lost the equally elaborate answer of the tall cleric, and when he listened again it was again Father Brown who was speaking:

'Reason and justice grip the remotest and the loneliest star. Look at those stars. Don't they look as if they were single diamonds and sapphires? Well, you can imagine any mad botany or geology you please. Think of forests of adamant with leaves of brilliants. Think the moon is a blue moon, a single elephantine sapphire. But don't fancy that all that frantic astronomy would make the smallest difference to the reason and justice of conduct. On plains of opal, under cliffs cut out of pearl, you would still find a notice-board, "Thou shalt not steal."'

Valentin was just in the act of rising from his rigid and crouching attitude and creeping away as softly as might be, felled by the one great folly of his life. But something in the very silence of the tall priest made him stop until the latter spoke. When at last he did speak, he said simply, his head bowed and his hands on his knees:

'Well, I still think that other worlds may perhaps rise higher than our reason. The mystery of heaven is unfathomable, and I for one can only bow my head.'

Then, with brow yet bent and without changing by the faintest shade his attitude or voice, he added:

'Just hand over that sapphire cross of yours, will you? We're all alone here, and I could pull you to pieces like a straw doll.'

The utterly unaltered voice and attitude added a strange violence to that shocking change of speech. But the guarder of the relic only seemed to turn his head by the smallest section of the compass. He seemed still to have a somewhat foolish face turned to the stars. Perhaps he had not understood. Or, perhaps, he had understood and sat rigid with terror.

'Yes,' said the tall priest, in the same low voice and in the same still posture, 'yes, I am Flambeau.'

Then, after a pause, he said:

'Come, will you give me that cross?'

'No,' said the other, and the monosyllable had an odd sound.

Flambeau suddenly flung off all his pontifical pretensions. The great robber leaned back in his seat and laughed low but long.

'No,' he cried; 'you won't give it me, you proud prelate. You won't give it me, you little celibate simpleton. Shall I tell you why you won't give it me? Because I've got it already in my own breast-pocket.'

The small man from Essex turned what seemed to be a dazed face in the dusk, and said, with the timid eagerness of 'The Private Secretary':*

'Are—are you sure?'

Flambeau yelled with delight.

'Really, you're as good as a three-act farce,' he cried. 'Yes, you turnip, I am quite sure. I had the sense to make a duplicate of the right parcel, and now, my friend, you've got the duplicate, and I've got the jewels. An old dodge, Father Brown—a very old dodge.'

'Yes,' said Father Brown, and passed his hand through his hair with the same strange vagueness of manner. 'Yes, I've heard of it before.'

The colossus of crime leaned over to the little rustic priest with a sort of sudden interest.

'*You* have heard of it?' he asked. 'Where have *you* heard of it?'

'Well, I mustn't tell you his name, of course,' said the little man simply. 'He was a penitent, you know. He had lived prosperously for about twenty years entirely on duplicate brown-paper parcels. And so, you see, when I began to suspect you, I thought of this poor chap's way of doing it at once.'

'Began to suspect me?' repeated the outlaw with increased intensity. 'Did you really have the gumption to suspect me just because I brought you up to this bare part of the heath?'

'No, no,' said Brown with an air of apology. 'You see, I suspected you when we first met. It's that little bulge up the sleeve where you people have the spiked bracelet.'*

'How in Tartarus,' cried Flambeau, 'did you ever hear of the spiked bracelet?'

'Oh, one's little flock, you know!' said Father Brown, arching his eyebrows rather blankly. 'When I was a curate in Hartlepool,* there were three of them with spiked bracelets. So, as I suspected you from the first, don't you see, I made sure that cross should go safe, anyhow. I'm afraid I watched you, you know. So at last I saw you change the parcels. Then, don't you see, I changed them back again. And then I left the right one behind.'

'Left it behind?' repeated Flambeau, and for the first time there was another note in his voice beside his triumph.

'Well, it was like this,' said the little priest, speaking in the same unaffected way. 'I went back to that sweet-shop and asked if I'd left a parcel, and gave them a particular address if it turned up. Well, I knew I hadn't; but when I went away again I did. So, instead of running after me with that valuable parcel, they have sent it flying to a friend of mine in Westminster.' Then he added rather sadly: 'I learnt that, too, from a poor fellow in Hartlepool. He used to do it with handbags he stole at railway stations, but he's in a monastery now. Oh, one gets to know, you know,' he added, rubbing his head again with the same sort of desperate apology. 'We can't help being priests. People come and tell us these things.'

Flambeau tore a brown-paper parcel out of his inner pocket and rent it in pieces. There was nothing but paper and sticks of lead inside it. He sprang to his feet with a gigantic gesture, and cried:

'I don't believe you. I don't believe a bumpkin like you could manage all that. I believe you've still got the stuff on you, and if you don't give it up—why, we're all alone, and I'll take it by force!'

'No,' said Father Brown simply, and stood up also; 'you won't take it by force. First, because I really haven't still got it. And, second, because we are not alone.'

Flambeau stopped in his stride forward.

'Behind that tree,' said Father Brown, pointing, 'are two strong policemen and the greatest detective alive. How did they come here, do you ask? Why, I brought them, of course! How did I do it? Why, I'll tell you if you like! Lord bless you, we have to know twenty such things when we work among the criminal classes! Well, I wasn't sure you were a thief, and it would never do to make a scandal against one of our own clergy. So I just tested you to see if anything would make you show yourself. A man generally makes a small scene if he finds salt in his coffee; if he doesn't, he has some reason for keeping quiet. I changed the salt and sugar, and *you* kept quiet. A man generally objects if his bill is three times too big. If he pays it, he has some motive for passing unnoticed. I altered your bill, and *you* paid it.'

The world seemed waiting for Flambeau to leap like a tiger. But he was held back as by a spell; he was stunned with the utmost curiosity.

'Well,' went on Father Brown, with lumbering lucidity, 'as you wouldn't leave any tracks for the police, of course somebody had to. At every place we went to, I took care to do something that would get us talked about for the rest of the day. I didn't do much harm—a splashed wall, spilt apples, a broken window; but I saved the cross, as the cross will always be saved. It is at Westminster by now. I rather wonder you didn't stop it with the Donkey's Whistle.'*

'With the what?' asked Flambeau.

'I'm glad you've never heard of it,' said the priest, making a face. 'It's a foul thing. I'm sure you're too good a man for a Whistler. I couldn't have countered it even with the Spots* myself; I'm not strong enough in the legs.'

'What on earth are you talking about?' asked the other.

'Well, I did think you'd know the Spots,' said Father Brown, agreeably surprised. 'Oh, you can't have gone so very wrong yet!'

'How in blazes do you know all these horrors?' cried Flambeau.

The shadow of a smile crossed the round, simple face of his clerical opponent.

'Oh, by being a celibate simpleton, I suppose,' he said. 'Has it never struck you that a man who does next to nothing but hear men's real sins is not likely to be wholly unaware of human evil? But, as a matter of fact, another part of my trade, too, made me sure you weren't a priest.'

'What?' asked the thief, almost gaping.

'You attacked reason,' said Father Brown. 'It's bad theology.'

And even as he turned away to collect his property, the three policemen came out from under the twilight trees. Flambeau was an artist and a sportsman. He stepped back and swept Valentin a great bow.

'Do not bow to me, *mon ami*,' said Valentin, with silver clearness. 'Let us both bow to our master.'

And they both stood an instant uncovered, while the little Essex priest blinked about for his umbrella.

THE SECRET GARDEN

ARISTIDE VALENTIN, Chief of the Paris Police, was late for his dinner, and some of his guests began to arrive before him. These were, however, reassured by his confidential servant, Ivan, the old man with a scar and a face almost as grey as his moustaches, who always sat at a table in the entrance hall—a hall hung with weapons. Valentin's house was perhaps as peculiar and celebrated as its master. It was an old house, with high walls and tall poplars almost overhanging the Seine; but the oddity—and perhaps the police value—of its architecture was this: that there was no ultimate exit at all except through this front door, which was guarded by Ivan and the armoury. The garden was large and elaborate, and there were many exits from the house into the garden. But there was no exit from the garden into the world outside; all round it ran a tall, smooth unscalable wall with special spikes at the top; no bad garden, perhaps, for a man to reflect in whom some hundred criminals had sworn to kill.

As Ivan explained to the guests, their host had telephoned that he was detained for ten minutes. He was, in truth, making some last arrangements about executions and such ugly things; and though these duties were rootedly repulsive to him, he always performed them with precision. Ruthless in the pursuit of criminals, he was very mild about their punishment. Since he had been supreme over French—and largely over European—police methods, his great influence had been honourably used for the mitigation of sentences and the purification of prisons. He was one of the great humanitarian French freethinkers; and the only thing wrong with them is that they make mercy even colder than justice.

When Valentin arrived he was already dressed in black clothes and the red rosette—an elegant figure, his dark beard already streaked with grey. He went straight through his house to his study, which opened on the grounds behind. The garden door of it was open, and after he had carefully locked his box in its official place, he stood for a few seconds at the open door looking out upon the garden. A sharp moon was fighting with the flying rags and tatters of a storm, and Valentin regarded it with a wistfulness unusual in such scientific natures as his. Perhaps such scientific natures have some psychic prevision of the most tremendous problem of their lives. From any such occult mood, at least, he quickly recovered, for he knew he was late and that his guests had already begun to arrive. A glance at his drawing-room when he entered it was enough to make certain that his principal guest was not there, at any rate. He saw all the other pillars of the little party: he saw Lord Galloway, the English Ambassador— a choleric old man with a russet face like an apple, wearing the blue ribbon of the Garter. He saw Lady Galloway, slim and thread-like, with silver hair and a face sensitive and superior. He saw her daughter, Lady Margaret Graham, a pale and pretty girl with an elfish face and copper-coloured hair. He saw the Duchess of Mont St Michel, black-eyed and opulent, and with her her two daughters, black-eyed and opulent also. He saw Dr Simon, a typical French scientist, with glasses, a pointed brown beard, and a forehead barred with those parallel wrinkles which are the penalty of superciliousness, since they come through constantly elevating the eyebrows. He saw Father Brown of Cobhole,* in Essex, whom he had recently met in England. He saw—perhaps with more interest than any of these—a tall man in uniform, who had bowed to the Galloways without receiving any very hearty acknowledgment, and who now advanced alone to pay his respects to his host. This was Commandant O'Brien, of the French Foreign Legion. He was a slim yet somewhat swaggering figure, clean-shaven, dark-haired, and blue-eyed, and as seemed natural in an officer of that famous regiment of victorious failures and successful suicides, he had an air at once dashing and melancholy. He was by birth an Irish gentleman, and in boyhood had known the Galloways—especially Margaret Graham. He had left his country after some crash of debts, and now expressed his complete freedom from British etiquette by swinging about in uniform, sabre and spurs. When he bowed to the Ambassador's family, Lord and Lady Galloway bent stiffly, and Lady Margaret looked away.

But for whatever old causes such people might be interested in each other, their distinguished host was not specially interested in them. No one of them at least was in his eyes the guest of the evening. Valentin was expecting, for special reasons, a man of world-wide fame, whose friendship he had secured during some of his great detective tours and triumphs in the United States. He was expecting Julius K. Brayne,* that multi-millionaire whose colossal and even crushing endowments of small religions have occasioned so much easy sport and easier solemnity for the American and English papers. Nobody could quite make out whether Mr Brayne was an atheist or a Mormon, or a Christian Scientist; but he was ready to pour money into any intellectual vessel, so long as it was an untried vessel. One of his hobbies was to wait for the American Shakespeare—a hobby more patient than angling. He admired Walt Whitman,* but thought that Luke P. Tanner, of Paris, Pa., was more 'progressive'* than Whitman any day. he liked anything that he thought 'progressive.' He thought Valentin 'progressive,' thereby doing him a grave injustice.

The solid appearance of Julius K. Brayne in the room was as decisive as a dinner bell. He had this great quality, which very few of us can claim, that his presence was as big as his absence. He was a huge fellow, as fat as he was tall, clad in complete evening black, without so much relief as a watch-chain or a ring. His hair was white and well brushed back like a German's; his face was red, fierce and cherubic, with one dark tuft under the lower lip that threw up that other-wise infantile visage with an effect theatrical and even Mephistophelean. Not long, however, did that *salon* merely stare at the celebrated American; his lateness had already become a domestic problem, and he was sent with all speed into the dining-room with Lady Galloway upon his arm.

Except on one point the Galloways were genial and casual enough. So long as Lady Mrgaret did not take the arm of that adventurer O'Brien her father was quite satisfied; and she had not done so; she had decorously gone in with Dr Simon. Nevertheless, old Lord Galloway was restless and almost rude. He was diplomatic enough during dinner, but when, over the cigars, three of the younger men—Simon the doctor, Brown the priest, and the detrimental O'Brien, the exile in a foreign uniform—all melted away to mix with the ladies or smoke in the conservatory, then the English diplomatist grew very undiplomatic indeed. He was stung every sixty seconds with the thought that the scamp O'Brien might be signalling to Margaret somehow; he did not attempt to imagine how. He was left over the coffee with Brayne, the hoary Yankee who believed in all religions, and Valentin, the grizzled Frenchman who believed in none. They could argue with each other, but neither could appeal to him. After a time this 'progressive' logomachy* had reached a crisis of tedium; Lord Galloway got up also and sought the drawing-room. He lost his way in long passages for some six or eight minutes: till he heard the high-pitched, didactic voice of the doctor, and then the dull voice of the priest, followed by general laughter. They also, he thought with a curse, were probably arguing about 'science and religion.' But the instant he opened the *salon* door he saw only one thing—he saw what was not there. He saw that Commandant O'Brien was absent, and that Lady Margaret was absent, too.

Rising impatiently from the drawing-room, as he had from the dining-room, he stamped along the passage once more. His notion of protecting his daughter from the Irish-Algerian ne'er-do-weel had become something central and even mad in his mind. As he went towards the back of the house, where was Valentin's study, he was surprised to meet his daughter, who swept past with a white, scornful face, which was a second enigma. If she had been with O'Brien, where was O'Brien? If she had not been with O'Brien, where had she been? With a sort of senile and passionate suspicion he groped his way to the dark back parts of the mansion, and eventually found a servants' entrance that opened on to the garden. The moon with her scimitar had now ripped up and rolled away all the storm-wrack. The argent light lit up all four corners of the garden. A tall figure in blue was striding across the lawn towards the study door; a glint of moonlit silver on his facings picked him out as Commandant O'Brien.

He vanished through the French windows into the house, leaving Lord Galloway in an indescribable temper, at once virulent and vague. The blue-and-silver garden, like a scene in a theatre, seemed to taunt him with all that tyrannic tenderness against which his worldly authority was at war. The length and grace of the Irishman's stride enraged him as if he were a rival instead of a father; the moonlight maddened him. He was trapped as if by magic into a garden of troubadours, a Watteau* fairyland; and, willing to shake off such amorous imbecilities by speech, he stepped briskly after his enemy. As he did so he tripped over some tree or stone in the grass; looked down at it first with irritation and then a second time with curiosity. The next instant the moon and the tall poplars looked at an unusual sight—an elderly English diplomatist running hard and crying or bellowing as he ran.

His hoarse shouts brought a pale face to the study door, the beaming glasses and worried brow of Dr Simon, who heard the nobleman's first clear words. Lord Galloway was crying: 'A corpse in the grass—a bloody corpse.' O'Brien at least had gone utterly from his mind.

'We must tell Valentin at once,' said the doctor, when the other had brokenly described all that he had dared to examine. 'It is fortunate that he is here'; and even as he spoke the great detective entered the study, attracted by the cry. It was almost amusing to note his typical transformation; he had come with the common concern of a host and a gentleman, fearing that some guest or servant was ill. When he was told the gory fact, he turned with all his gravity instantly bright and business-like; for this, however, abrupt and awful, was his business.

'Strange, gentlemen,' he said, as they hurried out into the garden, 'that I should have hunted mysteries all over the earth, and now one comes and settles in my own back-yard. But where is the place?' They crossed the lawn less easily, as a slight mist had begun to rise from the river; but under the guidance of the shaken Galloway they found the body sunken in deep grass—the body of a very tall and broad-shouldered man. He lay face downwards, so they could only see that his big shoulders were clad in black cloth, and that his big head was bald, except for a wisp or two of brown hair that clung to his skull like wet seaweed. A scarlet serpent of blood crawled from under his fallen face.

'At least,' said Simon, with a deep and singular intonation, 'he is none of our party.'

'Examine him, doctor,' cried Valentin rather sharply. 'He may not be dead.'

The doctor bent down. 'He is not quite cold, but I am afraid he is dead enough,' he answered. 'Just help me to lift him up.'

They lifted him carefully an inch from the ground, and all doubts as to his being really dead were settled at once and frightfully. The head fell away. It had been entirely sundered from the body; whoever had cut his throat had managed to sever the neck as well. Even Valentin was slightly shocked. 'He must have been as strong as a gorilla,' he muttered.

Not without a shiver, though he was used to anatomical abortions, Dr Simon lifted the head. It was slightly slashed about the neck and jaw, but the face was substantially unhurt. It was a ponderous, yellow face, at once sunken and swollen, with a hawk-like nose and heavy lids—the face of a wicked Roman emperor, with, perhaps, a distant touch of a Chinese emperor. All present seemed to look at it with the coldest eye of ignorance. Nothing else could be noted about the man except that, as they had lifted his body, they had seen underneath it the white gleam of a shirtfront defaced with a red gleam of blood. As Dr Simon said, the man had never been of their party. But he might very well have been trying to join it, for he had come dressed for such an occasion.

Valentin went down on his hands and knees and examined with his closest professional attention the grass and ground for some twenty yards round the body, in which he was assisted less skilfully by the doctor, and quite vaguely by the English lord. Nothing rewarded their grovellings except a few twigs, snapped or chopped into very small lengths, which Valentin lifted for an instant's examination, and then tossed away.

'Twigs', he said gravely; 'twigs, and a total stranger with his head cut off; that is all there is on this lawn.'

There was an almost creepy stillness, and then the unnerved Galloway called out sharply:

'Who's that? Who's that over there by the garden wall?'

A small figure with a foolishly large head drew waveringly near them in the moonlit haze; looked for an instant like a goblin, but turned out to be the harmless little priest whom they had left in the drawing-room.

'I say,' he said meekly, 'there are no gates to this garden, do you know.'

Valentin's black brows had come together somewhat crossly, as they did on principle at the sight of the cassock. But he was far too just a man to deny the relevance of the remark. 'You are right,' he said. 'Before we find out how he came to be killed, we may have to find out how he came to be here. Now listen to me, gentlemen. If it can be done without prejudice to my position and duty, we shall all agree that certain distinguished names might well be kept out of this. There are ladies, gentlemen, and there is a foreign ambassador. If we must mark it down as a crime, then it must be followed up as a crime. But till then I can use my own discretion. I am the head of the police; I am so public that I can afford to be private. Please Heaven, I will clear every one of my own guests before I call in my men to look for anybody else. Gentlemen, upon your honour, you will none of you leave the house till to-morrow at noon; there are bedrooms for all. Simon, I think you know where to find my man, Ivan, in the front hall; he is a confidential man. Tell him to leave another servant on guard and come to me at once. Lord Galloway, you are certainly the best person to tell the ladies what has happened, and prevent a panic. They also must stay. Father Brown and I will remain with the body.'

When this spirit of the captain spoke in Valentin he was obeyed like a bugle. Dr Simon went through to the armoury and routed out Ivan, the public detective's private detective. Galloway went to the drawing-room and told the terrible news tactfully enough, so that by the time the company assembled there the ladies were already startled and already soothed. Meanwhile the good priest and the good atheist stood at the head and foot of the dead man motionless in the moonlight, like symbolic statues of their two philosophies of death.

Ivan, the confidential man with the scar and the moustaches, came out of the house like a cannon ball, and came racing across the lawn to Valentin like a dog to his master. His livid face was quite lively with the glow of this domestic detective story, and it was with almost unpleasant eagerness that he asked his master's permission to examine the remains.

'Yes; look, if you like, Ivan,' said Valentin, 'but don't be long. We must go in and thrash this out in the house.'

Ivan lifted his head, and then almost let it drop.

'Why,' he gasped, 'it's—no, it isn't; it can't be. Do you know this man, sir?'

'No,' said Valentin indifferently; 'we had better go inside.'

Between them they carried the corpse to a sofa in the study, and then all made their way to the drawing-room.

The detective sat down at a desk quietly, and even with hesitation; but his eye was the iron eye of a judge at assize.* He made a few rapid notes upon paper in front of him, and then said shortly: 'Is everybody here?'

'Not Mr Brayne,' said the Duchess of Mont St Michel, looking round.

'No,' said Lord Galloway, in a hoarse, harsh voice. 'And not Mr Neil O'Brien, I fancy. I saw that gentleman walking in the garden when the corpse was still warm.'

'Ivan,' said the detective, 'go and fetch Commandant O'Brien and Mr Brayne. Mr Brayne, I know, is finishing a cigar in the dining-room; Commandant O'Brien, I think, is walking up and down the conservatory. I am not sure.'

The faithful attendant flashed from the room, and before anyone could stir or speak Valentin went on with the same soldierly swiftness of exposition.

'Everyone here knows that a dead man has been found in the garden, his head cut clean from his body. Dr Simon, you have examined it. Do you think that to cut a man's throat like that would need great force? Or, perhaps, only a very sharp knife?'

'I should say that it could not be done with a knife at all,' said the pale doctor.

'Have you any thought,' resumed Valentin, 'of a tool with which it could be done?'

'Speaking within modern probabilities, I really haven't,' said the doctor, arching his painful brows. 'It's not easy to hack a neck through even clumsily, and this was a very clean cut. It could be done with a battle-axe or an old headsman's axe, or an old two-handed sword.'

'But, good heavens!' cried the Duchess, almost in hysterics; 'there aren't any two-handed swords and battle-axes round here.'

Valentin was still busy with the paper in front of him. 'Tell me,' he said, still writing rapidly, 'could it have been done with a long French cavalry sabre?'

A low knocking came at the door, which for some unreasonable reason, curdled everyone's blood like the knocking in *Macbeth*. Amid that frozen silence Dr Simon managed to say: 'A sabre—yes, I suppose it could.'

'Thank you,' said Valentin, 'Come in, Ivan.'

The confidential Ivan opened the door and ushered in Commandant Neil O'Brien, whom he had found at last pacing the garden again.

The Irish officer stood disordered and defiant on the threshold. 'What do you want with me?' he cried.

'Please sit down,' said Valentin in pleasant, level tones. 'Why, you aren't wearing your sword! Where is it?'

'I left it on the library table,' said O'Brien, his brogue deepening in his disturbed mood. 'It was a nuisance, it was getting——'

'Ivan,' said Valentin: 'please go and get the Commandant's sword from the library.' Then, as the servant vanished: 'Lord Galloway says he saw you leaving the garden just before he found the corpse. What were you doing in the garden?'

The Commandant flung himself recklessly into a chair. 'Oh,' he cried in pure Irish; 'admirin' the moon. Communing with Nature, me boy.'

A heavy silence sank and endured, and at the end of it came again that trivial and terrible knocking. Ivan reappeared, carrying an empty steel scabbard. 'This is all I can find,' he said.

'Put it on the table,' said Valentin, without looking up.

There was an inhuman silence in the room, like that sea of inhuman silence round the dock of the condemned murderer. The Duchess's weak exclamations had long ago died away. Lord Galloway's swollen hatred was satisfied and even sobered. The voice that came was quite unexpected.

'I think I can tell you,' cried Lady Margaret, in that clear, quivering voice with which a courageous woman speaks publicly. 'I can tell you what Mr O'Brien was doing in the garden, since he is bound to silence. He was asking me to marry him. I refused; I said in my family circumstances I could give him nothing but my respect. He was a little angry at that; he did not seem to think much of my respect. I wonder,' she added, with rather a wan smile, 'if he will care at all for it now. For I offer it him now. I will swear anywhere that he never did a thing like this.'

Lord Galloway had edged up to his daughter, and was intimidating her in what he imagined to be an undertone. 'Hold your tongue, Maggie,' he said in a thunderous whisper. 'Why should you shield the fellow? Where's his sword? Where's his confounded bloody——'

He stopped because of the singular stare with which his daughter was regarding him, a look that was indeed a lurid magnet for the whole group.

'You old fool!' she said, in a low voice without pretence of piety; 'what do you suppose you are trying to prove? I tell you this man was innocent while with me. But if he wasn't innocent, he was still with me. If he murdered a man in the garden, who was it who must have seen—who must at least have known? Do you hate Neil so much as to put your own daughter——'

Lady Galloway screamed. Everyone else sat tingling at the touch of those satanic tragedies that have been between lovers before now. They saw the proud, white face of the Scotch aristocrat and her lover, the Irish adventurer, like old portraits in a dark house. The long silence was full of formless historical memories of murdered husbands and poisonous paramours.

In the centre of this morbid silence an innocent voice said: 'Was it a very long cigar?'

The change of thought was so sharp that they had to look round to see who had spoken.

'I mean,' said little Father Brown, from the corner of the room. 'I mean that cigar Mr Brayne is finishing. It seems nearly as long as a walking-stick.'

Despite the irrelevance there was assent as well as irritation in Valentin's face as he lifted his head.

'Quite right,' he remarked sharply. 'Ivan, go and see about Mr Brayne again, and bring him here at once.'

The instant the factotum had closed the door, Valentin addressed the girl with an entirely new earnestness.

'Lady Margaret,' he said, 'we all feel, I am sure, both gratitude and admiration for your act in rising above your lower dignity and explaining the Commandant's conduct. But there is a hiatus still. Lord Galloway, I understand, met you passing from the study to the drawing-room, and it was only some minutes afterwards that he found the garden and the Commandant still walking there.'

'You have to remember,' replied Margaret, with a faint irony in her voice, 'that I had just refused him, so we should scarcely have come back arm in arm. He is a gentleman, anyhow; and he loitered behind—and so got charged with murder.'

'In those few moments,' said Valentin gravely, 'he might really——'

The knock came again, and Ivan put in his scarred face.

'Beg pardon, sir,' he said, 'but Mr Brayne has left the house.'

'Left!' cried Valentin, and rose for the first time to his feet.

'Gone. Scooted. Evaporated,' replied Ivan, in humorous French. 'His hat and coat are gone, too; and I'll tell you something to cap it all. I ran outside the house to find any traces of him, and I found one, and a big trace, too.'

'What do you mean?' asked Valentin.

'I'll show you,' said his servant, and reappeared with a flashing naked cavalry sabre, streaked with blood about the point and edge. Everyone in the room eyed it as if it were a thunderbolt; but the experienced Ivan went on quite quietly:

'I found this,' he said, 'flung among the bushes fifty yards up the road to Paris. In other words, I found it just where your respectable Mr Brayne threw it when he ran away.'

There was again a silence, but of a new sort. Valentin took the sabre, examined it, reflected with unaffected concentration of thought, and then turned a respectful face to O'Brien. 'Commandant,' he said, 'we trust you will always produce this weapon if it is wanted for police examination. Meanwhile,' he added, slapping the steel back in the ringing scabbard, 'let me return you your sword.'

At the military symbolism of the action the audience could hardly refrain from applause.

For Neil O'Brien, indeed, that gesture was the turning-point of existence. By the time he was wandering in the mysterious garden again in the colours of the morning the tragic futility of his ordinary mien had fallen from him; he was a man with many reasons for happiness. Lord Galloway was a gentleman, and had offered him an apology. Lady Margaret was something better than a lady, a woman at least, and had perhaps given him something better than an apology, as they drifted among the old flower-beds before breakfast. The whole company was more light-hearted and humane, for though the riddle of the death remained, the load of suspicion was lifted off them all, and sent flying off to Paris with the strange millionaire—a man they hardly knew. The devil was cast out of the house—he had cast himself out.

Still, the riddle remained; and when O'Brien threw himself on a garden seat beside Dr Simon, that keenly scientific person at once resumed it. He did not get much talk out of O'Brien, whose thoughts were on pleasanter things.

'I can't say it interests me much,' said the Irishman frankly, 'especially as it seems pretty plain now. Apparently Brayne hated this stranger for some reason; lured him into the garden, and killed him with my sword. Then he fled to the city, tossing the sword away as he went. By the way, Ivan tells me the dead man had a Yankee dollar in his pocket. So he was a countryman of Brayne's, and that seems to clinch it. I don't see any difficulties about the business.'

'There are five colossal difficulties,' said the doctor quietly; 'like high walls within walls. Don't mistake me. I don't doubt that Brayne did it; his flight, I fancy, proves that. But as to how he did it. First difficulty: Why should a man kill another man with a great hulking sabre, when he can almost kill him with a pocket knife and put it back in his pocket? Second difficulty: Why was there no noise or outcry? Does a man commonly see another come up waving a scimitar and offer no remarks? Third difficulty: A servant watched the front door all the evening; and a rat cannot get into Valentin's garden anywhere. How did the dead man get into the garden? Fourth difficulty: Given the same conditions, how did Brayne get out of the garden?'

'And the fifth,' said Neil, with eyes fixed on the English priest, who was coming slowly up the path.

'Is a trifle, I suppose,' said the doctor, 'but I think an odd one. When I first saw how the head had been slashed, I supposed the assassin had struck more than once. But on examination I found many cuts across the truncated section; in other words, they were struck *after* the head was off. Did Brayne hate his foe so fiendishly that he stood sabring his body in the moonlight?'

'Horrible!' said O'Brien, and shuddered.

The little priest, Brown, had arrived while they were talking, and had waited, with characteristic shyness, till they had finished. Then he said awkwardly:

'I say, I'm sorry to interrupt. But I was sent to tell you the news!'

'News?' repeated Simon, and stared at him rather painfully through his glasses.

'Yes, I'm sorry,' said Father Brown mildly. 'There's been another murder, you know.'

Both men on the seat sprang up, leaving it rocking

'And, what's stranger still,' continued the priest, with his dull eyes on the rhododendrons, 'it's the same disgusting sort; it's another beheading. They found the second head actually bleeding in the river, a few yards along Brayne's road to Paris; so they suppose that he——'

'Great Heaven!' cried O'Brien. 'Is Brayne a monomaniac?'

'There are American vendettas,' said the priest impassively. Then he added: 'They want you to come to the library and see it.'

Commandant O'Brien followed the others towards the inquest, feeling decidedly sick. As a soldier, he loathed all this secretive carnage; where were these extravagant amputations going to stop? First one head was hacked off, and then another; in this case (he told himself bitterly) it was not true that two heads were better than one. As he crossed the study he almost staggered at a shocking coincidence. Upon Valentin's table lay the coloured picture of yet a third bleeding head; and it was the head of Valentin himself. A second glance showed him it was only a Nationalist paper, called *The Guillotine*,* which every week showed one of its political opponents with rolling eyes and writhing features just after execution; for Valentin was an anticlerical of some note. But O'Brien was an Irishman, with a kind of chastity even in his sins; and his gorge rose against that great brutality of the intellect which belongs only to France. He felt Paris as a whole, from the grotesques on the Gothic churches to the gross caricatures in the newspapers. He remembered the gigantic jests of the Revolution. He saw the whole city as one ugly energy, from the sanguinary sketch lying on Valentin's table up to where, above a mountain and forest of gargoyles, the great devil grins on Notre Dame.

The library was long, low, and dark; what light entered it shot from under low blinds and had still some of the ruddy tinge of morning. Valentin and his servant Ivan were waiting for them at the upper end of a long, slightly-sloping desk, on which lay the mortal remains, looking enormous in the twilight. The big black figure and yellow face of the man found in the garden confronted them essentially unchanged. The second head, which had been fished from among the river reeds that morning, lay streaming and dripping beside it; Valentin's men were still seeking to recover the rest of this second corpse, which was supposed to be afloat. Father Brown, who did not seem to share O'Brien's sensibilities in the least, went up to the second head and examined it with his blinking care. It was little more than a mop of wet, white hair, fringed with silver fire in the red and level morning light; the face, which seemed of an ugly, empurpled and perhaps criminal type, had been much battered against trees or stones as it tossed in the water. To O'Brien it seemed the last touch of that Parisian nightmare that the apish face had this halo of silver hair like a saint.

'Good morning, Commandant O'Brien,' said Valentin, with quiet cordiality. 'You have heard of Brayne's last experiment in butchery, I suppose?'

Father Brown was still bending over the head with white hair, and he said, without looking up:

'I suppose it is quite certain that Brayne cut off this head, too.'

'Well, it seems common sense,' said Valentin, with his hands in his pockets. 'Killed in the same way as the other. Found within a few yards of the other. And sliced by the same weapon which we know he carried away.'

'Yes, yes; I know,' replied Father Brown, submissively. 'Yet, you know, I doubt whether Brayne could have cut off this head.'

'Why not?' inquired Dr Simon, with a rational stare.

'Well, doctor,' said the priest, looking up blinking, 'can a man cut off his own head? I don't know.'

O'Brien felt an insane universe crashing about his ears; but the doctor sprang forward with impetuous practicality and pushed back the wet, white hair.

'Oh, there's no doubt it's Brayne,' said the priest quietly. 'He had exactly that chip in the left ear.'

The detective, who had been regarding the priest with steady and glittering eyes, opened his clenched mouth and said sharply: 'You seem to know a lot about him, Father Brown.'

'I do,' said the little man simply. 'I've been about with him for some weeks. He was thinking of joining our church.'

The star of the fanatic sprang into Valentin's eyes; he strode towards the priest with clenched hands. 'And, perhaps,' he cried, with a blasting sneer: 'perhaps he was also thinking of leaving all his money to your church.'

'Perhaps he was,' said Brown stolidly; 'it is possible.'

'In that case,' cried Valentin, with a dreadful smile: 'you may indeed know a great deal about him. About his life and about his——'

Commandant O'Brien laid a hand on Valentin's arm. 'Drop that slanderous rubbish, Valentin,' he said: 'or there may be more swords yet.'

But Valentin (under the steady, humble gaze of the priest) had already recovered himself. 'Well,' he said shortly: 'people's private opinions can wait. You gentlemen are still bound by your promise to stay; you must enforce it on yourselves—and on each other. Ivan here will tell you anything more you want to know; I must get to business and write to the authorities. We can't keep this quiet any longer. I shall be writing in my study if there is any more news.'

'Is there any more news, Ivan?' asked Dr Simon, as the chief of police strode out of the room.

'Only one more thing, I think, sir,' said Ivan, wrinkling up his grey old face; 'but that's important, too, in its way. There's that old buffer you found on the lawn,' and he pointed without pretence of reverence at the big black body with the yellow head. 'We've found out who he is, anyhow.'

'Indeed!' cried the astonished doctor; 'and who is he?'

'His name was Arnold Becker,' said the under-detective, 'though he went by many aliases. He was a wandering sort of scamp, and is known to have been in America; so that was where Brayne got his knife into him. We didn't have much to do with him ourselves, for he worked mostly in Germany. We've communicated, of course, with the German police. But, oddly enough, there was a twin brother of his, named Louis Becker, with whom we had a great deal to do. In fact, we found it necessary to guillotine him only yesterday. Well, it's a rum thing, gentlemen, but when I saw that fellow flat on the lawn I had the greatest jump of my life. If I hadn't seen Louis Becker guillotined with my own eyes, I'd have sworn it was Louis Becker lying there in the grass. Then, of course, I remembered his twin brother in Germany, and following up the clue——'

The explanatory Ivan stopped, for the excellent reason that nobody was listening to him. The Commandant and the doctor were both staring at Father Brown, who had sprung stiffly to his feet, and was holding his temples tight like a man in sudden and violent pain.

'Stop, stop, stop!' he cried; 'stop talking a minute, for I see half. Will God give me strength? Will my brain make the one jump and see all? Heaven help me! I used to be fairly good at thinking. I could paraphrase any page in Aquinas* once. Will my head split—or will it see? I see half—I only see half.'

He buried his head in his hands, and stood in a sort of rigid torture of thought or prayer, while the other three could only go on staring at this last prodigy of their wild twelve hours.

When Father Brown's hands fell they showed a face quite fresh and serious, like a child's. He heaved a huge sigh, and said: 'Let us get this said and done with as quickly as possible. Look here, this will be the quickest way to convince you all of the truth.' He turned to the doctor. 'Dr Simon,' he said, 'you have a strong head-piece, and I heard you this morning asking the five hardest questions about this business. Well, if you will now ask them again, I will answer them.'

Simon's pince-nez dropped from his nose in his doubt and wonder, but he answered at once. 'Well, the first question, you know, is why a man should kill another with a clumsy sabre at all when a man can kill with a bodkin?'

'A man cannot behead with a bodkin,' said Brown, calmly, 'and for *this* murder beheading was absolutely necessary.'

'Why?' asked O'Brien, with interest.

'And the next question?' asked Father Brown.

'Well, why didn't the man cry out or anything?' asked the doctor; 'sabres in gardens are certainly unusual.'

'Twigs,' said the priest gloomily, and turned to the window which looked on the scene of death. 'No one saw the point of the twigs. Why should they lie on that lawn (look at it) so far from any tree? They were not snapped off; they were chopped off. The murderer occupied his enemy with some tricks with the sabre, showing how he could cut a branch in mid-air, or whatnot. Then, while his enemy bent down to see the result, a silent slash, and the head fell.'

'Well,' said the doctor slowly, 'that seems plausible enough. But my next two questions will stump anyone.'

The priest still stood looking critically out of the window and waited.

'You know how all the garden was sealed up like an airtight chamber,' went on the doctor. 'Well, how did the strange man get into the garden?'

Without turning round, the little priest answered: 'There never was any strange man in the garden.'

There was a silence, and then a sudden cackle of almost childish laughter relieved the strain. The absurdity of Brown's remark moved Ivan to open taunts.

'Oh!' he cried; 'then we didn't lug a great fat corpse on to a sofa last night? He hadn't got into the garden, I suppose?'

'Got into the garden?' repeated Brown reflectively. 'No, not entirely.'

'Hang it all,' cried Simon, 'a man gets into a garden, or he doesn't.'

'Not necessarily,' said the priest, with a faint smile. 'What is the next question, doctor?'

'I fancy you're ill,' exclaimed Dr Simon sharply; 'but I'll ask the next question if you like. How did Brayne get out of the garden?'

'He didn't get out of the garden,' said the priest, still looking out of the window.

'Didn't get out of the garden?' exploded Simon.

'Not completely,' said Father Brown.

Simon shook his fists in a frenzy of French logic. 'A man gets out of a garden, or he doesn't,' he cried.

'Not always,' said Father Brown.

Dr Simon sprang to his feet impatiently. 'I have no time to spare on such senseless talk,' he cried angrily. 'If you can't understand a man being on one side of the wall or the other, I won't trouble you further.'

'Doctor,' said the cleric very gently, 'we have always got on very pleasantly together. If only for the sake of old friendship, stop and tell me your fifth question.'

The impatient Simon sank into a chair by the door and said briefly: 'The head and shoulders were cut about in a queer way. It seemed to be done after death.'

'Yes,' said the motionless priest, 'it was done so as to make you assume exactly the one simple falsehood that you did assume. It was done to make you take for granted that the head belonged to the body.'

The borderland of the brain, where all the monsters are made, moved horribly in the Gaelic O'Brien. He felt the chaotic presence of all the horse-men and fish-women that man's unnatural fancy has begotten. A voice older than his first fathers seemed saying in his ear: 'Keep out of the monstrous garden where grows the tree with double fruit. Avoid the evil garden where died the man with two heads.' Yet, while these shameful symbolic shapes passed across the ancient mirror of his Irish soul, his Frenchified intellect was quite alert, and was watching the odd priest as closely and incredulously as all the rest.

Father Brown had turned round at last, and stood against the window with his face in dense shadow; but even in that shadow they could see it was pale as ashes. Nevertheless, he spoke quite sensibly, as if there were no Gaelic souls on earth.

'Gentlemen,' he said; 'you did not find the strange body of Becker in the garden. You did not find any strange body in the garden. In face of Dr Simon's rationalism, I still affirm that Becker was only partly present. Look here!' (pointing to the black bulk of the mysterious corpse); 'you never saw that man in your lives. Did you ever see this man?'

He rapidly rolled away the bald-yellow head of the unknown, and put in its place the white-maned head beside it. And there, complete, unified, unmistakable, lay Julius K.

Brayne in his plain black clothes, exactly as they had seen him, large and laughing, in the drawing-room.

'The murderer,' went on Brown quietly, 'hacked off his enemy's head and flung the sword far over the wall. But he was too clever to fling the sword only. He flung the *head* over the wall also. Then he had only to clap on another head to the corpse, and (as he insisted on a private inquest) you all imagined a totally new man.'

'Clap on another head!' said O'Brien, staring. 'What other head? Heads don't grow on garden bushes, do they?'

'No,' said Father Brown huskily, and looking at his boots; 'there is only one place where they grow. They grow in the basket of the guillotine, beside which the Chief of Police, Aristide Valentin, was standing not an hour before the murder. Oh, my friends, hear me a minute more before you tear me in pieces. Valentin is an honest man, if being mad for an arguable cause is honesty. But did you ever see in that cold, grey eye of his that he is mad? He would do anything, *anything*, to break what he calls the superstition of the Cross. He has fought for it and starved for it, and now he has murdered for it. Brayne's crazy millions had hitherto been scattered among so many sects that they did little to alter the balance of things. But Valentin heard a whisper that Brayne, like so many scatter-brained sceptics, was drifting to us; and that was quite a different thing. Brayne would pour supplies into the impoverished and pugnacious Church of France; he would support six Nationalist newspapers like *The Guillotine*. The battle was already balanced on a point, and the fanatic took flame at the risk. He resolved to destroy the millionaire, and he did it as one would expect the greatest of detectives to commit his only crime. He abstracted the severed head of Becker on some criminological excuse, and took it home in his official box. He had that last argument with Brayne, that Lord Galloway did not hear the end of; that failing, he led him out into the sealed garden, talked about swordsmanship, used twigs and a sabre for illustration, and——'

Ivan of the Scar sprang up, as if startled out of a trance. The dull rapidity and clearness with which the priest had unfolded the frightful actuality had held them so far with a paralyzed attention, but when Ivan found his voice it was the voice of the convulsed company. 'You filthy lunatic!' he yelled; 'and if my master does hate such shovel-hatted liars as you I reckon he's pretty well right. Well, he'll know how to finish you. He'll not leave much of you, my man; and you'll go to him now if I take you by the scruff of the neck.'

'Why, I was going there,' said Brown heavily; 'I must ask him to confess, and all that. If he does, it is not so very bad, you know, after all.'

Driving the unhappy Brown before them like a hostage or human sacrifice, they rushed together towards the back part of the house and tumbled somehow into the sudden stillness of Valentin's study.

The great detective sat at his desk apparently too occupied to hear their turbulent entrance. They paused a moment, and then something in the look of that upright and elegant back made the doctor run forward suddenly. A touch and a glance showed him that there was a small box of pills at Valentin's elbow, and that Valentin was dead in his chair; and on the blind face of the suicide was more than the pride of Cato.*

THE QUEER FEET

IF you meet a member of that select club, 'The Twelve True Fishermen,' entering the Vernon Hotel for the annual club dinner, you will observe, as he takes off his overcoat, that his evening coat is green and not black. If (supposing that you have the star-defying audacity to address such a being) you ask him why, he will probably answer that he does it to avoid being mistaken for a waiter. You will then retire crushed. But you will leave behind you a mystery as yet unsolved and a tale worth telling.

If (to pursue the same vein of improbable conjecture) you were to meet a mild, hard-working little priest, named Father Brown, and were to ask him what he thought was the most singular luck of his life, he would probably reply that upon the whole his best stroke was at the Vernon Hotel, where he had averted a crime and, perhaps, saved a soul, merely by listening to a few footsteps in a passage. He is perhaps a little proud of this wild and wonderful guess of his, and it is possible that he might refer to it. But since it is immeasurably unlikely that you will ever rise high enough in the social world to find 'The Twelve True Fishermen', or that you will ever sink low enough among slums and criminals to find Father Brown, I fear you will never hear the story at all unless you hear it from me.

The Vernon Hotel, at which The Twelve True Fishermen held their annual dinners, was an institution such as can only exist in an oligarchical society which has almost gone mad on good manners. It was that topsy-turvy product—an 'exclusive' commercial enterprise. That is, it was a thing which paid, not by attracting people, but actually by turning people away. In the heart of a plutocracy tradesmen become cunning enough to be more fastidious than their customers. They positively create difficulties so that their wealthy and weary clients may spend money and diplomacy in overcoming them. If there were a fashionable hotel in London which no man could enter who was under six foot, society would meekly make up parties of six-foot men to dine in it. If there were an expensive restaurant which by a mere caprice of its proprietor was only open on Thursday afternoon, it would be crowded on Thursday afternoon. The Vernon Hotel stood, as if by accident, in the corner of a square in Belgravia.* It was a small hotel; and a very inconvenient one. But its very inconveniences were considered as walls protecting a particular class. One inconvenience, in particular, was held to be of vital importance: the fact that practically only twenty-four people could dine in the place at once. The only big dinner table was the celebrated terrace table, which stood open to the air on a sort of veranda overlooking one of the most exquisite old gardens in London. Thus it happened that even the twenty-four seats at this table could only be enjoyed in warm weather; and this making the enjoyment yet more difficult made it yet more desired. The existing owner of the hotel was a Jew named Lever; and he made nearly a million out of it, by making it difficult to get into. Of course he combined with this limitation in the scope of his enterprise the most careful polish in its performance. The wines and cooking were really as good as any in Europe, and the demeanour of the attendants exactly mirrored the fixed mood of the English upper class. The proprietor knew all his waiters like the fingers on his hand; there were only fifteen of them all told. It was much easier to become a Member of Parliament than to become a waiter in that hotel. Each waiter was trained in terrible silence and smoothness, as if he were a gentleman's servant. And, indeed, there was generally at least one waiter to every gentleman who dined.

The club of The Twelve True Fishermen would not have consented to dine anywhere but in such a place, for it insisted on a luxurious privacy; and would have been quite upset by the mere thought that any other club was even dining in the same building. On the occasion of their annual dinner the Fishermen were in the habit of exposing all their treasures, as if they were in a private house, especially the celebrated set of fish knives and forks which were, as it were, the insignia of the society, each being exquisitely wrought in silver in the form of a fish, and each loaded at the hilt with one large pearl. These were always laid out for the fish course, and the fish course was always the most magnificent in that magnificent repast. The society had a vast number of ceremonies and observances, but it had no history and no object; that was where it was so very aristocratic. You did not have to be anything in order to be one of the Twelve Fishers; unless you were already a certain sort of person, you never even heard of them. It had been in existence twelve years. Its president was Mr Audley. Its vice-president was the Duke of Chester.

If I have in any degree conveyed the atmosphere of this appalling hotel, the reader may feel a natural wonder as to how I came to know anything about it, and may even speculate as to how so ordinary a person as my friend Father Brown came to find himself in that golden gallery. As far as that is concerned, my story is simple, or even vulgar. There is in the world a very aged rioter and demagogue who breaks into the most refined retreats with the dreadful information that all men are brothers, and wherever this leveller went on his pale horse* it was Father Brown's trade to follow. One of the waiters, an Italian, had been struck down with a paralytic stroke that afternoon; and his Jewish employer, marvelling

mildly at such superstitions, had consented to send for
the nearest Popish priest. With what the waiter confessed to
Father Brown we are not concerned, for the excellent reason
that the cleric kept it to himself; but apparently it involved
him in writing out a note or statement for the conveying of
some message or the righting of some wrong. Father Brown,
therefore, with a meek impudence which he would have
shown equally in Buckingham Palace, asked to be provided
with a room and writing materials. Mr Lever was torn in two.
He was a kind man, and had also that bad imitation of
kindness, the dislike of any difficulty or scene. At the same
time the presence of one unusual stranger in his hotel that
evening was like a speck of dirt on something just cleaned.
There was never any borderland or ante-room in the Vernon
Hotel, no people waiting in the hall, no customers coming in
on chance. There were fifteen waiters. There were twelve
guests. It would be as startling to find a new guest in the hotel
that night as to find a new brother taking breakfast or tea in
one's own family. Moreover, the priest's appearance was
second-rate and his clothes muddy; a mere glimpse of him
afar off might precipitate a crisis in the club. Mr Lever at last
hit on a plan to cover, since he might not obliterate, the disgrace. When you enter (as you never will) the Vernon Hotel,
you pass down a short passage decorated with a few dingy
but important pictures, and come to the main vestibule and
lounge which opens on your right into passages leading to the
public rooms, and on your left to a similar passage pointing to
the kitchens and offices of the hotel. Immediately on your left
hand is the corner of a glass office, which abuts upon the
lounge—a house within a house, so to speak, like the old hotel
bar which probably once occupied its place.

In this office sat the representative of the proprietor (nobody in this place ever appeared in person if he could help it),
and just beyond the office, on the way to the servants' quarters, was the gentlemen's cloakroom, the last boundary of the
gentlemen's domain. But between the office and the cloak-
room was a small private room without other outlet, sometimes used by the proprietor for delicate and important
matters, such as lending a duke a thousand pounds or declin-

ing to lend him sixpence. It is a mark of the magnificent tolerance of Mr Lever that he permitted this holy place to be for about half an hour profaned by a mere priest, scribbling away on a piece of paper. The story which Father Brown was writing down was very likely a much better story than this one, only it will never be known. I can merely state that it was very nearly as long, and that the last two or three paragraphs of it were the least exciting and absorbing.

For it was by the time he had reached these that the priest began a little to allow his thoughts to wander and his animal senses, which were commonly keen, to awaken. The time of darkness and dinner was drawing on; his own forgotten little room was without a light, and perhaps the gathering gloom, as occasionally happens, sharpened the sense of sound. As Father Brown wrote the last and least essential part of his document, he caught himself writing to the rhythm of a recurrent noise outside, just as one sometimes thinks to the tune of a railway train. When he became conscious of the thing he found what it was: only the ordinary patter of feet passing the door, which in an hotel was no very unlikely matter. Nevertheless, he stared at the darkened ceiling, and listened to the sound. After he had listened for a few seconds dreamily, he got to his feet and listened intently, with his head a little on one side. Then he sat down again and buried his brow in his hands, now not merely listening, but listening and thinking also.

The footsteps outside at any given moment were such as one might hear in any hotel; and yet, taken as a whole, there was something very strange about them. There were no other footsteps. It was always a very silent house, for the few familiar guests went at once to their own apartments, and the well-trained waiters were told to be almost invisible until they were wanted. One could not conceive any place where there was less reason to apprehend anything irregular. But these footsteps were so odd that one could not decide to call them regular or irregular. Father Brown followed them with his finger on the edge of the table, like a man trying to learn a tune on the piano.

First, there came a long rush of rapid little steps, such as a light man might make in winning a walking race. At a certain point they stopped and changed to a sort of slow, swinging stamp, numbering not a quarter of the steps, but occupying about the same time. The moment the last echoing stamp had died away would come again the run or ripple of light, hurrying feet, and then again the thud of the heavier walking. It was certainly the same pair of boots, partly because (as has been said) there were no other boots about, and partly because they had a small but unmistakable creak in them. Father Brown had the kind of head that cannot help asking questions; and on this apparently trivial question his head almost split. He had seen men run in order to jump. He had seen men run in order to slide. But why on earth should a man run in order to walk? Or, again, why should he walk in order to run? Yet no other description would cover the antics of this invisible pair of legs. The man was either walking very fast down one half of the corridor in order to walk very slow down the other half; or he was walking very slow at one end to have the rapture of walking fast at the other. Neither suggestion seemed to make much sense. His brain was growing darker and darker, like his room.

Yet, as he began to think steadily, the very blackness of his cell seemed to make his thoughts more vivid; he began to see as in a kind of vision the fantastic feet capering along the corridor in unnatural or symbolic attitudes. Was it a heathen religious dance? Or some entirely new kind of scientific exercise? Father Brown began to ask himself with more exactness what the steps suggested. Taking the slow step first; it certainly was not the step of the proprietor. Men of his type walk with a rapid waddle, or they sit still. It could not be any servant or messenger waiting for directions. It did not sound like it. The poorer orders (in an oligarchy) sometimes lurch about when they are slightly drunk, but generally, and especially in such gorgeous scenes, they stand or sit in constrained attitudes. No; that heavy yet springy step, with a kind of careless emphasis, not specially noisy, yet not caring what noise it made, belonged to only one of the animals of this earth. It was a gentleman of western Europe, and probably one who had never worked for his living.

Just as he came to this solid certainty, the step changed to the quicker one, and ran past the door as feverishly as a rat.

The listener remarked that though this step was much swifter it was also much more noiseless, almost as if the man were walking on tiptoe. Yet it was not associated in his mind with secrecy, but with something else—something that he could not remember. He was maddened by one of those half-memories that make a man feel half-witted. Surely he had heard that strange, swift walking somewhere. Suddenly he sprang to his feet with a new idea in his head, and walked to the door. His room had no direct outlet on the passage, but let on one side into the glass office, and on the other into the cloak-room beyond. He tried the door into the office, and found it locked. Then he looked at the window, now a square pane full of purple cloud cleft by livid sunset, and for an instant he smelt evil as a dog smells rats.

The rational part of him (whether the wiser or not) regained its supremacy. He remembered that the proprietor had told him that he should lock the door, and would come later to release him. He told himself that twenty things he had not thought of might explain the eccentric sounds outside; he reminded himself that there was just enough light left to finish his own proper work. Bringing his paper to the window so as to catch the last stormy evening light, he resolutely plunged once more into the almost completed record. He had written for about twenty minutes, bending closer and closer to his paper in the lessening light; then suddenly he sat upright. He had heard the strange feet once more.

This time they had a third oddity. Previously the unknown man had walked, with levity indeed and lightning quickness, but he had walked. This time he ran. One could hear the swift, soft, bounding steps coming along the corridor, like the pads of a fleeing and leaping panther. Whoever was coming was a very strong, active man, in still yet tearing excitement. Yet, when the sound had swept up to the office like a sort of whispering whirlwind, it suddenly changed again to the old slow, swaggering stamp.

Father Brown flung down his paper, and, knowing the office door to be locked, went at once into the cloak-room on the other side. The attendant of this place was temporarily absent, probably because the only guests were at dinner, and his office was a sinecure. After groping through a grey forest of over-coats, he found that the dim cloak-room opened on the lighted corridor in the form of a sort of counter or half-door, like most of the counters across which we have all handed um-brellas and received tickets. There was a light immediately above the semi-circular arch of this opening. It threw little illumination on Father Brown himself, who seemed a mere dark outline against the dim sunset window behind him. But it threw an almost theatrical light on the man who stood outside the cloak-room in the corridor.

He was an elegant man in very plain evening-dress; tall, but with an air of not taking up much room; one felt that he could have slid along like a shadow where many smaller men would have been obvious and obstructive. His face, now flung back in the lamplight, was swarthy and vivacious, the face of a foreigner. His figure was good, his manners good-humoured and confident; a critic could only say that his black coat was a shade below his figure and manners, and even bulged and bagged in an odd way. The moment he caught sight of Brown's black silhouette against the sunset, he tossed down a scrap of paper with a number and called out with amiable authority: 'I want my hat and coat, please; I find I have to go away at once.'

Father Brown took the paper without a word, and obedi-ently went to look for the coat; it was not the first menial work he had done in his life. He brought it and laid it on the counter; meanwhile, the strange gentleman who had been feeling in his waistcoat pocket, said, laughing: 'I haven't got any silver; you can keep this.' And he threw down half a sovereign, and caught up his coat.

Father Brown's figure remained quite dark and still; but in that instant he had lost his head. His head was always most valuable when he had lost it. In such moments he put two and two together and made four million. Often the Catholic Church (which is wedded to common sense) did not approve of it. Often he did not approve of it himself. But it was a real inspiration—important at rare crises—when whosoever shall lose his head the same shall save it.*

'I think, sir,' he said civilly, 'that you have some silver in your pocket.'

The tall gentleman stared. 'Hang it,' he cried. 'If I give you gold, why should you complain?'

'Because silver is sometimes more valuable than gold,' said the priest mildly; 'that is, in large quantities.'

The stranger looked at him curiously. Then he looked still more curiously up the passage towards the main entrance. Then he looked back at Brown again, and then he looked very carefully at the window beyond Brown's head, still coloured with the after-glow of the storm. Then he seemed to make up his mind. He put one hand on the counter, vaulted over as easily as an acrobat and towered above the priest, putting one tremendous hand upon his collar.

'Stand still,' he said, in a hacking whisper. 'I don't want to threaten you, but——'

'I do want to threaten you,' said Father Brown, in a voice like a rolling drum. 'I want to threaten you with the worm that dieth not, and the fire that is not quenched.'

'You're a rum sort of cloak-room clerk,' said the other.

'I am a priest, Monsieur Flambeau,' said Brown, 'and I am ready to hear your confession.'

The other stood gasping for a few moments, and then staggered back into a chair.

The first two courses of the dinner of The Twelve True Fishermen had proceeded with placid success. I do not possess a copy of the menu; and if I did it would not convey anything to anybody. It was written in a sort of super-French employed by cooks, but quite unintelligible to Frenchmen. There was a tradition in the club that the *hors d'œuvres* should be various and manifold to the point of madness. They were taken seriously because they were avowedly useless extras, like the whole dinner and the whole club. There was also a tradition that the soup course should be light and unpretending—a sort of simple and austere vigil for the feast of fish that was to come. The talk was that strange, slight talk which governs the British Empire, which governs it in secret, and yet would scarcely enlighten an ordinary Englishman even if he could overhear it. Cabinet Ministers on both sides were alluded to by their Christian names with a sort of bored benignity. The Radical Chancellor of the Exchequer, whom the whole Tory party was supposed to be cursing for his extortions, was praised for his minor poetry, or his saddle in the hunting-field. The Tory leader, whom all Liberals were supposed to hate as a tyrant, was discussed and, on the whole, praised—as a Liberal. It seemed somehow that politicians were very import-ant. And yet, anything seemed important about them except their politics. Mr Audley, the chairman, was an amiable, eld-erly man who still wore Gladstone collars;* he was a kind of symbol of all that phantasmal and yet fixed society. He had never done anything—not even anything wrong. He was not fast; he was not even particularly rich. He was simply in the thing; and there was an end of it. No party could ignore him, and if he had wished to be in the Cabinet he certainly would have been put there. The Duke of Chester, the vice-president, was a young and rising politician. That is to say, he was a pleasant youth, with flat, fair hair and a freckled face, with moderate intelligence and enormous estates. In public his appearances were always successful and his principle was simple enough. When he thought of a joke he made it, and was called brilliant. When he could not think of a joke he said that this was no time for trifling, and was called able. In private, in a club of his own class, he was simply quite pleasantly frank and silly, like a schoolboy. Mr Audley, never having been in politics, treated them a little more seriously. Sometimes he even embarrassed the company by phrases suggesting that there was some difference between a Liberal and a Conservative. He, himself, was a Conservative, even in private life. He had a roll of grey hair over the back of his collar like certain old-fashioned statesmen, and seen from behind he looked like the man the Empire wants. Seen from the front he looked like a mild, self-indulgent bachelor, with rooms in the Albany*—which he was.

As has been remarked, there were twenty-four seats at the terrace table, and only twelve members of the club. Thus they could occupy the terrace in the most luxurious style of all, being ranged along the inner side of the table, with no one opposite, commanding an uninterrupted view of the garden, the colours of which were still vivid, though evening was closing in somewhat luridly for the time of year. The chairman sat in the centre of the line, and the vice-president at the right-hand end of it. When the twelve guests first trooped into their seats it was the custom (for some unknown reason) for all the fifteen waiters to stand lining the wall like troops presenting arms to the king, while the fat proprietor stood and bowed to the club with radiant surprise, as if he had never heard of them before. But before the first chink of knife and fork this army of retainers had vanished, only the one or two required to collect and distribute the plates darting about in deathly silence. Mr Lever, the proprietor, of course had disappeared in convulsions of courtesy long before. It would be exaggerative, indeed irreverent, to say that he ever positively appeared again. But when the important course, the fish course, was being brought on, there was—how shall I put it?—a vivid shadow, a projection of his personality, which told that he was hovering near. The sacred fish course consisted (to the eyes of the vulgar) in a sort of monstrous pudding, about the size and shape of a wedding cake, in which some considerable number of interesting fishes had finally lost the shapes which God had given to them. The Twelve True Fishermen took up their celebrated fish knives and fish forks, and approached it as gravely as if every inch of the pudding cost as much as the silver fork it was eaten with. So it did, for all I know. This course was dealt with in eager and devouring silence; and it was only when his plate was nearly empty that the young duke made the ritual remark: 'They can't do this anywhere but here.'

'Nowhere,' said Mr Audley, in a deep bass voice, turning to the speaker and nodding his venerable head a number of times. 'Nowhere, assuredly, except here. It was represented to me that at the Café Anglais——'

Here he was interrupted and even agitated for a moment by the removal of his plate, but he recaptured the valuable thread of his thoughts. 'It was represented to me that the same could be done at the Café Anglais. Nothing like it, sir,' he said, shaking his head ruthlessly, like a hanging judge. 'Nothing like it.'

'Overrated place,' said a certain Colonel Pound, speaking (by the look of him) for the first time for some months.

'Oh, I don't know,' said the Duke of Chester, who was an optimist, 'it's jolly good for some things. You can't beat it at——'

A waiter came swiftly along the room, and then stopped dead. His stoppage was as silent as his tread; but all those vague and kindly gentlemen were so used to the utter smoothness of the unseen machinery which surrounded and supported their lives, that a waiter doing anything unexpected was a start and a jar. They felt as you and I would feel if the inanimate world disobeyed—if a chair ran away from us.

The waiter stood staring a few seconds, while there deepened on every face at table a strange shame which is wholly the product of our time. It is the combination of modern humanitarianism with the horrible modern abyss between the souls of the rich and poor. A genuine historic aristocrat would have thrown things at the waiter, beginning with empty bottles, and very probably ending with money. A genuine democrat would have asked him, with a comrade-like clearness of speech, what the devil he was doing. But these modern plutocrats could not bear a poor man near to them, either as a slave or as a friend. That something had gone wrong with the servants was merely a dull, hot embarrassment. They did not want to be brutal, and they dreaded the need to be benevolent. They wanted the thing, whatever it was, to be over. It was over. The waiter, after standing for some seconds rigid, like a cataleptic, turned round and ran madly out of the room.

When he reappeared in the room, or rather in the doorway, it was in company with another waiter, with whom he whispered and gesticulated with southern fierceness. Then the first waiter went away, leaving the second waiter, and reappeared with a third waiter. By the time a fourth waiter had joined this hurried synod, Mr Audley felt it necessary to break the silence in the interests of Tact. He used a very loud cough, instead of the presidential hammer, and said: 'Splendid work young Moocher's doing in Burmah. Now, no other nation in the world could have——'

A fifth waiter had sped towards him like an arrow, and was whispering in his ear: 'So sorry. Important! Might the proprietor speak to you?'

The chairman turned in disorder, and with a dazed stare saw Mr Lever coming towards them with his lumbering quickness. The gait of the good proprietor was indeed his usual gait, but his face was by no means usual. Generally it was a genial copper-brown; now it was a sickly yellow.

'You will pardon me, Mr Audley,' he said, with asthmatic breathlessness. 'I have great apprehensions. Your fish-plates, they are cleared away with the knife and fork on them!'

'Well, I hope so,' said the chairman, with some warmth.

'You see him?' panted the excited hotel keeper; 'you see the waiter who took them away? You know him?'

'Know the waiter?' answered Mr Audley indignantly. 'Certainly not!'

Mr Lever opened his hands with a gesture of agony. 'I never send him,' he said. 'I know not when or why he come. I send my waiter to take away the plates, and he find them already away.'

Mr Audley still looked rather too bewildered to be really the man the Empire wants; none of the company could say anything except the man of wood—Colonel Pound—who seemed galvanized into an unnatural life. He rose rigidly from his chair, leaving all the rest sitting, screwed his eyeglass into his eye, and spoke in a raucous undertone as if he had half-forgotten how to speak. 'Do you mean,' he said, 'that somebody has stolen our silver fish service?'

The proprietor repeated the open-handed gesture with even greater helplessness; and in a flash all the men at the table were on their feet.

'Are all your waiters here?' demanded the colonel, in his low, harsh accent.

'Yes; they're all here. I noticed it myself,' cried the young duke, pushing his boyish face into the inmost ring. 'Always count 'em as I come in; they look so queer standing up against the wall.'

'But surely one cannot exactly remember,' began Mr Audley, with heavy hesitation.

'I remember exactly, I tell you,' cried the duke excitedly. 'There never have been more than fifteen waiters at this place, and there were no more than fifteen to-night, I'll swear; no more and no less.'

The proprietor turned upon him, quaking in a kind of palsy of surprise. 'You say—you say,' he stammered, 'that you see all my fifteen waiters?'

'As usual,' assented the duke. 'What is the matter with that?'

'Nothing,' said Lever, with a deepening accent, 'only you did not. For one of zem is dead upstairs.'

There was a shocking stillness for an instant in that room. It may be (so supernatural is the word death) that each of those idle men looked for a second at his soul, and saw it as a small dried pea. One of them—the duke, I think—even said with the idiotic kindness of wealth: 'Is there anything we can do?'

'He has had a priest,' said the Jew, not untouched.

Then, as to the clang of doom, they awoke to their own position. For a few weird seconds they had really felt as if the fifteenth waiter might be the ghost of the dead man upstairs. They had been dumb under that oppression, for ghosts were to them an embarrassment, like beggars. But the remembrance of the silver broke the spell of the miraculous; broke it abruptly and with a brutal reaction. The colonel flung over his chair and strode to the door. 'If there was a fifteenth man here, friends,' he said, 'that fifteenth fellow was a thief. Down at once to the front and back doors and secure everything; then we'll talk. The twenty-four pearls are worth recovering.'

Mr Audley seemed at first to hesitate about whether it was gentlemanly to be in such a hurry about anything; but, seeing the duke dash down the stairs with youthful energy, he followed with a more mature motion.

At the same instant a sixth waiter ran into the room, and declared that he had found the pile of fish plates on a sideboard, with no trace of the silver.

The crowd of diners and attendants that tumbled helter-skelter down the passages divided into two groups. Most of the Fishermen followed the proprietor to the front room to demand news of any exit. Colonel Pound, with the chairman, the vice-president, and one or two others, darted down the corridor leading to the servants' quarters, as the more likely line of escape. As they did so they passed the dim alcove or cavern of the cloak-room, and saw a short, black-coated figure, presumably an attendant, standing a little way back in the shadow of it.

'Hallo there!' called out the duke. 'Have you seen anyone pass?'

The short figure did not answer the question directly, but merely said: 'Perhaps I have got what you are looking for, gentlemen.'

They paused, wavering and wondering, while he quietly went to the back of the cloak-room, and came back with both hands full of shining silver, which he laid out on the counter as calmly as a salesman. It took the form of a dozen quaintly shaped forks and knives.

'You—you——' began the colonel, quite thrown off his balance at last. Then he peered into the dim little room and saw two things: first, that the short, black-clad man was dressed like a clergyman; and, second, that the window of the room behind him was burst, as if someone had passed violently through.

'Valuable things to deposit in a cloak-room, aren't they?' remarked the clergyman, with cheerful composure.

'Did—did you steal those things?' stammered Mr Audley, with staring eyes.

'If I did,' said the cleric pleasantly, 'at least I am bringing them back again.'

'But you didn't,' said Colonel Pound, still staring at the broken window.

'To make a clean breast of it, I didn't,' said the other, with some humour. And he seated himself quite gravely on a stool.

'But you know who did,' said the colonel.

'I don't know his real name,' said the priest placidly; 'but I know something of his fighting weight, and a great deal about his spiritual difficulties. I formed the physical estimate when he was trying to throttle me, and the moral estimate when he repented.'

'Oh, I say—repented!' cried young Chester, with a sort of crow of laughter.

Father Brown got to his feet, putting his hands behind him. 'Odd, isn't it,' he said, 'that a thief and a vagabond should repent, when so many who are rich and secure remain hard and frivolous, and without fruit for God or man? But there, if you will excuse me, you trespass a little upon my province. If you doubt the penitence as a practical fact, there are your knives and forks. You are The Twelve True Fishers, and there are all your silver fish. But He has made me a fisher of men.'*

'Did you catch this man?' asked the colonel, frowning.

Father Brown looked him full in his frowning face. 'Yes,' he said, 'I caught him, with an unseen hook and an invisible line which is long enough to let him wander to the ends of the world, and still to bring him back with a twitch upon the thread.'*

There was a long silence. All the other men present drifted away to carry the recovered silver to their comrades, or to consult the proprietor about the queer condition of affairs. But the grim-faced colonel still sat sideways on the counter. swinging his long, lank legs and biting his dark moustache.

At last he said quietly to the priest: 'He must have been a clever fellow, but I think I know a cleverer.'

'He was a clever fellow,' answered the other, 'but I am not quite sure of what other you mean.'

'I mean you,' said the colonel, with a short laugh. 'I don't want to get the fellow jailed; make yourself easy about that. But I'd give a good many silver forks to know exactly how you fell into this affair, and how you got the stuff out of him. I reckon you're the most up-to-date devil of the present company.'

Father Brown seemed rather to like the saturnine candour of the soldier. 'Well,' he said, smiling, 'I mustn't tell you anything of the man's identity, or his own story, of course; but there's no particular reason why I shouldn't tell you of the mere outside facts which I found out for myself.'

He hopped over the barrier with unexpected activity, and sat beside Colonel Pound, kicking his short legs like a little boy on a gate. He began to tell the story as easily as if he were telling it to an old friend by a Christmas fire.

'You see, colonel,' he said, 'I was shut up in that small room there doing some writing, when I heard a pair of feet in this passage doing a dance that was as queer as the dance of death.* First came quick, funny little steps, like a man walking on tiptoe for a wager; then came slow, careless, creaking steps, as of a big man walking about with a cigar. But they were both made by the same feet, I swear, and they came in rotation; first the run and then the walk, and then the run again. I wondered at first idly, and then wildly why a man should act these two parts at once. One walk I knew; it was just like yours, colonel. It was the walk of a well-fed gentleman waiting for something, who strolls about rather because he is physically alert than because he is mentally impatient. I knew that I knew the other walk, too, but I could not remember what it was. What wild creature had I met on my travels that tore along on tiptoe in that extraordinary style? Then I heard a clink of plates somewhere; and the answer stood up as plain as St Peter's.* It was the walk of a waiter—that walk with the body slanted forward, the eyes looking down, the ball of the toe spurning away the ground, the coat tails and napkin flying. Then I thought for a minute and a half more. And I believe I saw the manner of the crime, as clearly as if I were going to commit it.'

Colonel Pound looked at him keenly, but the speaker's mild grey eyes were fixed upon the ceiling with almost empty wistfulness.

'A crime,' he said slowly, 'is like any other work of art. Don't look surprised; crimes are by no means the only works of art that come from an infernal workshop. But every work of art, divine or diabolic, has one indispensable mark—I mean, that the centre of it is simple, however much the fulfilment may be complicated. Thus, in *Hamlet*, let us say, the grotesqueness of the grave-digger, the flowers of the mad girl, the fantastic finery of Osric, the pallor of the ghost and the grin of the skull are all oddities in a sort of tangled wreath round one plain tragic figure of a man in black. Well, this also,' he said, getting slowly down from his seat with a smile, 'this also is the plain tragedy of a man in black. Yes,' he went on, seeing the colonel look up in some wonder, 'the whole of this tale turns on a black coat. In this, as in *Hamlet*, there are the rococo excrescences—yourselves, let us say. There is the dead waiter, who was there when he could not be there. There is the invisible hand that swept your table clear of silver and melted into air. But every clever crime is founded ultimately on some one quite simple fact—some fact that is not itself mysterious. The mystification comes in covering it up, in leading men's thoughts away from it. This large and subtle and (in the ordinary course) most profitable crime, was built on the plain fact that a gentleman's evening dress is the same as a waiter's. All the rest was acting, and thundering good acting, too.'

'Still,' said the colonel, getting up and frowning at his boots. 'I am not sure that I understand.'

'Colonel,' said Father Brown, 'I tell you that this archangel of impudence who stole your forks walked up and down this passage twenty times in the blaze of all the lamps, in the glare of all the eyes. He did not go and hide in dim corners where suspicion might have searched for him. He kept constantly on the move in the lighted corridors, and everywhere that he went he seemed to be there by right. Don't ask me what he was like; you have seen him yourself six or seven times to-night. You were waiting with all the other grand people in the reception room at the end of the passage there, with the terrace just beyond. Whenever he came among you gentlemen, he came in the lightning style of a waiter, with bent head, flapping napkin and flying feet. He shot out on to the terrace, did something to the table-cloth, and shot back again towards the office and the waiters' quarters. By the time he had come under the eye of the office clerk and the waiters he had become another man in every inch of his body, in every instinctive gesture. He strolled among the servants with the absent-minded insolence which they have all seen in their patrons. It was no new thing to them that a swell from the dinner party should pace all parts of the house like an animal at the Zoo; they know that nothing marks the Smart Set more than a habit of walking where one chooses. When he was magnificently weary of walking down that particular passage he would wheel round and pace back past the office; in the shadow of the arch just beyond he was altered as by a blast of magic, and went hurrying forward again among the Twelve Fishermen, an obsequious attendant. Why should the gentlemen look at a chance waiter? Why should the waiters suspect a first-rate walking gentleman? Once or twice he played the coolest tricks. In the proprietor's private quarters he called out breezily for a syphon of soda water, saying he was thirsty. He said genially that he would carry it himself, and he did; he carried it quickly and correctly through the thick of you, a waiter with an obvious errand. Of course, it could not have been kept up long, but it only had to be kept up till the end of the fish course.

'His worst moment was when the waiters stood in a row; but even then he contrived to lean against the wall just around the corner in such a way that for that important instant the waiters thought him a gentleman, while the gentlemen thought him a waiter. The rest went like winking. If any waiter caught him away from the table, that waiter caught a languid aristocrat. He had only to time himself two minutes before the fish was cleared, become a swift servant, and clear it himself. He put the plates down on a sideboard, stuffed the silver in his breast pocket, giving it a bulgy look, and ran like a hare (I heard him coming) till he came to the cloak-room. There he had only to be a plutocrat again—a plutocrat called away suddenly on business. He had only to give his ticket to the cloak-room attendant, and go out again elegantly as he had come in. Only—only I happened to be the cloak-room attendant.'

'What did you do to him?' cried the colonel, with unusual intensity. 'What did he tell you?'

'I beg your pardon,' said the priest immovably, 'that is where the story ends.'

'And the interesting story begins,' muttered Pound. 'I think I understand his professional trick. But I don't seem to have got hold of yours.'

'I must be going,' said Father Brown.

They walked together along the passage to the entrance hall, where they saw the fresh, freckled face of the Duke of Chester, who was bounding buoyantly along towards them.

'Come along, Pound,' he cried breathlessly. 'I've been look-ing for you everywhere. The dinner's going again in spanking style, and old Audley has got to make a speech in honour of the forks being saved. We want to start some new ceremony, don't you know, to commemorate the occasion. I say, you really got the goods back, what do you suggest?'

'Why,' said the colonel, eyeing him with a certain sardonic approval. 'I should suggest that henceforward we wear green coats, instead of black. One never knows what mistakes may arise when one looks so like a waiter.'

'Oh, hang it all!' said the young man, 'a gentleman never looks like a waiter.'

'Nor a waiter like a gentleman, I suppose,' said Colonel Pound, with the same lowering laughter on his face. 'Reverend sir, your friend must have been very smart to act the gentle-man.'

Father Brown buttoned up his commonplace overcoat to the neck, for the night was stormy, and took his commonplace umbrella from the stand.

'Yes,' he said; 'it must be very hard work to be a gentleman; but, do you know, I have sometimes thought that it may be almost as laborious to be a waiter.'

And saying 'Good evening,' he pushed open the heavy doors of that palace of pleasures. The golden gates closed behind him, and he went at a brisk walk through the damp, dark streets in search of a penny omnibus.

THE FLYING STARS

'THE most beautiful crime I ever committed,' Flambeau would say in his highly moral old age, 'was also, by a singular coincidence, my last. It was committed at Christmas. As an artist I had always attempted to provide crimes suitable to the special season or landscapes in which I found myself, choosing this or that terrace or garden for a catastrophe, as if for a statuary group. Thus squires should be swindled in long rooms panelled with oak; while Jews, on the other hand, should rather find themselves unexpectedly penniless among the light and screens of the Café Riche. Thus, in England, if I wished to relieve a dean of his riches (which is not so easy as you might suppose), I wished to frame him, if I make myself clear, in the green lawns and grey towers of some cathedral town. Similarly, in France, when I had got money out of a rich and wicked peasant (which is almost impossible), it gratified me to get his indignant head relieved against a grey line of clipped poplars, and those solemn plains of Gaul over which broods the mighty spirit of Millet.*

'Well, my last crime was a Christmas crime, a cheery, cosy, English middle-class crime; a crime of Charles Dickens. I did it in a good old middle-class house near Putney,* a house with a crescent of carriage drive, a house with a stable by the side of it, a house with the name on the two outer gates, a house with a monkey tree.* Enough, you know the species. I really think my imitation of Dickens's style was dexterous and literary. It seems almost a pity I repented the same evening.'

Flambeau would then proceed to tell the story from the inside; and even from the inside it was odd. Seen from the outside it was perfectly incomprehensible, and it is from the outside that the stranger must study it. From this standpoint the drama may be said to have begun when the front doors of the house with the stable opened on the garden with the monkey tree, and a young girl came out with bread to feed the birds on the afternoon of Boxing Day.* She had a pretty face, with brave brown eyes; but her figure was beyond conjecture, for she was so wrapped up in brown furs that it was hard to say which was hair and which was fur. But for the attractive face she might have been a small toddling bear.

The winter afternoon was reddening towards evening, and already a ruby light was rolled over the bloomless beds, filling them, as it were, with the ghosts of the dead roses. On the one side of the house stood the stable, on the other an alley or cloister of laurels led to the larger garden behind. The young lady, having scattered bread for the birds (for the fourth or fifth time that day, because the dog ate it), passed unobtrusively down the lane of laurels and into a glimmering plantation of evergreens behind. Here she gave an exclamation of wonder, real or ritual, and looking up at the high garden wall above her, beheld it fantastically bestridden by a somewhat fantastic figure.

'Oh, don't jump, Mr Crook,' she called out in some alarm; 'it's much too high.'

The individual riding the party wall like an aerial horse was a tall, angular young man, with dark hair sticking up like a hair brush, intelligent and even distinguished lineaments, but a sallow and almost alien complexion. This showed the more plainly because he wore an aggressive red tie, the only part of his costume of which he seemed to take any care. Perhaps it was a symbol. He took no notice of the girl's alarmed adjuration, but leapt like a grasshopper to the ground beside her, where he might very well have broken his legs.

'I think I was meant to be a burglar,' he said placidly, 'and I have no doubt I should have been if I hadn't happened to be born in that nice house next door. I can't see any harm in it, anyhow.'

'How can you say such things?' she remonstrated.

'Well,' said the young man, 'if you're born on the wrong side of the wall, I can't see that it's wrong to climb over.'

'I never know what you will say or do next,' she said.

'I don't often know myself,' replied Mr Crook; 'but then I am on the right side of the wall now.'

'And which is the right side of the wall?' asked the young lady, smiling.

'Whichever side you are on,' said the young man named Crook.

As they went together through the laurels towards the front garden a motor horn sounded thrice, coming nearer and nearer, and a car of splendid speed, great elegance, and a pale green colour swept up to the front doors like a bird and stood throbbing.

'Hullo, hullo!' said the young man with the red tie; 'here's somebody born on the right side, anyhow. I didn't know, Miss Adams, that your Santa Claus was so modern as this.'

'Oh, that's my godfather, Sir Leopold Fischer. He always comes on Boxing Day.'

Then, after an innocent pause, which unconsciously betrayed some lack of enthusiasm, Ruby Adams added:

'He is very kind.'

John Crook, journalist, had heard of that eminent City magnate; and it was not his fault if the City magnate had not heard of him; for in certain articles in *The Clarion** or *The New Age** Sir Leopold had been dealt with austerely. But he said nothing and grimly watched the unloading of the motor-car, which was rather a long process. A large, neat chauffeur in green got out from the front, and a small, neat manservant in grey got out from the back, and between them they deposited Sir Leopold on the doorstep and began to unpack him, like some very carefully protected parcel. Rugs enough to stock a bazaar, furs of all the beasts of the forest, and scarves of all the colours of the rainbow were unwrapped one by one, till they revealed something resembling the human form; the form of a friendly, but foreign-looking old gentleman, with a grey goat-like beard and a beaming smile, who rubbed his big fur gloves together.

Long before this revelation was complete the two big doors of the porch had opened in the middle, and Colonel Adams (father of the furry young lady) had come out himself to invite his eminent guest inside. He was a tall, sunburnt and very silent man, who wore a red smoking-cap like a fez, making him look like one of the English Sirdars or Pashas* in Egypt. With him was his brother-in-law, lately come from Canada, a big and rather boisterous young gentleman-farmer, with a yellow beard, by name James Blount. With him also was the more insignificant figure of the priest from the neighbouring Roman church; for the colonel's late wife had been a Catholic, and the children, as is common in such cases, had been trained to follow her. Everything seemed undistinguished about the priest, even down to his name, which was Brown; yet the colonel had always found something companionable about him, and frequently asked him to such family gatherings.

In the large entrance hall of the house there was ample room even for Sir Leopold and the removal of his wraps. Porch and vestibule, indeed, were unduly large in proportion to the house, and formed, as it were, a big room with the front door at one end, and the bottom of the staircase at the other. In front of the large hall fire, over which hung the colonel's sword, the process was completed and the company, including the saturnine Crook, presented to Sir Leopold Fischer. That venerable financier, however, still seemed struggling with portions of his well-lined attire, and at length produced from a very interior tail-coat pocket, a black oval case which he radiantly explained to be his Christmas present for his goddaughter. With an unaffected vainglory that had something disarming about it he held out the case before them all; it flew open at a touch and half-blinded them. It was just as if a crystal fountain had spurted in their eyes. In a nest of orange velvet lay like three eggs, three white and vivid diamonds that seemed to set the very air on fire all round them. Fischer stood beaming benevolently and drinking deep of the astonishment and ecstasy of the girl, the grim admiration and gruff thanks of the colonel, the wonder of the whole group.

'I'll put 'em back now, my dear,' said Fischer, returning the case to the tails of his coat. 'I had to be careful of 'em coming down. They're the three great African diamonds called "The Flying Stars," because they've been stolen so often. All the big criminals are on the track; but even the rough men about in the streets and hotels could hardly have kept their hands off them. I might have lost them on the road here. It was quite possible.'

'Quite natural, I should say,' growled the man in the red tie. 'I shouldn't blame 'em if they had taken 'em. When they ask for bread, and you don't even give them a stone, I think they might take the stone for themselves.'

'I won't have you talking like that,' cried the girl, who was in a curious glow. 'You've only talked like that since you became a horrid what's-his-name. You know what I mean. What do you call a man who wants to embrace the chimney-sweep?'

'A saint,' said Father Brown.

'I think,' said Sir Leopold, with a supercilious smile, 'that Ruby means a Socialist.'

'A Radical does not mean a man who lives on radishes,' remarked Crook, with some impatience; 'and a Conservative does not mean a man who preserves jam. Neither, I assure you, does a Socialist mean a man who desires a social evening with the chimney-sweep. A Socialist means a man who wants all the chimneys swept and all the chimney-sweeps paid for it.'

'But who won't allow you,' put in the priest in a low voice, 'to own your own soot.'

Crook looked at him with an eye of interest and even respect. 'Does one want to own soot?' he asked.

'One might,' answered Brown, with speculation in his eye. 'I've heard that gardeners use it. And I once made six children happy at Christmas when the conjurer didn't come, entirely with soot—applied externally.'

'Oh, splendid,' cried Ruby. 'Oh, I wish you'd do it to this company.'

The boisterous Canadian, Mr Blount, was lifting his loud voice in applause, and the astonished financier his (in some considerable deprecation), when a knock sounded at the double front doors. The priest opened them, and they showed again the front garden of evergreens, monkey-tree and all, now gathering gloom against a gorgeous violet sunset. The scene thus framed was so coloured and quaint, like a back scene in a play, that they forgot for a moment the insignificant figure standing in the door. He was dusty-looking and in a frayed coat, evidently a common messenger. 'Any of you gentlemen Mr Blount?' he asked, and held forward a letter doubtfully. Mr Blount started, and stopped in his shout of assent. Ripping up the envelope with evident astonishment, he read it; his face clouded a little, and then cleared, and he turned to his brother-in-law and host.

'I'm sick at being such a nuisance, colonel,' he said, with the cheery colonial convention; 'but would it upset you if an old acquaintance called on me here to-night on business? In point of fact it's Florian, that famous French acrobat and comic actor; I knew him years ago out West (he was a French-Canadian by birth), and he seems to have business for me, though I hardly guess what.'

'Of course, of course,' replied the colonel carelessly. 'My dear chap, any friend of yours. No doubt he will prove an acquisition.'

'He'll black his face, if that's what you mean,' cried Blount, laughing. 'I don't doubt he'd black everyone else's eyes. I don't care; I'm not refined. I like the jolly old pantomime where a man sits on his top hat.'

'Not on mine, please,' said Sir Leopold Fischer, with dignity.

'Well, well,' observed Crook, airily, 'don't let's quarrel. There are lower jokes than sitting on a top hat.'

Dislike of the red-tied youth, both of his predatory opinions and evident intimacy with the pretty godchild, led Fischer to say, in his most sarcastic, magisterial manner: 'No doubt you have found something much lower than sitting on a top hat. What is it, pray?'

'Letting a top hat sit on you, for instance,' said the Socialist.

'Now, now, now,' cried the Canadian farmer with his bar-barian benevolence, 'don't let's spoil a jolly evening. What I say is, let's do something for the company to-night. Not blacking faces or sitting on hats, if you don't like those—but something of the sort. Why couldn't we have a proper old English pantomime*—clown, columbine, and so on. I saw one when I left England at twelve years old, and it's blazed in my brain like a bonfire ever since. I came back to the old country only last year, and I find the thing's extinct. Nothing but a lot of snivelling fairy plays. I want a hot poker and a policeman made into sausages, and they give me princesses moralizing by moonlight, Blue Birds,* or something. Blue Beard's* more in my line, and him I liked best when he turned into the pantaloon.'

'I'm all for making a policeman into sausages,' said John Crook. 'It's a better definition of Socialism than some recently given. But surely the get-up would be too big a business.'

'Not a scrap,' cried Blount, quite carried away. 'A harlequinade's the quickest thing we can do, for two reasons. First, one can gag to any degree; and, second, all the objects are household things—tables and towel-horses* and washing baskets, and things like that.'

'That's true,' admitted Crook, nodding eagerly and walking about. 'But I'm afraid I can't have my policeman's uniform! Haven't killed a policeman lately.'

Blount frowned thoughtfully a space, and then smote his thigh. 'Yes, we can!' he cried. 'I've got Florian's address here, and he knows every *costumier* in London. I'll 'phone him to bring a police dress when he comes.' And he went bounding away to the telephone.

'Oh, it's glorious, godfather,' cried Ruby, almost dancing. 'I'll be columbine and you shall be pantaloon.'

The millionaire held himself stiff with a sort of heathen solemnity. 'I think, my dear,' he said, 'you must get someone else for pantaloon.'

'I will be pantaloon, if you like,' said Colonel Adams, taking his cigar out of his mouth, and speaking for the first and last time.

'You ought to have a statue,' cried the Canadian, as he came back, radiant, from the telephone. 'There, we are all fitted. Mr Crook shall be clown; he's a journalist and knows all the oldest jokes. I can be harlequin, that only wants long legs and jumping about. My friend Florian 'phones he's bringing the police costume; he's changing on the way. We can act it in this very hall, the audience sitting on those broad stairs opposite, one row above another. These front doors can be the back scene, either open or shut. Shut, you see an English interior. Open, a moonlit garden. It all goes by magic.' And snatching a chance piece of billiard chalk from his pocket, he ran it across the hall floor, half-way between the front door and the staircase, to mark the line of the footlights.

How even such a banquet of bosh was got ready in the time remained a riddle. But they went at it with that mixture of recklessness and industry that lives when youth is in a house; and youth was in that house that night, though not all may have isolated the two faces and hearts from which it flamed. As always happens, the invention grew wilder and wilder through the very tameness of the *bourgeois* conventions from which it had to create. The columbine looked charming in an outstanding skirt that strangely resembled the large lamp-shade in the drawing-room. The clown and pantaloon made themselves white with flour from the cook, and red with rouge from some other domestic, who remained (like all true Christian benefactors) anonymous. The harlequin, already clad in silver paper out of cigar boxes, was, with difficulty, prevented from smashing the old Victorian lustre chandeliers, that he might cover himself with resplendent crystals. In fact he would certainly have done so, had not Ruby unearthed some old pantomime paste jewels she had worn at a fancy-dress party as the Queen of Diamonds. Indeed, her uncle, James Blount, was getting almost out of hand in his excitement; he was like a schoolboy. He put a paper donkey's head unexpectedly on Father Brown, who bore it patiently, and even found some private manner of moving his ears. He even essayed to put the paper donkey's tail to the coat-tails of Sir Leopold Fischer. This, however, was frowned down. 'Uncle is too absurd,' cried Ruby to Crook, round whose shoulders she had seriously placed a string of sausages. 'Why is he so wild?'

'He is harlequin to your columbine,' said Crook. 'I am only the clown who makes the old jokes.'

'I wish you were the harlequin,' she said, and left the string of sausages swinging.

Father Brown, though he knew every detail done behind the scenes, and had even evoked applause by his transformation of a pillow into a pantomime baby, went round to the front and sat among the audience with all the solemn expectation of a child at his first matinée. The spectators were few, relations, one or two local friends, and the servants; Sir Leopold sat in the front seat, his full and still fur-collared figure largely obscuring the view of the little cleric behind him; but it has never been settled by artistic authorities whether the cleric lost much. The pantomime was utterly chaotic, yet not contemptible; there ran through it a rage of improvisation which came chiefly from Crook the clown. Commonly he was a clever man, and he was inspired to-night with a wild omniscience, a folly wiser than the world, that which comes to a young man who has seen for an instant a particular expression on a particular face. He was supposed to be the clown, but he was really almost everything else, the author (so far as there was an author), the prompter, the scene-painter, the scene-shifter, and, above all, the orchestra. At abrupt intervals in the outrageous performance he would hurl himself in full costume at the piano and bang out some popular music equally absurd and appropriate.

The climax of this, as of all else, was the moment when the two front doors at the back of the scene flew open, showing the lovely moonlit garden, but showing more prominently the famous professional guest; the great Florian, dressed up as a policeman. The clown at the piano played the constabulary chorus in the *Pirates of Penzance*,* but it was drowned in the deafening applause, for every gesture of the great comic actor was an admirable though restrained version of the carriage and manner of the police. The harlequin leapt upon him and hit him over the helmet; the pianist playing 'Where did you get that hat?' he faced about in admirably simulated astonishment, and then the leaping harlequin hit him again (the pianist suggesting a few bars of 'Then we had another one'). Then the harlequin rushed right into the arms of the policeman and fell on top of him, amid a roar of applause. Then it was that the strange actor gave that celebrated imitation of a dead man, of which the fame still lingers round Putney. It was almost impossible to believe that a living person could appear so limp.

The athletic harlequin swung him about like a sack or twisted or tossed him like an Indian club; all the time to the most maddeningly ludicrous tunes from the piano. When the harlequin heaved the comic constable heavily off the floor the clown played 'I arise from dreams of thee.' When he shuffled him across his back, 'With my bundle on my shoulder,' and when the harlequin finally let fall the policeman with a most convincing thud, the lunatic at the instrument struck into a jingling measure with some words which are still believed to have been, 'I sent a letter to my love and on the way I dropped it.'

At about this limit of mental anarchy Father Brown's view was obscured altogether; for the City magnate in front of him rose to his full height and thrust his hands savagely into all his pockets. Then he sat down nervously, still fumbling, and then stood up again. For an instant it seemed seriously likely that he would stride across the footlights; then he turned a glare at the clown playing the piano; and then he burst in silence out of the room.

The priest had only watched for a few more minutes the absurd but not inelegant dance of the amateur harlequin over his splendidly unconscious foe. With real though rude art, the harlequin danced slowly backwards out of the door into the garden, which was full of moonlight and stillness. The vamped dress of silver paper and paste, which had been too glaring in the footlights, looked more and more magical and silvery as it danced away under a brilliant moon. The audience was closing in with a cataract of applause, when Brown felt his arm abruptly touched, and he was asked in a whisper to come into the colonel's study.

He followed his summoner with increasing doubt, which was not dispelled by a solemn comicality in the scene of the study. There sat Colonel Adams, still unaffectedly dressed as a pantaloon, with the knobbed whalebone nodding above his brow, but with his poor old eyes sad enough to have sobered a Saturnalia. Sir Leopold Fischer was leaning against the mantelpiece and heaving with all the importance of panic.

'This is a very painful matter, Father Brown,' said Adams. 'The truth is, those diamonds we all saw this afternoon seem to have vanished from my friend's tail-coat pocket. And as you——'

'As I,' supplemented Father Brown, with a broad grin, 'was sitting just behind him——'

'Nothing of the sort shall be suggested,' said Colonel Adams, with a firm look at Fischer, which rather implied that some such thing *had* been suggested. 'I only ask you to give me the assistance that any gentleman might give.'

'Which is turning out his pockets,' said Father Brown, and proceeded to do so, displaying seven and sixpence, a return ticket, a small silver crucifix, a small breviary, and a stick of chocolate.

The colonel looked at him long and then said: 'Do you know, I should like to see the inside of your head more than the inside of your pockets. My daughter is one of your people, I know; well, she has lately——' and he stopped.

'She has lately,' cried out old Fischer, 'opened her father's house to a cut-throat Socialist, who says openly he would steal anything from a richer man. This is the end of it. Here is the richer man—and none the richer.'

'If you want the inside of my head you can have it,' said Father Brown rather wearily. 'What it's worth you can say afterwards. But the first thing I find in that disused pocket is this; that men who mean to steal diamonds don't talk Socialism. They are more likely,' he added demurely, 'to denounce it.'

Both the others shifted sharply, and the priest went on:

'You see, we know these people, more or less. That Socialist would no more steal a diamond than a Pyramid. We ought to look at once to the one man we don't know. The fellow acting the policeman—Florian. Where is he exactly at this minute, I wonder?'

The pantaloon sprang erect and strode out of the room. An interlude ensued, during which the millionaire stared at the priest, and the priest at his breviary; then the pantaloon returned and said, with *staccato* gravity: 'The policeman is still lying on the stage. The curtain has gone up and down six times; he is still lying there.'

Father Brown dropped his book and stood staring with a look of blank mental ruin. Very slowly a light began to creep back in his grey eyes, and then he made the scarcely obvious answer.

'Please forgive me, colonel, but when did your wife die?'

'My wife!' replied the staring soldier, 'she died this year two months. Her brother James arrived just a week too late to see her.'

The little priest bounded like a rabbit shot. 'Come on!' he cried in quite unusual excitement. 'Come on! We've got to go and look at that policeman!'

They rushed on to the now curtained stage, breaking rudely past the columbine and clown (who seemed whispering quite contentedly), and Father Brown bent over the prostrate comic policeman.

'Chloroform,' he said as he rose; 'I only guessed it just now.'

There was a startled stillness, and then the colonel said slowly: 'Please say seriously what all this means.'

Father Brown suddenly shouted with laughter, then stopped, and only struggled with it for instants during the rest of his speech. 'Gentlemen,' he gasped, 'there's not much time to talk. I must run after the criminal. But this great French actor who played the policeman—this clever corpse the harlequin waltzed with and dandled and threw about—he was——' His voice again failed him, and he turned his back to run.

'He was?' called Fischer inquiringly.

'A real policeman,' said Father Brown, and ran away, into the dark.

There were hollows and bowers at the extreme end of that leafy garden, in which the laurels and other immortal shrubs showed against sapphire sky and silver moon, even in that midwinter, warm colours as of the south. The green gaiety of the waving laurels, the rich purple indigo of the night, the moon like a monstrous crystal, make an almost irresponsibly romantic picture; and among the top branches of the garden trees a strange figure is climbing, who looks not so much romantic as impossible. He sparkles from head to heel, as if clad in ten million moons; the real moon catches him at every movement and sets a new inch of him on fire. But he swings, flashing and successful, from the short tree in this garden to the tall, rambling tree in the other, and only stops there because a shade has slid under the smaller tree and has unmistakably called up to him.

'Well, Flambeau,' says the voice, 'you really look like a Flying Star; but that always means a Falling Star at last.'

The silver, sparkling figure above seems to lean forward in the laurels and, confident of escape, listens to the little figure below.

'You never did anything better, Flambeau. It was clever to come from Canada (with a Paris ticket, I suppose) just a week after Mrs Adams died, when no one was in a mood to ask questions. It was cleverer to have marked down the Flying Stars and the very day of Fischer's coming. But there's no cleverness, but mere genius, in what followed. Stealing the stones, I suppose, was nothing to you. You could have done it by sleight of hand in a hundred other ways besides that pretence of putting a paper donkey's tail to Fischer's coat. But in the rest you eclipsed yourself.'

The silvery figure among the green leaves seems to linger as if hypnotized, though his escape is easy behind him; he is staring at the man below.

'Oh, yes,' says the man below, 'I know all about it. I know you not only forced the pantomime, but put it to a double use. You were going to steal the stones quietly; news came by an accomplice that you were already suspected, and a capable police-officer was coming to rout you up that very night. A common thief would have been thankful for the warning and fled; but you are a poet. You already had the clever notion of hiding the jewels in a blaze of false stage jewellery. Now, you saw that if the dress were a harlequin's the appearance of a policeman would be quite in keeping. The worthy officer started from Putney police station to find you, and walked into the queerest trap ever set in this world. When the front door opened he walked straight on to the stage of a Christmas pantomime, where he could be kicked, clubbed, stunned and drugged by the dancing harlequin, amid roars of laughter from all the most respectable people in Putney. Oh, you will never do anything better. And now, by the way, you might give me back those diamonds.'

The green branch on which the glittering figure swung, rustled as if in astonishment; but the voice went on:

'I want you to give them back, Flambeau, and I want you to give up this life. There is still youth and honour and humour in you; don't fancy they will last in that trade. Men may keep a sort of level of good, but no man has ever been able to keep on one level of evil. That road goes down and down. The kind man drinks and turns cruel; the frank man kills and lies about it. Many a man I've known started like you to be an honest outlaw, a merry robber of the rich, and ended stamped into slime. Maurice Blum started out as an anarchist of principle, a father of the poor; he ended a greasy spy and tale-bearer that both sides used and despised. Harry Burke started his free money movement sincerely enough; now he's sponging on a half-starved sister for endless brandies and sodas. Lord Amber went into wild society in a sort of chivalry; now he's paying blackmail to the lowest vultures in London. Captain Barillon was the great gentleman-apache before your time; he died in a madhouse, screaming with fear of the 'narks'* and receivers that had betrayed him and hunted him down. I know the woods look very free behind you, Flambeau; I know that in a flash you could melt into them like a monkey. But some day you will be an old grey monkey, Flambeau. You will sit up in your tree forest cold at heart and close to death, and the tree-tops will be very bare.'

Everything continued still, as if the small man below held the other in the tree in some long invisible leash;* and he went on:

'Your downward steps have begun. You used to boast of doing nothing mean, but you are doing something mean to-night. You are leaving suspicion on an honest boy with a good deal against him already; you are separating him from the woman he loves and who loves him. But you will do meaner things than that before you die.'

Three flashing diamonds fell from the tree to the turf. The small man stooped to pick them up, and when he looked up again the green cage of the tree was emptied of its silver bird.

The restoration of the gems (accidentally picked up by Father Brown, of all people) ended the evening in uproarious triumph; and Sir Leopold, in his height of good humour, even told the priest that though he himself had broader views, he could respect those whose creed required them to be cloistered and ignorant of this world.

THE INVISIBLE MAN

IN the cool blue twilight of two steep streets in Camden Town, the shop at the corner, a confectioner's, glowed like the butt of a cigar. One should rather say, perhaps, like the butt of a firework, for the light was of many colours and some complexity, broken up by many mirrors and dancing on many gilt and gaily-coloured cakes and sweetmeats. Against this one fiery glass were glued the noses of many gutter-snipes, for the chocolates were all wrapped in those red and gold and green metallic colours which are almost better than chocolate itself; and the huge white wedding-cake in the window was somehow at once remote and satisfying, just as if the whole North Pole were good to eat. Such rainbow provocations could naturally collect the youth of the neighbourhood up to the ages of ten or twelve. But this corner was also attractive to youth at a later stage; and a young man, not less than twenty-four, was staring into the same shop window. To him, also, the shop was of fiery charm, but this attraction was not wholly to be explained by chocolates; which, however, he was far from despising.

He was a tall, burly, red-haired young man, with a resolute face but a listless manner. He carried under his arm a flat, grey portfolio of black-and-white sketches which he had sold with more or less success to publishers ever since his uncle (who was an admiral) had disinherited him for Socialism, because of a lecture which he had delivered against that economic theory. His name was John Turnbull Angus.*

Entering at last, he walked through the confectioner's shop into the back room, which was a sort of pastry-cook restaurant, merely raising his hat to the young lady who was serving there. She was a dark, elegant, alert girl in black, with a high colour and very quick, dark eyes; and after the ordinary interval she followed him into the inner room to take his order.

His order was evidently a usual one. 'I want, please,' he said with precision, 'one halfpenny bun and a small cup of black coffee.' An instant before the girl could turn away he added, 'Also, I want you to marry me.'

The young lady of the shop stiffened suddenly, and said: 'Those are jokes I don't allow.'

The red-haired young man lifted grey eyes of an unexpected gravity.

'Really and truly,' he said, 'it's as serious—as serious as the halfpenny bun. It is expensive, like the bun; one pays for it. It is indigestible, like the bun. It hurts.'

The dark young lady had never taken her dark eyes off him, but seemed to be studying him with almost tragic exactitude.

At the end of her scrutiny she had something like the shadow of a smile, and she sat down in a chair.

'Don't you think,' observed Angus, absently, 'that it's rather cruel to eat these halfpenny buns? They might grow up into penny buns. I shall give up these brutal sports when we are married.'

The dark young lady rose from her chair and walked to the window, evidently in a state of strong but not unsympathetic cogitation. When at last she swung round again with an air of resolution, she was bewildered to observe that the young man was carefully laying out on the table various objects from the shop-window. They included a pyramid of highly coloured sweets, several plates of sandwiches, and the two decanters containing that mysterious port and sherry which are peculiar to pastry-cooks. In the middle of this neat arrangement he had carefully let down the enormous load of white sugared cake which had been the huge ornament of the window.

'What on earth are you doing?' she asked.

'Duty, my dear Laura,' he began.

'Oh, for the Lord's sake, stop a minute,' she cried, 'and don't talk to me in that way. I mean what is all that?'

'A ceremonial meal, Miss Hope.'

'And what is *that*?' she asked impatiently, pointing to the mountain of sugar.

'The wedding-cake, Mrs Angus,' he said.

The girl marched to that article, removed it with some clatter, and put it back in the shop-window; she then returned, and, putting her elegant elbows on the table, regarded the young man not unfavourably, but with considerable exasperation.

'You don't give me any time to think,' she said.

'I'm not such a fool,' he answered; 'that's my Christian humility.'

She was still looking at him; but she had grown considerably graver behind the smile.

'Mr Angus,' she said steadily, 'before there is a minute more of this nonsense I must tell you something about myself as shortly as I can.'

'Delighted,' replied Angus gravely. 'You might tell me something about myself, too, while you are about it.'

'Oh, do hold your tongue and listen,' she said. 'It's nothing that I'm ashamed of, and it isn't even anything that I'm specially sorry about. But what would you say if there were something that is no business of mine and yet is my nightmare?'

'In that case,' said the man seriously, 'I should suggest that you bring back the cake.'

'Well, you must listen to the story first,' said Laura, persistently. 'To begin with, I must tell you that my father owned the inn called the "Red Fish" at Ludbury,* and I used to serve people in the bar.'

'I have often wondered,' he said, 'why there was a kind of a Christian air* about this one confectioner's shop.'

'Ludbury is a sleepy, grassy little hole in the Eastern Counties, and the only kind of people who ever came to the "Red Fish" were occasional commercial travellers, and for the rest, the most awful people you can see, only you've never seen them. I mean little, loungy men, who had just enough to live on, and had nothing to do but lean about in bar-rooms and bet on horses, in bad clothes that were just too good for them. Even these wretched young rotters were not very common at our house; but there were two of them that were a lot too common—common in every sort of way. They both lived on money of their own, and were wearisomely idle and overdressed. But yet I was a bit sorry for them, because I half believe they slunk into our little empty bar because each of them had a slight deformity; the sort of thing that some yokels laugh at. It wasn't exactly a deformity either; it was more an oddity. One of them was a surprisingly small man, something like a dwarf, or at least like a jockey. He was not at all jockeyish to look at, though; he had a round black head and a well-trimmed black beard, bright eyes like a bird's; he jingled money in his pockets; he jangled a great gold watch chain; and he never turned up except dressed just too much like a gentleman to be one. He was no fool, though, though a futile idler; he was curiously clever at all kinds of things that couldn't be the slightest use; a sort of impromptu conjuring;

making fifteen matches set fire to each other like a regular firework; or cutting a banana or some such thing into a dancing doll. His name was Isidore Smythe; and I can see him still, with his little dark face, just coming up to the counter, making a jumping kangaroo out of five cigars.

'The other fellow was more silent and more ordinary; but somehow he alarmed me much more than poor little Smythe. He was very tall and slight, and light-haired; his nose had a high bridge, and he might almost have been handsome in a spectral sort of way; but he had one of the most appalling squints I have ever seen or heard of. When he looked straight at you, you didn't know where you were yourself, let alone what he was looking at. I fancy this sort of disfigurement embittered the poor chap a little; for while Smythe was ready to show off his monkey tricks anywhere, James Welkin (that was the squinting man's name) never did anything except soak in our bar parlour, and go for great walks by himself in the flat, grey country all round. All the same, I think Smythe, too, was a little sensitive about being so small, though he carried it off more smartly. And so it was that I was really puzzled, as well as startled, and very sorry, when they both offered to marry me in the same week.

'Well, I did what I've since thought was perhaps a silly thing. But, after all, these freaks were my friends in a way; and I had a horror of their thinking I refused them for the real reason, which was that they were so impossibly ugly. So I made up some gas of another sort, about never meaning to marry anyone who hadn't carved his way in the world. I said it was a point of principle with me not to live on money that was just inherited like theirs. Two days after I had talked in this well-meaning sort of way, the whole trouble began. The first thing I heard was that both of them had gone off to seek their fortunes, as if they were in some silly fairy tale.

'Well, I've never seen either of them from that day to this. But I've had two letters from the little man called Smythe, and really they were rather exciting.'

'Ever heard of the other man?' asked Angus.

'No, he never wrote,' said the girl, after an instant's hesitation. 'Smythe's first letter was simply to say that he had started out walking with Welkin to London; but Welkin was such a good walker that the little man dropped out of it, and took a rest by the roadside. He happened to be picked up by some travelling show, and, partly becuase he was nearly a dwarf, and partly because he was really a clever little wretch, he got on quite well in the show business, and was soon sent up to the Aquarium, to do some tricks that I forgot. That was his first letter. His second was much more of a startler, and I only got it last week.'

The man called Angus emptied his coffee-cup and regarded her with mild and patient eyes. Her own mouth took a slight twist of laughter as she resumed: 'I suppose you've seen on the hoardings* all about this "Smythe's Silent Service"? Or you must be the only person that hasn't. Oh, I don't know much about it, it's some clockwork invention for doing all the housework by machinery. You know the sort of thing: "Press a button—A Butler who Never Drinks." "Turn a handle—Ten Housemaids who Never Flirt." You must have seen the advertisements. Well, whatever these machines are, they are making pots of money; and they are making it all for that little imp whom I knew down in Ludbury. I can't help feeling pleased the poor little chap has fallen on his feet; but the plain fact is, I'm in terror of his turning up any minute and telling me he's carved his way in the world—as he certainly has.'

'And the other man?' repeated Angus with a sort of obstinate quietude.

Laura Hope got to her feet suddenly. 'My friend,' she said: 'I think you are a witch. Yes, you are quite right. I have not seen a line of the other man's writing; and I have no more notion than the dead of what or where he is. But it is of him that I am frightened. It is he who is all about my path. It is he who has half driven me mad. Indeed, I think he has driven me mad; for I have felt him where he could not have been, and I have heard his voice when he could not have spoken.'

'Well, my dear,' said the young man, cheerfully, 'if he were Satan himself, he is done for now you have told somebody. One goes mad all alone, old girl. But when was it you fancied you felt and heard our squinting friend?'

'I heard James Welkin laugh as plainly as I hear you speak,' said the girl, steadily. 'There was nobody there, for I stood just outside the shop at the corner, and could see down both streets at once. I had forgotten how he laughed, though his laugh was as odd as his squint. I had not thought of him for nearly a year. But it's a solemn truth that a few seconds later the first letter came from his rival.'

'Did you ever make the spectre speak or squeak, or anything?' asked Angus, with some interest.

Laura suddenly shuddered, and then said with an unshaken voice: 'Yes. Just when I had finished reading the second letter from Isidore Smythe announcing his success, just then, I heard Welkin say: "He shan't have you, though." It was quite plain, as if he were in the room. It is awful; I think I must be mad.'

'If you really were mad,' said the young man, 'you would think you must be sane. But certainly there seems to me to be something a little rum about this unseen gentleman. Two heads are better than one—I spare you allusions to any other organs—and really, if you would allow me, as a sturdy, practical man, to bring back the wedding-cake out of the window——'

Even as he spoke, there was a sort of steely shriek in the street outside, and a small motor, driven at devilish speed, shot up to the door of the shop and stuck there. In the same flash of time a small man in a shiny top hat stood stamping in the outer room.

Angus, who had hitherto maintained hilarious ease from motives of mental hygiene, revealed the strain of his soul by striding abruptly out of the inner room and confronting the new-comer. A glance at him was quite sufficient to confirm the savage guesswork of a man in love. This very dapper but dwarfish figure, with the spike of black beard carried insolently forward, the clever unrestful eyes, the neat but very nervous fingers, could be none other than the man just described to him: Isidore Smythe, who made dolls out of banana skins and matchboxes: Isidore Smythe, who made millions out of undrinking butlers and unflirting housemaids of metal. For a moment the two men, instinctively understanding each other's air of possession, looked at each other with that curious cold generosity which is the soul of rivalry.

Mr Smythe, however, made no allusion to the ultimate ground of their antagonism, but said simply and explosively: 'Has Miss Hope seen that thing on the window?'

'On the window?' repeated the staring Angus.

'There's no time to explain other things,' said the small millionaire shortly. 'There's some tomfoolery going on here that has to be investigated.'

He pointed his polished walking-stick at the window, recently depleted by the bridal preparations of Mr Angus; and that gentleman was astonished to see along the front of the glass a long strip of paper pasted, which had certainly not been on the window when he had looked through it some time before. Following the energetic Smythe outside into the street, he found that some yard and a half of stamp paper* had been carefully gummed along the glass outside, and on this was written in straggly characters: 'If you marry Smythe, he will die.'

'Laura,' said Angus, putting his big red head into the shop, 'you're not mad.'

'It's the writing of that fellow Welkin,' said Smythe gruffly. 'I haven't seen him for years, but he's always bothering me. Five times in the last fortnight he's had threatening letters left at my flat, and I can't even find out who leaves them, let alone if it is Welkin himself. The porter of the flats swears that no suspicious characters have been seen, and here he has pasted up a sort of dado* on a public shop window, while the people in the shop——'

'Quite so,' said Angus modestly, 'while the people in the shop were having tea. Well, sir, I can assure you I appreciate your common sense in dealing so directly with the matter. We can talk about other things afterwards. The fellow cannot be very far off yet, for I swear there was no paper there when I went last to the window, ten or fifteen minutes ago. On the other hand, he's too far off to be chased, as we don't even know the direction. If you'll take my advice, Mr Smythe, you'll put this at once in the hands of some energetic inquiry man, private rather than public. I know an extremely clever fellow, who has set up in business five minutes from here in your car. His name's Flambeau, and though his youth was a bit stormy, he's a strictly honest man now, and his brains are worth money. He lives in Lucknow Mansions, Hampstead.'

'That is odd,' said the little man, arching his black eyebrows. 'I live myself in Himalaya Mansions round the corner. Perhaps you might care to come with me; I can go to my rooms and sort out these queer Welkin documents, while you run round and get your friend the detective.'

'You are very good,' said Angus politely. 'Well, the sooner we act the better.'

Both men, with a queer kind of impromptu fairness, took the same sort of formal farewell of the lady, and both jumped into the brisk little car. As Smythe took the wheel and they turned the great corner of the street, Angus was amused to see a gigantesque poster of 'Smythe's Silent Service,' with a picture of a huge headless iron doll, carrying a saucepan, with the legend, 'A Cook Who is Never Cross.'

'I use them in my own flat,' said the little black-bearded man, laughing, 'partly for advertisement, and partly for real convenience. Honestly, and all above board, those big clockwork dolls of mine do bring you coals or claret or a time-table quicker than any live servants I've ever known, if you know which knob to press. But I'll never deny, between ourselves, that such servants have their disadvantages, too.'

'Indeed?' said Angus; 'is there something they can't do?'

'Yes,' replied Smythe coolly; 'they can't tell me who left those threatening letters at my flat.'

The man's motor was small and swift like himself; in fact, like his domestic service, it was of his own invention. If he was an advertising quack, he was one who believed in his own wares. The sense of something tiny and flying was accentuated as they swept up long white curves of road in the dead but open daylight of evening. Soon the white curves came sharper and dizzier; they were upon ascending spirals, as they say in the modern religions. For, indeed, they were cresting a corner of London which is almost as precipitous as Edinburgh, if not quite so picturesque. Terrace rose above terrace, and the special tower of flats they sought, rose above them all to almost Egyptian height, gilt by the level sunset. The change, as they turned the corner and entered the crescent known as Himalaya Mansions, was as abrupt as the opening of a window; for they found that pile of flats sitting above London as above a green sea of slate. Opposite to the mansions, on the other side of the gravel crescent, was a bushy enclosure more like a steep hedge or dyke than a garden, and some way below that ran a strip of artificial water, a sort of canal, like the moat of that embowered fortress. As the car swept round the crescent it passed, at one corner, the stray stall of a man selling chestnuts; and right away at the other end of the curve, Angus could see a dim blue policeman walking slowly. These were the only human shapes in that high suburban solitude; but he had an irrational sense that they expressed the speechless poetry of London. He felt as if they were figures in a story.

The little car shot up to the right house like a bullet, and shot out its owner like a bomb shell. He was immediately inquiring of a tall commissionaire in shining braid, and a short porter in shirt sleeves, whether anybody or anything had been seeking his apartments. He was assured that nobody and nothing had passed these officials since his last inquiries; whereupon he and the slightly bewildered Angus were shot up in the lift like a rocket, till they reached the top floor.

'Just come in for a minute,' said the breathless Smythe. 'I want to show you those Welkin letters. Then you might run round the corner and fetch your friend.' He pressed a button concealed in the wall, and the door opened of itself.

It opened on a long, commodious ante-room, of which the only arresting features, ordinarily speaking, were the rows of tall half-human mechanical figures that stood up on both sides like tailors' dummies. Like tailors' dummies they were headless; and like tailors' dummies they had a handsome unnecessary humpiness in the shoulders, and a pigeon-breasted protuberance of chest; but barring this, they were not much much more like a human figure than any automatic machine at a station that is about the human height. They had two great hooks like arms, for carrying trays; and they were painted pea-green, or vermilion, or black for convenience of distinction; in every other way they were only automatic machines and nobody would have looked twice at them. On this occasion, at least, nobody did. For between the two rows of these domestic dummies lay something more interesting than most of the mechanics of the world. It was a white, tattered scrap of paper scrawled with red ink; and the agile inventor had snatched it up almost as soon as the door flew open. He handed it to Angus without a word. The red ink on it actually was not dry, and the message ran: 'If you have been to see her to-day, I shall kill you.'

There was a short silence, and then Isidore Smythe said quietly: 'Would you like a little whisky? I rather feel as if I should.'

'Thank you; I should like a little Flambeau,' said Angus, gloomily. 'This business seems to me to be getting rather grave. I'm going round at once to fetch him.'

'Right you are,' said the other, with admirable cheerfulness. 'Bring him round here as quick as you can.'

But as Angus closed the front door behind him he saw Smythe push back a button, and one of the clockwork images glided from its place and slid along a groove in the floor carrying a tray with syphon and decanter. There did seem something a trifle weird about leaving the little man alone among those dead servants, who were coming to life as the door closed.

Six steps down from Smythe's landing the man in shirt sleeves was doing something with a pail. Angus stopped to extract a promise, fortified with a prospective bribe, that he would remain in that place until the return with the detective, and would keep count of any kind of stranger coming up those stairs. Dashing down to the front hall he then laid similar charges of vigilance on the commissionaire at the front door, from whom he learned the simplifying circumstance that there was no back door. Not content with this, he captured the floating policeman and induced him to stand opposite the entrance and watch it; and finally paused an instant for a pennyworth of chestnuts, and an inquiry as to the probable length of the merchant's stay in the neighbourhood.

The chestnut seller, turning up the collar of his coat, told him he should probably be moving shortly, as he thought it was going to snow. Indeed, the evening was growing grey and bitter, but Angus, with all his eloquence, proceeded to nail the chestnut man to his post.

'Keep yourself warm on your own chestnuts,' he said earnestly. 'Eat up your whole stock; I'll make it worth your while. I'll give you a sovereign if you'll wait here till I come back, and then tell me whether any man, woman, or child has gone into that house where the commissionaire is standing.'

He then walked away smartly, with a last look at the besieged tower.

'I've made a ring round that room, anyhow,' he said. 'They can't all four of them be Mr Welkin's accomplices.'

Lucknow Mansions were, so to speak, on a lower platform of that hill of houses, of which Himalaya Mansions might be called the peak. Mr Flambeau's semi-official flat was on the ground floor, and presented in every way a marked contrast to the American machinery and cold hotel-like luxury of the flat of the Silent Service. Flambeau, who was a friend of Angus, received him in a rococo artistic den behind his office, of which the ornaments were sabres, harquebuses,* Eastern curiosities, flasks of Italian wine, savage cooking-pots, a plumy Persian cat, and a small dusty-looking Roman Catholic priest, who looked particularly out of place.

'This is my friend, Father Brown,' said Flambeau. 'I've often wanted you to meet him. Splendid weather, this; a little cold for Southerners like me.'

'Yes, I think it will keep clear,' said Angus, sitting down on a violet-striped Eastern ottoman.

'No,' said the priest quietly; 'it has begun to snow.'

And indeed, as he spoke, the first few flakes, foreseen by the man of chestnuts, began to drift across the darkening window-pane.

'Well,' said Angus heavily. 'I'm afraid I've come on business, and rather jumpy business at that. The fact is, Flambeau, within a stone's throw of your house is a fellow who badly wants your help; he's perpetually being haunted and threatened by an invisible enemy—a scoundrel whom nobody has even seen.' As Angus proceeded to tell the whole tale of Smythe and Welkin beginning with Laura's story, and going on with his own, the supernatural laugh at the corner of two empty streets, the strange distinct words spoken in an empty room, Flambeau grew more and more vividly concerned, and the little priest seemed to be left out of it, like a piece of furniture. When it came to the scribbled stamp-paper pasted on the window, Flambeau rose, seeming to fill the room with his huge shoulders.

'If you don't mind,' he said, 'I think you had better tell me the rest on the nearest road to this man's house. It strikes me, somehow, that there is no time to be lost.'

'Delighted,' said Angus, rising also, 'though he's safe enough for the present, for I've set four men to watch the only hole to his burrow.'

They turned out into the street, the small priest trundling after them with the docility of a small dog. He merely said, in a cheerful way, like one making conversation: 'How quick the snow gets thick on the ground.'

As they threaded the steep side streets already powdered with silver, Angus finished his story; and by the time they reached the crescent with the towering flats, he had leisure to turn his attention to the four sentinels. The chestnut seller, both before and after receiving a sovereign, swore stubbornly that he had watched the door and seen no visitor enter. The policeman was even more emphatic. He said he had had experience of crooks of all kinds, in top hats and in rags; he wasn't so green as to expect suspicious characters to look suspicious; he looked out for anybody, and, so help him, there had been nobody. And when all three men gathered round the gilded commissionaire, who still stood smiling astride of the porch, the verdict was more final still.

'I've got a right to ask any man, duke or dustman, what he wants in these flats,' said the genial and gold-laced giant, 'and I'll swear there's been nobody to ask since this gentleman went away.'

The unimportant Father Brown, who stood back, looking modestly at the pavement, here ventured to say meekly: 'Has nobody been up and down stairs, then, since the snow began to fall? It began while we were all round at Flambeau's.'

'Nobody's been in here, sir, you can take it from me,' said the official, with beaming authority.

'Then I wonder what that is?' said the priest, and stared at the ground blankly like a fish.

The others all looked down also; and Flambeau used a fierce exclamation and a French gesture. For it was unquestionably true that down the middle of the entrance guarded by the man in gold lace, actually between the arrogant, stretched legs of that colossus, ran a stringy pattern of grey footprints stamped upon the white snow.

'God!' cried Angus involuntarily, 'the Invisible Man!'

Without another word he turned and dashed up the stairs, with Flambeau following; but Father Brown still stood looking about him in the snow-clad street as if he had lost interest in his query.

Flambeau was plainly in a mood to break down the door with his big shoulder; but the Scotsman, with more reason, if less intuition, fumbled about on the frame of the door till he found the invisible button; and the door swung slowly open.

It showed substantially the same serried* interior; the hall had grown darker, though it was still struck here and there with the last crimson shafts of sunset, and one or two of the headless machines had been moved from their places for this or that purpose, and stood here and there about the twilit place. The green and red of their coats were all darkened in the dusk, and their likeness to human shapes slightly increased by their very shapelessness. But in the middle of them all, exactly where the paper with the red ink had lain, there lay something that looked very like red ink spilt out of its bottle. But it was not red ink.

With a French combination of reason and violence Flambeau simply said 'Murder!' and, plunging into the flat, had explored every corner and cupboard of it in five minutes. But if he expected to find a corpse he found none. Isidore Smythe simply was not in the place, either dead or alive. After the most tearing search the two men met each other in the outer hall with streaming faces and staring eyes. 'My friend,' said Flambeau, talking French in his excitement, 'not only is your murderer invisible, but he makes invisible also the murdered man.'

Angus looked round at the dim room full of dummies, and in some Celtic corner of his Scotch soul a shudder started. One of the life-size dolls stood immediately overshadowing the blood stain, summoned, perhaps, by the slain man an instant before he fell. One of the high-shouldered hooks that served the thing for arms, was a little lifted and Angus had suddenly the horrid fancy that poor Smythe's own iron child had struck him down. Matter had rebelled, and these machines had killed their master.* But even so, what had they done with him?

'Eaten him?' said the nightmare at his ear; and he sickened for an instant at the idea of rent, human remains absorbed and crushed into all that acephalous clockwork.

He recovered his mental health by an emphatic effort, and said to Flambeau: 'Well, there it is. The poor fellow has evaporated like a cloud and left a red streak on the floor. The tale does not belong to this world.'

'There is only one thing to be done,' said Flambeau, 'whether it belongs to this world or the other, I must go down and talk to my friend.'

They descended, passing the man with the pail, who again asseverated that he had let no intruder pass, down to the commissionaire and the hovering chestnut man, who rightly reasserted their own watchfulness. But when Angus looked round for his fourth confirmation he could not see it, and called out with some nervousness: 'Where is the policeman?'

'I beg your pardon,' said Father Brown; 'that is my fault. I just sent him down the road to investigate something—that I just thought worth investigating.'

'Well, we want him back pretty soon,' said Angus abruptly, 'for the wretched man upstairs has not only been murdered, but wiped out.'

'How?' asked the priest.

'Father,' said Flambeau, after a pause, 'upon my soul I believe it is more in your department than mine. No friend or foe has entered the house, but Smythe is gone, as if stolen by the fairies. If that is not supernatural, I——'

As he spoke they were all checked by an unusual sight; the big blue policeman came round the corner of the crescent running. He came straight up to Brown.

'You're right, sir,' he panted, 'they've just found poor Mr Smythe's body in the canal down below.'

Angus put his hand wildly to his head. 'Did he run down and drown himself?' he asked.

'He never came down, I'll swear,' said the constable, 'and he wasn't drowned either, for he died of a great stab over the heart.'

'And yet you saw no one enter?' said Flambeau in a grave voice.

'Let us walk down the road a little,' said the priest.

As they reached the other end of the crescent he observed abruptly: 'Stupid of me! I forgot to ask the policeman something. I wonder if they found a light brown sack.'

'Why a light brown sack?' asked Angus, astonished.

'Because if it was any other coloured sack, the case must begin over again,' said Father Brown; 'but if it was a light brown sack, why, the case is finished.'

'I am pleased to hear it,' said Angus with hearty irony. 'It hasn't begun, so far as I am concerned.'

'You must tell us all about it,' said Flambeau, with a strange heavy simplicity, like a child.

Unconsciously they were walking with quickening steps down the long sweep of road on the other side of the high crescent, Father Brown leading briskly, though in silence. At last he said with an almost touching vagueness: 'Well, I'm afraid you'll think it so prosy. We always begin at the abstract end of things, and you can't begin this story anywhere else.

'Have you ever noticed this—that people never answer what you say? They answer what you mean—or what they think you mean. Suppose one lady says to another in a country house, "Is anybody staying with you?" the lady doesn't answer "Yes; the butler, the three footmen, the parlourmaid, and so on," though the parlourmaid may be in the room, or the butler behind her chair. She says: "There is *nobody* staying with us," meaning nobody of the sort you mean. But suppose a doctor inquiring into an epidemic asks,

"Who is staying in the house?" then the lady will remember the butler, parlourmaid, and the rest. All language is used like that; you never get a question answered literally, even when you get it answered truly. When those four quite honest men said that no man had gone into the Mansions, they did not really mean that *no man* had gone into them. They meant no man whom they could suspect of being your man. A man did go into the house, and did come out of it, but they never noticed him.'

'An invisible man?' inquired Angus, raising his red eyebrows.

'A mentally invisible man,' said Father Brown.

A minute or two after he resumed in the same unassuming voice, like a man thinking his way. 'Of course, you can't think of such a man, until you do think of him. That's where his cleverness comes in. But I came to think of him through two or three little things in the tale Mr Angus told us. First, there was the fact that this Welkin went for long walks. And then there was the vast lot of stamp paper on the window. And then, most of all, there were the two things the young lady said—things that couldn't be true. Don't get annoyed,' he added hastily, noting a sudden movement of the Scotsman's head; 'she thought they were true all right, but they couldn't be true. A person *can't* be quite alone in a street a second before she receives a letter. She can't be quite alone in a street when she starts reading a letter just received. There must be somebody pretty near her; he must be mentally invisible.'

'Why must there be somebody near her?' asked Angus.

'Because,' said Father Brown: 'barring carrier-pigeons, somebody must have brought her the letter.'

'Do you really mean to say,' asked Flambeau, with energy, 'that Welkin carried his rival's letters to his lady?'

'Yes,' said the priest. 'Welkin carried his rival's letters to his lady. You see, he had to.'

'Oh, I can't stand much more of this,' exploded Flambeau. 'Who is this fellow? What does he look like. What is the usual get-up of a mentally invisible man?'

'He is dressed rather handsomely in red, blue and gold,' replied the priest promptly with decision, 'and in this striking, and even showy costume he entered Himalaya Mansions under eight human eyes; he killed Smythe in cold blood, and came down into the street again carrying the dead body in his arms——'

'Reverend sir,' cried Angus, standing still, 'are you raving mad, or am I?'

'You are not mad,' said Brown, 'only a little unobservant. You have not noticed such a man as this, for example.'

He took three quick strides forward, and put his hand on the shoulder of an ordinary passing postman who had bustled by them unnoticed under the shade of the trees.

'Nobody ever notices postmen, somehow,' he said thoughtfully; 'yet they have passions like other men, and even carry large bags where a small corpse can be stowed quite easily.'

The postman, instead of turning naturally, had ducked and tumbled against the garden fence. He was a lean fair-bearded man of very ordinary appearance, but as he turned an alarmed face over his shoulder, all three men were fixed with an almost fiendish squint.

Flambeau went back to his sabres, purple rugs and Persian cat, having many things to attend to. John Turnbull Angus went back to the lady at the shop, with whom that imprudent young man contrives to be extremely comfortable. But Father Brown walked those snow-covered hills under the stars for many hours with a murderer, and what they said to each other will never be known.

THE HONOUR OF ISRAEL GOW

A STORMY evening of olive and silver was closing in, as Father Brown, wrapped in a grey Scotch plaid, came to the end of a grey Scotch valley and beheld the strange castle of Glengyle. It stopped one end of the glen or hollow like a blind alley; and it looked like the end of the world. Rising in steep roofs and spires of seagreen slate in the manner of the old French-Scottish châteaux, it reminded an Englishman of the sinister steeple-hats of witches in fairy tales; and the pine woods that rocked round the green turrets looked, by comparison, as black as numberless flocks of ravens. This note of a dreamy, almost a sleepy devilry, was no mere fancy from the landscape. For there did rest on the place one of those clouds of pride and madness and mysterious sorrow which lie more heavily on the noble houses of Scotland than on any other of the children of men. For Scotland has a double dose of the poison called heredity; the sense of blood in the aristocrat, and the sense of doom in the Calvinist.

The priest had snatched a day from his business at Glasgow to meet his friend Flambeau, the amateur detective, who was at Glengyle Castle with another more formal officer investigating the life and death of the late Earl of Glengyle. That mysterious person was the last representative of a race whose valour, insanity, and violent cunning had made them terrible even among the sinister nobility of their nation in the sixteenth century. None were deeper in that labyrinthine ambition, in chamber within chamber of that palace of lies that was built up around Mary Queen of Scots.

The rhyme in the country-side attested the motive and the result of their machinations candidly:

'As green sap to the simmer trees
Is red gold to the Ogilvies.'

For many centuries there had never been a decent lord in Glengyle Castle; and with the Victorian era one would have thought that all eccentricities were exhausted. The last Glengyle, however, satisfied his tribal tradition by doing the only thing that was left for him to do; he disappeared. I do not mean that he went abroad; by all accounts he was still in the castle, if he was anywhere. But though his name was in the church register and the big red Peerage, nobody ever saw him under the sun.

If anyone saw him it was a solitary man-servant, something between a groom and a gardener. He was so deaf that the more business-like assumed him to be dumb; while the more penetrating declared him to be half-witted. A gaunt, red-haired labourer, with a dogged jaw and chin, but quite black-blue eyes, he went by the name of Israel Gow, and was the one silent servant on that deserted estate. But the energy with which he dug potatoes, and the regularity with which he disappeared into the kitchen gave people an impression that he was providing for the meals of a superior, and that the strange earl was still concealed in the castle. If society needed any further proof that he was there, the servant persistently asserted that he was not at home. One morning the provost and the minister (for the Glengyles were Presbyterian) were summoned to the castle. There they found that the gardener, groom and cook had added to his many professions that of an undertaker, and had nailed up his noble master in a coffin. With how much or how little further inquiry this odd fact was passed, did not as yet very plainly appear; for the thing had never been legally investigated till Flambeau had gone north two or three days before. By then the body of Lord Glengyle (if it was the body) had lain for some time in the little church-yard on the hill.

As Father Brown passed through the dim garden and came under the shadow of the château, the clouds were thick and the whole air damp and thundery. Against the last stripe of the green-gold sunset he saw a black human silhouette; a man in a chimney-pot hat,* with a big spade over his shoulder. The combination was queerly suggestive of a sexton; but when Brown remembered the deaf servant who dug potatoes, he thought it natural enough. He knew something of the Scotch peasant; he knew the respectability which might well feel it necessary to wear 'blacks' for an official inquiry; he knew also the economy that would not lose an hour's digging for that. Even the man's start and suspicious stare as the priest went by were consonant enough with the vigilance and jealousy of such a type.

The great door was opened by Flambeau himself, who had with him a lean man with iron-grey hair and papers in his hand: Inspector Craven from Scotland Yard.* The entrance hall was mostly stripped and empty; but the pale, sneering faces of one or two of the wicked Ogilvies looked down out of the black periwigs and blackening canvas.

Following them into an inner room, Father Brown found that the allies had been seated at a long oak table, of which their end was covered with scribbled papers, flanked with whisky and cigars. Through the whole of its remaining length it was occupied by detached objects arranged at intervals; objects about as inexplicable as any objects could be. One looked like a small heap of glittering broken glass. Another looked like a high heap of brown dust. A third appeared to be a plain stick of wood.

'You seem to have a sort of geological museum here,' he said, as he sat down, jerking his head briefly in the direction of the brown dust and the crystalline fragments.

'Not a geological museum,' replied Flambeau; 'say a psychological museum.'

'Oh, for the Lord's sake,' cried the police detective, laughing, 'don't let's begin with such long words.'

'Don't you know what psychology means?' asked Flambeau with friendly surprise. 'Psychology means being off your chump.'

'Still I hardly follow,' replied the official.

'Well,' said Flambeau, with decision; 'I mean that we've only found out one thing about Lord Glengyle. He was a maniac.'

The black silhouette of Gow with his top hat and spade passed the window, dimly outlined against the darkening sky. Father Brown stared passively at it and answered:

'I can understand there must have been something odd about the man, or he wouldn't have buried himself alive—nor been in such a hurry to bury himself dead. But what makes you think it was lunacy?'

'Well,' said Flambeau; 'you just listen to the list of things Mr Craven has found in the house.'

'We must get a candle,' said Craven, suddenly. 'A storm is getting up, and it's too dark to read.'

'Have you found any candles,' asked Brown smiling, 'among your oddities?'

Flambeau raised a grave face, and fixed his dark eyes on his friend.

'That is curious, too,' he said. 'Twenty-five candles, and not a trace of a candlestick.'

In the rapidly darkening room and rapidly rising wind, Brown went along the table to where a bundle of wax candles lay among the other scrappy exhibits. As he did so he bent accidentally over the heap of red-brown dust; and a sharp sneeze cracked the silence.

'Hullo!' he said; 'snuff!'

He took one of the candles, lit it carefully, came back and stuck it in the neck of the whisky bottle. The unrestful night air, blowing through the crazy window, waved the long flame like a banner. And on every side of the castle they could hear the miles and miles of black pine wood seething like a black sea around a rock.

'I will read the inventory,' began Craven gravely, picking up one of the papers, 'the inventory of what we found loose and unexplained in the castle. You are to understand that the place generally was dismantled and neglected; but one or two rooms had plainly been inhabited in a simple but not squalid style by somebody; somebody who was not the servant Gow. The list is as follows:

'First item. A very considerable hoard of precious stones, nearly all diamonds, and all of them loose, without any setting whatever. Of course, it is natural that the Ogilvies should have family jewels; but those are exactly the jewels that are almost always set in particular articles of ornament. The Ogilvies would seem to have kept theirs loose in their pockets, like coppers.

'Second item. Heaps and heaps of loose snuff, not kept in a horn, or even a pouch, but lying in heaps on the mantelpieces, on the sideboard, on the piano, anywhere. It looks as if the old gentleman would not take the trouble to look in a pocket or lift a lid.

'Third item. Here and there about the house curious little heaps of minute pieces of metal, some like steel springs and some in the form of microscopic wheels. As if they had gutted some mechanical toy.

'Fourth item. The wax candles, which have to be stuck in bottle necks because there is nothing else to stick them in. Now I wish you to note how very much queerer all this is than anything we anticipated. For the central riddle we are prepared; we have all seen at a glance that there was something wrong about the last earl. We have come here to find out whether he really lived here, whether he really died here, whether that red-haired scarecrow who did his burying had anything to do with his dying. But suppose the worst in all this, the most lurid or melodramatic solution you like. Suppose the servant really killed the master, or suppose the master isn't really dead, or suppose the master is dressed up as the servant, or suppose the servant is buried for the master; invent what Wilkie Collins's* tragedy you like, and you still have not explained a candle without a candlestick, or why an elderly gentleman of good family should habitually spill snuff on the piano. The core of the tale we could imagine; it is the fringes that are mysterious. By no stretch of fancy can the human mind connect together snuff and diamonds and wax and loose clockwork.'

'I think I see the connection,' said the priest. 'This Glengyle was mad against the French Revolution. He was an enthusiast for the *ancien régime*, and was trying to re-enact literally the family life of the last Bourbons. He had snuff because it was the eighteenth century luxury; wax candles, because they were the eighteenth century lighting; the mechanical bits of iron represent the locksmith hobby of Louis XVI;* the diamonds are for the Diamond Necklace* of Marie Antoinette.'

Both the other men were staring at him with round eyes. 'What a perfectly extraordinary notion!' cried Flambeau. 'Do you really think that is the truth?'

'I am perfectly sure it isn't,' answered Father Brown, 'only you said that nobody could connect snuff and diamonds and clockwork and candles. I give you that connection off-hand. The real truth, I am very sure, lies deeper.'

He paused a moment and listened to the wailing of the wind in the turrets. Then he said: 'The late Earl of Glengyle was a thief. He lived a second and darker life as a desperate house-breaker. He did not have any candlesticks because he only used these candles cut short in the little lantern he carried. The snuff he employed as the fiercest French criminals have used pepper: to fling it suddenly in dense masses in the face of a captor or pursuer. But the final proof is in the curious coincidence of the diamonds and the small steel wheels. Surely that makes everything plain to you? Diamonds and small steel wheels are the only two instruments with which you can cut out a pane of glass.'

The bough of a broken pine tree lashed heavily in the blast against the window-pane behind them, as if in parody of a burglar, but they did not turn round. Their eyes were fastened on Father Brown.

'Diamonds and small wheels,' repeated Craven ruminating. 'Is that all that makes you think it the true explanation?'

'I don't think it the true explanation,' replied the priest placidly; 'but you said that nobody could connect the four things. The true tale, of course, is something much more humdrum. Glengyle had found, or thought he had found, precious stones on his estate. Somebody had bamboozled him with those loose brilliants, saying they were found in the castle caverns. The little wheels are some diamond-cutting affair. He had to do the thing very roughly and in a small way, with the help of a few shepherds or rude fellows on these hills. Snuff is the one great luxury of such Scotch shepherds; it's the one thing with which you can bribe them. They didn't have candlesticks because they didn't want them; they held the candles in their hands when they explored the caves.'

'Is that all?' asked Flambeau after a long pause. 'Have we got to the dull truth at last?'

'Oh, no,' said Father Brown.

As the wind died in the most distant pine woods with a long hoot as of mockery, Father Brown, with an utterly impassive face, went on:

'I only suggested that because you said one could not plausibly connect snuff with clockwork or candles with bright stones. Ten false philosophies will fit the universe; ten false theories will fit Glengyle Castle. But we want the real explanation of the castle and the universe. But are there no other exhibits?'

Craven laughed, and Flambeau rose smiling to his feet and strolled down the long table.

'Items five, six, seven, etc.,' he said, 'are certainly more varied than instructive. A curious collection, not of lead pencils, but of the lead out of lead pencils. A senseless stick of bamboo, with the top rather splintered. It might be the instrument of the crime. Only, there isn't any crime. The only other things are a few old missals and little Catholic pictures, which the Ogilvies kept, I suppose, from the Middle Ages—their family pride being stronger than their Puritanism. We only put them in the museum because they seem curiously cut about and defaced.'

The heady tempest without drove a dreadful wrack of clouds across Glengyle and threw the long room into darkness as Father Brown picked up the little illuminated pages to examine them. He spoke before the drift of darkness had passed; but it was the voice of an utterly new man.

'Mr Craven,' said he, talking like a man ten years younger: 'you have got a legal warrant, haven't you, to go up and examine that grave? The sooner we do it the better, and get to the bottom of this horrible affair. If I were you I should start now.'

'Now,' repeated the astonished detective, 'and why now?'

'Because this is serious,' answered Brown; 'this is not spilt snuff or loose pebbles, that might be there for a hundred reasons. There is only one reason I know of for *this* being done; and the reason goes down to the roots of the world. These religious pictures are not just dirtied or torn or scrawled over, which might be done in idleness or bigotry, by children or by Protestants. These have been treated very carefully—and very queerly. In every place where the great ornamented name of God comes in the old illuminations it has been elaborately taken out. The only other thing that has been removed is the halo round the head of the Child Jesus. Therefore, I say, let us get our warrant and our spade and our hatchet, and go up and break open that coffin.'

'What *do* you mean?' demanded the London officer.

'I mean,' answered the little priest, and his voice seemed to rise slightly in the roar of the gale. 'I mean that the great devil of the universe may be sitting on the top tower of this castle at this moment, as big as a hundred elephants, and roaring like the Apocalypse. There is black magic somewhere at the bottom of this.'

'Black magic,' repeated Flambeau in a low voice, for he was too enlightened a man not to know of such things; 'but what can these other things mean?'

'Oh, something damnable, I suppose,' replied Brown impatiently. 'How should I know? How can I guess all their mazes down below? Perhaps you can make a torture out of snuff and bamboo. Perhaps lunatics lust after wax and steel filings. Perhaps there is a maddening drug made of lead pencils! Our shortest cut to the mystery is up the hill to the grave.'

His comrades hardly knew that they had obeyed and followed him till a blast of the night wind nearly flung them on their faces in the garden. Nevertheless they had obeyed him like automata; for Craven found a hatchet in his hand, and the warrant in his pocket; Flambeau was carrying the heavy spade of the strange gardener; Father Brown was carrying the little gilt book from which had been torn the name of God.

The path up the hill to the churchyard was crooked but short; only under the stress of wind it seemed laborious and long. Far as the eye could see, farther and farther as they mounted the slope, were seas beyond seas of pines, now all aslope one way under the wind. And that universal gesture seemed as vain as it was vast, as vain as if that wind were whistling about some unpeopled and purposeless planet. Through all that infinite growth of grey-blue forests sang, shrill and high, that ancient sorrow that is in the heart of all heathen things. One could fancy that the voices from the underworld of unfathomable foliage were cries of the lost and wandering pagan gods: gods who had gone roaming in that irrational forest, and who will never find their way back to heaven.

'You see,' said Father Brown in low but easy tone, 'Scotch people before Scotland existed were a curious lot. In fact, they're a curious lot still. But in the prehistoric times I fancy they really worshipped demons. That,' he added genially, 'is why they jumped at the Puritan theology.'

'My friend,' said Flambeau, turning in a kind of fury, 'what does all that snuff mean?'

'My friend,' replied Brown, with equal seriousness, 'there is one mark of all genuine religions: materialism. Now, devil-worship is a perfectly genuine religion.'

They had come up on the grassy scalp of the hill, one of the few bald spots that stood clear of the crashing and roaring pine forest. A mean enclosure, partly timber and partly wire, rattled in the tempest to tell them the border of the graveyard. But by the time Inspector Craven had come to the corner of the grave, and Flambeau had planted his spade point downwards and leaned on it, they were both almost as shaken as the shaky wood and wire. At the foot of the grave grew great tall thistles, grey and silver in their decay. Once or twice, when a ball of thistledown broke under the breeze and flew past him, Craven jumped slightly as if it had been an arrow.

Flambeau drove the blade of his spade through the whistling grass into the wet clay below. Then he seemed to stop and lean on it as on a staff.

'Go on,' said the priest very gently. 'We are only trying to find the truth. What are you afraid of?'

'I am afraid of finding it,' said Flambeau.

The London detective spoke suddenly in a high crowing voice that was meant to be conversational and cheery. 'I wonder why he really did hide himself like that. Something nasty, I suppose; was he a leper?'

'Something worse than that,' said Flambeau.

'And what do you imagine,' asked the other, 'would be worse than a leper?'

'I don't imagine it,' said Flambeau.

He dug for some dreadful minutes in silence, and then said in a choked voice: 'I'm afraid of his not being the right shape.'

'Nor was that piece of paper, you know,' said Father Brown quietly, 'and we survived even that piece of paper.'*

Flambeau dug on with a blind energy. But the tempest had shouldered away the choking grey clouds that clung to the hills like smoke and revealed grey fields of faint starlight before he cleared the shape of a rude timber coffin, and somehow tipped it up upon the turf. Craven stepped forward with his axe; a thistle-top touched him, and he flinched. Then he took a firmer stride, and hacked and wrenched with an energy like Flambeau's till the lid was torn off, and all that was there lay glimmering in the grey starlight.

'Bones,' said Craven; and then he added, 'but it is a man,' as if that were something unexpected.

'Is he,' asked Flambeau in a voice that went oddly up and down, 'is he all right?'

'Seems so,' said the officer huskily, bending over the obscure and decaying skeleton in the box. 'Wait a minute.'

A vast heave went over Flambeau's huge figure. 'And now I come to think of it,' he cried, 'why in the name of madness shouldn't he be all right? What is it gets hold of a man on these cursed cold mountains? I think it's the black, brainless repetition; all these forests, and over all an ancient horror of unconsciousness. It's like the dream of an atheist. Pine-trees and more pine-trees and millions more pine-trees——'

'God!' cried the man by the coffin; 'but he hasn't got a head.'

While the others stood rigid the priest, for the first time, showed a leap of startled concern.

'No head!' he repeated. '*No head?*' as if he had almost expected some other deficiency.

Half-witted visions of a headless baby born to Glengyle, of a headless youth hiding himself in the castle, of a headless man pacing those ancient halls or that gorgeous garden, passed in panorama through their minds. But even in that stiffened instant the tale took no root in them and seemed to have no reason in it. They stood listening to the loud woods and the shrieking sky quite foolishly, like exhausted animals. Thought seemed to be something enormous that had suddenly slipped out of their grasp.

'There are three headless men,' said Father Brown: 'standing round this open grave.'

The pale detective from London opened his mouth to speak, and left it open like a yokel, while a long scream of wind tore the sky; then he looked at the axe in his hands as if it did not belong to him, and dropped it.

'Father,' said Flambeau in that infantile and heavy voice he used very seldom, 'what are we to do?'

His friend's reply came with the pent promptitude of a gun going off.

'Sleep!' cried Father Brown. 'Sleep. We have come to the end of the ways. Do you know what sleep is? Do you know that every man who sleeps believes in God? It is a sacrament; for it is an act of faith and it is a food. And we need a sacrament, if only a natural one. Something has fallen on us that falls very seldom on men; perhaps the worst thing that can fall on them.'

Craven's parted lips came together to say: 'What do you mean'

The priest turned his face to the castle as he answered:

'We have found the truth; and the truth makes no sense.'

He went down the path in front of them with a plunging and reckless step very rare with him, and when they reached the castle again he threw himself upon sleep with the simplicity of a dog.

Despite his mystic praise of slumber, Father Brown was up earlier than anyone else except the silent gardener; and was found smoking a big pipe and watching that expert at his speechless labours in the kitchen garden. Towards daybreak the rocking storm had ended in roaring rains, and the day came with a curious freshness. The gardener seemed even to have been conversing, but at sight of the detectives he planted his spade sullenly in a bed and, saying something about his breakfast, shifted along the lines of cabbages and shut himself in the kitchen. 'He's a valuable man, that,' said Father Brown. 'He does the potatoes amazingly. Still,' he added, with a dispassionate charity, 'he has his faults; which of us hasn't? He doesn't dig this bank quite regularly. There, for instance,' and he stamped suddenly on one spot. 'I'm really very doubtful about that potato.'

'And why?' asked Craven, amused with the little man's new hobby.

'I'm doubtful about it,' said the other, 'because old Gow was doubtful about it himself. He put his spade in methodically in every place but just this. There must be a mighty fine potato just there.'

Flambeau pulled up the spade and impetuously drove it into the place. He turned up, under a load of soil, something that did not look like a potato, but rather like a monstrous, over-domed mushroom. But it struck the spade with a cold click; it rolled over like a ball, and grinned up at them.

'The Earl of Glengyle,' said Brown sadly, and looked down heavily at the skull.

Then, after a momentary meditation, he plucked the spade from Flambeau, and, saying: 'We must hide it again,' clamped the skull down in the earth. Then he leaned his little body and huge head on the great handle of the spade, that stood up stiffly in the earth, and his eyes were empty and his forehead full of wrinkles. 'If one could only conceive,' he muttered, 'the meaning of this last monstrosity.' And leaning on the large spade handle, he buried his brows in his hands, as men do in church.

All the corners of the sky were brightening into blue and silver; the birds were chattering in the tiny garden trees; so loud it seemed as if the trees themselves were talking. But the three men were silent enough.

'Well, I give it all up,' said Flambeau at last boisterously. 'My brain and this world don't fit each other; and there's an end of it. Snuff, spoilt Prayer Books, and the insides of musical boxes—what——'

Brown threw up his bothered brow and rapped on the spade handle with an intolerance quite unusual with him. 'Oh, tut, tut, tut, tut!' he cried. 'All that is as plain as a pikestaff. I understood the snuff and clockwork, and so on, when I first opened my eyes this morning. And since then I've had it out with old Gow, the gardener, who is neither so deaf nor so stupid as he pretends. There's nothing amiss about the loose items. I was wrong about the torn mass-book, too; there's no harm in that. But it's this last business. Desecrating graves and stealing dead men's heads—surely there's harm in that? Surely there's black magic still in that? That doesn't fit in to the quite simple story of the snuff and the candles.' And striding about again, he smoked moodily.

'My friend,' said Flambeau, with a grim humour, 'you must be careful with me and remember I was once a criminal. The great advantage of that estate was that I always made up the story myself, and acted it as quick as I chose. This detective business of waiting about is too much for my French impatience. All my life, for good or evil, I have done things at the instant; I always fought duels the next morning; I always paid bills on the nail;* I never even put off a visit to the dentist——'

Father Brown's pipe fell out of his mouth and broke into three pieces on the gravel path. He stood rolling his eyes, the exact picture of an idiot. 'Lord, what a turnip I am!' he kept saying. 'Lord, what a turnip!' Then, in a somewhat groggy kind of way, he began to laugh.

'The dentist!' he repeated. 'Six hours in the spiritual abyss, and all because I never thought of the dentist! Such a simple, such a beautiful and peaceful thought! Friends, we have passed a night in hell; but now the sun is risen, the birds are singing, and the radiant form of the dentist consoles the world.'

'I will get some sense out of this,' cried Flambeau, striding forward, 'if I use the tortures of the Inquisition.'

Father Brown repressed what appeared to be a momentary disposition to dance on the now sunlit lawn and cried quite piteously, like a child: 'Oh, let me be silly a little. You don't know how unhappy I have been. And now I know that there has been no deep sin in this business at all. Only a little lunacy, perhaps—and who minds that?'

He spun round once, then faced them with gravity.

'This is not a story of crime,' he said; 'rather it is the story of a strange and crooked honesty. We are dealing with the one man on earth, perhaps, who has taken no more than his due. It is a study in the savage living logic that has been the religion of this race.

'That old local rhyme about the house of Glengyle——

> "As green sap to the simmer trees
> Is red gold to the Ogilvies"——

was literal as well as metaphorical. It did not merely mean that the Glengyles sought for wealth; it was also true that they literally gathered gold; they had a huge collection of ornaments and utensils in that metal. They were, in fact, misers whose mania took that turn. In the light of that fact, run through all the things we found in the castle. Diamonds without their gold rings; candles without their gold candlesticks; snuff without the gold snuff-boxes; pencil-leads without the gold pencil-cases; a walking-stick without its gold top; clockwork without the gold clocks—or rather watches. And, mad as it sounds, because the halos and the name of God in the old missals were of real gold, these also were taken away.'

The garden seemed to brighten, the grass to grow gayer in the strengthening sun, as the crazy truth was told. Flambeau lit a cigarette as his friend went on.

'Were taken away,' continued Father Brown; 'were taken away—but not stolen. Thieves would never have left this mystery. Thieves would have taken the gold snuff-boxes, snuff and all; the gold pencil-cases, lead and all. We have to deal with a man with a peculiar conscience, but certainly a conscience. I found that mad moralist this morning in the kitchen garden yonder, and I heard the whole story.

'The late Archibald Ogilvie was the nearest approach to a good man ever born at Glengyle. But his bitter virtue took the turn of the misanthrope; he moped over the dishonesty of his ancestors, from which, somehow, he generalized a dishonesty of all men. More especially he distrusted philanthropy or freegiving; and he swore if he could find one man who took his exact rights he should have all the gold of Glengyle. Having delivered this defiance to humanity he shut himself up, without the smallest expectation of its being answered. One day, however, a deaf and seemingly senseless lad from a distant village brought him a belated telegram; and Glengyle, in his acrid pleasantry, gave him a new farthing. At least he thought he had done so, but when he turned over his change he found the new farthing still there and a sovereign gone. The accident offered him vistas of sneering speculation. Either way, the boy would show the greasy greed of the species. Either he would vanish, a thief stealing a coin; or he would sneak back with it virtuously, a snob seeking a reward. In the middle of the night Lord Glengyle was knocked up out of his bed—for he lived alone—and forced to open the door to the deaf idiot. The idiot brought with him, not the sovereign, but exactly nineteen shillings and eleven-pence three-farthings in change.

'Then the mad exactitude of this action took hold on the mad lord's brain like fire. He swore he was Diogenes, that had long sought an honest man, and at last had found one. He made a new will, which I have seen. He took the literal youth into his huge, neglected house, and trained him up as his solitary servant and—after an odd manner—his heir. And whatever that queer creature understands, he understood absolutely his lord's two fixed ideas: first, that the letter of right is everything; and second, that he himself was to have the gold of Glengyle. So far, that is all; and that is simple. He has stripped the house of gold, and taken not a grain that was not gold; not so much as a grain of snuff. He lifted the gold leaf off an old illumination, fully satisfied that he left the rest unspoilt. All that I understood; but I could not understand this skull business. I was really uneasy about that human head buried among the potatoes. It distressed me—till Flambeau said the right word—till the lovely word "dentist" rang out like the laughter of the fairies.

'It will be all right. He will put the skull back in the grave, when he has taken the gold out of the tooth.'

And, indeed, when Flambeau crossed the hill that morning, he saw that strange being, the just miser, digging at the desecrated grave, the plaid round his throat thrashing out in the mountain wind; the sober top hat on his head.

THE WRONG SHAPE

CERTAIN of the great roads going north out of London continue far into the country a sort of attenuated and interrupted spectre of a street, with great gaps in the building, but preserving the line. Here will be a group of shops, followed by a fenced field or paddock, and then a famous public-house, and then perhaps a market garden or a nursery garden, and then one large private house, and then another field and another inn, and so on. If anyone walks along one of these roads he will pass a house which will probably catch his eye, though he may not be able to explain its attraction. It is a long, low house, running parallel with the road, painted mostly white and pale green, with a veranda and sun-blinds, and porches capped with those quaint sort of cupolas like wooden umbrellas that one sees in some old-fashioned houses. In fact, it is an old-fashioned house, very English and very suburban in the good old wealthy Clapham sense. And yet the house has a look of having been built chiefly for the hot weather. Looking at its white paint and sun-blinds one thinks vaguely of pugarees* and even of palm trees. I cannot trace the feeling to its root; perhaps the place was built by an Anglo-Indian.

Anyone passing this house, I say, would be namelessly fascinated by it; would feel that it was a place about which some story was to be told. And he would have been right, as you shall shortly hear. For this is the story—the story of the strange things that did really happen in it in the Whitsuntide of the year 18—:

Anyone passing the house on the Thursday before Whit-Sunday at about half-past four p.m. would have seen the front door open, and Father Brown, of the small church of St Mungo,* come out smoking a large pipe in company with a very tall French friend of his called Flambeau, who was smoking a very small cigarette. These persons may or may not be of interest to the reader, but the truth is that they were not the only interesting things that were displayed when the front door of the white-and-green house was opened. There are further peculiarities about this house, which must be described to start with, not only that the reader may understand this tragic tale, but also that he may realize what it was that the opening of the door revealed.

The whole house was built upon the plan of a T, but a T with a very long cross piece and a very short tail piece. The long cross piece was the frontage that ran along in face of the street, with the front door in the middle; it was two stories high, and contained nearly all the important rooms. The short tail piece, which ran out at the back immediately opposite the front door, was one story high, and consisted only of two long rooms, the one leading into the other. The first of these two

rooms was the study in which the celebrated Mr Quinton*
wrote his wild Oriental poems and romances. The farther
room was a glass conservatory full of tropical blossoms of
quite unique and almost monstrous beauty, and on such afternoons as these was glowing with gorgeous sunlight. Thus
when the hall door was open, many a passer-by literally
stopped to stare and gasp; for he looked down a perspective of
rich apartments to something really like a transformation
scene in a fairy play: purple clouds and golden suns and
crimson stars that were at once scorchingly vivid and yet
transparent and far away.

Leonard Quinton, the poet, had himself most carefully arranged this effect; and it is doubtful whether he so perfectly
expressed his personality in any of his poems. For he was a
man who drank and bathed in colours, who indulged his lust
for colour somewhat to the neglect of form—even of good
form. This it was that had turned his genius so wholly to
Eastern art and imagery; to those bewildering carpets or
blinding embroideries in which all the colours seem fallen into
a fortunate chaos, having nothing to typify or to teach. He
had attempted, not perhaps with complete artistic success,
but with acknowledged imagination and invention, to
compose epics and love stories reflecting the riot of violent
and even cruel colour; tales of tropical heavens of burning
gold or blood-red copper; of Eastern heroes who rode with
twelve-turbaned mitres upon elephants painted purple or
peacock green; of gigantic jewels that a hundred negroes
could not carry, but which burned with ancient and strange-
hued fires.

In short (to put the matter from the more common point of
view), he dealt much in Eastern heavens, rather worse than
most western hells; in Eastern monarchs, whom we might
possibly call maniacs; and in Eastern jewels which a Bond
Street* jeweller (if the hundred staggering negroes brought
them into his shop) might possibly not regard as genuine.
Quinton was a genius, if a morbid one; and even his morbidity
appeared more in his life than in his work. In temperament he
was weak and waspish, and his health had suffered heavily
from Oriental experiments with opium. His wife—a hand-

some, hard-working, and, indeed, over-worked woman—objected to the opium, but objected much more to a live Indian hermit in white and yellow robes, whom her husband had insisted on entertaining for months together, a Virgil* to guide his spirit through the heavens and the hells of the East.

It was out of this artistic household that Father Brown and his friend stepped on to the door-step; and to judge from their faces, they stepped out of it with much relief. Flambeau had known Quinton in wild student days in Paris, and they had renewed the acquaintance for a week-end; but apart from Flambeau's more responsible developments of late, he did not get on well with the poet now. Choking oneself with opium and writing little erotic verses on vellum was not his notion of how a gentleman should go to the devil. As the two paused on the doorstep, before taking a turn in the garden, the front garden gate was thrown open with violence, and a young man with a billycock hat on the back of his head tumbled up the steps in his eagerness. He was a dissipated-looking youth with a gorgeous red necktie all awry, as if he had slept in it, and he kept fidgeting and lashing about with one of those little jointed canes.

'I say,' he said breathlessly, 'I want to see old Quinton. I must see him. Has he gone?'

'Mr Quinton is in, I believe,' said Father Brown, cleaning his pipe, 'but I do not know if you can see him. The doctor is with him at present.'

The young man, who seemed not to be perfectly sober, stumbled into the hall; and at the same moment the doctor came out of Quinton's study, shutting the door and beginning to put on his gloves.

'See Mr Quinton?' said the doctor coolly. 'No, I'm afraid you can't. In fact, you mustn't on any account. Nobody must see him; I've just given him his sleeping draught.'

'No, but look here, old chap,' said the youth in the red tie, trying affectionately to capture the doctor by the lapels of his coat. 'Look here. I'm simply sewn up, I tell you. I——'

'It's no good, Mr Atkinson,' said the doctor, forcing him to fall back; 'when you can alter the effects of a drug I'll alter my decision,' and, settling on his hat, he stepped out into the sunlight with the other two. He was a bull-necked, good-tempered little man with a small moustache, inexpressibly ordinary, yet giving an impression of capability.

The young man in the billycock, who did not seem to be gifted with any tact in dealing with people beyond the general idea of clutching hold of their coats, stood outside the door, as dazed as if he had been thrown out bodily, and silently watched the other three walk away together through the garden.

'That was a sound, spanking lie I told just now,' remarked the medical man, laughing. 'In point of fact, poor Quinton doesn't have his sleeping draught for nearly half an hour. But I'm not going to have him bothered with that little beast, who only wants to borrow money that he wouldn't pay back if he could. He's a dirty little scamp, though he is Mrs Quinton's brother, and she's as fine a woman as ever walked.'

'Yes,' said Father Brown. 'She's a good woman.'

'So I propose to hang about the garden till the creature has cleared off,' went on the doctor, 'and then I'll go in to Quinton with the medicine. Atkinson can't get in, because I locked the door.'

'In that case, Dr Harris,' said Flambeau, 'we might as well walk round at the back by the end of the conservatory. There's no entrance to it that way but it's worth seeing, even from the outside.'

'Yes, and I might get a squint at my patient,' laughed the doctor, 'for he prefers to lie on an ottoman right at the end of the conservatory amid all those blood-red poinsettias; it would give me the creeps. But what are you dong?'

Father Brown had stopped for a moment, and picked up out of the long grass, where it had almost been wholly hidden, a queer, crooked Oriental knife, inlaid exquisitely in coloured stones and metals.

'What is this?' asked Father Brown, regarding it with some disfavour.

'Oh, Quinton's, I suppose,' said Dr Harris carelessly; 'he has all sorts of Chinese knick-knacks about the place. Or perhaps it belongs to that mild Hindoo of his whom he keeps on a string.'

'What Hindoo?' asked Father Brown, still staring at the dagger in his hand.

'Oh, some Indian conjurer,' said the doctor lightly; 'a fraud, of course.'

'You don't believe in magic?' asked Father Brown without looking up.

'Oh crikey! magic!' said the doctor.

'It's very beautiful,' said the priest in a low, dreaming voice; 'the colours are very beautiful. But it's the wrong shape.'

'What for?' asked Flambeau, staring.

'For anything. It's the wrong shape in the abstract. Don't you ever feel that about Eastern art? The colours are intoxicatingly lovely; but the shapes are mean and bad— deliberately mean and bad. I have seen wicked things in a Turkey carpet.'

'*Mon Dieu!*' cried Flambeau, laughing.

'They are letters and symbols in a language I don't know; but I know they stand for evil words,' went on the priest, his voice growing lower and lower. 'The lines go wrong on purpose—like serpents doubling to escape.'

'What the devil are you talking about?' said the doctor with a loud laugh.

Flambeau spoke quietly to him in answer. 'The Father sometimes gets this mystic's cloud on him,' he said; 'but I give you fair warning that I have never known him have it except when there was some evil quite near.'

'Oh, rats!' said the scientist.

'Why, look at it,' cried Father Brown, holding out the crooked knife at arm's length, as if it were some glittering snake. 'Don't you see it is the wrong shape? Don't you see that it has no hearty and plain purpose? It does not point like a spear. It does not sweep like a scythe. It does not *look* like a weapon. It looks like an instrument of torture.'

'Well, as you don't seem to like it,' said the jolly Harris, 'it had better be taken back to its owner. Haven't we come to the end of this confounded conservatory yet? This house is the wrong shape, if you like.'

'You don't understand,' said Father Brown, shaking his head. 'The shape of this house is quaint—it is even laughable. But there is nothing *wrong* about it.'

As they spoke they came round the curve of glass that ended the conservatory, an uninterrupted curve, for there was neither door nor window by which to enter at that end. The glass, however, was clear, and the sun still bright, though beginning to set; and they could see not only the flamboyant blossoms inside, but the frail figure of the poet in a brown velvet coat lying languidly on the sofa, having, apparently, fallen half asleep over a book. He was a pale, slight man, with loose, chestnut hair and a fringe of beard that was the paradox of his face, for the beard made him look less manly. These traits were well known to all three of them; but even had it not been so, it may be doubted whether they would have looked at Quinton just then. Their eyes were riveted on another object.

Exactly in their path, immediately outside the round end of the glass building, was standing a tall man, whose drapery fell to his feet in faultless white, and whose bare, brown skull, face, and neck gleamed in the setting sun like splendid bronze. He was looking through the glass at the sleeper, and he was more motionless than a mountain.

'Who is that?' cried Father Brown, stepping back with a hissing intake of his breath.

'Oh, it is only that Hindoo humbug,' growled Harris; 'but I don't know what the deuce he's doing here.'

'It looks like hypnotism,' said Flambeau, biting his black moustache.

'Why are you unmedical fellows always talking bosh about hypnotism?' cried the doctor. 'It looks a deal more like burglary.'

'Well, we will speak to it, at any rate,' said Flambeau, who was always for action. One long stride took him to the place where the Indian stood. Bowing from his great height, which overtopped even the Oriental's, he said with placid impudence:

'Good evening, sir. Do you want anything?'

Quite slowly, like a great ship turning into a harbour, the great yellow face turned, and looked at last over its white shoulder. They where startled to see that its yellow eyelids were quite sealed, as in sleep. 'Thank you,' said the face in excellent English. 'I want nothing.' Then, half opening the lids, so as to show a slit of opalescent eyeball, he repeated, 'I want nothing.' Then he opened his eyes wide with a startling stare, said, 'I want nothing,' and went rustling away into the rapidly darkening garden.

'The Christian is more modest,' muttered Father Brown; 'he wants something.'

'What on earth was he doing?' asked Flambeau, knitting his black brows and lowering his voice.

'I should like to talk to you later,' said Father Brown.

The sunlight was still a reality, but it was the red light of evening, and the bulk of the garden trees and bushes grew blacker and blacker against it. They turned round the end of the conservatory, and walked in silence down the other side to get round to the front door. As they went they seemed to wake something, as one startles a bird, in the deeper corner between the study and the main building; and again they saw the white-robed fakir slide out of the shadow, and slip round towards the front door. To their surprise, however, he had not been alone. They found themselves abruptly pulled up and forced to banish their bewilderment by the appearance of Mrs Quinton, with her heavy golden hair and square pale face, advancing on them out of the twilight. She looked a little stern, but was entirely courteous.

'Good evening, Dr Harris,' was all she said.

'Good evening, Mrs Quinton,' said the little doctor heartily. 'I am just going to give your husband his sleeping draught.'

'Yes,' she said in a clear voice. 'I think it is quite time.' And she smiled at them, and went sweeping into the house.

'That woman's over-driven,' said Father Brown; 'that's the kind of woman that does her duty for twenty years, and then does something dreadful.'

The little doctor looked at him for the first time with an eye of interest. 'Did you ever study medicine?' he asked.

'You have to know something of the mind as well as the body,' answered the priest; 'we have to know something of the body as well as the mind.'

'Well,' said the doctor, 'I think I'll go and give Quinton his stuff.'

They had turned the corner of the front façade, and were approaching the front doorway. As they turned into it they saw the man in the white robe for the third time. He came so straight towards the front door that it seemed quite incredible that he had not just come out of the study opposite to it. Yet they knew that the study door was locked.

Father Brown and Flambeau, however, kept this weird contradiction to themselves, and Dr Harris was not a man to waste his thoughts on the impossible. He permitted the omnipresent Asiatic to make his exit, and then stepped briskly into the hall. There he found a figure which he had already forgotten. The inane Atkinson was still hanging about, humming and poking things with his knobby cane. The doctor's face had a spasm of disgust and decision, and he whispered rapidly to his companion: 'I must lock the door again, or this rat will get in. But I shall be out again in two minutes.'

He rapidly unlocked the door and locked it again behind him, just balking a blundering charge from the young man in the billycock. The young man threw himself impatiently on a hall chair. Flambeau looked at a Persian illumination on the wall; Father Brown, who seemed in a sort of daze, dully eyed the door. In about four minutes the door was opened again. Atkinson was quicker this time. He sprang forward, held the door open for an instant, and called out: 'Oh, I say, Quinton, I want——'

From the other end of the study came the clear voice of Quinton, in something between a yawn and a yell of weary laughter.

'Oh, I know what you want. Take it, and leave me in peace. I'm writing a song about peacocks.'

Before the door closed half a sovereign came flying through the aperture; and Atkinson, stumbling forward, caught it with singular dexterity.

'So that's settled,' said the doctor, and, locking the door savagely, he led the way out into the garden.

'Poor Leonard can get a little peace now,' he added to Father Brown; 'he's locked in all by himself for an hour or two.'

'Yes,' answered the priest; 'and his voice sounded jolly enough when we left him.' Then he looked gravely round the garden, and saw the loose figure of Atkinson standing and jingling the half-sovereign in his pocket, and beyond, in the purple twilight, the figure of the Indian sitting bolt upright upon a bank of grass with his face turned towards the setting sun. Then he said abruptly: 'Where is Mrs Quinton?'

'She has gone up to her room,' said the doctor. 'That is her shadow on the blind.'

Father Brown looked up, and frowningly scrutinized a dark outline at the gas-lit window.

'Yes,' he said, 'that is her shadow,' and he walked a yard or two and threw himself upon a garden seat.

Flambeau sat down beside him; but the doctor was one of those energetic people who live naturally on their legs. He walked away, smoking, into the twilight, and the two friends were left together.

'My father,' said Flambeau in French, 'what is the matter with you?'

Father Brown was silent and motionless for half a minute then he said: 'Superstition is irreligious, but there is something in the air of this place. I think it's that Indian—at least, partly.'

He sank into silence, and watched the distant outline of the Indian, who still sat rigid as if in prayer. At first sight he seemed motionless, but as Father Brown watched him he saw that the man swayed ever so slightly with a rhythmic movement, just as the dark tree-tops swayed ever so slightly in the little wind that was creeping up the dim garden paths and shuffling the fallen leaves a little.

The landscape was growing rapidly dark, as if for a storm, but they could still see all the figures in their various places. Atkinson was leaning against a tree, with a listless face; Quinton's wife was still at her window; the doctor had gone strolling round the end of the conservatory; they could see his cigar like a will-o'-the-wisp; and the fakir still sat rigid and yet rocking, while the trees above him began to rock and almost to roar. Storm was certainly coming.

'When that Indian spoke to us,' went on Brown in a conversational undertone, 'I had a sort of vision, a vision of him and all his universe. Yet he only said the same thing three times. When first he said, "I want nothing," it meant only that he was impenetrable, that Asia does not give itself away. Then he said again, "I want nothing," and I knew that he meant that he was sufficient to himself, like a cosmos, that he needed no God, neither admitted any sins. And when he said the third time, "I want nothing," he said it with blazing eyes. And I knew that he meant literally what he said; that nothing was his desire and his home; that he was weary for nothing as for wine; that annihilation, the mere destruction of everything or anything——'

Two drops of rain fell; and for some reason Flambeau started and looked up, as if they had stung him. And the same instant the doctor down by the end of the conservatory began running towards them, calling out something as he ran.

As he came among them like a bombshell the restless Atkinson happened to be taking a turn nearer to the house front; and the doctor clutched him by the collar in a convulsive grip. 'Foul play!' he cried; 'what have you been doing to him, you dog?'

The priest had sprung erect, and had the voice of steel of a soldier in command.

'No fighting,' he cried coolly; 'we are enough to hold anyone we want to. What is the matter, doctor?'

'Things are not right with Quinton,' said the doctor, quite white. 'I could just see him through the glass, and I don't like the way he's lying. It's not as I left him, anyhow.'

'Let us go in to him,' said Father Brown shortly. 'You can leave Mr Atkinson alone. I have had him in sight since we heard Quinton's voice.'

'I will stop here and watch him,' said Flambeau hurriedly. 'You go in and see.'

The doctor and the priest flew to the study door, unlocked it, and fell into the room. In doing so they nearly fell over the large mahogany table in the centre at which the poet usually wrote; for the place was lit only by a small fire kept for the invalid. In the middle of this table lay a single sheet of paper, evidently left there on purpose. The doctor snatched it up, glanced at it, handed it to Father Brown, and crying, 'Good God, look at that!' plunged towards the glass room beyond, where the terrible tropic flowers still seemed to keep a crimson memory of the sunset.

Father Brown read the words three times before he put down the paper. The words were: 'I die by my own hand; yet I die murdered!' They were in the quite inimitable, not to say illegible, handwriting of Leonard Quinton.

Then Father Brown, still keeping the paper in his hand, strode towards the conservatory, only to meet his medical friend coming back with a face of assurance and collapse. 'He's done it,' said Harris.

They went together through the gorgeous unnatural beauty of cactus and azalea and found Leonard Quinton, poet and romancer, with his head hanging downward off his ottoman and his red curls sweeping the ground. Inside his left side was thrust the queer dagger that they had picked up in the garden, and his limp hand still rested on the hilt.

Outside, the storm had come at one stride, like the night in Coleridge,* and garden and glass roof were darkening with driving rain. Father Brown seemed to be studying the paper more than the corpse; he held it close to his eyes; and seemed trying to read it in the twilight. Then he held it up against the faint light, and, as he did so, lightning stared at them for an instant so white that the paper looked black against it.

Darkness full of thunder followed, and after the thunder Father Brown's voice said out of the dark: 'Doctor, this paper is the wrong shape.'

'What do you mean?' asked Doctor Harris, with a frowning stare.

'It isn't square,' answered Brown. 'It has a sort of edge snipped off at the corner. What does it mean?'

'How the deuce should I know?' growled the doctor. 'Shall we move this poor chap, do you think? He's quite dead.'

'No,' answered the priest; 'we must leave him as he lies and send for the police.' But he was still scrutinizing the paper.

As they went back through the study he stopped by the table and picked up a small pair of nail scissors. 'Ah,' he said with a sort of relief; 'this is what he did it with. But yet——' And he knitted his brows.

'Oh, stop fooling with that scrap of paper,' said the doctor emphatically. 'It was a fad of his. He had hundreds of them. He cut all his paper like that,' as he pointed to a stack of sermon paper* still unused on another and smaller table.

Father Brown went up to it and held up a sheet. It was the same irregular shape.

'Quite so,' he said. 'And here I see the corners that were snipped off.' And to the indignation of his colleague he began to count them.

'That's all right,' he said, with an apologetic smile. 'Twenty-three sheets cut and twenty-two corners cut off them. And as I see you are impatient we will rejoin the others.'

'Who is to tell his wife?' asked Dr Harris. 'Will you go and tell her now, while I send a servant for the police?'

'As you will,' said Father Brown indifferently. And he went out to the hall door.

Here also he found a drama, though of a more grotesque sort. It showed nothing less than his big friend Flambeau in an attitude to which he had long been unaccustomed, while upon the pathway at the bottom of the steps was sprawling with his boots in the air the amiable Atkinson, his billycock hat and walking-cane sent flying in opposite directions along the path. Atkinson had at length wearied of Flambeau's almost paternal custody, and had endeavoured to knock him down, which was by no means a smooth game to play with the Roi des Apaches,* even after that monarch's abdication.

Flambeau was about to leap upon his enemy and secure him once more, when the priest patted him easily on the sholder.

'Make it up with Mr Atkinson, my friend,' he said. 'Beg a mutual pardon and say "Good night." We need not detain him any longer.' Then, as Atkinson rose somewhat doubtfully and gathered his hat and stick and went towards the garden gate, Father Brown said in a more serious voice: 'Where is that Indian?'

They all three (for the doctor had joined them) turned involuntarily towards the dim grassy bank amid the tossing trees, purple with twilight, where they had last seen the brown man swaying in his strange prayers. The Indian was gone.

'Confound him,' said the doctor, stamping furiously. 'Now I know that it was that nigger that did it.'

'I thought you didn't believe in magic,' said Father Brown quietly.

'No more I did,' said the doctor, rolling his eyes. 'I only know that I loathed that yellow devil when I thought he was a sham wizard. And I shall loathe him more if I come to think he was a real one.'

'Well, his having escaped is nothing,' said Flambeau. 'For we could have proved nothing and done nothing against him. One hardly goes to the parish constable with a story of suicide imposed by witchcraft or auto-suggestion.'

Meanwhile Father Brown had made his way into the house, and now went to break the news to the wife of the dead man.

When he came out again he looked a little pale and tragic; but what passed between them in that interview was never known, even when all was known.

Flambeau, who was talking quietly with the doctor, was surprised to see his friend reappear so soon at his elbow; but Brown took no notice, and merely drew the doctor apart. 'You have sent for the police, haven't you?' he asked.

'Yes,' answered Harris. 'They ought to be here in ten minutes.'

'Will you do me a favour?' said the priest quietly. 'The truth is, I make a collection of these curious stories, which often contain, as in the case of our Hindoo friend, elements which can hardly be put into a police report. Now, I want you to write out a report of this case for my private use. Yours is a clever trade,' he said, looking at the doctor gravely and steadily in the face. 'I sometimes think that you know some details of this matter which you have not thought fit to mention. Mine is a confidential trade like yours, and I will treat anything you write for me in strict confidence. But write the whole.'

The doctor, who had been listening thoughtfully with his head a little on one side, looked the priest in the face for an instant, and said: 'All right,' and went into the study, closing the door behind him.

'Flambeau,' said Father Brown, 'there is a long seat there under the veranda, where we can smoke, out of the rain. You are my only friend in the world, and I want to talk to you. Or, perhaps, be silent with you.'

They established themselves comfortably in the veranda seat; Father Brown, against his common habit, accepted a good cigar and smoked it steadily in silence, while the rain shrieked and rattled on the roof of the veranda.

'My friend,' he said at length, 'this is a very queer case. A very queer case.'

'I should think it was,' said Flambeau, with something like a shudder.

'You call it queer, and I call it queer,' said the other, 'and yet we mean quite opposite things. The modern mind always mixes up two different ideas: mystery in the sense of what is marvellous, and mystery in the sense of what is complicated. That is half its difficulty about miracles. A miracle is startling; but it is simple. It is simple because it *is* a miracle. It is power coming directly from God (or the devil) instead of indirectly through nature or human wills. Now you mean that this business is marvellous because it is miraculous, because it is witchcraft worked by a wicked Indian. Understand, I do not say that it was not spiritual or diabolic. Heaven and hell only know by what surrounding influences strange sins come into the lives of men. But for the present my point is this: If it was pure magic, as you think, then it is marvellous; but it is not mysterious—that is, it is not complicated. The quality of a miracle is mysterious, but its manner is simple. Now, the manner of this business has been the reverse of simple.'

The storm that had slackened for a little seemed to be swelling again, and there came heavy movements as of faint thunder. Father Brown let fall the ash of his cigar and went on:

'There has been in this incident,' he said, 'a twisted, ugly, complex quality that does not belong to the straight bolts either of heaven or hell. As one knows the crooked track of a snail, I know the crooked track of a man.'

The white lightning opened its enormous eye in one wink, the sky shut up again, and the priest went on:

'Of all these crooked things, the crookedest was the shape of that piece of paper. It was crookeder than the dagger that killed him.'

'You mean the paper on which Quinton confessed his suicide,' said Flambeau.

'I mean the paper on which Quinton wrote, "I die by my own hand,"' answered Father Brown. 'The shape of that paper, my friend, was the wrong shape; the wrong shape, if ever I have seen it in this wicked world.'

'It only had a corner snipped off,' said Flambeau, 'and I understand that all Quinton's paper was cut that way.'

'It was a very odd way,' said the other, 'and a very bad way, to my taste and fancy. Look here, Flambeau, this Quinton— God receive his soul!—was perhaps a bit of a cur in some ways, but he really was an artist, with the pencil as well as the pen. His handwriting, though hard to read, was bold and beautiful. I can't prove what I say; I can't prove anything. But I tell you with the full force of conviction that he could never have cut that mean little piece off a sheet of paper. If he had wanted to cut down paper for some purpose of fitting in, or binding up, or what not, he would have made quite a different slash with the scissors. Do you remember the shape? It was a mean shape. It was a wrong shape. Like this. Don't you remember?'

And he waved his burning cigar before him in the darkness, making irregular squares so rapidly that Flambeau really seemed to see them as fiery hieroglyphics upon the darkness— hieroglyphics such as his friend had spoken of, which are undecipherable, yet can have no good meaning.

'But,' said Flambeau, as the priest put his cigar in his mouth again and leaned back, staring at the roof. 'Suppose somebody else did use the scissors. Why should somebody else, cutting pieces off his sermon paper, make Quinton commit suicide?'

Father Brown was still leaning back and staring at the room, but he took his cigar out of his mouth and said: 'Quinton never did commit suicide.'

Flambeau stared at him. 'Why, confound it all,' he cried; 'then why did he confess to suicide?'

The priest leaned forward again, settled his elbows on his knees, looked at the ground, and said in a low distinct voice: 'He never did confess to suicide.'

Flambeau laid his cigar down. 'You mean,' he said, 'that the writing was forged?'

'No,' said Father Brown; 'Quinton wrote it all right.'

'Well, there you are,' said the aggravated Flambeau; 'Quinton wrote: "I die by my own hand," with his own hand on a plain piece of paper.'

'Of the wrong shape,' said the priest calmly.

'Oh, the shape be damned!' cried Flambeau. 'What has the shape to do with it?'

'There were twenty-three snipped papers,' resumed Brown unmoved, 'and only twenty-two pieces snipped off. Therefore one of the pieces had been destroyed, probably that from the written paper. Does that suggest anything to you?'

A light dawned on Flambeau's face, and he said: 'There was something else written by Quinton, some other words. "They will tell you I die by my own hand," or "Do not believe that——"'

'Hotter, as the children say,' said his friend. 'But the piece was hardly half an inch across; there was no room for one word, let alone five. Can you think of anything hardly bigger than a comma which the man with hell in his heart had to tear away as a testimony against him?'

'I can think of nothing,' said Flambeau at last.

'What about quotation marks?' said the priest, and flung his cigar far into the darkness like a shooting star.

All words had left the other man's mouth, and Father Brown, said, like one going back to fundamentals:

'Leonard Quinton was a romancer, and was writing an Oriental romance about wizardry and hypnotism. He——'

At this moment the door opened briskly behind them and the doctor came out with his hat on. He put a long envelope into the priest's hands.

'That's the document you wanted,' he said, 'and I must be getting home. Good night.'

'Good night,' said Father Brown, as the doctor walked briskly to the gate. He had left the front door open, so that a shaft of gaslight fell upon them. In the light of this Brown opened the envelope and read the following words:

'DEAR FATHER BROWN,—*Vicisti, Galilæe!** Otherwise, damn your eyes, which are very penetrating ones. Can it be possible that there is something in all that stuff of yours after all?

'I am a man who has ever since boyhood believed in Nature and in all natural functions and instincts, whether men called them moral or immoral. Long before I became a doctor, when

I was a schoolboy keeping mice and spiders, I believed that to be a good animal is the best thing in the world. But just now I am shaken; I have believed in Nature; but it seems as if Nature could betray a man. Can there be anything in your bosh? I am really getting morbid.

'I loved Quinton's wife. What was there wrong in that? Nature told me to, and it's love that makes the world go round. I also thought, quite sincerely, that she would be happier with a clean animal like me than with that tormenting little lunatic. What was there wrong in that? I was only facing facts, like a man of science. She would have been happier.

'Accoding to my own creed I was quite free to kill Quinton, which was the best thing for everybody, even himself. But as a healthy animal I had no notion of killing myself. I resolved, therefore, that I would never do it until I saw a chance that would leave me scot free. I saw that chance this morning.

'I have been three times, all told, into Quinton's study to-day. The first time I went in he would talk about nothing but the weird tale, called "The Curse of a Saint," which he was writing, which was all about how some Indian hermit made an English colonel kill himself by thinking about him. He showed me the last sheets, and even read me the last paragraph, which was something like this: "The conqueror of the Punjab, a mere yellow skeleton, but still gigantic, managed to lift himself on his elbow and gasp in his nephew's ear: 'I die by my own hand, yet I die murdered!'" It so happened, by one chance out of a hundred, that those last words were written at the top of a new sheet of paper. I left the room, and went out into the garden intoxicated with a frightful opportunity.

'We walked round the house, and two more things happened in my favour. You suspected an Indian, and you found a dagger which the Indian might most probably use. Taking the opportunity to stuff it in my pocket I went back to Quinton's study, locked the door, and gave him his sleeping draught. He was against answering Atkinson at all, but I urged him to call out and quiet the fellow, because I wanted a clear proof that Quinton was alive when I left the room for the second time. Quinton lay down in the conservatory, and I came through the study. I am a quick man with my hands, and in a minute and a half I had done what I wanted to do. I had emptied all the first part of Quinton's romance into the fire-place, where it burnt to ashes. Then I saw that the quotation marks wouldn't do, so I snipped them off, and to make it seem likelier, snipped the whole quire* to match. Then I came out with the knowledge that Quinton's confession of suicide lay on the front table, while Quinton lay alive, but asleep, in the conservatory beyond.

'The last act was a desperate one; you can guess it: I pre-tended to have seen Quinton dead and rushed to his room. I delayed you with the paper; and, being a quick man with my hands, killed Quinton while you were looking at his confes-sion of suicide. He was half-asleep, being drugged, and I put his own hand on the knife and drove it into his body. The knife was of so queer a shape that no one but an operator could have calculated the angle that would reach his heart. I wonder if you noticed this.

'When I had done it the extraordinary thing happened. Nature deserted me. I felt ill. I felt just as if I had done something wrong. I think my brain is breaking up; I feel some sort of desperate pleasure in thinking I have told the thing to somebody; that I shall not have to be alone with it if I marry and have children. What is the matter with me? . . . Madness . . . or can one have remorse, just as if one were in Byron's poems! I cannot write any more.—JAMES ERSKINE HARRIS.'

Father Brown carefully folded up the letter and put it in his breast pocket just as there came a loud peal at the gate bell, and the wet waterproofs of several policemen gleamed in the road outside.

THE HAMMER OF GOD

THE little village of Bohun Beacon* was perched on a hill so steep that the tall spire of its church seemed only like the peak of a small mountain. At the foot of the church stood a smithy, generally red with fires and always littered with hammers and scraps of iron; opposite to this, over a rude cross of cobbled paths, was 'The Blue Boar,' the only inn of the place. It was upon this crossway, in the lifting of a leaden and silver daybreak, that two brothers met in the street and spoke; though one was beginning the day and the other finishing it. The Rev. and Hon. Wilfred Bohun was very devout, and was making his way to some austere exercises of prayer or contemplation at dawn. Colonel the Hon. Norman Bohun, his elder brother, was by no means devout, and was sitting in evening-dress on the bench outside 'The Blue Boar,' drinking what the philosophic observer was free to regard either as his last glass on Tuesday or his first on Wednesday. The colonel was not particular.

The Bohuns were one of the very few aristocratic families really dating from the Middle Ages, and their pennon had actually seen Palestine. But it is a great mistake to suppose that such houses stand high in chivalric traditions. Few except the poor preserve traditions. Aristocrats live not in traditions but in fashions. The Bohuns had been Mohocks* under Queen Anne and Mashers* under Queen Victoria. But, like more than one of the really ancient houses, they had rotted in the last two centuries into mere drunkards and dandy degenerates, till there had even come a whisper of insanity. Certainly there was something hardly human about the colonel's wolfish pursuit of pleasure, and his chronic resolution not to go home till morning had a touch of the hideous clarity of insomnia. He was a tall, fine animal, elderly, but with hair startlingly yellow. He would have looked merely blond and leonine, but his blue eyes were sunk so deep in his face that they looked black. They were a little too close together. He had very long yellow moustaches, on each side of them a fold or furrow from nostril to jaw, so that a sneer seemed to cut into his face. Over his evening clothes he wore a curiously pale yellow coat that looked more like a very light dressing gown than an overcoat, and on the back of his head was stuck an extraordinary broad-brimmed hat of a bright green colour, evidently some Oriental curiosity caught up at random. He was proud of appearing in such incongruous attires—proud of the fact that he always made them look congruous.

His brother the curate had also the yellow hair and the elegance, but he was buttoned up to the chin in black, and his face was clean-shaven, cultivated and a little nervous. He seemed to live for nothing but his religion; but there were some who said (notably the blacksmith, who was a Presbyterian) that it was a love of Gothic architecture rather than of God, and that his haunting of the church like a ghost was only another and purer turn of the almost morbid thirst for beauty which sent his brother raging after women and wine. This charge was doubtful, while the man's practical piety was indubitable. Indeed, the charge was mostly an ignorant misunderstanding of the love of solitude and secret prayer, and was founded on his being often found kneeling, not before the altar, but in peculiar places, in the crypts or gallery, or even in the belfry. He was at the moment about to enter the church through the yard of the smithy, but stopped and frowned a little as he saw his brother's cavernous eyes staring in the same direction. On the hypothesis that the colonel was interested in the church he did not waste any speculations. There only remained the blacksmith's shop, and though the blacksmith was a Puritan and none of his people, Wilfred Bohun had heard some scandals about a beautiful and rather celebrated wife. He flung a suspicious look across the shed, and the colonel stood up laughing to speak to him.

'Good morning, Wilfred,' he said. 'Like a good landlord I am watching sleeplessly over my people. I am going to call on the blacksmith.'

Wilfred looked at the ground and said: 'The blacksmith is out. He is over at Greenford.'*

'I know,' answered the other with silent laughter; 'that is why I am calling on him.'

'Norman,' said the cleric, with his eye on a pebble in the road, 'are you ever afraid of thunderbolts?'

'What do you mean?' asked the colonel. 'Is your hobby meteorology?'

'I mean,' said Wilfred, without looking up, 'do you ever think that God might strike you in the street?'

'I beg your pardon,' said the colonel; 'I see your hobby is folklore.'

'I know your hobby is blasphemy,' retorted the religious man, stung in the one live place of his nature. 'But if you do not fear God, you have good reason to fear man.'

The elder raised his eyebrows politely. 'Fear man?' he said.

'Barnes the blacksmith is the biggest and strongest man for forty miles round,' said the clergyman sternly. 'I know you are no coward or weakling, but he could throw you over the wall.'

This struck home, being true, and the lowering line by mouth and nostril darkened and deepened. For a moment he stood with the heavy sneer on his face. But in an instant Colonel Bohun had recovered his own cruel good humour and laughed, showing two dog-like front teeth under his yellow moustache. 'In that case, my dear Wilfred,' he said quite carelessly, 'it was wise for the last of the Bohuns to come out partially in armour.'

And he took off the queer round hat covered with green, showing that it was lined within with steel. Wilfred recognized it indeed as a light Japanese or Chinese helmet torn down from a trophy that hung in the old family hall.

'It was the first to hand,' expained his brother airily; 'always the nearest hat—and the nearest woman.'

'The blacksmith is away at Greenford,' said Wilfred quietly; 'the time of his return is unsettled.'

And with that he turned and went into the church with bowed head, crossing himself like one who wishes to be quit of an unclean spirit. He was anxious to forget such grossness in the cool twilight of his tall Gothic cloisters; but on that morning it was fated that his still round of religious exercises should be everywhere arrested by small shocks. As he entered the church, hitherto always empty at that hour, a kneeling figure rose hastily to its feet and came towards the full daylight of the doorway. When the curate saw it he stood still with surprise. For the early worshipper was none other than the village idiot, a nephew of the blacksmith, one who neither would nor could care for the church or for anything else. He was always called 'Mad Joe,' and seemed to have no other name; he was a dark, strong, slouching lad, with a heavy white face, dark straight hair, and a mouth always open. As he passed the priest, his moon-calf countenance gave no hint of what he had been doing or thinking of. He had never been known to pray before. What sort of prayers was he saying now? Extraordinary prayers surely.

Wilfred Bohun stood rooted to the spot long enough to see the idiot go out into the sunshine, and even to see his dissolute brother hail him with a sort of avuncular jocularity. The last thing he saw was the colonel throwing pennies at the open mouth of Joe, with the serious appearance of trying to hit it.

This ugly sunlight picture of the stupidity and cruelty of the earth sent the ascetic finally to his prayers for purification and new thoughts. He went up to a pew in the gallery, which brought him under a coloured window which he loved and which always quieted his spirit; a blue window with an angel carrying lilies. There he began to think less about the half-wit, with his livid face and mouth like a fish. He began to think less of his evil brother, pacing like a lean lion in his horrible hunger. He sank deeper and deeper into those cold and sweet colours of silver blossoms and sapphire sky.

In this place half an hour afterwards he was found by Gibbs, the village cobbler, who had been sent for him in some haste. He got to his feet with promptitude, for he knew that no small matter would have brought Gibbs into such a place at all. The cobbler was, as in many villages, an atheist, and his appearance in church was a shade more extraordinary than Mad Joe's. It was a morning of theological enigmas.

'What is it?' asked Wilfred Bohun rather stiffly, but putting out a trembling hand for his hat.

The atheist spoke in a tone that, coming from him, was quite startlingly respectful, and even, as it were, huskily sympathetic.

'You must excuse me, sir,' he said in a hoarse whisper, 'but we didn't think it right not to let you know at once. I'm afraid a rather dreadful thing has happened, sir. I'm afraid your brother——'

Wilfred clenched his frail hands. 'What devilry has he done now?' he cried in involuntary passion.

'Why, sir,' said the cobbler, coughing, 'I'm afraid he's done nothing, and won't do anything. I'm afraid he's done for. You had really better come down, sir.'

The curate followed the cobbler down a short winding stair which brought them out at an entrance rather higher than the street. Bohun saw the tragedy in one glance, flat underneath him like a plan. In the yard of the smithy were standing five or six men, mostly in black, one in an inspector's uniform. They included the doctor, the Presbyterian minister, and the priest from the Roman Catholic chapel to which the blacksmith's wife belonged. The latter was speaking to her, indeed, very rapidly, in an undertone, as she, a magnificent woman with red-gold hair, was sobbing blindly on a bench. Between these two groups, and just clear of the main heap of hammers, lay a man in evening dress, spread-eagled and flat on his face. From the height above Wilfred could have sworn to every item of his costume and appearance, down to the Bohun rings upon his fingers; but the skull was only a hideous splash, like a star of blackness and blood.

Wilfred Bohun gave but one glance, and ran down the steps into the yard. The doctor, who was the family physician, saluted him, but he scarcely took any notice. He could only stammer out: 'My brother is dead. What does it mean? What is this horrible mystery?' There was an unhappy silence; and then the cobbler, the most outspoken man present, answered: 'Plenty of horror, sir,' he said, 'but not much mystery.'

'What do you mean?' asked Wilfred, with a white face.

'It's plain enough,' answered Gibbs. 'There is only one man for forty miles round that could have struck such a blow as that, and he's the man that had most reason to.'

'We must not prejudge anything,' put in the doctor, a tall, black-bearded man, rather nervously; 'but it is competent for me to corroborate what Mr Gibbs says about the nature of the blow, sir; it is an incredible blow. Mr Gibbs says that only one man in this district could have done it. I should have said myself that nobody could have done it.'

A shudder of superstition went through the slight figure of the curate. 'I can hardly understand,' he said.

'Mr Bohun,' said the doctor in a low voice, 'metaphors literally fail me. It is inadequate to say that the skull was smashed to bits like an egg-shell. Fragments of bone were driven into the body and the ground like bullets into a mud wall. It was the hand of a giant.'

He was silent a moment, looking grimly through his glasses; then he added: 'The thing has one advantage—that it clears most people of suspicion at one stroke. If you or I or any normally made man in the country were accused of this crime, we should be acquitted as an infant would be acquitted of stealing the Nelson Column.'*

'That's what I say,' repeated the cobbler obstinately, 'there's only one man that could have done it, and he's the man that would have done it. Where's Simeon Barnes, the blacksmith?'

'He's over at Greenford,' faltered the curate.

'More likely over in France,' muttered the cobbler.

'No; he is in neither of those places,' said a small and colourless voice, which came from the little Roman priest who had joined the group. 'As a matter of fact, he is coming up the road at this moment.'

The little priest was not an interesting man to look at, having stubbly brown hair and a round and stolid face. But if he had been as splendid as Apollo no one would have looked at him at that moment. Everyone turned round and peered at the pathway which wound across the plain below, along which was indeed walking, at his own huge stride and with a hammer on his shoulder, Simeon the smith. He was a bony and gigantic man, with deep, dark, sinister eyes and a dark chin beard. He was walking and talking quietly with two other men; and though he was never specially cheerful, he seemed quite at his ease.

'My God!' cried the atheistic cobbler; 'and there's the hammer he did it with.'

'No,' said the inspector, a sensible-looking man with a sandy moustache, speaking for the first time. 'There's the hammer he did it with, over there by the church wall. We have left it and the body exactly as they are.'

All glanced round, and the short priest went across and looked down in silence at the tool where it lay. It was one of the smallest and the lightest of the hammers, and would not have caught the eye among the rest; but on the iron edge of it were blood and yellow hair.

After a silence the short priest spoke without looking up, and there was a new note in his dull voice. 'Mr Gibbs was hardly right,' he said, 'in saying that there is no mystery. There is at least the mystery of why so big a man should attempt so big a blow with so little a hammer.'

'Oh, never mind that,' cried Gibbs, in a fever. 'What are we to do with Simeon Barnes?'

'Leave him alone,' said the priest quietly. 'He is coming here of himself. I know these two men with him. They are very good fellows from Greenford, and they have come over about the Presbyterian chapel.'

Even as he spoke the tall smith swung round the corner of the church and strode into his own yard. Then he stood there quite still, and the hammer fell from his hand. The inspector, who had preserved impenetrable propriety, immediately went up to him.

'I won't ask you, Mr Barnes,' he said, 'whether you know anything about what has happened here. You are not bound to say. I hope you don't know, and that you will be able to prove it. But I must go through the form of arresting you in the King's name for the murder of Colonel Norman Bohun.'

'You are not bound to say anything,' said the cobbler in officious excitement. 'They've got to prove everything. They haven't proved yet that it is Colonel Bohun, with the head all smashed up like that.'

'That won't wash,' said the doctor aside to the priest. 'That's out of detective stories. I was the colonel's medical man, and I knew his body better than he did. He had very fine hands, but quite peculiar ones. The second and third fingers were the same in length. Oh, that's the colonel right enough.'

As he glanced at the brained corpse upon the ground the iron eyes of the motionless blacksmith followed them and rested there also.

'Is Colonel Bohun dead?' said the smith quite calmly. 'Then he's damned.'

'Don't say anything! Oh, don't say anything,' cried the atheist cobbler, dancing about in an ecstasy of admiration of the English legal system. For no man is such a legalist as the good Secularist.

The blacksmith turned on him over his shoulder the august face of a fanatic.

'It is well for you infidels to dodge like foxes because the world's law favours you,' he said; 'but God guards His own in His pocket, as you shall see this day.'

Then he pointed to the colonel and said: 'When did this dog die in his sins?'

'Moderate your language,' said the doctor.

'Moderate the Bible's language, and I'll moderate mine. When did he die?'

'I saw him alive at six o'clock this morning,' stammered Wilfred Bohun.

'God is good,' said the smith. 'Mr Inspector, I have not the slightest objection to being arrested. It is you who may object to arresting me. I don't mind leaving the court without a stain on my character. You do mind, perhaps, leaving the court with a bad set-back in your career.'

The solid inspector for the first time looked at the blacksmith with a lively eye—as did everybody else, except the short, strange priest, who was still looking down at the little hammer that had dealt the dreadful blow.

'There are two men standing outside this shop,' went on the blacksmith with ponderous lucidity, 'good tradesmen in Greenford whom you all know, who will swear that they saw me from before midnight till daybreak and long after in the committee-room of our Revival Mission, which sits all night, we save souls so fast. In Greenford itself twenty people could swear to me for all that time. If I were a heathen, Mr Inspector, I would let you walk on to your downfall; but, as a Christian man, I feel bound to give you your chance and ask you whether you will hear my alibi now or in court.'

The inspector seemed for the first time disturbed and said: 'Of course I should be glad to clear you altogether now.'

The smith walked out of his yard with the same long and easy stride, and returned to his two friends from Greenford, who were indeed friends of nearly everyone present. Each of them said a few words which no one ever thought of disbelieving. When they had spoken the innocence of Simeon stood up as solid as the great church above them.

One of those silences struck the group which are more strange and insufferable than any speech. Madly, in order to make conversation, the curate said to the Catholic priest:

'You seem very much interested in that hammer, Father Brown.'

'Yes, I am,' said Father Brown; 'why is it such a small hammer?'

The doctor swung round on him.

'By George, that's true,' he cried; 'who would use a little hammer with ten larger hammers lying about?'

Then he lowered his voice in the curate's ear and said: 'Only the kind of person that can't lift a large hammer. It is not a question of force or courage between the sexes. It's a question of lifting power in the shoulders. A bold woman could commit ten murders with a light hammer and never turn a hair. She could not kill a beetle with a heavy one.'

Wilfred Bohun was staring at him with a sort of hypnotized horror, while Father Brown listened with his head a little on one side, really interested and attentive. The doctor went on with more hissing emphasis:

'Why do those idiots always assume that the only person who hates the wife's lover is the wife's husband? Nine times out of ten the person who most hates the wife's lover is the wife. Who knows what insolence or treachery he had shown her—look there?'

He made a momentary gesture towards the red-haired woman on the bench. She had lifted her head at last and the tears were drying on her splendid face. But the eyes were fixed on the corpse with an electric glare that had in it something of idiocy.

The Rev. Wilfred Bohun made a limp gesture as if waving away all desire to know; but Father Brown, dusting off his sleeve some ashes blown from the furnace, spoke in his indifferent way.

'You are like so many doctors,' he said; 'your mental science is really suggestive. It is your physical science that is utterly impossible. I agree that the woman wants to kill the co-respondent much more than the petitioner does. And I agree that a woman will always pick up a small hammer instead of a big one. But the difficulty is one of physical impossibility. No woman ever born could have smashed a man's skull out flat like that.' Then he added reflectively, after a pause: 'These people haven't grasped the whole of it. The man was actually wearing an iron helmet, and the blow scattered it like broken glass. Look at that woman. Look at her arms.'

Silence held them all up again, and then the doctor said rather sulkily: 'Well, I may be wrong; there are objections to everything. But I stick to the main point. No man but an idiot would pick up that little hammer if he could use a big hammer.'

With that the lean and quivering hands of Wilfred Bohun went up to his head and seemed to clutch his scanty yellow hair. After an instant they dropped, and he cried: 'That was the word I wanted; you have said the word.'

Then he continued, mastering his discomposure: 'The words you said were, "No man but an idiot would pick up the small hammer."'

'Yes,' said the doctor. 'Well?'

'Well,' said the curate, 'no man but an idiot did.' The rest stared at him with eyes arrested and riveted, and he went on in a febrile and feminine agitation.

'I am a priest,' he cried unsteadily, 'and a priest should be no shedder of blood. I—I mean that he should bring no one to the gallows. And I thank God that I see the criminal clearly now—because he is a criminal who cannot be brought to the gallows.'

'You will not denounce him?' inquired the doctor.

'He would not be hanged if I did denounce him,' answered Wilfred, with a wild but curiously happy smile. 'When I went into the church this morning I found a madman praying there—that poor Joe, who has been wrong all his life. God knows what he prayed; but with such strange folk it is not incredible to suppose that their prayers are all upside down. Very likely a lunatic would pray before killing a man. When I last saw poor Joe he was with my brother. My brother was mocking him.'

'By Jove!' cried the doctor, 'this is talking at last. But how do you explain——'

The Rev. Wilfred was almost trembling with the excitement of his own glimpse of the truth. 'Don't you see; don't you see,' he cried feverishly, 'that is the only theory that covers both the queer things, that answers both the riddles. The two riddles are the little hammer and the big blow. The smith might have struck the big blow, but he would not have chosen the little hammer. His wife would have chosen the little hammer, but she could not have struck the big blow. But the madman might have done both. As for the little hammer—why, he was mad and might have picked up anything. And for the big blow, have you never heard, doctor, that a maniac in his paroxysm may have the strength of ten men?'

The doctor drew a deep breath and then said: 'By golly, I believe you've got it.'

Father Brown had fixed his eyes on the speaker so long and steadily as to prove that his large grey, ox-like eyes were not quite so insignificant as the rest of his face. When silence had fallen he said with marked respect: 'Mr Bohun, yours is the only theory yet propounded which holds water every way and is essentially unassailable. I think, therefore, that you deserve to be told, on my positive knowledge, that it is not the true one.' And with that the odd little man walked away and stared again at the hammer.

'That fellow seems to know more than he ought to,' whispered the doctor peevishly to Wilfred. 'Those popish priests are deucedly sly.'

'No, no,' said Bohun, with a sort of wild fatigue. 'It was the lunatic. It was the lunatic.'

The group of the two clerics and the doctor had fallen away from the more official group containing the inspector and the man he had arrested. Now, however, that their own party had broken up, they heard voices from the others. The priest looked up quietly and then looked down again as he heard the blacksmith say in a loud voice:

'I hope I've convinced you, Mr Inspector. I'm a strong man, as you say, but I couldn't have flung my hammer bang here from Greenford. My hammer hasn't any wings that it should come flying half a mile over hedges and fields.'

The inspector laughed amicably and said: 'No; I think you can be considered out of it, though it's one of the rummiest coincidences I ever saw. I can only ask you to give us all the assistance you can in finding a man as big and strong as yourself. By George! you might be useful, if only to hold him! I suppose you yourself have no guess at the man?'

'I may have a guess,' said the pale smith, 'but it is not at a man.' Then, seeing the scared eyes turn towards his wife on the bench, he put his huge hand on her shoulder and said: 'Nor a woman either.'

'What do you mean?' asked the inspector jocularly. 'You don't think cows use hammers, do you?'

'I think no thing of flesh held that hammer,' said the black-smith in a stifled voice; 'mortally speaking, I think the man died alone.'

Wilfred made a sudden forward movement and peered at him with burning eyes.

'Do you mean to say, Barnes,' came the sharp voice of the cobbler, 'that the hammer jumped up of itself and knocked the man down?'

'Oh, you gentlemen may stare and snigger,' cried Simeon; 'you clergymen who tell us on Sunday in what a stillness the Lord smote Sennacherib.* I believe that One who walks invisible in every house defended the honour of mine, and laid the defiler dead before the door of it. I believe the force in that blow was just the force there is in earthquakes, and no force less.'

Wilfred said, with a voice utterly undescribable: 'I told Norman myself to beware of the thunderbolt.'

'That agent is outside my jurisdiction,' said the inspector with a slight smile.

'You are not outside His,' answered the smith; 'see you to it.' And, turning his broad back, he went into the house.

The shaken Wilfred was led away by Father Brown, who had an easy and friendly way with him. 'Let us get out of this horrid place, Mr Bohun,' he said. 'May I look inside your church? I hear it's one of the oldest in England. We take some interest, you know,' he added with a comical grimace, 'in old English churches.'

Wilfred Bohun did not smile, for humour was never his strong point. But he nodded rather eagerly, being only too ready to explain the Gothic splendours to someone more likely to be sympathetic than the Presbyterian blacksmith or the atheist cobbler.

'By all means,' he said; 'let us go in at this side.' And he led the way into the high side entrance at the top of the flight of steps. Father Brown was mounting the first step to follow him when he felt a hand on his shoulder, and turned to behold the dark, thin figure of the doctor, his face darker yet with suspicion.

'Sir,' said the physician harshly, 'you appear to know some secrets in this black business. May I ask if you are going to keep them to yourself?'

'Why, doctor,' answered the priest, smiling quite pleasantly, 'there is one very good reason why a man of my trade would keep things to himself when he is not sure of them, and that is that it is so constantly his duty to keep them to himself when he is sure of them. But if you think I have been discourteously reticent with you or anyone, I will go to the extreme limit of my custom. I will give you two very large hints.'

'Well, sir?' said the doctor gloomily.

'First,' said Father Brown quietly, 'the thing is quite in your own province. It is a matter of physical science. The blacksmith is mistaken, not perhaps in saying that the blow was divine, but certainly in saying that it came by a miracle. It was no miracle, doctor, except in so far as man is himself a miracle, with his strange and wicked and yet half-heroic heart. The force that smashed that skull was a force well known to scientists—one of the most frequently debated of the laws of nature.'

The doctor, who was looking at him with frowning intentness, only said: 'And the other hint?'

'The other hint is this,' said the priest: 'Do you remember the blacksmith, though he believes in miracles, talking scornfully of the impossible fairy tale that his hammer had wings and flew half a mile across country?'

'Yes,' said the doctor, 'I remember that.'

'Well,' added Father Brown, with a broad smile, 'that fairy tale was the nearest thing to the real truth that has been said to-day.' And with that he turned his back and stumped up the steps after the curate.

The Reverend Wilfred, who had been waiting for him, pale and impatient, as if this little delay were the last straw for his nerves, led him immediately to his favourite corner of the church, that part of the gallery closest to the carved roof and lit by the wonderful window with the angel. The little Latin priest explored and admired everything exhaustively, talking cheerfully but in a low voice all the time. When in the course of his investigation he found the side exit and the winding stair down which Wilfred had rushed to find his brother dead, Father Brown ran not down but up, with the agility of a monkey, and his clear voice came from an outer platform above.

'Come up here, Mr Bohun,' he called. 'The air will do you good.'

Bohun followed him, and came out on a kind of stone gallery or balcony outside the building, from which one could see the illimitable plain in which their small hill stood, wooded away to the purple horizon and dotted with villages and farms. Clear and square, but quite small beneath them, was the blacksmith's yard, where the inspector still stood taking notes and the corpse still lay like a smashed fly.

'Might be the map of the world, mightn't it?' said Father Brown.

'Yes,' said Bohun very gravely, and nodded his head.

Immediately beneath and about them the lines of the Gothic building plunged outwards into the void with a sickening swiftness akin to suicide. There is that element of Titan energy in the architecture of the Middle Ages that, from whatever aspect it be seen, it always seems to be rushing away, like the strong back of some maddened horse. This church was hewn out of ancient and silent stone, bearded with old fungoids and stained with the nests of birds. And yet, when they saw it from below, it sprang like a fountain at the stars; and when they saw it, as now, from above, it poured like a cataract into a voiceless pit. For these two men on the tower were left alone with the most terrible aspect of the Gothic: the monstrous foreshortening and disproportion, the dizzy perspectives, the glimpses of great things small and small things great; a topsy-turvydom of stone in the mid-air. Details of stone, enormous by their proximity, were relieved against a pattern of fields and farms, pygmy in their distance. A carved bird or beast at a corner seemed like some vast walking or flying dragon wasting the pastures and villages below. The whole atmosphere was dizzy and dangerous, as if men were upheld in air amid the gyrating wings of colossal genii; and the whole of that old church, as tall and rich as a cathedral, seemed to sit upon the sunlit country like a cloud-burst.

'I think there is something rather dangerous about standing on these high places even to pray,' said Father Brown. 'Heights were made to be looked at, not to be looked from.'

'Do you mean that one may fall over?' asked Wilfred.

'I mean that one's soul may fall if one's body doesn't,' said the other priest.

'I scarcely understand you,' remarked Bohun indistinctly.

'Look at that blacksmith, for instance,' went on Father Brown calmly; 'a good man, but not a Christian—hard, imperious, unforgiving. Well, his Scotch religion was made up by men who prayed on hills and high crags, and learnt to look down on the world more than to look up at heaven. Humility is the mother of giants. One sees great things from the valley; only small things from the peak.'

'But he—he didn't do it,' said Bohun tremulously.

'No,' said the other in an odd voice; 'we know he didn't do it.'

After a moment he resumed, looking tranquilly out over the plain with his pale grey eyes. 'I knew a man,' he said, 'who began by worshipping with others before the altar, but who grew fond of high and lonely places to pray from, corners or niches in the belfry or the spire. And once in one of those dizzy places, where the whole world seemed to turn under him like a wheel, his brain turned also, and he fancied he was God. So that though he was a good man, he committed a great crime.'

Wilfred's face was turned away, but his bony hands turned blue and white as they tightened on the parapet of stone.

'He thought it was given to *him* to judge the world and strike down the sinner. He would never have had such a thought if he had been kneeling with other men upon a floor. But he saw all men walking about like insects. He saw one especially strutting just below him, insolent and evident by a bright green hat—a poisonous insect.'

Rooks cawed round the corners of the belfry; but there was no other sound till Father Brown went on.

'This also tempted him, that he had in his hand one of the most awful engines of nature; I mean gravitation, that mad and quickening rush by which all earth's creatures fly back to her heart when released. See, the inspector is strutting just below us in the smithy. If I were to toss a pebble over this parapet it would be something like a bullet by the time it struck him. If I were to drop a hammer—even a small hammer——'

Wilfred Bohun threw one leg over the parapet, and Father Brown had him in a minute by the collar.

'Not by that door,' he said quite gently; 'that door leads to hell.'

Bohun staggered back against the wall, and stared at him with frightful eyes.

'How do you know all this?' he cried. 'Are you a devil?'

'I am a man,' answered Father Brown gravely; 'and therefore have all devils in my heart. Listen to me,' he said after a short pause. 'I know what you did—at least, I can guess the great part of it. When you left your brother you were racked with no unrighteous rage to the extent even that you snatched up the small hammer, half inclined to kill him with his foulness on his mouth. Recoiling, you thrust it under your buttoned coat instead, and rushed into the church. You pray wildly in many places, under the angel window, upon the platform above, and on a higher platform still, from which you could see the colonel's Eastern hat like the back of a green beetle crawling about. Then something snapped in your soul, and you let God's thunderbolt fall.'

Wilfred put a weak hand to his head, and asked in a low voice: 'How did you know that his hat looked like a green beetle?'

'Oh, that,' said the other with the shadow of a smile, 'that was common sense. But hear me further. I say I know all this; but no one else shall know it. The next step is for you; I shall take no more steps; I will seal this with the seal of confession.

If you ask me why, there are many reasons, and only one that concerns you. I leave things to you because you have not yet gone very far wrong, as assassins go. You did not help to fix the crime on the smith when it was easy; or on his wife, when that was easy. You tried to fix it on the imbecile, because you knew that he could not suffer. That was one of the gleams that it is my business to find in assassins. And now come down into the village, and go your own way as free as the wind; for I have said my last word.'

They went down the winding stairs in utter silence, and came out into the sunlight by the smithy. Wilfred Bohun carefully unlatched the wooden gate of the yard, and going up to the inspector, said: 'I wish to give myself up; I have killed my brother.'

THE EYE OF APOLLO

THAT singular smoky sparkle, at once a confusion and a transparency, which is the strange secret of the Thames, was changing more and more from its grey to its glittering extreme as the sun climbed to the zenith over Westminster, and the two men crossed Westminster Bridge. One man was very tall and the other very short; they might even have been fantastically compared to the arrogant clock-tower of Parliament and the humbler humped shoulders of the Abbey, for the short man was in clerical dress. The official description of the tall man was M. Hercule Flambeau,* private detective, and he was going to his new offices in a new pile of flats facing the Abbey entrance. The official description of the short man was the Rev. J. Brown, attached to St Francis Xavier's Church, Camberwell,* and he was coming from a Camberwell death-bed to see the new offices of his friend.

The building was American in its sky-scraping altitude, and American also in the oiled elaboration of its machinery of telephones and lifts. But it was barely finished and still under-staffed: only three tenants had moved in; the office just above Flambeau was occupied, as also was the office just below him;

the two floors above that and the three floors below were entirely bare. But the first glance at the new tower of flats caught something much more arresting. Save for a few relics of scaffolding, the one glaring object was erected outside the office just above Flambeau's. It was an enormous gilt effigy of the human eye, surrounded with rays of gold, and taking up as much room as two or three office windows.

'What on earth is that?' asked Father Brown, and stood still.

'Oh, a new religion,' said Flambeau, laughing; 'one of those new religions that forgive your sins by saying you never had any. Rather like Christian Science,* I should think. The fact is that a fellow calling himself Kalon* (I don't know what his name is, except that it can't be that) has taken the flat just above me. I have two lady typewriters* underneath me, and this enthusiastic old humbug on top. He calls himself the New Priest of Apollo, and he worships the sun.'

'Let him look out,' said Father Brown. 'The sun was the cruellest of all the gods. But what does that monstrous eye mean?'

'As I understand it, it is a theory of theirs,' answered Flambeau, 'that a man can endure anything if his mind is quite steady. Their two great symbols are the sun and the open eye; for they say that if a man were really healthy he could stare at the sun.'

'If a man were really healthy,' said Father Brown, 'he would not bother to stare at it.'

'Well, that's all I can tell you about the new religion,' went on Flambeau carelessly. 'It claims, of course, that it can cure all physical diseases.'

'Can it cure the one spiritual disease?' asked Father Brown, with a serious curiosity.

'And what is the one spiritual disease?' asked Flambeau, smiling.

'Oh, thinking one is quite well,' said his friend.

Flambeau was more interested in the quiet little office below him than in the flamboyant temple above. He was a lucid Southerner, incapable of conceiving himself as anything but a Catholic or an atheist; and new religions of a bright and pallid sort were not much in his line. But humanity was always in his line, especially when it was good-looking; moreover, the ladies downstairs were characters in their way. The office was kept by two sisters, both slight and dark, one of them tall and striking. She had a dark, eager and aquiline profile, and was one of those women whom one always thinks of in profile, as of the clean-cut edge of some weapon. She seemed to cleave her way through life. She had eyes of startling brilliancy, but it was the brilliancy of steel rather than of diamonds; and her straight, slim figure was a shade too stiff for its grace. Her younger sister was like her shortened shadow, a little greyer, paler, and more insignificant. They both wore a business-like black, with little masculine cuffs and collars. There are thousands of such curt, strenuous ladies in the offices of London, but the interest of these lay rather in their real than their apparent position.

For Pauline Stacey, the elder, was actually the heiress of a crest and half a county, as well as great wealth; she had been brought up in castles and gardens, before a frigid fierceness (peculiar to the modern woman) had driven her to what she considered a harsher and a higher existence. She had not, indeed, surrendered her money; in that there would have been a romantic or monkish abandon quite alien to her masterful utilitarianism. She held her wealth, she would say, for use upon practical social objects. Part of it she had put into her business, the nucleus of a model typewriting emporium; part of it was distributed in various leagues and causes for the advancement of such work among women. How far Joan, her sister and partner, shared this slightly prosaic idealism no one could be very sure. But she followed her leader with a dog-like affection which was somehow more attractive—with its touch of tragedy—than the hard, high spirits of the elder. For Pauline Stacey had nothing to say to tragedy; she was understood to deny its existence.

Her rigid rapidity and cold impatience had amused Flambeau very much on the first occasion of his entering the flats. He had lingered outside the lift in the entrance-hall waiting for the lift-boy, who generally conducts strangers to the various floors. But this bright-eyed falcon of a girl had openly refused to endure such official delay. She said sharply that she knew all about the lift, and was not dependent on boys—or on men either. Though her flat was only three floors above, she managed in the few seconds of ascent to give Flambeau a great many of her fundamental views in an off-hand manner; they were to the general effect that she was a modern working woman and loved modern working machinery. Her bright black eyes blazed with abstract anger against those who rebuke mechanic science and ask for the return of romance. Everyone, she said, ought to be able to manage machines, just as she could manage the lift. She seemed almost to resent the fact of Flambeau opening the lift-door for her; and that gentleman went up to his own apartments smiling with somewhat mingled feelings at the memory of such spitfire self-dependence.

She certainly had a temper, of a snappy, practical sort; the gestures of her thin, elegant hands were abrupt or even destructive. Once Flambeau entered her office on some typewriting business, and found she had just flung a pair of spectacles belonging to her sister into the middle of the floor and stamped on them. She was already in the rapids of an ethical tirade about the 'sickly medical notions' and the morbid admission of weakness implied in such an apparatus. She dared her sister to bring such artificial, unhealthy rubbish into the place again. She asked if she was expected to wear wooden legs or false hair or glass eyes; and as she spoke her eyes sparkled like the terrible crystal.

Flambeau, quite bewildered with this fanaticism, could not refrain from asking Miss Pauline (with direct French logic) why a pair of spectacles was a more morbid sign of weakness than a lift, and why, if science might help us in the one effort, it might not help us in the other.

'That is *so* different,' said Pauline Stacey loftily. 'Batteries and motors and all those things are marks of the force of man—yes, Mr Flambeau, and the force of women, too! We shall take our turn at these great engines that devour distance and defy time. That is high and splendid—that is really science. But these nasty props and plasters the doctors sell—why, they are just badges of poltroonery. Doctors stick on legs and arms as if we were born cripples and sick slaves. But I was free-born, Mr Flambeau! People only think they need these things because they have been trained in fear instead of being trained in power and courage, just as the silly nurses tell children not to stare at the sun, and so they can't do it without blinking. But why among the stars should there be one star I may not see? The sun is not my master, and I will open my eyes and stare at him, whenever I choose.'

'Your eyes,' said Flambeau, with a foreign bow, 'will dazzle the sun.'* He took pleasure in complimenting this strange stiff beauty, partly because it threw her a little off her balance. But as he went upstairs to his floor he drew a deep breath and whistled, saying to himself: 'So she has got into the hands of that conjurer upstairs with his golden eye.' For, little as he knew or cared about the new religion of Kalon, he had heard of his special notion about sun-gazing.

He soon discovered that the spiritual bond between the floors above and below him was close and increasing. The man who called himself Kalon was a magnificent creature, worthy, in a physical sense, to be the pontiff of Apollo. He was nearly as tall even as Flambeau, and very much better looking, with a golden beard, strong blue eyes, and a mane flung back like a lion's. In structure he was the blond beast of Nietzsche,* but all this animal beauty was heightened, brightened and softened by genuine intellect and spirituality. If he looked like one of the great Saxon kings, he looked like one of the kings that were also saints. And this despite the cockney incongruity of his surroundings; the fact that he had an office half-way up a building in Victoria Street; that the clerk (a commonplace youth in cuffs and collars) sat in the outer room, between him and the corridor; that his name was on a brass plate, and the gilt emblem of his creed hung above the street, like the advertisement of an oculist. All this vulgarity could not take away from the man called Kalon the vivid oppression and inspiration that came from his soul and body. When all was said, a man in the presence of this quack did feel in the presence of a great man. Even in the loose jacket-suit of linen that he wore as a workshop dress in his office he was a fascinating and formidable figure; and when robed in the white vestments and crowned with the golden circlet, in which he daily saluted the sun, he really looked so splendid that the laughter of the street people sometimes died suddenly on their lips. For three times in the day the new sun-worshipper went out on his little balcony, in the face of all Westminster, to say some litany to his shining lord: once at daybreak, once at sunset, and once at the shock of noon.* And it was while the shock of noon still shook faintly from the towers of Parliament and parish church that Father Brown, the friend of Flambeau, first looked up and saw the white priest of Apollo.

Flambeau had seen quite enough of these daily salutations of Phœbus, and plunged into the porch of the tall building without even looking for his clerical friend to follow. But Father Brown, whether from a professional interest in ritual or a strong individual interest in tomfoolery, stopped and stared up at the balcony of the sun-worshipper, just as he might have stopped and stared up at a Punch and Judy. Kalon the Prophet was already erect, with argent garments and uplifted hands, and the sound of his strangely penetrating voice could be heard all the way down the busy street uttering his solar litany. He was already in the middle of it; his eyes were fixed upon the flaming disk. It is doubtful if he saw anything or anyone on this earth; it is substantially certain that he did not see a stunted, round-faced priest who, in the crowd below, looked up at him with blinking eyes. That was perhaps the most startling difference between even these two far-divided men. Father Brown could not look at anything without blinking; but the priest of Apollo could look on the blaze at noon without a quiver of the eyelid.

'O sun,' cried the prophet, 'O star that art too great to be allowed among the stars! O fountain that flowest quietly in that secret spot that is called space. White father of all white unwearied things, white flames and white flowers and white peaks. Father, who art more innocent than all thy most innocent and quiet children; primal purity, into the peace of which——'

A rush and crash like the reversed rush of a rocket was cloven with a strident and incessant yelling. Five people rushed into the gate of the mansions as three people rushed out, and for an instant they all deafened each other. The sense of some utterly abrupt horror seemed for a moment to fill half the street with bad news—bad news that was all the worse because no one knew what it was. Two figures remained still after the crash of commotion: the fair priest of Apollo on the balcony above, and the ugly priest of Christ below him.

At last the tall figure and titanic energy of Flambeau appeared in the doorway of the mansions and dominated the little mob. Talking at the top of his voice like a fog-horn, he told somebody or anybody to go for a surgeon; and as he turned back into the dark and thronged entrance his friend Father Brown slipped in insignificantly after him. Even as he ducked and dived through the crowd he could still hear the magnificent melody and monotony of the solar priest still calling on the happy god who is the friend of fountains and flowers.

Father Brown found Flambeau and some six other people standing round the enclosed space into which the lift commonly descended. But the lift had not descended. Something else had descended; something that ought to have come by a lift.

For the last four minutes Flambeau had looked down on it; had seen the brained and bleeding figure of that beautiful woman who denied the existence of tragedy. He had never had the slightest doubt that it was Pauline Stacey; and, though he had sent for a doctor, he had not the slightest doubt that she was dead.

He could not remember for certain whether he had liked her or disliked her; there was so much both to like and dislike. But she had been a person to him, and the unbearable pathos of details and habit stabbed him with all the small daggers of bereavement. He remembered her pretty face and priggish speeches with a sudden secret vividness which is all the bitterness of death. In an instant, like a bolt from the blue, like a thunderbolt from nowhere, that beautiful and defiant body had been dashed down the open well of the lift to death at the bottom. Was it suicide? With so insolent an optimist it seemed impossible. Was it murder? But who was there in those hardly-inhabited flats to murder anybody? In a rush of raucous words, which he meant to be strong and suddenly found weak, he asked where was that fellow Kalon. A voice, habitually heavy, quiet and full, assured him that Kalon for the last fifteen minutes had been away up on his balcony worshipping his god. When Flambeau heard the voice, and felt the hand of Father Brown, he turned his swarthy face and said abruptly:

'Then, if he has been up there all the time, who can have done it?'

'Perhaps,' said the other, 'we might go upstairs and find out. We have half an hour before the police will move.'

Leaving the body of the slain heiress in charge of the surgeons, Flambeau dashed up the stairs to the typewriting office, found it utterly empty, and dashed up to his own. Having entered that, he returned with a new and white face to his friend.

'Her sister,' he said, with an unpleasant seriousness, 'her sister seems to have gone out for a walk.'

Father Brown nodded. 'Or, she may have gone up to the office of that sun man,' he said. 'If I were you I should just verify that, and then let us talk it over in your office. No,' he added suddenly, as if remembering something; 'shall I ever get over that stupidity of mine? Of course, in their office downstairs.'

Flambeau stared; but he followed the little father downstairs to the empty flat of the Staceys, where that impenetrable pastor took a large red-leather chair in the very entrance, from which he could see the stairs and landings, and waited. He did not wait very long. In about four minutes three figures descended the stairs, alike only in their solemnity. The first was Joan Stacey,* the sister of the dead woman—evidently she *had* been upstairs in the temporary temple of Apollo; the second was the priest of Apollo himself, his litany finished, sweeping down the empty stairs in utter magnificence—something in his white robes, beard and parted hair had the look of Doré's Christ* leaving the Pretorium;* the third was Flambeau, black-browed and somewhat bewildered.

Miss Joan Stacey, dark, with a drawn face and hair prematurely touched with grey, walked straight to her own desk and set out her papers with a practical flap. The mere action rallied everyone else to sanity. If Miss Joan Stacey was a criminal, she was a cool one. Father Brown regarded her for some time with an odd little smile, and then, without taking his eyes off her, addressed himself to somebody else.

'Prophet,' he said, presumably addressing Kalon, 'I wish you would tell me a lot about your religion.'

'I shall be proud to do it,' said Kalon, inclining his still crowned head, 'but I am not sure that I understand.'

'Why, it's like this,' said Father Brown, in his frankly doubtful way. 'We are taught that if a man has really bad first principles, that must be partly his fault. But, for all that, we can make some difference between a man who insults his quite clear conscience and a man with a conscience more or less crowded with sophistries. Now, do you really think that murder is wrong at all?'

'Is this an accusation?' asked Kalon very quietly.

'No,' answered Brown, equally gently, 'it is the speech for the defence.'

In the long and startled stillness of the room the prophet of Apollo slowly rose and really it was like the rising of the sun. He filled that room with his light and life in such a manner that a man felt he could as easily have filled Salisbury Plain.* His robed form seemed to hang the whole room with classic draperies; his epic gesture seemed to extend it into grander perspectives, till the little black figure of the modern cleric seemed to be a fault and an intrusion, a round, black blot upon some splendour of Hellas.*

'We meet at last, Caiaphas,'* said the prophet. 'Your church and mine are the only realities on this earth. I adore the sun, and you the darkening of the sun; you are the priest of the dying, and I of the living God. Your present work of suspicion and slander is worthy of your coat and creed. All your church is but a black police; you are only spies and detectives seeking to tear from men confessions of guilt, whether by treachery or torture. You would convict men of crime, I would convict them of innocence. You would convince them of sin, I would convince them of virtue.

'Reader of the books of evil, one more word before I blow away your baseless nightmares for ever. Not even faintly could you understand how little I care whether you can convict me or no. The things you call disgrace and horrible hanging are to me no more than an ogre in a child's toybook to a man once grown up. You said you were offering the speech for the defence. I care so little for the cloud-land of this life that I will offer you the speech for the prosecution. There is but one thing that can be said against me in this matter, and I will say it myself. The woman that is dead was my love and my bride; not after such manner as your tin chapels call lawful, but by a law purer and sterner than you will ever understand. She and I walked another world from yours, and trod palaces of crystal while you were plodding through tunnels and corridors of brick. Well, I know that policemen, theological and otherwise, always fancy that where there has been love there must soon be hatred; so there you have the first point made for the prosecution. But the second point is stronger; I do not grudge it you. Not only is it true that Pauline loved me, but it is also true that this very morning, before she died, she wrote at that table a will leaving me and my new church half a million. Come, where are the handcuffs? Do you suppose I care what foolish things you do with me? Penal servitude will only be like waiting for her at a wayside station. The gallows will only be going to her in a headlong car.'

He spoke with the brain-shaking authority of an orator, and Flambeau and Joan Stacey stared at him in an amazed admiration. Father Brown's face seemed to express nothing but extreme distress; he looked at the ground with one wrinkle of pain across his forehead. The prophet of the sun leaned easily against the mantelpiece and resumed:

'In a few words I have put before you the whole case against me—the only possible case against me. In fewer words still I will blow it to pieces, so that not a trace of it remains. As to whether I have committed this crime, the truth is in one sentence: I could not have committed this crime. Pauline Stacey fell from this floor to the ground at five minutes past twelve. A hundred people will go into the witness-box and say that I was standing out upon the balcony of my own rooms above from just before the stroke of noon to a quarter-past—the usual period of my public prayers. My clerk (a respectable youth from Clapham, with no sort of connection with me) will swear that he sat in my outer office all the morning, and that no communication passed through. He will swear that I arrived a full ten minutes before the hour, fifteen minutes before any whisper of the accident, and that I did not leave the office or the balcony all that time. No one ever had so complete an alibi: I could subpœna half Westminster. I think you had better put the handcuffs away again. The case is at an end.

'But last of all, that no breath of this idiotic suspicion remain in the air, I will tell you all you want to know. I believe I do know how my unhappy friend came by her death. You can, if you choose, blame me for it, or my faith and philosophy at least; but you certainly cannot lock me up. It is well known to all students of the higher truths that certain adepts and *illuminati* have in history attained the power of levitation—that is, of being self-sustained upon the empty air. It is but a part of that general conquest of matter which is the main element in our occult wisdom. Poor Pauline was of an impulsive and ambitious temper. I think, to tell the truth, she thought herself somewhat deeper in the mysteries than she was; and she has often said to me, as we went down in the lift together, that if one's will were strong enough, one could float down as harmlessly as a feather. I solemnly believe that in some ecstasy of noble thoughts she attempted the miracle. Her will, or faith, must have failed her at the crucial instant, and the lower law of matter had its horrible revenge. There is the whole story, gentlemen, very sad and, as you think, very presumptuous and wicked, but certainly not criminal or in any way connected with me. In the shorthand of the police-courts, you had better call it suicide. I shall always call it heroic failure for the advance of science and the slow scaling of heaven.'

It was the first time Flambeau had ever seen Father Brown vanquished. He still sat looking at the ground, with a painful and corrugated brow, as if in shame. It is impossible to avoid the feeling which the prophet's winged words had fanned, that here was a sullen, professional suspector of men overwhelmed by a prouder and purer spirit of natural liberty and health. At last he said, blinking as if in bodily distress: 'Well, if that is so, sir, you need do no more than take the testamentary paper you spoke of and go. I wonder where the poor lady left it.'

'It will be over there on her desk by the door, I think,' said Kalon, with that massive innocence of manner that seemed to acquit him wholly. 'She told me specially she would write it this morning, and I actually saw her writing as I went up in the lift to my own room.'

'Was her door open then?' asked the priest, with his eye on a corner of the matting.

'Yes,' said Kalon calmly.

'Ah! it has been open ever since,' said the other, and resumed his silent study of the mat.

'There is a paper over here,' said the grim Miss Joan, in a somewhat singular voice. She had passed over to her sister's desk by the doorway, and was holding a sheet of blue foolscap in her hand. There was a sour smile on her face that seemed unfit for such a scene or occasion, and Flambeau looked at her with a darkening brow.

Kalon the prophet stood away from the paper with that royal unconsciousness that had carried him through. But Flambeau took it out of the lady's hand and read it with the utmost amazement. It did, indeed, begin in the formal manner of a will, but after the words 'I give and bequeath all of which I die possessed' the writing abruptly stopped with a set of scratches, and there was no trace of the name of any legatee. Flambeau, in wonder, handed this truncated testament to his clerical friend, who glanced at it and silently gave it to the priest of the sun.

An instant afterwards that pontiff, in his splendid sweeping draperies, had crossed the room in two great strides, and was towering over Joan Stacey, his blue eyes standing from his head.

'What monkey tricks have you been playing here?' he cried. 'That's not all Pauline wrote.'

They were startled to hear him speak in quite a new voice, with a Yankee shrillness in it; all his grandeur and good English had fallen from him like a cloak.

'That is the only thing on her desk,' said Joan, and confronted him steadily with the same smile of evil favour.

Of a sudden the man broke out into blasphemies and cat-aracts of incredulous words. There was something shocking about the dropping of his mask; it was like a man's real face falling off.

'See here!' he cried in broad American, when he was breath-less with cursing; 'I may be an adventurer, but I guess you're a murderess. Yes, gentlemen, here's your death explained, and without any levitation. The poor girl is writing a will in my favour; her cursed sister comes in, struggles for the pen, drags her to the well, and throws her down before she can finish it. Sakes! I reckon we want the handcuffs after all.'

'As you have truly remarked,' replied Joan, with ugly calm, 'your clerk is a very respectable young man, who knows the nature of an oath; and he will swear in any court that I was up in your office arranging some typewriting work for five min-utes before and five minutes after my sister fell. Mr Flambeau will say he found me there.'

There was a silence.

'Why, then,' cried Flambeau, 'Pauline was alone when she fell, and it was suicide!'

'She was alone when she fell,' said Father Brown, 'but it was not suicide.'

'Then how did she die?' asked Flambeau impatiently.

'She was murdered.'

'But she was all alone,' objected the detective.

'She was murdered when she was all alone,' answered the priest.

All the rest stared at him, but he remained sitting in the same old dejected attitude, with a wrinkle in his round fore-head and an appearance of impersonal shame and sorrow; his voice was colourless and sad.

'What I want to know,' cried Kalon, with an oath, 'is when the police are coming for this bloody and wicked sister. She's killed her flesh and blood; she's robbed me of half a million that was just as sacredly mine as——'

'Come, come, prophet,' interrupted Flambeau, with a kind of sneer; 'remember that all this world is a cloud-land.'

The hierophant of the sun-god made an effort to climb back on to his pedestal. 'It is not the mere money,' he cried, 'though that would equip the cause throughout the world. It is also my beloved one's wishes. To Pauline all this was holy. In Pauline's eyes——'

Father Brown suddenly sprang erect, so that his chair fell over flat behind him. He was deathly pale, yet he seemed fired with a hope; his eyes shone.

'That's it!' he cried in a clear voice. 'That's the way to begin. In Pauline's eyes——'

The tall prophet retreated before the tiny priest in an almost mad disorder. 'What do you mean? How dare you?' he cried repeatedly.

'In Pauline's eyes,' repeated the priest, his own shining more and more. 'Go on—in God's name, go on. The foulest crime the fiends ever prompted feels lighter after confession; and I implore you to confess. Go on, go on—in Pauline's eyes——'

'Let me go, you devil!' thundered Kalon, struggling like a giant in bonds. 'Who are you, you cursed spy, to weave your spiders' webs round me, and peep and peer? Let me go.'

'Shall I stop him?' asked Flambeau, bounding towards the exit, for Kalon had already thrown the door wide open.

'No; let him pass,' said Father Brown, with a strange deep sigh that seemed to come from the depths of the universe. 'Let Cain pass by, for he belongs to God.'

There was a long-drawn silence in the room when he had left it, which was to Flambeau's fierce wits one long agony of interrogation. Miss Joan Stacey very coolly tidied the papers on her desk.

'Father,' said Flambeau at last, 'it is my duty, not my curiosity only—it is my duty to find out, if I can, who committed the crime.'

'Which crime?' asked Father Brown.

'The one we are dealing with, of course,' replied his impatient friend.

'We are dealing with two crimes,' said Brown; 'crimes of very different weight—and by very different criminals.'

Miss Joan Stacey, having collected and put away her papers, proceeded to lock up her drawer. Father Brown went on, noticing her as little as she noticed him.

'The two crimes,' he observed, 'were committed against the same weakness of the same person, in a struggle for her money. The author of the larger crime found himself thwarted by the smaller crime; the author of the smaller crime got the money.'

'Oh, don't go on like a lecturer,' groaned Flambeau; 'put it in a few words.'

'I can put it in one word,' answered his friend.

Miss Joan Stacey skewered her business-like black hat on to her head with a business-like black frown before a little mirror, and, as the conversation proceeded, took her handbag and umbrella in an unhurried style, and left the room.

'The truth is in one word, and a short one,' said Father Brown. 'Pauline Stacey was blind.'

'Blind!' repeated Flambeau, and rose slowly to his whole huge stature.

'She was subject to it by blood,' Brown proceeded. 'Her sister would have started eyeglasses if Pauline would have let her; but it was her special philosophy or fad that one must not encourage such diseases by yielding to them. She would not admit the cloud; or she tried to dispel it by will. So her eyes got worse and worse with straining; but the worst strain was to come. It came with this precious prophet, or whatever he calls himself, who taught her to stare at the hot sun with the naked eye. It was called accepting Apollo. Oh, if these new pagans would only be old pagans, they would be a little wiser! The old pagans knew that mere naked Nature-worship has a cruel side. They knew that the eye of Apollo can blast and blind.'

There was a pause, and the priest went on in a gentle and even broken voice: 'Whether or no that devil deliberately made her blind, there is no doubt that he deliberately killed her through her blindness. The very simplicity of the crime is sickening. You know he and she went up and down in those lifts without official help; you know also how smoothly and silently the lifts side. Kalon brought the lift to the girl's landing, and saw her, through the open door, writing in her slow, sightless way the will she had promised him. He called out to her cheerily that he had the lift ready for her, and she was to come out when she was ready. Then he pressed a button and shot soundlessly up to his own floor, walked through his own office, out on to his own balcony, and was safely praying before the crowded street when the poor girl, having finished her work, ran gaily out to where her lover and lift were to receive her, and stepped——'

'Don't!' cried Flambeau.

'He ought to have got half a million by pressing that button,' continued the little father in the colourless voice in which he talked of such horrors; 'but that went smash. It went smash because there happened to be another person who also wanted the money, and who also knew the secret about poor Pauline's sight. There was one thing about that will that I think nobody noticed: although it was unfinished and without a signature, the other Miss Stacey and some servant of hers had already signed it as witnesses. Joan had signed first, saying Pauline could finish it later, with a typical feminine contempt for legal forms. Therefore, Joan wanted her sister to sign the will without real witnesses. Why? I thought of the blindness, and felt sure she had wanted Pauline to sign in solitude because she had wanted her not to sign at all.

'People like the Staceys always use fountain pens; but this was specially natural to Pauline. By habit and her strong will and her memory she could still write almost as well as if she saw; but she could not tell when her pen needed dipping. Therefore, her fountain pens were carefully filled by her sister—all except this fountain pen. This was carefully *not* filled by her sister; the remains of the ink held out for a few lines and then failed altogether. And the prophet lost five hundred thousand pounds and committed one of the most brutal and brilliant murders in human history for nothing.'

Flambeau went to the open door and heard the official police ascending the stairs. He turned and said: 'You must have followed everything devilish close to have traced the crime to Kalon in ten minutes.'

Father Brown gave a sort of start.

'Oh! to him,' he said. 'No; I had to follow rather close to find out about Miss Joan and the fountain pen. But I knew Kalon was the criminal before I came into the front door.'

'You must be joking!' cried Flambeau.

'I'm quite serious,' answered the priest. 'I tell you I knew he had done it, even before I knew what he had done.'

'But why?'

'These pagan stoics,' said Brown reflectively, 'always fail by their strength. There came a crash and a scream down the street, and the priest of Apollo did not start or look round. I did not know what it was; but I knew that he was expecting it.'

THE SIGN OF THE BROKEN SWORD

THE thousand arms of the forest were grey, and its million fingers silver. In a sky of dark green-blue-like slate the stars were bleak and brilliant like splintered ice. All that thickly wooded and sparsely tenanted countryside was stiff with a bitter and brittle frost. The black hollows between the trunks of the trees looked like bottomless, black caverns of that heartless Scandinavian hell, a hell of incalculable cold. Even the square stone tower of the church looked northern to the point of heathenry, as if it were some barbaric tower among the sea rocks of Iceland. It was a queer night for anyone to explore a churchyard. But, on the other hand, perhaps it was worth exploring.

It rose abruptly out of the ashen wastes of forest in a sort of hump or shoulder of green turf that looked grey in the star-light. Most of the graves were on a slant, and the path leading up to the church was as steep as a staircase. On the top of the hill, in the one flat and prominent place, was the monument for which the place was famous. It contrasted strangely with the featureless graves all round, for it was the work of one of the greatest sculptors of modern Europe; and yet his fame was at once forgotten in the fame of the man whose image he had made. It showed, by touches of the small silver pencil of starlight, the massive metal figure of a soldier recumbent, the strong hands sealed in an everlasting worship, the great head pillowed upon a gun. The venerable face was bearded, or rather whiskered, in the old, heavy Colonel Newcome* fashion. The uniform, though suggested with the few strokes of simplicity, was that of modern war. By his right side lay a sword, of which the tip was broken off; on the left side lay a Bible. On glowing summer afternoons wagonettes* came full of Americans and cultured suburbans to see the sepulchre; but even then they felt the vast forest land with its one dumpy dome of churchyard and church as a place oddly dumb and neglected. In this freezing darkness of mid-winter one would think he might be left alone with the stars. Nevertheless, in the stillness of those stiff woods a wooden gate creaked, and two dim figures dressed in black climbed up the little path to the tomb.

So faint was that frigid starlight that nothing could have been traced about them except that while they both wore black, one man was enormously big, and the other (perhaps by contrast) almost startlingly small. They went up to the great graven tomb of the historic warrior, and stood for a few minutes staring at it. There was no human, perhaps no living, thing for a wide circle; and a morbid fancy might well have wondered if they were human themselves. In any case, the beginning of their conversation might have seemed strange. After the first silence the small man said to the other:

'Where does a wise man hide a pebble?'

And the tall man answered in a low voice: 'On the beach.'

The small man nodded, and after a short silence said: 'Where does a wise man hide a leaf?'

And the other answered: 'In the forest.'

There was another stillness, and then the tall man resumed: 'Do you mean that when a wise man has to hide a real diamond he has been known to hide it among sham ones?'*

'No, no,' said the little man with a laugh, 'we will let bygones be bygones.'

He stamped his cold feet for a second or two and then said: 'I'm not thinking of that at all, but of something else; something rather peculiar. Just strike a match, will you?'

The big man fumbled in his pocket, and soon a scratch and a flare painted gold the whole flat side of the monument. On it was cut in black letters the well-known words which so many Americans had reverently read: 'Sacred to the Memory of General Sir Arthur St Clare, Hero and Martyr, who Always Vanquished his Enemies and Always Spared Them, and Was Treacherously Slain by Them at Last. May God in Whom he Trusted both Reward and Revenge him.'

The match burnt the big man's fingers, blackened, and dropped. He was about to strike another, but his small companion stopped him. 'That's all right, Flambeau, old man; I saw what I wanted. Or, rather, I didn't see what I didn't want. And now we must walk a mile and a half along the road to the next inn, and I will try to tell you all about it. For Heaven knows a man should have fire and ale when he dares tell such a story.'

They descended the precipitous path, they re-latched the rusty gate, and set off at a stamping, ringing walk down the frozen forest road. They had gone a full quarter of a mile before the smaller man spoke again. He said: 'Yes; the wise man hides a pebble on the beach. But what does he do if there is no beach? Do you know anything of the great St Clare trouble?'

'I know nothing about English generals, Father Brown,' answered the large man, laughing, 'though a little about English policemen. I only know that you have dragged me a precious long dance to all the shrines of this fellow, whoever he is. One would think he got buried in six different places. I've seen a memorial to General St Clare in Westminster Abbey; I've seen a ramping equestrian statue of General St Clare on the Embankment;* I've seen a medallion of General St Clare in the street he was born in; and another in the street he lived in; and now you drag me after dark to his coffin in the village churchyard. I am beginning to be a bit tired of his magnificent personality, especially as I don't in the least know who he was. What are you hunting for in all these crypts and effigies?'

'I am only looking for one word,' said Father Brown. 'A word that isn't there.'

'Well,' asked Flambeau, 'are you going to tell me anything about it?'

'I must divide it into two parts,' remarked the priest. 'First there is what everybody knows; and then there is what I know.

Now, what everybody knows is short and plain enough. It is also entirely wrong.'

'Right you are,' said the big man called Flambeau cheerfully. 'Let's begin at the wrong end. Let's begin with what everybody knows, which isn't true.'

'If not wholly untrue, it is at least very inadequate,' continued Brown; 'for in point of fact, all that the public knows amounts precisely to this: The public knows that Arthur St Clare was a great and successful English general. It knows that after splendid yet careful campaigns both in India and Africa he was in command against Brazil* when the great Brazilian patriot Olivier* issued his ultimatum. It knows that on that occasion St Clare with a very small force attacked Olivier with a very large one, and was captured after heroic resistance. And it knows that after his capture, and to the abhorrence of the civilized world, St Clare was hanged on the nearest tree. He was found swinging there after the Brazilians had retired, with his broken sword hung round his neck.'

'And that popular story is untrue?' suggested Flambeau.

'No,' said his friend quietly; 'that story is quite true, so far as it goes.'

'Well, I think it goes far enough!' said Flambeau, 'but if the popular story is true, what is the mystery?'

They had passed many hundreds of grey and ghostly trees before the little priest answered. Then he bit his finger reflectively and said: 'Why, the mystery is a mystery of psychology. Or, rather, it is a mystery of two psychologies. In that Brazilian business two of the most famous men of modern history acted flat against their characters. Mind you, Olivier and St Clare were both heroes—the old thing, and no mistake; it was like the fight between Hector and Achilles. Now, what would you say to an affair in which Achilles was timid and Hector was treacherous?'*

'Go on,' said the large man impatiently as the other bit his finger again.

'Sir Arthur St Clare was a soldier of the old religious type— the type that saved us during the Mutiny,* continued Brown. 'He was always more for duty than for dash; and with all his personal courage was decidedly a prudent commander, particularly indignant at any needless waste of soldiers. Yet, in this last battle, he attempted something that a baby could see was absurd. One need not be a strategist to see it was as wild as wind; just as one need not be a strategist to keep out of the way of a motor-bus. Well, that is the first mystery; what had become of the English general's head? The second riddle is, what had become of the Brazilian general's heart? President Olivier might be called a visionary or a nuisance; but even his enemies admitted that he was magnanimous to the point of knight errantry. Almost every other prisoner he had ever captured had been set free, or even loaded with benefits. Men who had really wronged him came away touched by his simplicity and sweetness. Why the deuce should he diabolically revenge himself only once in his life; and then for the one particular blow that could not have hurt him? Well, there you have it. One of the wisest men in the world acted like an idiot for no reason. One of the best men in the world acted like a fiend for no reason. That's the long and short of it; and I leave it to you, my boy.'

'No, you don't,' said the other with a snort. 'I leave it to you; and you jolly well tell me all about it.'

'Well,' resumed Father Brown, 'it's not fair to say that the public impression is just what I've said, without adding that two things have happened since. I can't say they threw a new light, for nobody can make sense of them. But they threw a new kind of darkness, they threw the darkness in new directions. The first was this. The family physician of the St Clares quarrelled with that family and began publishing a violent series of articles, in which he said that the late general was a religious maniac; but as far as the tale went, this seemed to mean little more than a religious man. Anyhow, the story fizzled out. Everyone knew, of course, that St Clare had some of the eccentricities of puritan piety. The second incident was much more arresting. In the luckless and unsupported regiment which made that rash attempt at the Black River there was a certain Captain Keith, who was at that time engaged to St Clare's daughter, and who afterwards married her. He was one of those who were captured by Olivier, and, like all the rest except the general, appears to have been bounteously treated and promptly set free. Some twenty years afterwards this man, then Lieutenant-Colonel Keith, published a sort of autobiography called "A British Officer in Burmah and Brazil." In the place where the reader looks eagerly for some account of the mystery of St Clare's disaster may he found the following words: "Everywhere else in this book I have narrated things exactly as they occurred, holding as I do the old-fashioned opinion that the glory of England is old enough to take care of itself. The exception I shall make is in this matter of the defeat by the Black River; and my reasons, though private, are honourable and compelling. I will, however, add this in justice to the memories of two distinguished men. General St Clare has been accused of incapacity on this occasion; I can at least testify that this action, properly understood, was one of the most brilliant and sagacious of his life. President Olivier by similar report is charged with savage injustice. I think it due to the honour of an enemy to say that he acted on this occasion with even more than his characteristic good feeling. To put the matter popularly, I can assure my countrymen that St Clare was by no means such a fool, nor Olivier such a brute as he looked. This is all I have to say; nor shall any earthly consideration induce me to add a word to it."'

A large frozen moon like a lustrous snowball began to show through the tangle of twigs in front of them, and by its light the narrator had been able to refresh his memory of Captain Keith's text from a scrap of printed paper. As he folded it up and put it back in his pocket Flambeau threw up his hand with a French gesture.

'Wait a bit, wait a bit,' he cried excitedly. 'I believe I can guess it at the first go.'

He strode on, breathing hard, his black head and bull neck forward, like a man winning a walking race. The little priest, amused and interested, had some trouble in trotting beside him. Just before them the trees fell back a little to left and right, and the road swept downwards across a clear, moonlit valley, till it dived again like a rabbit into the wall of another wood. The entrance to the farther forest looked small and round, like the black hole of a remote railway tunnel. But it was within some hundred yards, and gaped like a cavern before Flambeau spoke again.

'I've got it,' he cried at last, slapping his thigh with his great hand. 'Four minutes' thinking, and I can tell you the whole story myself.'

'All right,' assented his friend. 'You tell it.'

Flambeau lifted his head, but lowered his voice. 'General Sir Arthur St Clare,' he said, 'came of a family in which madness was hereditary; and his whole aim was to keep this from his daughter, and even, if possible, from his future son-in-law. Rightly or wrongly, he thought the final collapse was close, and resolved on suicide. Yet ordinary suicide would blazon the very idea he dreaded. As the campaign approached the clouds came thicker on his brain, and at last in a mad moment he sacrificed his public duty to his private. He rushed rashly into battle, hoping to fall by the first shot. When he found that he had only attained capture and discredit, the sealed bomb in his brain burst, and he broke his own sword and hanged himself.'

He stared firmly at the grey façade of forest in front of him, with the one black gap in it, like the mouth of the grave, into which their path plunged. Perhaps something menacing in the road thus suddenly swallowed reinforced his vivid vision of the tragedy, for he shuddered.

'A horrid story', he said.

'A horrid story,' repeated the priest with bent head; 'but not the real story.'

Then he threw back his head with a sort of despair and cried: 'Oh, I wish it had been.'

The tall Flambeau faced round and stared at him.

'Yours is a clean story,' cried Father Brown, deeply moved. 'A sweet, pure, honest story, as open and white as that moon. Madness and despair are innocent enough. There are worse things, Flambeau.'

Flambeau looked up wildly at the moon thus invoked; and from where he stood one black tree-bough curved across it exactly like a devil's horn.

'Father—Father,' cried Flambeau with the French gesture and stepping yet more rapidly forward, 'do you mean it was worse than that?'

'Worse than that,' said the priest like a grave echo. And they plunged into the black cloister of the woodland, which ran by them in a dim tapestry of trunks, like one of the dark corridors in a dream.

They were soon in the most secret entrails of the wood, and felt close about them the foliage that they could not see, when the priest said again:

'Where does a wise man hide a leaf? In the forest. But what does he do if there is no forest?'

'Well—well,' cried Flambeau irritably, 'what does he do?'

'He grows a forest to hide it in,' said the priest in an obscure voice. 'A fearful sin.'

'Look here,' cried his friend impatiently, for the dark wood and the dark sayings got a little on his nerves; 'will you tell me this story or not? What other evidence is there to go on?'

'There are three more bits of evidence,' said the other, 'that I have dug up in holes and corners, and I will give them in logical rather than chronological order. First of all, of course, our authority for the issue and event of the battle is in Olivier's own despatches, which are lucid enough. He was entrenched with two or three regiments on the heights that swept down to the Black River, on the other side of which was lower and more marshy ground. Beyond this again was gently rising country, on which was the first English outpost, supported by others which lay, however, considerably in its rear. The British forces as a whole were greatly superior in numbers; but this particular regiment was just far enough from its base to make Olivier consider the project of crossing the river to cut it off. By sunset, however, he had decided to retain his own position, which was a specially strong one. At daybreak next morning he was thunderstruck to see that this stray handful of English, entirely unsupported from their rear, had flung themselves across the river, half by a bridge to the right, and the other half by a ford higher up, and were massed upon the marshy bank below him.

'That they should attempt an attack with such numbers against such a position was incredible enough; but Olivier noticed something yet more extraordinary. For instead of attempting to seize more solid ground, this mad regiment, having put the river in its rear by one wild charge, did nothing more, but stuck there in the mire like flies in treacle. Needless to say, the Brazilians blew great gaps in them with artillery, which they could only return with spirited but lessening rifle fire. Yet they never broke; and Olivier's curt account ends with a strong tribute of admiration for the mystic valour of these imbeciles. "Our line then advanced finally," writes Olivier, "and drove them into the river; we captured General St Clare himself and several other officers. The colonel and the major had both fallen in the battle. I cannot resist saying that few finer sights can have been seen in history than the last stand of this extraordinary regiment; wounded officers picking up the rifles of dead soldiers, and the general himself facing us on horseback bare-headed and with a broken sword." On what happened to the general afterwards Olivier is as silent as Captain Keith.'

'Well,' grunted Flambeau, 'get on to the next bit of evidence.'

'The next evidence,' said Father Brown, 'took some time to find, but it will not take long to tell. I found at last, in an almshouse down in the Lincolnshire Fens,* an old soldier who not only was wounded at the Black River, but had actually knelt beside the colonel of the regiment when he died. This latter was a certain Colonel Clancy, a big bull of an Irishman; and it would seem that he died almost as much of rage as of bullets. He, at any rate, was not responsible for that ridiculous raid; it must have been imposed on him by the general. His last edifying words, according to my informant, were these: "And there goes the damned old donkey with the end of his sword knocked off. I wish it was his head." You will remark that everyone seems to have noticed this detail about the broken sword blade, though most people regard it somewhat more reverently than did the late Colonel Clancy. And now for the third fragment.'

Their path through the woodland began to go upward, and the speaker paused a little for breath before he went on. Then he continued in the same business-like tone:

'Only a month or two ago a certain Brazilian official died in England, having quarrelled with Olivier and left his country.

He was a well-known figure both here and on the Continent, a Spaniard named Espado; I knew him myself, a yellow-faced old dandy, with a hooked nose. For various private reasons I had permission to see the documents he had left; he was a Catholic, of course, and I had been with him towards the end. There was nothing of his that lit up any corner of the black St Clare business, except five or six common exercise books filled with the diary of some English soldier. I can only suppose that it was found by the Brazilians on one of those that fell. Anyhow, it stopped abruptly the night before the battle.

'But the account of that last day in the poor fellow's life was certainly worth reading. I have it on me; but it's too dark to read it here, and I will give you a résumé. The first part of that entry is full of jokes, evidently flung about among the men, about somebody called the Vulture. It does not seem as if this person, whoever he was, was one of themselves, nor even an Englishman; neither is he exactly spoken of as one of the enemy. It sounds rather as if he were some local go-between and non-combatant; perhaps a guide or a journalist. He has been closeted with old Colonel Clancy; but is more often seen talking to the major. Indeed, the major is somewhat promi-nent in this soldier's narrative; a lean, dark-haired man, appar-ently, of the name of Murray—a north of Ireland man and a Puritan. There are continual jests about the contrast between this Ulsterman's austerity and the conviviality of Colonel Clancy. There is also some joke about the Vulture wearing bright-coloured clothes.

'But all these levities are scattered by what may well be called the note of a bugle. Behind the English camp, and almost parallel to the river, ran one of the few great roads of that district. Westward the road curved round towards the river, which it crossed by the bridge before mentioned. To the east the road swept backwards into the wilds, and some two miles along it was the next English outpost. From this direc-tion there came along the road that evening a glitter and clatter of light cavalry, in which even the simple diarist could recognize with astonishment the general with his staff. He rode the great white horse which you have seen so often in illustrated papers and Academy pictures; and you may be sure that the salute they gave him was not merely ceremonial. He, at least, wasted no time on ceremony, but, springing from the saddle immediately, mixed with the group of officers, and fell into emphatic though confidential speech. What struck our friend the diarist most was his special disposition to discuss matters with Major Murray; but, indeed, such a selection, so long as it was not marked, was in no way unnatural. The two men were made for sympathy; they were men who "read their Bibles";* they were both the old Evangelical type of officer. However this may be, it is certain that when the general mounted again he was still talking earnestly to Murray; and that as he walked his horse slowly down the road towards the river, the tall Ulsterman still walked by his bridle-rein in earnest debate. The soldiers watched the two until they vanished behind a clump of trees where the road turned towards the river. The colonel had gone back to his tent, and the men to their pickets; the man with the diary lingered for another four minutes, and saw a marvellous sight.

'The great white horse which had marched slowly down the road, as it had marched in so many processions, flew back, galloping up the road towards them as if it were mad to win a race. At first they thought it had run away with the man on its back; but they soon saw that the general, a fine rider, was himself urging it to full speed. Horse and man swept up to them like a whirlwind; and then, reining up the reeling charger, the general turned on them a face like flame, and called for the colonel like the trumpet that wakes the dead.

'I conceive that all the earthquake events of that catastrophe tumbled on top of each other rather like lumber in the minds of men such as our friend with the diary. With the dazed excitement of a dream, they found themselves falling—literally falling—into their ranks, and learned that an attack was to be led at once across the river. The general and the major, it was said, had found out something at the bridge, and there was only just time to strike for life. The major had gone back at once to call up the reserve along the road behind; it was doubtful if even with that prompt appeal help could reach them in time. But they must pass the stream that night, and seize the heights by morning. It is with the very stir and throb of that romantic nocturnal march that the diary suddenly ends.'

Father Brown had mounted ahead; for the woodland path grew smaller, steeper, and more twisted, till they felt as if they were ascending a winding staircase. The priest's voice came from above out of the darkness.

'There was one other little and enormous thing. When the general urged them to their chivalric charge he drew half his sword from the scabbard; and then, as if ashamed of such melodrama, thrust it back again. The sword again, you see.'

A half-light broke through the network of boughs above them, flinging the ghost of a net about their feet; for they were mounting again to the faint luminosity of the naked night. Flambeau felt truth all round him as an atmosphere, but not as an idea. He answered with bewildered brain: 'Well, what's the matter with the sword? Officers generally have swords, don't they?'

'They are not often mentioned in modern war,' said the other dispassionately; 'but in this affair one falls over the blessed sword everywhere.'

'Well, what is there in that?' growled Flambeau; 'it was a twopence coloured sort of incident; the old man's blade breaking in his last battle. Anyone might bet the papers would get hold of it, as they have. On all these tombs and things it's shown broken at the point. I hope you haven't dragged me through this Polar expedition merely because two men with an eye for a picture saw St Clare's broken sword.'

'No,' cried Father Brown, with a sharp voice like a pistol shot; 'but who saw his unbroken sword?'

'What do you mean?' cried the other, and stood still under the stars. They had come abruptly out of the grey gates of the wood.

'I say, who saw his unbroken sword?' repeated Father Brown obstinately. 'Not the writer of the diary, anyhow; the general sheathed it in time.'

Flambeau looked about him in the moonlight, as a man struck blind might look in the sun; and his friend went on for the first time with eagerness:

'Flambeau,' he cried, 'I cannot prove it, even after hunting through the tombs. But I am sure of it. Let me add just one more tiny fact that tips the whole thing over. The colonel, by a strange chance, was one of the first struck by a bullet. He was struck long before the troops came to close quarters. But he saw St Clare's sword broken. Why was it broken? How was it broken? My friend, it was broken before the battle.'

'Oh!' said his friend, with a sort of forlorn jocularity; 'and pray where is the other piece?'

'I can tell you,' said the priest promptly. 'In the north-east corner of the cemetery of the Protestant Cathedral at Belfast.'

'Indeed?' inquired the other. 'Have you looked for it?'

'I couldn't,' replied Brown, with frank regret. 'There's a great marble monument on top of it; a monument to the heroic Major Murray, who fell fighting gloriously at the famous Battle of the Black River.'

Flambeau seemed suddenly galvanized into existence. 'You mean,' he cried hoarsely, 'that General St Clare hated Murray, and murdered him on the field of battle because——'

'You are still full of good and pure thoughts,' said the other. 'It was worse than that.'

'Well,' said the large man, 'my stock of evil imagination is used up.'

The priest seemed really doubtful where to begin, and at last he said again:

'Where would a wise man hide a leaf? In the forest.'

The other did not answer.

'If there were no forest, he would make a forest. And if he wished to hide a dead leaf, he would make a dead forest.'

There was still no reply, and the priest added still more mildly and quietly:

'And if a man had to hide a dead body, he would make a field of dead bodies to hide it in.'

Flambeau began to stamp forward with an intolerance of delay in time or space; but Father Brown went on as if he were continuing the last sentence:

'Sir Arthur St Clare, as I have already said, was a man who read his Bible. That was what was the matter with *him*. When will people understand that it is useless for a man to read his Bible unless he also reads everybody else's Bible? A printer reads a Bible for misprints. A Mormon reads his Bible and finds polygamy; a Christian Scientist reads his and finds we have no arms and legs. St Clare was an old Anglo-Indian Protestant soldier. Now, just think what that might mean; and, for Heaven's sake, don't cant about it. It might mean a man physically formidable living under a tropic sun in an Oriental society, and soaking himself without sense or guidance in an Oriental book. Of course, he read the Old Testament rather than the New. Of course, he found in the Old Testament anything that he wanted—lust, tyranny, treason. Oh, I dare say he was honest, as you call it. But what is the good of a man being honest in his worship of dishonesty?

'In each of the hot and secret countries to which that man went he kept a harem, he tortured witnesses, he amassed shameful gold; but certainly he would have said with steady eyes that he did it to the glory of the Lord. My own theology is sufficiently expressed by asking which Lord? Anyhow, there is this about such evil, that it opens door after door in hell, and always into smaller and smaller chambers. This is the real case against crime, that a man does not become wilder and wilder, but only meaner and meaner. St Clare was soon suffocated by difficulties of bribery and blackmail; and needed more and more cash. And by the time of the battle of the Black River he had fallen from world to world to that place which Dante makes the lowest floor of the universe.'

'What do you mean?' asked his friend again.

'I mean *that*,' retorted the cleric, and suddenly pointed at a puddle sealed with ice that shone in the moon. 'Do you remember whom Dante put in the last circle of ice?'

'The traitors,' said Flambeau, and shuddered. As he looked round at the inhuman landscape of trees, with taunting and almost obscene outlines, he could almost fancy he was Dante, and the priest with the rivulet of a voice was, indeed, a Virgil leading him through a land of eternal sins.

The voice went on: 'Olivier, as you know, was quixotic, and would not permit a secret service and spies. The thing, however, was done, like many other things, behind his back. It was managed by my old friend Espado; he was the bright-clad fop, whose hook nose got him called the Vulture. Posing as a sort of philanthropist at the front, he felt his way through the

English Army, and at last got his fingers on its one corrupt man—please God!—and that man at the top. St Clare was in foul need of money, and mountains of it. The discredited family doctor was threatening those extraordinary exposures that afterwards began and were broken off; tales of monstrous and prehistoric things in Park Lane;* things done by an English Evangelical that smelt like human sacrifice and hordes of slaves. Money was wanted, too, for his daughter's dowry; for to him the fame of wealth was as sweet as wealth itself. He snapped the last thread, whispered the word to Brazil, and wealth poured in from the enemies of England. But another man had talked to Espado the Vulture as well as he. Somehow the dark, grim young major from Ulster had guessed the hideous truth; and when they walked slowly together down that road towards the bridge Murray was telling the general that he must resign instantly, or be court-martialled and shot. The general temporized with him till they came to the fringe of tropic trees by the bridge; and there by the singing river and the sunlit palms (for I can see the picture) the general drew his sabre and plunged it through the body of the major.'

The wintry road curved over a ridge in cutting frost, with cruel black shapes of bush and thicket; but Flambeau fancied that he saw beyond it faintly the edge of an aureole that was not starlight and moonlight, but some fire such as is made by men. He watched it as the tale drew to its close.

'St Clare was a hell-hound, but he was a hound of breed. Never, I'll swear, was he so lucid and so strong as when poor Murray lay a cold lump at his feet. Never in all his triumphs, as Captain Keith said truly, was the great man so great as he was in this last world-despised defeat. He looked coolly at his weapon to wipe off the blood; he saw the point he had planted between his victim's shoulders had broken off in the body. He saw quite calmly, as through a club window-pane, all that must follow. He saw that men must find the unaccountable corpse; must extract the unaccountable sword-point; must notice the unaccountable broken sword—or absence of sword. He had killed, but not silenced. But his imperious intellect rose against the facer—there was one way yet. He could make the corpse less unaccountable. He could create a hill of corpses to cover this one. In twenty minutes eight hundred English soldiers were marching down to their death.'

The warmer glow behind the black winter wood grew richer and brighter, and Flambeau strode on to reach it. Father Brown also quickened his stride; but he seemed merely absorbed in his tale.

'Such was the valour of that English thousand, and such the genius of their commander, that if they had at once attacked the hill, even their mad march might have met some luck. But the evil mind that played with them like pawns had other aims and reasons. They must remain in the marshes by the bridge at least till British corpses should be a common sight there. Then for the last grand scene: the silver-haired soldier-saint would give up his shattered sword to save further slaughter. Oh, it was well organized for an impromptu. But I think (I cannot prove), I think that it was while they stuck there in the bloody mire that someone doubted—and someone guessed.'

He was mute a moment, and then said: 'There is a voice from nowhere that tells me the man who guessed was the lover . . . the man to wed the old man's child.'

'But what about Olivier and the hanging?' asked Flambeau.

'Olivier, partly from chivalry, partly from policy, seldom encumbered his march with captives,' explained the narrator. 'He released everybody in most cases. He released everybody in this case.'

'Everybody but the general,' said the tall man.

'Everybody,' said the priest.

Flambeau knitted his black brows. 'I don't grasp it all yet,' he said.

'There is another picture, Flambeau,' said Brown in his more mystical undertone. 'I can't prove it; but I can do more— I can see it. There is a camp breaking up on the bare, torrid hills at morning, and Brazilian uniforms massed in blocks and columns to march. There is the red shirt and long black beard of Olivier, which blows as he stands, his broad-brimmed hat in his hand. He is saying farewell to the great enemy he is setting free—the simple, snow-headed English veteran, who thanks him in the name of his men. The English remnant stand behind at attention; beside them are stores and vehicles for the retreat. The drums roll; the Brazilians are moving; the English are still like statues. So they abide till the last hum and flash of the enemy have faded from the tropic horizon. Then they alter their postures all at once, like dead men coming to life; they turn their fifty faces upon the general—faces not to be forgotten.'

Flambeau gave a great jump. 'Ah,' he cried. 'You don't mean——'

'Yes,' said Father Brown in a deep, moving voice. 'It was an English hand that put the rope round St Clare's neck; I believe the hand that put the ring on his daughter's finger. They were English hands that dragged him up to the tree of shame; the hands of men that had adored him and followed him to victory. And they were English souls (God pardon and endure us all!) who stared at him swinging in that foreign sun on the green gallows of palm, and prayed in their hatred that he might drop off it into hell.'

As the two topped the ridge there burst on them the strong scarlet light of a red-curtained English inn. It stood sideways in the road, as if standing aside in the amplitude of hospitality. Its three doors stood open with invitation; and even where they stood they could hear the hum and laughter of humanity happy for a night.

'I need not tell you more,' said Father Brown. 'They tried him in the wilderness and destroyed him; and then, for the honour of England and of his daughter, they took an oath to seal up for ever the story of the traitor's purse and the assassin's sword blade. Perhaps—Heaven help them—they tried to forget it. Let us try to forget it, anyhow; here is our inn.'

'With all my heart,' said Flambeau, and was just striding into the bright, noisy bar when he stepped back and almost fell on the road.

'Look there, in the devil's name!' he cried, and pointed rigidly at the square wooden sign that overhung the road. It showed dimly the crude shape of a sabre hilt and a shortened blade; and was inscribed in false archaic lettering, 'The Sign of the Broken Sword.'

'Were you not prepared?' asked Father Brown gently. 'He is the god of this country; half the inns and parks and streets are named after him and his story.'

'I thought we had done with the leper,' cried Flambeau, and spat on the road.

'You will never have done with him in England,' said the priest, looking down, 'while brass is strong and stone abides. His marble statues will erect the souls of proud, innocent boys for centuries, his village tomb will smell of loyalty as of lilies. Millions who never knew him shall love him like a father— this man whom the last few that knew him dealt with like dung. He shall be a saint; and the truth shall never be told of him, because I have made up my mind at last. There is so much good and evil in breaking secrets, that I put my conduct to a test. All these newspapers will perish; the anti-Brazil boom is already over; Olivier is already honoured everywhere. But I told myself that if anywhere, by name, in metal or marble that will endure like the pyramids, Colonel Clancy, or Captain Keith, or President Olivier, or any innocent man was wrongly blamed, then I would speak. If it were only that St Clare was wrongly praised, I would be silent. And I will.'

They plunged into the red-curtained tavern, which was not only cosy, but even luxurious inside. On a table stood a silver model of the tomb of St Clare, the silver head bowed, the silver sword broken. On the walls were coloured photographs of the same scene, and of the system of wagonettes that took tourists to see it. They sat down on the comfortable padded benches.

'Come, it's cold,' cried Father Brown; 'let's have some wine or beer.'

'Or brandy,' said Flambeau.

THE DUEL OF DR HIRSCH

M. MAURICE BRUN and M. Armand Armagnac were crossing the sunlit Champs Élysées with a kind of vivacious respectability. They were both short, brisk and bold. They both had black beards that did not seem to belong to their faces, after the strange French fashion which makes real hair look like artificial. M. Brun had a dark wedge of beard apparently affixed under his lower lip. M. Armagnac, by way of a change, had two beards; one sticking out from each corner of his emphatic chin. They were both young. They were both atheists, with a depressing fixity of outlook but great mobility of exposition. They were both pupils of the great Dr Hirsch, scientist, publicist and moralist.

M. Brun had become prominent by his proposal that the common expression 'Adieu' should be obliterated from all the French classics, and a slight fine imposed for its use in private life. 'Then,' he said, 'the very name of your imagined God will have echoed for the last time in the ear of man.' M. Armagnac specialized rather in a resistance to militarism, and wished the chorus of the Marseillaise altered from 'Aux armes, citoyens' to 'Aux grèves, citoyens.'* But his antimilitarism was of a peculiar and Gallic sort. An eminent and very wealthy English Quaker, who had come to see him to arrange for the disarmament of the whole planet, was rather distressed by Armagnac's proposal that (by way of beginning) the soldiers should shoot their officers.

And indeed it was in this regard that the two men differed most from their leader and father in philosophy. Dr Hirsch, though born in France and covered with the most triumphant favours of French education, was temperamentally of another type—mild, dreamy, humane; and, despite his sceptical system, not devoid of transcendentalism. He was, in short, more like a German than a Frenchman; and much as they admired him, something in the subconsciousness of these Gauls was irritated at his pleading for peace in so peaceful a manner. To their party throughout Europe, however, Paul Hirsch was a saint of science. His large and daring cosmic theories advertised his austere life and innocent, if somewhat frigid, morality; he held something of the position of Darwin doubled with the position of Tolstoy. But he was neither an anarchist nor an antipatriot; his views on disarmament were moderate and evolutionary—the Republican Government put considerable confidence in him as to various chemical improvements. He had lately even discovered a noiseless explosive, the secret of which the Government was carefully guarding.

His house stood in a handsome street near the Élysée*—a street which in that strong summer seemed almost as full of foliage as the park itself; a row of chestnuts shattered the sunshine, interrupted only in one place where a large café ran out into the street. Almost opposite to this were the white and green blinds of the great scientist's house, an iron balcony, also painted green, running along in front of the first-floor windows. Beneath this was the entrance into a kind of court, gay with shrubs and tiles, into which the two Frenchmen passed in animated talk.

The door was opened to them by the doctor's old servant Simon, who might very well have passed for a doctor himself, having a strict suit of black, spectacles, grey hair, and a confidential manner. In fact, he was a far more presentable man of science than his master, Dr Hirsch, who was a forked radish* of a fellow, with just enough bulb of a head to make his body insignificant. With all the gravity of a great physician handling a prescription, Simon handed a letter to M. Armagnac. That gentleman ripped it up with a racial impatience, and rapidly read the following:

'I cannot come down to speak to you. There is a man in this house whom I refuse to meet. He is a Chauvinist* officer, Dubosc. He is sitting on the stairs. He has been kicking the furniture about in all the other rooms; I have locked myself in my study, opposite that café. If you love me, go over to the café and wait at one of the tables outside. I will try to send him over to you. I want you to answer him and deal with him. I cannot meet him myself. I cannot: I will not.

'There is going to be another Dreyfus case.*

'P. HIRSCH.'

M. Armagnac looked at M. Brun. M. Brun borrowed the letter, read it, and looked at M. Armagnac. Then both betook themselves briskly to one of the little tables under the chestnuts opposite, where they procured two tall glasses of horrible green absinthe, which they could drink apparently in any weather and at any time. Otherwise the café seemed empty, except for one soldier drinking coffee at one table, and at another a large man drinking a small syrup and a priest drinking nothing.

Maurice Brun cleared his throat and said: 'Of course we must help the master in every way, but——'

There was an abrupt silence, and Armagnac said: 'He may have excellent reasons for not meeting the man himself, but——'

Before either could complete a sentence, it was evident that the invader had been expelled from the house opposite. The shrubs under the archway swayed and burst apart, as that unwelcome guest was shot out of them like a cannon-ball.

He was a sturdy figure in a small and tilted Tyrolean felt hat, a figure that had indeed something generally Tyrolean about it. The man's shoulders were big and broad, but his legs were neat and active in knee-breeches and knitted stockings. His face was brown like a nut; he had very bright and restless brown eyes; his dark hair was brushed back stiffly in front and cropped close behind, outlining a square and powerful skull; and he had a huge black moustache like the horns of a bison. Such a substantial head is generally based on a bull neck; but this was hidden by a big coloured scarf, swathed round up the man's ears and falling in front inside his jacket like a sort of fancy waistcoat. It was a scarf of strong dead colours, dark red and old gold and purple, probably of Oriental fabrication. Altogether the man had something a shade barbaric about him; more like a Hungarian squire than an ordinary French officer. His French, however, was obviously that of a native; and his French patriotism was so impulsive as to be slightly absurd. His first act when he burst out of the archway was to call in a clarion voice down the street, 'Are there any Frenchmen here?' as if he were calling for Christians in Mecca.

Armagnac and Brun instantly stood up; but they were too late. Men were already running from the street corners; there was a small but ever-clustering crowd. With the prompt French instinct for the politics of the street, the man with the black moustache had already run across to a corner of the café, sprung on one of the tables, and seizing a branch of chestnut to steady himself, shouted as Camille Desmoulins* once shouted when he scattered the oak-leaves among the populace.

'Frenchmen!' he volleyed; 'I cannot speak! God help me, that is why I am speaking! The fellows in their filthy parliaments who learn to speak also learn to be silent—silent as that spy cowering in the house opposite! Silent as he is when I beat on his bedroom door! Silent as he is now, though he hears my voice across this street and shakes where he sits! Oh, they can be silent eloquently—the politicians! But the time has come when we that cannot speak *must* speak. You are betrayed to the Prussians. Betrayed at this moment. Betrayed by that man. I am Jules Dubosc, Colonel of Artillery, Belfort. We caught a German spy in the Vosges yesterday, and a paper was found on him—a paper I hold in my hand. Oh, they tried to hush it up; but I took it direct to the man who wrote it—the man in that house! It is in his hand. It is signed with his initials. It is a direction for finding the secret of this new Noiseless Powder. Hirsch invented it; Hirsch wrote this note about it. This note is in German, and was found in a German's pocket. "Tell the man the formula for powder is in grey envelope in first drawer to the left of Secretary's desk, War Office, in red ink. He must be careful. P.H."'

He rattled short sentences like a quick-firing gun, but he was plainly the sort of man who is either mad or right. The mass of the crowd was Nationalist, and already in threatening uproar; and a minority of equally angry Intellectuals, led by Armagnac and Brun, only made the majority more militant.

'If this is a military secret,' shouted Brun, 'why do you yell about it in the street?'

'I will tell you why I do!' roared Dubosc above the roaring crowd. 'I went to this man in straight and civil style. If he had any explanation it could have been given in complete confidence. He refuses to explain. He refers me to two strangers in a café as to two flunkeys. He has thrown me out of the house, but I am going back into it, with the people of Paris behind me!'

A shout seemed to shake the very façade of mansions and two stones flew, one breaking a window above the balcony. The indignant Colonel plunged once more under the archway and was heard crying and thundering inside. Every instant the human sea grew wider and wider; it surged up against the

rails and steps of the traitor's house; it was already certain
that the place would be burst into like the Bastille, when
the broken French window opened and Dr Hirsch came
out on the balcony. For an instant the fury half turned to
laughter; for he was an absurd figure in such a scene. His
long bare neck and sloping shoulders were the shape of a
champagne bottle, but that was the only festive thing about
him. His coat hung on him as on a peg; he wore his
carrot-coloured hair long and weedy; his cheeks and chin were
fully fringed with one of those irritating beards that begin
far from the mouth. He was very pale, and he wore blue
spectacles.

Livid as he was, he spoke with a sort of prim decision, so
that the mob fell silent in the middle of his third sentence.

'. . . only two things to say to you now. The first is to my
foes, the second to my friends. To my foes I say: It is true I will
not meet M. Dubosc, though he is storming outside this very
room. It is true I have asked two other men to confront him
for me. And I will tell you why! Because I will not and must
not see him—because it would be against all rules of dignity
and honour to see him. Before I am triumphantly cleared
before a court, there is another arbitration this gentleman
owes me as a gentleman, and in referring him to my seconds
I am strictly——'

Armagnac and Brun were waving their hats wildly, and even
the Doctor's enemies roared applause at this unexpected defiance. Once more a few sentences were inaudible, but they
could hear him say: 'To my friends—I myself should always
prefer weapons purely intellectual, and to these an evolved
humanity will certainly confine itself. But our own most
precious truth is the fundamental force of matter and heredity.
My books are successful; my theories are unrefuted; but I
suffer in politics from a prejudice almost physical in the
French. I cannot speak like Clemenceau* and Déroulède,* for
their words are like echoes of their pistols. The French ask for
a duellist as the English ask for a sportsman. Well, I give my
proofs: I will pay this barbaric bribe, and then go back to
reason for the rest of my life.'

Two men were instantly found in the crowd itself to offer
their services to Colonel Dubosc, who came out presently,

satisfied. One was the common soldier with the coffee, who said simply: 'I will act for you, sir. I am the Duc de Valognes.' The other was the big man, whom his friend the priest sought at first to dissuade; and then walked away alone.

In the early evening a light dinner was spread at the back of the Café Charlemagne. Though unroofed by any glass or gilt plaster, the guests were nearly all under a delicate and irregular roof of leaves; for the ornamental trees stood so thick around and among the tables as to give something of the dimness and the dazzle of a small orchard. At one of the central tables a very stumpy little priest sat in complete solitude, and applied himself to a pile of whitebait with the gravest sort of enjoyment. His daily living being very plain, he had a peculiar taste for sudden and isolated luxuries; he was an abstemious epicure. He did not lift his eyes from his plate, round which red pepper, lemons, brown bread and butter, etc., were rigidly ranked, until a tall shadow fell across the table, and his friend Flambeau sat down opposite. Flambeau was gloomy.

'I'm afraid I must chuck this business,' said he heavily. 'I'm all on the side of the French soldiers like Dubosc, and I'm all against the French atheists like Hirsch; but it seems to me in this case we've made a mistake. The Duke and I thought it as well to investigate the charge, and I must say I'm glad we did.'

'Is the paper a forgery, then?' asked the priest.

'That's just the odd thing,' replied Flambeau. 'It's exactly like Hirsch's writing, and nobody can point out any mistake in it. But it wasn't written by Hirsch. If he's a French patriot he didn't write it, because it gives information to Germany. And if he's a German spy he didn't write it, well—because it doesn't give information to Germany.'

'You mean the information is wrong?' asked Father Brown.

'Wrong,' replied the other, 'and wrong exactly where Dr Hirsch would have been right—about the hiding-place of his own secret formula in his own official department. By favour of Hirsch and the authorities, the Duke and I have actually been allowed to inspect the secret drawer at the War Office where the Hirsch formula is kept. We are the only people who have ever known it, except the inventor himself and the Minister for War; but the Minister permitted it to save Hirsch from fighting. After that we really can't support Dubosc if his revelation is a mare's nest.'

'And it is?' asked Father Brown.

'It is,' said his friend gloomily. 'It is a clumsy forgery by somebody who knew nothing of the real hiding-place. It says the paper is in the cupboard on the right of the Secretary's desk. As a fact the cupboard with the secret drawer is some way to the left of the desk. It says the grey envelope contains a long document written in red ink. It isn't written in red ink, but in ordinary black ink. It's manifestly absurd to say that Hirsch can have made a mistake about a paper that nobody knew of but himself; or can have tried to help a foreign thief by telling him to fumble in the wrong drawer. I think we must chuck it up and apologize to old Carrots.'

Father Brown seemed to cogitate; he lifted a little whitebait on his fork. 'You are sure the grey envelope was in the left cupboard?' he asked.

'Positive,' replied Flambeau. 'The grey envelope—it was a white envelope really—was——'

Father Brown put down the small silver fish and the fork and stared across at his companion. 'What?' he asked, in an altered voice.

'Well, what?' repeated Flambeau, eating heartily.

'It was *not* grey,' said the priest, 'Flambeau, you frighten me.'

'What the deuce are you frightened of?'

'I'm frightened of a white envelope,' said the other seriously. 'If it had only just been grey! Hang it all, it might as well have been grey. But if it was white, the whole business is black. The Doctor has been dabbling in some of the old brimstone after all.'

'But I tell you he couldn't have written such a note!' cried Flambeau. 'The note is utterly wrong about the facts. And innocent or guilty, Dr Hirsch knew all about the facts.'

'The man who wrote that note knew all about the facts,' said his clerical companion soberly. 'He could never have got 'em so wrong without knowing about 'em. You have to know an awful lot to be wrong on every subject—like the devil.'

'Do you mean——?'

'I mean a man telling lies on chance would have told some of the truth,' said his friend firmly. 'Suppose someone sent you to find a house with a green door and a blue blind, with a front garden but no back garden, with a dog but no cat, and where they drank coffee but not tea. You would say if you found no such house that it was all made up. But I say no. I say if you found a house where the door was blue and the blind green, where there was a back garden and no front garden, where cats were common and dogs instantly shot, where tea was drunk in quarts and coffee forbidden— then you would know you had found the house. The man must have known that particular house to be so accurately inaccurate.'

'But what could it mean?' demanded the diner opposite.

'I can't conceive,' said Brown; 'I don't understand this Hirsch affair at all. As long as it was only the left drawer instead of the right, and red ink instead of black, I thought it must be the chance blunders of a forger, as you say. But three is a mystical number; it finishes things. It finishes this. That the direction about the drawer, the colour of ink, the colour of envelope, should *none* of them be right by accident, that *can't* be a coincidence. It wasn't.'

'What was it, then? Treason?' asked Flambeau, resuming his dinner.

'I don't know that either,' answered Brown, with a face of blank bewilderment. 'The only thing I can think of. . . . Well, I never understood that Dreyfus case. I can always grasp moral evidence easier than the other sorts. I go by a man's eyes and voice, don't you know, and whether his family seems happy, and by what subjects he chooses—and avoids. Well, I was puzzled in the Dreyfus case. Not by the horrible things imputed both ways; I know (though it's not modern to say so) that human nature in the highest places is still capable of being Cenci or Borgia.* No; what puzzled me was the *sincerity* of both parties. I don't mean the political parties; the rank and file are always roughly honest, and often duped. I mean the persons of the play. I mean the conspirators, if they were conspirators. I mean the traitor, if he was a traitor. I mean the men who *must* have known the truth. Now Dreyfus went on like a man who *knew* he was a wronged man. And yet the French statesmen and soldiers went on as if they *knew* he wasn't a wronged man but simply a wrong 'un. I don't mean they behaved well; I mean they behaved as if they were sure. I can't describe these things; I know what I mean.'

'I wish I did,' said his friend. 'And what has it to do with old Hirsch?'

'Suppose a person in a position of trust,' went on the priest, 'began to give the enemy information because it was false information. Suppose he even thought he was saving his country by misleading the foreigner. Suppose this brought him into spy circles, and little loans were made to him, and little ties tied on to him. Suppose he kept up his contradictory position in a confused way by never telling the foreign spies the truth, but letting it more and more be guessed. The better part of him (what was left of it) would still say: "I have not helped the enemy; I said it was the left drawer." The meaner part of him would already be saying: "But they may have the sense to see that means the right." I think it is psychologically possible—in an enlightened age, you know.'

'It may be psychologically possible,' answered Flambeau, 'and it certainly would explain Dreyfus being certain he was wronged and his judges being sure he was guilty. But it won't wash historically, because Dreyfus's document (if it was his document) was literally correct.'

'I wasn't thinking of Dreyfus,' said Father Brown.

Silence had sunk around them with the emptying of the tables; it was already late, though the sunlight still clung to everything, as if accidentally entangled in the trees. In the stillness Flambeau shifted his seat sharply—making an isolated and echoing noise—and threw his elbow over the angle of it. 'Well,' he said, rather harshly, 'if Hirsch is not better than a timid treason-monger. . . .'

'You mustn't be too hard on them,' said Father Brown gently. 'It's not entirely their fault; but they have no instincts. I mean those things that make a woman refuse to dance with a man or a man to touch an investment. They've been taught that it's all a matter of degree.'

'Anyhow,' cried Flambeau impatiently, 'he's not a patch on my principal; and I shall go through with it. Old Dubosc may be a bit mad, but he's a sort of patriot after all.'

Father Brown continued to consume whitebait.

Something in the stolid way he did so caused Flambeau's fierce black eyes to ramble over his companion afresh. 'What's the matter with you?' Flambeau demanded. 'Dubosc's all right in that way. You don't doubt him?'

'My friend,' said the small priest, laying down his knife and fork in a kind of cold despair, 'I doubt everything. Everything, I mean, that has happened to-day. I doubt the whole story, though it has been acted before my face. I doubt every sight that my eyes have seen since morning. There is something in this business quite different from the ordinary police mystery where one man is more or less lying and the other man more or less telling the truth. Here both men. . . . Well! I've told you the only theory I can think of that could satisfy anybody. It doesn't satisfy me.'

'Nor me either,' replied Flambeau frowning, while the other went on eating fish with an air of entire resignation. 'If all you can suggest is that notion of a message conveyed by contraries, I call it uncommonly clever, but . . . well, what would you call it?'

'I should call it thin,' said the priest promptly. 'I should call it uncommonly thin. But that's the queer thing about the whole business. The lie is like a schoolboy's. There are only three versions, Dubosc's and Hirsch's and that fancy of mine. Either that note was written by a French officer to ruin a French official; or it was written by the French official to help German officers; or it was written by the French official to mislead German officers. Very well. You'd expect a secret paper passing between such people, officials or officers, to look quite different from that. You'd expect, probably a cipher, certainly abbreviations; most certainly scientific and strictly professional terms. But this thing's elaborately simple, like a penny dreadful: "In the purple grotto you will find the golden casket." It looks as if . . . as if it were meant to be seen through at once.'

Almost before they could take it in a short figure in French uniform had walked up to their table like the wind, and sat down with a sort of thump.

'I have extraordinary news,' said the Duc de Valognes. 'I have just come from this Colonel of ours. He is packing up to leave the country, and he asks us to make his excuses *sur le terrain*.'*

'What?' cried Flambeau, with an incredulity quite frightful—'*apologize?*'

'Yes,' said the Duke gruffly; 'then and there—before everybody—when the swords are drawn. And you and I have to do it while he is leaving the country.'

'But what *can* this mean?' cried Flambeau. 'He can't be afraid of that little Hirsch! Confound it!' he cried, in a kind of rational rage; 'nobody *could* be afraid of Hirsch!'

'I believe it's some plot!' snapped Valognes—'some plot of the Jews and Freemasons. It's meant to work up glory for Hirsch. . . .'

The face of Father Brown was commonplace, but curiously contented; it could shine with ignorance as well as with knowledge. But there was always one flash when the foolish mask fell, and the wise mask fitted itself in its place; and Flambeau, who knew his friend, knew that his friend had suddenly understood. Brown said nothing, but finished his plate of fish.

'Where did you last see our precious Colonel?' asked Flambeau, irritably.

'He's round at the Hôtel Saint Louis by the Élysée, where we drove with him. He's packing up, I tell you.'

'Will he be there still, do you think?' asked Flambeau, frowning at the table.

'I don't think he can get away yet,' replied the Duke; 'he's packing to go a long journey. . . .'

'No,' said Father Brown, quite simply, but suddenly standing up, 'for a very short journey. For one of the shortest, in fact. But we may still be in time to catch him if we go there in a motor-cab.'

Nothing more could be got out of him until the cab swept round the corner by the Hôtel Saint Louis, where they got out, and he led the party up a side lane already in deep shadow with the growing dusk. Once, when the Duke impatiently asked whether Hirsch was guilty of treason or not, he answered rather absently: 'No; only of ambition—like Cæsar.' Then he somewhat inconsequently added: 'He lives a very lonely life; he has had to do everything for himself.'

'Well, if he's ambitious, he ought to be satisfied now,' said Flambeau rather bitterly. 'All Paris will cheer him now our cursed Colonel has turned tail.'

'Don't talk so loud,' said Father Brown, lowering his voice; 'your cursed Colonel is just in front.'

The other two started and shrank farther back into the shadow of the wall, for the sturdy figure of their runaway principal could indeed be seen shuffling along in the twilight in front, a bag in each hand. He looked much the same as when they first saw him, except that he had changed his picturesque mountaineering knickers for a conventional pair of trousers. It was clear he was already escaping from the hotel.

The lane down which they followed him was one of those that seem to be at the back of things, and look like the wrong side of the stage scenery. A colourless, continuous wall ran down one flank of it, interrupted at intervals by dull-hued and dirt-stained doors, all shut fast and featureless save for the chalk scribbles of some passing *gamin*.* The tops of trees, mostly rather depressing evergreens, showed at intervals over the top of the wall, and beyond them in the grey and purple gloaming could be seen the back of some long terrace of tall Parisian houses, really comparatively close, but somehow looking as inaccessible as a range of marble mountains. On the other side of the lane ran the high gilt railings of a gloomy park.

Flambeau was looking round him in rather a weird way. 'Do you know,' he said, 'there is something about this place that——'

'Hullo!' called out the Duke sharply; 'that fellow's disappeared. Vanished, like a blasted fairy!'

'He has a key,' explained their clerical friend. 'He's only gone into one of these garden doors,' and as he spoke they heard one of the dull wooden doors close again with a click in front of them.

Flambeau strode up to the door thus shut almost in his face, and stood in front of it for a moment, biting his black moustache in a fury of curiosity. Then he threw up his long arms and swung himself aloft like a monkey and stood on the top of the wall, his enormous figure dark against the purple sky, like the dark tree-tops.

The Duke looked at the priest. 'Dubosc's escape is more elaborate than we thought,' he said; 'but I suppose he is escaping from France.'

'He is escaping from everywhere,' answered Father Brown.

Valognes's eyes brightened, but his voice sank. 'Do you mean suicide?' he asked.

'You will not find his body,' replied the other.

A kind of cry came from Flambeau on the wall above. 'My God,' he exclaimed in French, 'I know what this place is now! Why, it's the back of the street where old Hirsch lives. I thought I could recognize the back of a house as well as the back of a man.'

'And Dubosc's gone in there!' cried the Duke, smiting his hip. 'Why, they'll meet after all!' And with sudden Gallic vivacity he hopped up on the wall beside Flambeau and sat there positively kicking his legs with excitement. The priest alone remained below, leaning against the wall, with his back to the whole theatre of events, and looking wistfully across to the park palings and the twinkling, twilit trees.

The Duke, however stimulated, had the instincts of an aristocrat, and desired rather to stare at the house than to spy on it; but Flambeau, who had the instincts of a burglar (and a detective), had already swung himself from the wall into the fork of a straggling tree from which he could crawl quite close to the only illuminated window in the back of the high dark house. A red blind had been pulled down over the light, but pulled crookedly, so that it gaped on one side, and by risking his neck along a branch that looked as treacherous as a twig, Flambeau could just see Colonel Dubosc walking about in a brilliantly-lighted and luxurious bedroom. But close as

Flambeau was to the house, he heard the words of his colleagues by the wall, and repeated them in a low voice.

'Yes, they will meet now after all!'

'They will never meet,' said Father Brown. 'Hirsch was right when he said that in such an affair the principals must not meet. Have you read a queer psychological story* by Henry James, of two persons who so perpetually missed meeting each other by accident that they began to feel quite frightened of each other, and to think it was fate? This is something of the kind, but more curious.'

'There are people in Paris who will cure them of such morbid fancies,' said Valognes vindictively. 'They will jolly well have to meet if we capture them and force them to fight.'

'They will not meet on the Day of Judgment,' said the priest. 'If God Almighty held the truncheon of the lists, if St Michael blew the trumpet for the swords to cross—even then, if one of them stood ready, the other would not come.'

'Oh, what does all this mysticism mean?' cried the Duc de Valognes, impatiently; 'why on earth shouldn't they meet like other people?'

'They are the opposite of each other,' said Father Brown, with a queer kind of smile. 'They contradict each other. They cancel out, so to speak.'

He continued to gaze at the darkening trees opposite, but Valognes turned his head sharply at a suppressed exclamation from Flambeau. That investigator, peering into the lighted room, had just seen the Colonel, after a pace or two, proceed to take his coat off. Flambeau's first thought was that this really looked like a fight; but he soon dropped the thought for another. The solidity and squareness of Dubosc's chest and shoulders was all a powerful piece of padding and came off with his coat. In his shirt and trousers he was a comparatively slim gentleman, who walked across the bedroom to the bathroom with no more pugnacious purpose than that of washing himself. He bent over a basin, dried his dripping hands and face on a towel, and turned again so that the strong light fell on his face. His brown complexion had gone, his big black moustache had gone; he was clean-shaven and very pale.

Nothing remained of the Colonel but his bright, hawk-like, brown eyes. Under the wall Father Brown was going on in heavy meditation, as if to himself.

'It is all just like what I was saying to Flambeau. These opposites won't do. They don't work. They don't fight. If it's white instead of black, and solid instead of liquid, and so on all along the line—then there's something wrong, Monsieur, there's something wrong. One of these men is fair and the other dark, one stout and the other slim, one strong and the other weak. One has a moustache and no beard, so you can't see his mouth; the other has a beard and no moustache, so you can't see his chin. One has hair cropped to his skull, but a scarf to hide his neck; the other has low shirt-collars, but long hair to hide his skull. It's all too neat and correct, Monsieur, and there's something wrong. Things made so opposite are things that cannot quarrel. Wherever the one sticks out the other sinks in. Like a face and a mask, like a lock and a key. . . .'

Flambeau was peering into the house with a visage as white as a sheet. The occupant of the room was standing with his back to him, but in front of a looking-glass, and had already fitted round his face a sort of framework of rank red hair, hanging disordered from the head and clinging round the jaws and chin while leaving the mocking mouth uncovered. Seen thus in the glass the white face looked like the face of Judas laughing horribly* and surrounded by capering flames of hell. For a spasm Flambeau saw the fierce, red-brown eyes dancing, then they were covered with a pair of blue spectacles. Slipping on a loose black coat, the figure vanished towards the front of the house. A few moments later a roar of popular applause from the street beyond announced that Dr Hirsch had once more appeared upon the balcony.

THE MAN IN THE PASSAGE

Two men appeared simultaneously at the two ends of a sort of passage running along the side of the Apollo Theatre in the Adelphi.* The evening daylight in the streets was large and

luminous, opalescent and empty. The passage was comparatively long and dark, so each man could see the other as a
mere black silhouette at the other end. Nevertheless, each man
knew the other, even in that inky outline; for they were both
men of striking appearance and they hated each other.

The covered passage opened at one end on one of the steep
streets of the Adelphi, and at the other on a terrace overlooking the sunset-coloured river. One side of the passage was a
blank wall, for the building it supported was an old unsuccessful theatre restaurant, now shut up. The other side of the
passage contained two doors, one at each end. Neither was
what was commonly called the stage door; they were a sort of
special and private stage doors used by very special performers, and in this case by the star actor and actress in the
Shakespearean performance of the day. Persons of that eminence often like to have such private exits and entrances, for
meeting friends or avoiding them.

The two men in question were certainly two such friends,
men who evidently knew the doors and counted on their
opening, for each approached the door at the upper end with
equal coolness and confidence. Not, however, with equal
speed; but the man who walked fast was the man from the
other end of the tunnel, so they both arrived before the secret
stage door almost at the same instant. They saluted each other
with civility, and waited a moment before one of them, the
sharper walker who seemed to have the shorter patience,
knocked at the door.

In this and everything else each man was opposite and
neither could be called inferior. As private persons both were
handsome, capable and popular. As public persons, both were
in the first public rank. But everything about them, from their
glory to their good looks, was of a diverse and incomparable
kind. Sir Wilson Seymour was the kind of man whose importance is known to everybody who knows. The more you mixed
with the innermost ring in every polity or profession, the more
often you met Sir Wilson Seymour. He was the one intelligent
man on twenty unintelligent committees—on every sort of
subject, from the reform of the Royal Academy to the project
of bimetallism for Greater Britain. In the Arts especially he

was omnipotent. He was so unique that nobody could quite decide whether he was a great aristocrat who had taken up Art, or a great artist whom the aristocrats had taken up. But you could not meet him for five minutes without realizing that you had really been ruled by him all your life.

His appearance was 'distinguished' in exactly the same sense; it was at once conventional and unique. Fashion could have found no fault with his high silk hat; yet it was unlike anyone else's hat—a little higher, perhaps, and adding something to his natural height. His tall, slender figure had a slight stoop, yet it looked the reverse of feeble. His hair was silver-grey, but he did not look old; it was worn longer than the common yet he did not look effeminate; it was curly but it did not look curled. His carefully pointed beard made him look more manly and militant than otherwise, as it does in those old admirals of Velazquez* with whose dark portraits his house was hung. His grey gloves were a shade bluer, his silver-knobbed cane a shade longer than scores of such gloves and canes flapped and flourished about the theatres and the restaurants.

The other man was not so tall, yet would have struck nobody as short, but merely as strong and handsome. His hair also was curly, but fair and cropped close to a strong, massive head—the sort of head you break a door with, as Chaucer said of the Miller's.* His military moustache and the carriage of his shoulders showed him a soldier, but he had a pair of those peculiar frank and piercing blue eyes which are more common in sailors. His face was somewhat square, his jaw was square, his shoulders were square, even his jacket was square. Indeed, in the wild school of caricature then current, Mr Max Beerbohm* had represented him as a proposition in the fourth book of Euclid.

For he also was a public man, though with quite another sort of success. You did not have to be in the best society to have heard of Captain Cutler, of the siege of Hong-Kong, and the great march across China. You could not get away from hearing of him wherever you were; his portrait was on every other postcard; his maps and battles in every other illustrated paper; songs in his honour in every other music-hall turn or on every other barrel-organ. His fame, though probably more temporary, was ten times more wide, popular and spontaneous than the other man's. In thousands of English homes he appeared enormous above England, like Nelson. Yet he had infinitely less power in England than Sir Wilson Seymour.

The door was opened to them by an aged servant or 'dresser,' whose broken-down face and figure and black shabby coat and trousers contrasted queerly with the glittering interior of the great actress's dressing-room. It was fitted and filled with looking-glasses at every angle of refraction, so that they looked like the hundred facets of one huge diamond—if one could get inside a diamond. The other features of luxury, a few flowers, a few coloured cushions, a few scraps of stage costume, were multiplied by all the mirrors into the madness of the Arabian Nights, and danced and changed places perpetually as the shuffling attendant shifted a mirror outwards or shot one back against the wall.

They both spoke to the dingy dresser by name, calling him Parkinson, and asking for the lady as Miss Aurora Rome. Parkinson said she was in the other room, but he would go and tell her. A shade crossed the brow of both visitors; for the other room was the private room of the great actor with whom Miss Aurora was performing, and she was of the kind that does not inflame admiration without inflaming jealousy. In about half a minute, however, the inner door opened, and she entered as she always did, even in private life, so that the very silence seemed to be a roar of applause, and one well deserved. She was clad in a somewhat strange garb of peacock green and peacock blue satins, that gleamed like blue and green metals, such as delight children and æsthetes, and her heavy, hot brown hair framed one of those magic faces which are dangerous to all men, but especially to boys and to men growing grey. In company with her male colleague, the great American actor, Isidore Bruno, she was producing a particularly poetical and fantastic interpretation of the *Midsummer Night's Dream*: in which the artistic prominence was given to Oberon and Titania, or in other words to Bruno and herself. Set in dreamy and exquisite scenery, and moving in mystical dances, the green costume, like burnished beetle-wings, expressed all the elusive individuality of an elfin queen. But when personally confronted in what was still broad daylight, a man looked only at the woman's face.

She greeted both men with the beaming and baffling smile which kept so many males at the same just dangerous distance from her. She accepted some flowers from Cutler, which were as tropical and expensive as his victories; and another sort of present from Sir Wilson Seymour, offered later on and more nonchalantly by that gentleman. For it was against his breeding to show eagerness, and against his conventional unconventionality to give anything so obvious as flowers. He had picked up a trifle, he said, which was rather a curiosity; it was an ancient Greek dagger of the Mycenæan Epoch, and might well have been worn in the time of Theseus and Hippolyta. It was made of brass like all the Heroic weapons, but, oddly enough, sharp enough to prick anyone still. He had really been attracted to it by the leaf-like shape; it was as perfect as a Greek vase. If it was of any interest to Miss Rome or could come in anywhere in the play, he hoped she would——

The inner door burst open and a big figure appeared, who was more of a contrast to the explanatory Seymour than even Captain Cutler. Nearly six-foot-six, and of more than theatrical thews and muscles, Isidore Bruno, in the gorgeous leopard skin and golden-brown garments of Oberon, looked like a barbaric god. He leaned on a sort of hunting-spear, which across a theatre looked a slight, silvery wand, but which in the small and comparatively crowded room looked as plain as a pikestaff—and as menacing. His vivid black eyes rolled volcanically, his bronzed face, handsome as it was, showed at that moment a combination of high cheekbones with set white teeth, which recalled certain American conjectures about his origin in the Southern plantations.

'Aurora,' he began, in that deep voice like a drum of passion that had moved so many audiences, 'will you——'

He stopped indecisively because a sixth figure had suddenly presented itself just inside the doorway—a figure so incongruous in the scene as to be almost comic. It was a very short man in the black uniform of the Roman secular clergy, and looking (especially in such a presence as Bruno's and Aurora's) rather like the wooden Noah* out of an ark. He did not, however, seem conscious of any contrast, but said with dull civility: 'I believe Miss Rome sent for me.'

A shrewd observer might have remarked that the emotional temperature rather rose at so unemotional an interruption. The detachment of a professional celibate seemed to reveal to the others that they stood round the woman as a ring of amorous rivals; just as a stranger coming in with frost on his coat will reveal that a room is like a furnace. The presence of the one man who did not care about her increased Miss Rome's sense that everybody else was in love with her, and each in a somewhat dangerous way: the actor with all the appetite of a savage and a spoilt child; the soldier with all the simple selfishness of a man of will rather than mind; Sir Wilson with that daily hardening concentration with which old Hedonists take to a hobby; nay, even the abject Parkinson, who had known her before her triumphs, and who followed her about the room with eyes or feet, with the dumb fascination of a dog.

A shrewd person might also have noted a yet odder thing. The man like a black wooden Noah (who was not wholly without shrewdness) noted it with a considerable but contained amusement. It was evident that the great Aurora, though by no means indifferent to the admiration of the other sex, wanted at this moment to get rid of all the men who admired her and be left alone with the man who did not— did not admire her in that sense at least; for the little priest did admire and even enjoy the firm feminine diplomacy with which she set about her task. There was, perhaps, only one thing that Aurora Rome was clever about, and that was one half of humanity—the other half. The little priest watched, like a Napoleonic campaign, the swift precision of her policy for expelling all while banishing none. Bruno, the big actor, was so babyish that it was easy to send him off in brute sulks, banging the door. Cutler, the British officer, was pachydermatous to ideas, but punctilious about behaviour. He would ignore all hints, but he would die rather than ignore a definite commission from a lady. As to old Seymour, he had to be treated differently; he had to be left to the last. The only way to move him was to appeal to him in confidence as an old friend, to let him into the secret of the clearance. The priest did really admire Miss Rome as she achieved all these three objects in one selected action.

She went across to Captain Cutler and said in her sweetest manner: 'I shall value all these flowers, because they must be your favourite flowers. But they won't be complete, you know, without *my* favourite flower. *Do* go over to that shop round the corner and get me some lilies-of-the-valley, and then it will be *quite lovely.*'

The first object of her diplomacy, the exit of the enraged Bruno, was at once achieved. He had already handed his spear in a lordly style, like a sceptre, to the piteous Parkinson, and was about to assume one of the cushioned seats like a throne. But at this open appeal to his rival there glowed in his opal eyeballs all the sensitive insolence of the slave; he knotted his enormous brown fists for an instant, and then, dashing open the door, disappeared into his own apartments beyond. But meanwhile Miss Rome's experiment in mobilizing the British Army had not succeeded so simply as seemed probable. Cutler had indeed risen stiffly and suddenly, and walked towards the door, hatless, as if at a word of command. But perhaps there was something ostentatiously elegant about the languid figure of Seymour leaning against one of the looking-glasses that brought him up short at the entrance, turning his head this way and that like a bewildered bulldog.

'I must show this stupid man where to go,' said Aurora in a whisper to Seymour, and ran out to the threshold to speed the parting guest.

Seymour seemed to be listening, elegant and unconscious as was his posture, and he seemed relieved when he heard the lady call out some last instructions to the Captain, and then turn sharply and run laughing down the passage towards the other end, the end on the terrace above the Thames. Yet a second or two after Seymour's brow darkened again. A man in his position has so many rivals, and he remembered that at the other end of the passage was the corresponding entrance to Bruno's private room. He did not lose his dignity; he said some civil words to Father Brown about the revival of Byzantine architecture in the Westminster Cathedral, and then, quite naturally, strolled out himself into the upper end of the passage. Father Brown and Parkinson were left alone, and they were neither of them men with a taste for superfluous conversation. The dresser went round the room, pulling out looking-glasses and pushing them in again, his dingy dark coat and trousers looking all the more dismal since he was still holding the festive fairy spear of King Oberon. Every time he pulled out the frame of a new glass, a new black figure of Father Brown appeared; the absurd glass chamber was full of Father Browns, upside down in the air like angels, turning somersaults like acrobats, turning their backs to everybody like very rude persons.

Father Brown seemed quite unconscious of this cloud of witnesses, but followed Parkinson with an idly attentive eye till he took himself and his absurd spear into the farther room of Bruno. Then he abandoned himself to such abstract meditations as always amused him—calculating the angles of the mirrors,* the angles of each refraction, the angle at which each must fit into the wall . . . when he heard a strong but strangled cry.

He sprang to his feet and stood rigidly listening. At the same instant Sir Wilson Seymour burst back into the room, white as ivory. 'Who's that man in the passage?' he cried. 'Where's that dagger of mine?'

Before Father Brown could turn in his heavy boots Seymour was plunging about the room looking for the weapon. And before he could possibly find that weapon or any other, a brisk running of feet broke upon the pavement outside, and the square face of Cutler was thrust into the same doorway. He was still grotesquely grasping a bunch of lilies-of-the-valley. 'What's this?' he cried. 'What's that creature down the passage? Is this some of your tricks?'

'My tricks!' hissed his pale rival, and made a stride towards him.

In the instant of time in which all this happened Father Brown stepped out into the top of the passage, looked down it, and at once walked briskly towards what he saw.

At this the other two men dropped their quarrel and darted after him, Cutler calling out: 'What are you doing? Who are you?'

'My name is Brown,' said the priest sadly, as he bent over something and straightened himself again. 'Miss Rome sent for me, and I came as quickly as I could. I have come too late.'

The three men looked down, and in one of them at least the life died in that late light of afternoon. It ran along the passage like a path of gold, and in the midst of it Aurora Rome lay lustrous in her robes of green and gold, with her dead face turned upwards. Her dress was torn away as in a struggle, leaving the right shoulder bare, but the wound from which the blood was welling was on the other side. The brass dagger lay flat and gleaming a yard or so away.

There was a blank stillness for a measurable time, so that they could hear far off a flower-girl's laugh outside Charing Cross, and someone whistling furiously for a taxicab in one of the streets off the Strand. Then the Captain, with a movement so sudden that it might have been passion or play-acting, took Sir Wilson Seymour by the throat.

Seymour looked at him steadily without either fight or fear. 'You need not kill me,' he said in a voice quite cold; 'I shall do that on my own account.'

The Captain's hand hesitated and dropped; and the other added with the same icy candour: 'If I find I haven't the nerve to do it with that dagger I can do it in a month with drink.'

'Drink isn't good enough for me,' replied Cutler, 'but I'll have blood for this before I die. Not yours—but I think I know whose.'

And before the others could appreciate his intention he snatched up the dagger, sprang at the other door at the lower end of the passage, burst it open, bolt and all, and confronted Bruno in his dressing-room. As he did so, old Parkinson tottered in his wavering way out of the door and caught sight of the corpse lying in the passage. He moved shakily towards it; looked at it weakly with a working face; then moved shakily back into the dressing-room again, and sat down suddenly on one of the richly cushioned chairs. Father Brown instantly ran across to him, taking no notice of Cutler and the colossal actor, though the room already rang with their blows and they began to struggle for the dagger. Seymour, who retained some practical sense, was whistling for the police at the end of the passage.

When the police arrived it was to tear the two men from an almost ape-like grapple; and, after a few formal inquiries, to arrest Isidore Bruno upon a charge of murder, brought against him by his furious opponent. The idea that the great national hero of the hour had arrested a wrongdoer with his own hand doubtless had its weight with the police, who are not without elements of the journalist. They treated Cutler with a certain solemn attention, and pointed out that he had got a slight slash on the hand. Even as Cutler bore him back across tilted chair and table, Bruno had twisted the dagger out of his grasp and disabled him just below the wrist. The injury was really slight, but till he was removed from the room the half-savage prisoner stared at the running blood with a steady smile.

'Looks a cannibal sort of chap, don't he?' said the constable confidentially to Cutler.

Cutler made no answer, but said sharply a moment after: 'We must attend to the . . . the death . . .' and his voice escaped from articulation.

'The two deaths,' came in the voice of the priest from the farther side of the room. 'This poor fellow was gone when I got across to him.' And he stood looking down at old Parkinson, who sat in a black huddle on the gorgeous chair. He also had paid his tribute, not without eloquence, to the woman who had died.

The silence was first broken by Cutler, who seemed not untouched by a rough tenderness. 'I wish I was him,' he said huskily. 'I remember he used to watch her wherever she walked more than—anybody. She was his air, and he's dried up. He's just dead.'

'We are all dead,' said Seymour in a strange voice, looking down the road.

They took leave of Father Brown at the corner of the road, with some random apologies for any rudeness they might have shown. Both their faces were tragic, but also cryptic.

The mind of the little priest was always a rabbit-warren of wild thoughts that jumped too quickly for him to catch them. Like the white tail of a rabbit he had the vanishing thought that he was certain of their grief, but not so certain of their innocence.

'We had better all be going,' said Seymour heavily; 'we have done all we can to help.'

'Will you understand my motives,' asked Father Brown quietly, 'If I say you have done all you can to hurt?'

They both started as if guiltily, and Cutler said sharply: 'To hurt whom?'

'To hurt yourselves,' answered the priest. 'I would not add to your troubles if it weren't common justice to warn you. You've done nearly everything you could do to hang yourselves, if this actor should be acquitted. They'll be sure to subpœna me; I shall be bound to say that after the cry was heard each of you rushed into the room in a wild state and began quarrelling about a dagger. As far as my words on oath can go, you might either of you have done it. You hurt yourselves with that; and then Captain Cutler must have hurt himself with the dagger.'

'Hurt myself!' exclaimed the Captain, with contempt. 'A silly little scratch.'

'Which drew blood,' replied the priest, nodding. 'We know there's blood on the brass now. And so we shall never know whether there was blood on it before.'

There was a silence; and then Seymour said, with an emphasis quite alien to his daily accent: 'But I saw a man in the passage.'

'I know you did,' answered the cleric Brown with a face of wood, 'so did Captain Cutler. That's what seems so improbable.'

Before either could make sufficient sense of it even to answer, Father Brown had politely excused himself and gone stumping up the road with his stumpy old umbrella.

As modern newspapers are conducted, the most honest and most important news is the police news. If it be true that in the twentieth century more space is given to murder than to politics, it is for the excellent reason that murder is a more serious subject. But even this would hardly explain the enormous omnipresence and widely distributed detail of 'The Bruno Case,' or 'The Passage Mystery,' in the Press of London and the provinces. So vast was the excitement that for some weeks the Press really told the truth; and the reports of examination and cross-examination, if interminable, even if intolerable, are at least reliable. The true reason, of course, was the coincidence of persons. The victim was a popular actress; the accused was a popular actor; and the accused had been caught red-handed, as it were, by the most popular soldier of the patriotic season. In those extraordinary circumstances the Press was paralysed into probity and accuracy; and the rest of this somewhat singular business can practically be recorded from the reports of Bruno's trial.

The trial was presided over by Mr Justice Monkhouse, one of those who are jeered at as humorous judges,* but who are generally much more serious than the serious judges, for their levity comes from a living impatience of professional solemnity; while the serious judge is really filled with frivolity, because he is filled with vanity. All the chief actors being of a worldly importance, the barristers were well balanced; the prosecutor for the Crown was Sir Walter Cowdray, a heavy but weighty advocate of the sort that knows how to seem English and trustworthy, and how to be rhetorical with reluctance. The prisoner was defended by Mr Patrick Butler, KC,* who was mistaken for a mere *flâneur** by those who misunderstood the Irish character—and those who had not been examined by him. The medical evidence involved no contradictions, the doctor whom Seymour had summoned on the spot, agreeing with the eminent surgeon who had later examined the body. Aurora Rome had been stabbed with some sharp instrument such as a knife or dagger; some instrument, at least, of which the blade was short. The wound was just over the heart, and she had died instantly. When the doctor first saw her she could hardly have been dead for twenty minutes. Therefore when Father Brown found her she could hardly have been dead for three.

Some official detective evidence followed, chiefly concerned with the presence or absence of any proof of a struggle; the only suggestion of this was the tearing of the dress at the shoulder, and this did not seem to fit in particularly well with the direction and finality of the blow. When these details had been supplied, though not explained, the first of the important witnesses was called.

Sir Wilson Seymour gave evidence as he did everything else that he did at all—not only well, but perfectly. Though himself much more of a public man than the judge, he conveyed exactly the fine shade of self-effacement before the King's Justice; and though everyone looked at him as they would at the Prime Minister or the Archbishop of Canterbury, they could have said nothing of his part in it but that it was that of a private gentleman, with an accent on the noun. He was also refreshingly lucid, as he was on the committees. He had been calling on Miss Rome at the theatre; he had met Captain Cutler there; they had been joined for a short time by the accused, who had then returned to his own dressing-room; they had then been joined by a Roman Catholic priest, who asked for the deceased lady and said his name was Brown. Miss Rome had then gone just outside the theatre to the entrance of the passage, in order to point out to Captain Cutler a flower-shop at which he was to buy her some more flowers; and the witness had remained in the room, exchanging a few words with the priest. He had then distinctly heard the deceased, having sent the Captain on his errand, turn round laughing and run down the passage towards its other end, where was the prisoner's dressing-room. In idle curiosity as to the rapid movements of his friends, he had strolled out to the head of the passage himself and looked down it towards the prisoner's door. Did he see anything in the passage? Yes; he saw something in the passage.

Sir Walter Cowdray allowed an impressive interval, during which the witness looked down, and for all his usual composure seemed to have more than his usual pallor. Then the barrister said in a lower voice, which seemed at once sympathetic and creepy: 'Did you see it distinctly?'

Sir Wilson Seymour, however moved, had his excellent brains in full working-order. 'Very distinctly as regards its outline, but quite indistinctly, indeed not at all, as regards the details inside the outline. The passage is of such length that anyone in the middle of it appears quite black against the light at the other end.' The witness lowered his steady eyes once more and added: 'I had noticed the fact before, when Captain Cutler first entered it.' There was another silence, and the judge leaned forward and made a note.

'Well,' said Sir Walter patiently, 'what was the outline like? Was it, for instance, like the figure of the murdered woman?'

'Not in the least,' answered Seymour quietly.

'What did it look like to you?'

'It looked to me,' replied the witness, 'like a tall man.'

Everyone in court kept his eyes riveted on his pen or his umbrella-handle or his book or his boots or whatever he happened to be looking at. They seemed to be holding their eyes away from the prisoner by main force; but they felt his figure in the dock, and they felt it as gigantic. Tall as Bruno was to the eye, he seemed to swell taller and taller when all eyes had been torn away from him.

Cowdray was resuming his seat with his solemn face, smoothing his black silk robes, and white silk whiskers. Sir Wilson was leaving the witness-box, after a few final particulars to which there were many other witnesses, when the counsel for the defence sprang up and stopped him.

'I shall only detain you a moment,' said Mr Butler, who was a rustic-looking person with red eyebrows and an expression of partial slumber. 'Will you tell his lordship how you knew it was a man?'

A faint, refined smile seemed to pass over Seymour's features. 'I'm afraid it is the vulgar test of trousers,' he said. 'When I saw daylight between the long legs I was sure it was a man, after all.'

Butler's sleepy eyes opened as suddenly as some silent explosion. 'After all!' he repeated slowly. 'So you did think at first it was a woman?'

Seymour looked troubled for the first time. 'It is hardly a point of fact,' he said, 'but if his lordship would like me to answer for my impression, of course I shall do so. There was something about the thing that was not exactly a woman and yet was not quite a man; somehow the curves were different. And it had something that looked like long hair.'

'Thank you,' said Mr Butler, KC, and sat down suddenly, as if he had got what he wanted.

Captain Cutler was a far less plausible and composed witness than Sir Wilson, but his account of the opening incidents was solidly the same. He described the return of Bruno to his dressing-room, the dispatching of himself to buy a bunch of lilies-of-the-valley, his return to the upper end of the passage, the thing he saw in the passage, his suspicion of Seymour, and his struggle with Bruno. But he could give little artistic assistance about the black figure that he and Seymour had seen. Asked about its outline, he said he was no art critic—with a somewhat too obvious sneer at Seymour. Asked if it was a man or a woman, he said it looked more like a beast—with a too obvious snarl at the prisoner. But the man was plainly shaken with sorrow and sincere anger, and Cowdray quickly excused him from confirming facts that were already fairly clear.

The defending counsel also was again brief in his cross-examination; although (as was his custom) even in being brief, he seemed to take a long time about it. 'You used a rather remarkable expression,' he said, looking at Cutler sleepily. 'What do you mean by saying that it looked more like a beast than a man or a woman?'

Cutler seemed seriously agitated. 'Perhaps I oughtn't to have said that,' he said; 'but when the brute has huge humped shoulders like a chimpanzee, and bristles sticking out of its head like a pig——'

Mr Butler cut short his curious impatience in the middle. 'Never mind whether its hair was like a pig's,' he said, 'was it like a woman's?'

'A woman's!' cried the soldier. 'Great Scott, no!'

'The last witness said it was,' commented the counsel, with unscrupulous swiftness. 'And did the figure have any of those serpentine and semi-feminine curves to which eloquent allusion has been made? No? No feminine curves? The figure, if I understand you, was rather heavy and square than otherwise?'

'He may have been bending forward,' said Cutler, in a hoarse and rather faint voice.

'Or again, he may not,' said Mr Butler, and sat down suddenly for the second time.

The third witness called by Sir Walter Cowdray was the little Catholic clergyman, so little, compared with the others, that his head seemed hardly to come above the box, so that it was like cross-examining a child. But unfortunately Sir Walter had somehow got it into his head (mostly by some ramifications of his family's religion) that Father Brown was on the side of the prisoner, because the prisoner was wicked and foreign and even partly black. Therefore he took Father Brown up sharply whenever that proud pontiff tried to explain anything; and told him to answer yes or no, and tell the plain facts without any jesuitry. When Father Brown began, in his simplicity, to say who he thought the man in the passage was, the barrister told him that he did not want his theories.

'A black shape was seen in the passage. And you say you saw the black shape. Well, what shape was it?'

Father Brown blinked as under rebuke; but he had long known the literal nature of obedience. 'The shape,' he said, 'was short and thick, but had two sharp, black projections curved upwards on each side of the head or top, rather like horns, and——'

'Oh! the devil with horns, no doubt,' ejaculated Cowdray, sitting down in triumphant jocularity. 'It was the devil come to eat Protestants.'

'No,' said the priest dispassionately; 'I know who it was.'

Those in court had been wrought up to an irrational, but real sense of some monstrosity. They had forgotten the figure in the dock and thought only of the figure in the passage. And the figure in the passage, described by three capable and respectable men who had all seen it, was a shifting nightmare: one called it a woman, and the other a beast, and the other a devil. . . .

The judge was looking at Father Brown with level and piercing eyes. 'You are a most extraordinary witness,' he said; 'but there is something about you that makes me think you are trying to tell the truth. Well, who was the man you saw in the passage?'

'He was myself,' said Father Brown.

Butler, KC, sprang to his feet in an extraordinary stillness, and said quite calmly: 'Your lordship will allow me to cross-examine?' And then, without stopping, he shot at Brown the apparently disconnected question: 'You have heard about this dagger; you know the experts say the crime was committed with a short blade?'

'A short blade,' assented Brown, nodding solemnly like an owl, 'but a very long hilt.'

Before the audience could quite dismiss the idea that the priest had really seen himself doing murder with a short dagger with a long hilt (which seemed somehow to make it more horrible), he had himself hurried on to explain.

'I mean daggers aren't the only things with short blades. Spears have short blades. And spears catch at the end of the steel just like daggers, if they're that sort of fancy spear they had in theatres; like the spear poor old Parkinson killed his wife with, just when she'd sent for me to settle their family troubles—and I came just too late, God forgive me! But he died penitent—he just died of being penitent. He couldn't bear what he'd done.'

The general impression in court was that the little priest, who was gabbling away, had literally gone mad in the box. But the judge still looked at him with bright and steady eyes of interest; and the counsel for the defence went on with his questions unperturbed.

'If Parkinson did it with that pantomime spear,' said Butler, 'he must have thrust from four yards away. How do you account for signs of struggle, like the dress dragged off the shoulder?' He had slipped into treating this mere witness as an expert; but no one noticed it now.

'The poor lady's dress was torn,' said the witness, 'because it was caught in a panel that slid to just behind her. She struggled to free herself, and as she did so Parkinson came out of the prisoner's room and lunged with the spear.'

'A panel?' repeated the barrister in a curious voice.

'It was a looking-glass on the other side,' explained Father Brown. 'When I was in the dressing-room I noticed that some of them could probably be slid out into the passage.'

There was another vast and unnatural silence, and this time it was the judge who spoke. 'So you really mean that when you looked down that passage, the man you saw was yourself—in a mirror?'

'Yes, my lord; that was what I was trying to say,' said Brown, 'but they asked me for the shape; and our hats have corners just like horns, and so I——'

The judge leaned forward, his old eyes yet more brilliant, and said in specially distinct tones: 'Do you really mean to say that when Sir Wilson Seymour saw that wild what-you-call-him with curves and a woman's hair and a man's trousers, what he saw was Sir Wilson Seymour?'

'Yes, my lord,' said Father Brown.

'And you mean to say that when Captain Cutler saw that chimpanzee with humped shoulders and hog's bristles, he simply saw himself?'

'Yes, my lord.'

The judge leaned back in his chair with a luxuriance in which it was hard to separate the cynicism and the admiration. 'And can you tell us why,' he asked, 'you should know your own figure in a looking-glass, when two such distinguished men don't?'

Father Brown blinked even more painfully than before; then he stammered: 'Really, my lord, I don't know . . . unless it's because I don't look at it so often.'

THE GOD OF THE GONGS

IT was one of those chilly and empty afternoons in early winter, when the daylight is silver rather than gold and pewter rather than silver. If it was dreary in a hundred bleak offices and yawning drawing-rooms, it was drearier still along the edges of the flat Essex coast, where the monotony was the more inhuman for being broken at very long intervals by a lamp-post that looked less civilized than a tree, or a tree that looked more ugly than a lamp-post. A light fall of snow had half-melted into a few strips, also looking leaden rather than silver, when it had been fixed again by the seal of frost; no fresh snow had fallen, but a ribbon of the old snow ran along the very margin of the coast, so as to parallel the pale ribbon of the foam.

The line of the sea looked frozen in the very vividness of its violet-blue, like the vein of a frozen finger. For miles and miles, forward and back, there was no breathing soul, save two pedestrians, walking at a brisk pace, though one had much longer legs and took much longer strides than the other.

It did not seem a very appropriate place or time for a holiday, but Father Brown had few holidays, and had to take them when he could, and he always preferred, if possible, to take them in company with his old friend Flambeau, ex-criminal and ex-detective. The priest had had a fancy for visiting his old parish at Cobhole, and was going north-eastward along the coast.

After walking a mile or two farther, they found that the shore was beginning to be formally embanked, so as to form something like a parade; the ugly lamp-posts became less few and far between and more ornamental, though quite equally ugly. Half a mile farther on Father Brown was puzzled first by little labyrinths of flowerless flower-pots, covered with the low, flat, quiet-coloured plants that look less like a garden than a tessellated pavement, between weak curly paths studded with seats with curly backs. He faintly sniffed the atmosphere of a certain sort of seaside town that he did not specially care about, and, looking ahead along the parade by the sea, he saw something that put the matter beyond a doubt. In the grey distance the big bandstand of a watering-place stood up like a giant mushroom with six legs.

'I suppose,' said Father Brown, turning up his coat-collar and drawing a woollen scarf rather closer round his neck, 'that we are approaching a pleasure resort.'

'I fear,' answered Flambeau, 'a pleasure resort to which few people just now have the pleasure of resorting. They try to revive these places in the winter, but it never succeeds except with Brighton and the old ones. This must be Seawood, I think—Lord Pooley's experiment; he had the Sicilian Singers down at Christmas, and there's talk about holding one of the great glove-fights here. But they'll have to chuck the rotten place into the sea; it's as dreary as a lost railway-carriage.'

They had come under the big bandstand, and the priest was looking up at it with a curiosity that had something rather odd about it, his head a little on one side, like a bird's. It was the conventional, rather tawdry kind of erection for its purpose: a flattened dome or canopy, gilt here and there, and lifted on six slender pillars of painted wood, the whole being raised about five feet above the parade on a round wooden platform like a drum. But there was something fantastic about the snow combined with something artificial about the gold that haunted Flambeau as well as his friend with some association he could not capture, but which he knew was at once artistic and alien.

'I've got it,' he said at last. 'It's Japanese. It's like those fanciful Japanese prints, where the snow on the mountain looks like sugar, and the gilt on the pagodas is like gilt on gingerbread. It looks just like a little pagan temple.'

'Yes,' said Father Brown. 'Let's have a look at the god.' And with an agility hardly to be expected of him, he hopped up on to the raised platform.

'Oh, very well,' said Flambeau, laughing; and the next instant his own towering figure was visible on that quaint elevation.

Slight as was the difference of height, it gave in those level wastes a sense of seeing yet farther and farther across land and sea. Inland the little wintry gardens faded into a confused grey copse; beyond that, in the distance, were long low barns of a lonely farmhouse, and beyond that nothing but the long East Anglian plains. Seawards there was no sail or sign of life save a few seagulls: and even they looked like the last snowflakes, and seemed to float rather than fly.

Flambeau turned abruptly at an exclamation behind him. It seemed to come from lower down than might have been expected, and to be addressed to his heels rather than his head. He instantly held out his hand, but he could hardly help laughing at what he saw. For some reason or other the plat-form had given way under Father Brown, and the unfortunate little man had dropped through to the level of the parade. He was just tall enough, or short enough, for his head alone to stick out of the hole in the broken wood, looking like St John the Baptist's head* on a charger. The face wore a disconcerted expression, as did, perhaps, that of St John the Baptist.

In a moment he began to laugh a little. 'This wood must be rotten,' said Flambeau. 'Though it seems odd it should bear me, and you go through the weak place. Let me help you out.'

But the little priest was looking rather curiously at the corners and edges of the wood alleged to be rotten, and there was a sort of trouble on his brow.

'Come along,' cried Flambeau impatiently, still with his big brown hand extended. 'Don't you want to get out?'

The priest was holding a splinter of the broken wood between his finger and thumb, and did not immediately reply. At last he said thoughtfully: 'Want to get out? Why, no. I rather think I want to get in.' And he dived into the darkness under the wooden floor so abruptly as to knock off his big curved clerical hat and leave it lying on the boards above, without any clerical head in it.

Flambeau looked once more inland and out to sea, and once more could see nothing but seas as wintry as the snows, and snows as level as the sea.

There came a scurrying noise behind him, and the little priest came scrambling out of the hole faster than he had fallen in. His face was no longer disconcerted, but rather resolute, and, perhaps only through the reflections of the snow, a trifle paler than usual.

'Well?' asked his tall friend. 'Have you found the god of the temple?'

'No,' answered Father Brown. 'I have found what was sometimes more important. The Sacrifice.'

'What the devil do you mean?' cried Flambeau, quite alarmed.

Father Brown did not answer. He was staring, with a knot in his forehead, at the landscape; and he suddenly pointed at it. 'What's that house over there?' he asked.

Following his finger, Flambeau saw for the first time the corners of a building nearer than the farmhouse, but screened for the most part with a fringe of trees. It was not a large building, and stood well back from the shore; but a glint of ornament on it suggested that it was part of the same watering-place scheme of decoration as the bandstand, the little gardens and the curly-backed iron seats.

Father Brown jumped off the bandstand, his friend following; and as they walked in the direction indicated the trees fell away to right and left, and they saw a small, rather flashy hotel, such as is common in resorts—the hotel of the Saloon Bar rather than the Bar Parlour. Almost the whole frontage was of gilt plaster and figured glass, and between that grey seascape and the grey, witch-like trees, its gimcrack quality had something spectral in its melancholy. They both felt vaguely that if any food or drink were offered at such a hostelry, it would be the pasteboard ham and empty mug of the pantomime.

In this, however, they were not altogether confirmed. As they drew nearer and nearer to the place they saw in front of the buffet, which was apparently closed, one of the iron garden-seats with curly backs that had adorned the gardens, but much longer, running almost the whole length of the frontage. Presumably, it was placed so that visitors might sit there and look at the sea, but one hardly expected to find anyone doing it in such weather.

Nevertheless, just in front of the extreme end of the iron seat stood a small round restaurant table, and on this stood a small bottle of Chablis and a plate of almonds and raisins. Behind the table and on the seat sat a dark-haired young man, bareheaded, and gazing at the sea in a state of almost astonishing immobility.

But though he might have been a waxwork when they were within four yards of him, he jumped up like a jack-in-the-box when they came within three, and said in a deferential, though not undignified, manner: 'Will you step inside, gentlemen? I have no staff at present, but I can get you anything simple myself.'

'Much obliged,' said Flambeau. 'So you are the proprietor?'

'Yes,' said the dark man, dropping back a little into his motionless manner. 'My waiters are all Italians, you see, and I thought it only fair they should see their countryman beat the black, if he really can do it. You know the great fight between Malvoli and Nigger Ned is coming off after all?'

'I'm afraid we can't wait to trouble your hospitality seriously,' said Father Brown. 'But my friend would be glad of a glass of sherry, I'm sure, to keep out the cold and drink success to the Latin champion.'

Flambeau did not understand the sherry, but he did not object to it in the least. He could only say amiably: 'Oh, thank you very much.'

'Sherry, sir—certainly,' said their host, turning to his hostel. 'Excuse me if I detain you a few minutes. As I told you, I have no staff——' And he went towards the black windows of his shuttered and unlighted inn.

'Oh, it doesn't really matter,' began Flambeau, but the man turned to reassure him.

'I have the keys,' he said. 'I could find my way in the dark.'

'I didn't mean——' began Father Brown.

He was interrupted by a bellowing human voice that came out of the bowels of the uninhabited hotel. It thundered some foreign name loudly but inaudibly, and the hotel proprietor moved more sharply towards it than he had done for Flambeau's sherry. As instant evidence proved, the proprietor had told, then and after, nothing but the literal truth. But both Flambeau and Father Brown have often confessed that, in all their (often outrageous) adventures, nothing had so chilled their blood as that voice of an ogre, sounding suddenly out of a silent and empty inn.

'My cook!' cried the proprietor hastily. 'I had forgotten my cook. He will be starting presently. Sherry, sir?'

And, sure enough, there appeared in the doorway a big white bulk with white cap and white apron, as befits a cook, but with the needless emphasis of a black face. Flambeau had often heard that negroes made good cooks. But somehow something in the contrast of colour and caste increased his surprise that the hotel proprietor should answer the call of the cook, and not the cook the call of the proprietor. But he reflected that head cooks are proverbially arrogant; and, besides, the host had come back with the sherry, and that was the great thing.

'I rather wonder,' said Father Brown, 'that there are so few people about the beach, when this big fight is coming on after all. We only met one man for miles.'

The hotel proprietor shrugged his shoulders. 'They come from the other end of the town, you see—from the station, three miles from here. They are only interested in the sport, and will stop in hotels for the night only. After all, it is hardly weather for basking on the shore.'

'Or on the seat,' said Flambeau, and pointed to the little table.

'I have to keep a look-out,' said the man with the motion-less face. He was a quiet, well-featured fellow, rather sallow; his dark clothes had nothing distinctive about them, except that his black necktie was worn rather high, like a stock, and secured by a gold pin with some grotesque head to it. Nor was there anything notable in the face, except something that was probably a mere nervous trick—a habit of opening one eye more narrowly than the other, giving the impression that the other was larger or was, perhaps, artificial.

The silence that ensued was broken by their host saying quietly: 'Whereabouts did you meet the one man on your march?'

'Curiously enough,' answered the priest, 'close by here— just by that bandstand.'

Flambeau, who had sat on the long iron seat to finish his sherry, put it down and rose to his feet, staring at his friend in amazement. He opened his mouth to speak, and then shut it again.

'Curious,' said the dark-haired man thoughtfully. 'What was he like?'

'It was rather dark when I saw him,' began Father Brown, 'but he was——'

As has been said, the hotel-keeper can be proved to have told the precise truth. His phrase that the cook was starting presently was fulfilled to the letter, for the cook came out, pulling his gloves on, even as they spoke.

But he was a very different figure from the confused mass of white and black that had appeared for an instant in the doorway. He was buttoned and buckled up to his bursting eyeballs in the most brilliant fashion. A tall black hat was tilted on his broad black head—a hat of the sort that the French wit has compared to eight mirrors. But somehow the black man was like the black hat. He also was black, and yet his glossy skin flung back the light at eight angles or more. It is needless to say that he wore white spats and a white slip inside his waistcoat. The red flower stood up in his buttonhole aggressively, as if it had suddenly grown there. And in the way he carried his cane in one hand and his cigar in the other there was a certain attitude—an attitude we must always remember when we talk of racial prejudices: something innocent and insolent—the Cake-Walk.*

'Sometimes,' said Flambeau, looking after him, 'I'm not surprised that they lynch them.'

'I am never surprised,' said Father Brown, 'at any work of hell. But as I was saying,' he resumed, as the negro, still ostentatiously pulling on his yellow gloves, betook himself briskly towards the watering-place, a queer music-hall figure against that grey and frosty scene—'as I was saying, I couldn't describe the man very minutely, but he had a flourish and old-fashioned whiskers and moustachios, dark or dyed, as in the pictures of foreign financiers; round his neck was wrapped a long purple scarf that thrashed out in the wind as he walked. It was fixed at the throat rather in the way that nurses fix children's comforters with a safety-pin. Only this,' added the priest, gazing placidly out to sea, 'was not a safety-pin.'

The man sitting on the long iron bench was also gazing placidly out to sea. Now he was once more in repose, Flambeau felt quite certain that one of his eyes was naturally larger than the other. Both were now well opened, and he could almost fancy the left eye grew larger as he gazed.

'It was a very long gold pin, and had the carved head of a monkey or some such thing,' continued the cleric; 'and it was fixed in a rather odd way—he wore pince-nez and a broad black——'

The motionless man continued to gaze at the sea, and the eyes in his head might have belonged to two different men. Then he made a movement of blinding swiftness.

Father Brown had his back to him, and in that flash might have fallen dead on his face. Flambeau had no weapon, but his large brown hands were resting on the end of the long iron seat. His shoulders abruptly altered their shape, and he heaved the whole huge thing high over his head, like a headsman's axe about to fall. The mere height of the thing, as he held it vertical, looked like a long iron ladder by which he was inviting men to climb towards the stars. But the long shadow, in the level evening light, looked like a giant brandishing the Eiffel Tower. It was the shock of that shadow, before the shock of the iron crash, that made the stranger quail and dodge, and then dart into his inn, leaving the flat and shining dagger he had dropped exactly where it had fallen.

'We must get away from here instantly,' cried Flambeau, flinging the huge seat away with furious indifference on the beach. He caught the little priest by the elbow and ran him down a grey perspective of barren back garden, at the end of which there was a closed back-garden door. Flambeau bent over it an instant in violent silence, and then said: 'The door is locked.'

As he spoke a black feather from one of the ornamental firs fell, brushing the brim of his hat. It startled him more than the small and distant detonation that had come just before. Then came another distant detonation, and the door he was trying to open shook under the bullet buried in it. Flambeau's shoulders again filled out and altered suddenly. Three hinges and a lock burst at the same instant, and he went out into the empty path behind, carrying the great garden door with him, as Samson carried the gates of Gaza.*

Then he flung the garden door over the garden wall, just as a third shot picked up a spurt of snow and dust behind his heel. Without ceremony he snatched up the little priest, slung him astraddle on his shoulders, and went racing towards Seawood as fast as his long legs could carry him. It was not until nearly two miles farther on that he set his small companion down. It had hardly been a dignified escape, in spite of the classic model of Anchises,* but Father Brown's face only wore a broad grin.

'Well,' said Flambeau, after an impatient silence, as they resumed their more conventional tramp through the streets on the edge of the town, where no outrage need be feared, 'I don't know what all this means, but I take it I may trust my own eyes that you never met the man you have so accurately described.'

'I did meet him in a way,' Brown said, biting his finger rather nervously—'I did really. And it was too dark to see him properly, because it was under that bandstand affair. But I'm afraid I didn't describe him so very accurately after all, for his pince-nez was broken under him, and the long gold pin wasn't stuck through his purple scarf but through his heart.'

'And I suppose,' said the other in a lower voice, 'that glass-eyed guy had something to do with it.'

'I had hoped he had only a little,' answered Brown in a rather troubled voice, 'and I may have been wrong in what I did. I acted on impulse. But I fear this business has deep roots and dark.'

They walked on through some streets in silence. The yellow lamps were beginning to be lit in the cold blue twilight, and they were evidently approaching the more central parts of the town. Highly coloured bills announcing the glove-fight between Nigger Ned and Malvoli were slapped about the walls.

'Well,' said Flambeau, 'I never murdered anyone, even in my criminal days, but I can almost sympathize with anyone doing it in such a dreary place. Of all God-forsaken dustbins of Nature, I think the most heart-breaking are places like that bandstand, that were meant to be festive and are forlorn. I can fancy a morbid man feeling he must kill his rival in the solitude and irony of such a scene. I remember once taking a tramp in your glorious Surrey hills, thinking of nothing but gorse and skylarks, when I came out on a vast circle of land, and over me lifted a vast, voiceless structure, tier above tier of seats, as huge as a Roman amphitheatre and as empty as a new letter-rack. A bird sailed in heaven over it. It was the Grand Stand at Epsom. And I felt that no one would ever be happy there again.'

'It's odd you should mention Epsom,' said the priest. 'Do you remember what was called the Sutton Mystery, because two suspected men—ice-cream men, I think—happened to live at Sutton? They were eventually released. A man was found strangled, it was said, on the Downs round that part. As a fact, I know (from an Irish policeman who is a friend of

mine) that he was found close up to the Epsom Grand Stand—
in fact, only hidden by one of the lower doors being pushed
back.'

'That is queer,' assented Flambeau. 'But it rather confirms
my view that such pleasure places look awfully lonely out of
season, or the man wouldn't have been murdered there.'

'I'm not so sure he——' began Brown, and stopped.

'Not so sure he was murdered?' queried his companion.

'Not so sure he was murdered out of the season,' answered
the little priest, with simplicity. 'Don't you think there's something rather tricky about this solitude, Flambeau? Do you feel
sure a wise murderer would always *want* the spot to be
lonely? It's very, very seldom a man is *quite* alone. And, short
of that, the more alone he is, the more certain he is to be seen.
No; I think there must be some other—— Why, here we are at
the Pavilion or Palace, or whatever they call it.'

They had emerged on a small square, brilliantly lighted, of
which the principal building was gay with gilding, gaudy with
posters, and flanked with two giant photographs of Malvoli
and Nigger Ned.

'Hallo!' cried Flambeau in great surprise, as his clerical
friend stumped straight up the broad steps. 'I didn't know
pugilism was your latest hobby. Are you going to see the
fight?'

'I don't think there will be any fight,' replied Father Brown.

They passed rapidly through ante-rooms and inner rooms;
they passed through the hall of combat itself, raised, roped,
and padded with innumerable seats and boxes, and still the
cleric did not look round or pause till he came to a clerk at a
desk outside a door marked 'Committee.' There he stopped
and asked to see Lord Pooley.

The attendant observed that his lordship was very busy, as
the fight was coming on soon, but Father Brown had a good-
tempered tedium of reiteration for which the official mind is
generally not prepared. In a few moments the rather baffled
Flambeau found himself in the presence of a man who was
still shouting directions to another man going out of the room.
'Be careful, you know, about the ropes after the fourth——
Well, and what do you want, I wonder!'

Lord Pooley was a gentleman, and, like most of the few remaining to our race, was worried—especially about money. He was half grey and half flaxen, and he had the eyes of fever and a high-bridged, frost-bitten nose.

'Only a word,' said Father Brown. 'I have come to prevent a man being killed.'

Lord Pooley bounded off his chair as if a spring had flung him from it. 'I'm damned if I'll stand any more of this!' he cried. 'You and your committees and parsons and petitions! Weren't there parsons in the old days, when they fought without gloves? Now they're fighting with the regulation gloves, and there's not the rag of a possibility of either of the boxers being killed.'

'I didn't mean either of the boxers,' said the little priest.

'Well, well, well!' said the nobleman, with a touch of frosty humour. 'Who's going to be killed? The referee?'

'I don't know who's going to be killed,' replied Father Brown, with a reflective stare. 'If I did I shouldn't have to spoil your pleasure. I could simply get him to escape. I never could see anything wrong about prize-fights. As it is, I must ask you to announce that the fight is off for the present.'

'Anything else?' jeered the gentleman with feverish eyes. 'And what do you say to the two thousand people who have come to see it?'

'I say there will be one thousand nine hundred and ninety-nine of them left alive when they have seen it,' said Father Brown.

Lord Pooley looked at Flambeau. 'Is your friend mad?' he asked.

'Far from it,' was the reply.

'And look here,' resumed Pooley in his restless way, 'it's worse than that. A whole pack of Italians have turned up to back Malvoli—swarthy, savage fellows of some country, anyhow. You know what these Mediterranean races are like. If I send out word that it's off we shall have Malvoli storming in here at the head of a whole Corsican clan.'

'My lord, it is a matter of life and death,' said the priest. 'Ring your bell. Give your message. And see whether it is Malvoli who answers.'

The nobleman struck the bell on the table with an odd air of new curiosity. He said to the clerk who appeared almost instantly in the doorway: 'I have a serious announcement to make to the audience shortly. Meanwhile, would you kindly tell the two champions that the fight will have to be put off.'

The clerk stared for some seconds as if at a demon and vanished.

'What authority have you for what you say?' ssked Lord Pooley abruptly. 'Whom did you consult?'

'I consulted a bandstand,' said Father Brown, scratching his head. 'But, no, I'm wrong; I consulted a book, too. I picked it up on a bookstall in London—very cheap, too.'

He had taken out of his pocket a small, stout, leather-bound volume, and Flambeau, looking over his shoulder, could see that it was some book of old travels, and had a leaf turned down for reference.

'"The only form in which Voodoo*——"' began Father Brown, reading aloud.

'In which what?' inquired his lordship.

'"In which Voodoo,"' repeated the reader, almost with relish, '"is widely organized outside Jamaica itself is in the form known as the Monkey, or the God of the Gongs, which is powerful in many parts of the two American continents, especially among half-breeds, many of whom look exactly like white men. It differs from most other forms of devil-worship and human sacrifice in the fact that the blood is not shed formally on the altar, but by a sort of assassination among the crowd. The gongs beat with a deafening din as the doors of the shrine open and the monkey-god is revealed; almost the whole congregation rivet ecstatic eyes on him. But after——"'

The door of the room was flung open, and the fashionable negro stood framed in it, his eyeballs rolling, his silk hat still insolently tilted on his head. 'Huh!' he cried, showing his apish teeth. 'What this? Huh! Huh! You steal a coloured gentleman's prize—prize his already—yo' think yo' jes' save that white 'Talian trash——'

'The matter is only deferred,' said the nobleman quietly. 'I will be with you to explain in a minute or two.'

'Who you to——' shouted Nigger Ned, beginning to storm.

'My name is Pooley,' replied the other, with a creditable coolness. 'I am the organizing secretary, and I advise you just now to leave the room.'

'Who this fellow?' demanded the dark champion, pointing to the priest disdainfully.

'My name is Brown,' was the reply. 'And I advise you just now to leave the country.'

The prize-fighter stood glaring for a few seconds, and then, rather to the surprise of Flambeau and the others, strode out, sending the door to with a crash behind him.

'Well,' asked Father Brown, rubbing his dusty hair up, 'what do you think of Leonardo da Vinci? A beautiful Italian head.'

'Look here,' said Lord Pooley, 'I've taken a considerable responsibility on your bare word. I think you ought to tell me more about this.'

'You are quite right, my lord,' answered Brown. 'And it won't take long to tell.' He put the little leather book in his overcoat pocket. 'I think we know all that this can tell us, but you shall look at it to see if I'm right. That negro who has just swaggered out is one of the most dangerous men on earth, for he has the brains of a European, with the instincts of a cannibal. He has turned what was clean, common-sense butchery among his fellow-barbarians into a very modern and scientific secret society of assassins. He doesn't know I know it, nor, for the matter of that, that I can't prove it.'

There was a silence, and the little man went on.

'But if I want to murder somebody, will it really be the best plan to make sure I'm alone with him?'

Lord Pooley's eyes recovered their frosty twinkle as he looked at the little clergyman. He only said: 'If you *want* to murder somebody, I should advise it.'

Father Brown shook his head, like a murderer of much riper experience. 'So Flambeau said,' he replied, with a sigh. 'But consider. The more a man feels lonely the less he can be sure he is alone. It must mean empty spaces round him, and they are just what make him obvious. Have you never seen one ploughman from the heights, or one shepherd from the valleys? Have you never walked along a cliff, and seen one man walking along the sands? Didn't you know when he'd killed a crab, and wouldn't you have known if it had been a creditor? No! No! No! For an intelligent murderer, such as you or I might be, it is an impossible plan to make sure that nobody is looking at you.'

'But what other plan is there?'

'There is only one,' said the priest. 'To make sure that everybody is looking at something else. A man is throttled close by the big stand at Epsom. Anybody might have seen it done while the stand stood empty—any tramp under the hedges or motorist among the hills. But nobody would have seen it when the stand was crowded and the whole ring roaring, when the favourite was coming in first—or wasn't. The twisting of a neck-cloth, the thrusting of a body behind a door could be done in an instant—so long as it was *that* instant. It was the same, of course,' he continued turning to Flambeau, 'with that poor fellow under the bandstand. He was dropped through the hole (it wasn't an accidental hole) just at some very dramatic moment of the entertainment, when the bow of some great violinist or the voice of some great singer opened or came to its climax. And here, of course, when the knock-out blow came—it would not be the only one. That is the little trick Nigger Ned has adopted from his old God of Gongs.'

'By the way, Malvoli——' Pooley began.

'Malvoli,' said the priest, 'has nothing to do with it. I dare say he has some Italians with him, but our amiable friends are not Italians. They are octoroons and African half-bloods of various shades, but I fear we English think all foreigners are much the same so long as they are dark and dirty. 'Also,' he added, with a smile, 'I fear the English decline to draw any fine distinction between the moral character produced by my religion and that which blooms out of Voodoo.'

The blaze of the spring season had burst upon Seawood, littering its foreshore with families and bathing-machines, with nomadic preachers and nigger minstrels, before the two friends saw it again, and long before the storm of pursuit after the strange secret society had died away. Almost on every hand the secret of their purpose perished with them. The man of the hotel was found drifting dead on the sea like so much seaweed; his right eye was closed in peace, but his left eye was wide open, and glistened like glass in the moon. Nigger Ned had been overtaken a mile or two away, and murdered three policemen with his closed left hand. The remaining officer was surprised—nay, pained—and the negro got away. But this was enough to set all the English papers in a flame, and for a month or two the main purpose of the British Empire was to prevent the buck nigger (who was so in both senses) escaping by any English port. Persons of a figure remotely reconcilable with his were subjected to quite extraordinary inquisitions, made to scrub their faces before going on board ship, as if each white complexion were made up like a mask of grease-paint. Every negro in England was put under special regulations and made to report himself; the outgoing ships would no more have taken a nigger than a basilisk.* For people had found out how fearful and vast and silent was the force of the savage secret society, and by the time Flambeau and Father Brown were leaning on the parade parapet in April, the Black Man* meant in England almost what he once meant in Scotland.

'He must be still in England,' observed Flambeau, 'and horridly well hidden, too. They must have found him at the ports if he had only whitened his face.'

'You see, he is really a clever man,' said Father Brown apologetically. 'And I'm sure he wouldn't whiten his face.'

'Well, but what would he do?'

'I think,' said Father Brown, 'he would blacken his face.'

Flambeau, leaning motionless on the parapet, laughed and said: 'My dear fellow!'

Father Brown, also leaning motionless on the parapet, moved one finger for an instant into the direction of the soot-masked niggers singing on the sands.

THE STRANGE CRIME OF JOHN BOULNOIS

MR CALHOUN KIDD was a very young gentleman with a very old face, a face dried up with its own eagerness, framed in blue-black hair and a black butterfly tie. He was the emissary in England of the colossal American daily called *The Western Sun*—also humorously described as the 'Rising Sunset.' This was in allusion to a great journalistic declaration (attributed to Mr Kidd himself) that 'he guessed the sun would rise in the west yet, if American citizens did a bit more hustling.'* Those, however, who mock American journalism from the standpoint of somewhat mellower traditions forget a certain paradox which partly redeems it. For while the journalism of the States permits a pantomimic vulgarity long past anything English, it also shows a real excitement about the most earnest mental problems, of which English papers are innocent, or rather incapable. The *Sun* was full of the most solemn matters treated in the most farcical way. William James* figured there as well as 'Weary Willie,' and pragmatists alternated with pugilists in the long procession of its portraits.

Thus, when a very unobtrusive Oxford man named John Boulnois wrote in a very unreadable review called the *Natural Philosophy Quarterly* a series of articles on alleged weak points in Darwinian evolution, it fluttered no corner of the English papers; though Boulnois's theory (which was that of a comparatively stationary universe visited occasionally by convulsions of change) had some rather faddy fashionableness at Oxford, and got so far as to be named 'Catastrophism.' But many American papers seized on the challenge as a great event; and the *Sun* threw the shadow of Mr Boulnois quite gigantically across its pages. By the paradox already noted, articles of valuable intelligence and enthusiasm were presented with headlines apparently written by an illiterate maniac; headlines such as 'Darwin Chews Dirt; Critic Boulnois says He Jumps the Shocks'—or 'Keep Catastrophic, says Thinker Boulnois.' And Mr Calhoun Kidd, of *The Western Sun*, was bidden to take his butterfly tie and lugubrious visage down to the little house outside Oxford where Thinker Boulnois lived in happy ignorance of such a title.

That fated philosopher had consented, in a somewhat dazed manner, to receive the interviewer, and had named the hour of nine that evening. The last of a summer sunset clung about Cumnor and the low wooded hills; the romantic Yankee was both doubtful of his road and inquisitive about his surroundings; and seeing the door of a genuine feudal old-country inn, The Champion Arms, standing open, he went in to make inquiries.

In the bar parlour he rang the bell, and had to wait some little time for a reply to it. The only other person present was a lean man with close red hair and loose, horsey-looking clothes, who was drinking very bad whisky, but smoking a very good cigar. The whisky, of course, was the choice brand of The Champion Arms; the cigar he had probably brought with him from London. Nothing could be more different than his cynical *négligé* from the dapper dryness of the young American; but something in his pencil and open notebook, and perhaps in the expression of his alert blue eye, caused Kidd to guess, correctly, that he was a brother journalist.

'Could you do me the favour,' asked Kidd, with the courtesy of his nation, 'of directing me to the Grey Cottage, where Mr Boulnois lives, as I understand?'

'It's a few yards down the road,' said the red-haired man, removing his cigar; 'I shall be passing it myself in a minute, but I'm going on to Pendragon Park to try and see the fun.'

'What is Pendragon Park?' asked Calhoun Kidd.

'Sir Claude Champion's place—haven't you come down for that, too?' asked the other pressman, looking up. 'You're a journalist, aren't you?'

'I have come to see Mr Boulnois,' said Kidd.

'I've come to see Mrs Boulnois,' replied the other. 'But I shan't catch her at home.' And he laughed rather unpleasantly.

'Are you interested in Catastrophism?' asked the wondering Yankee.

'I'm interested in catastrophes; and there are going to be some,' replied his companion gloomily. 'Mine's a filthy trade, and I never pretend it isn't.'

With that he spat on the floor; yet somehow in the very act and instant one could realize that the man had been brought up as a gentleman.

The American pressman considered him with more attention. His face was pale and dissipated, with the promise of formidable passions yet to be loosed; but it was a clever and sensitive face; his clothes were coarse and careless, but he had a good seal ring on one of his long, thin fingers. His name, which came out in the course of talk, was James Dalroy; he was the son of a bankrupt Irish landlord, and attached to a pink paper which he heartily despised, called *Smart Society*, in the capacity of reporter and of something painfully like spy.

Smart Society, I regret to say, felt none of that interest in Boulnois on Darwin which was such a credit to the head and hearts of *The Western Sun*. Dalroy had come down, it seemed, to snuff up the scent of a scandal which might very well end in the Divorce Court, but which was at present hovering between Grey Cottage and Pendragon Park.

Sir Claude Champion was known to the readers of *The Western Sun* as well as Mr Boulnois. So were the Pope and the Derby Winner; but the idea of their intimate acquaintanceship would have struck Kidd as equally incongruous. He had heard of (and written about, nay, falsely pretended to know) Sir Claude Champion, as 'one of the brightest and wealthiest of England's Upper Ten'; as the great sportsman who raced yachts round the world; as the great traveller who wrote books about the Himalayas, as the politician who swept constituencies with a startling sort of Tory Democracy, and as the great dabbler in art, music, literature, and, above all, acting. Sir Claude was really rather magnificent in other than American eyes. There was something of the Renascence Prince about his omnivorous culture and restless publicity; he was not only a great amateur, but an ardent one. There was in him none of that antiquarian frivolity that we convey by the word 'dilettante.'

That faultless falcon profile with purple-black Italian eye, which had been snap-shotted so often both for *Smart Society* and *The Western Sun*, gave everyone the impression of a man eaten by ambition as by a fire, or even a disease. But though Kidd knew a great deal about Sir Claude—a great deal more, in fact, than there was to know—it would never have crossed his wildest dreams to connect so showy an aristocrat with the newly-unearthed founder of Catastrophism, or to guess that Sir Claude Champion and John Boulnois could be intimate friends. Such, according to Dalroy's account, was nevertheless the fact. The two had hunted in couples at school and college, and, though their social destinies had been very different (for Champion was a great landlord and almost a millionaire, while Boulnois was a poor scholar and, until just lately, an unknown one), they still kept in very close touch with each other. Indeed, Boulnois's cottage stood just outside the gates of Pendragon Park.

But whether the two men could be friends much longer was becoming a dark and ugly question. A year or two before, Boulnois had married a beautiful and not unsuccessful actress, to whom he was devoted in his own shy and ponderous style; and the proximity of the household to Champion's had given that flighty celebrity opportunities for behaving in a way that could not but cause painful and rather base excitement. Sir Claude had carried the arts of publicity to perfection; and he seemed to take a crazy pleasure in being equally ostentatious in an intrigue that could do him no sort of honour. Footmen from Pendragon were perpetually leaving bouquets for Mrs Boulnois; carriages and motor-cars were perpetually calling at the cottage for Mrs Boulnois; balls and masquerades perpetually filled the grounds in which the baronet paraded Mrs Boulnois, like the Queen of Love and Beauty at a tournament. That very evening, marked by Mr Kidd for the exposition of Catastrophism, had been marked by Sir Claude Champion for an open-air rendering of *Romeo and Juliet*, in which he was to play Romeo to a Juliet it was needless to name.

'I don't think it can go on without a smash,' said the young man with red hair, getting up and shaking himself. 'Old Boulnois may be squared—or he may be square. But if he's square he's thick—what you might call cubic. But I don't believe it's possible.'

'He is a man of grand intellectual powers,' said Calhoun Kidd in a deep voice.

'Yes,' answered Dalroy; 'but even a man of grand intellectual powers can't be such a blighted fool as all that. Must you be going on? I shall be following myself in a minute or two.'

But Calhoun Kidd, having finished a milk and soda, betook himself smartly up the road towards the Grey Cottage, leaving his cynical informant to his whisky and tobacco. The last of the daylight had faded; the skies were of a dark, green-grey, like slate, studded here and there with a star, but lighter on the left side of the sky, with the promise of a rising moon.

The Grey Cottage, which stood entrenched, as it were, in a square of stiff, high thorn-hedges, was so close under the pines and palisades of the Park that Kidd at first mistook it for the Park Lodge. Finding the name on the narrow wooden gate, however, and seeing by his watch that the hour of the 'Thinker's' appointment had just struck, he went in and knocked at the front door. Inside the garden hedge, he could see that the house, though unpretentious enough, was larger and more luxurious than it looked at first, and was quite a different kind of place from a porter's lodge. A dog-kennel and a beehive stood outside, like symbols of old English country-life; the moon was rising behind a plantation of prosperous pear trees; the dog that came out of the kennel was reverend-looking and reluctant to bark; and the plain, elderly manservant who opened the door was brief but dignified.

'Mr Boulnois asked me to offer his apologies, sir,' he said, 'but he has been obliged to go out suddenly.'

'But see here, I had an appointment,' said the interviewer, with a rising voice. 'Do you know where he went to?'

'To Pendragon Park, sir,' said the servant, rather sombrely, and began to close the door.

Kidd started a little.

'Did he go with Mrs——with the rest of the party?' he asked rather vaguely.

'No, sir,' said the man shortly; 'he stayed behind, and then went out alone.' And he shut the door, brutally, but with an air of duty not done.

The American, that curious compound of impudence and sensitiveness, was annoyed. He felt a strong desire to hustle them all along a bit and teach them business habits; the hoary old dog and the grizzled, heavy-faced old butler with his prehistoric shirt-front, and the drowsy old moon, and above all the scatter-brained old philosopher who couldn't keep an appointment.

'If that's the way he goes on he deserves to lose his wife's purest devotion,' said Mr Calhoun Kidd. 'But perhaps he's gone over to make a row. In that case I reckon a man from *The Western Sun* will be on the spot.'

And turning the corner by the open lodge-gates, he set off, stumping up the long avenue of black pine-woods that pointed in abrupt perspective towards the inner gardens of Pendragon Park. The trees were as black and orderly as plumes upon a hearse; there were still a few stars. He was a man with more literary than direct natural associations; the word 'Ravenswood' came into his head repeatedly. It was partly the raven colour of the pine-woods; but partly also an indescribable atmosphere almost described in Scott's great tragedy;* the smell of something that died in the eighteenth century; the smell of dank gardens and broken urns; of wrongs that will never now be righted; of something that is none the less incurably sad because it is strangely unreal.*

More than once, as he went up that trim, black road of tragic artifice, he stopped startled, thinking he heard steps in front of him. He could see nothing in front but the twin sombre walls of pine and the wedge of starlit sky above them. At first he thought he must have fancied it or been mocked by a mere echo of his own tramp. But as he went on he was more and more inclined to conclude, with the remains of his reason, that there really were other feet upon the road. He thought hazily of ghosts; and was surprised how swiftly he could see the image of an appropriate and local ghost, one with a face as white as Pierrot's, but patched with black. The apex of the triangle of dark-blue sky was growing brighter and bluer, but he did not realize as yet that this was because he was coming nearer to the lights of the great house and garden. He only felt that the atmosphere was growing more intense; there was in the sadness more violence and secrecy—more—he hesitated for the word, and then said it with a jerk of laughter—Catastrophism.

More pines, more pathway slid past him, and then he stood rooted as by a blast of magic. It is vain to say that he felt as if he had got into a dream; but this time he felt quite certain that he had got into a book. For we human beings are used to inappropriate things; we are accustomed to the clatter of the incongruous; it is a tune to which we can go to sleep. If one appropriate thing happens, it wakes us up like the pang of a perfect chord. Something happened such as would have happened in such a place in a forgotten tale.

Over the black pine-wood came flying and flashing in the moon a naked sword—such a slender and sparkling rapier as may have fought many an unjust duel in that ancient park. It fell on the pathway far in front of him and lay there glistening like a large needle. He ran like a hare and bent to look at it. Seen at close quarters it had rather a showy look: the big red jewels in the hilt and guard were a little dubious. But there were other red drops upon the blade which were not dubious.

He looked round wildly in the direction from which the dazzling missile had come, and saw that at this point the sable façade of fir and pine was interrupted by a smaller road at right angles; which, when he turned it, brought him in full view of the long, lighted house, with a lake and fountains in front of it. Nevertheless, he did not look at this, having something more interesting to look at.

Above him, at the angle of the steep green bank of the terraced garden, was one of those small picturesque surprises common in the old landscape gardening; a kind of small round hill or dome of grass, like a giant mole-hill, ringed and crowned with three concentric fences of roses, and having a sundial in the highest point in the centre. Kidd could see the finger of the dial stand up dark against the sky like the dorsal fin of a shark, and the vain moonlight clinging to that idle clock. But he saw something else clinging to it also, for one wild moment—the figure of a man.

Though he saw it there only for a moment, though it was outlandish and incredible in costume, being clad from neck to heel in tight crimson, with glints of gold, yet he knew in one flash of moonlight who it was. That white face flung up to heaven, clean-shaven and so unnaturally young, like Byron with a Roman nose, those black curls already grizzled—he had seen the thousand public portraits of Sir Claude Champion. The wild red figure reeled an instant against the sundial; the next it had rolled down the steep bank and lay at the

American's feet, faintly moving one arm. A gaudy, unnatural gold ornament on the arm suddenly reminded Kidd of *Romeo and Juliet*; of course the tight crimson suit was part of the play. But there was a long red stain down the bank from which the man had rolled—that was no part of the play. He had been run through the body.

Mr Calhoun Kidd shouted and shouted again. Once more he seemed to hear phantasmal footsteps, and started to find another figure already near him. He knew the figure, and yet it terrified him. The dissipated youth who had called himself Dalroy had a horribly quiet way with him; if Boulnois failed to keep appointments that had been made, Dalroy had a sinister air of keeping appointments that hadn't. The moonlight discoloured everything; against Dalroy's red hair his wan face looked not so much white as pale green.

All this morbid impressionism must be Kidd's excuse for having cried out, brutally and beyond all reason: 'Did you do this, you devil?'

James Dalroy smiled his unpleasing smile; but before he could speak, the fallen figure made another movement of the arm, waving vaguely towards the place where the sword fell; then came a moan, and then it managed to speak.

'Boulnois . . . Boulnois, I say . . . Boulnois did it . . . jealous of me . . . he was jealous, he was, he was. . . .'

Kidd bent his head down to hear more, and just managed to catch the words:

'Boulnois . . . with my own sword . . . he threw it. . . .'

Again the failing hand waved towards the sword, and then fell rigid with a thud. In Kidd rose from its depth all that acrid humour that is the strange salt of the seriousness of his race.

'See here,' he said sharply and with command, 'you must fetch a doctor. This man's dead.'

'And a priest, too, I suppose,' said Dalroy in an undecipherable manner. 'All these Champions are papists.'

The American knelt down by the body, felt the heart, propped up the head and used some last efforts at restoration; but before the other journalist reappeared, followed by a doctor and a priest, he was already prepared to assert they were too late.

'Were you too late also?' asked the doctor, a solid prosper-ous-looking man, with conventional moustache and whiskers, but a lively eye, which darted over Kidd dubiously.

'In one sense,' drawled the representative of the *Sun*. 'I was too late to save the man, but I guess I was in time to hear something of importance. I heard the dead man denounce his assassin.'

'And who was the assassin?' asked the doctor, drawing his eyebrows together.

'Boulnois,' said Calhoun Kidd, and whistled softly.

The doctor stared at him gloomily with a reddening brow; but he did not contradict. Then the priest, a shorter figure in the background, said mildly: 'I understood that Mr Boulnois was not coming to Pendragon Park this evening.'

'There again,' said the Yankee grimly, 'I may be in a posi-tion to give the old country a fact or two. Yes, *sir*, John Boulnois was going to stay in all this evening; he fixed up a real good appointment there with me. But John Boulnois changed his mind; John Boulnois left his home abruptly and all alone, and came over to this derned Park an hour or so ago. His butler told me so. I think we hold what the all-wise police call a clue—have you sent for them?'

'Yes,' said the doctor; 'but we haven't alarmed anyone else yet.'

'Does Mrs Boulnois know?' asked James Dalroy; and again Kidd was conscious of an irrational desire to hit him on his curling mouth.

'I have not told her,' said the doctor gruffly; 'but here come the police.'

The little priest had stepped out into the main avenue, and now returned with the fallen sword, which looked ludicrously large and theatrical when attached to his dumpy figure, at once clerical and commonplace. 'Just before the police come,' he said apologetically, 'has anyone got a light?'

The Yankee journalist took an electric torch from his pocket, and the priest held it close to the middle part of the blade, which he examined with blinking care. Then, without glancing at the point or pommel, he handed the long weapon to the doctor.

'I fear I'm no use here,' he said, with a brief sigh. 'I'll say good night to you, gentlemen.' And he walked away up the dark avenue towards the house, his hands clasped behind him and his big head bent in cogitation.

The rest of the group made increased haste towards the lodge-gates, where an inspector and two constables could already be seen in consultation with the lodge-keeper. But the little priest only walked slower and slower in the dim cloister of pine, and at last stopped dead, on the steps of the house. It was his silent way of acknowledging an equally silent approach; for there came towards him a presence that might have satisfied even Calhoun Kidd's demands for a lovely and aristocratic ghost. It was a young woman in silvery satins of a Renascence design; she had golden hair in two long shining ropes, and a face so startlingly pale between them that she might have been chryselephantine—made, that is, like some old Greek statues, out of ivory and gold. But her eyes were very bright, and her voice, though low, was confident.

'Father Brown?' she said.

'Mrs Boulnois?' he replied gravely. Then he looked at her and immediately said: 'I see you know about Sir Claude.'

'How do you know I know?' she asked steadily.

He did not answer the question, but asked another: 'Have you seen your husband?'

'My husband is at home,' she said. 'He has nothing to do with this.'

Again he did not answer; and the woman drew nearer to him, with a curiously intense expression on her face.

'Shall I tell you something more?' she said, with a rather fearful smile. 'I don't think he did it, and *you* don't either.'

Father Brown returned her gaze with a long, grave stare, and then nodded, yet more gravely.

'Father Brown,' said the lady, 'I am going to tell you all I know, but I want you to do me a favour first. Will you tell me *why* you haven't jumped to the conclusion of poor John's guilt, as all the rest have done? Don't mind what you say: I— I know about the gossip and the appearances that are against him.'

Father Brown looked honestly embarrassed, and passed his hand across his forehead. 'Two very little things,' he said, 'At least, one's very trivial and the other very vague. But such as they are, they don't fit in with Mr Boulnois being the murderer.'

He turned his blank, round face up to the stars and continued absent-mindedly: 'To take the vague idea first. I attach a good deal of importance to vague ideas. All those things that "aren't evidence" are what convince me. I think a moral impossibility the biggest of all impossibilities. I know your husband only slightly, but I think this crime of his, as generally conceived, something very like a moral impossibility. Please do not think I mean that Boulnois could not be so wicked. Anybody can be wicked—as wicked as he chooses. We can direct our moral wills; but we can't generally change our instinctive tastes and ways of doing things. Boulnois might commit a murder, but not this murder. He would not snatch Romeo's sword from its romantic scabbard; or slay his foe on the sundial as on a kind of altar; or leave his body among the roses; or fling the sword away among the pines. If Boulnois killed anyone he'd do it quietly and heavily, as he'd do any other doubtful thing—take a tenth glass of port, or read a loose Greek poet. No, the romantic setting is not like Boulnois. It's more like Champion.'

'Ah!' she said, and looked at him with eyes like diamonds.

'And the trivial thing was this,' said Brown. 'There were finger-prints on that sword; finger-prints can be detected quite a time after they are made if they're on some polished surface like glass or steel. These were on a polished surface. They were half-way down the blade of the sword. Whose prints they were I have no earthly clue; but why should anybody hold a sword half-way down? It was a long sword, but length is an advantage in lunging at an enemy. At least, at most enemies. At all enemies except one.'

'Except one!' she repeated.

'There is only one enemy,' said Father Brown, 'whom it is easier to kill with a dagger than a sword.'

'I know,' said the woman. 'Oneself.'

There was a long silence, and then the priest said quietly but abruptly: 'Am I right, then? Did Sir Claude kill himself?'

'Yes,' she said, with a face like marble. 'I saw him do it.'

'He died,' said Father Brown, 'for love of you?'

An extraordinary expression flashed across her face, very different from pity, modesty, remorse, or anything her companion had expected: her voice became suddenly strong and full. 'I don't believe,' she said, 'he ever cared about me a rap. He hated my husband.'

'Why?' asked the other, and turned his round face from the sky to the lady.

'He hated my husband because . . . it is so strange I hardly know how to say it . . . because. . . .'

'Yes?' said Brown patiently.

'Because my husband wouldn't hate him.'

Father Brown only nodded, and seemed still to be listening; he differed from most detectives in fact and fiction in a small point—he never pretended not to understand when he understood perfectly well.

Mrs Boulnois drew near once more with the same contained glow of certainty. 'My husband,' she said, 'is a great man. Sir Claude Champion was not a great man: he was a celebrated and successful man. My husband has never been celebrated or successful; and it is the solemn truth that he has never dreamed of being so. He no more expects to be famous for thinking than for smoking cigars. On all that side he has a sort of splendid stupidity. He has never grown up. He still liked Champion exactly as he liked him at school; he admired him as he would admire a conjuring trick done at the dinner-table. But he couldn't be got to conceive the notion of *envying* Champion. *And Champion wanted to be envied.* He went mad and killed himself for that.'

'Yes,' said Father Brown; 'I think I begin to understand.'

'Oh, don't you see?' she cried; 'the whole picture is made for that—the place is planned for it. Champion put John in a little house at his very door, like a dependant—to make him *feel* a failure. He never felt it. He thinks no more about such things than—than an absent-minded lion. Champion would burst in on John's shabbiest hours or homeliest meals with some dazzling present or announcement or expedition that made it like the visit of Haroun Alraschid,* and John would accept or refuse amiably with one eye off, so to speak, like one lazy schoolboy agreeing or disagreeing with another. After five years of it John had not turned a hair; and Sir Claude Champion was a monomaniac.'

'And Haman began to tell them,' said Father Brown, 'of all the things wherein the king had honoured him; and he said: "All these things profit me nothing while I see Mordecai the Jew* sitting in the gate."'

'The crisis came,' Mrs Boulnois continued, 'when I persuaded John to let me take down some of his speculations and send them to a magazine. They began to attract attention, especially in America, and one paper wanted to interview him. When Champion (who was interviewed nearly every day) heard of this late little crumb of success falling to his unconscious rival, the last link snapped that held back his devilish hatred. Then he began to lay that insane siege to my own love and honour which has been the talk of the shire. You will ask me why I allowed such atrocious attentions. I answer that I could not have declined them except by explaining to my husband, and there are some things the soul cannot do, as the body cannot fly. Nobody could have explained to my husband. Nobody could do it now. If you said to him in so many words, "Champion is stealing your wife," he would think the joke a little vulgar; that it could be anything but a joke—that notion could find no crack in his great skull to get in by. Well, John was to come and see us act this evening, but just as we were starting he said he wouldn't; he had got an interesting book and a cigar. I told this to Sir Claude, and it was his death-blow. The monomaniac suddenly saw despair. He stabbed himself, crying out like a devil that Boulnois was slaying him; he lies there in the garden dead of his own jealousy to produce jealousy; and John is sitting in the dining-room reading a book.'

There was another silence, and then the little priest said: 'There is only one weak point, Mrs Boulnois, in all your very vivid account. Your husband is not sitting in the dining-room reading a book. That American reporter told me he had been to your house, and your butler told him Mr Boulnois had gone to Pendragon Park after all.'

Her bright eyes widened to an almost electric glare; and yet it seemed rather bewilderment than confusion or fear. 'Why, what *can* you mean?' she cried. 'All the servants were out of the house, seeing the theatricals. And we don't keep a butler, thank goodness!'

Father Brown started and spun half round like an absurd teetotum. 'What, what?' he cried seeming galvanized into sudden life. 'Look here—I say—can I make your husband hear if I go to the house?'

'Oh, the servants will be back by now,' she said, wondering.

'Right, right!' rejoined the cleric energetically, and set off scuttling up the path towards the Park gates. He turned once to say: 'Better get hold of that Yankee, or "Crime of John Boulnois" will be all over the Republic in large letters.'*

'You don't understand,' said Mrs Boulnois. 'He wouldn't mind. I don't think he imagines that America really is a place.'

When Father Brown reached the house with the beehive and the drowsy dog, a small and neat maid-servant showed him into the dining-room, where Boulnois sat reading by a shaded lamp, exactly as his wife described him. A decanter of port and a wineglass were at his elbow; and the instant the priest entered he noted the long ash stand out unbroken on his cigar.

'He has been here for half an hour at least,' thought Father Brown. In fact, he had the air of sitting where he had sat when his dinner was cleared away.

'Don't get up, Mr Boulnois,' said the priest in his pleasant, prosaic way. 'I shan't interrupt you a moment. I fear I break in on some of your scientific studies.'

'No,' said Boulnois; 'I was reading *The Bloody Thumb*.' He said it with neither frown nor smile, and his visitor was conscious of a certain deep and virile indifference in the man which his wife had called greatness. He laid down a gory yellow 'shocker' without even feeling its incongruity enough to comment on it humorously. John Boulnois was a big, slow-moving man with a massive head, partly grey and partly bald, and blunt, burly features. He was in shabby and very old-fashioned evening-dress, with a narrow triangular opening of shirt-front: he had assumed it that evening in his original purpose of going to see his wife act Juliet.

'I won't keep you long from 'The Bloody Thumb' or any other catastrophic affairs,' said Father Brown, smiling. 'I only came to ask you about the crime you committed this evening.'

Boulnois looked at him steadily, but a red bar began to show across his broad brow; and he seemed like one discovering embarrassment for the first time.

'I know it was a strange crime,' assented Brown in a low voice. 'Stranger than murder perhaps—to you. The little sins are sometimes harder to confess than the big ones—but that's why it's so important to confess them. Your crime is committed by every fashionable hostess six times a week: and yet you find it stick to your tongue like a nameless atrocity.'

'It makes one feel,' said the philosopher slowly, 'such a damned fool.'

'I know,' assented the other, 'but one often has to choose between feeling a damned fool and being one.'

'I can't analyse myself well,' went on Boulnois; 'but sitting in that chair with that story I was as happy as a schoolboy on a half-holiday. It was security, eternity—I can't convey it . . . the cigars were within reach . . . the matches were within reach . . . the *Thumb* had four more appearances to . . . it was not only a peace, but a plenitude. Then that bell rang, and I thought for one long, mortal minute that I couldn't get out of that chair—literally, physically, muscularly couldn't. Then I did it like a man lifting the world, because I knew all the servants were out. I opened the front door, and there was a little man with his mouth open to speak and his notebook open to write in. I remembered the Yankee interviewer I had forgotten. His hair was parted in the middle, and I tell you that murder——'

'I understand,' said Father Brown. 'I've seen him.'

'I didn't commit murder,' continued the Catastrophist mildly, 'but only perjury. I said I had gone across to Pendragon Park and shut the door in his face. That is my crime, Father Brown, and I don't know what penance you would inflict for it.'

'I shan't inflict any penance,' said the clerical gentleman, collecting his heavy hat and umbrella with an air of some amusement; 'quite the contrary. I came here specially to let you off the little penance which would otherwise have followed your little offence.'

'And what,' asked Boulnois, smiling, 'is the little penance I have so luckily been let off?'

'Being hanged,' said Father Brown.

THE FAIRY TALE OF FATHER BROWN

THE picturesque city and state of Heiligwaldenstein* was one of those toy kingdoms of which certain parts of the German Empire still consist. It had come under the Prussian hegemony quite late in history—hardly fifty years before* the fine summer day when Flambeau and Father Brown found themselves sitting in its gardens and drinking its beer. There had been not a little of war and wild justice* there within living memory, as soon will be shown. But in merely looking at it one could not dismiss that impression of childishness which is the most charming side of Germany—those little pantomime, paternal monarchies in which a king seems as domestic as a cook. The German soldiers by the innumerable sentry-boxes looked strangely like German toys, and the clean-cut battlements of the castle, gilded by the sunshine, looked the more like gilt gingerbread. For it was brilliant weather. The sky was as Prussian a blue as Potsdam* itself could require, but it was yet more like that lavish and glowing use of the colour which a child extracts from a shilling paint-box. Even the grey-ribbed trees looked young, for the pointed buds on them were still pink, and in a pattern against the strong blue looked like innumerable childish figures.

Despite his prosaic appearance and generally practical walk of life, Father Brown was not without a certain streak of romance in his composition, though he generally kept his day-dreams to himself, as many children do. Amid the brisk, bright colours of such a day, and in the heraldic framework of such a town, he did feel rather as if he had entered a fairy tale. He took a childish pleasure, as a younger brother might, in the formidable sword-stick which Flambeau always flung as he walked, and which now stood upright beside his tall mug of Munich.* Nay, in his sleepy irresponsibility, he even found himself eyeing the knobbed and clumsy head of his own shabby umbrella, with some faint memories of the ogre's club in a coloured toy-book. But he never composed anything in the form of fiction, unless it be the tale that follows:

'I wonder,' he said, 'whether one would have real adventures in a place like this, if one put oneself in the way? It's a splendid back-scene for them, but I always have a kind of feeling that they would fight you with pasteboard sabres more than real, horrible swords.'

'You are mistaken,' said his friend. 'In this place they not only fight with swords, but kill without swords. And there's worse than that.'

'Why, what do you mean?' asked Father Brown.

'Why,' replied the other, 'I should say this was the only place in Europe where a man was ever shot without firearms.'

'Do you mean a bow and arrow?' asked Brown in some wonder.

'I mean a bullet in the brain,' replied Flambeau. 'Don't you know the story of the late Prince of this place? It was one of the great police mysteries about twenty years ago. You remember, of course, that this place was forcibly annexed at the time of Bismarck's very earliest schemes of consolidation—forcibly, that is, but not at all easily. The empire (or what wanted to be one) sent Prince Otto of Grossenmark to rule the place in the Imperial interests. We saw his portrait in the gallery there—a handsome old gentleman if he'd had any hair or eyebrows, and hadn't been wrinkled all over like a vulture; but he had things to harass him, as I'll explain in a minute. He was a soldier of distinguished skill and success, but he didn't have altogether an easy job with this little place. He was defeated in several battles by the celebrated Arnhold brothers—the three guerrilla patriots to whom Swinburne wrote a poem, you remember:

"Wolves with the hair of the ermine,*
    Crows that are crowned and kings—
These things be many as vermin,
    Yet Three shall abide these things."

Or something of that kind. Indeed, it is by no means certain that the occupation would ever have been successful had not one of the three brothers, Paul, despicably, but very decisively declined to abide these things any longer, and, by surrendering all the secrets of the insurrection, ensured its overthrow and his own ultimate promotion to the post of chamberlain to Prince Otto. After this, Ludwig, the one genuine hero among Mr Swinburne's heroes, was killed, sword in hand, in the capture of the city; and the third, Heinrich, who, though not a traitor, had always been tame and even timid compared with his active brothers, retired into something like a hermitage, became converted to a Christian quietism which was almost Quakerish, and never mixed with men except to give nearly all he had to the poor. They tell me that not long ago he could still be seen about the neighbourhood occasionally, a man in a black cloak, nearly blind, with very wild, white hair, but a face of astonishing softness.'

'I know,' said Father Brown. 'I saw him once.'

His friend looked at him in some surprise. 'I didn't know you'd been here before,' he said. 'Perhaps you know as much about it as I do. Anyhow, that's the story of the Arnholds, and he was the last survivor of them. Yes, and of all the men who played parts in that drama.'

'You mean that the Prince, too, died long before?'

'Died,' repeated Flambeau, 'and that's about as much as we can say. You must understand that towards the end of his life he began to have those tricks of the nerves not uncommon with tyrants. He multiplied the ordinary daily and nightly guard round his castle till there seemed to be more sentry-boxes than houses in the town, and doubtful characters were shot without mercy. He lived almost entirely in a little room that was in the very centre of the enormous labyrinth of all the other rooms, and even in this he erected another sort of central cabin or cupboard, lined with steel, like a safe or a battleship. Some say that under the floor of this again was a secret hole in the earth, no more than large enough to hold him, so that, in his anxiety to avoid the grave, he was willing to go into a place pretty much like it. But he went further yet. The populace had been supposed to be disarmed ever since the suppression of the revolt, but Otto now insisted, as governments very seldom insist, on an absolute and literal disarmament. It was carried out, with extraordinary thoroughness and severity, by very well-organized officials over a small and familiar area, and, so far as human strength and science can be absolutely certain of anything, Prince Otto was absolutely certain that nobody could introduce so much as a toy pistol into Heiligwaldenstein.'

'Human science can never be quite certain of things like that,' said Father Brown, still looking at the red budding of the branches over his head, 'if only because of the difficulty about definition and connotation. What is a *weapon*? People have been murdered with the mildest domestic comforts; certainly with tea-kettles, probably with tea-cosies. On the other hand, if you showed an Ancient Briton a revolver, I doubt if he would know it was a weapon—until it was fired into him, of course. Perhaps somebody introduced a firearm so new that it didn't even look like a firearm. Perhaps it looked like a thimble or something. Was the bullet at all peculiar?'

'Not that I ever heard of,' answered Flambeau; 'but all my information is fragmentary, and only comes from my old friend Grimm.* He was a very able detective in the German service, and he tried to arrest me; I arrested him instead, and we had many interesting chats. He was in charge here of the inquiry about Prince Otto, but I forgot to ask him anything about the bullet. According to Grimm, what happened was this.' He paused a moment to drain the greater part of his dark lager at a draught, and then resumed:

'On the evening in question, it seems, the Prince was expected to appear in one of the outer rooms, because he had to receive certain visitors whom he really wished to meet. They were geological experts sent to investigate the old question of the alleged supply of gold from the rocks round here, upon which (as it was said) the small city-state had so long maintained its credit and been able to negotiate with its neighbours

even under the ceaseless bombardment of bigger armies.
Hitherto it had never been found by the most exacting inquiry
which could——'

'Which could be quite certain of discovering a toy pistol,'
said Father Brown with a smile. 'But what about the brother
who ratted? Hadn't he anything to tell the Prince?'

'He always asseverated that he did not know,' replied
Flambeau; 'that this was the one secret his brothers had not
told him. It is only right to say that it received some support
from fragmentary words spoken by the great Ludwig in the
hour of death, when he looked at Heinrich but pointed at
Paul, and said, "You have not told *him* . . ." and was soon
afterwards incapable of speech. Anyhow, the deputation of
distinguished geologists and mineralogists from Paris and
Berlin were there in the most magnificent and appropriate
dress, for there are no men who like wearing their decorations
so much as the men of science—as anybody knows who has
ever been to a soirée of the Royal Society. It was a brilliant
gathering, but very late, and gradually the Chamberlain—you
saw his portrait, too: a man with black eyebrows, serious
eyes, and a meaningless sort of smile underneath—the Chamberlain, I say, discovered there was everything there except
the Prince himself. He searched all the outer *salons*; then,
remembering the man's mad fits of fear, hurried to the inmost
chamber. That also was empty, but the steel turret or cabin
erected in the middle of it took some time to open. When it did
open it was empty, too. He went and looked into the hole in
the ground, which seemed deeper and somehow all the more
like a grave—this is his account, of course. And even as he did
so he heard a burst of cries and tumult in the long rooms and
corridors without.

'First it was a distant din and thrill of something unthinkable on the horizon of the crowd, even beyond the castle. Next
it was a wordless clamour startingly close, and loud enough to
be distinct if each word had not killed the other. Next came
words of a terrible clearness, coming nearer, and next one
man, rushing into the room and telling the news as briefly as
such news is told.

'Otto, Prince of Heiligwaldenstein and Grossenmark, was
lying in the dews of the darkening twilight in the woods

beyond the castle, with his arms flung out and his face flung up to the moon. The blood still pulsed from his shattered temple and jaw, but it was the only part of him that moved like a living thing. He was clad in his full white and yellow uniform, as to receive his guests within, except that the sash or scarf had been unbound and lay rather crumpled by his side. Before he could be lifted he was dead. But, dead or alive, he was a riddle—he who had always hidden in the inmost chamber out there in the wet woods, unarmed and alone.'

'Who found his body?' asked Father Brown.

'Some girl attached to the Court named Hedwig von something or other,' replied his friend, 'who had been out in the wood picking wild flowers.'

'Had she picked any?' asked the priest, staring rather vacantly at the veil of the branches above him.

'Yes,' replied Flambeau. 'I particularly remember that the Chamberlain, or old Grimm or somebody, said how horrible it was, when they came up at her call, to see a girl holding spring flowers and bending over that—that bloody collapse. However, the main point is that before help arrived he was dead, and the news, of course, had to be carried back to the castle. The consternation it created was something beyond even that natural in a Court at the fall of a potentate. The foreign visitors, especially the mining experts, were in the wildest doubt and excitement, as well as many important Prussian officials, and it soon began to be clear that the scheme for finding the treasure bulked much bigger in the business than people had supposed. Experts and officials had been promised great prizes or international advantages, and some even said that the Prince's secret apartments and strong military protection were due less to fear of the populace than to the pursuit of some private investigation of——'

'Had the flowers got long stalks?' asked Father Brown.

Flambeau stared at him. 'What an odd person you are!' he said. 'That's exactly what old Grimm said. He said the ugliest part of it, he thought—uglier than the blood and bullet—was that the flowers were quite short, plucked close under the head.'

'Of course,' said the priest, 'when a grown up girl is *really* picking flowers, she picks them with plenty of stalk. If she just pulled their heads off, as a child does, it looks as if——' And he hesitated.

'Well?' inquired the other.

'Well, it looks rather as if she had snatched them nervously, to make an excuse for being there after—well, after she was there.'

'I know what you're driving at,' said Flambeau rather gloomily. 'But that and every other suspicion breaks down on the one point—the want of a weapon. He could have been killed, as you say, with lots of other things—even with his own military sash; but we have to explain not how he was killed, but how he was shot. And the fact is we can't. They had the girl most ruthlessly searched; for, to tell the truth, she was a little suspect, though the niece and ward of the wicked old Chamberlain, Paul Arnhold. But she was very romantic, and was suspected of sympathy with the old revolutionary enthusiasm in her family. All the same, however romantic you are, you can't imagine a big bullet into a man's jaw or brain without using a gun or pistol. And there was no pistol, though there were two pistol shots. I leave it to you, my friend.'

'How do you know there were two shots?' asked the little priest

'There was only one in his head,' said his companion, 'but there was another bullet-hole in the sash.'

Father Brown's smooth brow became suddenly constricted. 'Was the other bullet found?' he demanded.

Flambeau started a little. 'I don't think I remember,' he said.

'Hold on! Hold on! Hold on!' cried Brown, frowning more and more, with a quite unusual concentration of curiosity. 'Don't think me rude. Let me think this out for a moment.'

'All right,' said Flambeau, laughing, and finished his beer. A slight breeze stirred the budding trees and blew up into the sky cloudlets of white and pink that seemed to make the sky bluer and the whole coloured scene more quaint. They might have been cherubs flying home to the casements of a sort of celestial nursery. The oldest tower of the castle, the Dragon Tower, stood up as grotesque as the ale-mug, but as homely. Only beyond the tower glimmered the wood in which the man had lain dead.

'What became of this Hedwig eventually?' asked the priest at last.

'She is married to General Schwartz,' said Flambeau. 'No doubt you've heard of his career, which was rather romantic. He had distinguished himself even before his exploits at Sadowa* and Gravelotte;* in fact, he rose from the ranks, which is very unusual even in the smallest of the German——'

Father Brown sat up suddenly.

'Rose from the ranks!' he cried, and made a mouth as if to whistle. 'Well, well, what a queer story! What a queer way of killing a man; but I suppose it was the only one possible. But to think of hate so patient——'

'What do you mean?' demanded the other. 'In what way did they kill the man?'

'They killed him with the sash,' said Brown carefully; and then, as Flambeau protested: 'Yes, yes, I know about the bullet. Perhaps I ought to say he died of having a sash. I know it doesn't sound like having a disease.'

'I suppose,' said Flambeau, 'that you've got some notion in your head, but it won't easily get the bullet out of his. As I explained before, he *might* easily have been strangled. But he *was* shot. By whom? By what?'

'He was shot by his own orders,' said the priest.

'You mean he committed suicide?'

'I didn't say by his own wish,' replied Father Brown. 'I said by his own orders.'

'Well, anyhow, what is your theory?'

Father Brown laughed. 'I am only on my holiday,' he said. 'I haven't got any theories. Only this place reminds me of fairy stories, and, if you like, I'll tell you a story.'

The little pink clouds, that looked rather like sweet-stuff, had floated up to crown the turrets of the gilt gingerbread castle, and the pink baby fingers of the budding trees seemed spreading and stretching to reach them; the blue sky began to take a bright violet of evening, when Father Brown suddenly spoke again:

'It was on a dismal night, with rain still dropping from the trees and dew already clustering, that Prince Otto of

Grossenmark stepped hurriedly out of a side door of the castle and walked swiftly into the wood. One of the innumerable sentries saluted him, but he did not notice it. He had no wish to be specially noticed himself. He was glad when the great trees, grey and already greasy with rain, swallowed him up like a swamp. He had deliberately chosen the least frequented side of his palace, but even that was more frequented than he liked. But there was no particular chance of officious or diplomatic pursuit, for his exit had been a sudden impulse. All the full-dressed diplomatists he left behind were unimportant. He had realized suddenly that he could do without them.

'His great passion was not the much nobler dread of death, but the strange desire of gold. For this legend of the gold he had left Grossenmark and invaded Heiligwaldenstein. For this and only this he had bought the traitor and butchered the hero, for this he had long questioned and cross-questioned the false Chamberlain, until he had come to the conclusion that, touching his ignorance, the renegade really told the truth. For this he had, somewhat reluctantly, paid and promised money on the chance of gaining the larger amount; and for this he had stolen out of his palace like a thief in the rain, for he had thought of another way to get the desire of his eyes, and to get it cheap.

'Away at the upper end of a rambling mountain path to which he was making his way, among the pillared rocks along the ridge that hangs above the town, stood the hermitage, hardly more than a cavern fenced with thorn, in which the third of the great brethren had long hidden himself from the world. He, thought Prince Otto, could have no real reason for refusing to give up the gold. He had known its place for years, and made no effort to find it, even before his new ascetic creed had cut him off from property or pleasures. True, he had been an enemy, but he now professed a duty of having no enemies. Some concession to his cause, some appeal to his principles, would probably get the mere money secret out of him. Otto was no coward, in spite of his net-work of military pre-cautions, and, in any case, his avarice was stronger than his fears. Nor was there much cause for fear. Since he was certain there were no private arms in the whole principality, he was a hundred times more certain there were none in the Quaker's little hermitage on the hill, where he lived on herbs, with two old rustic servants, and with no other voice of man for year after year. Prince Otto looked down with something of a grim smile at the bright, square labyrinths of the lamp-lit city below him. For as far as the eye could see there ran the rifles of his friends, and not one pinch of powder for his enemies. Rifles ranked so close even to that mountain path that a cry from him would bring the soldiers rushing up the hill, to say nothing of the fact that the wood and ridge were patrolled at regular intervals; rifles so far away, in the dim woods, dwarfed by distance, beyond the river, that an enemy could not slink into the town by any detour. And round the palace rifles at the west door and the east door, at the north door and the south, and all along the four façades linking them. He was safe.

'It was all the more clear when he had crested the ridge and found how naked was the nest of his old enemy. He found himself on a small platform of rock, broken abruptly by the three corners of precipice. Behind was the black cave, masked with green thorn, so low that it was hard to believe that a man could enter it. In front was the fall of the cliffs and the vast but cloudy vision of the valley. On the small rock platform stood an old bronze lectern or reading-stand, groaning under a great German Bible. The bronze or copper of it had grown green with the eating airs of that exalted place, and Otto had instantly the thought, "Even if they had arms, they must be rusted by now." Moonrise had already made a deathly dawn behind the crests and crags, and the rain had ceased.

'Behind the lectern, and looking across the valley, stood a very old man in a black robe that fell as straight as the cliffs around him, but whose white hair and weak voice seemed alike to waver in the wind. He was evidently reading some daily lesson as part of his religious exercises. "They trust in their horses..."

'"Sir," said the Prince of Heiligwaldenstein, with quite unusual courtesy, "I should like only one word with you." ·

'"... and in their chariots," went on the old man weakly, "but we will trust in the name of the Lord of Hosts...."* His last words were inaudible, but he closed the book reverently and, being nearly blind, made a groping movement and gripped the reading-stand. Instantly his two servants slipped out of the low-browed cavern and supported him. They wore dull-black gowns like his own, but they had not the frosty silver on the hair, nor the frost-bitten refinement of the features. They were peasants, Croat or Magyar, with broad, blunt visages and blinking eyes. For the first time something troubled the Prince, but his courage and diplomatic sense stood firm.

' "I fear we have not met," he said, "since that awful cannonade in which your poor brother died."

' "All my brothers died," said the old man, still looking across the valley. Then, for one instant turning on Otto his drooping, delicate features, and the wintry hair that seemed to drip over his eyebrows like icicles, he added: "You see, I am dead, too."

' "I hope you'll understand," said the Prince, controlling himself almost to a point of conciliation, "that I do not come here to haunt you, as a mere ghost of those great quarrels. We will not talk about who was right or wrong in that, but at least there was one point on which we were never wrong, because you were always right. Whatever is to be said of the policy of your family, no one for one moment imagines that you were moved by the mere gold; you have proved yourself above the suspicion that——"

'The old man in the old black gown had hitherto continued to gaze at him with watery blue eyes and a sort of weak wisdom in his face. But when the word "gold" was said he held out his hand as if in arrest of something, and turned away his face to the mountains.

' "He has spoken of gold," he said. "He has spoken of things not lawful. Let him cease to speak."

'Otto had the vice of his Prussian type and tradition, which is to regard success not as an incident but as a quality. He conceived himself and his like as perpetually conquering peoples who were perpetually being conquered. Consequently, he was ill acquainted with the emotion of surprise, and ill prepared for the next movement, which startled and stiffened him. He had opened his mouth to answer the hermit, when the mouth was stopped and the voice strangled by a strong, soft gag suddenly twisted round his head like a tourniquet. It was fully forty seconds before he even realized that the two Hungarian servants had done it, and that they had done it with his own military scarf.

'The old man went again weakly to his great brazen-supported Bible, turned over the leaves, with a patience that had something horrible about it, till he came to the Epistle of St James,* and then began to read: "The tongue is a little member, but——"

'Something in the very voice made the Prince turn suddenly and plunge down the mountain-path he had climbed. He was half-way towards the gardens of the palace before he even tried to tear the strangling scarf from his neck and jaws. He tried again and again, and it was impossible; the men who had knotted that gag knew the difference between what a man can do with his hands in front of him and what he can do with his hands behind his head. His legs were free to leap like an antelope on the mountains, his arms were free to use any gesture or wave any signal, but he could not speak. A dumb devil was in him.

'He had come close to the woods that walled in the castle before he had quite realized what his wordless state meant and was meant to mean. Once more he looked down grimly at the bright, square labyrinths of the lamplit city below him, and he smiled no more. He felt himself repeating the phrases of his former mood with a murderous irony. Far as the eye could see ran the rifles of his friends, every one of whom would shoot him dead if he could not answer the challenge. Rifles were so near that the wood and ridge could be patrolled at regular intervals; therefore it was useless to hide in the wood till morning. Rifles were ranked so far away that an enemy could not slink into the town by any detour; therefore it was vain to return to the city by any remote course. A cry from him would bring his soldiers rushing up the hill. But from him no cry would come.

'The moon had risen in strengthening silver, and the sky showed in stripes of bright, nocturnal blue between the black stripes of the pines about the castle. Flowers of some wide and feathery sort—for he had never noticed such things before—were at once made luminous and discoloured by the moonshine, and seemed indescribably fantastic as they clustered, as if crawling about the roots of the trees. Perhaps his reason had been suddenly unseated by the unnatural captivity he carried with him, but in that wood he felt something unfathomably German—the fairy tale. He knew with half his mind that he was drawing near to the castle of an ogre—he had forgotten that he was the ogre. He remembered asking his mother if bears lived in the old park at home. He stooped to pick a flower, as if it were a charm against enchantment. The stalk was stronger than he expected, and broke with a slight snap. Carefully trying to place it in his scarf, he heard the halloo, "Who goes there?" Then he remembered the scarf was not in its usual place.

'He tried to scream, and was silent. The second challenge came; and then a shot that shrieked as it came and then was stilled suddenly by impact. Otto of Grossenmark lay very peacefully among the fairy trees, and would do no more harm either with gold or steel; only the silver pencil of the moon would pick out and trace here and there the intricate ornament of his uniform, or the old wrinkles on his brow. May God have mercy on his soul.

'The sentry who had fired, according to the strict orders of the garrison, naturally ran forward to find some trace of his quarry. He was a private named Schwartz, since not unknown in his profession, and what he found was a bald man in uniform, but with his face so bandaged by a kind of mask made of his own military scarf that nothing but open, dead eyes could be seen, glittering stonily in the moonlight. The bullet had gone through the gag into the jaw; that is why there was a shot-hole in the scarf, but only one shot. Naturally, if not correctly, young Schwartz tore off the mysterious silken mask and cast it on the grass; and then he saw whom he had slain.

'We cannot be certain of the next phase. But I incline to believe that there was a fairy tale, after all, in that little wood, horrible as was its occasion. Whether the young lady named

Hedwig had any previous knowledge of the soldier she saved and eventually married, or whether she came accidentally upon the accident and their intimacy began that night, we shall probably never know. But we can know, I fancy, that this Hedwig was a heroine, and deserved to marry a man who became something of a hero. She did the bold and the wise thing. She persuaded the sentry to go back to his post, in which place there was nothing to connect him with the disaster; he was but one of the most loyal and orderly of fifty such sentries within call. She remained by the body and gave the alarm; and there was nothing to connect her with the disaster either, since she had not got, and could not have, any firearms.

'Well,' said Father Brown rising cheerfully 'I hope they're happy.'

'Where are you going?' asked his friend.

'I'm going to have another look at that portrait of the Chamberlain, the Arnhold who betrayed his brethren,' answered the priest. 'I wonder what part——I wonder if a man is less a traitor when he is twice a traitor?'

And he ruminated long before the portrait of a white-haired man with black eyebrows and a pink, painted sort of smile that seemed to contradict the black warning in his eyes.

THE ORACLE OF THE DOG

'YES,' said Father Brown, 'I always like a dog, so long as he isn't spelt backwards.'*

Those who are quick in talking are not always quick in listening. Sometimes even their brilliancy produces a sort of stupidity. Father Brown's friend and companion was a young man with a stream of ideas and stories, an enthusiastic young man named Fiennes, with eager blue eyes and blond hair that seemed to be brushed back, not merely with a hair-brush but with the wind of the world as he rushed through it. But he stopped in the torrent of his talk in a momentary bewilderment before he saw the priest's very simple meaning.

'You mean that people make too much of them?' he said. 'Well, I don't know. They're marvellous creatures. Sometimes I think they know a lot more than we do.'

Father Brown said nothing, but continued to stroke the head of the big retriever in a half-abstracted but apparently soothing fashion.

'Why,' said Fiennes, warming again to his monologue, 'there was a dog in the case I've come to see you about: what they call the "Invisible Murder Case," you know. It's a strange story, but from my point of view the dog is about the strangest thing in it. Of course, there's the mystery of the crime itself, and how old Druce can have been killed by somebody else when he was all alone in the summer-house——'

The hand stroking the dog stopped for a moment in its rhythmic movement, and Father Brown said calmly: 'Oh, it was a summer-house, was it?'

'I thought you'd read all about it in the papers,' answered Fiennes. 'Stop a minute; I believe I've got a cutting that will give you all the particulars.' He produced a strip of newspaper from his pocket and handed it to the priest, who began to read it, holding it close to his blinking eyes with one hand while the other continued its half-conscious caresses of the dog. It looked like the parable of a man not letting his right hand know what his left hand did.*

'Many mystery stories, about men murdered behind locked doors and windows, and murderers escaping without means of entrance and exit, have come true in the course of the extraordinary events at Cranston on the coast of Yorkshire, where Colonel Druce was found stabbed from behind by a dagger that has entirely disappeared from the scene, and apparently even from the neighbourhood.

'The summer-house in which he died was indeed accessible at one entrance, the ordinary doorway which looked down the central walk of the garden towards the house. But, by a combination of events almost to be called a coincidence, it appears that both the path and the entrance were watched during the crucial time, and there is a chain of witnesses who confirm each other. The summer-house stands at the extreme end of the garden, where there is no exit or entrance of any kind. The central garden path is a lane between two ranks of tall delphiniums, planted so close that any stray step off the path would leave its traces; and both path and plants run right up to the very mouth of the summer-house, so that no straying from that straight path could fail to be observed, and no other mode of entrance can be imagined.

'Patrick Floyd, secretary of the murdered man, testified that he had been in a position to overlook the whole garden from the time when Colonel Druce last appeared alive in the doorway to the time when he was found dead; as he, Floyd, had been on the top of a step-ladder clipping the garden hedge. Janet Druce, the dead man's daughter, confirmed this, saying that she had sat on the terrace of the house throughout that time and had seen Floyd at his work. Touching some part of the time, this is again supported by Donald Druce, her brother—who overlooked the garden—standing at his bedroom window in his dressing-gown, for he had risen late. Lastly, the account is consistent with that given by Dr Valentine, a neighbour, who called for a time to talk with Miss Druce on the terrace, and by the Colonel's solicitor, Mr Aubrey Traill, who was apparently the last to see the murdered man alive—presumably with the exception of the murderer.

'All are agreed that the course of events was as follows: About half-past three in the afternoon, Miss Druce went down the path to ask her father when he would like tea; but he said he did not want any and was waiting to see Traill, his lawyer, who was to be sent to him in the summer-house. The girl then came away and met Traill coming down the path; she directed him to her father and he went in as directed. About half an hour afterwards he came out again, the Colonel coming with him to the door and showing himself to all appearance in health and even high spirits. He had been somewhat annoyed earlier in the day by his son's irregular hours, but seemed to recover his temper in a perfectly normal fashion, and had been rather markedly genial in receiving other visitors, including two of his nephews, who came over for the day. But as these were out walking during the whole period of the tragedy, they had no evidence to give. It is said, indeed, that the Colonel was not on very good terms with Dr Valentine, but that gentleman only had a brief interview with the daughter of the house, to whom he is supposed to be paying serious attentions.

'Traill, the solicitor, says he left the Colonel entirely alone in the summer-house, and this is confirmed by Floyd's bird's-eye view of the garden, which showed nobody else passing the only entrance. Ten minutes later, Miss Druce again went down the garden and had not reached the end of the path when she saw her father, who was conspicuous by his white linen coat, lying in a heap on the floor. She uttered a scream which brought others to the spot, and on entering the place they found the Colonel lying dead beside his basket-chair, which was also upset. Dr Valentine, who was still in the immediate neighbourhood, testified that the wound was made by some sort of stiletto, entering under the shoulder-blade and piercing the heart. The police have searched the neighbourhood for such a weapon, but no trace of it can be found.'

'So Colonel Druce wore a white coat, did he?' said Father Brown as he put down the paper.

'Trick he learnt in the tropics,' replied Fiennes, with some wonder. 'He'd had some queer adventures there, by his own account; and I fancy his dislike of Valentine was connected with the doctor coming from the tropics, too. But it's all an infernal puzzle. The account there is pretty accurate; I didn't see the tragedy, in the sense of the discovery; I was out walking with the young nephews and the dog—the dog I wanted to tell you about. But I saw the stage set for it as described; the straight lane between the blue flowers right up to the dark entrance, and the lawyer going down it in his blacks and his silk hat, and the red head of the secretary showing high above the green hedge as he worked on it with his shears. Nobody could have mistaken that red head at any distance; and if people say they saw it there all the time, you may be sure they did. This red-haired secretary, Floyd, is quite a character; a breathless, bounding sort of fellow, always doing everybody's work as he was doing the gardener's. I think he is an American; he's certainly got the American view of life—what they call the view-point, bless 'em.'

'What about the lawyer?' asked Father Brown.

There was a silence and then Fiennes spoke quite slowly for him. 'Traill struck me as a singular man. In his fine black clothes he was almost foppish, yet you can hardly call him fashionable. For he wore a pair of long, luxuriant black whiskers such as haven't been seen since Victorian times. He had rather a fine grave face and a fine grave manner, but every now and then he seemed to remember to smile. And when he showed his white teeth he seemed to lose a little of his dignity, and there was something faintly fawning about him. It may have been only embarrassment, for he would also fidget with his cravat and his tie-pin, which were at once handsome and unusual, like himself. If I could think of anybody—but what's the good, when the whole thing's impossible? Nobody knows who did it. Nobody knows how it could be done. At least there's only one exception I'd make, and that's why I really mentioned the whole thing. The dog knows.'

Father Brown sighed and then said absently: 'You were there as a friend of young Donald, weren't you? He didn't go on your walk with you?'

'No,' replied Fiennes smiling. 'The young scoundrel had gone to bed that morning and got up that afternoon. I went with his cousins, two young officers from India, and our conversation was trivial enough. I remember the elder, whose name I think is Herbert Druce and who is an authority on horse-breeding, talked about nothing but a mare he had bought and the moral character of the man who sold her; while his brother Harry seemed to be brooding on his bad luck at Monte Carlo. I only mention it to show you, in the light of what happened on our walk, that there was nothing psychic about us. The dog was the only mystic in our company.'

'What sort of a dog was he?' asked the priest.

'Same breed as that one,' answered Fiennes. 'That's what started me off on the story, your saying you didn't believe in believing in a dog. He's a big black retriever, named Nox,* and a suggestive name, too; for I think what he did a darker mystery than the murder. You know Druce's house and garden are by the sea; we walked about a mile from it along the sands and then turned back, going the other way. We passed a rather curious rock called the Rock of Fortune, famous in the neighbourhood because it's one of those examples of one stone barely balanced on another, so that a touch would knock it over. It is not really very high but the hanging outline of it makes it look a little wild and sinister; at least it made it look so to me, for I don't imagine my jolly young companions were afflicted with the picturesque. But it may be that I was beginning to feel an atmosphere; for just then the question arose of whether it was time to go back to tea, and even then I think I had a premonition that time counted for a good deal in the business. Neither Herbert Druce nor I had a watch, so we called out to his brother, who was some paces behind, having stopped to light his pipe under the hedge. Hence it happened that he shouted out the hour, which was twenty past four, in his big voice through the growing twilight; and somehow the loudness of it made it sound like the proclamation of something tremendous. His unconsciousness seemed to make it all the more so; but that was always the way with omens; and particular ticks of the clock were really very ominous things that afternoon. According to Dr Valentine's testimony, poor Druce had actually died just about half-past four.

'Well, they said we needn't go home for ten minutes, and we walked a little farther along the sands, doing nothing in particular—throwing stones for the dog and throwing sticks into the sea for him to swim after. But to me the twilight seemed to grow oddly oppressive, and the very shadow of the top-heavy Rock of Fortune lay on me like a load. And then the curious thing happened. Nox had just brought back Herbert's walking-stick out of the sea and his brother had thrown his in also. The dog swam out again, but just about what must have been the stroke of the half-hour, he stopped swimming. He came back again on to the shore and stood in front of us. Then he suddenly threw up his head and sent up a howl or wail of woe, if ever I heard one in the world.

' "What the devil's the matter with the dog?" asked Herbert; but none of us could answer. There was a long silence after the brute's wailing and whining died away on the desolate shore; and then the silence was broken. As I live, it was broken by a faint and far-off shriek, like the shriek of a woman from beyond the hedges inland. We didn't know what it was then; but we knew afterwards. It was the cry the girl gave when she first saw the body of her father.'

'You went back, I suppose,' said Father Brown patiently. 'What happened then?'

'I'll tell you what happened then,' said Fiennes with a grim emphasis. 'When we got back into that garden the first thing we saw was Traill, the lawyer; I can see him now with his black hat and black whiskers relieved against the perspective of the blue flowers stretching down to the summer-house, with the sunset and the strange outline of the Rock of Fortune in the distance. His face and figure were in shadow against the sunset; but I swear the white teeth were showing in his head and he was smiling.

'The moment Nox saw that man the dog dashed forward and stood in the middle of the path barking at him madly, murderously, volleying out curses that were almost verbal in their dreadful distinctness of hatred. And the man doubled up and fled along the path between the flowers.'

Father Brown sprang to his feet with a startling impatience.

'So the dog denounced him, did he?' he cried. 'The oracle of the dog condemned him. Did you see what birds were flying, and are you sure whether they were on the right hand or the left? Did you consult the augurs about the sacrifices? Surely you didn't omit to cut open the dog and examine his entrails. That is the sort of scientific test you heathen humanitarians seem to trust when you are thinking of taking away the life and honour of a man.'

Fiennes sat gaping for an instant before he found breath to say: 'Why, what's the matter with you? What have I done now?'

A sort of anxiety came back into the priest's eyes—the anxiety of a man who has run against a post in the dark and wonders for a moment whether he has hurt it.

'I'm most awfully sorry,' he said with sincere distress. 'I beg your pardon for being so rude; pray forgive me.'

Fiennes looked at him curiously. 'I sometimes think you are more of a mystery than any of the mysteries,' he said. 'But anyhow, if you don't believe in the mystery of the dog, at least you can't get over the mystery of the man. You can't deny that at the very moment when the beast came back from the sea and bellowed, his master's soul was driven out of his body by the blow of some unseen power that no mortal man can trace or even imagine. And as for the lawyer—I don't go only by the dog—there are other curious details, too. He struck me as a smooth, smiling, equivocal sort of person; and one of his tricks seemed like a sort of hint. You know the doctor and the police were on the spot very quickly; Valentine was brought back when walking away from the house, and he telephoned instantly. That, with the secluded house, small numbers, and enclosed space, made it pretty possible to search everybody who could have been near; and everybody was thoroughly searched—for a weapon. The whole house, garden, and shore were combed for a weapon. The disappearance of the dagger is almost as crazy as the disappearance of the man.'

'The disappearance of the dagger,' said Father Brown, nodding. He seemed to have become suddenly attentive.

'Well,' continued Fiennes, 'I told you that man Traill had a trick of fidgeting with his tie and tie-pin—especially his tie-pin. His pin, like himself, was at once showy and old-fashioned. It had one of those stones with concentric coloured rings that look like an eye; and his own concentration on it got on my nerves, as if he had been a Cyclops with one eye in the middle of his body. But the pin was not only large but long; and it occurred to me that his anxiety about its adjustment was because it was even longer than it looked; as long as a stiletto in fact.'

Father Brown nodded thoughtfully. 'Was any other instrument ever suggested?' he asked.

'There was another suggestion,' answered Fiennes, 'from one of the young Druces—the cousins, I mean. Neither Herbert nor Harry Druce would have struck one at first as likely to be of assistance in scientific detection; but while Herbert was really the traditional type of heavy Dragoon, caring for nothing but horses and being an ornament to the Horse Guards, his younger brother Harry had been in the Indian Police and knew something about such things. Indeed, in his own way he was quite clever; and I rather fancy he had been too clever; I mean he had left the police through breaking some red-tape regulations and taking some sort of risk and responsibility of his own. Anyhow, he was in some sense a detective out of work, and threw himself into this business with more than the ardour of an amateur. And it was with him that I had an argument about the weapon—an argument that led to something new. It began by his countering my description of the dog barking at Traill; and he said that a dog at his worst didn't bark, but growled.'

'He was quite right there,' observed the priest.

'This young fellow went on to say that, if it came to that, he'd heard Nox growling at other people before then; and among others at Floyd, the secretary. I retorted that his own argument answered itself; for the crime couldn't be brought home to two or three people, and least of all to Floyd, who was as innocent as a harum-scarum schoolboy, and had been seen by everybody all the time perched above the garden hedge with his fan of red hair as conspicuous as a scarlet cockatoo. "I know there's difficulties anyhow," said my colleague; "but I wish you'd come with me down the garden a minute. I want to show you something I don't think any one else has seen," This was on the very day of the discovery, and the garden was just as it had been. The step-ladder was still standing by the hedge, and just under the hedge my guide stopped and disentangled something from the deep grass. It was the shears used for clipping the hedge, and on the point of one of them was a smear of blood.'

There was a short silence, and then Father Brown said suddenly. 'What was the lawyer there for?'

'He told us the Colonel sent for him to alter his will,' answered Fiennes. 'And, by the way, there was another thing about the business of the will that I ought to mention. You see, the will wasn't actually signed in the summer-house that afternoon.'

'I suppose not,' said Father Brown; 'there would have to be two witnesses.'

'The lawyer actually came down the day before and it was signed then; but he was sent for again next day because the old man had a doubt about one of the witnesses and had to be reassured.'

'Who were the witnesses?' asked Father Brown.

'That's just the point,' replied his informant eagerly, 'the witnesses were Floyd, the secretary, and this Dr Valentine, the foreign sort of surgeon or whatever he is; and the two have a quarrel. Now I'm bound to say that the secretary is something of a busybody. He's one of those hot and headlong people whose warmth of temperament has unfortunately turned mostly to pugnacity and bristling suspicion; to distrusting people instead of to trusting them. That sort of red-haired red-hot fellow is always either universally credulous or universally incredulous; and sometimes both. He was not only a Jack-of-all-trades, but he knew better than all tradesmen. He not only knew everything, but he warned everybody against everybody. All that must be taken into account in his suspicions about Valentine; but in that particular case there seems to have been something behind it. He said the name of Valentine was not really Valentine. He said he had seen him elsewhere known by the name of De Villon. He said it would invalidate the will; of course he was kind enough to explain to the lawyer what the law was on that point. They were both in a frightful wax.'

Father Brown laughed. 'People often are when they are to witness a will,' he said; 'for one thing, it means that they can't have any legacy under it. But what did Dr Valentine say? No doubt the universal secretary knew more about the doctor's name than the doctor did. But even the doctor might have some information about his own name.'

Fiennes paused a moment before he replied.

'Dr Valentine took it in a curious way. Dr Valentine is a curious man. His appearance is rather striking but very foreign. He is young but wears a beard cut square; and his face is very pale, dreadfully pale and dreadfully serious. His eyes have a sort of ache in them, as if he ought to wear glasses, or had given himself a headache with thinking; but he is quite handsome and always very formally dressed, with a top hat and a dark coat and a little red rosette. His manner is rather cold and haughty, and he has a way of staring at you which is very disconcerting. When thus charged with having changed his name, he merely stared like a sphinx and then said with a little laugh that he supposed Americans had no names to change. At that I think the Colonel also got into a fuss and said all sorts of angry things to the doctor; all the more angry because of the doctor's pretensions to a future place in his family. But I shouldn't have thought much of that but for a few words that I happened to hear later, early in the afternoon of the tragedy. I don't want to make a lot of them, for they weren't the sort of words on which one would like, in the ordinary way, to play the eavesdropper. As I was passing out towards the front gate with my two companions and the dog, I heard voices which told me that Dr Valentine and Miss Druce had withdrawn for a moment into the shadow of the house, in an angle behind a row of flowering plants, and were talking to each other in passionate whisperings—sometimes almost like hissings; for it was something of a lovers' quarrel as well as a lovers' tryst. Nobody repeats the sort of things they said for the most part; but in an unfortunate business like this I'm bound to say that there was repeated more than once a phrase about killing somebody. In fact, the girl seemed to be begging him not to kill somebody, or saying that no provocation could justify killing anybody; which seems an unusual sort of talk to address to a gentleman who has dropped in to tea.'

'Do you know,' asked the priest, 'whether Dr Valentine seemed to be very angry after the scene with the secretary and the Colonel—I mean about witnessing the will?'

'By all accounts,' replied the other, 'he wasn't half so angry as the secretary was. It was the secretary who went away raging after witnessing the will.'

'And now,' said Father Brown, 'what about the will itself?'

'The Colonel was a very wealthy man, and his will was important. Traill wouldn't tell us the alteration at that stage, but I have since heard, only this morning in fact—that most of the money was transferred from the son to the daughter. I told you that Druce was wild with my friend Donald over his dissipated hours.'

'The question of motive has been rather over-shadowed by the question of method,' observed Father Brown thoughtfully.

'At that moment, apparently, Miss Druce was the immediate gainer by the death.'

'Good God! What a cold-blooded way of talking,' cried Fiennes, staring at him. 'You don't really mean to hint that she——'

'Is she going to marry that Dr Valentine?' asked the other.

'Some people are against it,' answered his friend. 'But he is liked and respected in the place and is a skilled and devoted surgeon.'

'So devoted a surgeon,' said Father Brown, 'that he had surgical instruments with him when he went to call on the young lady at tea-time. For he must have used a lancet or something, and he never seems to have gone home.'

Fiennes sprang to his feet and looked at him in a heat of inquiry. 'You suggest he might have used the very same lancet——'

Father Brown shook his head. 'All these suggestions are fancies just now,' he said. 'The problem is not who did it or what did it, but how it was done. We might find many men and even many tools—pins and shears and lancets. But how did a man get into the room? How did even a pin get into it?'

He was staring reflectively at the ceiling as he spoke, but as he said the last words his eye cocked in an alert fashion as if he had suddenly seen a curious fly on the ceiling.

'Well, what would you do about it?' asked the young man. 'You have a lot of experience; what would you advise now?'

'I'm afraid I'm not much use,' said Father Brown with a sigh. 'I can't suggest very much without having ever been near the place or the people. For the moment you can only go on with local inquiries. I gather that your friend from the Indian Police is more or less in charge of your inquiry down there. I should run down and see how he is getting on. See what he's been doing in the way of amateur detection. There may be news already.'

As his guests, the biped and the quadruped, disappeared, Father Brown took up his pen and went back to his interrupted occupation of planning a course of lectures on the Encyclical *Rerum Novarum*.* The subject was a large one and he had to re-cast it more than once, so that he was somewhat similarly employed some two days later when the big black dog again came bounding into the room and sprawled all over him with enthusiasm and excitement. The master who followed the dog shared the excitement if not the enthusiasm. He had been excited in a less pleasant fashion, for his blue eyes seemed to start from his head and his eager face was even a little pale.

'You told me,' he said abruptly and without preface, 'to find out what Harry Druce was doing. Do you know what he's done?'

The priest did not reply, and the young man went on in jerky tones:

'I'll tell you what he's done. He's killed himself.'

Father Brown's lips moved only faintly, and there was nothing practical about what he was saying—nothing that has anything to do with this story or this world.

'You give me the creeps sometimes,' said Fiennes. 'Did you—did you expect this?'

'I thought it possible,' said Father Brown; 'that was why I asked you to go and see what he was doing. I hoped you might not be too late.'

'It was I who found him,' said Fiennes rather huskily. 'It was the ugliest and most uncanny thing I ever knew. I went down that old garden again, and I knew there was something new and unnatural about it besides the murder. The flowers still tossed about in blue masses on each side of the black entrance into the old grey summer-house; but to me the blue flowers looked like blue devils dancing before some dark cavern of the underworld. I looked all round, everything seemed to be in its ordinary place. But the queer notion grew on me that there was something wrong with the very shape of the sky. And then I saw what it was. The Rock of Fortune always rose in the background beyond the garden hedge and against the sea. And the Rock of Fortune was gone.'

Father Brown had lifted his head and was listening intently.

'It was as if a mountain had walked away out of a landscape or a moon fallen from the sky; though I knew, of course, that a touch at any time would have tipped the thing over. Something possesed me and I rushed down that garden path like the wind and went crashing through that hedge as if it were a spider's web. It was a thin hedge really, though its undisturbed trimness had made it serve all the purposes of a wall. On the shore I found the loose rock fallen from its pedestal; and poor Harry Druce lay like a wreck underneath it. One arm was thrown round it in a sort of embrace as if he had pulled it down on himself; and on the broad brown sands beside it, in large crazy lettering, he had scrawled the words: "The Rock of Fortune falls on the Fool."'

'It was the Colonel's will that did that,' observed Father Brown. 'The young man had staked everything on profiting himself by Donald's disgrace, especially when his uncle sent for him on the same day as the lawyer, and welcomed him with so much warmth. Otherwise he was done; he'd lost his police job; he was beggared at Monte Carlo. And he killed himself when he found he'd killed his kinsman for nothing.'

'Here, stop a minute!' cried the staring Fiennes. 'You're going too fast for me.'

'Talking about the will, by the way,' continued Father Brown calmly 'before I forget it, or we go on to bigger things, there was a simple explanation, I think, of all that business about the doctor's name. I rather fancy I have heard both names before somewhere. The doctor is really a French nobleman with the title of the Marquis de Villon. But he is also an ardent Republican and has abandoned his title and fallen back on the forgotten family surname. "With your Citizen Riquetti* you have puzzled Europe for ten days."'

'What is that?' asked the young man blankly.

'Never mind,' said the priest. 'Nine times out of ten it is a rascally thing to change one's name; but this was a piece of fine fanaticism. That's the point of his sarcasm about Americans having no names—that is, no titles. Now in England the Marquis of Hartington is never called Mr Hartington; but in France the Marquis de Villon is called M. de Villon. So it might well look like a change of name. As for the talk about killing. I fancy that also was a point of French etiquette. The doctor was talking about challenging Floyd to a duel, and the girl was trying to dissuade him.'

'Oh, I *see*,' cried Fiennes slowly. 'Now I understand what she meant.'

'And what is that about?' asked his companion, smiling.

'Well,' said the young man, 'it was something that happened to me just before I found that poor fellow's body; only the catastrophe drove it out of my head. I suppose it's hard to remember a little romantic idyll when you've just come on top of a tragedy. But as I went down the lanes leading to the Colonel's old place I met his daughter walking with Dr Valentine. She was in mourning, of course, and he always wore black as if he were going to a funeral; but I can't say that their faces were very funereal. Never have I seen two people looking in their own way more respectably radiant and cheerful. They stopped and saluted me, and then she told me they were married and living in a little house on the outskirts of the town, where the doctor was continuing his practice. This rather surprised me, because I knew that her old father's will had left her his property; and I hinted at it delicately by saying I was going along to her father's old place and had half expected to meet her there. But she only laughed and said: "Oh, we've given up all that. My husband doesn't like heiresses." And I discovered with some astonishment they really had insisted on restoring the property to poor Donald; so I hope he's had a healthy shock and will treat it sensibly. There was never much really the matter with him; he was very young and his father was not very wise. But it was in connexion with that that she said something I didn't understand at the time; but now I'm sure it must be as you say. She said with a sort of sudden and splendid arrogance that was entirely altruistic:

' "I hope it'll stop that red-haired fool from fussing any more about the will. Does he think my husband, who has given up a crest and a coronet as old as the Crusades for his principles, would kill an old man in a summer-house for a legacy like that?" Then she laughed again and said, "My husband isn't killing anybody except in the way of business.

Why, he didn't even ask his friends to call on the secretary." Now, of course, I see what she meant.'

'I see part of what she meant, of course,' said Father Brown. 'What did she mean exactly by the secretary fussing about the will?'

Fiennes smiled as he answered. 'I wish you knew the secretary, Father Brown. It would be a joy to you to watch him make things hum, as he calls it. He made the house of mourning hum. He filled the funeral with all the snap and zip of the brightest sporting event. There was no holding him, after something had really happened. I've told you how he used to oversee the gardener as he did the garden, and how he instructed the lawyer in the law. Needless to say, he also instructed the surgeon in the practice of surgery; and as the surgeon was Dr Valentine, you may be sure it ended in accusing him of something worse than bad surgery. The secretary got it fixed in his red head that the doctor had committed the crime, and when the police arrived he was perfectly sublime. Need I say that he became, on the spot, the greatest of all amateur detectives? Sherlock Holmes never towered over Scotland Yard with more Titanic intellectual pride and scorn than Colonel Druce's private secretary over the police investigating Colonel Druce's death. I tell you it was a joy to see him. He strode about with an abstracted air, tossing his scarlet crest of hair and giving curt impatient replies. Of course it was his demeanour during these days that made Druce's daughter so wild with him. Of course he had a theory. It's just the sort of theory a man would have in a book; and Floyd is the sort of man who ought to be in a book. He'd be better fun and less bother in a book.'

'What was his theory?' asked the other.

'Oh, it was full of pep,' replied Fiennes gloomily. 'It would have been glorious copy if it could have held together for ten minutes longer. He said the Colonel was still alive when they found him in the summer-house, and the doctor killed him with the surgical instrument on pretence of cutting the clothes.'

'I see,' said the priest. 'I suppose he was lying flat on his face on the mud floor as a form of siesta.'

'It's wonderful; what hustle will do,' continued his informant. 'I believe Floyd would have got his great theory into the
papers at any rate, and perhaps had the doctor arrested, when
all these things were blown sky high as if by dynamite by the
discovery of that dead body lying under the Rock of Fortune.
And that's what we come back to after all. I suppose the
suicide is almost a confession. But nobody will ever know the
whole story.'

There was a silence, and then the priest said modestly: 'I
rather think I know the whole story.'

Fiennes stared. 'But look here,' he cried; 'how do you come
to know the whole story, or to be sure it's the true story?
You've been sitting here a hundred miles away writing a
sermon; do you mean to tell me you really know what happened already? If you've really come to the end, where in the
world do you begin? What started you off with your own
story?'

Father Brown jumped up with a very unusual excitement
and his first exclamation was like an explosion.

'The dog!' he cried. 'The dog, of course! You had the whole
story in your hands in the business of the dog on the beach, if
you'd only noticed the dog properly.'

Fiennes stared still more. 'But you told me before that my
feelings about the dog were all nonsense, and the dog had
nothing to do with it.'

'The dog had everything to do with it,' said Father Brown,
'as you'd have found out if you'd only treated the dog as a
dog, and not as God Almighty judging the souls of men.'

He paused in an embarrassed way for a moment, and then
said, with a rather pathetic air of apology: 'The truth is, I
happen to be awfully fond of dogs. And it seemed to me that
in all this lurid halo of dog superstitions nobody was really
thinking about the poor dog at all. To begin with a small
point, about his barking at the lawyer or growling at the
secretary. You asked how I could guess things a hundred miles
away; but honestly it's mostly to your credit, for you described
people so well that I know the types. A man like Traill, who
frowns usually and smiles suddenly, a man who fiddles with
things, especially at his throat, is a nervous, easily embar-

rassed man. I shouldn't wonder if Floyd, the efficient secretary, is nervy and jumpy, too; those Yankee hustlers often are.
Otherwise he wouldn't have cut his fingers on the shears and
dropped them when he heard Janet Druce scream.

'Now dogs hate nervous people. I don't know whether they
make the dog nervous, too; or whether, being after all a brute,
he is a bit of a bully; or whether his canine vanity (which is
colossal) is simply offended at not being liked. But anyhow
there was nothing in poor Nox protesting against those
people, except that he disliked them for being afraid of him.
Now I know you're awfully clever, and nobody of sense sneers
at cleverness. But I sometimes fancy, for instance, that you are
too clever to understand animals. Sometimes you are too
clever to understand men, especially when they act almost as
simply as animals. Animals are very literal; they live in a world
of truisms. Take this case: a dog barks at a man and a man
runs away from a dog. Now you do not seem to be quite
simple enough to see the fact: that the dog barked because he
disliked the man and the man fled because he was frightened
of the dog. They had no other motives and they needed none;
but you must read psychological mysteries into it and suppose
the dog had super-normal vision, and was a mysterious
mouthpiece of doom. You must suppose the man was running
away, not from the dog but from the hangman. And yet, if you
come to think of it, all this deeper psychology is exceedingly
improbable. If the dog really could completely and consciously realize the murderer of his master he wouldn't stand
yapping as he might at a curate at a tea-party; he's much more
likely to fly at his throat. And on the other hand, do you really
think a man who had hardened his heart to murder an old
friend and then walk about smiling at the old friend's family,
under the eyes of his old friend's daughter and post-mortem
doctor—do you think a man like that would be doubled up by
mere remorse because a dog barked? He might feel the tragic
irony of it; it might shake his soul, like any other tragic trifle.
But he wouldn't rush madly the length of a garden to escape
from the only witness whom he knew to be unable to talk.
People have a panic like that when they are frightened, not of
tragic ironies, but of teeth. The whole thing is simpler than
you can understand.

'But when we come to that business by the seashore, things are much more interesting. As you stated them, they were much more puzzling. I didn't understand that tale of the dog going in and out of the water; it didn't seem to me a doggy thing to do. If Nox had been very much upset about something else, he might possibly have refused to go after the stick at all. He'd probably go off nosing in whatever direction he suspected the mischief. But when once a dog is actually chasing a thing, a stone or a stick or a rabbit, my experience is that he won't stop for anything but the most peremptory command, and not always for that. That he should turn round because his mood changed seems to me unthinkable.'

'But he did turn round,' insisted Fiennes; 'and came back without the stick.'

'He came back without the stick for the best reason in the world,' replied the priest. 'He came back because he couldn't find it. He whined because he couldn't find it. That's the sort of thing a dog really does whine about. A dog is a devil of a ritualist. He is as particular about the precise routine of a game as a child about the precise repetition of a fairy-tale. In this case something had gone wrong with the game. He came back to complain seriously of the conduct of the stick. Never had such a thing happened before. Never had an eminent and distinguished dog been so treated by a rotten old walking-stick.'

'Why, what had the walking-stick done?' inquired the young man.

'It had sunk,' said Father Brown.

Fiennes said nothing, but continued to stare; and it was the priest who continued:

'It had sunk because it was not really a stick, but a rod of steel with a very thin shell of cane and a sharp point. In other words, it was a sword-stick. I suppose a murderer never gets rid of a bloody weapon so oddly and yet so naturally as by throwing it into the sea for a retriever.'

'I begin to see what you mean,' admitted Fiennes; 'but even if a sword-stick was used, I have no guess of how it was used.'

'I had a sort of guess,' said Father Brown, 'right at the beginning when you said the word summer-house. And another when you said that Druce wore a white coat. As long as everybody was looking for a short dagger, nobody thought of it; but if we admit a rather long blade like a rapier, it's not so impossible.'

He was leaning back, looking at the ceiling, and began like one going back to his own first thoughts and fundamentals.

'All that discussion about detective stories like the Yellow Room,* about a man found dead in sealed chambers which no one could enter, does not apply to the present case, because it is a summer-house. When we talk of a Yellow Room, or any room, we imply walls that are really homogeneous and impenetrable. But a summer-house is not made like that; it is often made, as it was in this case, of closely interlaced but separate boughs and strips of wood, in which there are chinks here and there. There was one of them just behind Druce's back as he sat in his chair up against the wall. But just as the room was a summer-house, so the chair was a basket-chair. That also was a lattice of loopholes. Lastly, the summer-house was close up under the hedge; and you have just told me that it was really a thin hedge. A man standing outside it could easily see, amid a network of twigs and branches and canes, one white spot of the Colonel's coat as plain as the white of a target.

'Now, you left the geography a little vague; but it was possible to put two and two together. You said the Rock of Fortune was not really high; but you also said it could be seen dominating the garden like a mountain-peak. In other words, it was very near the end of the garden, though your walk had taken you a long way round to it. Also, it isn't likely the young lady really howled so as to be heard half a mile. She gave an ordinary involuntary cry, and yet you heard it on the shore. And among other interesting things that you told me, may I remind you that you said Harry Druce had fallen behind to light his pipe under a hedge.'

Fiennes shuddered slightly. 'You mean he drew his blade there and sent it through the hedge at the white spot. But surely it was a very odd chance and a very sudden choice. Besides, he couldn't be certain the old man's money had passed to him, and as a fact it hadn't.'

Father Brown's face became animated.

'You misunderstand the man's character,' he said, as if he himself had known the man all his life. 'A curious but not unknown type of character. If he had really *known* the money would come to him, I seriously believe he wouldn't have done it. He would have seen it as the dirty thing it was.'

'Isn't that rather paradoxical?' asked the other.

'This man was a gambler,' said the priest, 'and a man in disgrace for having taken risks and anticipated orders. It was probably for something pretty unscrupulous, for every imperial police is more like a Russian secret police than we like to think. But he had gone beyond the line and failed. Now, the temptation of that type of man is to do a mad thing precisely because the risk will be wonderful in retrospect. He wants to say. "Nobody but I could have seized that chance or seen that it was then or never. What a wild and wonderful guess it was, when I put all those things together; Donald in disgrace; and the lawyer being sent for; and Herbert and I sent for at the same time—and then nothing more but the way the old man grinned at me and shook hands. Anybody would say I was mad to risk it; but that is how fortunes are made, by the man mad enough to have a little foresight." In short, it is the vanity of guessing. It is the megalomania of the gambler. The more incongruous the coincidence, the more instantaneous the decision, the more likely he is to snatch the chance. The accident, the very triviality of the white speck and the hole in the hedge intoxicated him like a vision of the world's desire. Nobody clever enough to see such a combination of accidents could be cowardly enough not to use them! That is how the devil talks to the gambler. But the devil himself would hardly have induced that unhappy man to go down in a dull, deliberate way and kill an old uncle from whom he'd always had expectations. It would be too respectable.'

He paused a moment, and then went on with a certain quiet emphasis.

'And now try to call up the scene, even as you saw it yourself. As he stood there, dizzy with his diabolical opportunity, he looked up and saw that strange outline that might have been the image of his own tottering soul; the one great crag poised perilously on the other like a pyramid on its point, and remembered that it was called the Rock of Fortune. Can you guess how such a man at such a moment would read such a signal? I think it strung him up to action and even to vigilance. He who would be a tower must not fear to be a toppling tower. Anyhow, he acted; his next difficulty was to cover his tracks. To be found with a sword-stick, let alone a blood-stained sword-stick, would be fatal in the search that was certain to follow. If he left it anywhere, it would be found and probably traced. Even if he threw it into the sea the action might be noticed, and thought noticeable—unless indeed he could think of some more natural way of covering the action. As you know, he did think of one, and a very good one. Being the only one of you with a watch, he told you it was not yet time to return, strolled a little farther and started the game of throwing in sticks for the retriever. But how his eyes must have rolled darkly over all that desolate sea-shore before they alighted on the dog!'

Fiennes nodded, gazing thoughtfully into space. His mind seemed to have drifted back to a less practical part of the narrative.

'It's queer,' he said, 'that the dog really was in the story after all.'

'The dog could almost have told you the story, if he could talk,' said the priest. 'All I complain of is that because he couldn't talk, you made up his story for him, and made him talk with the tongues of men and angels. It's part of something I've noticed more and more in the modern world, appearing in all sorts of newspaper rumours and conversational catchwords; something that's arbitrary without being authoritative. People readily swallow the untested claims of this, that, or the other. It's drowning all your old rationalism and scepticism, it's coming in like a sea; and the name of it is superstition.' He stood up abruptly, his face heavy with a sort of frown, and went on talking almost as if he were alone. 'It's the first effect of not believing in God that you lose your common sense and can't see things as they are. Anything that anybody talks about, and says there's a good deal in it, extends itself indefinitely like a vista in a nightmare. And a dog is an omen, and a cat is a mystery, and a pig is a mascot and a beetle is a scarab, calling up all the menagerie of polytheism from Egypt and old India; Dog Anubis* and great green-eyed Pasht* and all the holy howling Bulls of Bashan;* reeling back to the bestial gods of the beginning, escaping into elephants and snakes and crocodiles; and all because you are frightened of four words: "He was made Man".'

The young man got up with a little embarrassment, almost as if he had overheard a soliloquy. He called to the dog and left the room with vague but breezy farewells. But he had to call the dog twice; for the dog had remained behind quite motionless for a moment, looking up steadily at Father Brown as the wolf looked at St Francis.*

THE DAGGER WITH WINGS

FATHER BROWN, at one period of his life, found it difficult to hang his hat on a hat-peg without repressing a slight shudder. The origin of this idiosyncrasy was indeed a mere detail in much more complicated events; but it was perhaps the only detail that remained to him in his busy life to remind him of the whole business. Its remote origin was to be found in the facts which led Dr Boyne,* the medical officer attached to the police force, to send for the priest on a particular frosty morning in December.

Dr Boyne was a big dark Irishman, one of those rather baffling Irishmen to be found all over the world, who will talk scientific scepticism, materialism and cynicism at length and at large, but who never dream of referring anything touching the ritual of religion to anything except the traditional religion of their native land. It would be hard to say whether their creed is a very superficial varnish or a very fundamental substratum; but most probably it is both, with a mass of materialism in between. Anyhow, when he thought that matters of that sort might be involved, he asked Father Brown to call, though he made no pretence of preference for that aspect of them.

'I'm not sure I want you, you know,' was his greeting. 'I'm not sure about anything yet. I'm hanged if I can make out whether it's a case for a doctor, or a policeman, or a priest.'

'Well,' said Father Brown with a smile, 'as I suppose you're both a policeman and a doctor, I seem to be rather in a minority.'

'I admit you're what politicians call an instructed minority,' replied the doctor. 'I mean, I know you've had to do a little in our line as well as your own. But it's precious hard to say whether this business is in your line or ours, or merely in the line of the Commissioners in Lunacy.* We've just had a message from a man living near here, in that white house on the hill, asking for protection against a murderous persecution. We've gone into the facts as far as we could, and perhaps I'd better tell you the story, as it is supposed to have happened, from the beginning.

'It seems that a man named Aylmer, who was a wealthy landowner in the West Country, married rather late in life and had three sons, Philip, Stephen and Arnold. But in his bachelor days, when he thought he would have no heir, he had adopted a boy whom he thought very brilliant and promising, who went by the name of John Strake. His origin seems to be vague; they say he was a foundling; some say he was a gipsy. I think the last notion is mixed up with the fact that Aylmer in his old age dabbled in all sorts of dingy occultism, including palmistry and astrology, and his three sons say that Strake encouraged him in it. But they said a great many other things besides that. They said Strake was an amazing scoundrel, and especially an amazing liar; a genius in inventing lies on the spur of the moment, and telling them so as to deceive a detective. But that might very well be a natural prejudice, in the light of what happened. Perhaps you can more or less imagine what happened. The old man left practically everything to the adopted son; and when he died the three real sons disputed the will. They said their father had been frightened into surrender and, not to put too fine a point on it, into gibbering idiocy. They said Strake had the strangest and most cunning ways of getting at him, in spite of the nurses and the family, and terrorizing him on his death-bed. Anyhow, they seemed to have proved something about the dead man's mental condition, for the courts set aside the will and the sons inherited. Strake is said to have broken out in the most dreadful fashion, and sworn he would kill all three of them, one after another, and that nothing could hide them from his vengeance. It is the third or last of the brothers, Arnold Aylmer, who is asking for police protection.'

'Third and last,' said the priest, looking at him gravely.

'Yes,' said Boyne. 'The other two are dead.'

There was a silence before he continued. 'That is where the doubt comes in. There is no proof they were murdered, but they might possibly have been. The eldest, who took up his position as squire, was supposed to have committed suicide in his garden. The second, who went into trade as a manufacturer, was knocked on the head by the machinery in his factory; he might very well have taken a false step and fallen. But if Strake did kill them, he is certainly very cunning in his way of getting to work and getting away. On the other hand, it's more than likely that the whole thing is a mania of conspiracy founded on a coincidence. Look here, what I want is this. I want somebody of sense, who isn't an official, to go up and have a talk to this Mr Arnold Aylmer, and form an impression of him. You know what a man with a delusion is like, and how a man looks when he is telling the truth. I want you to be the advance guard, before we take the matter up.'

'It seems rather odd,' said Father Brown, 'that you haven't had to take it up before. If there is anything in this business, it seems to have been going on for a good time. Is there any particular reason why he should send for you just now, any more than any other time?'

'That had occurred to me, as you may imagine,' answered Dr Boyne. 'He does give a reason, but I confess it is one of the things that make me wonder whether the whole thing isn't only the whim of some half-witted crank. He declares that all his servants have suddenly gone on strike and left him, so that he is obliged to call on the police to look after his house. And on making inquiries, I certainly do find that there has been a general exodus of servants from that house on the hill; and of course the town is full of tales, very one-sided tales I dare say. Their account of it seems to be that their employer had become quite impossible in his fidgets and fears and exactions; that he wanted them to guard the house like sentries, or sit up like night nurses in a hospital; that they could never be left alone because he must never be left alone. So they all announced in a loud voice that he was a lunatic, and left. Of course that does not prove he is a lunatic; but it seems rather rum nowadays for a man to expect his valet or his parlourmaid to act as an armed guard.'

'And so,' said the priest with a smile, 'he wants a policeman to act as his parlour-maid because his parlour-maid won't act as a policeman.'

'I thought that rather thick, too,' agreed the doctor; 'but I can't take the responsibility of a flat refusal till I've tried a compromise. You are the compromise.'

'Very well,' said Father Brown simply. 'I'll go and call on him now if you like.'

The rolling country round the little town was sealed and bound with frost, and the sky was as clear and cold as steel, except in the north-east, where clouds with lurid haloes were beginning to climb up the sky. It was against these darker and more sinister colours that the house on the hill gleamed with a row of pale pillars, forming a short colonnade of the classical sort. A winding road led up to it across the curve of the down, and plunged into a mass of dark bushes. Just before it reached the bushes the air seemed to grow colder and colder, as if he were approaching an ice-house or the North Pole. But he was a highly practical person, never entertaining such fancies except as fancies. And he merely cocked his eye at the great livid cloud crawling up over the house, and remarked cheerfully:

'It's going to snow.'

Through a low ornamental iron gateway of the Italianate pattern he entered a garden having something of that desolation which only belongs to the disorder of orderly things. Deep-green growths were grey with the faint powder of the frost, large weeds had fringed the fading pattern of the flower-beds as if in a ragged frame; and the house stood as if waist-high in a stunted forest of shrubs and bushes. The vegetation consisted largely of evergreens or very hardy plants; and though it was thus thick and heavy, it was too northern to be called luxuriant. It might be described as an Arctic jungle. So it was in some sense with the house itself, which had a row of columns and a classical façade, which might have looked out on the Mediterranean; but which seemed now to be withering in the wind of the North Sea. Classical ornament here and there accentuated the contrast; caryatides* and carved masks of comedy or tragedy looked down from corners of the building upon the grey confusion of the garden paths; but the faces seemed to be frost-bitten. The very volutes of the capitals might have curled up with the cold.

Father Brown went up the grassy steps to a square porch flanked by big pillars and knocked at the door. About four minutes afterwards he knocked again. Then he stood still patiently waiting with his back to the door and looked out on the slowly darkening landscape. It was darkening under the shadow of that one great continent of cloud that had come flying out of the north; and even as he looked out beyond the pillars of the porch, which seemed huge and black above him in the twilight, he saw the opalescent crawling rim of the great cloud as it sailed over the roof and bowed over the porch like a canopy. The grey canopy with its faintly coloured fringes seemed to sink lower and lower upon the garden beyond, until what had recently been a clear and pale-hued winter sky was left in a few silver ribbons and rags like a sickly sunset. Father Brown waited, and there was no sound within.

Then he betook himself briskly down the steps and round the house to look for another entrance. He eventually found one, a side door in the flat wall, and on this also he hammered and outside this also he waited. Then he tried the handle and found the door apparently bolted or fastened in some fashion; and then he moved along that side of the house, musing on the possibilities of the position, and wondering whether the eccentric Mr Aylmer had barricaded himself too deep in the house to hear any kind of summons; or whether perhaps he would barricade himself all the more, on the assumption that any summons must be the challenge of the avenging Strake. It might be that the decamping servants had only unlocked one door when they left in the morning, and that their master had locked that; but whatever he might have done it was unlikely that they, in the mood of that moment, had looked so carefully to the defences. He continued his prowl round the place; it was not really a large place, though perhaps a little pretentious; and in a few moments he found he had made the complete circuit. A moment after he found what he suspected and sought. The French window of one room, curtained and shadowed with creeper, stood open by a crack, doubtless accidently left ajar, and he found himself in a central room, comfortably upholstered in a rather old-fashioned way, with a staircase leading up from it on one side and a door leading out of it on the other. Immediately opposite him was another door with red glass let into it, a little gaudily for later tastes; something that looked like a red-robed figure in cheap stained glass. On a round table to the right stood a sort of aquarium—a great bowl full of greenish water, in which fishes and similar things moved about as in a tank; and just opposite it a plant of the palm variety with very large green leaves. All this looked so very dusty and Early Victorian that the telephone, visible in the curtained alcove, was almost a surprise.

'Who is that?' a voice called out sharply and rather suspiciously from behind the stained-glass door.

'Could I see Mr Aylmer?' asked the priest apologetically.

The door opened and a gentleman in a peacock-green dressing-gown came out with an inquiring look. His hair was rather rough and untidy, as if he had been in bed or lived in a state of slowly getting up, but his eyes were not only awake but alert, and some would have said alarmed. Father Brown knew that the contradiction was likely enough in a man who had rather run to seed under the shadow either of a delusion or a danger. He had a fine aquiline face when seen in profile, but when seen full face the first impression was of the untidiness and even the wilderness of his loose brown beard.

'I am Mr Aylmer,' he said, 'but I have got out of the way of expecting visitors.'

Something about Mr Aylmer's unrestful eye prompted the priest to go straight to the point. If the man's persecution was only a monomania, he would be the less likely to resent it.

'I was wondering,' said Father Brown softly, 'whether it is quite true that you never expect visitors.'

'You are right,' replied his host steadily. 'I always expect one visitor. And he may be the last.'

'I hope not,' said Father Brown, 'but at least I am relieved to infer that I do not look very like him.'

Mr Aylmer shook himself with a sort of savage laugh. 'You certainly do not,' he said.

'Mr Aylmer,' said Father Brown frankly, 'I apologize for the liberty, but some friends of mine have told me about your trouble, and asked me to see if I could do anything for you. The truth is, I have some little experience in affairs like this.'

'There are no affairs like this,' said Aylmer.

'You mean,' observed Father Brown, 'that the tragedies in your unfortunate family were not normal deaths?'

'I mean they were not even normal murders,' answered the other. 'The man who is hounding us all to death is a hell-hound, and his power is from hell.'

'All evil has one origin,' said the priest gravely. 'But how do you know they were not normal murders?'

Aylmer answered with a gesture which offered his guest a chair; then he seated himself slowly in another, frowning, with his hands on his knees; but when he looked up his expression had grown milder and more thoughtful, and his voice was quite cordial and composed.

'Sir,' he said, 'I don't want you to imagine that I'm in the least an unreasonable person. I have come to these conclusions by reason, because unfortunately reason really leads there. I have read a great deal on these subjects; for I was the only one who inherited my father's scholarship in somewhat obscure matters, and I have since inherited his library. But what I tell you does not rest on what I have read but on what I have seen.'

Father Brown nodded, and the other proceeded, as if picking his words:

'In my elder brother's case I was not certain at first. There were no marks or footprints where he was found shot, and the pistol was left beside him. But he had just received a threatening letter, certainly from our enemy, for it was marked with a sign like a winged dagger, which was one of his infernal cabalistic* tricks. And a servant said she had seen something moving along the garden wall in the twilight that was much too large to be a cat. I leave it there; all I can say is that if the murderer came, he managed to leave no traces of his coming. But when my brother Stephen died it was different; and since then I have known. A machine was working in an open scaffolding under the factory tower; I scaled the platform a moment after he had fallen under the iron hammer that struck him; I did not see anything else strike him, but I saw what I saw.

'A great drift of factory smoke was rolling between me and the factory tower; but through a rift of it I saw on the top of it a dark human figure wrapped in what looked like a black cloak. Then the sulphurous smoke drove between us again; and when it cleared I looked up at the distant chimney—there was nobody there. I am a rational man, and I will ask all rational men how he had reached that dizzy unapproachable turret, and how he left it.'

He stared across at the priest with a sphinx-like challenge; then after a silence he said abruptly:

'My brother's brains were knocked out, but his body was not much damaged. And in his pocket we found one of those warning messages dated the day before and stamped with the flying dagger.

'I am sure,' he went on gravely, 'that the symbol of the winged dagger is not merely arbitrary or accidental. Nothing about that abominable man is accidental. He is all design; though it is indeed a most dark and intricate design. His mind is woven not only out of elaborate schemes but out of all sorts of secret languages and signs, and dumb signals and wordless pictures which are the names of nameless things. He is the worst sort of man that the world knows: he is the wicked mystic. Now, I don't pretend to penetrate all that is conveyed by this symbol; but it seems surely that it must have a relation to all that was most remarkable, or even incredible, in his movements as he had hovered round my unfortunate family. Is there no connexion between the idea of a winged weapon and the mystery by which Philip was struck dead on his own lawn without the lightest touch of any footprint having disturbed the dust or grass? Is there no connexion between the plumed poignard flying like a feathered arrow and that figure which hung on the far top of the toppling chimney, clad in a cloak for pinions?'

'You mean,' said Father Brown thoughtfully, 'that he is in a perpetual state of levitation.'

'Simon Magus* did it,' replied Aylmer, 'and it was one of the commonest predictions of the Dark Ages that Antichrist* would be able to fly. Anyhow, there was the flying dagger on the document; and whether or no it could fly, it could certainly strike.'

'Did you notice what sort of paper it was on?' asked Father Brown, 'Common paper?'

The sphinx-like face broke abruptly into a harsh laugh.

'You can see what they're like,' said Aylmer grimly, 'for I got one myself this morning.'

He was leaning back in his chair now, with his long legs thrust out from under the green dressing-gown, which was a little short for him, and his bearded chin pillowed on his chest. Without moving otherwise, he thrust his hand deep in the dressing-gown pocket and held out a fluttering scrap of paper at the end of a rigid arm. His whole attitude was suggestive of a sort of paralysis, that was both rigidity and collapse. But the next remark of the priest had a curious effect of rousing him.

Father Brown was blinking in his short-sighted way at the paper presented to him. It was a singular sort of paper, rough without being common, as from an artist's sketch-book; and on it was drawn boldly in red ink a dagger decorated with wings like the rod of Hermes, with the written words, 'Death comes the day after this, as it came to your brothers.'

Father Brown tossed the paper on the floor and sat bolt upright in his chair.

'You mustn't let that sort of stuff stupefy you,' he said sharply. 'These devils always try to make us helpless by making us hopeless.'

Rather to his surprise, an awakening wave went over the prostrate figure, which sprang from its chair as if startled out of a dream.

'You're right, you're right!' cried Aylmer with a rather uncanny animation; 'and the devils shall find I'm not so hopeless after all, nor so helpless either. Perhaps I have more hope and better help than you fancy.'

He stood with his hands in his pockets, frowning down at the priest, who had a momentary doubt, during that strained silence, about whether the man's long peril had not touched the man's brain. But when he spoke it was quite soberly.

'I believe my unfortunate brothers failed because they used the wrong weapons. Philip carried a revolver, and that was how his death came to be called suicide. Stephen had police protection, but he also had a sense of what made him ridiculous; and he could not allow a policeman to climb up a ladder after him to a scaffolding where he stood only a moment. They were both scoffers, reacting into scepticism from the strange mysticism of my father's last days. But I always knew there was more in my father than they understood. It is true that by studying magic he fell at last under the blight of black magic; the black magic of this scoundrel Strake. But my brothers were wrong about the antidote. The antidote to black magic is not brute materialism or worldly wisdom. The antidote to black magic is white magic.'

'It rather depends,' said Father Brown, 'what you mean by white magic.'

'I mean silver magic,' said the other, in a low voice, like one speaking of a secret revelation. Then after a silence he said: 'Do you know what I mean by silver magic? Excuse me a moment.'

He turned and opened the central door with the red glass and went into a passage beyond it. The house had less depth than Brown had supposed; instead of the door opening into interior rooms, the corridor it revealed ended in another door on the garden. The door of one room was on one side of the passage; doubtless, the priest told himself, the proprietor's bedroom, whence he had rushed out in his dressing-gown. There was nothing else on that side but an ordinary hat-stand with the ordinary dingy cluster of old hats and overcoats; but on the other side was something more interesting: a very dark old oak sideboard laid out with some old silver, and overhung by a trophy or ornament of old weapons. It was by this that Arnold Aylmer halted, looking up at a long, antiquated pistol with a bell-shaped mouth.

The door at the end of the passage was barely open, and through the crack came a streak of white daylight. The priest had very quick instincts about natural things, and something in the unusual brilliancy of that white line told him what had happened outside. It was indeed what he had prophesied when he was approaching the house. He ran past his rather startled host and opened the door; to face something that was at once a blank and a blaze. What he had seen shining through the crack was not only the most negative whiteness of daylight but the positive whiteness of snow. All round, the sweeping fall of the country was covered with that shining pallor that seems at once hoary and innocent.

'Here is white magic anyhow,' said Father Brown in his cheerful voice. Then, as he turned back into the hall, he murmured, 'And silver magic too, I suppose,' for the white lustre touched the silver with splendour and lit up the old steel here and there in the darkling armoury. The shaggy head of the brooding Aylmer seemed to have a halo of silver fire, as he turned with his face in shadow and the outlandish pistol in his hand.

'Do you know why I choose this sort of old blunderbuss?' he asked. 'Because I can load it with this sort of bullet.'

He had picked up a small apostle spoon from the sideboard, and by sheer violence broke off the small figure at the top. 'Let us go back into the other room,' he added.

'Did you ever read about the death of Dundee?' he asked when they had reseated themselves. He had recovered from his momentary annoyance at the priest's restlessness. 'Graham of Claverhouse, you know, who persecuted the Covenanters* and had a black horse that could ride straight up a precipice. Don't you know he could only be shot with a silver bullet, because he had sold himself to the Devil? That's one comfort about you; at least you know enough to believe in the Devil.'

'Oh, yes,' replied Father Brown, 'I believe in the Devil. What I don't believe in is the Dundee. I mean the Dundee of Covenanting legends, with his nightmare of a horse. John

Graham was simply a seventeenth-century professional soldier, rather better than most. If he dragooned them it was because he was a dragoon, but not a dragon. Now my experience is that it's not that sort of swaggering blade who sells himself to the Devil. The devil-worshippers I've known were quite different. Not to mention names, which might cause a social flutter, I'll take a man in Dundee's own day. Have you ever heard of Dalrymple of Stair?'*

'No,' replied the other gruffly.

'You've heard of what he did,' said Father Brown, 'and it was worse than anything Dundee ever did; yet he escapes the infamy by oblivion. He was the man who made the Massacre of Glencoe.* He was a very learned man and lucid lawyer, a statesman with very serious and enlarged ideas of statesmanship, a quiet man with a very refined and intellectual face. That's the sort of man who sells himself to the Devil.'

Aylmer half started from his chair with an enthusiasm of eager assent.

'By God! you are right,' he cried. 'A refined intellectual face! That is the face of John Strake.'

Then he raised himself and stood looking at the priest with a curious concentration. 'If you will wait here a little while,' he said, 'I will show you something.'

He went back through the central door, closing it after him; going, the priest presumed, to the old sideboard or possibly to his bedroom. Father Brown remained seated, gazing abstractedly at the carpet, where a faint red glimmer shone from the glass in the doorway. Once it seemed to brighten like a ruby and then darkened again, as if the sun of that stormy day had passed from cloud to cloud. Nothing moved except the aquatic creatures which floated to and fro in the dim green bowl. Father Brown was thinking hard.

A minute or two afterwards he got up and slipped quietly to the alcove of the telephone, where he rang up his friend Dr Boyne, at the official headquarters. 'I wanted to tell you about Aylmer and his affairs,' he said quietly. 'It's a queer story, but I rather think there's something in it. If I were you I'd send some men up here straight away; four or five men, I think, and surround the house. If anything does happen there'll probably be something startling in the way of an escape.'

Then he went back and sat down again, staring at the dark carpet, which again glowed blood-red with the light from the glass door. Something in that filtered light set his mind drifting on certain borderlands of thought, with the first white daybreak before the coming of colour, and all that mystery which is alternately veiled and revealed in the symbol of windows and of doors.

An inhuman howl in a human voice came from beyond the closed doors; almost simultaneously with the noise of firing. Before the echoes of the shot had died away the door was violently flung open and his host staggered into the room, the dressing-gown half torn from his shoulder and the long pistol smoking in his hand. He seemed to be shaking in every limb, yet he was shaken in part with an unnatural laughter.

'Glory be to the White Magic!' he cried; 'Glory be to the silver bullet! The hell-hound has hunted once too often, and my brothers are avenged at last.'

He sank into a chair and the pistol slid from his hand and fell on the floor. Father Brown darted past him, slipped through the glass door and went down the passage. As he did so he put his hand on the handle of the bedroom door, as if half intending to enter; then he stooped a moment, as if examining something—and then he ran to the outer door and opened it.

On the field of snow, which had been so blank a little while before, lay one black object. At the first glance it looked a little like an enormous bat. A second glance showed that it was, after all, a human figure; fallen on its face, the whole head covered by a broad black hat having something of a Latin-American look; while the appearance of bat-wings came from the two flaps or loose sleeves of a very vast black cloak spread out, perhaps by accident, to their utmost length on either side. Both the hands were hidden, though Father Brown thought he could detect the position of one of them, and saw close to it, under the edge of the cloak, the glimmer of some metallic weapon. The main effect, however, was curiously like that of the simple extravagances of heraldry; like a black eagle displayed on a white ground. But by walking round it and peering under the hat the priest got a glimpse of the face, which was indeed what his host had called refined and intellectual; even sceptical and austere: the face of John Strake.

'Well, I'm jiggered,' muttered Father Brown. 'It really does look like some vast vampire that has swooped down like a bird.'

'How else could he have come?' came a voice from the doorway, and Father Brown looked up to see Aylmer once more standing there.

'Couldn't he have walked?' replied Father Brown evasively.

Aylmer stretched out his arm and swept the white landscape with a gesture.

'Look at the snow,' he said in a deep voice that had a sort of roll and thrill in it. 'Is not the snow unspotted—pure as the white magic you yourself called it? Is there a speck on it for miles, save that one foul black blot that has fallen there? There are no footprints, but a few of yours and mine; there are none approaching the house from anywhere.'

Then he looked at the little priest for a moment with a concentrated and curious expression, and said:

'I will tell you something else. That cloak he flies with is too long to walk with. He was not a very tall man, and it would trail behind him like a royal train. Stretch it out over his body, if you like, and see.'

'What happened to you both?' asked Father Brown abruptly.

'It was too swift to describe,' answered Aylmer. 'I had looked out of the door and was turning back when there came a kind of rushing of wind all around me, as if I were being buffeted by a wheel revolving in mid-air. I spun round somehow and fired blindly; and then I saw nothing but what you see now. But I am morally certain you wouldn't see it if I had not had a silver shot in my gun. It would have been a different body lying there in the snow.'

'By the way,' remarked Father Brown, 'shall we leave it lying there in the snow? Or would you like it taken into your room—I suppose that's your bedroom in the passage?'

'No, no,' replied Aylmer hastily; 'we must leave it there till the police have seen it. Besides, I've had as much of such things as I can stand for the moment. Whatever else happens,

I'm going to have a drink. After that, they can hang me if they like.'

Inside the central apartment, between the palm plant and the bowl of fishes, Aylmer tumbled into a chair. He had nearly knocked the bowl over as he lurched into the room, but he had managed to find the decanter of brandy after plunging his hand rather blindly into several cupboards and corners. He did not at any time look like a methodical person; but at this moment his distraction must have been extreme. He drank with a long gulp and began to talk rather feverishly, as if to fill up a silence.

'I see you are still doubtful,' he said, 'though you have seen the thing with your own eyes. Believe me, there was something more behind the quarrel between the spirit of Strake and the spirit of the house of Aylmer. Besides, you have no business to be an unbeliever. You ought to stand for all the things these stupid people call superstitions. Come now, don't you think there's a lot in those old wives' tales about luck and charms and so on, silver bullets included? What do you say about them as a Catholic?'

'I say I'm an agnostic,' replied Father Brown, smiling.

'Nonsense,' said Aylmer impatiently. 'It's your business to believe things.'

'Well, I do believe some things, of course,' conceded Father Brown; 'and therefore, of course, I don't believe other things.'

Aylmer was leaning forward, and looking at him with a strange intensity that was almost like that of a mesmerist.

'You do believe it,' he said. 'You do believe everything. We all believe everything, even when we deny everything. The deniers believe. The unbelievers believe. Don't you feel in your heart that these contradictions do not really contradict: that there is a cosmos that contains them all? The soul goes round upon a wheel of stars and all things return; perhaps Strake and I have striven in many shapes, beast against beast and bird against bird, and perhaps we shall strive for ever. But since we seek and need each other, even that eternal hatred is an eternal love. Good and evil go round in a wheel that is one thing and not many. Do you not realize in your heart, do you not believe behind all your beliefs, that there is but one reality and we are its shadows; and that all things are but aspects of one thing: a centre where men melt into Man and Man into God?'

'No,' said Father Brown.

Outside, twilight had begun to fall, in that phase of such a snow-laden evening when the land looks brighter than the sky. In the porch of the main entrance, visible through a half-curtained window, Father Brown could dimly see a bulky figure standing. He glanced casually at the French windows through which he had originally entered, and saw they were darkened with two equally motionless figures. The inner door with the coloured glass stood slightly ajar; and he could see in the short corridor beyond, the ends of two long shadows, exaggerated and distorted by the level light of evening, but still like grey caricatures of the figures of men. Dr Boyne had already obeyed his telephone message. The house was surrounded.

'What is the good of saying no?' insisted his host, still with the same hypnotic stare. 'You have seen part of that eternal drama with your own eyes. You have seen the threat of John Strake to slay Arnold Aylmer by black magic. You have seen Arnold Aylmer slay John Strake by white magic. You see Arnold Aylmer alive and talking to you now. And yet you do not believe it.'

'No, I do not believe it,' said Father Brown, and rose from his chair like one terminating a visit.

'Why not?' asked the other.

The priest only lifted his voice a little, but it sounded in every corner of the room like a bell.

'Because you are not Arnold Aylmer,' he said. 'I know who you are. Your name is John Strake; and you have murdered the last of the brothers, who is lying outside in the snow.'

A ring of white showed round the iris of the other man's eyes; he seemed to be making, with bursting eyeballs, a last effort to mesmerize and master his companion. Then he made a sudden movement sideways; and even as he did so the door behind him opened and a big detective in plain clothes put one hand quietly on his shoulder. The other hand hung down, but it held a revolver. The man looked wildly round, and saw plain-clothes men in all corners of the quiet room.

That evening Father Brown had another and longer conversation with Dr Boyne about the tragedy of the Aylmer family. By that time there was no longer any doubt of the central fact of the case, for John Strake had confessed his identity and even confessed his crimes; only it would be truer to say that he boasted of his victories. Compared to the fact that he had rounded off his life's work with the last Aylmer lying dead, everything else, including existence itself, seemed to be indifferent to him.

'The man is a sort of monomaniac,' said Father Brown. 'He is not interested in any other matter; not even in any other murder. I owe him something for that; for I had to comfort myself with the reflection a good many times this afternoon. As has doubtless occurred to you, instead of weaving all that wild but ingenious romance about winged vampires and silver bullets, he might have put an ordinary leaden bullet into me, and walked out of the house. I assure you it occurred quite frequently to me.'

'I wonder why he didn't,' observed Boyne. 'I don't understand it; but I don't understand anything yet. How on earth did you discover it, and what in the world did you discover?'

'Oh, you provided me with very valuable information,' replied Father Brown modestly, 'especially the one piece of information that really counted. I mean the statement that Strake was a very inventive and imaginative liar, with great presence of mind in producing his lies. This afternoon he needed it; but he rose to the occasion. Perhaps his only mistake was in choosing a preternatural story; he had the notion that because I am a clergyman I should believe anything. Many people have little notions of that kind.'

'But I can't make head or tail of it,' said the doctor. 'You must really begin at the beginning.'

'The beginning of it was a dressing-gown,' said Father Brown simply. 'It was the one really good disguise I've ever known. When you meet a man in a house with a dressing-gown on, you assume quite automatically that he's in his own house. I assumed it myself; but afterwards queer little things began to happen. When he took the pistol down he clicked it at arm's length, as a man does to make sure a strange weapon isn't loaded; of course he would know whether the pistols in his own hall were loaded or not. I didn't like the way he looked for the brandy, or the way he nearly barged into the bowl of fishes. For a man who has a fragile thing of that sort as a fixture in his rooms gets a quite mechanical habit of avoiding it. But these things might possibly have been fancies; the first real point was this. He came out from the little passage between the two doors; and in that passage there's only one other door leading to a room; so I assumed it was the bedroom he had just come from. I tried the handle; but it was locked. I thought this odd; and looked through the keyhole. It was an utterly bare room, obviously deserted; no bed, no anything. Therefore he had not come from inside any room, but from outside the house. And when I saw that, I think I saw the whole picture.

'Poor Arnold Aylmer doubtless slept and perhaps lived upstairs, and came down in his dressing-gown and passed through the red glass door. At the end of the passage, black against the winter daylight, he saw the enemy of his house. He saw a tall bearded man in a broad-brimmed black hat and a large flapping black cloak. He did not see much more in this world. Strake sprang on him, throttling or stabbing him; we cannot be sure till the inquest. Then Strake, standing in the narrow passage between the hat-stand and the old sideboard, and looking down in triumph on the last of his foes, heard something he had not expected. He heard footsteps in the parlour beyond. It was myself entering by the french windows.

'His masquerade was a miracle of promptitude. It involved not only a disguise but a romance—an impromptu romance. He took off his big black hat and cloak and put on the dead man's dressing-gown. Then he did a rather grisly thing; at least a thing that affects my fancy as more grisly than the rest. He hung the corpse like a coat on one of the hatpegs. He draped it in his own long cloak, and found it hung well below the heels; he covered the head entirely with his own wide hat. It was the only possible way of hiding it in that little passage with the locked door; but it was really a very clever one. I myself walked past the hat-stand once without knowing it was anything but a hat-stand. I think that unconsciousness of mine will always give me a shiver.

'He might perhaps have left it at that; but I might have discovered the corpse at any minute; and, hung where it was, it was a corpse calling for what you might call an explanation. He adopted the bolder stroke of discovering it himself and explaining it himself.

'Then there dawned on this strange and frightfully fertile mind the conception of a story of substitution; the reversal of the parts. He had already assumed the part of Arnold Aylmer. Why should not his dead enemy assume the part of John Strake? There must have been something in that topsy-turvydom to take the fancy of that darkly fanciful man. It was like some frightful fancy-dress ball to which the two mortal enemies were to go dressed up as each other. Only, the fancy-dress ball was to be a dance of death; and one of the dancers would be dead. That is why I can imagine that man putting it in his own mind, and I can imagine him smiling.'

Father Brown was gazing into vacancy with his large grey eyes, which, when not blurred by his trick of blinking, were the one notable thing in his face. He went on speaking simply and seriously.

'All things are from God; and above all, reason and imagination and the great gifts of the mind. They are good in themselves; and we must not altogether forget their origin even in their perversion. Now this man had in him a very noble power to be perverted; the power of telling stories. He was a great novelist; only he had twisted his fictive power to practical and to evil ends; to deceiving men with false fact instead of with true fiction. It began with his deceiving old Aylmer with elaborate excuses and ingeniously detailed lies; but even that may have been, at the beginning, little more than the tall stories and tarradiddles of the child who may say equally he has seen the King of England or the King of the Fairies. It grew strong in him through the vice that perpetuates all vices, pride; he grew more and more vain of his promptitude in producing stories, of his originality and subtlety in developing them. That is what the young Aylmers meant by saying that he could always cast a spell over their father; and it was true. It was the sort of spell that the story-teller cast over the tyrant in the Arabian Nights.* And to the last he walked the world with the pride of a poet, and with the false yet unfathomable courage of a great liar. He could always produce more Arabian Nights if ever his neck was in danger. And to-day his neck was in danger.

'But I am sure, as I say, that he enjoyed it as a fantasy as well as a conspiracy. He set about the task of telling the true story the wrong way round: of treating the dead man as living and the live man as dead. He had already got into Aylmer's dressing-gown; he proceeded to get into Aylmer's body and soul. He looked at the corpse as if it were his own corpse lying cold in the snow. Then he spread-eagled it in that strange fashion to suggest the sweeping descent of a bird of prey, and decked it out not only in his own dark and flying garments but in a whole dark fairy-tale about the black bird that could only fall by the silver bullet. I do not know whether it was the silver glittering on the sideboard or the snow shining beyond the door that suggested to his intensely artistic temperament the theme of white magic and the white metal used against magicians. But whatever its origin, he made it his own like a poet; and did it very promptly, like a practical man. He completed the exchange and reversal of parts by flinging the corpse out on to the snow as the corpse of Strake. He did his best to work up a creepy conception of Strake as something hovering in the air everywhere, a harpy with wings of speed and claws of death; to explain the absence of footprints and other things. For one piece of artistic impudence I hugely admire him. He actually turned one of the contradictions in his case into an argument for it; and said that the man's cloak being too long for him proved that he never walked on the ground like an ordinary mortal. But he looked at me very hard while he said that; and something told me that he was at that moment trying a very big bluff.'

Dr Boyne looked thoughtful. 'Had you discovered the truth by then?' he asked. 'There is something very queer and close to the nerves, I think, about notions affecting identity. I don't know whether it would be more weird to get a guess like that swiftly or slowly. I wonder when you suspected and when you were sure.'

'I think I really suspected when I telephoned to you,' replied his friend. 'And it was nothing more than the red light from the closed door brightening and darkening on the carpet. It looked like a splash of blood that grew vivid as it cried for vengeance. Why should it change like that? I knew the sun had not come out; it could only be because the second door behind it had been opened and shut on the garden. But if he had gone out and seen his enemy then, he would have raised the alarm then; and it was some time afterwards that the fracas occurred. I began to feel he had gone out to do something . . . to prepare something . . . but as to when I was certain, that is a different matter. I knew that right at the end he was trying to hypnotize me, to master me by the black art of eyes like talismans and a voice like an incantation. That's what he used to do with old Aylmer, no doubt. But it wasn't only the way he said it, it was what he said. It was the religion and philosophy of it.'

'I'm afraid I'm a practical man,' said the doctor with gruff humour, 'and I don't bother much about religion and philosophy.'

'You'll never be a practical man till you do,' said Father Brown. 'Look here, doctor; you know me pretty well; I think you know I'm not a bigot. You know I know there are all sorts in all religions; good men in bad ones and bad men in good ones. But there's just one little fact I've learned simply as a practical man, an entirely practical point, that I've picked up by experience, like the tricks of an animal or the trademark of a good wine. I've scarcely ever met a criminal who philosophized at all, who didn't philosophize along those lines of orientalism and recurrence and reincarnation, and the wheel of destiny and the serpent biting its own tail. I have found merely in practice that there is a curse on the servants of that serpent; on their belly shall they go and the dust shall they eat;* and there was never a blackguard or a profligate born who could not talk that sort of spirituality. It may not be like that in its real religious origins; but here in our working world it is the religion of rascals; and I knew it was a rascal who was speaking.'

'Why,' said Boyne, 'I should have thought that a rascal could pretty well profess any religion he chose.'

'Yes,' assented the other; 'he could profess any religion; that is he could pretend to any religion, if it was all a pretence. If it was mere mechanical hypocrisy and nothing else, no doubt it could be done by a mere mechanical hypocrite. Any sort of mask can be put on any sort of face. Anybody can learn certain phrases or state verbally that he holds certain views. I can go out into the street and state that I am a Wesleyan Methodist* or a Sandemanian,* though I fear in no very convincing accent. But we are talking about an artist; and for the enjoyment of the artist the mask must be to some extent moulded on the face. What he makes outside him must correspond to something inside him; he can only make his effects out of some of the materials of his soul. I suppose he could have said he was a Wesleyan Methodist; but he could never be an eloquent Methodist as he can be an eloquent mystic and fatalist. I am talking of the sort of ideal such a man thinks of if he really tries to be idealistic. It was his whole game with me to be as idealistic as possible; and whenever that is attempted by that sort of man, you will generally find it is that sort of ideal. That sort of man may be dripping with gore; but he will always be able to tell you quite sincerely that Buddhism is better than Christianity. Nay, he will tell you quite sincerely that Buddhism is more Christian than Christianity. That alone is enough to throw a hideous and ghastly ray of light on his notion of Christianity.'

'Upon my soul,' said the doctor, laughing, 'I can't make out whether you're denouncing or defending him.'

'It isn't defending a man to say he is a genius,' said Father Brown. 'Far from it. And it is simply a psychological fact that an artist will betray himself by some sort of sincerity. Leonardo da Vinci cannot draw as if he couldn't draw. Even if he tried, it will always be a strong parody of a weak thing. This man would have made something much too fearful and wonderful out of the Wesleyan Methodist.'

When the priest went forth again and set his face homeward, the cold had grown more intense and yet was somehow intoxicating. The trees stood up like silver candelabra of some incredible cold candlemas of purification. It was a piercing cold, like that silver sword of pure pain that once pierced the very heart of purity. But it was not a killing cold, save in the sense of seeming to kill all the mortal obstructions to our immortal and immeasurable vitality. The pale green sky of twilight, with one star like the star of Bethlehem,* seemed by some strange contradiction to be a cavern of clarity. It was as if there could be a green furnace of cold which wakened all things to life like warmth, and that the deeper they went into those cold crystalline colours the more were they light like winged creatures and clear like coloured glass. It tingled with truth and it divided truth from error with a blade like ice; but all that was left had never felt so much alive. It was as if all joy were a jewel in the heart of an iceberg. The priest hardly understood his own mood as he advanced deeper and deeper into the green gloaming, drinking deeper and deeper draughts of that virginal vivacity of the air. Some forgotten muddle and morbidity seemed to be left behind, or wiped out as the snow had painted out the footprints of the man of blood. As he shuffled homewards through the snow, he muttered to himself: 'And yet he is right enough about there being a white magic, if he only knows where to look for it.'

THE GHOST OF GIDEON WISE

FATHER BROWN always regarded the case as the queerest example of the theory of an alibi: the theory by which it is maintained, in defiance of the mythological Irish bird, that it is impossible for anybody to be in two places at once. To begin with, James Byrne, being an Irish journalist, was perhaps the nearest approximation to the Irish bird. He came as near as anybody could to being in two places at once: for he was in two places at the opposite extremes of the social and political world within the space of twenty minutes. The first was in the Babylonian halls of the big hotel, which was the meeting place of the three commercial magnates concerned with arranging for a coal lock-out and denouncing it as a coal-strike; the second was in a curious tavern, having the façade of a grocery store, where met the more subterranean triumvirate of those who would have been very glad to turn the lock-out into a strike—and the strike into a revolution. The reporter passed to and fro between the three millionaires and the three Bolshevist leaders with the immunity of the modern herald or the new ambassador.

He found the three mining magnates hidden in a jungle of flowering plants and a forest of fluted and florid-columns of gilded plaster; gilded birdcages hung high under the painted domes amid the highest leaves of the palms; and in them were birds of motley colours and varied cries. No bird in the wilderness ever sang more unheeded, and no flower ever wasted its sweetness* on the desert air more completely than the blossoms of those tall plants wasted theirs upon the brisk and breathless business men, mostly American, who talked and ran to and fro in that place. And there, amid a riot of rococo ornament that nobody ever looked at, and a chatter of expensive foreign birds that nobody ever heard, and a mass of gorgeous upholstery and a labyrinth of luxurious architecture, the three men sat and talked of how success was founded on the thought and thrift and a vigilance of economy and self-control. One of them indeed did not talk so much as the others; but he watched with very bright and motionless eyes, which seemed to be pinched together by his pince-nez, and the permanent smile under his small black moustache was rather like a permanent sneer. This was the famous Jacob P. Stein, and he did not speak till he had something to say. But his companion, old Gallup the Pennsylvanian, a huge fat fellow with reverend grey hair but a face like a pugilist, talked a great deal. He was in a jovial mood and was half rallying, half bullying the third millionaire, Gideon Wise—a hard, dried, angular old bird of the type that his countrymen compare to hickory,* with a stiff grey chin-beard and the manners and clothes of any old farmer from the central plains. There was an old argument between Wise and Gallup about combination and competition. For old Wise still retained, with the manners of the old backwoodsman, something of his opinions of the old individualist; he belonged, as we should say in England, to the Manchester School;* and Gallup was always trying to persuade him to cut out competition and pool the resources of the world.

'You'll have to come in, old fellow, sooner or later,' Gallup was saying genially as Byrne entered. 'It's the way the world is going, and we can't go back to the one man business now. We've all got to stand together.'

'If I might say a word,' said Stein, in his tranquil way, 'I would say there is something a little more urgent even than standing together commercially. Anyhow, we must stand together politically; and that's why I've asked Mr Byrne to meet us here to-day. On the political issue we must combine, for the simple reason that all our most dangerous enemies are already combined.'

'Oh, I quite agree about political combination,' grumbled Gideon Wise.

'See here,' said Stein to the journalist; 'I know you have the run of these queer places, Mr Byrne, and I want you to do something for us unofficially. You know where these men meet; there are only two or three of them that count, John Elias and Jake Halket, who does all the spouting, and perhaps that poet fellow, Horne.'

'Why, Horne used to be a friend of Gideon,' said the jeering Mr Gallup; 'used to be in his Sunday School class or something.'

'He was a Christian, then,' said old Gideon solemnly; 'but when a man takes up with atheists you never know. I still meet him now and then. I was quite ready to back him against war and conscription and all that, of course, but when it comes to all the goldarn bolshies in creation——'

'Excuse me,' interposed Stein, 'the matter is rather urgent, so I hope you will excuse me putting it before Mr Byrne at once. Mr Byrne, I may tell you in confidence that I hold information, or rather evidence, that would land at least two of those men in prison for long terms, in connection with conspiracies during the late war. I don't want to use that evidence. But I want you to go to them quietly and tell them that I shall use it, and use it to-morrow, unless they alter their attitude.'

'Well,' replied Byrne, 'what you propose would certainly be called compounding a felony and might be called blackmail. Don't you think it is rather dangerous?'

'I think it is rather dangerous for them,' said Stein with a snap; 'and I want you to go and tell them so.'

'Oh, very well,' said Byrne standing up, with a half humorous sigh. 'It's all in the day's work; but if I get into trouble, I warn you I shall try to drag you into it.'

'You will try, boy,' said old Gallup with a hearty laugh.

For so much still lingers of that great dream of Jefferson* and the thing that men have called Democracy that in his country, while the rich rule like tyrants, the poor do not talk like slaves; but there is candour between the oppressor and the oppressed.

The meeting-place of the revolutionists was a queer, bare, whitewashed place, on the walls of which were one or two distorted uncouth sketches in black and white, in the style of something that was supposed to be Proletarian Art, of which not one proletarian in a million could have made head or tail. Perhaps the one point in common to the two council chambers was that both violated the American Constitution by the display of strong drink. Cocktails of various colours had stood before the three millionaires. Halket, the most violent of the Bolshevists, thought it only appropiate to drink vodka. He was a long, hulking fellow with a menacing stoop, and his very profile was aggressive like a dog's, the nose and lips thrust out together, the latter carrying a ragged red moustache and the whole curling outwards with perpetual scorn. John Elias was a dark watchful man in spectacles, with a black pointed beard; and he had learnt in many European cafés a taste for absinthe. The journalist's first and last feeling was how very like each other, after all, were John Elias and Jacob P. Stein. They were so like in face and mind and manner, that the millionaire might have disappeared down a trap-door in the Babylon Hotel and come up again in the stronghold of the Bolshevists.

The third man also had a curious taste in drinks, and his drink was symbolic of him. For what stood in front of the poet Horne was a glass of milk, and its very mildness seemed in that setting to have something sinister about it, as if its opaque and colourless colour were of some leprous paste more poisonous than the dead sick green of absinthe. Yet in truth the mildness was so far genuine enough; for Henry Horne came to the camp of revolution along a very different road and from very different origins from those of Jake, the common tub-thumper, and Elias, the cosmopolitan wire-puller. He had had what is called a careful upbringing, had gone to chapel in his childhood, and carried through life a teetotalism which he could not shake off when he cast away such trifles as Christianity and marriage. He had fair hair and a fine face that might have looked like Shelley, if he had not weakened the chin with a little foreign fringe of beard. Somehow the beard made him look more like a woman; it was as if those few golden hairs were all he could do.

When the journalist entered, the notorious Jake was talking as he generally was. Horne had uttered some casual and conventional phrase about 'Heaven forbid' something or other, and this was quite enough to set Jake off with a torrent of profanity.

'Heaven forbid! and that's about all it bally well does do,' he said. 'Heaven never does anything but forbid this, that and the other; forbids us to strike, and forbids us to fight, and forbids us to shoot the damned usurers and blood-suckers where they sit. Why doesn't Heaven forbid *them* something for a bit? Why don't your damned priests and parsons stand up and tell the truth about these brutes for a change? Why doesn't their precious God——'

Elias allowed a gentle sigh, as of faint fatigue, to escape him.

'Priests,' he said, 'belonged, as Marx has shown, to the feudal stage of economic development and are therefore no longer really any part of the problem. The part once played by the priest is now played by the capitalist expert and——'

'Yes,' interrupted the journalist, with his grim and ironic impartiality, 'and it's about time you knew that some of them are pretty expert in playing it.' And without moving his own eyes from the bright but dead eyes of Elias, he told him of the threat of Stein.

'I was prepared for something of that sort,' said the smiling Elias without moving; 'I may say quite prepared.'

'Dirty dogs!' exploded Jake. 'If a poor man said a thing like that he'd go to penal servitude. But I reckon they'll go somewhere worse before they guess. If they don't go to hell, I don't know where the hell they'll go to——'

Horne made a movement of protest, perhaps not so much at what the man was saying as at what he was going to say, and Elias cut the speech short with cold exactitude.

'It is quite unnecessary for us,' he said, looking at Byrne steadily through his spectacles, 'to bandy threats with the other side. It is quite sufficient that their threats are quite ineffective so far as we are concerned. We also have made all our own arrangements, and some of them will not appear until they appear in action. So far as we are concerned, an immediate rupture and an extreme trial of strength will be quite according to plan.'

As he spoke in a quite quiet and dignified fashion, something in his motionless yellow face and his great goggles started a faint fear creeping up the journalist's spine. Halket's savage face might seem to have a snarl in its very silhouette when seen sideways; but when seen face to face, the smouldering rage in his eyes had also something of anxiety, as if the ethical and economic riddle were after all a little too much for him; and Horne seemed even more hung on wires of worry and self-criticism. But about this third man with the goggles, who spoke so sensibly and simply, there was something uncanny; it was like a dead man talking at the table.

As Byrne went out with his message of defiance, and passed along the very narrow passage beside the grocery store, he found the end of it blocked by a strange though strangely familiar figure: short and sturdy, and looking rather quaint when seen in dark outline with its round head and wide hat.

'Father Brown!' cried the astonished journalist. 'I think you must have come into the wrong door. You're not likely to be in this little conspiracy.'

'Mine is a rather older conspiracy,' replied Father Brown smiling, 'but it is quite a widespread conspiracy.'

'Well,' replied Byrne, 'you can't imagine any of the people here being within a thousand miles of your concern.'

'It's not always easy to tell,' replied the priest equably; 'but as a matter of fact, there is one person here who's within an inch of it.'

He disappeared into the dark entrance and the journalist went on his way very much puzzled. He was still more puzzled by a small incident that happened to him as he turned into the hotel to make his report to his capitalist clients. The bower of blossoms and bird-cages in which those crabbed old gentlemen were embosomed was approached by a flight of marble steps, flanked by gilded nymphs and tritons. Down these steps ran an active young man with black hair, a snub nose and a flower in his buttonhole, who seized him and drew him aside before he could ascend the stair.

'I say,' whispered the young man, 'I'm Potter—old Gid's secretary, you know: now, between ourselves, there is a sort of a thunderbolt being forged, isn't there, now?'

'I came to the conclusion,' replied Byrne cautiously, 'that the Cyclops* had something on the anvil. But always remember that the Cyclops is a giant, but he has only one eye. I think Bolshevism is——'

While he was speaking the secretary listened with a face that had a certain almost Mongolian immobility, despite the liveliness of his legs and his attire. But when Byrne said the word 'Bolshevism,' the young man's sharp eyes shifted and he said quickly: 'What has that—oh yes, that sort of thunderbolt; so sorry, my mistake. So easy to say anvil when you mean ice-box.'

With which the extraordinary young man disappeared down the steps and Byrne continued to mount them, more and more mystification clouding his mind.

He found the group of three augmented to four by the presence of a hatchet-faced person with very thin straw-coloured hair and a monocle, who appeared to be a sort of adviser to old Gallup, possibly his solicitor, though he was not definitely so called. His name was Nares, and the questions which he directed towards Byrne referred chiefly, for some reason or other, to the number of those probably enrolled in the revolutionary organization. Of this, as Byrne knew little, he said less; and the four men eventually rose from their seats, the last word being with the man who had been most silent.

'Thank you, Mr Byrne,' said Stein, folding up his eyeglasses. 'It only remains to say that everything is ready; on that point I quite agree with Mr Elias. To-morrow, before noon, the police will have arrested Mr Elias, on evidence I shall by then have put before them, and those three at least will be in jail before night. As you know, I attempted to avoid this course. I think that is all, gentlemen.'

But Mr Jacob P. Stein did not lay his formal information next day, for a reason that has often interrupted the activities of such industrious characters. He did not do it because he happened to be dead; and none of the rest of the programme was carried out, for a reason which Byrne found displayed in gigantic letters when he opened his morning paper: 'Terrific Triple Murder: Three Millionaires Slain in One Night.' Other exclamatory phrases followed in smaller letters, only about four times the size of normal type, which insisted on the special feature of the mystery: the fact that the three men had been killed not only simultaneously but in three widely separated places—Stein in his artistic and luxurious country seat a hundred miles inland, Wise outside the little bungalow on the coast where he lived on sea breezes and the simple life, and old Gallup in a thicket just outside the lodge-gates of his great house at the other end of the county. In all three cases there could be no doubt about the scenes of violence that had preceded death, though the actual body of Gallup was not found till the second day, where it hung, huge and horrible, amid the broken forks and branches of the little wood into which its weight had crashed, like a bison rushing on the spears; while Wise had clearly been flung over the cliff into the sea, not without a struggle, for his scraping and slipping footprints could still be traced upon the very brink. But the first signal of the tragedy had been the sight of his large limp straw hat, floating far out upon the waves and conspicuous from the cliffs above. Stein's body also had at first eluded search, till a faint trail of blood led the investigators to a bath on the ancient Roman model he had been constructing in his garden; for he had been a man of an experimental turn of mind with a taste for antiquities.

Whatever he might think, Byrne was bound to admit that there was no legal evidence against anybody as things stood. A motive for murder was not enough. Even a moral aptitude for murder was not enough. And he could not conceive that pale young pacifist, Henry Horne, butchering another man by brutal violence, though he might imagine the blaspheming Jake and even the sneering Jew as capable of anything. The police, and the man who appeared to be assisting them (who was no other than the rather mysterious man with the monocle, who had been introduced as Mr Nares), realized the position quite as clearly as the journalist. They knew that at the moment the Bolshevist conspirators could not be prosecuted and convicted, and that it would be a highly sensational failure if they were prosecuted and acquitted. Nares started with an artful candour by calling them in some sense to the council, inviting them to a private conclave and asking them to give their opinions freely in the interests of humanity. He had started his investigations at the nearest scene of tragedy, the bungalow by the sea; and Byrne was permitted to be present at a curious scene, which was at once a peaceful parley of diplomatists and a veiled inquisition or putting of suspects to the question. Rather to Byrne's surprise the incongruous company, seated round the table in the seaside bungalow, included the dumpy figure and owlish head of Father Brown, though his connexion with the affair did not appear until some time afterwards. The presence of young Potter, the dead man's secretary, was more natural; yet somehow his demeanour was not quite so natural. He alone was quite familiar with their meeting-place, and was even in some grim sense their host; yet he offered little assistance or information. His round snub-nosed face wore an expression more like sulks than sorrow.

Jake Halket as usual talked most; and a man of his type could not be expected to keep up the polite fiction that he and his friends were not accused. Young Horne, in his more refined way, tried to restrain him when he began to abuse the men who had been murdered; but Jake was always quite as ready to roar down his friends as his foes. In a spout of blasphemies he relieved his soul of a very unofficial obituary notice of the late Gideon Wise. Elias sat quite still and apparently indifferent behind those spectacles that masked his eyes.

'It would be useless, I suppose,' said Nares coldly, 'to tell you that your remarks are indecent. It may affect you more if I tell you they are imprudent. You practically admit that you hated the dead man.'

'Going to put me in quod for that, are you?' jeered the demagogue. 'All right. Only you'll have to build a prison for a million men if you're going to jail all the poor people who had reason to hate Gid Wise. And you know it's God's truth as well as I do.'

Nares was silent; and nobody spoke until Elias interposed with his clear though faintly lisping drawl.

'This appears to me to be a highly unprofitable discussion on both sides,' he said. 'You have summoned us here either to ask us for information or to subject us to cross-examination. If you trust us, we tell you we have no information. If you distrust us, you must tell us of what we are accused, or have the politeness to keep the fact to yourselves. Nobody has been able to suggest the faintest trace of evidence connecting any one of us with these tragedies any more than with the murder of Julius Cæsar. You dare not arrest us, and you will not believe us. What is the good of our remaining here?'

And he rose, calmly buttoning his coat, his friends following his example. As they went towards the door, young Horne turned back and faced the investigators for a moment with his pale fanatical face.

'I wish to say,' he said, 'that I went to a filthy jail during the whole war because I would not consent to kill a man.'

With that they passed out, and the members of the group remaining looked grimly at each other.

'I hardly think,' said Father Brown, 'that we remain entirely victorious, in spite of the retreat.'

'I don't mind anything,' said Nares, 'except being bully-ragged by that blasphemous blackguard Halket. Horne is a gentleman, anyhow. But whatever they say, I am dead certain they know; they are in it, or most of them are. They almost admitted it. They taunted us with not being able to prove we're right, much more than with being wrong. What do you think, Father Brown?'

The person addressed looked across at Nares with a gaze almost disconcertingly mild and meditative.

'It is quite true,' he said, 'that I have formed an idea that one particular person knows more than he has told us. But I think it would be well if I did not mention his name just yet.'

Nare's eyeglass dropped from his eye, and he looked up sharply. 'This is unofficial so far,' he said. 'I suppose you know that at a later stage if you withhold information, your position may be serious.'

'My position is simple,' replied the priest. 'I am here to look after the legitimate interests of my friend Halket. I think it will be in his interest, under the circumstances, if I tell you I think he will before long sever his connexion with this organization, and cease to be a Socialist in that sense. I have every reason to believe he will probably end as a Catholic.'

'Halket!' exploded the other incredulously. 'Why, he cursed priests from morning till night!'

'I don't think you quite understand that kind of man,' said Father Brown mildly. 'He curses priests for failing (in his opinion) to defy the whole world for justice. Why should he expect them to defy the whole world for justice, unless he had already begun to assume they were—what they are? But we haven't met here to discuss the psychology of conversion. I only mention this because it may simplify your task—perhaps narrow your search.'

'If it's true, it would jolly well narrow it to that narrow-faced rascal Elias—and I shouldn't wonder, for a more creepy, cold-blooded, sneering devil I never saw.'

Father Brown sighed. 'He always reminded me of poor Stein,' he said, 'in fact I think he was some relation.'

'Oh, I say,' began Nares, when his protest was cut short by the door being flung open, revealing once more the long loose figure and pale face of young Horne; but it seemed as if he had not merely his natural, but a new and unnatural pallor.

'Hullo,' cried Nares, putting up his single eyeglass, 'why have you come back again?'

Horne crossed the room rather shakily without a word and sat down heavily in a chair. Then he said, as in a sort of daze: 'I missed the others . . . I lost my way. I thought I'd better come back.'

The remains of evening refreshments were on the table, and Henry Horne, that lifelong Prohibitionist, poured himself out a wine-glassful of liqueur brandy and drank it at a gulp.

'You seem upset,' said Father Brown.

Horne had put his hands to his forehead and spoke as from under the shadow of it: he seemed to be speaking to the priest only, in a low voice.

'I may as well tell you. I have seen a ghost.'

'A ghost!' repeated Nares in astonishment. 'Whose ghost?'

'The ghost of Gideon Wise, the master of this house,' answered Horne more firmly, 'standing over the abyss into which he fell.'

'Oh, nonsense!' said Nares; 'no sensible person believes in ghosts.'

'That is hardly exact,' said Father Brown, smiling a little. 'There is really quite as good evidence for many ghosts as there is for most crimes.'

'Well, it's my business to run after the criminals,' said Nares rather roughly, 'and I will leave other people to run away from the ghosts. If anybody at this time of day chooses to be frightened of ghosts it's his affair.'

'I didn't say I was frightened of them, though I dare say I might be,' said Father Brown. 'Nobody knows till he tries. I said I believed in them, at any rate, enough to want to hear more about this one. What, exactly, did you see, Mr Horne?'

'It was over there on the brink of those crumbling cliffs; you know there is a sort of gap or crevice just about the spot where he was thrown over. The others had gone on ahead, and I was crossing the moor towards the path along the cliff. I often went that way, for I liked seeing the high seas dash up against the crags. I thought little of it to-night, beyond wondering that the sea should be so rough on this sort of clear moonlight night. I could see the pale crests of spray appear and disappear as the great waves leapt up at the headland. Thrice I saw the momentary flash of foam in the moonlight and then I saw something inscrutable. The fourth flash of the silver foam seemed to be fixed in the sky. It did not fall; I waited with insane intensity for it to fall. I fancied I was mad, and that time had been for me mysteriously arrested or prolonged. Then I drew nearer, and then I think I screamed aloud. For that suspended spray, like unfallen snowflakes, had fitted together into a face and a figure, white as the shining leper in a legend and terrible as the fixed lightning.'

'And it was Gideon Wise, you say?'

Horne nodded without speech; there was a silence broken abruptly by Nares rising to his feet; so abruptly indeed that he knocked a chair over.

'Oh, this is all nonsense,' he said, 'but we'd better go out and see.'

'I won't go,' said Horne with sudden violence. 'I'll never walk by that path again.'

'I think we must all walk by that path to-night,' said the priest gravely, 'though I will never deny it has been a perilous path . . . to more people than one.'

'I will not . . . God, how you all goad me,' cried Horne, and his eyes began to roll in a strange fashion. He had risen with the rest, but he made no motion towards the door.

'Mr Horne,' said Nares firmly, 'I am a police-officer, and this house, though you may not know it, is surrounded by the police. I have tried to investigate in a friendly fashion, but I must investigate everything, even anything so silly as a ghost. I must ask you to take me to the spot you speak of.'

There was another silence while Horne stood heaving and panting as with indescribable fears. Then he suddenly sat down on his chair again and said with an entirely new and much more composed voice:

'I can't do it. You may just as well know why. You will know it sooner or later. I killed him.'

For an instant there was the stillness of a house struck by a thunderbolt and full of corpses. Then the voice of Father Brown sounded in that enormous silence strangely small like the squeak of a mouse.

'Did you kill him deliberately?' he asked.

'How can one answer such a question?' answered the man in the chair, moodily gnawing his finger. 'I was mad, I suppose. He was intolerable and insolent, I know. I was on his land and I believe he struck me; anyhow, we came to a grapple and he went over the cliff. When I was well away from the scene it burst upon me that I had done a crime that cut me off from men; the brand of Cain* throbbed on my brow and my very brain; I realized for the first time that I had indeed killed a man. I knew I should have to confess it sooner or later.' He sat suddenly erect in his chair. 'But I will say nothing against anybody else. It is no use asking me about plots or accomplices—I will say nothing.'

'In the light of the other murders,' said Nares, 'it is difficult to believe that the quarrel was quite so unpremeditated. Surely somebody sent you there?'

'I will say nothing against anybody I worked with,' said Horne proudly. 'I am a murderer, but I will not be a traitor.'

Nares stepped between the man and the door and called out in an official fashion to someone outside.

'We will all go to the place, anyhow,' he said in a low voice to the secretary; 'but this man must go in custody.'

The company generally felt that to go spook-hunting on a sea-cliff was a very silly anti-climax after the confession of the murderer. But Nares, though the most sceptical and scornful of all, thought it his duty to leave no stone unturned; as one might say, no gravestone unturned. For, after all, that crumbling cliff was the only gravestone over the watery grave of poor Gideon Wise. Nares locked the door, being the last out of the house, and followed the rest across the moor to the cliff, when he was astonished to see young Potter, the secretary, coming back quickly towards them, his face in the moonlight looking white as a moon.

'By God, sir,' he said, speaking for the first time that night, 'there really is something there. It—it's just like him.'

'Why, you're raving,' gasped the detective, 'Everybody's raving.'

'Do you think I don't know him when I see him?' cried the secretary with singular bitterness. 'I have reason to.'

'Perhaps,' said the detective sharply, 'you are one of those who had reason to hate him, as Halket said.'

'Perhaps,' said the secretary; 'anyhow, I know him, and I tell you I can see him standing there stark and staring under this hellish moon.'

And he pointed towards the crack in the cliffs, where they could already see something that might have been a moonbeam or a streak of foam, but which was already beginning to look a little more solid. They had crept a hundred yards nearer, and it was still motionless; but it looked like a statue in silver.

Nares himself looked a little pale and seemed to stand debating what to do. Potter was frankly as much frightened as Horne himself; and even Byrne, who was a hardened reporter, was rather reluctant to go any nearer if he could help it. He could not help considering it a little quaint, therefore, that the only man who did not seem to be frightened of a ghost was the man who had said openly that he might be. For Father Brown was advancing as steadily, at his stumping pace, as if he were going to consult a notice-board.

'It don't seem to bother you much,' said Byrne to the priest; 'and yet I thought you were the only one who believed in spooks.'

'If it comes to that,' replied Father Brown, 'I thought you were one who didn't believe in them. But believing in ghosts is one thing, and believing in a ghost is quite another.'

Byrne looked rather ashamed of himself, and glanced almost covertly at the crumbling headlands in the cold moonlight which were the haunts of the vision or delusion.

'I didn't believe in it till I saw it,' he said.

'And I did believe in it till I saw it,' said Father Brown.

The journalist stared after him as he went stumping across the great waste ground that rose towards the cloven headland like the sloping side of a hill cut in two. Under the discolouring moon the grass looked like long grey hair all combed one way by the wind and seeming to point towards the place where the breaking cliff showed pale gleams of chalk in the grey-green turf, and where stood the pale figure or shining shade that none could yet understand. As yet that pale figure dominated a desolate landscape that was empty except for the black square back and business-like figure of the priest advancing alone towards it. Then the prisoner Horne broke suddenly from his captors with a piercing cry and ran ahead of the priest, falling on his knees before the spectre.

'I have confessed,' they heard him crying. 'Why have you come to tell them I killed you?'

'I have come to tell them you did not,' said the ghost, and stretched forth a hand to him. Then the kneeling man sprang up with quite a new kind of scream; and they knew it was the hand of flesh.

It was the most remarkable escape from death in recent records, said the experienced detective and the no less experienced journalist. Yet, in a sense, it had been very simple after all. Flakes and shards of the cliff were continually falling away, and some had caught in the gigantic crevice, so as to form what was really a ledge or pocket in what was supposed to be a sheer drop through darkness to the sea. The old man, who was a very tough and wiry old man, had fallen on this lower shoulder of rock and had passed a pretty terrible twenty-four hours in trying to climb back by crags that constantly collapsed under him, but at length formed by their very ruins a sort of stairway of escape. This might be the explanation of Horne's optical illusion about a white wave that appeared and disappeared, and finally came to stay. But anyhow, there was Gideon Wise, solid in bone and sinew, with his white hair and white dusty country clothes and harsh country features, which were, however, a great deal less harsh than usual. Perhaps it is good for millionaires to spend twenty-four hours on a ledge of rock within a foot of eternity. Anyhow, he not only disclaimed all malice against the criminal, but gave an account of the matter which considerably modified the crime. He declared that Horne had not thrown him over at all; that the continually breaking ground had given way under him, and that Horne had even made some movement as of attempted rescue.

'On that providential bit of rock down there,' he said solemnly, 'I promised the Lord to forgive my enemies; and the

Lord would think it mighty mean if I didn't forgive a little accident like that.'

Horne had to depart under police supervision, of course, but the detective did not disguise from himself that the prisoner's detention would probably be short, and his punishment, if any, trifling. It is not every murderer who can put the murdered man in the witness-box to give him a testimonial.

'It's a strange case,' said Byrne, as the detective and the others hastened along the cliff path towards the town.

'It is,' said Father Brown. 'It's no business of ours; but I wish you'd stop with me and talk it over.'

There was a silence and then Byrne complied by saying suddenly: 'I suppose you were thinking of Horne already, when you said somebody wasn't telling all he knew.'

'When I said that,' replied his friend, 'I was thinking of the exceedingly silent Mr Potter, the secretary of the no longer late or (shall we say) lamented Mr Gideon Wise.'

'Well, the only time Potter ever spoke to me I thought he was a lunatic,' said Byrne, staring, 'but I never thought of his being a criminal. He said something about it all having to do with an ice-box.'

'Yes, I thought he knew something about it,' said Father Brown reflectively. 'I never said he had anything to do with it. . . . I suppose old Wise really is strong enough to have climbed out of that chasm.'

'What do you mean?' asked the astonished reporter. 'Why, of course he got out of that chasm; for there he is.'

The priest did not answer the question but asked abruptly:

'What do you think of Horne?'

'Well, one can't call him a criminal exactly,' answered Byrne. 'He never was at all like any criminal I ever knew, and I've had some experience; and, of course, Nares has had much more. I don't think we ever quite believed him a criminal.'

'And I never believed in him in another capacity,' said the priest quietly. 'You may know more about criminals. But there's one class of people I probably do know more about than you do, or even Nares for that matter. I've known quite a lot of them, and I know their little ways.'

'Another class of people,' repeated Byrne, mystified. 'Why, what class do you know about?'

'Penitents,' said Father Brown.

'I don't quite understand,' objected Byrne. 'Do you mean you don't believe in his crime?'

'I don't believe in his confession,' said Father Brown. 'I've heard a good many confessions, and there was never a genuine one like that. It was romantic; it was all out of books. Look how he talked about having the brand of Cain. That's out of books. It's not what anyone would feel who had in his own person done a thing hitherto horrible to him. Suppose you were an honest clerk or shop-boy shocked to feel that for the first time you'd stolen money. Would you immediately reflect that your action was the same as that of Barabbas?* Suppose you'd killed a child in some ghastly anger. Would you go back through history, till you could identify your action with that of an Idumean* potentate named Herod? Believe me, our own crimes are far too hideously private and prosaic to make our first thoughts turn towards historical parallels, however apt. And why did he go out of his way to say he would not give his colleagues away? Even in saying so, he was giving them away. Nobody had asked him so far to give away anything or anybody. No; I don't think he was genuine, and I wouldn't give him absolution. A nice state of things, if people started getting absolved for what they hadn't done.' And Father Brown, his head turned away, looked steadily out to sea.

'But I don't understand what you're driving at,' cried Byrne. 'What's the good of buzzing round him with suspicions when he's pardoned? He's out of it anyhow. He's quite safe.'

Father Brown spun round like a teetotum and caught his friend by the coat with unexpected and inexplicable excitement.

'That's it,' he cried emphatically. 'Freeze on to that! He's quite safe. He's out of it. That's why he's the key of the whole puzzle.'

'Oh, help,' said Byrne feebly.

'I mean,' persisted the little priest, 'he's in it because he's out of it. That's the whole explanation.'

'And a very lucid explanation too,' said the journalist with feeling.

They stood looking out to sea for a time in silence, and then Father Brown said cheerfully:

'And so we come back to the ice-box. Where you have all gone wrong from the first in this business is where a good many of the papers and the public men do go wrong. It's because you assumed that there is nothing whatever in the modern world to fight about except Bolshevism. This story has nothing whatever to do with Bolshevism; except perhaps as a blind.'

'I don't see how that can be,' remonstrated Byrne. 'Here you have the three millionaires in that one business murdered——'

'No!' said the priest in a sharp ringing voice. 'You do not. That is just the point. You do not have three millionaires murdered. You have two millionaires murdered; and you have the third millionaire very much alive and kicking and quite ready to kick. And you have that third millionaire freed for ever from the threat that was thrown at his head before your very face, in playfully polite terms, and in that conversation you described as taking place in the hotel. Gallup and Stein threatened the more old-fashioned and independent old huckster that if he would not come into their combine they would freeze him out. Hence the ice-box, of course.'

After a pause he went on. 'There is undoubtedly a Bolshevist movement in the modern world, and it must undoubtedly be resisted, though I do not believe very much in your way of resisting it. But what nobody notices is that there is another movement equally modern and equally moving: the great movement towards monopoly or the turning of all trades into trusts. That also is a revolution. That also produces what all revolutions produce. Men will kill for that and against that, as they do for and against Bolshevism. It has its ultimatums and its invasions and its executions. These trust magnates have their courts like kings; they have their bodyguard and bravos; they have their spies in the enemy camp. Horne was one of old Gideon's spies in one of the enemy camps; but he was used here against another enemy: the rivals who were ruining him for standing out.'

'I still don't quite see how he was used,' said Byrne, 'or what was the good of it.'

'Don't you see,' cried Father Brown sharply, 'that they gave each other an alibi?'

Byrne still looked at him a little doubtfully, though understanding was dawning on his face.

'That's what I mean,' continued the other, 'when I say they were in it because they were out of it. Most people would say they must be out of the other two crimes, because they were in this one. As a fact, they were in the other two because they were out of this one; because this one never happened at all. A very queer, improbable sort of alibi, of course; improbable and therefore impenetrable. Most people would say a man who confesses a murder must be sincere; a man who forgives his murderer must be sincere. Nobody would think of the notion that the thing never happened, so that one man had nothing to forgive and the other nothing to fear. They were fixed here for that night by a story against themselves. But they were not here that night; for Horne was murdering old Gallup in the wood, while Wise was strangling that little Jew in his Roman bath. That's why I ask whether Wise was really strong enough for the climbing adventure.'

'It was quite a good adventure,' said Byrne regretfully. 'It fitted into the landscape, and was really very convincing.'

'Too convincing to convince,' said Father Brown, shaking his head 'How very vivid was that moonlit foam flung up and turning to a ghost. And how very literary! Horne is a sneak and a skunk, but do not forget that, like many other sneaks and skunks in history, he is also a poet.'

THE MIRROR OF THE MAGISTRATE*

JAMES BAGSHAW and Wilfred Underhill were old friends, and were fond of rambling through the streets at night, talking interminably as they turned corner after corner in the silent and seemingly lifeless labyrinth of the large suburb in which they lived. The former, a big, dark, good-humoured man with a strip of black moustache, was a professional police detective; the latter, a sharp-faced, sensitive-looking gentleman with light hair, was an amateur interested in detection. It will come as a shock to the readers of the best scientific romance to learn that it was the policeman who was talking and the amateur who was listening, even with a certain respect.

'Ours is the only trade,' said Bagshaw, 'in which the professional is always supposed to be wrong. After all, people don't write stories in which hairdressers can't cut hair and have to be helped by a customer; or in which a cabman can't drive a cab until his fare explains to him the philosophy of cab-driving. For all that, I'd never deny that we often tend to get into a rut: or, in other words, have the disadvantages of going by a rule. Where the romancers are wrong is, that they don't allow us even the advantages of going by a rule.'

'Surely,' said Underhill, 'Sherlock Holmes would say that he went by a logical rule.'

'He may be right,' answered the other; 'but I mean a collective rule. It's like the staff work of an army. We pool our information.'

'And you don't think detective stories allow for that?' asked his friend.

'Well, let's take any imaginary case of Sherlock Holmes, and Lestrade, the official detective. Sherlock Holmes, let us say, can guess that a total stranger crossing the street is a foreigner, merely because he seems to look for the traffic to go to the right instead of the left. I'm quite ready to admit Holmes might guess that. I'm quite sure Lestrade wouldn't guess anything of the kind. But what they leave out is the fact that the policeman, who couldn't guess, might very probably know. Lestrade might know the man was a foreigner merely because his department has to keep an eye on all foreigners; some would say on all natives, too. As a policeman I'm glad the police know so much; for every man wants to do his own job well. But as a citizen, I sometimes wonder whether they don't know too much.'

'You don't seriously mean to say,' cried Underhill incredulously, 'that you know anything about strange people in a strange street. That if a man walked out of that house over there, you would know anything about him?'

'I should if he was the householder,' answered Bagshaw. 'That house is rented by a literary man of Anglo-Roumanian extraction, who generally lives in Paris, but is over here in connexion with some poetical play of his. His name's Osric Orm, one of the new poets, and pretty steep to read, I believe.'

'But I mean all the people down the road,' said his companion. 'I was thinking how strange and new and nameless everything looks, with these high blank walls and these houses lost in large gardens. You can't know all of them.'

'I know a few,' answered Bagshaw. 'This garden wall we're walking under is at the end of the grounds of Sir Humphrey Gwynne, better known as Mr Justice Gwynne, the old judge who made such a row about spying during the war. The house next door to it belongs to a wealthy cigar merchant. He comes from Spanish-America and looks very swarthy and Spanish himself; but he bears the very English name of Buller. The house beyond that—did you hear that noise?'

'I heard something,' said Underhill, 'but I really don't know what it was.'

'I know what it was,' replied the detective, 'it was a rather heavy revolver, fired twice, followed by a cry for help. And it came straight out of the back garden of Mr Justice Gwynne, that paradise of peace and legality.'

He looked up and down the street sharply and then added:

'And the only gate of the back garden is half a mile round on the other side. I wish this wall were a little lower, or I were a little lighter; but it's got to be tried.'

'It is lower a little farther on,' said Underhill, 'and there seems to be a tree that looks helpful.'

They moved hastily along and found a place where the wall seemed to stoop abruptly, almost as if it had half-sunk into the earth; and a garden tree, flamboyant with the gayest garden blossom, straggled out of the dark enclosure and was gilded by the gleam of a solitary street-lamp. Bagshaw caught the crooked branch and threw one leg over the low wall; and the next moment they stood knee-deep amid the snapping plants of a garden border.

The garden of Mr Justice Gwynne by night was rather a singular spectacle. It was large and lay on the empty edge of the suburb, in the shadow of a tall, dark house that was the last in its line of houses. The house was literally dark, being shuttered and unlighted, at least on the side overlooking the garden. But the garden itself, which lay in its shadow and should have been a tract of absolute darkness, showed a random glitter, like that of fading fireworks; as if a giant rocket had fallen in fire among the trees. As they advanced they were able to locate it as the light of several coloured lamps, entangled in the trees like the jewel fruits of Aladdin,* and especially as the light from a small, round lake or pond, which gleamed with pale colours as if a lamp were kindled under it.

'Is he having a party?' asked Underhill. 'The garden seems to be illuminated.'

'No,' answered Bagshaw. 'It's a hobby of his, and I believe he prefers to do it when he's alone. He likes playing with a little plant of electricity that he works from that bungalow or hut over there, where he does his work and keeps his papers. Buller, who knows him very well, says the coloured lamps are rather more often a sign he's not to be disturbed.'

'Sort of red danger signals,' suggested the other.

'Good Lord! I'm afraid they are danger signals!' and he began suddenly to run.

A moment after, Underhill saw what he had seen. The opalescent ring of light, like the halo of the moon, round the sloping sides of the pond, was broken by two black stripes or streaks which soon proved themselves to be the long, black legs of a figure fallen head downwards into the hollow, with the head in the pond.

'Come on,' cried the detective sharply, 'that looks to me like——'

His voice was lost, as he ran on across the wide lawn, faintly luminous in the artificial light, making a bee-line across the big garden for the pool and the fallen figure. Underhill was trotting steadily in that straight track, when something happened that startled him for the moment. Bagshaw, who was travelling as steadily as a bullet towards the black figure by the luminous pool, suddenly turned at a sharp angle and began to run even more rapidly towards the shadow of the house.

Underhill could not imagine what he meant by the altered direction. The next moment, when the detective had vanished into the shadow of the house, there came out of that obscurity the sound of a scuffle and a curse; and Bagshaw returned lugging with him a little struggling man with red hair. The captive had evidently been escaping under the shelter of the building, when the quicker ears of the detective had heard him rustling like a bird among the bushes.

'Underhill,' said the detective, 'I wish you'd run on and see what's up by the pool. And now, who are you?' he asked, coming to a halt. 'What's your name?'

'Michael Flood,' said the stranger in a snappy fashion. He was an unnaturally lean little man, with a hooked nose too large for his face, which was colourless, like parchment, in contrast with the ginger colour of his hair. 'I've got nothing to do with this. I found him lying dead and I was scared; but I only came to interview him for a paper.'

'When you interview celebrities for the Press,' said Bagshaw, 'do you generally climb over the garden wall?'

And he pointed grimly to a trail of footprints coming and going along the path towards the flower bed.

The man calling himself Flood wore an expression equally grim.

'An interviewer might very well get over the wall,' he said, 'for I couldn't make anybody hear at the front door. The servant had gone out.'

'How do you know he'd gone out?' asked the detective suspiciously.

'Because,' said Flood, with an almost unnatural calm, 'I'm not the only person who gets over garden walls. It seems just possible that you did it yourself. But, anyhow, the servant did; for I've just this moment seen him drop over the wall, away on the other side of the garden, just by the garden door.'

'Then why didn't he use the garden door?' demanded the cross-examiner.

'How should I know?' retorted Flood. 'Because it was shut, I suppose. But you'd better ask him, not me; he's coming towards the house at this minute.'

There was, indeed, another shadowy figure beginning to be visible through the fire-shot gloaming, a squat, square-headed figure, wearing a red waistcoat as the most conspicuous part of a rather shabby livery. He appeared to be making with unobtrusive haste towards a side-door in the house, until Bagshaw hallooed to him to halt. He drew nearer to them very reluctantly, revealing a heavy, yellow face, with a touch of something Asiatic which was consonant with his flat, blue-black hair.

Bagshaw turned abruptly to the man called Flood. 'Is there anybody in this place,' he said, 'who can testify to your identity?'

'Not many, even in this country,' growled Flood. 'I've only just come from Ireland; the only man I know round here is the priest at St Dominic's Church—Father Brown.'

'Neither of you must leave this place,' said Bagshaw, and then added to the servant: 'But you can go into the house and ring up St Dominic's Presbytery and ask Father Brown if he would mind coming round here at once. No tricks, mind.'

While the energetic detective was securing the potential fugitives, his companion, at his direction, had hastened on to the actual scene of the tragedy. It was a strange enough scene; and, indeed, if the tragedy had not been tragic it would have been highly fantastic. The dead man (for the briefest examination proved him to be dead) lay with his head in the pond, where the glow of the artificial illumination encircled the head with something of the appearance of an unholy halo. The face was gaunt and rather sinister, the brow bald, and the scanty curls dark grey, like iron rings; and, despite the damage done by the bullet wound in the temple, Underhill had no difficulty in recognizing the features he had seen in the many portraits of Sir Humphrey Gwynne. The dead man was in evening-dress, and his long, black legs, so thin as to be almost spidery, were sprawling at different angles up the steep bank from which he had fallen. As by some weird whim of diabolical arabesque,* blood was eddying out, very slowly, into the luminous water in snaky rings, like the transparent crimson of sunset clouds.

Underhill did not know how long he stood staring down at this macabre figure, when he looked up and saw a group of four figures standing above him on the bank. He was prepared for Bagshaw and his Irish captive, and he had no difficulty in guessing the status of the servant in the red waistcoat. But the fourth figure had a sort of grotesque solemnity that seemed strangely congruous to that incongruity. It was a stumpy figure with a round face and a hat like a black halo. He realized that it was, in fact, a priest; but there was something about it that reminded him of some quaint old black woodcut at the end of a Dance of Death.*

Then he heard Bagshaw saying to the priest:

'I'm glad you can identify this man; but you must realize that he's to some extent under suspicion. Of course, he may be innocent; but he did enter the garden in an irregular fashion.'

'Well, I think he's innocent myself,' said the little priest in a colourless voice. 'But, of course, I may be wrong.'

'Why do you think he is innocent?'

'Because he entered the garden in an irregular fashion,' answered the cleric. 'You see, I entered it in a regular fashion myself. But I seem to be almost the only person who did. All the best people seem to get over garden walls nowadays.'

'What do you mean by a regular fashion?' asked the detective.

'Well,' said Father Brown, looking at him with limpid gravity, 'I came in by the front door. I often come into houses that way.'

'Excuse me,' said Bagshaw, 'but does it matter very much how you came in, unless you propose to confess to the murder?'

'Yes, I think it does,' said the priest mildly. 'The truth is, that when I came in at the front door I saw something I don't think any of the rest of you have seen. It seems to me it might have something to do with it.'

'What did you see?'

'I saw a sort of general smash-up,' said Father Brown in his mild voice. 'A big looking-glass broken, and a small palm tree knocked over, and the pot smashed all over the floor. Somehow, it looked to me as if something had happened.'

'You are right,' said Bagshaw after a pause. 'If you saw that, it certainly looks as if it had something to do with it.'

'And if it had anything to do with it,' said the priest very gently, 'it looks as if there was one person who had nothing to do with it; and that is Mr Michael Flood, who entered the garden over the wall in an irregular fashion, and then tried to leave it in the same irregular fashion. It is his irregularity that makes me believe in his innocence.'

'Let us go into the house,' said Bagshaw abruptly.

As they passed in at the side-door, the servant leading the way, Bagshaw fell back a pace or two and spoke to his friend.

'Something odd about that servant,' he said. 'Says his name is Green, though he doesn't look it; but there seems no doubt he's really Gwynne's servant, apparently the only regular servant he had. But the queer thing is, that he flatly denied that his master was in the garden at all, dead or alive. Said the old judge had gone out to a grand legal dinner and couldn't be home for hours, and gave that as his excuse for slipping out.'

'Did he,' asked Underhill, 'give any excuse for his curious way of slipping in?'

'No, none that I can make sense of,' answered the detective. 'I can't make him out. He seems to be scared of something.'

Entering by the side-door, they found themselves at the inner end of the entrance hall, which ran along the side of the house and ended with the front door, surmounted by a dreary fanlight of the old-fashioned pattern. A faint, grey light was beginning to outline its radiation upon the darkness, like some dismal and discoloured sunrise; but what light there was in the hall came from a single, shaded lamp, also of an antiquated sort, that stood on a bracket in a corner. By the light of this Bagshaw could distinguish the debris of which Brown had spoken. A tall palm, with long sweeping leaves, had fallen full length, and its dark red pot was shattered into shards. They lay littered on the carpet, along with pale and gleaming fragments of a broken mirror, of which the almost empty frame hung behind them on the wall at the end of the vestibule. At right angles to this entrance, and directly opposite the side-door as they entered, was another and similar passage leading into the rest of the house. At the other end of it could be seen the telephone which the servant had used to summon the priest; and a half-open door, showing, even through the crack, the serried ranks of great leather-bound books, marked the entrance to the judge's study.

Bagshaw stood looking down at the fallen pot and the mingled fragments at his feet.

'You're quite right,' he said to the priest; 'there's been a struggle here. And it must have been a struggle between Gwynne and his murderer.'

'It seemed to me,' said Father Brown modestly, 'that something had happened here.'

'Yes; it's pretty clear what happened,' assented the detective. 'The murderer entered by the front door and found Gwynne; probably Gwynne let him in. There was a death grapple, possibly a chance shot, that hit the glass, though they might have broken it with a stray kick or anything. Gwynne managed to free himself and fled into the garden, where he was pursued and shot finally by the pond. I fancy that's the whole story of the crime itself; but, of course, I must look round the other rooms.'

The other rooms, however, revealed very little, though Bagshaw pointed significantly to the loaded automatic pistol that he found in a drawer of the library desk.

'Looks as if he was expecting this,' he said; 'yet it seems queer he didn't take it with him when he went out into the hall.'

Eventually they returned to the hall, making their way towards the front door, Father Brown letting his eye rove around in a rather absent-minded fashion. The two corridors, monotonously papered in the same grey and faded pattern, seemed to emphasize the dust and dingy floridity of the few early Victorian ornaments, the green rust that devoured the bronze of the lamp, the dull gold that glimmered in the frame of the broken mirror.

'They say it's bad luck to break a looking-glass,' he said. 'This looks like the very house of ill-luck. There's something about the very furniture——'

'That's rather odd,' said Bagshaw sharply. 'I thought the front door would be shut, but it's left on the latch.'

There was no reply; and they passed out of the front door into the front garden, a narrower and more formal plot of flowers, having at one end a curiously clipped hedge with a hole in it, like a green cave, under the shadow of which some broken steps peeped out.

Father Brown strolled up to the hole and ducked his head under it. A few moments after he had disappeared they were astonished to hear his quiet voice in conversation above their heads, as if he were talking to somebody at the top of a tree. The detective followed, and found that the curious covered stairway led to what looked like a broken bridge, over-hanging the darker and emptier spaces of the garden. It just curled round the corner of the house, bringing in sight the field of coloured lights beyond and beneath. Probably it was the relic of some abandoned architectural fancy of building a sort of terrace on arches across the lawn. Bagshaw thought it a curious cul-de-sac in which to find anybody in the small hours between night and morning; but he was not looking at the details of it just then. He was looking at the man who was found.

As the man stood with his back turned—a small man in light grey clothes—the one outstanding feature about him was a wonderful head of hair, as yellow and radiant as the head of a huge dandelion. It was literally outstanding like a halo, and something in that association made the face, when it was slowly and sulkily turned on them, rather a shock of contrast. That halo should have enclosed an oval face of the mildly angelic sort; but the face was crabbed and elderly with a powerful jowl and a short nose that somehow suggested the broken nose of a pugilist.

'This is Mr Orm,* the celebrated poet, I understand,' said Father Brown, as calmly as if he were introducing two people in a drawing-room.

'Whoever he is,' said Bagshaw, 'I must trouble him to come with me and answer a few questions.'

Mr Osric Orm, the poet, was not a model of self-expression when it came to the answering of questions. There, in that corner of the old garden, as the grey twilight before dawn began to creep over the heavy hedges and the broken bridge, and afterwards in a succession of circumstances and stages of legal inquiry that grew more and more ominous, he refused to say anything except that he had intended to call on Sir Humphrey Gwynne, but had not done so because he could not get anyone to answer the bell. When it was pointed out that the door was practically open, he snorted. When it was hinted that the hour was somewhat late, he snarled. The little that he said was obscure, either because he really knew hardly any English, or because he knew better than to know any. His opinions seemed to be of a nihilistic and destructive sort, as was indeed the tendency of his poetry for those who could follow it; and it seemed possible that his business with the judge, and perhaps his quarrel with the judge, had been something in the anarchist line. Gwynne was known to have had something of a mania about Bolshevist spies, as he had about German spies. Anyhow, one coincidence, only a few moments after his capture, confirmed Bagshaw in the impression that the case must be taken seriously. As they went out of the front gate into the street, they so happened to encounter yet another neighbour, Buller, the cigar merchant from next door, conspicuous by his brown, shrewd face and the unique orchid in his buttonhole; for he had a name in that branch of horticulture. Rather to the surprise of the rest, he hailed his neighbour, the poet, in a matter-of-fact manner, almost as if he had expected to see him.

'Hallo, here we are again,' he said, 'Had a long talk with old Gwynne, I suppose?'

'Sir Humphrey Gwynne is dead,' said Bagshaw. 'I am investigating the case and I must ask you to explain.'

Buller stood as still as the lamp-post beside him, possibly stiffened with surprise. The red end of his cigar brightened and darkened rhythmically, but his brown face was in shadow; when he spoke it was with quite a new voice.

'I only mean,' he said, 'that when I passed two hours ago Mr Orm was going in at this gate to see Sir Humphrey.'

'He says he hasn't seen him yet,' observed Bagshaw, 'or even been into the house.'

'It's a long time to stand on the door-step,' observed Buller.

'Yes,' said Father Brown; 'it's rather a long time to stand in the street.'

'I've been home since then,' said the cigar merchant. 'Been writing letters and came out again to post them.'

'You'll have to tell all that later,' said Bagshaw. 'Good night—or good morning.'

The trial of Osric Orm for the murder of Sir Humphrey Gwynne, which filled the newspapers for so many weeks, really turned entirely on the same crux as that little talk under the lamp-post, when the grey-green dawn was breaking about the dark streets and gardens. Everything came back to the enigma of those two empty hours between the time when Buller saw Orm going in at the garden gate, and the time when Father Brown found him apparently still lingering in the garden. He had certainly had the time to commit six murders, and might almost have committed them for want of something to do; for he could give no coherent account of what he was doing. It was argued by the prosecution that he had also the opportunity, as the front door was unlatched, and the side-door into the larger garden left standing open. The court followed, with considerable interest, Bagshaw's clear reconstruction of the struggle in the passage, of which the traces were so evident; indeed, the police had since found the shot that had shattered the glass. Finally, the hole in the hedge to which he had been tracked, had very much the appearance of a hiding-place. On the other hand, Sir Matthew Blake, the very able counsel for the defence, turned this last argument the other way: asking why any man should entrap himself in a place without possible exit, when it would obviously be much more sensible to slip out into the street. Sir Matthew Blake also made effective use of the mystery that still rested upon the motive for the murder. Indeed, upon this point, the passages between Sir Matthew Blake and Sir Arthur Travers, the equally brilliant advocate for the prosecution, turned rather to the advantage of the prisoner. Sir Arthur could only throw out suggestions about a Bolshevist conspiracy which sounded a little thin. But when it came to investigating the facts of Orm's mysterious behaviour that night he was considerably more effective.

The prisoner went into the witness-box, chiefly because his astute counsel calculated that it would create a bad impression if he did not. But he was almost as uncommunicative to his own counsel as to the prosecuting counsel. Sir Arthur Travers made all possible capital out of his stubborn silence, but did not succeed in breaking it. Sir Arthur was a long, gaunt man, with a long, cadaverous face, in striking contrast to the sturdy figure and bright, bird-like eye of Sir Matthew Blake. But if Sir Matthew suggested a very cocksure sort of cock-sparrow, Sir Arthur might more truly have been compared to a crane or stork; as he leaned forward, prodding the poet with questions, his long nose might have been a long beak.

'Do you mean to tell the jury,' he asked, in tones of grating incredulity, 'that you never went in to see the deceased gentleman at all?'

'No!' replied Orm shortly.

'You wanted to see him, I suppose. You must have been very anxious to see him. Didn't you wait two whole hours in front of his front door?'

'Yes,' replied the other.

'And yet you never even noticed the door was open?'

'No,' said Orm.

'What in the world were you doing for two hours in somebody's else's front garden?' insisted the barrister. 'You were doing something I suppose?'

'Yes,'

'Is it a secret?' asked Sir Arthur, with adamantine jocularity.

'It's a secret from you,' answered the poet.

It was upon this suggestion of a secret that Sir Arthur seized in developing his line of accusation. With a boldness which some thought unscrupulous, he turned the very mystery of the motive, which was the strongest part of his opponent's case, into an argument for his own. He gave it as the first fragmentary hint of some far-flung and elaborate conspiracy, in which a patriot had perished like one caught in the coils of an octopus.

'Yes,' he cried in a vibrating voice, 'my learned friend is perfectly right! We do not know the exact reason why this honourable public servant was murdered. We shall not know the reason why the next public servant is murdered. If my learned friend himself falls a victim to his eminence, and the hatred which the hellish powers of destruction feel for the guardians of law, he will be murdered, and he will not know the reason. Half the decent people in this court will be butchered in their beds, and we shall not know the reason. And we shall never know the reason and never arrest the massacre, until it has depopulated our country, so long as the defence is permitted to stop all proceedings with this stale tag about "motive," when every other fact in the case, every glaring incongruity, every gaping silence, tells us that we stand in the presence of Cain.'

'I never knew Sir Arthur so excited,' said Bagshaw to his group of companions afterwards. 'Some people are saying he went beyond the usual limit and that the prosecutor in a murder case oughtn't to be so vindictive. But I must say there was something downright creepy about that little goblin with the yellow hair, that seemed to play up to the impression. I was vaguely recalling, all the time, something that De Quincey* says about Mr Williams, that ghastly criminal who slaughtered two whole families almost in silence. I think he says that Williams had hair of a vivid, unnatural yellow; and that he thought it had been dyed by a trick learned in India, where they dye horses green or blue. Then there was his queer, stony silence, like a troglodyte's;* I'll never deny that it all worked me up until I felt there was a sort of monster in the dock. If that was only Sir Arthur's eloquence, then he certainly took a heavy responsibility in putting so much passion into it.'

'He was a friend of poor Gwynne's, as a matter of fact,' said Underhill, more gently; 'a man I know saw them hobnobbing together after a great legal dinner lately. I dare say that's why he feels so strongly in this case. I suppose it's doubtful whether a man ought to act in such a case on mere personal feeling.'

'He wouldn't,' said Bagshaw. 'I bet Sir Arthur Travers wouldn't act only on feeling, however strongly he felt. He's got a very stiff sense of his own professional position. He's one of those men who are ambitious even when they've satisfied their ambition. I know nobody who'd take more trouble to keep his position in the world. No; you've got hold of the wrong moral to his rather thundering sermon. If he lets himself go like that, it's because he thinks he can get a conviction, anyhow, and wants to put himself at the head of some political movement against the conspiracy he talks about. He must have some very good reason for wanting to convict Orm and some very good reason for thinking he can do it. That means that the facts will support him. His confidence doesn't look well for the prisoner.' He became conscious of an insignificant figure in the group.

'Well, Father Brown,' he said with a smile; 'what do you think of our judicial procedure?'

'Well,' replied the priest rather absently, 'I think the thing that struck me most was how different men look in their wigs. You talk about the prosecuting barrister being so tremendous. But I happened to see him take his wig off for a minute, and he really looks quite a different man. He's quite bald, for one thing.'

'I'm afraid that won't prevent his being tremendous,' answered Bagshaw. 'You don't propose to found the defence on the fact that the prosecuting counsel is bald, do you?'

'Not exactly,' said Father Brown good-humouredly. 'To tell the truth, I was thinking how little some kinds of people know about other kinds of people. Suppose I went among some remote people who had never even heard of England. Suppose I told them that there is a man in my country who won't ask a question of life and death, until he has put an erection made of horse-hair on the top of his head, with little tails behind, and grey corkscrew curls at the side, like an Early Victorian old woman. They would think he must be rather eccentric; but he isn't at all eccentric; he's only conventional. They would think so, because they don't know anything about English barristers; because they don't know what a barrister is. Well, that barrister doesn't know what a poet is. He doesn't understand that a poet's eccentricities wouldn't seem eccentric to other poets. He thinks it odd that Orm should walk about in a beautiful garden for two hours, with nothing to do. God bless my soul! a poet would think nothing of walking about in the same backyard for ten hours if he had a poem to do. Orm's own counsel was quite as stupid. It never occurred to him to ask Orm the obvious question.'

'What question do you mean?' asked the other.

'Why, what poem he was making up, of course,' said Father Brown rather impatiently. 'What line he was stuck at, what epithet he was looking for, what climax he was trying to work up to. If there were any educated people in court, who know what literature is, they would have known well enough whether he had had anything genuine to do. You'd have asked a manufacturer about the conditions of his factory; but nobody seems to consider the conditions under which poetry is manufactured. It's done by doing nothing.'

'That's all very well,' replied the detective; 'but why did he hide? Why did he climb up that crooked little stairway and stop there; it led nowhere.'

'Why, because it led nowhere, of course,' cried Father Brown explosively. 'Anybody who clapped eyes on that blind alley ending in mid-air might have known an artist would want to go there, just as a child would.'

He stood blinking for a moment, and then said apologetically: 'I beg your pardon; but it seems odd that none of them understand these things. And then there was another thing. Don't you know that everything has, for an artist, one aspect or angle that is exactly *right*? A tree, a cow, and a cloud, in a certain relation only, mean something; as three letters, in one order only, mean a word. Well, the view of that illuminated garden from that unfinished bridge was the right view of it. It was as unique as the fourth dimension. It was a sort of fairy foreshortening; it was like looking *down* at heaven and seeing all the stars growing on trees and that luminous pond like a moon fallen flat on the fields in some happy nursery tale. He could have looked at it for ever. If you told him the path led nowhere, he would tell you it had led him to the country at the end of the world. But do you expect him to tell you that in the witness-box? What would you say to him if he did? You talk about a man having a jury of his peers. Why don't you have a jury of poets?'

'You talk as if you were a poet yourself,' said Bagshaw.

'Thank your stars I'm not,' said Father Brown. 'Thank your lucky stars a priest has to be more charitable than a poet. Lord have mercy on us, if you knew what a crushing, what a cruel contempt he feels for the lot of you, you'd feel as if you were under Niagara.'

'You may know more about the artistic temperament than I do,' said Bagshaw after a pause; 'but, after all, the answer is simple. You can only show that he might have done what he did, without committing the crime. But it's equally true that he might have committed the crime. And who else could have committed it?'

'Have you thought about the servant, Green?' asked Father Brown, reflectively. 'He told a rather queer story.'

'Ah,' cried Bagshaw quickly, 'you think Green did it, after all.'

'I'm quite sure he didn't,' replied the other. 'I only asked if you'd thought about his queer story. He only went out for some trifle, a drink or an assignation or what not. But he went out by the garden door and came back over the garden wall. In other words, he left the door open, but he came back to find it shut. Why? Because Somebody Else had already passed out that way.'

'The murderer,' muttered the detective doubtfully. 'Do you know who he was?'

'I know what he looked like,' answered Father Brown quietly. 'That's the only thing I do know. I can almost see him as he came in at the front door, in the gleam of the hall lamp; his figure, his clothes, even his face!'

'What's all this?'

'He looked like Sir Humphrey Gwynne,' said the priest.

'What the devil do you mean?' demanded Bagshaw. 'Gwynne was lying dead with his head in the pond.'

'Oh, yes,' said Father Brown.

After a moment he went on: 'Let's go back to that theory of yours, which was a very good one, though I don't quite agree with it. You suppose the murderer came in at the front door, met the judge in the front hall, struggling with him and breaking the mirror; that the judge then retreated into the garden, where he was finally shot. Somehow, it doesn't sound natural to me. Granted he retreated down the hall, there are two exits at the end, one into the garden and one into the house. Surely, he would be more likely to retreat into the house? His gun was there; his telephone was there; his servant, so far as he knew, was there. Even the nearest neighbours were in that direction. Why should he stop to open the garden door and go out alone on the deserted side of the house?'

'But we know he did go out of the house,' replied his companion, puzzled. 'We know he went out of the house, because he was found in the garden.'

'He never went out of the house, because he never was in the house,' said Father Brown. 'Not that evening, I mean. He was sitting in that bungalow. I read *that* lesson in the dark, at the beginning, in red and golden stars across the garden. They were worked from the hut; they wouldn't have been burning at all if he hadn't been in the hut. He was trying to run across to the house, and the telephone, when the murderer shot him beside the pond.'

'But what about the pot and the palm and the broken mirror?' cried Bagshaw. 'Why, it was you who found them! It was you yourself who said there must have been a struggle in the hall.'

The priest blinked rather painfully. 'Did I?' he muttered. 'Surely, I didn't say that. I never thought that. What I think I said, was that something had happened in the hall. And something did happen; but it wasn't a struggle.'

'Then what broke the mirror?' asked Bagshaw shortly.

'A bullet broke the mirror,' answered Father Brown gravely; 'a bullet fired by the criminal. The big fragments of falling glass were quite enough to knock over the pot and the palm.'

'Well, what else could he have been firing at except Gwynne?' asked the detective.

'It's rather a fine metaphysical point,' answered his clerical companion almost dreamily. 'In one sense, of course, he was firing at Gwynne. But Gwynne wasn't there to be fired at. The criminal was alone in the hall.'

He was silent for a moment, and then went on quietly. 'Imagine the looking-glass at the end of the passage, before it was broken, and the tall palm arching over it. In the half-light, reflecting these monochrome walls, it would look like the end of the passage. A man reflected in it would look like a man coming from inside the house. It would look like the master of the house—if only the reflection were a little like him.'

'Stop a minute,' cried Bagshaw. 'I believe I begin——'

'You begin to see,' said Father Brown. 'You begin to see why all the suspects in this case must be innocent. Not one of them could possibly have mistaken his own reflection for old Gwynne. Orm would have known at once that his bush of yellow hair was not a bald head. Flood would have seen his own red head, and Green his own red waistcoat. Besides, they're all short and shabby; none of them could have thought his own image was a tall, thin, old gentleman in evening-dress. We want another, equally tall and thin, to match him. That's what I meant by saying that I knew what the murderer looked like.'

'And what do you argue from that?' asked Bagshaw, looking at him steadily.

The priest uttered a sort of sharp, crisp laugh, oddly different from his ordinary mild manner of speech.

'I am going to argue,' he said, 'the very thing that you said was so ludicrous and impossible.'

'What do you mean?'

'I'm going to base the defence,' said Father Brown, 'on the fact that the prosecuting counsel has a bald head.'

'Oh, my God!' said the detective quietly, and got to his feet, staring.

Father Brown had resumed his monologue in an unruffled manner.

'You've been following the movements of a good many people in this business; you policemen were prodigiously interested in the movements of the poet, and the servant, and the Irishman. The man whose movements seem to have been rather forgotten is the dead man himself. His servant was quite honestly astonished at finding his master had returned. His master had gone to a great dinner of all the leaders of the legal profession, but had left it abruptly and come home. He was not ill, for he summoned no assistance; he had almost certainly quarrelled with some leader of the legal profession. It's among the leaders of that profession that we should have looked first for his enemy. He returned, and shut himself up in the bungalow, where he kept all his private documents about treasonable practices. But the leader of the legal profession, who knew there was something against him in those documents, was thoughtful enough to follow his accuser home; he also being in evening-dress, but with a pistol in his pocket. That is all; and nobody could ever have guessed it except for the mirror.'

He seemed to be gazing into vacancy for a moment, and then added:

'A queer thing is a mirror; a picture frame that holds hundreds of different pictures, all vivid and all vanished for ever. Yet, there was something specially strange about the glass that hung at the end of that grey corridor under that green palm. It is as if it was a magic glass and had a different fate from others, as if its picture could somehow survive it, hanging in the air of that twilight house like a spectre; or at least like an abstract diagram, the skeleton, of an argument. We could, at least, conjure out of the void the thing that Sir Arthur Travers saw. By the way, there was one very true thing that you said about him.'

'I'm glad to hear it,' said Bagshaw with grim good-nature. 'And what was it?'

'You said,' observed the priest, 'that Sir Arthur must have some good reason for wanting to get Orm hanged.'

A week later the priest met the police detective once more, and learned that the authorities had already been moving on the new lines of inquiry when they were interrupted by a sensational event.

'Sir Arthur Travers,' began Father Brown.

'Sir Arthur Travers is dead,' said Bagshaw, briefly.

'Ah!' said the other, with a little catch in his voice; 'you mean that he——'

'Yes,' said Bagshaw, 'he shot at the same man again, but not in a mirror.'

THE ACTOR AND THE ALIBI

MR MUNDON MANDEVILLE, the theatrical manager, walked briskly through the passages behind the scenes, or rather below the scenes. His attire was smart and festive, perhaps a little too festive; the flower in his buttonhole was festive; the very varnish on his boots was festive; but his face was not at all festive. He was a big, bull-necked, black-browed man, and at the moment his brow was blacker than usual. He had in any case, of course, the hundred botherations that besiege a man in such a position; and they ranged from large to small and from new to old. It annoyed him to pass through the passages where the old pantomime scenery was stacked; because he had successfully begun his career at that theatre with very popular pantomimes, and had since been induced to gamble in more serious and classical drama over which he had dropped a good deal of money. Hence, to see the sapphire Gates of Bluebeard's Blue Palace, or portions of the Enchanted Grove of Golden Orange Trees, leaning up against the wall to be festooned with cobwebs or nibbled by mice, did not give him that soothing sense of a return to simplicity which we all ought to have when given a glimpse of that wonderland of our childhood. Nor had he any time to drop a tear where he had dropped the money, or to dream of this Paradise of Peter Pan;* for he had been summoned hurriedly to settle a practical problem, not of the past but of the moment. It was the sort of thing that does sometimes happen in that strange world behind the scenes; but it was big enough to be serious. Miss Maroni, the talented young actress of Italian parentage, who had undertaken to act an important part in the play that was to be rehearsed that afternoon and performed that evening, had abruptly and even violently refused at the last moment to do anything of the kind. He had not even seen the exasperating lady yet; and as she had locked herself up in her dressing-room and defied the world through the door, it seemed unlikely, for the present, that he would. Mr Mundon Mandeville was sufficiently British to explain it by murmuring that all foreigners were mad; but the thought of his good fortune in inhabiting the only sane island of the planet did not suffice to soothe him any more than the memory of the Enchanted Grove. All these things, and many more, were annoying; and yet a very intimate observer might have suspected that something was wrong with Mr Mandeville that went beyond annoyance.

If it be possible for a heavy and healthy man to look haggard, he looked haggard. His face was full, but his eye-sockets were hollow; his mouth twitched as if it were always trying to bite the black strip of moustache that was just too short to be bitten. He might have been a man who had begun to take drugs; but even on that assumption there was something that suggested that he had a reason for doing it; that the drug was not the cause of the tragedy, but the tragedy the cause of the drug. Whatever was his deeper secret, it seemed to inhabit that dark end of the long passage where was the entrance to his own little study; and as he went along the empty corridor, he threw back a nervous glance now and then.

However, business is business; and he made his way to the opposite end of the passage where the blank green door of Miss Maroni defied the world. A group of actors and other people involved were already standing in front of it, conferring and considering, one might almost fancy, the advisability of a battering-ram. The group contained one figure, at least, who was already well enough known; whose photograph was on many mantelpieces and his autograph in many albums. For though Norman Knight was playing the hero in a theatre that was still a little provincial and old-fashioned and capable of calling him the first walking gentleman, he, at least, was certainly on the way to wider triumphs. He was a good-looking man with a long cleft chin and fair hair low on his forehead, giving him a rather Neronian* look that did not altogether correspond to his impulsive and plunging movements. The group also contained Ralph Randall, who generally acted elderly character parts, and had a humorous hatchet face, blue with shaving, and discoloured with grease paint. It contained Mandeville's second walking gentleman, carrying on the not yet wholly vanished tradition of Charles's Friend, a dark, curly-haired youth of somewhat Semitic profile bearing the name of Aubrey Vernon.

It included Mr Mundon Mandeville's wife's maid or dresser, a very powerful-looking person with tight red hair and a hard wooden face. It also, incidentally, included Mandeville's wife, a quiet woman in the background, with a pale, patient face, the lines of which had not lost a classical symmetry and severity, but which looked all the paler because her very eyes were pale, and her pale yellow hair lay in two plain bands like some very archaic Madonna. Not everybody knew that she had once been a serious and successful actress in Ibsen and the intellectual drama. But her husband did not think much of problem plays; and certainly at the moment was more interested in the problem of getting a foreign actress out of a locked room; a new version of the conjuring trick of the Vanishing Lady.

'Hasn't she come out yet?' he demanded, speaking to his wife's business-like attendant rather than to his wife.

'No, sir,' answered the woman—who was known as Mrs Sands—in a sombre manner.

'We are beginning to get a little alarmed,' said old Randall. 'She seemed quite unbalanced, and we're afraid she might even do herself some mischief.'

'Hell!' said Mandeville in his simple and artless way. 'Advertisement's very good, but we don't want that sort of advertisement. Hasn't she any friends here? Has nobody any influence with her?'

'Jarvis thinks the only man who might manage her is her own priest round the corner,' said Randall; 'and in case she does start hanging herself on a hat peg, . I really thought perhaps he'd better be here. Jarvis has gone to fetch him . . . and, as a matter of fact, here he comes.'

Two more figures appeared in that subterranean passage under the stage: the first was Ashton Jarvis, a jolly fellow who generally acted villains, but who had surrendered that high vocation for the moment to the curly-headed youth with the nose. The other figure was short and square and clad all in black; it was Father Brown from the church round the corner.

Father Brown seemed to take it quite naturally and even casually, that he should be called in to consider the queer conduct of one of his flock, whether she was to be regarded as a black sheep or only as a lost lamb. But he did not seem to think much of the suggestion of suicide.

'I suppose there was some reason for her flying off the handle like that,' he said. 'Does anybody know what it was?'

'Dissatisfied with her part, I believe,' said the older actor.

'They always are,' growled Mr Mundon Mandeville. 'And I thought my wife would look after those arrangements.'

'I can only say,' said Mrs Mundon Mandeville rather wearily, 'that I gave her what ought to be the best part. It's supposed to be what stage-struck young women want, isn't it—to act the beautiful young heroine and marry the beautiful young hero in a shower of bouquets and cheers from the gallery? Women of my age naturally have to fall back on acting respectable matrons, and I was careful to confine myself to that.'

'It would be devilish awkward to alter the parts now, anyhow,' said Randall.

'It's not to be thought of,' declared Norman Knight firmly. 'Why, I could hardly act—but anyhow it's much too late.'

Father Brown had slipped forward and was standing outside the locked door listening.

'Is there no sound?' asked the manager anxiously; and then added in a lower voice: 'Do you think she can have done herself in?'

'There is a certain sound,' replied Father Brown calmly. 'I should be inclined to deduce from the sound that she is engaged in breaking windows or looking-glasses, probably with her feet. No; I do not think there is much danger of her going on to destroy herself. Breaking looking-glasses with your feet is a very unusual prelude to suicide. If she had been a German, gone away to think quietly about metaphysics and *weltschmerz*,* I should be all for breaking the door down. These Italians don't really die so easily; and are not liable to kill themselves in a rage. Somebody else, perhaps . . . yes, possibly . . . it might be well to take ordinary precautions if she comes out with a leap.'

'So you're not in favour of forcing the door?' asked Mandeville.

'Not if you want her to act in your play,' replied Father Brown. 'If you do that, she'll raise the roof and refuse to stay in the place; if you leave her alone she'll probably come out from mere curiosity. If I were you, I should just leave somebody to guard the door, more or less, and trust to time for an hour or two.'

'In that case,' said Mandeville, 'we can only get on with rehearsing the scenes where she doesn't appear. My wife will arrange all that is necessary for scenery just now. After all, the fourth act is the main business. You had better get on with that.'

'Not a dress rehearsal,' said Mandeville's wife to the others.

'Very well,' said Knight, 'not a dress rehearsal, of course. I wish the dresses of the infernal period weren't so elaborate.'

'What is the play?' asked the priest with a touch of curiosity.

'*The School for Scandal*,'*said Mandeville. 'It may be literature, but I want plays. My wife likes what she calls classical comedies. A long sight more classic than comic.'

At this moment, the old doorkeeper known as Sam, and the solitary inhabitant of the theatre during off-hours, came waddling up to the manager with a card, to say that Lady Miriam Marden wished to see him. He turned away, but Father Brown continued to blink steadily for a few seconds in the direction of the manager's wife, and saw that her wan face wore a faint smile; not altogether a cheerful smile.

Father Brown moved off in company with the man who had brought him in, who happened, indeed, to be a friend and person of a similar persuasion, which is not uncommon among actors. As he moved off, however, he heard Mrs Mandeville give quiet directions to Mrs Sands that she should take up the post of watcher beside the closed door.

'Mrs Mandeville seems to be an intelligent woman,' said the priest to his companion, 'though she keeps so much in the background.'

'She was once a highly intellectual woman,' said Jarvis sadly; 'rather washed-out and wasted, some would say, by marrying a bounder like Mandeville. She has the very highest ideals of the drama, you know; but, of course, it isn't often she can get her lord and master to look at anything in that light. Do you know, he actually wanted a woman like that to act as a pantomime boy? Admitted that she was a fine actress, but said pantomimes paid better. That will give you about a measure of his psychological insight and sensibility. But she never complained. As she said to me once: "Complaint always comes back in an echo from the ends of the world; but silence strengthens us." If only she were married to somebody who understood her ideas she might have been one of the great actresses of the age; indeed, the highbrow critics still think a lot of her. As it is, she is married to that.'

And he pointed to where the big black bulk of Mandeville stood with his back to them, talking to the ladies who had summoned him forth into the vestibule. Lady Miriam was a very long and languid and elegant lady, handsome in a recent fashion largely modelled on Egyptian mummies; her dark hair cut low and square, like a sort of helmet, and her lips very painted and prominent and giving her a permanent expression of contempt. Her companion was a very vivacious lady with an ugly attractive face and hair powdered with grey. She was a Miss Theresa Talbot and she talked a great deal, while her companion seemed too tired to talk at all. Only, just as the two men passed, Lady Miriam summoned up the energy to say:

'Plays are a bore; but I've never seen a rehearsal in ordinary clothes. Might be a bit funny. Somehow, nowadays, one can never find a thing one's never seen.'

'Now, Mr Mandeville,' said Miss Talbot, tapping him on the arm with animated persistence, 'you simply must let us see that rehearsal. We can't come to-night, and we don't want to. We want to see all the funny people in the wrong clothes.'

'Of course I can give you a box if you wish it,' said Mandeville hastily. 'Perhaps your ladyship would come this way.' And he led them off down another corridor.

'I wonder,' said Jarvis in a meditative manner, 'whether even Mandeville prefers *that* sort of woman.'

'Well,' asked his clerical companion, 'have you any reason to suppose that Mandeville does prefer her?'

Jarvis looked at him steadily for an instant before answering.

'Mandeville is a mystery,' he said gravely. 'Oh, yes, I know that he looks about as commonplace a cad as ever walked down Piccadilly. But he really is a mystery for all that. There's something on his conscience. There's a shadow in his life. And I doubt whether it has anything more to do with a few fashionable flirtations than it has with his poor neglected wife. If it has, there's something more in them than meets the eye. As a matter of fact, I happen to know rather more about it than anyone else does, merely by accident. But even I can't make anything of what I know, except a mystery.'

He looked around him in the vestibule to see that they were alone and then added, lowering his voice:

'I don't mind telling you, because I know you are a tower of silence where secrets are concerned. But I had a curious shock the other day; and it has been repeated several times since. You know that Mandeville always works in that little room at the end of the passage, just under the stage. Well, twice over I happened to pass by there when everyone thought he was alone; and what's more, when I myself happened to be able to account for all the women in the company, and all the women likely to have to do with him, being absent or at their usual posts.'

'All the women?' remarked Father Brown inquiringly.

'There was a woman with him,' said Jarvis almost in a whisper. 'There is some woman who is always visiting him; somebody that none of us knows. I don't even know how she comes there, since it isn't down the passage to the door; but I think I once saw a veiled or cloaked figure passing out into the twilight at the back of the theatre, like a ghost. But she can't be a ghost. And I don't believe she's even an ordinary "affair." I don't think it's love-making. I think it's blackmail.'

'What makes you think that?' asked the other.

'Because,' said Jarvis, his face turning from grave to grim, 'I once heard sounds like a quarrel; and then the strange woman said in a metallic, menacing voice, four words: "I am your wife."'

'You think he's a bigamist,' said Father Brown reflectively. 'Well, bigamy and blackmail often go together, of course. But she may be bluffing as well as blackmailing. She may be mad. These theatrical people often have monomaniacs running after them. You may be right, but I shouldn't jump to conclusions. . . . And talking about theatrical people, isn't the rehearsal going to begin, and aren't you a theatrical person?'

'I'm not on in this scene,' said Jarvis with a smile. 'They're only doing one act, you know, until your Italian friend comes to her senses.'

'Talking about my Italian friend,' observed the priest, 'I should rather like to know whether she has come to her senses.'

'We can go back and see, if you like,' said Jarvis; and they descended again to the basement and the long passage, at one end of which was Mandeville's study and at the other the closed door of Signora Maroni. The door seemed to be still closed; and Mrs Sands sat grimly outside it, as motionless as a wooden idol.

Near the other end of the passage they caught a glimpse of some of the other actors in the scene mounting the stairs to the stage just above. Vernon and old Randall went ahead, running rapidly up the stairs; but Mrs Mandeville went more slowly, in her quietly dignified fashion, and Norman Knight seemed to linger a little to speak to her. A few words fell on the ears of the unintentional eavesdroppers as they passed.

'I tell you a woman visits him,' Knight was saying violently.

'Hush!' said the lady in her voice of silver that still had in it something of steel. 'You must not talk like this. Remember, he is my husband.'

'I wish to God I could forget it,' said Knight, and rushed up the stairs to the stage.

The lady followed him, still pale and calm, to take up her own position there.

'Somebody else knows it,' said the priest quietly; 'but I doubt whether it is any business of ours.'

'Yes,' muttered Jarvis; 'it seems as if everybody knows it and nobody knows anything about it.'

They proceeded along the passage to the other end, where the rigid attendant sat outside the Italian's door.

'No; she ain't come out yet,' said the woman in her sullen way; 'and she ain't dead, for I heard her moving about now and then. I dunno what tricks she's up to.'

'Do you happen to know, ma'am,' said Father Brown with abrupt politeness, 'where Mr Mandeville is just now?'

'Yes,' she replied promptly. 'Saw him go into his little room at the end of the passage a minute or two ago; just before the prompter called and the curtain went up. Must be there still, for I ain't seen him come out.'

'There's no other door to his office, you mean,' said Father Brown in an off-hand way. 'Well, I suppose the rehearsal's going in full swing now, for all the Signora's sulking.'

'Yes,' said Jarvis after a moment's silence; 'I can just hear the voices on the stage from here. Old Randall has a splendid carrying voice.'

They both remained for an instant in a listening attitude, so that the booming voice of the actor on the stage could indeed be heard rolling faintly down the stairs and along the passage. Before they had spoken again or resumed their normal poise, their ears were filled with another sound. It was a dull but heavy crash and it came from behind the closed door of Mundon Mandeville's private room.

Father Brown went racing along the passage like an arrow from the bow and was struggling with the door-handle before Jarvis had wakened with a start and begun to follow him.

'The door is locked,' said the priest, turning a face that was a little pale. 'And I am all in favour of breaking down *this* door.'

'Do you mean,' asked Jarvis with a rather ghastly look, 'that the unknown visitor has got in here again? Do you think it's . . . anything serious?' After a moment he added: 'I may be able to push back the bolt; I know the fastening on these doors.'

He knelt down and pulled out a pocket-knife with a long steel implement, manipulated it for a moment, and the door swung open on the manager's study. Almost the first thing they noticed was that there was no other door and even no window, but a great electric lamp stood on the table. But it was not quite the first thing that they noticed; for even before that they had seen that Mandeville was lying flat on his face in the middle of the room and the blood was crawling out from under his fallen face like a pattern of scarlet snakes that glittered evilly in that unnatural subterranean light.

They did not know how long they had been staring at each other when Jarvis said, like one letting loose something that he had held back with his breath:

'If the stranger got in somehow, she has gone somehow.'

'Perhaps we think too much about the stranger,' said Father Brown. 'There are so many strange things in this strange theatre that you rather tend to forget some of them.'

'Why, which things do you mean?' asked his friend quickly.

'There are many,' said the priest. 'There is the other locked door, for instance.'

'But the other door *is* locked,' cried Jarvis staring.

'But you forgot it all the same,' said Father Brown.

A few moments afterwards he said thoughtfully:

'That Mrs Sands is a grumpy and gloomy sort of card.'

'Do you mean,' asked the other in a lowered voice, 'that she's lying and the Italian did come out?'

'No,' said the priest calmly; 'I think I meant it more or less as a detached study of character.'

'You can't mean,' cried the actor, 'that Mrs Sands did it herself?'

'I didn't mean a study of *her* character,' said Father Brown.

While they had been exchanging these abrupt reflections, Father Brown had knelt down by the body and ascertained that it was beyond any hope or question a dead body. Lying beside it, though not immediately visible from the doorway, was a dagger of the theatrical sort; lying as if it had fallen from the wound or from the hand of the assassin. According to Jarvis, who recognized the instrument, there was not very much to be learned from it, unless the experts could find some finger-prints. It was a property dagger; that is, it was nobody's property. It had been kicking about the theatre for a long time, and anybody might have picked it up. Then the priest rose and looked gravely round the room.

'We must send for the police,' he said; 'and for a doctor, though the doctor comes too late . . . looking at this room, by the way, I don't see how our Italian friend could manage it.'

'The Italian!' cried his friend; 'I should think not. I should have thought she had an alibi, if anybody had. Two separate rooms, both locked, at opposite ends of a long passage, with a fixed witness watching it.'

'No,' said Father Brown. 'Not quite. The difficulty is how she could have got in this end. I think she might have got out the other end.'

'And why?' asked the other.

'I told you,' said Father Brown, 'that it sounded as if she was breaking glass—mirrors or windows. Stupidly enough I forgot something I knew quite well; that she is pretty superstitious. She wouldn't be likely to break a mirror; so I suspect she broke a window. It's true that all this is under the ground floor; but it might be a skylight or a window opening on an area. But there don't seem to be any skylights or areas here.' And he stared at the ceiling very intently for a considerable time.

Suddenly he came back to conscious life again with a start. 'We must go upstairs and telephone and tell everybody. It is pretty painful. . . . My God, can you hear those actors still shouting and ranting upstairs? The play is still going on. I suppose that's what they mean by tragic irony.'

When it was fated that the theatre should be turned into a house of mourning, an opportunity was given to the actors to show many of the real virtues of their type and trade. They did, as the phrase goes, behave like gentlemen; and not only like first walking gentlemen. They had not all of them liked or trusted Mandeville, but they knew exactly the right things to say about him; they showed not only sympathy but delicacy in their attitude to his widow. She had become, in a new and very different sense, a tragedy queen—her lightest word was law and while she moved about slowly and sadly, they ran her many errands.

'She was always a strong character,' said old Randall rather huskily; 'and had the best brains of any of us. Of course poor Mandeville was never on her level in education and so on; but she always did her duty splendidly. It was quite pathetic the way she would sometimes say she wished she had more intellectual life; but Mandeville—well, *nil nisi bonum*,* as they say.' And the old gentleman went away wagging his head sadly.

'*Nil nisi bonum* indeed,' said Jarvis grimly. 'I don't think Randall at any rate has heard of the story of the strange lady visitor. By the way, don't you think it probably *was* the strange woman?'

'It depends,' said the priest, 'whom you mean by the strange woman.'

'Oh! I don't mean the Italian woman,' said Jarvis hastily. 'Though, as a matter of fact, you were quite right about her, too. When they went in the skylight was smashed and the room was empty; but so far as the police can discover, she simply went home in the most harmless fashion. No, I mean the woman who was heard threatening him at that secret meeting; the woman who said she was his wife. Do you think she really was his wife?'

'It is possible,' said Father Brown, staring blankly into the void, 'that she really was his wife.'

'That would give us the motive of jealousy over his bigamous remarriage,' reflected Jarvis, 'for the body was not robbed in any way. No need to poke about for thieving servants or even impecunious actors. But as for that, of course, you've noticed the outstanding and peculiar thing about the case?'

'I have noticed several peculiar things,' said Father Brown. 'Which one do you mean?'

'I mean the corporate alibi,' said Jarvis gravely. 'It's not often that practically a whole company has a public alibi like that; an alibi on a lighted stage and all witnessing to each other. As it turns out it is jolly lucky for our friends here that poor Mandeville did put those two silly society women in the box to watch the rehearsal. They can bear witness that the whole act was performed without a hitch, with the characters on the stage all the time. They began long before Mandeville was last seen going into his room. They went on at least five or ten minutes after you and I found his dead body. And, by a lucky coincidence, the moment we actually heard him fall was during the time when all the characters were on the stage together.'

'Yes, that is certainly very important and simplifies everything,' agreed Father Brown. 'Let us count the people covered by the alibi. There was Randall: I rather fancy Randall practically hated the manager, though he is very properly covering his feelings just now. But he is ruled out; it was his voice we heard thundering over our heads from the stage. There is our *jeune premier*,* Mr Knight: I have rather good reason to suppose he was in love with Mandeville's wife and not concealing that sentiment so much as he might; but he is out of it, for he was on the stage at the same time, being thundered at. There was that amiable Jew who calls himself Aubrey Vernon, he's out of it; and there's Mrs Mandeville, she's out of it. Their corporate alibi, as you say, depends chiefly on Lady Miriam and her friend in the box; though there is the general common-sense corroboration that the act had to be gone through and the routine of the theatre seems to have suffered no interruption. The legal witnesses, however, are Lady Miriam and her friend, Miss Talbot. I suppose you feel sure *they* are all right?'

'Lady Miriam?' said Jarvis in surprise. 'Oh, yes. . . . I suppose you mean that she looks a queer sort of vamp. But you've no notion what even the ladies of the best families are looking like nowadays. Besides, is there any particular reason for doubting their evidence?'

'Only that it brings us up against a blank wall,' said Father Brown. 'Don't you see that this collective alibi practically covers everybody? Those four were the only performers in the theatre at the time; and there were scarcely any servants in the theatre; none indeed, except old Sam, who guards the only regular entrance, and the woman who guarded Miss Maroni's door. There is nobody else left available but you and me. We certainly might be accused of the crime, especially as we found the body. There seems nobody else who can be accused. You didn't happen to kill him when I wasn't looking, I suppose?'

Jarvis looked up with a slight start and stared a moment, then the broad grin returned to his swarthy face. He shook his head.

'You didn't do it,' said Father Brown; 'and we will assume for the moment, merely for the sake of argument, that I didn't do it. The people on the stage being out of it, it really leaves the Signora behind her locked door, the sentinel in front of her door, and old Sam. Or are you thinking of the two ladies in the box? Of course they might have slipped out of the box.'

'No,' said Jarvis; 'I am thinking of the unknown woman who came and told Mandeville she was his wife.'

'Perhaps she was,' said the priest; and this time there was a note in his steady voice that made his companion start to his feet once more and lean across the table.

'We said,' he observed in a low, eager voice, 'that this first wife might have been jealous of the other wife.'

'No,' said Father Brown; 'she might have been jealous of the Italian girl, perhaps, or of Lady Miriam Marden. But she was not jealous of the other wife.'

'And why not?'

'Because there was no other wife,' said Father Brown. 'So far from being a bigamist, Mr Mandeville seems to me to have been a highly monogamous person. His wife was almost too much with him; so much with him that you all charitably suppose that she must be somebody else. But I don't see how she could have been with him when he was killed, for we agree that she was acting all the time in front of the footlights. Acting an important part, too. . . .'

'Do you really mean,' cried Jarvis, 'that the strange woman who haunted him like a ghost was only the Mrs Mandeville we know?' But he received no answer; for Father Brown was staring into vacancy with a blank expression almost like an idiot's. He always did look most idiotic at the instant when he was most intelligent.

The next moment he scrambled to his feet, looking very harassed and distressed. 'This is awful,' he said. 'I'm not sure it isn't the worst business I ever had; but I've got to go through with it. Would you go and ask Mrs Mandeville if I may speak to her in private?'

'Oh, certainly,' said Jarvis, as he turned towards the door. 'But what's the matter with you?'

'Only being a born fool,' said Father Brown; 'a very common complaint in this vale of tears. I was fool enough to forget altogether that the play was *The School for Scandal.*'

He walked restlessly up and down the room until Jarvis reappeared at the door with an altered and even alarmed face.

'I can't find her anywhere,' he said. 'Nobody seems to have seen her.'

'They haven't seen Norman Knight either, have they?' asked Father Brown dryly. 'Well, it saves me the most painful interview of my life. Saving the grace of God, I was very nearly frightened of that woman. But she was frightened of me, too; frightened of something I'd seen or said. Knight was always begging her to bolt with him. Now she's done it; and I'm devilish sorry for him.'

'For him?' inquired Jarvis.

'Well, it can't be very nice to elope with a murderess,' said the other dispassionately. 'But as a matter of fact she was something very much worse than a murderess.'

'And what is that?'

'An egoist,' said Father Brown. 'She was the sort of person who had looked in the mirror before looking out of the window, and it is the worst calamity of mortal life. The looking-glass was unlucky for her, all right; but rather because it wasn't broken.'

'I can't understand what all this means,' said Jarvis. 'Everybody regarded her as a person of the most exalted ideals, almost moving on a higher spiritual plane than the rest of us. . . .'

'She regarded herself in that light,' said the other; 'and she knew how to hypnotize everybody else into it. Perhaps I hadn't known her long enough to be wrong about her. But I knew the sort of person she was five minutes after I clapped eyes on her.'

'Oh, come!' cried Jarvis; 'I'm sure her behaviour about the Italian was beautiful.'

'Her behaviour always was beautiful,' said the other. 'I've heard from everybody here all about her refinements and subtleties and spiritual soarings above poor Mandeville's head. But all these spiritualities and subtleties seem to me to boil themselves down to the simple fact that she certainly was a lady and he most certainly was not a gentleman. But, do you know, I have never felt quite sure that St Peter will make that the only test at the gate of heaven.

'As for the rest,' he went on with increasing animation, 'I knew from the very first words she said that she was not really being fair to the poor Italian, with all her fine airs of frigid magnanimity. And again, I realized it when I knew that the play was *The School for Scandal*.'

'You are going rather too fast for me,' said Jarvis in some bewilderment. 'What does it matter what the play was?'

'Well,' said the priest, 'she said she had given the girl the part of the beautiful heroine and had retired into the background herself with the older part of a matron. Now that might have applied to almost any play; but it falsifies the facts about that particular play. She can only have meant that she gave the other actress the part of Maria, which is hardly a part at all. And the part of the obscure and self-effacing married woman, if you please, must have been the part of Lady Teazle, which is the only part any actress wants to act. If the Italian was a first-rate actress who had been promised a first-rate part, there was really some excuse, or at least some cause, for her mad Italian rage. There generally is for mad Italian rages: Latins are logical and have a reason for going mad. But that one little thing let in daylight for me on the meaning of her magnanimity. And there was another thing, even then. You laughed when I said that the sulky look of Mrs Sands was a study in character; but not in the character of Mrs Sands. But it was true. If you want to know what a lady is really like, don't look at her; for she may be too clever for you. Don't look at the men round her, for they may be too silly about her. But look at some other woman who is always near to her, and especially one who is under her. You will see in that mirror her real face, and the face mirrored in Mrs Sands was very ugly.

'And as for all the other impressions, what were they? I heard a lot about the unworthiness of poor old Mandeville; but it was all about his being unworthy of her, and I am pretty certain it came indirectly from her. And, even so, it betrayed itself. Obviously, from what every man said, she had confided in every man about her confounded intellectual loneliness. You yourself said she never complained; and then quoted her about how her uncomplaining silence strengthened her soul. And that is just the note; that's the unmistakable style. People who complain are just jolly, human, Christian nuisances; I don't mind them. But people who complain that they never complain are the devil. They are really the devil; isn't that swagger of stoicism the whole point of the Byronic cult of Satan? I heard all this; but for the life of me I couldn't hear of anything tangible she had to complain of. Nobody pretended that her husband drank, or beat her, or left her without money, or even was unfaithful, until the rumour about the secret meetings, which were simply her own melodramatic habit of pestering him with curtain-lectures in his own business office. And when one looked at the facts, apart from the atmospheric impression of martyrdom she contrived to spread, the facts were really quite the other way. Mandeville left off making money on pantomimes to please her; he started losing money on classical drama to please her. She arranged the scenery and furniture as she liked. She wanted Sheridan's play and she had it; she wanted the part of Lady Teazle and she had it; she wanted a rehearsal without costume at that particular hour and she had it. It may be worth remarking on the curious fact that she wanted that.'

'But what is the use of all this tirade?' asked the actor, who had hardly ever heard his clerical friend make so long a speech before. 'We seem to have got a long way from the murder in all this psychological business. She may have eloped with Knight; she may have bamboozled Randall; she may have bamboozled me. But she can't have murdered her husband— for everyone agrees she was on the stage through the whole scene. She may be wicked; but she isn't a witch.'

'Well, I wouldn't be so sure,' said Father Brown, with a smile. 'But she didn't need to use any witchcraft in this case. I know now that she did it, and very simply indeed.'

'Why are you so sure of that?' asked Jarvis, looking at him in a puzzled way.

'Because the play was *The School for Scandal*,' replied Father Brown, 'and that particular act of *The School for Scandal*. I should like to remind you, as I said just now, that she always arranged the furniture how she liked. I should also like to remind you that this stage was built and used for pantomimes; it would naturally have trap-doors and trick exits of that sort. And when you say that witnesses could attest to having seen all the performers on the stage, I should like to remind you that in the principal scene of *The School for Scandal* one of the principal performers remains for a considerable time on the stage, but is *not* seen. She is technically "on," but she might practically be very much "off." That is the Screen of Lady Teazle and the Alibi of Mrs Mandeville.'

There was a silence and then the actor said: 'You think she slipped through a trap-door behind a screen down to the floor below, where the manager's room was?'

'She certainly slipped away in some fashion; and that is the most probable fashion,' said the other. 'I think it all the more probable because she took the opportunity of an undress rehearsal, and even indeed arranged for one. It is a guess; but I fancy if it had been a dress rehearsal it might have been more difficult to get through a trap-door in the hoops of the eighteenth century. There are many little difficulties, of course, but I think they could all be met in time and in turn.'

'What I can't meet is the big difficulty,' said Jarvis, putting his head on his hand with a sort of groan. 'I simply can't bring myself to believe that a radiant and serene creature like that could so lose, so to speak, her bodily balance, to say nothing of her moral balance. Was any motive strong enough? Was she very much in love with Knight?'

'I hope so,' replied his companion; 'for really it would be the most human excuse. But I'm sorry to say that I have my doubts. She wanted to get rid of her husband, who was an old-fashioned provincial hack, not even making much money. She wanted to have a career as the brilliant wife of a brilliant and rapidly-rising actor. But she didn't want in that sense to act in *The School for Scandal*. She wouldn't have run away with a man except in the last resort. It wasn't a human passion with her, but a sort of hellish respectability. She was always dogging her husband in secret and badgering him to divorce himself or otherwise get out of the way; and as he refused he paid at last for his refusal. There's another thing you've got to remember. You talk about these highbrows having a higher art and a more philosophical drama. But remember what a lot of the philosophy is! Remember what sort of conduct those highbrows often present to the highest! All about the Will to Power and the Right to Live and the Right to Experience ... damned nonsense and more than damned nonsense—nonsense that can damn.'

Father Brown frowned, which he did very rarely; and there was still a cloud on his brow as he put on his hat and went out into the night.

THE WORST CRIME IN THE WORLD

FATHER BROWN was wandering through a picture gallery with an expression that suggested that he had not come there to look at the pictures. Indeed, he did not want to look at the pictures, though he liked pictures well enough. Not that there

was anything immoral or improper about those highly modern pictorial designs. He would indeed be of an inflammable
temperament who was stirred to any of the more pagan
passions by the display of interrupted spirals, inverted cones
and broken cylinders with which the art of the future inspired
or menaced mankind. The truth is that Father Brown was
looking for a young friend who had appointed that somewhat
incongruous meeting-place, being herself of a more futuristic
turn. The young friend was also a young relative,* one of the
few relatives that he had. Her name was Elizabeth Fane,
simplified into Betty, and she was the child of a sister who had
married into a race of refined but impoverished squires. As the
squire was dead as well as impoverished, Father Brown stood
in the relation of a protector as well as a priest, and in some
sense a guardian as well as an uncle. At the moment, however,
he was blinking about at the groups in the gallery without
catching sight of the familiar brown hair and bright face of his
niece. Nevertheless, he saw some people he knew and a
number of people he did not know, including some that, as a
mere matter of taste, he did not much want to know.

Among the people the priest did not know and who yet
aroused his interest was a lithe and alert young man, very
beautifully dressed and looking rather like a foreigner, because, while his beard was cut in a spade shape like an old
Spaniard's, his dark hair was cropped so close as to look like
a tight black skull-cap. Among the people the priest did not
particularly want to know was a very dominant-looking lady,
sensationally clad in scarlet, with a mane of yellow hair too
long to be called bobbed, but too loose to be called anything
else. She had a powerful and rather heavy face of a pale and
rather unwholesome complexion, and when she looked at
anybody she cultivated the fascinations of a basilisk. She
towed in attendance behind her a short man with a big beard
and a very broad face, with long sleepy slits of eyes. The
expression of his face was beaming and benevolent, if only
partially awake; but his bull neck, when seen from behind,
looked a little brutal.

Father Brown gazed at the lady, feeling that the appearance
and approach of his niece would be an agreeable contrast. Yet

he continued to gaze, for some reason, until he reached the point of feeling that the appearance of anybody would be an agreeable contrast. It was therefore with a certain relief, though with a slight start as of awakening, that he turned at the sound of his name and saw another face that he knew.

It was the sharp but not unfriendly face of a lawyer named Granby, whose patches of grey hair might almost have been the powder from a wig, so incongruous were they with his youthful energy of movement. He was one of those men in the City who run about like schoolboys in and out of their offices. He could not run round the fashionable picture gallery quite in that fashion; but he looked as if he wanted to, and fretted as he glanced to left and right, seeking somebody he knew.

'I didn't know,' said Father Brown, smiling, 'that you were a patron of the New Art.'

'I didn't know that you were,' retorted the other. 'I came here to catch a man.'

'I hope you will have good sport,' answered the priest. 'I'm doing much the same.'

'Said he was passing through to the Continent,' snorted the solicitor, 'and could I meet him in this cranky place.' He ruminated a moment, and said abruptly: 'Look here, I know you can keep a secret. Do you know Sir John Musgrave?'

'No,' answered the priest; 'but I should hardly have thought he was a secret, though they say he does hide himself in a castle. Isn't he the old man they tell all those tales about—how he lives in a tower with a real portcullis and drawbridge, and generally refuses to emerge from the Dark Ages? Is he one of your clients?'

'No,' replied Granby shortly: 'it's his son, Captain Musgrave, who has come to us. But the old man counts for a good deal in the affair, and I don't know him; that's the point. Look here, this is confidential, as I say, but I can confide in you.' He dropped his voice and drew his friend apart into a side gallery containing representations of various real objects, which was comparatively empty.

'This young Musgrave,' he said, 'wants to raise a big sum from us on a *post obit** on his old father in Northumberland. The old man's long past seventy and presumably will *obit* some time or other; but what about the *post*, so to speak? What will happen afterwards to his cash and castles and portcullises and all the rest? It's a very fine old estate, and still worth a lot, but strangely enough it isn't entailed. So you see how we stand. The question is, as the man said in Dickens, is the old man friendly?'*

'If he's friendly to his son you'll feel all the friendlier,' observed Father Brown. 'No, I'm afraid I can't help you. I never met Sir John Musgrave, and I understand very few people do meet him nowadays. But it seems obvious you have a right to an answer on that point before you lend the young gentleman your firm's money. Is he the sort that people cut off with a shilling?'

'Well, I'm doubtful,' answered the other. 'He's very popular and brilliant and a great figure in society; but he's a great deal abroad, and he's been a journalist.'

'Well,' said Father Brown, 'that's not a crime. At least not always.'

'Nonsense!' said Granby curtly. 'You know what I mean—he's rather a rolling stone, who's been a journalist and a lecturer and an actor, and all sorts of things. I've got to know where I stand. . . . Why, there he is.'

And the solicitor, who had been stamping impatiently about the emptier gallery, turned suddenly and darted into the more crowded room at a run. He was running towards the tall and well-dressed young man with the short hair and the foreign-looking beard.

The two walked away together talking, and for some moments afterwards Father Brown followed them with his screwed, short-sighted eyes. His gaze was shifted and recalled, however, by the breathless and even boisterous arrival of his niece, Betty. Rather to the surprise of her uncle, she led him back into the emptier room and planted him on a seat that was like an island in that sea of floor.

'I've got something I must tell you,' she said. 'It's so silly that nobody else will understand it.'

'You overwhelm me,' said Father Brown. 'Is it about this business your mother started telling me about? Engagements and all that; not what the military historians call a general engagement.'

'You know,' she said, 'that she wants me to be engaged to Captain Musgrave.'

'I didn't,' said Father Brown with resignation; 'but Captain Musgrave seems to be quite a fashionable topic.'

'Of course we're very poor,' she said, 'and it's no good saying it makes no difference.'

'Do you want to marry him?' asked Father Brown, looking at her through his half-closed eyes.

She frowned at the floor, and answered in a lower tone:

'I thought I did. At least I think I thought I did. But I've just had rather a shock.'

'Then tell us all about it.'

'I heard him laugh,' she said.

'It is an excellent social accomplishment,' he replied.

'You don't understand,' said the girl. 'It wasn't social at all. That was just the point of it—that it wasn't social.'

She paused a moment, and then went on firmly:

'I came here quite early, and saw him sitting quite alone in the middle of that gallery with the new pictures, that was quite empty then. He had no idea I or anybody was near; he was sitting quite alone, and he laughed.'

'Well, no wonder,' said Father Brown. 'I'm not an art critic myself, but as a general view of the pictures taken as a whole——'

'Oh, you *won't* understand,' she said almost angrily. 'It wasn't a bit like that. He wasn't looking at the pictures. He was staring right up at the ceiling; but his eyes seemed to be turned inwards, and he laughed so that my blood ran cold.'

The priest had risen and was pacing the room with his hands behind him. 'You mustn't be hasty in a case of this sort,' he began. 'There are two kinds of men—but we can hardly discuss him just now, for here he is.'

Captain Musgrave entered the room swiftly and swept it with a smile. Granby, the lawyer, was just behind him, and his legal face bore a new expression of relief and satisfaction.

'I must apologize for everything I said about the Captain,' he said to the priest as they drifted together towards the door. 'He's a thoroughly sensible fellow and quite sees my point. He asked me himself why I didn't go north and see his old father; I could hear from the old man's own lips how it stood about the inheritance. Well, he couldn't say fairer than that, could he? But he's so anxious to get the thing settled that he offered to take me up in his own car to Musgrave Moss. That's the name of the estate. I suggested that, if he was so kind, we might go together; and we're starting to-morrow morning.'

As they spoke Betty and the Captain came through the doorway together, making in that framework at least a sort of picture that some would be sentimental enough to prefer to cones and cylinders. Whatever their other affinities, they were both very good-looking; and the lawyer was moved to a remark on the fact, when the picture abruptly altered.

Captain James Musgrave looked out into the main gallery, and his laughing and triumphant eyes were riveted on something that seemed to change him from head to foot. Father Brown looked round as under an advancing shadow of premonition; and he saw the lowering, almost livid face of the large woman in scarlet under its leonine yellow hair. She always stood with a slight stoop like a bull lowering its horns and the expression of her pale pasty face was so oppressive and hypnotic that they hardly saw the little man with the large beard standing beside her.

Musgrave advanced into the centre of the room towards her, almost like a beautifully dressed wax-work wound up to walk. He said a few words to her that could not be heard. She did not answer; but they turned away together, walking down the long gallery as if in debate, the short, bull-necked man with the beard bringing up the rear like some grotesque goblin page.

'Heaven help us!' muttered Father Brown, frowning after them. 'Who in the world is that woman?'

'No pal of mine, I'm happy to say,' replied Granby with grim flippancy. 'Looks as if a little flirtation with her might end fatally, doesn't it?'

'I don't think he's flirting with her,' said Father Brown.

Even as he spoke the group in question turned at the end of the gallery and broke up, and Captain Musgrave came back to them in hasty strides.

'Look here,' he cried, speaking naturally enough, though they fancied his colour was changed. 'I'm awfully sorry, Mr Granby, but I find I can't come north with you to-morrow. Of course, you will take the car all the same. Please do; I shan't want it. I—I have to be in London for some days. Take a friend with you if you like.'

'My friend, Father Brown——' began the lawyer.

'If Captain Musgrave is really so kind,' said Father Brown gravely. 'I may explain that I have some status in Mr Granby's inquiry, and it would be a great relief to my mind if I could go.'

Which was how it came about that a very elegant car, with an equally elegant chauffeur, shot north the next day over the Yorkshire moors, bearing the incongruous burden of a priest who looked rather like a black bundle, and a lawyer who had the habit of running about on his feet instead of racing on somebody else's wheels.

They broke their journey very agreeably in one of the great dales of the West Riding,* dining and sleeping at a comfortable inn, and starting early next day, began to run along the Northumbrian coast till they reached a country that was a maze of sand dunes and rank sea meadows, somewhere in the heart of which lay the old Border castle which had remained so unique and yet so secretive a monument of the old Border wars. They found it at last, by following a path running beside a long arm of the sea that ran inland, and turned eventually into a sort of rude canal ending in the moat of the castle. The castle really was a castle, of the square, embattled plan that the Normans built everywhere from Galilee to the Grampians.* It did really and truly have a portcullis and a drawbridge, and they were very realistically reminded of the fact by an accident that delayed their entrance.

They waded amid long coarse grass and thistle to the bank of the moat which ran in a ribbon of black with dead leaves and scum upon it, like ebony inlaid with a pattern of gold. Barely a yard or two beyond the black ribbon was the other green bank and the big stone pillars of the gateway. But so little, it would seem, had this lonely fastness been approached from outside that when the impatient Granby halloed across to the dim figures behind the portcullis, they seemed to have considerable difficulty even in lowering the great rusty draw-bridge. It started on its way, turning over like a great falling tower above them, and then stuck, sticking out in mid-air at a threatening angle.

The impatient Granby, dancing upon the bank, called out to his companion:

'Oh, I can't stand these stick-in-the-mud ways! Why, it'd be less trouble to jump.'

And with characteristic impetuosity he did jump, landing with a slight stagger in safety on the inner shore. Father Brown's short legs were not adapted to jumping. But his temper was more adapted than most people's to falling with a splash into very muddy water. By the promptitude of his companion he escaped falling in very far. But as he was being hauled up the green, slimy bank, he stopped with bent head, peering at a particular point upon the grassy slope.

'Are you botanizing?' asked Granby irritably. 'We've got no time for you to collect rare plants after your last attempt as a diver among the wonders of the deep. Come on, muddy or no, we've got to present ourselves before the baronet.'

When they had penetrated into the castle, they were re-ceived courteously enough by an old servant, the only one in sight, and after indicating their business were shown into a long oak-panelled room with latticed windows of antiquated pattern. Weapons of many different centuries hung in bal-anced patterns on the dark walls, and a complete suit of fourteenth-century armour stood like a sentinel beside the large fireplace. In another long room beyond could be seen, through the half-open door, the dark colours of the rows of family portraits.

'I feel as if I'd got into a novel instead of a house,' said the lawyer. 'I'd no idea anybody did really keep up the "Mysteries of Udolpho"* in this fashion.'

'Yes; the old gentleman certainly carries out his historical craze consistently,' answered the priest; 'and these things are not fakes, either. It's not done by somebody who thinks all mediæval people lived at the same time. Sometimes they make up suits of armour out of different bits; but that suit all covered one man, and covered him very completely. You, see it's the late sort of tilting-armour.'

'I think he's a late sort of host, if it comes to that,' grumbled Granby. 'He's keeping us waiting the devil of a time.'

'You must expect everything to go slowly in a place like this,' said Father Brown. 'I think it's very decent of him to see us at all: two total strangers come to ask him highly personal questions.'

And, indeed, when the master of the house appeared they had no reason to complain of their reception; but rather became conscious of something genuine in the traditions of breeding and behaviour that could retain their native dignity without difficulty in that barbarous solitude, and after those long years of rustication and moping. The baronet did not seem either surprised or embarrassed at the rare visitation; though they suspected that he had not had a stranger in his house for a quarter of a life-time, he behaved as if he had been bowing out duchesses a moment before. He showed neither shyness nor impatience when they touched on the very private matter of their errand; after a little leisurely reflection he seemed to recognize their curiosity as justified under the circumstances. He was a thin, keen-looking old gentleman, with black eyebrows and a long chin, and though the carefully-curled hair he wore was undoubtedly a wig, he had the wisdom to wear the grey wig of an elderly man.

'As regards the question that immediately concerns you,' he said, 'the answer is very simple indeed. I do most certainly propose to hand on the whole of my property to my son, as my father handed it on to me; and nothing—I say advisedly, nothing—would induce me to take any other course.'

'I am most profoundly grateful for the information,' answered the lawyer. 'But your kindness encourages me to say that you are putting it very strongly. I would not suggest that it is in the least likely that your son would do anything to make you doubt his fitness for the charge. Still he might——'

'Exactly,' said Sir John Musgrave dryly, 'he might. It is rather an under-statement to say that he might. Will you be good enough to step into the next room with me for a moment.'

He led them into the further gallery, of which they had already caught a glimpse, and gravely paused before a row of the blackened and lowering portraits.

'This is Sir Roger Musgrave,' he said, pointing to a long-faced person in a black periwig. 'He was one of the lowest liars and rascals in the rascally time of William of Orange, a traitor to two kings and something like the murderer of two wives. That is his father, Sir Robert, a perfectly honest old cavalier. That is his son, Sir James, one of the noblest of the Jacobite martyrs and one of the first men to attempt some reparation to the Church and the poor. Does it matter that the House of Musgrave, the power, the honour, the authority, descended from one good man to another good man through the interval of a bad one? Edward I governed England well. Edward III covered England with glory. And yet the second glory came from the first glory through the infamy and imbecility of Edward II, who fawned upon Gaveston and ran away from Bruce. Believe me, Mr Granby, the greatness of a great house and history is something more than these accidental individuals who carry it on, even though they do not grace it. From father to son our heritage has come down, and from father to son it shall continue. You may assure yourselves, gentlemen, and you may assure my son, that I shall not leave my money to a home for lost cats. Musgrave shall leave it to Musgrave till the heavens fall.'

'Yes,' said Father Brown thoughtfully; 'I see what you mean.'

'And we shall be only too glad,' said the solicitor, 'to convey such a happy assurance to your son.'

'You may convey the assurance,' said their host gravely. 'He is secure in any event of having the castle, the title, the land and the money. There is only a small and merely private addition to that arrangement. Under no circumstances whatever will I ever see or speak to him as long as I live.'

The lawyer remained in the same respectful attitude, but he was now respectfully staring.

'Why, what on earth has he——'

'I am a private gentleman,' said Musgrave, 'as well as the custodian of a great inheritance. And my son did something so horrible that he has ceased to be—I will not say a gentleman—but even a human being. It is the worst crime in the world. Do you remember what Douglas said when Marmion, his guest,* offered to shake hands with him?'

'Yes,' said Father Brown.

'"My castles are my king's alone, from turret to foundation stone,"' said Musgrave. '"The hand of Douglas is his own."'

He turned towards the other room and showed his rather dazed visitors back into it.

'I hope you will take some refreshment,' he said, in the same equable fashion. 'If you have any doubt about your movements, I should be delighted to offer you the hospitality of the castle for the night.'

'Thank you, Sir John,' said the priest in a dull voice, 'but I think we had better go.'

'I will have the bridge lowered at once,' said their host; and in a few moments the creaking of that huge and absurdly antiquated apparatus filled the castle like the grinding of a mill. Rusty as it was, however, it worked successfully this time, and they found themselves standing once more on the grassy bank beyond the moat.

Granby was suddenly shaken by a shudder.

'What in hell was it that his son did?' he cried.

Father Brown made no answer. But when they had driven off again in their car and pursued their journey to a village not far off, called Graystones, where they alighted at the inn of the Seven Stars, the lawyer learned with a little mild surprise that the priest did not propose to travel much farther; in other words, that he had apparently every intention of remaining in the neighbourhood.

'I cannot bring myself to leave it like this,' he said gravely. 'I will send back the car, and you, of course, may very naturally want to go with it. Your question is answered; it is simply whether your firm can afford to lend money on young Musgrave's prospects. But my question isn't answered; it is whether he is a fit husband for Betty. I must try to discover whether he's really done something dreadful, or whether it's the delusion of an old lunatic.'

'But,' objected the lawyer, 'if you want to find out about him, why don't you go after him? Why should you hang about in this desolate hole where he hardly ever comes?'

'What would be the use of my going after him?' asked the other. 'There's no sense in going up to a fashionable young man in Bond Street and saying: "Excuse me, but have you committed a crime too horrible for a human being?" If he's bad enough to do it, he's certainly bad enough to deny it. And we don't even know what it is. No, there's only one man that knows, and *may* tell, in some further outburst of dignified eccentricity. I'm going to keep near him for the present.'

And in truth Father Brown did keep near the eccentric baronet, and did actually meet him on more than one occasion, with the utmost politeness on both sides. For the baronet, in spite of his years, was very vigorous and a great walker, and could often be seen stumping through the village, and along the country lanes. Only the day after their arrival, Father Brown, coming out of the inn on to the cobbled market-place, saw the dark and distinguished figure stride past in the direction of the post office. He was very quietly dressed in black, but his strong face was even more arresting in the strong sunlight; with his silvery hair, swarthy eyebrows and long chin, he had something of a reminiscence of Henry Irving, or some other famous actor. In spite of his hoary hair, his figure as well as his face suggested strength, and he carried his stick more like a cudgel than a crutch. He saluted the priest, and spoke with the same air of coming fearlessly to the point which had marked his revelations of yesterday.

'If you are still interested in my son,' he said, using the term with an icy indifference, 'you will not see very much of him. He has just left the country. Between ourselves, I might say fled the country.'

'Indeed,' said Father Brown with a grave stare.

'Some people I never heard of, called Grunov, have been pestering me, of all people, about his whereabouts,' said Sir John; 'and I've just come in to send off a wire to tell them that, so far as I know, he's living in the Poste Restante, Riga. Even that has been a nuisance. I came in yesterday to do it, but was five minutes too late for the post office. Are you staying long? I hope you will pay me another visit.'

When the priest recounted to the lawyer his little interview with old Musgrave in the village, the lawyer was both puzzled and interested.

'Why has the Captain bolted?' he asked. 'Who are the other people who want him? Who on earth are the Grunovs?'

'For the first, I don't know,' replied Father Brown. 'Possibly his mysterious sin has come to light. I should rather guess that the other people are blackmailing him about it. For the third, I think I do know. That horrible fat woman with yellow hair is called Madame Grunov, and that little man passes as her husband.'

The next day Father Brown came in rather wearily, and threw down his black bundle of an umbrella with the air of a pilgrim laying down his staff. He had an air of some depression. But it was as it was so often in his criminal investigations. It was not the depression of failure, but the depression of success.

'It's rather a shock,' he said in a dull voice; 'but I ought to have guessed it. I ought to have guessed it when I first went in and saw the thing standing there.'

'When you saw what?' asked Granby impatiently.

'When I saw there was only one suit of armour,' answered Father Brown.

There was a silence during which the lawyer only stared at his friend, and then the friend resumed.

'Only the other day I was just going to tell my niece that there are two types of men who can laugh when they are alone. One might almost say the man who does it is either very good or very bad. You see, he is either confiding the joke to God or confiding it to the Devil. But anyhow he has an inner life. Well, there really is a kind of man who confides the joke to the Devil. He does not mind if nobody sees the joke; if nobody can safely be allowed even to know the joke. The joke is enough in itself, if it is sufficiently sinister and malignant.'

'But what are you talking about?' demanded Granby. '*Whom* are you talking about? Which of them, I mean? *Who* is this person who is having a sinister joke with his Satanic Majesty?'

Father Brown looked across at him with a ghastly smile.

'Ah,' he said, 'that's the joke.'

There was another silence, but this time the silence seemed to be rather full and oppressive than merely empty; it seemed to settle down on them like the twilight that was gradually turning from dusk to dark. Father Brown went on speaking in a level voice, sitting stolidly with his elbows on the table.

'I've been looking up the Musgrave family,' he said. 'They are vigorous and long-lived stock, and even in the ordinary way I should think you would wait a good time for your money.'

'We're quite prepared for that,' answered the solicitor; 'but anyhow it can't last indefinitely. The old man is nearly eighty, though he still walks about, and the people at the inn here laugh and say they don't believe he will ever die.'

Father Brown jumped up with one of his rare but rapid movements, but remained with his hands on the table, leaning forward and looking his friend in the face.

'That's it,' he cried in a low but excited voice. 'That's the only problem. That's the only real difficulty. How will he die? How on earth is he to die?'

'What on earth do you mean?' asked Granby.

'I mean,' came the voice of the priest out of the darkening room, 'that I know the crime that James Musgrave committed.'

His tones had such a chill in them that Granby could hardly repress a shiver; he murmured a further question.

'It was really the worst crime in the world,' said Father Brown. 'At least, many communities and civilizations have accounted it so. It was always from the earliest times marked out in tribe and village for tremendous punishment. But anyhow, I know now what young Musgrave really did and why he did it.'

'And what did he do?' asked the lawyer.

'He killed his father,' answered the priest.

The lawyer in his turn rose from his seat and gazed across the table with wrinkled brows.

'But his father is at the castle,' he cried in sharp tones.

'His father is in the moat,' said the priest, 'and I was a fool not to have known it from the first when something bothered me about that suit of armour. Don't you remember the look of that room? How very carefully it was arranged and decorated? There were two crossed battle-axes hung on one side of the fire-place, two crossed battle-axes on the other. There was a round Scottish shield on one wall, a round Scottish shield on the other. And there was a stand of armour guarding one side of the hearth, and an empty space on the other. Nothing will make me believe that a man who arranged all the rest of that room with that exaggerated symmetry left that one feature of it lopsided. There was almost certainly another man in armour. And what has become of him?'

He paused a moment, and then went on in a more matter-of-fact tone:

'When you come to think of it, it's a very good plan for a murder, and meets the permanent problem of the disposal of the body. The body could stand inside that complete tilting-armour for hours, or even days, while servants came and went, until the murderer could simply drag it out in the dead of night and lower it into the moat, without even crossing the bridge. And then what a good chance he ran! As soon as the body was at all decayed in the stagnant water there would sooner or later be nothing but a skeleton in fourteenth-century armour, a thing very likely to be found in the moat of an old Border castle. It was unlikely that anybody would look for anything there, but if they did, that would soon be all they would find. And I got some confirmation of that. That was when you said I was looking for a rare plant; it was a plant in a good many senses, if you'll excuse the jest. I saw the marks of two feet sunk so deep into the solid bank I was sure that the man was either very heavy or was carrying something very heavy. Also, by the way, there's another moral from that little incident when I made my celebrated graceful and cat-like leap.'

'My brain is rather reeling,' said Granby, 'but I begin to have some notion of what all this nightmare is about. What about you and your cat-like leap?'

'At the post office to-day,' said Father Brown, 'I casually confirmed the statement the baronet made to me yesterday, that he had been there just after closing-time on the day previous—that is, not only on the very day we arrived, but at the very time we arrived. Don't you see what that means? It means that he was actually out when we called, and came back while we were waiting; and that was why we had to wait so long. And when I saw that, I suddenly saw a picture that told the whole story.'

'Well,' asked the other impatiently, 'and what about it?'

'An old man of eighty can walk,' said Father Brown. 'An old man can even walk a good deal, pottering about in country lanes. But an old man can't *jump*. He would be an even less graceful jumper than I was. Yet, if the baronet came back while we were waiting, he must have come in as we came in—by jumping the moat—for the bridge wasn't lowered till later. I rather guess he had hampered it himself to delay inconvenient visitors, to judge by the rapidity with which it was repaired. But that doesn't matter. When I saw that fancy picture of the black figure with the grey hair taking a flying leap across the moat I knew instantly that it was a young man dressed up as an old man. And there you have the whole story.'

'You mean,' said Granby slowly, 'that this pleasing youth killed his father, hid the corpse first in the armour and then in the moat, disguised himself and so on?'

'They happened to be almost exactly alike,' said the priest. 'You could see from the family portraits how strong the likeness ran. And then you talk of his disguising himself. But in a sense everybody's dress is a disguise. The old man disguised himself in a wig, and the young man in a foreign beard. When he shaved and put the wig on his cropped head he was exactly like his father, with a little make-up. Of course, you understand now why he was so very polite about getting you to come up next day here by car. It was because he himself was coming up that night by train. He got in front of you, committed his crime, assumed his disguise, and was ready for the legal negotiations.'

'Ah,' said Granby thoughtfully, 'the legal negotiations! You mean, of course, that the real old baronet would have negotiated very differently.'

'He would have told you plainly that the Captain would never get a penny,' said Father Brown. 'The plot, queer as it sounds, was really the only way of preventing his telling you so. But I want you to appreciate the cunning of what the fellow did tell you. His plan answered several purposes at once. He was being blackmailed by these Russians for some villainy; I suspect for treason during the war. He escaped from them at a stroke, and probably sent them chasing off to Riga after him. But the most beautiful refinement of all was that theory he enunciated about recognizing his son as an heir, but not as a human being. Don't see that while it secured the *post obit*, it also provided some sort of answer to what would soon be the greatest difficulty of all?'

'I see several difficulties,' said Granby; 'which one do you mean?'

'I mean that if the son was not even disinherited, it would look rather odd that the father and son never met. The theory of a private repudiation answered that. So there only remained one difficulty, as I say, which is probably perplexing the gentleman now. How on earth is the old man to die?'

'I know how he ought to die,' said Granby.

Father Brown seemed to be a little bemused, and went on in a more abstracted fashion.

'And yet there is something more in it than that,' he said. 'There was something about that theory that he liked in a way that is more—well, more theoretical. It gave him an insane intellectual pleasure to tell you in one character that he had committed a crime in another character—when he really had. That is what I mean by the infernal irony; by the joke shared with the Devil. Shall I tell you something that sounds like what they call a paradox? Sometimes it is a joy in the very heart of hell to tell the truth. And above all, to tell it so that everybody misunderstands it. That is why he liked that antic of pretending to be somebody else, and then painting himself as black—as he was. And that was why my niece heard him laughing to himself all alone in the picture gallery.'

Granby gave a slight start, like a person brought back to common things with a bump.

'Your niece,' he cried. 'Didn't her mother want her to marry Musgrave? A question of wealth and position, I suppose.'

'Yes,' said Father Brown dryly; 'her mother was all in favour of a prudent marriage.'

THE CHIEF MOURNER OF MARNE

A BLAZE of lightning blanched the grey woods tracing all the wrinkled foliage down to the last curled leaf, as if every detail were drawn in silverpoint or graven in silver. The same strange trick of lightning by which it seems to record millions of minute things in an instant of time, picked out everything, from the elegant litter of the picnic spread under the spreading tree to the pale lengths of winding road, at the end of which a white car was waiting. In the distance a melancholy mansion with four towers like a castle, which in the grey evening had been but a dim and distant huddle of walls like a crumbling cloud, seemed to spring into the foreground, and stood up with all its embattled roofs and blank and staring windows. And in this, at least, the light had something in it of revelation. For to some of those grouped under the tree that castle was, indeed, a thing faded and almost forgotten, which was to prove its power to spring up again in the foreground of their lives.

The light also clothed for an instant, in the same silver splendour, at least one human figure that stood up as motionless as one of the towers. It was that of a tall man standing on a rise of ground above the rest, who were mostly sitting on the grass or stooping to gather up the hamper and crockery. He wore a picturesque short cloak or cape clasped with a silver clasp and chain, which blazed like a star when the flash touched it; and something metallic in his motionless figure was emphasized by the fact that his closely-curled hair was of

the burnished yellow that can be really called gold; and had
the look of being younger than his face, which was handsome
in a hard aquiline fashion, but looked, under the strong light,
a little wrinkled and withered. Possibly it had suffered from
wearing a mask of make-up, for Hugo Romaine was the
greatest actor of his day. For that instant of illumination the
golden curls and ivory mask and silver ornament made his
figure gleam like that of a man in armour; the next instant his
figure was a dark and even black silhouette against the sickly
grey of the rainy evening sky.

But there was something about its stillness, like that of a
statue, that distinguished it from the group at his feet. All the
other figures around him had made the ordinary involuntary
movement at the unexpected shock of light; for though the
skies were rainy it was the first flash of the storm. The only
lady present, whose air of carrying grey hair gracefully, as if
she were really proud of it, marked her a matron of the United
States, unaffectedly shut her eyes and uttered a sharp cry. Her
English husband, General Outram, a very stolid Anglo-Indian,
with a bald head and black moustache and whiskers of antiquated pattern, looked up with one stiff movement and then
resumed his occupation of tidying up. A young man of the
name of Mallow, very big and shy, with brown eyes like a
dog's, dropped a cup and apologized awkwardly. A third man,
much more dressy, with a resolute head, like an inquisitive
terrier's, and grey hair brushed stiffly back, was no other than
the great newspaper proprietor, Sir John Cockspur;* he cursed
freely, but not in an English idiom or accent, for he came from
Toronto. But the tall man in the short cloak stood up literally
like a statue in the twilight; his eagle face under the full glare
had been like the bust of a Roman Emperor, and the carved
eyelids had not moved.

A moment after, the dark dome cracked across with thunder, and the statue seemed to come to life. He turned his head
over his shoulder and said casually;

'About a minute and half between the flash and the bang,
but I think the storm's coming nearer. A tree is not supposed
to be a good umbrella for the lightning, but we shall want it
soon for the rain. I think it will be a deluge.'

The young man glanced at the lady a little anxiously and said: 'Can't we get shelter anywhere? There seems to be a house over there.'

'There is a house over there,' remarked the general, rather grimly; 'but not quite what you'd call a hospitable hotel.'

'It's curious,' said his wife sadly, 'that we should be caught in a storm with no house near but that one, of all others.'

Something in her tone seemed to check the younger man, who was both sensitive and comprehending; but nothing of that sort daunted the man from Toronto.

'What's the matter with it?' he asked. 'Looks rather like a ruin.'

'That place,' said the general dryly, 'belongs to the Marquis of Marne.'

'Gee!' said Sir John Cockspur. 'I've heard all about that bird, anyhow; and a queer bird, too. Ran him as a front-page mystery in the *Comet* last year. "The Nobleman Nobody Knows."'

'Yes, I've heard of him, too,' said young Mallow in a low voice. 'There seem to be all sorts of weird stories about why he hides himself like that. I've heard that he wears a mask because he's a leper. But somebody else told me quite seriously that there's a curse on the family; a child born with some frightful deformity that's kept in a dark room.'

'The Marquis of Marne has three heads,' remarked Romaine quite gravely. 'Once in every three hundred years a three-headed nobleman adorns the family tree. No human being dares approach the accursed house except a silent procession of hatters, sent to provide an abnormal number of hats. But'—and his voice took one of those deep and terrible turns, that could cause such a thrill in the theatre—'my friends, *those hats are of no human shape.*'

The American lady looked at him with a frown and a slight air of distrust, as if that trick of voice had moved her in spite of herself.

'I don't like your ghoulish jokes,' she said; 'and I'd rather you didn't joke about this, anyhow.'

'I hear and obey,' replied the actor; 'but am I, like the Light Brigade, forbidden even to reason why?'

'The reason,' she replied, 'is that he isn't the Nobleman Nobody Knows. I know him myself, or, at least, I knew him very well when he was an attaché at Washington thirty years ago, when we were all young. And he didn't wear a mask, at least, he didn't wear it with me. He wasn't a leper, though he may be almost as lonely. And he had only one head and only one heart, and that was broken.'

'Unfortunate love affair, of course,' said Cockspur. 'I should like that for the *Comet*.'

'I suppose it's a compliment to us,' she replied thoughtfully, 'that you always assume a man's heart is broken by a woman. But there are other kinds of love and bereavement. Have you never read "In Memoriam"?* Have you never heard of David and Jonathan?* What broke poor Marne up was the death of his brother; at least, he was really a first cousin, but had been brought up with him like a brother, and was much nearer than most brothers. James Mair, as the marquis was called when I knew him, was the elder of the two, but he always played the part of worshipper, with Maurice Mair as a god. And, by his account, Maurice Mair was certainly a wonder. James was no fool, and very good at his own political job; but it seems that Maurice could do that and everything else; that he was a brilliant artist and amateur actor and musician, and all the rest of it. James was very good-looking himself, long and strong and strenuous, with a high-bridged nose; though I suppose the young people would think he looked very quaint with his beard divided into two bushy whiskers in the fashion of those Victorian times. But Maurice was clean-shaven, and, by the portraits shown to me, certainly quite beautiful; though he looked a little more like a tenor than a gentleman ought to look. James was always asking me again and again whether his friend was not a marvel, whether any woman wouldn't fall in love with him, and so on, until it became rather a bore, except that it turned so suddenly into a tragedy. His whole life seemed to be in that idolatry, and one day the idol tumbled down, and was broken like any china doll. A chill caught at the seaside, and it was all over.'

'And after that,' asked the young man, 'did he shut himself up like this?'

'He went abroad at first,' she answered; 'away to Asia and the Cannibal Islands and Lord knows where. These deadly strokes take different people in different ways. It took him in the way of an utter sundering or severance from everything, even from tradition and as far as possible from memory. He could not bear a reference to the old tie; a portrait or an anecdote or even an association. He couldn't bear the business of a great public funeral. He longed to get away. He stayed away for ten years. I heard some rumour that he had begun to revive a little at the end of the exile; but when he came back to his own home he relapsed completely. He settled down into religious melancholia, and that's practically madness.'

'The priests got hold of him, they say,' grumbled the old general. 'I know he gave thousands to found a monastery, and lives himself rather like a monk—or, at any rate, a hermit. Can't understand what good they think that will do.'

'Goddarned superstition,' snorted Cockspur; 'that sort of thing ought to be shown up. Here's a man that might have been useful to the Empire and the world, and these vampires get hold of him and suck him dry. I bet with their unnatural notions they haven't even let him marry.'

'No, he has never married,' said the lady. 'He was engaged when I knew him, as a matter of fact, but I don't think it ever came first with him, and I think it went with the rest when everything else went. Like Hamlet and Ophelia—he lost hold of love because he lost hold of life. But I knew the girl; indeed, I know her still. Between ourselves, it was Viola Grayson, daughter of the old admiral. She's never married either.'

'It's infamous! It's infernal!' cried Sir John, bounding up. 'It's not only a tragedy, but a crime. I've got a duty to the public, and I mean to see all this nonsensical nightmare . . . in the twentieth century——'

He was almost choked with his own protest, and then, after a silence, the old soldier said:

'Well, I don't profess to know much about those things, but I think these religious people need to study a text which says: "Let the dead bury their dead."'

'Only, unfortunately, that's just what it looks like,' said his wife with a sigh. 'It's just like some creepy story of a dead man burying another dead man, over and over again for ever.'

'The storm has passed over us,' said Romaine, with a rather inscrutable smile. 'You will not have to visit the inhospitable house after all.'

She suddenly shuddered.

'Oh, I'll never do that again!' she exclaimed.

Mallow was staring at her.

'Again! Have you tried it before?' he cried.

'Well, I did once,' she said, with a lightness not without a touch of pride; 'but we needn't go back on all that. It's not raining now, but I think we'd better be moving back to the car.'

As they moved off in procession, Mallow and the general brought up the rear; and the latter said abruptly, lowering his voice:

'I don't want that little cad Cockspur to hear but as you've asked you'd better know. It's the one thing I can't forgive Marne; but I suppose these monks have drilled him that way. My wife, who had been the best friend he ever had in America, actually came to that house when he was walking in the garden. He was looking at the ground like a monk, and hidden in a black hood that was really as ridiculous as any mask. She had sent her card in, and stood there in his very path. And he walked past her without a word or a glance, as if she had been a stone. He wasn't human; he was like some horrible automaton. She may well call him a dead man.'

'It's all very strange,' said the young man rather vaguely. 'It isn't like—like what I should have expected.'

Young Mr Mallow, when he left that rather dismal picnic, took himself thoughtfully in search of a friend. He did not know any monks, but he knew one priest, whom he was very much concerned to confront with the curious revelations he had heard that afternoon. He felt he would very much like to know the truth about the cruel superstition that hung over the house of Marne, like the black thundercloud he had seen hovering over it.

After being referred from one place to another, he finally ran his friend Father Brown to earth in the house of another friend, a Roman Catholic friend with a large family. He entered somewhat abruptly to find Father Brown sitting on the floor with a serious expression, and attempting to pin the somewhat florid hat belonging to a wax doll on to the head of a teddy bear.

Mallow felt a faint sense of incongruity; but he was far too full of his problem to put off the conversation if he could help it. He was staggering from a sort of set-back in a subconscious process that had been going on for some time. He poured out the whole tragedy of the house of Marne as he had heard it from the general's wife, along with most of the comments of the general and the newspaper proprietor. A new atmosphere of attention seemed to be created with the mention of the newspaper proprietor.

Father Brown neither knew nor cared that his attitudes were comic or commonplace. He continued to sit on the floor, where his large head and short legs made him look very like a baby playing with toys. But there came into his great grey eyes a certain expression that has been seen in the eyes of many men in many centuries through the story of nineteen hundred years; only the men were not generally sitting on floors, but at council tables, or on the seats of chapters, or the thrones of bishops and cardinals; a far-off, watchful look, heavy with the humility of a charge too great for men. Something of that anxious and far-reaching look is found in the eyes of sailors and of those who have steered through so many storms the ship of St Peter.

'It's very good of you to tell me this,' he said. 'I'm really awfully grateful, for we may have to do something about it. If it were only people like you and the general, it might be only a private matter; but if Sir John Cockspur is going to spread some sort of scare in his papers—well, he's a Toronto Orangeman,* and we can hardly keep out of it.'

'But what will you say about it?' asked Mallow anxiously.

'The first thing I should say about it,' said Father Brown, 'is that, as you tell it, it doesn't sound like life. Suppose, for the sake of argument, that we are all pessimistic vampires blight-

ing all human happiness. Suppose I'm a pessimistic vampire.'
He scratched his nose with the teddy bear, became faintly
conscious of the incongruity, and put it down. 'Suppose we do
destroy all human and family ties. Why should we entangle a
man again in an old family tie just when he showed signs of
getting loose from it? Surely it's a little unfair to charge us
both with crushing such affection and encouraging such
infatuation. I don't see why even a religious maniac should
be that particular sort of monomaniac, or how religion
could increase that mania, except by brightening it with a
little hope.'

Then he said, after a pause: 'I should like to talk to that
general of yours.'

'It was his wife who told me,' said Mallow.

'Yes,' replied the other; 'but I'm more interested in what he
didn't tell you than in what she did.'

'You think he knows more than she does?'

'I think he knows more than she says,' answered Father
Brown. 'You tell me he used a phrase about forgiving everything except the rudeness to his wife. After all, what else was
there to forgive?'

Father Brown had risen and shaken his shapeless clothes,
and stood looking at the young man with screwed up eyes and
a slightly quizzical expression. The next moment he had
turned, and picking up his equally shapeless umbrella and
large shabby hat, went stumping down the street.

He plodded through a variety of wide streets and squares
till he came to a handsome old-fashioned house in the West
End, where he asked the servant if he could see General
Outram. After some little palaver he was shown into a study,
fitted out less with books than with maps and globes, where
the bald-headed, black-whiskered Anglo-Indian sat smoking a
long, thin, black cigar and playing with pins on a chart.

'I am sorry to intrude,' said the priest, 'and all the more
because I can't help the intrusion looking like interference. I
want to speak to you about a private matter, but only in the
hope of keeping it private. Unfortunately, some people are
likely to make it public. I think, general, that you know Sir
John Cockspur.'

The mass of black moustache and whisker served as a sort of mask for the lower half of the old general's face; it was always hard to see whether he smiled, but his brown eyes often had a certain twinkle.

'Everybody knows him, I suppose,' he said. 'I don't know him very well.'

'Well, you know everybody knows whatever he knows.' said Father Brown, smiling, 'when he thinks it convenient to print it. And I understand from my friend Mr Mallow, whom, I think, you know, that Sir John is going to print some scorching anti-clerical articles founded on what he would call the Marne Mystery. "Monks Drive Marquis Mad," etc.'

'If he is,' replied the general, 'I don't see why you should come to me about it. I ought to tell you I'm a strong Protestant.'

'I'm very fond of strong Protestants,' said Father Brown. 'I came to you because I was sure you would tell the truth. I hope it is not uncharitable to feel less sure of Sir John Cockspur.'

The brown eyes twinkled again, but the general said nothing.

'General,' said Father Brown, 'suppose Cockspur or his sort were going to make the world ring with tales against your country and your flag. Suppose he said your regiment ran away in battle, or your staff were in the pay of the enemy. Would you let anything stand between you and the facts that would refute him? Wouldn't you get on the track of the truth at all costs to anybody? Well, I have a regiment, and I belong to an army. It is being discredited by what I am certain is a fictitious story; but I don't know the true story. Can you blame me for trying to find it out?'

The soldier was silent, and the priest continued:

'I have heard the story Mallow was told yesterday, about Marne retiring with a broken heart through the death of his more than brother. I am sure there was more in it than that. I came to ask you if you know any more.'

'No,' said the general shortly; 'I cannot tell you any more.'

'General,' said Father Brown with a broad grin, 'you would have called me a Jesuit if I had used that equivocation.'

The soldier laughed gruffly, and then growled with much greater hostility.

'Well, I won't tell you, then,' he said. 'What do you say to that?'

'I only say,' said the priest mildly, 'that in that case I shall have to tell you.'

The brown eyes stared at him; but there was no twinkle in them now. He went on:

'You compel me to state, less sympathetically perhaps than you could, why it is obvious that there is more behind. I am quite sure the marquis has better cause for his brooding and secretiveness than merely having lost an old friend. I doubt whether priests have anything to do with it; I don't even know if he's a convert or merely a man comforting his conscience with charities; but I'm sure he's something more than a chief mourner. Since you insist, I will tell you one or two of the things that made me think so.

'First, it was stated that James Mair was engaged to be married, but somehow became unattached again after the death of Maurice Mair. Why should an honourable man break off his engagement merely because he was depressed by the death of a third party? He's much more likely to have tuned for consolation to it; but, anyhow, he was bound in decency to go through with it.'

The general was biting his black moustache, and his brown eyes had become very watchful and even anxious, but he did not answer.

'A second point,' said Father Brown, frowning at the table. 'James Mair was always asking his lady friend whether his cousin Maurice was not very fascinating, and whether women would not admire him. I don't know if it occurred to the lady that there might be another meaning to that inquiry.'

The general got to his feet and began to walk or stamp about the room.

'Oh, damn it all,' he said, but without any air of animosity.

'The third point,' went on Father Brown, 'is James Mair's curious manner of mourning—destroying all relics, veiling all portraits, and so on. It does sometimes happen, I admit; it might mean mere affectionate bereavement. But it might mean something else.'

'Confound you,' said the other. 'How long are you going on piling this up?'

'The fourth and fifth points are pretty conclusive,' said the priest calmly, 'especially if you take them together. The first is that Maurice Mair seems to have had no funeral in particular, considering he was a cadet of a great family. He must have been buried hurriedly; perhaps secretly. And the last point is, that James Mair instantly disappeared to foreign parts; fled, in fact, to the ends of the earth.

'And so,' he went on, still in the same soft voice, 'when you would blacken my religion to brighten the story of the pure and perfect affection of two brothers, it seems——'

'Stop!' cried Outram in a tone like a pistol shot. 'I must tell you more, or you will fancy worse. Let me tell you one thing to start with. It was a fair fight.'

'Ah,' said Father Brown, and seemed to exhale a huge breath.

'It was a duel,' said the other. 'It was probably the last duel fought in England, and it is long ago now.'

'That's better,' said Father Brown. 'Thank God; that's a great deal better.'

'Better than the ugly things you thought of, I suppose?' said the general gruffly. 'Well, it's all very well for you to sneer at the pure and perfect affection; but it was true for all that. James Mair really was devoted to his cousin, who'd grown up with him like a younger brother. Elder brothers and sisters do sometimes devote themselves to a child like that, especially when he's a sort of infant phenomenon. But James Mair was the sort of simple character in whom even hate is in a sense unselfish. I mean that even when his tenderness turns to rage it is still objective, directed outwards to its object; he isn't conscious of himself. Now poor Maurice Mair was just the opposite. He was far more friendly and popular; but his success had made him live in a house of mirrors. He was first in every sort of sport and art and accomplishment; he nearly always won and took his winning amiably. But if ever, by any chance, he lost, there was just a glimpse of something not so

amiable; he was a little jealous. I needn't tell you the whole
miserable story of how he was a little jealous of his cousin's
engagement; how he couldn't keep his restless vanity from
interfering. It's enough to say that one of the few things in
which James Mair was admittedly ahead of him was marks-
manship with a pistol; and with that the tragedy ended.'

'You mean the tragedy began,' replied the priest. 'The tragedy of the survivor. I thought he did not need any monkish
vampires to make him miserable.'

'To my mind he's more miserable than he need be,' said the
general. 'After all, as I say, it was a ghastly tragedy, but it was
a fair fight. And Jim had great provocation.'

'How do you know all this?' asked the priest.

'I know it because I saw it,' answered Outram stolidly. 'I
was James Mair's second, and I saw Maurice Mair shot dead
on the sands before my very eyes.'

'I wish you would tell me more about it,' said Father Brown
reflectively. 'Who was Maurice Mair's second?'

'He had a more distinguished backing,' replied the general
grimly. 'Hugo Romaine was his second; the great actor, you
know. Maurice was mad on acting and had taken up Romaine
(who was then a rising but still a struggling man), and
financed the fellow and his ventures in return for taking
lessons from the professional in his own hobby of amateur
acting. But Romaine was then, I suppose, practically dependent on his rich friend; though he's richer now than any
aristocrat. So his serving as second proves very little about
what he thought of the quarrel. They fought in the English
fashion, with only one second apiece; I wanted at least to have
a surgeon, but Maurice boisterously refused it, saying the
fewer people who knew, the better; and at the worst we could
immediately get help. "There's a doctor in the village not half
a mile away," he said; "I know him and he's got the fastest
horse in the country. He could be brought here in no time; but
there's no need to bring him here till we know." Well, we all
knew that Maurice ran most risk, as the pistol was not his
weapon; so when he refused aid nobody liked to ask for it.
The duel was fought on a flat stretch of sand on the east coast
of Scotland; and both the sight and sound of it were masked

from the hamlets inland by a long rampart of sandhills patched with rank grass; probably part of the links, though in those days no Englishman had heard of golf. There was one deep, crooked cranny in the sandhills through which we came out on the sands. I can see them now; first a wide strip of dead yellow, and beyond, a narrower strip of dark red; a dark red that seemed already like the long shadow of a deed of blood.

'The thing itself seemed to happen with horrible speed; as if a whirlwind had struck the sand. With the very crack of sound Maurice Mair seemed to spin like a teetotum and pitch upon his face like a ninepin. And queerly enough, while I'd been worrying about him up to that moment, the instant he was dead all my pity was for the man who killed him; as it is to this day and hour. I knew that with that, the whole huge terrible pendulum of my friend's life-long love would swing back; and that whatever cause others might find to pardon him, he would never pardon himself for ever and ever. And so, some-how, the really vivid thing, the picture that burns in my memory so that I can't forget it, is not that of the catastrophe, the smoke and the flash and the falling figure. That seemed to be all over, like the noise that wakes a man up. What I saw, what I shall always see, is poor Jim hurrying across towards his fallen friend and foe; his brown beard looking black against the ghastly pallor of his face, with its high features cut out against the sea; and the frantic gestures with which he waved me to run for the surgeon in the hamlet behind the sandhills. He had dropped his pistol as he ran; he had a glove in one hand and the loose and fluttering fingers of it seemed to elongate and emphasize his wild pantomime of pointing or hailing for help. That is the picture that really remains with me; and there is nothing else in that picture, except the striped background of sands and sea and the dark, dead body lying still as a stone, and the dark figure of the dead man's second standing grim and motionless against the horizon.'

'Did Romaine stand motionless?' asked the priest. 'I should have thought he would have run even quicker towards the corpse.'

'Perhaps he did when I had left,' replied the general. 'I took in that undying picture in an instant and the next instant I had dived among the sandhills, and was far out of sight of the others. Well, poor Maurice had made a good choice in the matter of doctors; though the doctor came too late, he came quicker than I should have thought possible. This village surgeon was a very remarkable man, redhaired, irascible, but extraordinarily strong in promptitude and presence of mind. I saw him but for a flash as he leapt on his horse and went thundering away to the scene of death, leaving me far behind. But in that flash I had so strong a sense of his personality that I wished to God he had really been called in before the duel began; for I believe on my soul he would have prevented it somehow. As it was, he cleaned up the mess with marvellous swiftness; long before I could trail back to the sea-shore on my two feet his impetuous practicality had managed everything; the corpse was temporarily buried in the sandhills and the unhappy homicide had been persuaded to do the only thing he could do—to flee for his life. He slipped along the coast till he came to a port and managed to get out of the country. You know the rest; poor Jim remained abroad for many years; later, when the whole thing had been hushed up or forgotten, he returned to his dismal castle and automatically inherited the title. I have never seen him from that day to this, and yet I know what is written in red letters in the inmost darkness of his brain.'

'I understand,' said Father Brown, 'that some of you have made efforts to see him?'

'My wife never relaxed her efforts,' said the general. 'She refuses to admit that such a crime ought to cut a man off for ever; and I confess I am inclined to agree with her. Eighty years before it would have been thought quite normal; and really it was manslaughter rather than murder. My wife is a great friend of the unfortunate lady who was the occasion of the quarrel and she has an idea that if Jim would consent to see Viola Grayson once again, and receive her assurance that old quarrels are buried, it might restore his sanity. My wife is calling a sort of council of old friends to-morrow, I believe. She is very energetic.'

Father Brown was playing with the pins that lay beside the general's map; he seemed to listen rather absent-mindedly. He had the sort of mind that sees things in pictures; and the picture which had coloured even the prosaic mind of the practical soldier took on tints yet more significant and sinister in the more mystical mind of the priest. He saw the dark-red desolation of sand, the very hue of Aceldama,* and the dead man lying in a dark heap, and the slayer, stooping as he ran, gesticulating with a glove in demented remorse, and always his imagination came back to the third thing that he could not yet fit into any human picture: the second of the slain man standing motionless and mysterious, like a dark statue on the edge of the sea. It might seem to some a detail; but for him it was that stiff figure that stood up like a standing note of interrogation.

Why had not Romaine moved instantly? It was the natural thing for a second to do, in common humanity, let alone friendship. Even if there were some double-dealing or darker motive not yet understood, one would think it would be done for the sake of appearances. Anyhow, when the thing was all over, it would be natural for the second to stir long before the other second had vanished beyond the sandhills.

'Does this man Romaine move very slowly?' he asked.

'It's queer you should ask that,' answered Outram, with a sharp glance. 'No, as a matter of fact he moves very quickly when he moves at all. But, curiously enough, I was just thinking that only this afternoon I saw him stand exactly like that, during the thunderstorm. He stood in that silver-clasped cape of his, and with one hand on his hip, exactly and in every line as he stood on those bloody sands long ago. The lightning blinded us all, but he did not blink. When it was dark again he was standing there still.'

'I suppose he isn't standing there now?' inquired Father Brown. 'I mean, I suppose he moved sometime?'

'No, he moved quite sharply when the thunder came,' replied the other. 'he seemed to have been waiting for it, for he told us the exact time of the interval . . . is anything the matter?'

'I've pricked myself with one of your pins,' said Father Brown. 'I hope I haven't damaged it.' But his eyes had snapped and his mouth abruptly shut.

'Are you ill?' inquired the general, staring at him.

'No,' answered the priest; 'I'm only not quite so stoical as your friend Romaine. I can't help blinking when I see light.'

He turned to gather up his hat and umbrella; but when he had got to the door he seemed to remember something and turned back. Coming up close to Outram, he gazed up into his face with a rather helpless expression, as of a dying fish, and made a motion as if to hold him by the waistcoat.

'General,' he almost whispered, 'for God's sake don't let your wife and that other woman insist on seeing Marne again. Let sleeping dogs lie, or you'll unleash all the hounds of hell.'

The general was left alone with a look of bewilderment in his brown eyes, as he sat down again to play with his pins.

Even greater, however, was the bewilderment which attended the successive stages of the benevolent conspiracy of the general's wife, who had assembled her little group of sympathizers to storm the castle of the misanthrope. The first surprise she encountered was the unexplained absence of one of the actors in the ancient tragedy. When they assembled by agreement at a quiet hotel quite near the castle, there was no sign of Hugo Romaine, until a belated telegram from a lawyer told them that the great actor had suddenly left the country. The second surprise, when they began the bombardment by sending up word to the castle with an urgent request for an interview, was the figure which came forth from those gloomy gates to receive the deputation in the name of the noble owner. It was no such figure as they would have conceived suitable to those sombre avenues or those almost feudal formalities. It was not some stately steward or major-domo, nor even a dignified butler or tall and ornamental footman. The only figure that came out of the cavernous castle doorway was the short and shabby figure of Father Brown.

'Look here,' he said, in his simple, bothered fashion. 'I told you you'd much better leave him alone. He knows what he's doing and it'll only make everybody unhappy.'

Lady Outram, who was accompanied by a tall and quietly-dressed lady, still very handsome, presumably the original Miss Grayson, looked at the little priest with cold contempt.

'Really sir,' she said; 'this is a very private occasion, and I don't understand what you have to do with it.'

'Trust a priest to have to do with a private occasion,' snarled Sir John Cockspur. 'Don't you know they live behind the scenes like rats behind a wainscot burrowing their way into everybody's private rooms. See how he's already in possession of poor Marne.' Sir John was slightly sulky, as his aristocratic friends had persuaded him to give up the great scoop of publicity in return for the privilege of being really inside a Society secret. It never occurred to him to ask himself whether *he* was at all like a rat in a wainscot.

'Oh, that's all right,' said Father Brown, with the impatience of anxiety. 'I've talked it over with the marquis and the only priest he's ever had anything to do with; his clerical tastes have been much exaggerated. I tell you he knows what he's about; and I do implore you all to leave him alone.'

'You mean to leave him to this living death of moping and going mad in a ruin!' cried Lady Outram, in a voice that shook a little. 'And all because he had the bad luck to shoot a man in a duel more than a quarter of a century ago. Is that what you call Christian charity?

'Yes,' answered the priest stolidly; 'that is what I call Christian charity.'

'It's about all the Christian charity you'll ever get out of these priests,' cried Cockspur bitterly. 'That's their only idea of pardoning a poor fellow for a piece of folly; to wall him up alive and starve him to death with fasts and penances and pictures of hell-fire. And all because a bullet went wrong.'

'Really, Father Brown,' said General Outram, 'do you honestly think he deserves this? Is that your Christianity?'

'Surely the true Christianity,' pleaded his wife more gently, 'is that which knows all and pardons all; the love that can remember—and forget.'

'Father Brown,' said young Mallow, very earnestly, 'I generally agree with what you say; but I'm hanged if I can follow you here. A shot in a duel, followed instantly by remorse, is not such an awful offence.'

'I admit,' said Father Brown dully, 'that I take a more serious view of his offence.'

'God soften your hard heart,' said the strange lady speaking for the first time. 'I am going to speak to my old friend.'

Almost as if her voice had raised a ghost in that great grey house, something stirred within and a figure stood in the dark doorway at the top of the great stone flight of steps. It was clad in dead black, but there was something wild about the blanched hair and something in the pale features that was like the wreck of a marble statue.

Viola Grayson began calmly to move up the great flight of steps; and Outram muttered in his thick black moustache: 'He won't cut her dead as he did my wife, I fancy.'

Father Brown, who seemed in a collapse of resignation, looked up at him for a moment.

'Poor Marne has enough on his conscience,' he said. 'Let us acquit him of what we can. At least he never cut your wife.'

'What do you mean by that?'

'He never knew her,' said Father Brown.

As they spoke, the tall lady proudly mounted the last step and came face to face with the Marquis of Marne. His lips moved, but something happened before he could speak.

A scream rang across the open space and went wailing away in echoes along those hollow walls. By the abruptness and agony with which it broke from the woman's lips it might have been a mere inarticulate cry. But it was an articulated word; and they all heard it with a horrible distinctness.

'Maurice!'

'What is it, dear?' cried Lady Outram, and began to run up the steps; for the other woman was swaying as if she might fall down the whole stone flight. Then she faced about and began to descend, all bowed and shrunken and shuddering. 'Oh, my God,' she was saying. 'Oh, my God . . . it isn't Jim at all . . . it's Maurice!'

'I think, Lady Outram,' said the priest gravely, 'you had better go with your friend.'

As they turned, a voice fell on them like a stone from the top of the stone stair, a voice that might have come out of an open grave. It was hoarse and unnatural, like the voices of men who are left alone with wild birds on desert islands. It was the voice of the Marquis of Marne, and it said: 'Stop!'

'Father Brown,' he said, 'before your friends disperse I authorize you to tell them all I have told you. Whatever follows, I will hide from it no longer.'

'You are right,' said the priest, 'and it shall be counted to you.'

'Yes,' said Father Brown quietly to the questioning company afterwards. 'He has given me the right to speak; but I will not tell it as he told me, but as I found it out for myself. Well, I knew from the first that the blighting monkish influence was all nonsense out of novels. Our people might possibly, in certain cases, encourage a man to go regularly into a monastery, but certainly not to hang about in a mediæval castle. In the same way, they certainly wouldn't want him to dress up as a monk when he wasn't a monk. But it struck me that he might himself want to wear a monk's hood or even a mask. I had heard of him as a mourner, and then as a murderer; but already I had hazy suspicions that his reason for hiding might not only be concerned with what he was, but with who he was.'

'Then came the general's vivid description of the duel; and the most vivid thing in it to me was the figure of Mr Romaine in the background; it was vivid because it was in the background. Why did the general leave behind him on the sand a dead man, whose friend stood yards away from him like a stock or a stone? Then I heard something, a mere trifle, about a trick habit that Romaine has of standing quite still when he is waiting for something to happen; as he waited for the thunder to follow the lightning. Well, that automatic trick in this case betrayed everything. Hugo Romaine on that old occasion, also, was waiting for something.'

'But it was all over,' said the general. 'What could he have been waiting for?'

'He was waiting for the duel,' said Father Brown.

'But I tell you I saw the duel!' cried the general.

'And I tell you you didn't see the duel,' said the priest.

'Are you mad?' demanded the other. 'Or why should you think I am blind?'

'Because you were blinded—that you might not see,' said the priest. 'Because you are a good man and God had mercy on your innocence, and he turned your face away from that unnatural strife. He set a wall of sand and silence between you and what really happened on that horrible red shore, abandoned to the raging spirits of Judas and of Cain.'

'Tell us what happened!' gasped the lady impatiently.

'I will tell it as I found it,' proceeded the priest. 'The next thing I found was that Romaine the actor had been training Maurice Mair in all the tricks of the trade of acting. I once had a friend who went in for acting. He gave me a very amusing account of how his first week's training consisted entirely of falling down; of learning how to fall flat without a stagger, as if he were stone dead.'

'God have mercy on us!' cried the general, and gripped the arms of his chair as if to rise.

'Amen,' said Father Brown. 'You told me how quickly it seemed to come; in fact, Maurice fell before the bullet flew, and lay perfectly still, waiting. And his wicked friend and teacher stood also in the background, waiting.'

'We are waiting,' said Cockspur, 'and I feel as if I couldn't wait.'

'James Mair, already broken with remorse, rushed across to the fallen man and bent over to lift him up. He had thrown away his pistol like an unclean thing; but Maurice's pistol still lay under his hand and it was undischarged. Then as the elder man bent over the younger, the younger lifted himself on his left arm and shot the elder through the body. He knew he was not so good a shot, but there was no question of missing the heart at that distance.'

The rest of the company had risen and stood staring down at the narrator with pale faces. 'Are you sure of this?' asked Sir John at last, in a thick voice.

'I am sure of it,' said Father Brown, 'and now I leave Maurice Mair, the present Marquis of Marne, to your Christian charity. You have told me something to-day about Christian charity. You seemed to me to give it almost too large a place; but how fortunate it is for poor sinners like this man that you err so much on the side of mercy, and are ready to be reconciled to all mankind.'

'Hang it all,' exploded the general; 'if you think I'm going to be reconciled to a filthy viper like that, I tell you I wouldn't say a word to save him from hell. I said I could pardon a regular decent duel, but of all the treacherous assassins——'

'He ought to be lynched,' cried Cockspur excitedly. 'He ought to burn alive like a nigger in the States. And if there is such a thing as burning for ever, he jolly well——'

'I wouldn't touch him with a barge-pole myself,' said Mallow.

'There is a limit to human charity,' said Lady Outram, trembling all over.

'There is,' said Father Brown dryly; 'and that is the real difference between human charity and Christian charity. You must forgive me if I was not altogether crushed by your contempt for my uncharitableness to-day; or by the lectures you read me about pardon for every sinner. For it seems to me that you only pardon the sins that you don't really think sinful. You only forgive criminals when they commit what you don't regard as crimes, but rather as conventions. So you tolerate a conventional duel, just as you tolerate a conventional divorce. You forgive because there isn't anything to be forgiven.'

'But, hang it all,' cried Mallow, 'you don't expect us to be able to pardon a vile thing like this?'

'No,' said the priest; 'but *we* have to be able to pardon it.'

He stood up abruptly and looked round at them.

'We have to touch such men, not with a barge-pole, but with a benediction,' he said. 'We have to say the word that will save them from hell. We alone are left to deliver them from despair when your human charity deserts them. Go on your own primrose path pardoning all your favourite vices and being generous to your fashionable crimes; and leave us in the darkness, vampires of the night, to console those who really need consolation; who do things really indefensible, things that neither the world nor they themselves can defend; and none but a priest will pardon. Leave us with the men who commit the mean and revolting and real crimes; mean as St Peter when the cock crew,* and yet the dawn came.'

'The dawn,' repeated Mallow doubtfully. 'You mean hope—for *him*?'

'Yes,' replied the other. 'Let me ask you one question. You are great ladies and men of honour and secure of yourselves; you would never, you can tell yourselves, stoop to such squalid treason as that. But tell me this. If any of you had so stooped, which of you, years afterwards, when you were old and rich and safe, would have been driven by conscience or confessor to tell such a story of yourself? You say you could not commit so base a crime. Could you confess so base a crime?'

The others gathered their possessions together and drifted by twos and threes out of the room in silence. And Father Brown, also in silence, went back to the melancholy castle of Marne.

THE QUICK ONE

THE strange story of the incongruous strangers is still remembered along that strip of the Sussex coast, where the large and quiet hotel called the Maypole and Garland looks across its own gardens to the sea. Two quaintly assorted figures did, indeed, enter that quiet hotel on that sunny afternoon; one being conspicuous in the sunlight, and visible over the whole shore, by the fact of wearing a lustrous green turban, surrounding a brown face and a black beard; the other would have seemed to some even more wild and weird, by reason of his wearing a soft black clergyman's hat with a yellow moustache and yellow hair of leonine length. He at least had often been seen preaching on the sands or conducting Band of Hope* services with a little wooden spade; only he had certainly never been seen going into the bar of an hotel. The arrival of these quaint companions was the climax of the story, but not the beginning of it; and, in order to make a rather mysterious story as clear as possible, it is better to begin at the beginning.

Half an hour before those two conspicuous figures entered the hotel, and were noticed by everybody, two other very inconspicuous figures had also entered it, and been noticed by nobody. One was a large man, and handsome in a heavy style, but he had a knack of taking up very little room, like a background; only an almost morbidly suspicious examination of his boots would have told anybody that he was an Inspector of Police in plain clothes; in very plain clothes. The other was a drab and insignificant little man, also in plain clothes, only that they happened to be clerical clothes; but nobody had ever seen *him* preaching on the sands.

These travellers also found themselves in a sort of large smoking-room with a bar, for a reason which determined all the events of that tragic afternoon. The truth is that the respectable hotel called the Maypole and Garland was being 'done-up.' Those who had liked it in the past were moved to say that it was being done down; or possibly done in. This was the opinion of the local grumbler, Mr Raggley, the eccentric old gentleman who drank cherry brandy in a corner and cursed. Anyhow, it was being carefully stripped of all the stray indications that it had once been an English inn; and being busily turned, yard by yard and room by room, into something resembling the sham palace of a Levantine usurer in an American film. It was, in short, being 'decorated'; but the only part where the decoration was complete, and where customers could yet be made comfortable, was this large room leading out of the hall. It had once been honourably known as a Bar Parlour and was now mysteriously known as a Saloon Lounge, and was newly 'decorated,' in the manner of an Asiatic Divan. For Oriental ornament pervaded the new scheme; and where there had once been a gun hung on hooks, and sporting prints and a stuffed fish in a glass case, there were now festoons of Eastern drapery and trophies of scimitars,* tulwars* and yataghans,* as if in unconscious preparation for the coming of the gentleman with the turban. The practical point was, however, that the few guests who did arrive had to be shepherded into this lounge, now swept and garnished, because all the more regular and refined parts of the hotel were still in a state of transition. Perhaps that was also the reason why even those few guests were somewhat neglected, the manager and others being occupied with explanations or exhortations elsewhere. Anyhow, the first two travellers who arrived had to kick their heels for some time unattended.

The bar was at the moment entirely empty, and the Inspector rang and rapped impatiently on the counter; but the little clergyman had already dropped into a lounge seat and seemed in no hurry for anything. Indeed his friend the policeman, turning his head, saw that the round face of the little cleric had gone quite blank, as it had a way of doing sometimes; he seemed to be staring through his moonlike spectacles at the newly decorated wall.

'I may as well offer you a penny for your thoughts,' said Inspector Greenwood, turning from the counter with a sigh, 'as nobody seems to want my pennies for anything else. This seems to be the only room in the house that isn't full of ladders and whitewash; and this is so empty that there isn't even a potboy to give me a pot of beer.'

'Oh . . . my thoughts are not worth a penny, let alone a pot of beer,' answered the cleric, wiping his spectacles, 'I don't know why . . . but I was thinking how easy it would be to commit a murder here.'

'It's all very well for you, Father Brown,' said the Inspector good-humouredly. 'You've had a lot more murders than your fair share; and we poor policemen sit starving all our lives, even for a little one. But why should you say . . . Oh I see, you're looking at all those Turkish daggers on the wall. There are plenty of things to commit a murder *with*, if that's what you mean. But not more than there are in any ordinary kitchen: carving-knives or pokers or whatnot. That isn't where the snag of a murder comes in.'

Father Brown seemed to recall his rambling thoughts in some bewilderment; and said that he supposed so.

'Murder is always easy,' said Inspector Greenwood. 'There can't possibly be anything more easy than murder. I could murder you at this minute—more easily than I can get a drink in this damned bar. The only difficulty is committing a murder without committing oneself as a murderer. It's this shyness about owning up to a murder; it's this silly modesty of murderers about their own masterpieces, that makes the trouble. They will stick to this extraordinary fixed idea of killing people without being found out; and that's what restrains them, even in a room full of daggers. Otherwise every cutler's shop would be piled with corpses. And that, by the way, explains the one kind of murder that really *can't* be prevented. Which is why, of course, we poor bobbies are always blamed for not preventing it. When a madman murders a King or a President, it can't be prevented. You can't make a King live in a coal-cellar, or carry about a President in a steel box. Anybody can murder him who does not mind being a murderer. That is where the madman is like the martyr—sort of beyond this world. A real fanatic can always kill anybody he likes.'

Before the priest could reply, a joyous band of bagmen rolled into the room like a shoal of porpoises; and the magnificent bellow of a big, beaming man, with an equally big and beaming tie-pin, brought the eager and obsequious manager running like a dog to the whistle, with a rapidity which the police in plain clothes had failed to inspire.

'I'm sure I'm very sorry, Mr Jukes,' said the manager, who wore a rather agitated smile and a wave or curl of very varnished hair across his forehead. 'We're rather understaffed at present; and I had to attend to something in the hotel, Mr Jukes.'

Mr Jukes was magnanimous, but in a noisy way; and ordered drinks all round, conceding one even to the almost cringing manager. Mr Jukes was a traveller for a very famous and fashionable wine and spirits firm; and may have conceived himself as lawfully the leader in such a place. Anyhow, he began a boisterous monologue, rather tending to tell the manager how to manage his hotel; and the others seemed to accept him as an authority. The policeman and the priest had retired to a low bench and small table in the background, from which they watched events, up to that rather remarkable moment when the policeman had very decisively to intervene.

For the next thing that happened, as already narrated, was the astonishing apparition of a brown Asiatic in a green turban, accompanied by the (if possible) more astonishing apparition of a Nonconformist minister; omens such as appear before a doom. In this case there was no doubt about evidence for the portent. A taciturn but observant boy cleaning the steps for the last hour (being a leisurely worker), the dark, fat, bulky bar-attendant, even the diplomatic but distracted manager, all bore witness to the miracle.

The apparitions, as the sceptics say, were due to perfectly natural causes. The man with the mane of yellow hair and the semi-clerical clothes was not only familiar as a preacher on the sands, but as a propagandist throughout the modern world. He was no less a person than the Rev. David Pryce-Jones, whose far-resounding slogan was Prohibition and Purification for Our Land and the Britains Overseas. He was an excellent public speaker and organizer; and an idea had occurred to him that ought to have occurred to Prohibitionists long ago. It was the simple idea that, if Prohibition is right, some honour is due to the Prophet who was perhaps the first Prohibitionist. He had corresponded with the leaders of Mahommedan religious thought, and had finally induced a distinguished Moslem (one of whose names was Akbar and the rest an untranslatable ululation of Allah with attributes) to come and lecture in England on the ancient Moslem veto on wine. Neither of them certainly had been in a public-house bar before; but they had come there by the process already described; driven from the genteel tea-rooms, shepherded into the newly-decorated saloon. Probably all would have been well, if the great Prohibitionist, in his innocence, had not advanced to the counter and asked for a glass of milk.

The commercial travellers, though a kindly race, emitted involuntary noises of pain; a murmur of suppressed jests was heard, as 'Shun the bowl,' or 'Better bring out the cow.' But the magnificent Mr Jukes, feeling it due to his wealth and tie-pin to produce more refined humour, fanned himself as one about to faint, and said pathetically: 'They know they can knock me down with a feather. They know a breath will blow me away. They know my doctor says I'm not to have these shocks. And they come and drink cold milk in cold blood, before my very eyes.'

The Rev. David Pryce-Jones, accustomed to deal with hecklers at public meetings, was so unwise as to venture on remonstrance and recrimination, in this very different and much more popular atmosphere. The Oriental total abstainer abstained from speech as well as spirits; and certainly gained in dignity by doing so. In fact, so far as he was concerned, the Moslem culture certainly scored a silent victory; he was obviously so much more of a gentleman than the commercial gentlemen, that a faint irritation began to arise against his aristocratic aloofness; and when Mr Pryce-Jones began to refer in argument to something of the kind, the tension became very acute indeed.

'I ask you, friends,' said Mr Pryce-Jones, with expansive platform gestures, 'why does our friend here set an example to us Christians in truly Christian self-control and brotherhood? Why does he stand here as a model of true Christianity, of real refinement, of genuine gentlemanly behaviour, amid all the quarrels and riots of such places as these? Because, whatever the doctrinal differences between us, at least in his soil the evil plant, the accursed hop or vine, has never——'

At this crucial moment of the controversy it was that John Raggley, the stormy petrel of a hundred storms of controversy, red-faced, white-haired, his antiquated top-hat on the back of his head, his stick swinging like a club, entered the house like an invading army.

John Raggley was generally regarded as a crank. He was the sort of man who writes letters to the newspaper, which generally do not appear in the newspaper; but which do appear afterwards as pamphlets, printed (or misprinted) at his own expense; and circulated to a hundred waste-paper baskets. He had quarrelled alike with the Tory squires and the Radical County Councils; he hated Jews; and he distrusted nearly everything that is sold in shops, or even in hotels. But there was a backing of fact behind his fads; he knew the county in every corner and curious detail; and he was a sharp observer. Even the manager, a Mr Wills, had a shadowy respect for Mr Raggley, having a nose for the sort of lunacy allowed in the gentry; not indeed the prostrate reverence which he had for the jovial magnificence of Mr Jukes, who was really good for trade, but at least a disposition to avoid quarrelling with the old grumbler, partly perhaps out of fear of the old grumbler's tongue.

'And you will have your usual, Sir,' said Mr Wills, leaning and leering across the counter.

'It's the only decent stuff you've still got,' snorted Mr Raggley, slapping down his queer and antiquated hat. 'Damn it, I sometimes think the only English thing left in England is cherry brandy. Cherry brandy does taste of cherries. Can you find me any beer that tastes of hops, or any cider that tastes of apples, or any wine that has the remotest indication of being made out of grapes? There's an infernal swindle going on now in every inn in the country, that would have raised a revolution in any other country. I've found out a thing or two about it, I can tell you. You wait till I can get it printed, and people will sit up. If I could stop our people being poisoned with all this bad drink——'

Here again the Rev. David Pryce-Jones showed a certain failure in tact; though it was a virtue he almost worshipped. He was so unwise as to attempt to establish an alliance with Mr Raggley, by a fine confusion between the idea of bad drink and the idea that drink is bad. Once more he endeavoured to drag his stiff and stately Eastern friend into the argument, as a refined foreigner superior to our rough English ways. He was even so foolish as to talk of a broad theological outlook; and ultimately to mention the name of Mahomet,* which was echoed in a sort of explosion.

'God damn your soul!' roared Mr Raggley, with a less broad theological outlook. 'Do you mean that Englishmen mustn't drink English beer, because wine was forbidden in a damned desert by that dirty old humbug Mahomet?'

In an instant, the Inspector of Police had reached the middle of the room with a stride. For, the instant before that, a remarkable change had taken place in the demeanour of the Oriental gentleman, who had hitherto stood perfectly still, with steady and shining eyes. He now proceeded, as his friend had said, to set an example in truly Christian self-control and brotherhood by reaching the wall with the bound of a tiger, tearing down one of the heavy knives hanging there and sending it smack like a stone from a sling, so that it stuck quivering in the wall exactly half an inch above Mr Raggley's ear. It would undoubtedly have stuck quivering in Mr Raggley, if Inspector Greenwood had not been just in time to jerk the arm and deflect the aim. Father Brown continued in his seat, watching the scene with screwed-up eyes and a screw of something almost like a smile at the corners of his mouth, as if he saw something beyond the mere momentary violence of the quarrel.

And then the quarrel took a curious turn; which may not be understood by everybody, until men like Mr John Raggley are better understood than they are. For the red-faced old fanatic was standing up and laughing uproariously as if it were the best joke he had ever heard. All his snapping vituperation and bitterness seemed to have gone out of him; and he regarded the other fanatic, who had just tried to murder him, with a sort of boisterous benevolence.

'Blast your eyes,' he said, 'you're the first man I've met in twenty years!'

'Do you charge this man, Sir?' said the Inspector, looking doubtful.

'Charge him, of course not,' said Raggley. 'I'd stand him a drink if he were allowed any drinks. I hadn't any business to insult his religion; and I wish to God all you skunks had the guts to kill a man, I won't say for insulting your religion, because you haven't got any, but for insulting anything—even your beer.'

'Now he's called us all skunks,' said Father Brown to Greenwood, 'peace and harmony seem to be restored. I wish that teetotal lecturer could get himself impaled on his friend's knife; it was he who made all the mischief.'

As he spoke, the odd groups in the room were already beginning to break up; it had been found possible to clear the commercial room for the commercial travellers, and they adjourned to it, the potboy carrying a new round of drinks after them on a tray. Father Brown stood for a moment gazing at the glasses left on the counter; recognizing at once the ill-omened glass of milk, and another which smelt of whisky; and then turned just in time to see the parting between those two quaint figures, fanatics of the East and West. Raggley was still ferociously genial; there was still something a little darkling and sinister about the Moslem, which was perhaps natural;

but he bowed himself out with grave gestures of dignified reconciliation; and there was every indication that the trouble was really over.

Some importance, however, continued attached, in the mind of Father Brown at least, to the memory and interpretation of those last courteous salutes between the combatants. Because, curiously enough, when Father Brown came down very early next morning, to perform his religious duties in the neighbourhood, he found the long saloon bar, with its fantastic Asiatic decoration, filled with a dead white light of daybreak in which every detail was distinct; and one of the details was the dead body of John Raggley bent and crushed into a corner of the room, with the heavy-hilted crooked dagger rammed through his heart.

Father Brown went very softly upstairs again and summoned his friend the Inspector; and the two stood beside the corpse, in a house in which no one else was as yet stirring.

'We mustn't either assume or avoid the obvious,' said Greenwood after a silence, 'but it is well to remember, I think, what I was saying to you yesterday afternoon. It's rather odd, by the way, that I should have said it—yesterday afternoon.'

'I know,' said the priest, nodding with an owlish stare.

'I said,' observed Greenwood, 'that the one sort of murder we can't stop is murder by somebody like a religious fanatic. That brown fellow probably thinks that if he's hanged, he'll go straight to Paradise for defending the honour of the Prophet.'

'There is that, of course,' said Father Brown. 'It would be very reasonable, so to speak, of our Moslem friend to have stabbed him. And you may say we don't know of anybody else yet, who could at all reasonably have stabbed him. But . . . but I was thinking . . .' And his round face suddenly went blank again and all speech died on his lips.

'What's the matter now?' asked the other.

'Well, I know it sounds funny,' said Father Brown in a forlorn voice. 'But I was thinking . . . I was thinking, in a way, it doesn't much matter who stabbed him.'

'Is this the New Morality?' asked his friend. 'Or the old Casuistry, perhaps. Are the Jesuits really going in for murder?'

'I didn't say it didn't matter who murdered him,' said Father Brown. 'Of course the man who stabbed him might possibly be the man who murdered him. But it might be quite a different man. Anyhow, it was done at quite a different time. I suppose you'll want to work on the hilt for finger-prints; but don't take too much notice of them. I can imagine other reasons for other people sticking this knife in the poor old boy. Not very edifying reasons, of course, but quite distinct from the murder. You'll have to put some more knives into him, before you find out about that.'

'You mean——' began the other, watching him keenly.

'I mean the autopsy,' said the priest, 'to find the real cause of death.'

'You're quite right, I believe,' said the Inspector, 'about the stabbing, anyhow. We must wait for the doctor; but I'm pretty sure he'll say you're right. There isn't blood enough. This knife was stuck in the corpse when it had been cold for hours. But why?'

'Possibly to put the blame on the Mahommedan,' answered Father Brown. 'Pretty mean, I admit, but not necessarily murder. I fancy there are people in this place trying to keep secrets, who are not necessarily the murderers.'

'I haven't speculated on that line yet,' said Greenwood. 'What makes you think so?'

'What I said yesterday, when we first came into this horrible room. I said it would be easy to commit a murder here. But I wasn't thinking about all those stupid weapons, though you thought I was. About something quite different.'

For the next few hours the Inspector and his friend conducted a close and thorough investigation into the goings and comings of everybody for the last twenty-four hours, the way the drinks had been distributed, the glasses that were washed or unwashed, and every detail about every individual involved, or apparently not involved. One might have supposed they thought that thirty people had been poisoned, as well as one.

It seemed certain that nobody had entered the building except by the big entrance that adjoined the bar; all the others were blocked in one way or another by the repairs. A boy had been cleaning the steps outside this entrance; but he had nothing very clear to report. Until the amazing entry of the Turk in the Turban, with his teetotal lecturer, there did not seem to have been much custom of any kind, except for the commercial travellers who came in to take what they called 'quick ones'; and they seemed to have moved together, like Wordsworth's Cloud;* there was a slight difference of opinion between the boy outside and the men inside about whether one of them had not been abnormally quick in obtaining a quick one, and come out on the doorstep by himself; but the manager and the barman had no memory of any such independent individual. The manager and the barman knew all the travellers quite well, and there was no doubt about their movements as a whole. They had stood at the bar chaffing and drinking; they had been involved, through their lordly leader, Mr Jukes, in a not very serious altercation with Mr Pryce-Jones; and they had witnessed the sudden and very serious altercation between Mr Akbar and Mr Raggley. Then they were told they could adjourn to the Commercial Room, and did so, their drinks being borne after them like a trophy.

'There's precious little to go on,' said Inspector Greenwood. 'Of course a lot of officious servants must do their duty as usual, and wash out all the glasses; including old Raggley's glass. If it weren't for everybody else's efficiency, we detectives might be quite efficient.'

'I know,' said Father Brown, and his mouth took on again the twisted smile. 'I sometimes think criminals invented hygiene. Or perhaps hygienic reformers invented crime; they look like it, some of them. Everybody talks about foul dens and filthy slums in which crime can run riot; but it's just the other way. They are called foul, not because crimes are committed, but because crimes are discovered. It's in the neat, spotless, clean and tidy places that crime can run riot; no mud to make footprints; no dregs to contain poison; kind servants washing out all traces of the murder; and the murderer killing and cremating six wives and all for want of a little Christian dirt. Perhaps I express myself with too much warmth—but look here. As it happens, I do remember one glass, which has doubtless been cleaned since, but I should like to know more about it.'

'Do you mean Raggley's glass?' asked Greenwood.

'No; I mean Nobody's glass,' replied the priest. 'It stood near that glass of milk and it still held an inch or two of whisky. Well, you and I had no whisky. I happen to remember that the manager, when treated by the jovial Jukes, had "a drop of gin." I hope you don't suggest that our Moslem was a whisky-drinker disguised in a green turban; or that the Rev. David Pryce-Jones managed to drink whisky and milk together, without noticing it.'

'Most of the commercial travellers took whisky,' said the Inspector. 'They generally do.'

'Yes; and they generally see they get it too,' answered Father Brown. 'In this case, they had it all carefully carted after them to their own room. But this glass was left behind.'

'An accident, I suppose,' said Greenwood, doubtfully. 'The man could easily get another in the Commercial Room afterwards.'

Father Brown shook his head. 'You've got to see people as they are. Now these sort of men—well, some call them vulgar and some common; but that's all likes and dislikes. I'd be content to say that they are mostly simple men. Lots of them very good men, very glad to go back to the missus and the kids; some of them might be blackguards; might have had several missuses; or even murdered several missuses. But most of them are simple men; and, mark you, just the least tiny little bit drunk. Not much; there's many a duke or don at Oxford drunker; but when that sort of man is at that stage of conviviality, he simply can't help noticing things, and noticing them very loud. Don't you observe that the least little incident jerks them into speech; if the beer froths over, they froth over with it, and have to say, "Whoa, Emma," or, "Doing me proud, aren't you?" Now I should say it's flatly impossible for five of these festive beings to sit round a table in the Commercial Room, and have only four glasses set before them, the fifth man being left out, without making a shout about it. Probably they would all make a shout about it. Certainly *he* would make a shout about it. He wouldn't wait, like an Englishman of another class, till he could get a drink quietly later. The air would resound with things like, "And what about little me?" or, "Here, George, have I joined the Band of Hope?" or, "Do you see any green in my turban, George?" But the barman heard no such complaints. I take it as certain that the glass of whisky left behind had been nearly emptied by somebody else; somebody we haven't thought about yet.'

'But can you think of any such person?' asked the other.

'It's because the manager and the barman won't hear of any such person, that you dismiss the one really independent piece of evidence; the evidence of that boy outside cleaning the steps. He says that a man, who may well have been a bagman, but who did not, in fact, stick to the other bagmen, went in and came out again almost immediately. The manager and the barman never saw him; or say they never saw him. But he got a glass of whisky from the bar somehow. Let us call him, for the sake of argument, The Quick One. Now you know I don't often interfere with your business, which I know you do better than I should do it, or should want to do it. I've never had anything to do with setting police machinery at work, or running down criminals, or anything like that. But, for the first time in my life, I want to do it now. I want you to find The Quick One; to follow The Quick One to the ends of the earth; to set the whole infernal official machinery at work like a drag-net across the nations, and jolly well recapture The Quick One. Because he is the man we want.'

Greenwood made a despairing gesture. 'Has he face or form or any visible quality except quickness?' he inquired.

'He was wearing a sort of Inverness cape,'* said Father Brown, 'and he told the boy outside he must reach Edinburgh by next morning. That's all the boy outside remembers. But I know your organization has got on to people with less clue than that.'

'You seem very keen on this,' said the Inspector, a little puzzled.

The priest looked puzzled also, as if at his own thoughts; he sat with knotted brow and then said abruptly:

'You see, it's so easy to be misunderstood. All men matter. You matter. I matter. It's the hardest thing in theology to believe.'

The Inspector stared at him without comprehension; but he proceeded.

'We matter to God—God only knows why. But that's the only possible justification of the existence of policemen.' The policeman did not seem enlightened as to his own cosmic justification. 'Don't you see, the law really is right in a way, after all. If all men matter, all murders matter. That which He has so mysteriously created, we must not suffer to be mysteriously destroyed. But——'

He said the last word sharply, like one taking a new step in decision.

'*But*, when once I step off that mystical level of equality, I don't see that most of your important murders are particularly important. You are always telling me that this case and that is important. As a plain, practical man of the world, I must realize that it is the Prime Minister who has been murdered. As a plain, practical man of the world, I don't think that the Prime Minister matters at all. As a mere matter of human importance, I should say he hardly exists at all. Do you suppose if he and the other public men were shot dead to-morrow, there wouldn't be other people to stand up and say that every avenue was being explored, or that the Government had the matter under the gravest consideration? The masters of the modern world don't matter. Even the real masters don't matter much. Hardly anybody you ever read about in a newspaper matters at all.'

He stood up, giving the table a small rap: one of his rare gestures; and his voice changed again.

'But Raggley did matter. He was one of a great line of some half a dozen men who might have saved England. They stand up stark and dark like disregarded sign-posts, down all that smooth descending road which has ended in this swamp of merely commercial collapse. Dean Swift* and Dr Johnson* and old William Cobbett;* they had all without exception the name of being surly or savage, and they were all loved by their friends, and they all deserved to be. Didn't you see how that old man, with the heart of a lion, stood up and forgave his enemy as only fighters can forgive? He jolly well *did* do what that temperance lecturer talked about; he set an example to us Christians and was a model of Christianity. And when there is foul and secret murder of a man like that—then I do think it matters, matters so much that even the modern machinery of police will be a thing that any respectable person may make use of . . . Oh, don't mention it. And so, for once in a way, I really do want to make use of you.'

And so, for some stretch of those strange days and nights, we might almost say that the little figure of Father Brown drove before him into action all the armies and engines of the police forces of the Crown, as the little figure of Napoleon drove the batteries and the battle-lines of the vast strategy that covered Europe. Police stations and post offices worked all night; traffic was stopped, correspondence was intercepted, inquiries were made in a hundred places, in order to track the flying trail of that ghostly figure, without face or name, with an Inverness cape and an Edinburgh ticket.

Meanwhile, of course, the other lines of investigation were not neglected. The full report of the *post-mortem* had not yet come in; but everybody seemed certain that it was a case of poisoning. This naturally threw the primary suspicion upon the cherry brandy; and this again naturally threw the primary suspicion on the hotel.

'Most probably on the manager of the hotel,' said Greenwood gruffly. 'He looks a nasty little worm to me. Of course it might be something to do with some servant, like the barman; he seems rather a sulky specimen, and Raggley might have cursed him a bit, having a flaming temper, though he was generally generous enough afterwards. But, after all, as I say, the primary responsibility, and therefore the primary suspicion, rests on the manager.'

'Oh, I knew the primary suspicion would rest on the manager,' said Father Brown. 'That was why I didn't suspect him. You see, I rather fancied somebody else must have known that the primary suspicion would rest on the manager; or the servants of the hotel. That is why I said it would be easy to kill anybody in the hotel. . . . But you'd better go and have it out with him, I suppose.'

The Inspector went; but came back again after a surprisingly short interview, and found his clerical friend turning over some papers that seemed to be a sort of *dossier* of the stormy career of John Raggley.

'This is a rum go,' said the Inspector. 'I thought I should spend hours cross-examining that slippery little toad there, for we haven't legally got a thing against him. And instead of that, he went to pieces all at once, and I really think he's told me all he knows in sheer funk.'

'I know,' said Father Brown. 'That's the way he went to pieces when he found Raggley's corpse apparently poisoned in his hotel. That's why he lost his head enough to do such a clumsy thing as decorate the corpse with a Turkish knife, to put the blame on the nigger, as he would say. There never is anything the matter with him but funk; he's the very last man that ever would really stick a knife into a live person. I bet he had to nerve himself to stick it into a dead one. But he's the very first person to be frightened of being charged with what he didn't do; and to make a fool of himself, as he did.'

'I suppose I must see the barman too,' observed Greenwood.

'I suppose so,' answered the other. 'I don't believe myself it was any of the hotel people—well, because it was made to look as if it *must* be the hotel people. . . . But look here, have you seen any of this stuff they've got together about Raggley? He had a jolly interesting life; I wonder whether anyone will write his biography.'

'I took a note of everything likely to affect an affair like this,' answered the official. 'He was a widower; but he did once have a row with a man about his wife; a Scotch landagent then in these parts; and Raggley seems to have been pretty violent. They say he hated Scotchmen; perhaps that's the reason. . . . Oh, I know what you are smiling grimly about. A Scotchman. . . . Perhaps an Edinburgh man.'

'Perhaps,' said Father Brown. 'It's quite likely, though, that he did dislike Scotchmen, apart from private reasons. It's an odd thing, but all that tribe of Tory Radicals, or whatever you call them, who resisted the Whig mercantile movement, all of them did dislike Scotchmen. Cobbett did; Dr Johnson did; Swift described their accent in one of his deadliest passages; even Shakespeare has been accused of the prejudice. But the prejudices of great men generally have something to do with principles. And there was a reason, I fancy. The Scot came from a poor agricultural land, that became a rich industrial land. He was able and active; he thought he was bringing industrial civilization from the north; he simply didn't know that there had been for centuries a rural civilization in the south. His own grandfather's land was highly rural but not civilized. . . . Well, well; I suppose we can only wait for more news.'

'I hardly think you'll get the latest news out of Shakespeare and Dr Johnson,' grinned the police officer. 'What Shakespeare thought of Scotchmen isn't exactly evidence.'

Father Brown cocked an eyebrow, as if a new thought had surprised him. 'Why, now I come to think of it,' he said, 'there might be better evidence, even out of Shakespeare. He doesn't often mention Scotchmen. But he was rather fond of making fun of Welshmen.'*

The Inspector was searching his friend's face; for he fancied he recognized an alertness behind its demure expression.

'By Jove,' he said. 'Nobody thought of turning the suspicions *that* way, anyhow.'

'Well,' said Father Brown, with broad-minded calm, 'you started by talking about fanatics; and how a fanatic could do anything. Well, I suppose we had the honour of entertaining, in this bar-parlour yesterday, about the biggest and loudest and most fat-headed fanatic in the modern world. If being a pig-headed idiot with one idea is the way to murder, I put in a claim for my reverend brother Pryce-Jones, the Prohibitionist, in preference to all the fakirs in Asia, and it's perfectly true, as I told you, that his horrible glass of milk was standing side by side on the counter with the mysterious glass of whisky.'

'Which you think was mixed up with the murder,' said Greenwood staring. 'Look here, I don't know whether you're really serious or not.'

Even as he was looking steadily in his friend's face, finding something still inscrutable in its expression, the telephone rang stridently behind the bar. Lifting the flap in the counter

Inspector Greenwood passed rapidly inside, unhooked the receiver, listened for an instant, and then uttered a shout; not addressed to his interlocutor, but to the universe in general. Then he listened still more attentively and said explosively at intervals, 'Yes, yes. . . . Come round at once; bring him round if possible. . . . Good piece of work. . . . Congratulate you.'

Then Inspector Greenwood came back into the outer lounge, like a man who has renewed his youth, sat down squarely on his seat, with his hands planted on his knees, stared at his friend, and said:

'Father Brown, I don't know how you do it. You seem to have known he was a murderer before anybody else knew he was a man. He was nobody; he was nothing; he was a slight confusion in the evidence; nobody in the hotel saw him; the boy on the steps could hardly swear to him; he was just a fine shade of doubt founded on an extra dirty glass. But we've got him, and he's the man we want.'

Father Brown had risen with the sense of the crisis, mechanically clutching the papers destined to be so valuable to the biographer of Mr Raggley; and stood staring at his friend. Perhaps this gesture jerked his friend's mind to fresh confirmations.

'Yes, we've got The Quick One. And very quick he was, like quicksilver, in making his get-away; we only just stopped him—off on a fishing trip to Orkney, he said. But he's the man, all right; he's the Scotch land-agent who made love to Raggley's wife; he's the man who drank Scotch whisky in this bar and then took a train for Edinburgh. And nobody would have known it but for you.'

'Well, what I meant,' began Father Brown, in a rather dazed tone; and at that instant there was a rattle and rumble of heavy vehicles outside the hotel; and two or three other and subordinate policemen blocked the bar with their presence. One of them, invited by his superior to sit down, did so in an expansive manner, like one at once happy and fatigued; and he also regarded Father Brown with admiring eyes.

'Got the murderer, sir, oh yes,' he said; 'I know he's a murderer, 'cause he bally nearly murdered me. I've captured some tough characters before now; but never one like this—

hit me in the stomach like the kick of a horse and nearly got away from five men. Oh, you've got a real killer this time, Inspector.'

'Where is he?' asked Father Brown, staring.

'Outside in the van, in handcuffs,' replied the policeman, 'and, if you're wise, you'll leave him there—for the present.'

Father Brown sank into a chair in a sort of soft collapse; and the papers he had been nervously clutching were shed around him, shooting and sliding about the floor like sheets of breaking snow. Not only his face, but his whole body, conveyed the impression of a punctured balloon.

'Oh . . . Oh,' he repeated, as if any further oath would be inadequate. 'Oh . . . I've done it again.'

'If you mean you've caught the criminal again,' began Greenwood. But his friend stopped him with a feeble explosion, like that of expiring soda-water.

'I mean,' said Father Brown, 'that it's always happening; and really, I don't know why. I always try to say what I mean. But everybody else means such a lot by what I say.'

'What in the world is the matter now?' cried Greenwood, suddenly exasperated.

'Well, I say things,' said Father Brown in a weak voice, which could alone convey the weakness of the words. 'I say things, but everybody seems to know they mean more than they say. Once I saw a broken mirror and said "Something has happened,"* and they all answered, "Yes, yes, as you truly say, two men wrestled and one ran into the garden," and so on. I don't understand it, "Something happened," and "Two men wrestled," don't seem to me at all the same; but I dare say I read old books of logic. Well, it's like that here. You seem to be all certain this man is a murderer. But I never said he was a murderer. I said he was the man we wanted. He is. I want him very much. I want him frightfully. I want him as the one thing we haven't got in the whole of this horrible case—a witness!'

They all stared at him, but in a frowning fashion, like men trying to follow a sharp new turn of the argument; and it was he who resumed the argument.

'From the first minute I entered that big empty bar or saloon, I knew that what was the matter with all this business was emptiness; solitude; too many chances for anybody to be alone. In a word, the absence of witnesses. All we knew was that when we came in, the manager and the barman were not in the bar. But when *were* they in the bar? What chance was there of making any sort of time-table of when anybody was anywhere? The whole thing was blank for want of witnesses. I rather fancy the barman or somebody was in the bar just before we came; and that's how the Scotchman got his Scotch whisky. He certainly didn't get it after we came. But we can't begin to inquire whether anybody in the hotel poisoned poor Raggley's cherry brandy, till we really know who was in the bar and when. Now I want you to do me another favour, in spite of this stupid muddle, which is probably all my fault. I want you to collect all the people involved in this room—I think they're all still available, unless the Asiatic has gone back to Asia—and then take the poor Scotchman out of his handcuffs, and bring him in here, and let him tell us who did serve him with whisky, and who was in the bar, and who else was in the room, and all the rest. He's the only man whose evidence can cover just that period when the crime was done. I don't see the slightest reason for doubting his word.'

'But look here,' said Greenwood. 'This brings it all back to the hotel authorities; and I thought you agreed that the manager isn't the murderer. Is it the barman, or what?'

'I don't know,' said the priest blankly. 'I don't know for certain even about the manager. I don't know anything about the barman. I fancy the manager might be a bit of a conspirator, even if he wasn't a murderer. But I do know there's one solitary witness on earth who may have seen something; and that's why I set all your police dogs on his trail to the ends of the earth.'

The mysterious Scotchman, when he finally appeared before the company thus assembled, was certainly a formidable figure; tall, with a hulking stride and a long sardonic hatchet face, with tufts of red hair; and wearing not only an Inverness cape but a Glengarry bonnet.* He might well be excused for a somewhat acrid attitude; but anybody could see he was of the sort to resist arrest, even with violence. It was not surprising that he had come to blows with a fighting fellow like Raggley. It was not even surprising that the police had been convinced, by the mere details of capture, that he was a tough and a typical killer. But he claimed to be a perfectly respectable farmer, in Aberdeenshire, his name being James Grant; and somehow not only Father Brown, but Inspector Greenwood, a shrewd man with a great deal of experience, was pretty soon convinced that the Scot's ferocity was the fury of innocence rather than guilt.

'Now what we want from you, Mr Grant,' said the Inspector gravely dropping without further parley into tones of courtesy, 'is simply your evidence on one very important fact. I am greatly grieved at the misunderstanding by which you have suffered, but I am sure you wish to serve the ends of justice. I believe you came into this bar just after it opened, at half-past five, and were served with a glass of whisky. We are not certain what servant of the hotel, whether the barman or the manager or some subordinate, was in the bar at that time. Will you look round the room, and tell me whether the bar-attendant who served you is present here.'

'Aye, he's present,' said Mr Grant, grimly smiling, having swept the group with a shrewd glance. 'I'd know him anywhere; and ye'll agree he's big enough to be seen. Do ye have all your inn-servants as grand as yon?'

The Inspector's eye remained hard and steady, and his voice colourless and continuous; the face of Father Brown was a blank; but on many other faces there was a cloud; the barman was not particularly big and not at all grand; and the manager was decidedly small.

'We only want the barman identified,' said the Inspector calmly. 'Of course we know him; but we should like you to verify it independently. You mean . . . ?' And he stopped suddenly.

'Weel, there he is plain enough,' said the Scotchman wearily; and made a gesture, and with that gesture the gigantic Jukes, the prince of commercial travellers, rose like a trumpeting elephant; and in a flash had three policemen fastened on him like hounds on a wild beast.

'Well, all that was simple enough,' said Father Brown to his friend afterwards. 'As I told you, the instant I entered the empty bar-room, my first thought was that, if the barman left the bar unguarded like that, there was nothing in the world to stop you or me or anybody else lifting the flap and walking in, and putting poison in any of the bottles standing waiting for customers. Of course, a practical poisoner would probably do it as Jukes did, by substituting a poisoned bottle for the ordinary bottle; that could be done in a flash. It was easy enough for him, as he travelled in bottles, to carry a flask of cherry brandy prepared and of the same pattern. Of course, it requires one condition; but it's a fairly common condition. It would hardly do to start poisoning the beer or whisky that scores of people drink; it would cause a massacre. But when a man is well known as drinking only one special thing, like cherry brandy, that isn't very widely drunk, it's just like poisoning him in his own home. Only it's a jolly sight safer. For practically the whole suspicion instantly falls on the hotel, or somebody to do with the hotel; and there's no earthly argument to show that it was done by anyone out of a hundred customers that might come into the bar; even if people realized that a customer could do it. It was about as absolutely anonymous and irresponsible a murder as a man could commit.'

'And why exactly did the murderer commit it?' asked his friend.

Father Brown rose and gravely gathered the papers which he had previously scattered in a moment of distraction.

'May I recall your attention,' he said smiling, 'to the materials of the forthcoming Life and Letters of the Late John Raggley? Or, for that matter, to his own spoken words? He said in this very bar that he was going to expose a scandal about the management of hotels; and the scandal was the pretty common one of a corrupt agreement between hotel proprietors and a salesman who took and gave secret commissions, so that his business had a monopoly of all the drink sold in the place. It wasn't even an open slavery like an ordinary tied house; it was a swindle at the expense of everybody the manager was supposed to serve. It was a legal offence. So the ingenious Jukes, taking the first moment when the bar was empty, as it often was, stepped inside and made the exchange of bottles; unfortunately at that very moment a Scotchman in an Inverness cape came in harshly demanding whisky. Jukes saw his only chance was to pretend to be the barman and serve the customer. He was very much relieved that the customer was a Quick One.'

'I think you're rather a Quick One yourself,' observed Greenwood; 'if you say you smelt something at the start, in the mere air of an empty room. Did you suspect Jukes at all at the start?'

'Well, he sounded rather rich somehow,' answered Father Brown vaguely. 'You know when a man has a rich voice. And I did sort of ask myself why he should have such a disgustingly rich voice, when all those honest fellows were fairly poor. But I think I knew he was a sham when I saw that big shining breast-pin.'

'You mean because it was sham?' asked Greenwood doubtfully.

'Oh, no; because it was genuine,' said Father Brown.

THE BLAST OF THE BOOK

PROFESSOR OPENSHAW always lost his temper, with a loud bang, if anybody called him a Spiritualist; or a believer in Spiritualism. This, however, did not exhaust his explosive elements; for he also lost his temper if anybody called him a disbeliever in Spiritualism. It was his pride to have given his whole life to investigating Psychic Phenomena; it was also his pride never to have given a hint of whether he thought they were really psychic or merely phenomenal. He enjoyed nothing so much as to sit in a circle of devout Spiritualists and give devastating descriptions of how he had exposed medium after medium and detected fraud after fraud: for indeed he was a man of much detective talent and insight, when once he had fixed his eye on an object, and he always fixed his eye on a medium, as a highly suspicious object. There was a story of his having spotted the same Spiritualistic mountebank under three different disguises: dressed as a woman, a white-bearded old man, and a Brahmin of a rich chocolate brown. These recitals made the true believers rather restless, as indeed they were intended to do; but they could hardly complain, for no Spiritualist denies the existence of fraudulent mediums: only the Professor's flowing narrative might well seem to indicate that all mediums were fraudulent.

But woe to the simple-minded and innocent Materialist (and Materialists as a race are rather innocent and simple-minded) who, presuming on this narrative tendency, should advance the thesis that ghosts were against the laws of nature, or that such things were only old superstitions; or that it was all tosh, or, alternately, bunk. Him would the Professor, suddenly reversing all his scientific batteries, sweep from the field with a cannonade of unquestionable cases and unexplained phenomena, of which the wretched rationalist had never heard in his life, giving all the dates and details, stating all the attempted and abandoned natural explanations; stating everything, indeed, except whether he, John Oliver Openshaw, did or did not believe in Spirits; and that neither Spiritualist nor Materialist could ever boast of finding out.

Professor Openshaw, a lean figure with pale leonine hair and hypnotic blue eyes, stood exchanging a few words with Father Brown, who was a friend of his, on the steps outside the hotel where both had been breakfasting that morning and sleeping the night before. The Professor had come back rather late from one of his grand experiments, in general exasperation, and was still tingling with the fight that he always waged alone and against both sides.

'Oh, I don't mind you,' he said laughing. 'You don't believe in it even if it's true. But all these people are perpetually asking me what I'm trying to prove. They don't seem to understand that I'm a man of science. A man of science isn't trying to prove anything. He's trying to find out what will prove itself.'

'But he hasn't found out yet,' said Father Brown.

'Well, I have some little notions of my own, that are not quite so negative as most people think,' answered the Professor, after an instant of frowning silence; 'anyhow, I've begun to fancy that if there is something to be found, they're looking for it along the wrong line. It's all too theatrical; it's showing off, all their shiny ectoplasm and trumpets and voices and the rest; all on the model of old melodramas and mouldy historical novels about the Family Ghost. If they'd go to history instead of historical novels, I'm beginning to think they'd really find something. But not Apparitions.'

'After all,' said Father Brown, 'Apparitions are only Appearances. I suppose you'd say the Family Ghost is only keeping up appearances.'

The Professor's gaze, which had commonly a fine abstracted character, suddenly fixed and focussed itself as it did on a dubious medium. It had rather the air of a man screwing a strong magnifying-glass into his eye. Not that he thought the priest was in the least like a dubious medium; but he was startled into attention by his friend's thought following so closely on his own.

'Appearances!' he muttered, 'crikey, but it's odd you should say that just now. The more I learn, the more I fancy they lose by merely looking for appearances. Now if they'd look a little into Disappearances——'

'Yes,' said Father Brown, 'after all, the real fairy legends weren't so very much about the appearance of famous fairies; calling up Titania or exhibiting Oberon* by moonlight. But there were no end of legends about people *disappearing*, because they were stolen by the fairies. Are you on the track of Kilmeny* or Thomas the Rhymer?'*

'I'm on the track of ordinary modern people you've read of in the newspapers,' answered Openshaw. 'You may well stare; but that's my game just now; and I've been on it for a long time. Frankly, I think a lot of psychic appearances could be explained away. It's the disappearances I can't explain, unless they're psychic. These people in the newspapers who vanish and are never found—if you knew the details as I do . . . and now only this morning I got confirmation; an extraordinary letter from an old missionary, quite a respectable old boy. He's coming to see me at my office this morning. Perhaps you'd lunch with me or something; and I'd tell the results—in confidence.'

'Thanks; I will—unless,' said Father Brown modestly, 'the fairies have stolen me by then.'

With that they parted and Openshaw walked round the corner to a small office he rented in the neighbourhood; chiefly for the publication of a small periodical, of psychical and psychological notes of the driest and most agnostic sort. He had only one clerk, who sat at a desk in the outer office, totting up figures and facts for the purposes of the printed report; and the Professor paused to ask if Mr Pringle had called. The clerk answered mechanically in the negative and went on mechanically adding up figures; and the Professor turned towards the inner room that was his study. 'Oh, by the way, Berridge,' he added, without turning round, 'if Mr Pringle comes, send him straight in to me. You needn't interrupt your work; I rather want those notes finished to-night if possible. You might leave them on my desk to-morrow, if I am late.'

And he went into his private office, still brooding on the problem which the name of Pringle had raised; or rather, perhaps, had ratified and confirmed in his mind. Even the most perfectly balanced of agnostics is partially human; and it is possible that the missionary's letter seemed to have greater weight as promising to support his private and still tentative hypothesis. He sat down in his large and comfortable chair, opposite the engraving of Montaigne;* and read once more the short letter from the Rev. Luke Pringle, making the appointment for that morning. No man knew better than Professor Openshaw the marks of the letter of the crank; the crowded details; the spidery handwriting; the unnecessary length and repetition. There were none of these things in this case; but a brief and businesslike typewritten statement that the writer had encountered some curious cases of Disappearance, which seemed to fall within the province of the Professor as a student of psychic problems. The Professor was favourably impressed; nor had he any unfavourable impression, in spite of a slight movement of surprise, when he looked up and saw that the Rev. Luke Pringle was already in the room.

'Your clerk told me I was to come straight in,' said Mr Pringle apologetically, but with a broad and rather agreeable grin. The grin was partly masked by masses of reddish-grey beard and whiskers; a perfect jungle of a beard, such as is sometimes grown by white men living in the jungles; but the eyes above the snub nose had nothing about them in the least wild or outlandish. Openshaw had instantly turned on them that concentrated spotlight or burning-glass of sceptical scrutiny which he turned on many men to see if they were mountebanks or maniacs; and, in this case, he had a rather unusual sense of reassurance. The wild beard might have belonged to a crank, but the eyes completely contradicted the beard; they were full of that quite frank and friendly laughter which is never found in the faces of those who are serious frauds or serious lunatics. He would have expected a man with those eyes to be a Philistine, a jolly sceptic, a man who shouted out shallow but hearty contempt for ghosts and spirits; but anyhow, no professional humbug could afford to look as frivolous as that. The man was buttoned up to the throat in a shabby old cape, and only his broad limp hat suggested the cleric; but missionaries from wild places do not always bother to dress like clerics.

'You probably think all this is another hoax, Professor,' said Mr Pringle, with a sort of abstract enjoyment, 'and I hope you will forgive my laughing at your very natural air of disapproval. All the same, I've got to tell my story to somebody who knows, because it's true. And, all joking apart, it's tragic as well as true. Well, to cut it short, I was missionary in Nya-Nya, a station in West Africa, in the thick of the forests, where almost the only other white man was the officer in command of the district, Captain Wales; and he and I grew rather thick. Not that he liked missions; he was, if I may say so, thick in many ways; one of those square-headed, square-shouldered men of action who hardly need to think, let alone believe. That's what makes it all the queerer. One day he came back to his tent in the forest, after a short leave, and said he had gone through a jolly rum experience, and didn't know what to do about it. He was holding a rusty old book in a leather binding, and he put it down on a table beside his revolver and an old Arab sword he kept, probably as a curiosity. He said this book had belonged to a man on the boat he had just come off; and the man swore that nobody must open the book, or look inside it; or else they would be carried off by the devil, or disappear, or something. Wales said this was all nonsense, of course; and they had a quarrel; and the upshot seems to have been that this man, taunted with cowardice or superstition, actually did look into the book; and instantly dropped it; walked to the side of the boat——'

'One moment,' said the Professor, who had made one or two notes. 'Before you tell me anything else. Did this man tell Wales where he had got the book, or who it originally belonged to?'

'Yes,' replied Pringle, now entirely grave. 'It seems he said he was bringing it back to Dr Hankey, the Oriental traveller now in England, to whom it originally belonged, and who had warned him of its strange properties. Well, Hankey is an able man and a rather crabbed and sneering sort of man; which makes it queerer still. But the point of Wales's story is much simpler. It is that the man who had looked into the book walked straight over the side of the ship, and was never seen again.'

'Do you believe it yourself?' asked Openshaw after a pause.

'Well, I do,' replied Pringle. 'I believe it for two reasons. First, that Wales was an entirely unimaginative man; and he added one touch that only an imaginative man could have added. He said that the man walked straight over the side on a still and calm day; but there was no splash.'

The Professor looked at his notes for some seconds in silence; and then said: 'And your other reason for believing it?'

'My other reason,' answered the Rev. Luke Pringle, 'is what I saw myself.'

There was another silence; until he continued in the same matter-of-fact way. Whatever he had, he had nothing of the eagerness with which the crank, or even the believer, tried to convince others.

'I told you that Wales put down the book on the table beside the sword. There was only one entrance to the tent; and it happened that I was standing in it, looking out into the forest, with my back to my companion. He was standing by the table grumbling and growling about the whole business; saying it

was tomfoolery in the twentieth century to be frightened of
opening a book; asking why the devil he shouldn't open it
himself. Then some instinct stirred in me and I said that he
had better not do that, it had better be returned to Dr Hankey.
"What harm could it do?" he said restlessly. "What harm did
it do?" I answered obstinately. "What happened to your
friend on the boat?" He didn't answer, indeed I didn't know
what he could answer; but I pressed my logical advantage in
mere vanity. "If it comes to that," I said, "what is your version
of what really happened on the boat?" Still he didn't answer;
and I looked round and saw that he wasn't there.

'The tent was empty. The book was lying on the table; open,
but on its face, as if he had turned it downwards. But the
sword was lying on the ground near the other side of the tent;
and the canvas of the tent showed a great slash, as if somebody had hacked his way out with the sword. The gash in the
tent gaped at me; but showed only the dark glimmer of the
forest outside. And when I went across and looked through
the rent I could not be certain whether the tangle of the tall
plants and the undergrowth had been bent or broken; at least
not farther than a few feet. I have never seen or heard of
Captain Wales from that day.

'I wrapped the book up in brown paper, taking good care
not to look at it; and I brought it back to England, intending
at first to return it to Dr Hankey. Then I saw some notes in
your paper suggesting a hypothesis about such things; and I
decided to stop on the way and put the matter before you; as
you have a name for being balanced and having an open
mind.'

Professor Openshaw laid down his pen and looked steadily
at the man on the other side of the table; concentrating in that
single stare all his long experience of many entirely different
types of humbug, and even some eccentric and extraordinary
types of honest men. In the ordinary way, he would have
begun with the healthy hypothesis that the story was a pack of
lies. On the whole he did incline to assume that it was a pack
of lies. And yet he could not fit the man into his story; if it
were only that he could not see that sort of liar telling that sort
of lie. The man was not trying to look honest on the surface,

as most quacks and impostors do; somehow, it seemed all the
other way; as if the man *was* honest, in spite of something else
that was merely on the surface. He thought of a good man
with one innocent delusion; but again the symptoms were not
the same; there was even a sort of virile indifference; as if the
man did not care much about his delusion, if it was a delusion.

'Mr Pringle,' he said sharply, like a barrister making a
witness jump, 'where is this book of yours now?'

The grin reappeared on the bearded face which had grown
grave during the recital.

'I left it outside,' said Mr Pringle. 'I mean in the outer office.
It was a risk, perhaps; but the less risk of the two.'

'What do you mean?' demanded the Professor. 'Why didn't
you bring it straight in here?'

'Because,' answered the missionary, 'I knew that as soon as
you saw it, you'd open it—before you had heard the story. I
thought it possible you might think twice about opening it—
after you'd heard the story.'

Then after a silence he added: 'There was nobody out there
but your clerk; and he looked a stolid steady-going specimen,
immersed in business calculations.'

Openshaw laughed unaffectedly. 'Oh, Babbage,'* he cried,
'your magic tomes are safe enough with him, I assure you. His
name's Berridge—but I often call him Babbage; because he's so
exactly like a Calculating Machine. No human being, if you
can call him a human being, would be less likely to open other
people's brown paper parcels. Well, we may as well go and
bring it in now; though I assure you I will consider seriously
the course to be taken with it. Indeed, I tell you frankly,' and
he stared at the man again, 'that I'm not quite sure whether we
ought to open it here and now, or send it to this Dr Hankey.'

The two had passed together out of the inner into the outer
office; and even as they did so, Mr Pringle gave a cry and ran
forward towards the clerk's desk. For the clerk's desk was
there; but not the clerk. On the clerk's desk lay a faded old
leather book, torn out of its brown-paper wrappings, and
lying closed, but as if it had just been opened. The clerk's desk
stood against the wide window that looked out into the street;
and the window was shattered with a huge ragged hole in the

glass; as if a human body had been shot through it into the world without. There was no other trace of Mr Berridge.

Both the two men left in the office stood as still as statues; and then it was the Professor who slowly came to life. He looked even more judicial than he had ever looked in his life, as he slowly turned and held out his hand to the missionary.

'Mr Pringle,' he said, 'I beg your pardon. I beg your pardon only for thoughts that I have had; and half-thoughts at that. But nobody could call himself a scientific man and not face a fact like this.'

'I suppose,' said Pringle doubtfully, 'that we ought to make some inquiries. Can you ring up his house and find out if he has gone home?'

'I don't know that he's on the telephone,' answered Openshaw, rather absently; 'he lives somewhere up Hampstead way, I think. But I suppose somebody will inquire here, if his friends or family miss him.'

'Could we furnish a description,' asked the other, 'if the police want it?'

'The police!' said the Professor, starting from his reverie. 'A description. . . . Well, he looked awfully like everybody else, I'm afraid, except for goggles. One of those clean-shaven chaps. But the police . . . look here, what *are* we to do about this mad business?'

'I know what I ought to do,' said the Rev. Mr Pringle firmly, 'I am going to take this book straight to the only original Dr Hankey, and ask him what the devil it's all about. He lives not very far from here, and I'll come straight back and tell you what he says.'

'Oh, very well,' said the Professor at last, as he sat down rather wearily; perhaps relieved for the moment to be rid of the responsibility. But long after the brisk and ringing foot-steps of the little missionary had died away down the street, the Professor sat in the same posture, staring into vacancy like a man in a trance.

He was still in the same seat and almost in the same atti-tude, when the same brisk footsteps were heard on the pave-ment without and the missionary entered, this time, as a glance assured him, with empty hands.

'Dr Hankey,' said Pringle gravely, 'wants to keep the book for an hour and consider the point. Then he asks us both to call, and he will give us his decision. He specially desired, Professor, that you should accompany me on the second visit.'

Openshaw continued to stare in silence; then he said, suddenly:

'Who the devil is Dr Hankey?'

'You sound rather as if you meant he was the devil,' said Pringle, smiling, 'and I fancy some people have thought so. He had quite a reputation in your own line; but he gained it mostly in India, studying local magic and so on, so perhaps he's not so well known here. He is a yellow skinny little devil with a lame leg, and a doubtful temper; but he seems to have set up in an ordinary respectable practice in these parts, and I don't know anything definitely wrong about him—unless it's wrong to be the only person who can possibly know anything about all this crazy affair.'

Professor Openshaw rose heavily and went to the telephone; he rang up Father Brown, changing the luncheon engagement to a dinner, that he might hold himself free for the expedition to the house of the Anglo-Indian doctor; after that he sat down again, lit a cigar and sank once more into his own unfathomable thoughts.

Father Brown went round to the restaurant appointed for dinner, and kicked his heels for some time in a vestibule full of mirrors and palms in pots; he had been informed of Openshaw's afternoon engagement, and, as the evening closed-in dark and stormy round the glass and the green plants, guessed that it had produced something unexpected and unduly prolonged. He even wondered for a moment whether the Professor would turn up at all, but when the Professor eventually did, it was clear that his own more general guesses had been justified. For it was a very wild-eyed and even wild-haired Professor who eventually drove back with Mr Pringle from the expedition to the North of London, where suburbs are still fringed with heathy wastes and scraps of common, looking more sombre under the rather thunderous sunset. Nevertheless, they had apparently found the house, standing a little apart though within hail of other houses; they had verified the brass-plate duly engraved: 'J. I. Hankey, MD, MRCS.'* Only they did not find J. I. Hankey, MD, MRCS. They found only what a nightmare whisper had already subconsciously prepared them to find: a commonplace parlour with the accursed volume lying on the table, as if it had just been read; and beyond, a backdoor burst open and a faint trail of footsteps that ran a little way up so steep a garden-path that it seemed that no lame man could have run up so lightly. But it was a lame man who had run; for in those few steps there was the misshapen unequal mark of some sort of surgical boot; then two marks of that boot alone (as if the creature had hopped) and then nothing. There was nothing further to be learnt from Dr J. I. Hankey, except that he had made his decision. He had read the oracle and received the doom.

When the two came into the entrance under the palms, Pringle put the book down suddenly on a small table, as if it burned his fingers. The priest glanced at it curiously; there was only some rude lettering on the front with a couplet:

> They that looked into this book
> Them the Flying Terror took

and underneath, as he afterwards discovered, similar warnings in Greek, Latin and French. The other two had turned away with a natural impulsion towards drinks, after their exhaustion and bewilderment; and Openshaw had called to the waiter, who brought cocktails on a tray.

'You will dine with us, I hope,' said the Professor to the missionary; but Mr Pringle amiably shook his head.

'If you'll forgive me,' he said, 'I'm going off to wrestle with this book and this business by myself somewhere. I suppose I couldn't use your office for an hour or so?'

'I suppose—I'm afraid it's locked,' said Openshaw in some surprise.

'You forget there's a hole in the window.' The Rev. Luke Pringle gave the very broadest of all his broad grins and vanished into the darkness without.

'A rather odd fellow, that, after all,' said the Professor, frowning.

He was rather surprised to find Father Brown talking to the waiter who had brought the cocktails, apparently about the waiter's most private affairs; for there was some mention of a baby who was now out of danger. He commented on the fact with some surprise, wondering how the priest came to know the man; but the former only said, 'Oh, I dine here every two or three months, and I've talked to him now and then.'

The Professor, who himself dined there about five times a week, was conscious that he had never thought of talking to the man; but his thoughts were interrupted by a strident ringing and a summons to the telephone. The voice on the telephone said it was Pringle; it was rather a muffled voice, but it might well be muffled in all those bushes of beard and whisker. Its message was enough to establish identity.

'Professor,' said the voice, 'I can't stand it any longer. I'm going to look for myself. I'm speaking from your office and the book is in front of me. If anything happens to me, this is to say good-bye. No—it's no good trying to stop me. You wouldn't be in time anyhow. I'm opening the book now. I . . .'

Openshaw thought he heard something like a sort of thrilling or shivering yet almost soundless crash; then he shouted the name of Pringle again and again; but he heard no more. He hung up the receiver, and, restored to a superb academic calm, rather like the calm of despair, went back and quietly took his seat at the dinner-table. Then, as coolly as if he were describing the failure of some small silly trick at a séance, he told the priest every detail of this monstrous mystery.

'Five men have now vanished in this impossible way,' he said. 'Every one is extraordinary; and yet the one case I simply can't get over is my clerk, Berridge. It's just because he was the quietest creature that he's the queerest case.'

'Yes,' replied Father Brown, 'it was a queer thing for Berridge to do, anyway. He was awfully conscientious. He was always so jolly careful to keep all the office business separate from any fun of his own. Why, hardly anybody knew he was quite a humorist at home and——'

'Berridge!' cried the Professor. 'What on earth are you talking about? Did you know him?'

'Oh no,' said Father Brown carelessly, 'only as you say I know the waiter. I've often had to wait in your office, till you turned up; and of course I passed the time of day with poor Berridge. He was rather a card. I remember he once said he would like to collect valueless things, as collectors did the silly things they thought valuable. You know the old story about the woman who collected valueless things.'

'I'm not sure I know what you're talking about,' said Openshaw. 'But even if my clerk was eccentric (and I never knew a man I should have thought less so), it wouldn't explain what happened to him; and it certainly wouldn't explain the others.'

'What others?' asked the priest.

The Professor stared at him and spoke distinctly, as if to a child:

'My dear Father Brown, Five Men have disappeared.'

'My dear Professor Openshaw, no men have disappeared.'

Father Brown gazed back at his host with equal steadiness and spoke with equal distinctness. Nevertheless, the Professor required the words repeated, and they were repeated as distinctly.

'I say that no men have disappeared.'

After a moment's silence, he added, 'I suppose the hardest thing is to convince anybody that O + O + O = O. Men believe the oddest things if they are in a series; that is why Macbeth* believed the three words of the three witches; though the first was something he knew himself; and the last something he could only bring about himself. But in your case the middle term is the weakest of all.'

'What do you mean?'

'You saw nobody vanish. You did not see the man vanish from the boat. You did not see the man vanish from the tent. All that rests on the word of Mr Pringle, which I will not discuss just now. But you'll admit this; you would never have taken his word yourself, *unless* you had seen it confirmed by your clerk's disappearance; just as Macbeth would never have believed he would be king, if he had not been confirmed in believing he would be Cawdor.'

'That may be true,' said the Professor, nodding slowly. 'But *when* it was confirmed, I knew it was the truth. You say I saw nothing myself. But I did; I saw my own clerk disappear. Berridge did disappear.'

'Berridge did not disappear,' said Father Brown. 'On the contrary.'

'What the devil do you mean by "on the contrary"?'

'I mean,' said Father Brown, 'that he never disappeared. He appeared.'

Openshaw stared across at his friend, but the eyes had already altered in his head, as they did when they concentrated on a new presentation of a problem. The priest went on:

'He appeared in your study, disguised in a bushy red beard and buttoned up in a clumsy cape, and announced himself as the Rev. Luke Pringle. And you had never noticed your own clerk enough to know him again, when he was in so rough-and-ready a disguise.'

'But surely,' began the Professor.

'Could you describe him for the police?' asked Father Brown. 'Not you. You probably knew he was clean-shaven and wore tinted glasses; and merely taking off those glasses was a better disguise than putting on anything else. You had never seen his eyes any more than his soul; jolly laughing eyes. He had planted his absurd book and all the properties; then he calmly smashed the window, put on the beard and cape and walked into your study; knowing that you had never looked at him in your life.'

'But why should he play me such an insane trick?' demanded Openshaw.

'Why, *because* you had never looked at him in your life,' said Father Brown; and his hand slightly curled and clinched, as if he might have struck the table, if he had been given to gesture. 'You called him the Calculating Machine, because that was all you ever used him for. You never found out even what a stranger strolling into your office could find out, in five minutes' chat: that he was a character; that he was full of antics; that he had all sorts of views on you and your theories and your reputation for "spotting" people. Can't you understand his itching to prove that you couldn't spot your own clerk? He has nonsense notions of all sorts. About collecting useless things, for instance. Don't you know the story of the woman who bought the two most useless things: an old doctor's brass-plate and a wooden leg? With those your ingenious clerk created the character of the remarkable Dr Hankey; as easily as the visionary Captain Wales. Planting them in his own house——'

'Do you mean that place we visited beyond Hampstead was Berridge's own house?' asked Openshaw.

'Did *you* know his house—or even his address?' retorted the priest. 'Look here, don't think I'm speaking disrespectfully of you or your work. You are a great servant of truth and you know I could never be disrespectful to that. You're seen through a lot of liars, when you put your mind to it. But don't *only* look at liars. Do, just occasionally, look at honest men— like the waiter.'

'Where is Berridge now?' asked the Professor, after a long silence.

'I haven't the least doubt,' said Father Brown, 'that he is back in your office. In fact, he came back into your office at the exact moment when the Rev. Luke Pringle read the awful volume and faded into the void.'

There was another long silence and then Professor Openshaw laughed; with the laugh of a great man who is great enough to look small. Then he said abruptly:

'I suppose I do deserve it; for not noticing the nearest helpers I have. But you must admit the accumulation of incidents was rather formidable. Did you *never* feel just a momentary awe of the awful volume?'

'Oh, that,' said Father Brown. 'I opened it as soon as I saw it lying there. It's all blank pages. You see, I am not superstitious.'

THE GREEN MAN

A YOUNG man in knickerbockers, with an eager sanguine profile, was playing golf against himself on the links that lay parallel to the sand and sea, which were all growing grey with twilight. He was not carelessly knocking a ball about, but rather practising particular strokes with a sort of microscopic fury; like a neat and tidy whirlwind. He had learned many games quickly, but he had a disposition to learn them a little more quickly than they can be learnt. He was rather prone to be a victim of those remarkable invitations by which a man may learn the Violin in Six Lessons—or acquire a perfect French accent by a Correspondence Course. He lived in the breezy atmosphere of such hopeful advertisement and adventure. He was at present the private secretary of Admiral Sir Michael Craven, who owned the big house behind the park abutting on the links. He was ambitious, and had no intention of continuing indefinitely to be private secretary to anybody. But he was also reasonable; and he knew that the best way of ceasing to be a secretary was to be a good secretary. Consequently he was a very good secretary; dealing with the ever-accumulating arrears of the Admiral's correspondence with the same swift centripetal concentration with which he addressed the golf-ball. He had to struggle with the correspondence alone and at his own discretion at present; for the Admiral had been with his ship for the last six months; and, though now returning, was not expected for hours, or possibly days.

With an athletic stride, the young man, whose name was Harold Harker, crested the rise of turf that was the rampart of the links and, looking out across the sands to the sea, saw a strange sight. He did not see it very clearly; for the dusk was darkening every minute under stormy clouds; but it seemed to him, by a sort of momentary illusion, like a dream of days long past or a drama played by ghosts, out of another age in history.

The last of the sunset lay in long bars of copper and gold above the last dark strip of sea that seemed rather black than blue. But blacker still against this gleam in the west, there passed in sharp outline, like figures in a shadow pantomime, two men with three-cornered cocked hats and swords; as if they had just landed from one of the wooden ships of Nelson. It was not at all the sort of hallucination that would have come natural to Mr Harker, had he been prone to hallucinations. He was of the type that is at once sanguine and scientific; and would be more likely to fancy the flying-ships of the future than the fighting-ships of the past. He therefore very sensibly came to the conclusion that even a futurist can believe his eyes.

His illusion did not last more than a moment. On the second glance, what he saw was unusual but not incredible. The two men who were striding in single file across the sands, one some fifteen yards behind the other, were ordinary modern naval officers; but naval officers wearing that almost extravagant full-dress uniform which naval officers never do wear if they can possibly help it; only on great ceremonial occasions such as the visits of Royalty. In the man walking in front, who seemed more or less unconscious of the man walking behind, Harker recognized at once the high-bridged nose and spike-shaped beard of his own employer the Admiral. The other man following in his tracks he did not know. But he did know something about the circumstances connected with the ceremonial occasion. He knew that when the Admiral's ship put in at the adjacent port, it was to be formally visited by a Great Personage; which was enough, in that sense, to explain the officers being in full dress. But he did also know the officers; or at any rate the Admiral. And what could have possessed the Admiral to come on shore in that rig-out, when one could swear he would seize five minutes to change into mufti or at least into undress uniform, was more than his secretary could conceive. It seemed somehow to be the very last thing he would do. It was indeed to remain for many weeks one of the chief mysteries of this mysterious business. As it was, the outline of these fantastic court uniforms against the empty scenery, striped with dark sea and sand, had something suggestive of comic opera; and reminded the spectator of *Pinafore*.*

The second figure was much more singular; somewhat singular in appearance, despite his correct lieutenant's uniform, and still more extraordinary in behaviour. He walked in a strangely irregular and uneasy manner; sometimes quickly and sometimes slowly; as if he could not make up his mind whether to overtake the Admiral or not. The Admiral was

rather deaf and certainly heard no footsteps behind him on the
yielding sand; but the footsteps behind him, if traced in the
detective manner, would have given rise to twenty conjectures
from a limp to a dance. The man's face was swarthy as well as
darkened with shadow and every now and then the eyes in it
shifted and shone, as if to accent his agitation. Once he began
to run and then abruptly relapsed into a swaggering slowness
and carelessness. Then he did something which Mr Harker
could never have conceived any normal naval officer in His
Britannic Majesty's Service doing, even in a lunatic asylum.
He drew his sword.

It was at this bursting-point of the prodigy that the two
passing figures disappeared behind a headland on the shore.
The staring secretary had just time to notice the swarthy
stranger, with a resumption of carelessness, knock off a head
of sea-holly* with his glittering blade. He seemed then to have
abandoned all idea of catching the other man up. But Mr
Harold Harker's face became very thoughtful indeed; and he
stood there ruminating for some time before he gravely took
himself inland, towards the road that ran past the gates of the
great house and so by a long curve down to the sea.

It was up this curving road from the coast that the Admiral
might be expected to come, considering the direction in which
he had been walking, and making the natural assumption
that he was bound for his own door. The path along the
sands, under the links, turned inland just beyond the headland
and solidifying itself into a road, returned towards Craven
House. It was down this road, therefore, that the secretary
darted, with characteristic impetuosity, to meet his patron
returning home. But the patron was apparently not returning
home. What was still more peculiar, the secretary was not
returning home either; at least until many hours later; a
delay quite long enough to arouse alarm and mystification at
Craven House.

Behind the pillars and palms of that rather too palatial
country house, indeed, there was expectancy gradually changing to uneasiness. Gryce the butler, a big bilious man abnormally silent below as well as above stairs, showed a certain
restlessness as he moved about the main front-hall and occasionally looked out of the side windows of the porch, on the

white road that swept towards the sea. The Admiral's sister Marion, who kept house for him, had her brother's high nose with a more sniffy expression; she was voluble, rather rambling, not without humour, and capable of sudden emphasis as shrill as a cockatoo. The Admiral's daughter Olive was dark, dreamy, and as a rule abstractedly silent, perhaps melancholy; so that her aunt generally conducted most of the conversation, and that without reluctance. But the girl also had a gift of sudden laughter that was very engaging.

'I can't think why they're not here already,' said the elder lady. 'The postman distinctly told me he'd seen the Admiral coming along the beach; along with that dreadful creature Rook. Why in the world they call him Lieutenant Rook——'

'Perhaps,' suggested the melancholy young lady, with a momentary brightness, 'perhaps they call him Lieutenant because he is a Lieutenant.'

'I can't think why the Admiral keeps him,' snorted her aunt, as if she were talking of a housemaid. She was very proud of her brother and always called him the Admiral; but her notions of a commission in the Senior Service were inexact.

'Well, Roger Rook is sulky and unsociable and all that,' replied Olive, 'but of course that wouldn't prevent him being a capable sailor.'

'Sailor!' cried her aunt with one of her rather startling cockatoo notes, 'he isn't my notion of a sailor. The Lass that Loved a Sailor, as they used to sing when I was young. . . . Just think of it! He's not gay and free and whatsitsname. He doesn't sing chanties or dance a hornpipe.'

'Well,' observed her niece with gravity. 'The Admiral doesn't very often dance a hornpipe.'

'Oh, you know what I mean—he isn't bright or breezy or anything,' replied the old lady. 'Why, that secretary fellow could do better than that.'

Olive's rather tragic face was transfigured by one of her good and rejuvenating waves of laughter.

'I'm sure Mr Harker would dance a hornpipe for you,' she said, 'and say he had learnt it in half an hour from the book of instructions. He's always learning things of that sort.'

She stopped laughing suddenly and looked at her aunt's rather strained face.

'I can't think why Mr Harker doesn't come,' she added.

'I don't care about Mr Harker,' replied the aunt, and rose and looked out of the window.

The evening light had long turned from yellow to grey and was now turning almost to white under the widening moonlight, over the large flat landscape by the coast; unbroken by any features save a clump of sea-twisted trees round a pool and beyond, rather gaunt and dark against the horizon, the shabby fishermen's tavern on the shore that bore the name of the Green Man.* And all that road and landscape was empty of any living thing. Nobody had seen the figure in the cocked hat that had been observed, earlier in the evening, walking by the sea; or the other and stranger figure that had been seen trailing after him. Nobody had even seen the secretary who saw them.

It was after midnight when the secretary at last burst in and aroused the household; and his face, white as a ghost, looked all the paler against the background of the stolid face and figure of a big Inspector of Police. Somehow that red, heavy, indifferent face looked, even more than the white and harassed one, like a mask of doom. The news was broken to the two women with such consideration or concealments as were possible. But the news was that the body of Admiral Craven had been eventually fished out of the foul weeds and scum of the pool under the trees; and that he was drowned and dead.

Anybody acquainted with Mr Harold Harker, secretary, will realize that, whatever his agitation, he was by morning in a mood to be tremendously on the spot. He hustled the Inspector, whom he had met the night before on the road down by the Green Man, into another room for private and practical consultation. He questioned the Inspector rather as the Inspector might have questioned a yokel. But Inspector Burns was a stolid character; and was either too stupid or too clever to resent such trifles. It soon began to look as if he were by no means so stupid as he looked; for he disposed of Harker's eager questions in a manner that was slow but methodical and rational.

'Well,' said Harker (his head full of many manuals with titles like 'Be a Detective in Ten Days'). 'Well, it's the old triangle, I suppose. Accident, Suicide or Murder.'

'I don't see how it could be accident,' answered the policeman. 'It wasn't even dark yet and the pool's fifty yards from the straight road that he knew like his own doorstep. He'd no more have got into that pond than he'd go and carefully lie down in a puddle in the street. As for suicide, it's rather a responsibility to suggest it, and rather improbable too. The Admiral was a pretty spry and successful man and frightfully rich, nearly a millionaire in fact; though of course that doesn't prove anything. He seemed to be pretty normal and comfortable in his private life too; he's the last man I should suspect of drowning himself.'

'So that we come,' said the secretary, lowering his voice with the thrill, 'I suppose we come to the third possibility.'

'We won't be in too much of a hurry about that,' said the Inspector to the annoyance of Harker, who was in a hurry about everything. 'But naturally there are one or two things one would like to know. One would like to know about his property, for instance. Do you know who's likely to come in for it? You're his private secretary; do you know anything about his will?'

'I'm not so private a secretary as all that,' answered the young man. 'His solicitors are Messrs. Willis, Hardman and Dyke, over in Suttford High Street; and I believe the will is in their custody.'

'Well, I'd better get round and see them pretty soon,' said the Inspector.

'Let's get round and see them at once,' said the impatient secretary.

He took a turn or two restlessly up and down the room and then exploded in a fresh place.

'What have you done about the body, Inspector?' he asked.

'Dr Straker is examining it now at the Police Station. His report ought to be ready in an hour or so.'

'It can't be ready too soon,' said Harker. 'It would save time if we could meet him at the lawyer's.' Then he stopped and his impetuous tone changed abruptly to one of some embarrassment.

'Look here,' he said, 'I want . . . we want to consider the young lady, the poor Admiral's daughter, as much as possible just now. She's got a notion that may be all nonsense; but I wouldn't like to disappoint her. There's some friend of hers she wants to consult, staying in the town at present. Man of the name of Brown; priest or parson of some sort; she's given me his address. I don't take much stock in priests or parsons, but——'

The Inspector nodded. 'I don't take any stock in priests or parsons; but I take a lot of stock in Father Brown,' he said. 'I happened to have to do with him in a queer sort of society jewel case. He ought to have been a policeman instead of a parson.'

'Oh, all right,' said the breathless secretary as he vanished from the room. 'Let him come to the lawyer's too.'

Thus it happened that, when they hurried across to the neighbouring town to meet Dr Straker at the solicitor's office, they found Father Brown already seated there, with his hands folded on his heavy umbrella, chatting pleasantly to the only available member of the firm. Dr Straker also had arrived, but apparently only at that moment, as he was carefully placing his gloves in his top-hat and his top-hat on a side-table. And the mild and beaming expression of the priest's moonlike face and spectacles, together with the silent chuckles of the jolly old grizzled lawyer, to whom he was talking, were enough to show that the doctor had not yet opened his mouth to bring the news of death.

'A beautiful morning after all,' Father Brown was saying. 'That storm seems to have passed over us. There were some big black clouds, but I notice that not a drop of rain fell.'

'Not a drop,' agreed the solicitor toying with a pen; he was the third partner, Mr Dyke; 'there's not a cloud in the sky now. It's the sort of day for a holiday.' Then he realized the newcomers and looked up, laying down the pen and rising. 'Ah, Mr Harker, how are you? I hear the Admiral is expected home soon.' Then Harker spoke, and his voice rang hollow in the room.

'I am sorry to say we are the bearers of bad news. Admiral Craven was drowned before reaching home.'

There was a change in the very air of the still office, though not in the attitudes of the motionless figures; both were staring at the speaker as if a joke had been frozen on their lips. Both repeated the word 'drowned' and looked at each other, and then again at their informant. Then there was a small hubbub of questions.

'When did this happen?' asked the priest.

'Where was he found?' asked the lawyer.

'He was found,' said the Inspector, 'in that pool by the coast, not far from the Green Man, and dragged out all covered with green scum and weeds so as to be almost unrecognizable. But Dr Straker here has——What is the matter, Father Brown? Are you ill?'

'The Green Man,' said Father Brown with a shudder. 'I'm so sorry . . . I beg your pardon for being upset.'

'Upset by what?' asked the staring officer.

'By his being covered with green scum, I suppose,' said the priest, with a rather shaky laugh. Then he added rather more firmly, 'I thought it might have been seaweed.'

By this time everybody was looking at the priest, with a not unnatural suspicion that he was mad; and yet the next crucial surprise was not to come from him. After a dead silence, it was the doctor who spoke.

Dr Straker was a remarkable man, even to look at. He was very tall and angular, formal and professional in his dress; yet retaining a fashion that has hardly been known since Mid-Victorian times. Though comparatively young, he wore his brown beard very long and spreading over his waistcoat; in contrast with it, his features, which were both harsh and handsome, looked singularly pale. His good looks were also diminished by something in his deep eyes that was not squinting, but like the shadow of a squint. Everybody noticed these things about him, because the moment he spoke, he gave forth an indescribable air of authority. But all he said was:

'There is one more thing to be said, if you come to details, about Admiral Craven being drowned.' Then he added reflectively, 'Admiral Craven was not drowned.'

The Inspector turned with quite a new promptitude and shot a question at him.

'I have just examined the body,' said Dr Straker, 'the cause of death was a stab through the heart with some pointed blade like a stiletto. It was after death, and even some little time after, that the body was hidden in the pool.'

Father Brown was regarding Dr Straker with a very lively eye, such as he seldom turned upon anybody; and when the group in the office began to break up, he managed to attach himself to the medical man for a little further conversation, as they went back down the street. There had not been very much else to detain them except the rather formal question of the will. The impatience of the young secretary had been somewhat tried by the professional etiquette of the old lawyer. But the latter was ultimately induced, rather by the tact of the priest than the authority of the policeman, to refrain from making a mystery where there was no mystery at all. Mr Dyke admitted, with a smile, that the Admiral's will was a very normal and ordinary document, leaving everything to his only child Olive; and that there really was no particular reason for concealing the fact.

The doctor and the priest walked slowly down the street that struck out of the town in the direction of Craven House. Harker had plunged on ahead of him with all his native eagerness to get somewhere; but the two behind seemed more interested in their discussion than their direction. It was in rather an enigmatic tone that the tall doctor said to the short cleric beside him:

'Well, Father Brown, what do you think of a thing like this?'

Father Brown looked at him rather intently for an instant and then said: 'Well, I've begun to think of one or two things; but my chief difficulty is that I only knew the Admiral slightly; though I've seen something of his daughter.'

'The Admiral,' said the doctor with a grim immobility of feature, 'was the sort of man of whom it is said that he had not an enemy in the world.'

'I suppose you mean,' answered the priest, 'that there's something else that will not be said.'

'Oh, it's no affair of mine,' said Straker hastily but rather harshly. 'He had his moods, I suppose. He once threatened me with a legal action about an operation; but I think he thought better of it. I can imagine his being rather rough with a subordinate.'

Father Brown's eyes were fixed on the figure of the secretary striding far ahead; and as he gazed he realized the special cause of his hurry. Some fifty yards farther ahead the Admiral's daughter was dawdling along the road towards the Admiral's house. The secretary soon came abreast of her; and for the remainder of the time Father Brown watched the silent drama of two human backs as they diminished into the distance. The secretary was evidently very much excited about something; but if the priest guessed what it was, he kept it to himself. When he came to the corner leading to the doctor's house, he only said briefly: 'I don't know if you have anything more to tell us.'

'Why should I?' answered the doctor very abruptly; and striding off, left it uncertain whether he was asking why he should have anything to tell, or why he should tell it.

Father Brown went stumping on alone, in the track of the two young people; but when he came to the entrance and avenues of the Admiral's park, he was arrested by the action of the girl, who turned suddenly and came straight towards him; her face unusually pale and her eyes bright with some new and as yet nameless emotion.

'Father Brown,' she said in a low voice, 'I must talk to you as soon as possible. You must listen to me, I can't see any other way out.'

'Why certainly,' he replied, as coolly as if a gutter-boy had asked him the time. 'Where shall we go and talk?'

The girl led him at random to one of the rather tumbledown arbours in the grounds; and they sat down behind a screen of large ragged leaves. She began instantly, as if she must relieve her feelings or faint.

'Harold Harker,' she said, 'has been talking to me about things. Terrible things.'

The priest nodded and the girl went on hastily. 'About Roger Rook. Do you know about Roger?'

'I've been told,' he answered, 'that his fellow-seamen call him The Jolly Roger, because he is never jolly; and looks like the pirate's skull and crossbones.'

'He was not always like that,' said Olive in a low voice. 'Something very queer must have happened to him. I knew him well when we were children; we used to play over there on the sands. He was harum-scarum and always talking about being a pirate; I dare say he was the sort they say might take to crime through reading shockers; but there was something poetical in his way of being piratical. He really was a Jolly Roger then. I suppose he was the last boy who kept up the old legend of really running away to sea; and at last his family had to agree to his joining the Navy. Well . . .'

'Yes,' said Father Brown patiently.

'Well,' she admitted, caught in one of her rare moments of mirth, 'I suppose poor Roger found it disappointing. Naval officers so seldom carry knives in their teeth or wave bloody cutlasses and black flags. But that doesn't explain the change in him. He just stiffened; grew dull and dumb, like a dead man walking about. He always avoids me; but that doesn't matter. I supposed some great grief that's no business of mine had broken him up. And now—well, if what Harold says is true, the grief is neither more nor less than going mad; or being possessed of a devil.'

'And what does Harold say?' asked the priest.

'It's so awful I can hardly say it,' she answered. 'He swears he saw Roger creeping behind my father that night; hesitating and then drawing his sword . . . and the doctor says father was stabbed with a steel point. . . . I *can't* believe Roger Rook had anything to do with it. His sulks and my father's temper sometimes led to quarrels; but what are quarrels? I can't exactly say I'm standing up for an old friend; because he isn't even friendly. But you can't help feeling sure of some things, even about an old acquaintance. And yet Harold swears that he——'

'Harold seems to swear a great deal,' said Father Brown.

There was a sudden silence; after which she said in a different tone:

'Well, he does swear other things too. Harold Harker proposed to me just now.'

'Am I to congratulate you, or rather him?' inquired her companion.

'I told him he must wait. He isn't good at waiting.' She was caught again in a ripple of her incongruous sense of the comic: 'He said I was his ideal and his ambition and so on. He had lived in the States; but somehow I never remember it when he is talking about dollars; only when he is talking about ideals.'

'And I suppose,' said Father Brown very softly, 'that it is because you have to decide about Harold that you want to know the truth about Roger.'

She stiffened and frowned, and then equally abruptly smiled, saying: 'Oh, you know too much.'

'I know very little, especially in this affair,' said the priest gravely. 'I only know who murdered your father.' She started up and stood staring down at him stricken white. Father Brown made a wry face as he went on: 'I made a fool of myself when I first realized it; when they'd just been asking where he was found, and went on talking about green scum and the Green Man.'

Then he also rose; clutching his clumsy umbrella with a new resolution, he addressed the girl with a new gravity.

'There is something else that I know, which is the key to all these riddles of yours; but I won't tell you yet. I suppose it's bad news; but it's nothing like so bad as the things you have been fancying.' He buttoned up his coat and turned towards the gate. 'I'm going to see this Mr Rook of yours. In a shed by the shore, near where Mr Harker saw him walking. I rather think he lives there.' And he went bustling off in the direction of the beach.

Olive was an imaginative person; perhaps too imaginative to be safely left to brood over such hints as her friend had thrown out; but he was in rather a hurry to find the best relief for her broodings. The mysterious connexion between Father Brown's first shock of enlightenment and the chance language about the pool and the inn, hag-rode her fancy in a hundred forms of ugly symbolism. The Green Man became a ghost trailing loathsome weeds and walking the countryside under the moon; the sign of the Green Man became a human figure hanging as from a gibbet; and the tarn itself became a tavern, a dark subaqueous tavern for the dead sailors. And yet he had taken the most rapid method to overthrow all such nightmares, with a burst of blinding daylight which seemed more mysterious than the night.

For before the sun had set, something had come back into her life that turned her whole world topsy-turvy once more; something she had hardly known that she desired until it was abruptly granted; something that was, like a dream, old and familiar, and yet remained incomprehensible and incredible. For Roger Rook had come striding across the sands, and even when he was a dot in the distance, she knew he was transfigured; and as he came nearer and nearer, she saw that his dark face was alive with laughter and exultation. He came straight towards her, as if they had never parted, and seized her shoulders saying: 'Now I can look after you, thank God.'

She hardly knew what she answered; but she heard herself questioning rather wildly why he seemed so changed and so happy.

'Because I am happy,' he answered. 'I have heard the bad news.'

All parties concerned, including some who seemed rather unconcerned, found themselves assembled on the garden path leading to Craven House, to hear the formality, now truly formal, of the lawyer's reading of the will; and the probable, and more practical, sequel of the lawyer's advice upon the crisis. Besides the grey-haired solicitor himself, armed with the testamentary document, there was the Inspector armed with more direct authority touching the crime, and Lieutenant Rook in undisguised attendance on the lady; some were rather mystified on seeing the tall figure of the doctor, some smiled a little on seeing the dumpy figure of the priest. Mr Harker, that Flying Mercury,* had shot down to the lodge-gates to meet them, led them back on to the lawn, and then dashed ahead of them again to prepare their reception. He said he would be back in a jiffy; and anyone observing his piston-rod of energy could well believe it; but, for the moment, they were left rather stranded on the lawn outside the house.

'Reminds me of somebody making runs at cricket,' said the Lieutenant.

'That young man,' said the lawyer, 'is rather annoyed that the law cannot move quite so quickly as he does. Fortunately Miss Craven understands our professional difficulties and delays. She has kindly assured me that she still has confidence in my slowness.'

'I wish,' said the doctor, suddenly, 'that I had as much confidence in his quickness.'

'Why, what do you mean?' asked Rook, knitting his brows; 'do you mean that Harker is too quick?'

'Too quick and too slow,' said Dr Straker, in his rather cryptic fashion. 'I know one occasion at least when he was not so very quick. Why was he hanging about half the night by the pond and the Green Man, before the Inspector came down and found the body? Why did he meet the Inspector? Why should he expect to meet the Inspector outside the Green Man?'

'I don't understand you,' said Rook. 'Do you mean that Harker wasn't telling the truth?'

Dr Straker was silent. The grizzled lawyer laughed with grim good humour.

'I have nothing more serious to say against the young man,' he said, 'than that he made a prompt and praiseworthy attempt to teach me my own business.'

'For that matter, he made an attempt to teach me mine,' said the Inspector, who had just joined the group in front. 'But that doesn't matter. If Dr Straker means anything by his hints, they do matter. I must ask you to speak plainly, doctor. It may be my duty to question him at once.'

'Well, here he comes,' said Rook, as the alert figure of the secretary appeared once more in the doorway.

At this point Father Brown, who had remained silent and inconspicuous at the tail of the procession, astonished everybody very much; perhaps especially those who knew him. He not only walked rapidly to the front, but turned facing the whole group with an arresting and almost threatening expression, like a sergeant bringing soldiers to the halt.

'Stop!' he said almost sternly. 'I apologize to everybody; but it's absolutely necessary that I should see Mr Harker first. I've got to tell him something I know; and I don't think anybody else knows; something he's got to hear. It may save a very tragic misunderstanding with somebody later on.'

'What on earth do you mean?' asked old Dyke the lawyer.

'I mean the bad news,' said Father Brown.

'Here, I say,' began the Inspector indignantly; and then suddenly caught the priest's eye and remembered strange things he had seen in other days. 'Well, if it were anyone in the world but you I should say of all the infernal cheek——'

But Father Brown was already out of hearing, and a moment afterwards was plunged in talk with Harker in the porch. They walked to and fro together for a few paces and then disappeared into the dark interior. It was about twelve minutes afterwards that Father Brown came out alone.

To their surprise he showed no disposition to re-enter the house, now that the whole company were at last about to enter it. He threw himself down on the rather rickety seat in the leafy arbour, and as the procession disappeared through the doorway, lit a pipe and proceeded to stare vacantly at the long ragged leaves about his head and to listen to the birds. There was no man who had a more hearty and enduring appetite for doing nothing.

He was apparently in a cloud of smoke and a dream of abstraction, when the front-doors were once more flung open and two or three figures came out helter-skelter, running towards him, the daughter of the house and her young admirer Mr Rook being easily winners in the race. Their faces were alight with astonishment; and the face of Inspector Burns, who advanced more heavily behind them, like an elephant shaking the garden, was inflamed with some indignation as well.

'What *can* all this mean?' cried Olive, as she came panting to a halt. 'He's gone!'

'Bolted!' said the Lieutenant explosively. 'Harker's just managed to pack a suitcase and bolted! Gone clean out of the back door and over the garden-wall to God knows where. What *did* you say to him?'

'Don't be silly!' said Olive, with a more worried expression. 'Of course you told him you'd found him out, and now he's gone. I never could have believed he was wicked like that?'

'Well!' gasped the Inspector, bursting into their midst. 'What have you done now? What have you let me down like this for?'

'Well,' repeated Father Brown, 'what have I done?'

'You have let a murderer escape,' cried Burns, with a decision that was like a thunderclap in the quiet garden; 'you have *helped* a murderer to escape. Like a fool I let you warn him; and now he is miles away.'

'I have helped a few murderers in my time, it is true,' said Father Brown; then he added, in careful distinction, 'not, you will understand, helped them to commit the murder.'

'But you knew all the time,' insisted Olive. 'You guessed from the first that it must be he. That's what you meant about being upset by the business of finding the body. That's what the doctor meant by saying my father might be disliked by a subordinate.'

'That's what I complain of,' said the official indignantly. 'You knew even then that he was the——'

'You knew even then,' insisted Olive, 'that the murderer was——'

Father Brown nodded gravely. 'Yes,' he said. 'I knew even then that the murderer was old Dyke.'

'Was *who*?' repeated the Inspector and stopped amid a dead silence; punctuated only by the occasional pipe of birds.

'I mean Mr Dyke, the solicitor,' explained Father Brown, like one explaining something elementary to an infant class. 'That gentleman with grey hair who's supposed to be going to read the will.'

They all stood like statues staring at him, as he carefully filled his pipe again and struck a match. At last Burns rallied his vocal powers to break the strangling silence with an effort resembling violence.

'But, in the name of heaven, *why*?'

'Ah, why?' said the priest and rose thoughtfully, puffing at his pipe. 'As to why he did it. . . . Well, I suppose the time has come to tell you, or those of you who don't know, the fact that is the key of all this business. It's a great calamity; and it's a great crime; but it's not the murder of Admiral Craven.'

He looked Olive full in the face and said very seriously:

'I tell you the bad news bluntly and in few words; because I think you are brave enough, and perhaps happy enough, to take it well. You have the chance, and I think the power, to be something like a great woman. You are not a great heiress.'

Amid the silence that followed it was he who resumed his explanation.

'Most of your father's money, I am sorry to say, has gone. It went by the financial dexterity of the grey-haired gentleman named Dyke, who is (I grieve to say) a swindler. Admiral Craven was murdered to silence him about the way in which he was swindled. The fact that he was ruined and you were disinherited is the single simple clue, not only to the murder, but to all the other mysteries in this business.' He took a puff or two and then continued.

'I told Mr Rook you were disinherited and he rushed back to help you. Mr Rook is a rather remarkable person.'

'Oh, chuck it,' said Mr Rook with a hostile air.

'Mr Rook is a monster,' said Father Brown with scientific calm. 'He is an anachronism, an atavism, a brute survival of the Stone Age. If there was one barbarous superstition we all supposed to be utterly extinct and dead in these days, it was that notion about honour and independence. But then I get mixed up with so many dead superstitions. Mr Rook is an extinct animal. He is a plesiosaurus. He did not want to live on his wife or have a wife who could call him a fortune-hunter. Therefore he sulked in a grotesque manner and only came to life again when I brought him the good news that you were ruined. He wanted to work for his wife and not be kept by her. Disgusting, isn't it? Let us turn to the brighter topic of Mr Harker.

'I told Mr Harker you were disinherited and he rushed away in a sort of panic. Do not be too hard on Mr Harker. He really had better as well as worse enthusiasms; but he had them all mixed up. There is no harm in having ambitions; but he had ambitions and called them ideals. The old sense of honour taught men to suspect success; to say, "This is a benefit; it may be a bribe." The new nine-times-accursed nonsense about Making Good teaches men to identify being good with making money. That was all that was the matter with him; in every other way he was a thoroughly good fellow, and there are thousands like him. Gazing at the stars and rising in the world were all Uplift. Marrying a good wife and marrying a rich wife were all Making Good. But he was not a cynical scoundrel; or he would simply have come back and jilted or cut you as the case might be. He could not face you; while you were there, half of his broken ideal was left.

'I did not tell the Admiral; but somebody did. Word came to him somehow, during the last grand parade on board, that his friend the family lawyer had betrayed him. He was in such a towering passion that he did what he could never have done in his senses; came straight on shore in his cocked hat and gold lace to catch the criminal; he wired to the police station, and that was why the Inspector was wandering round the Green Man. Lieutenant Rook followed him on shore because he suspected some family trouble and had half a hope he might help and put himself right. Hence his hesitating behaviour. As for his drawing his sword when he dropped behind and thought he was alone, well that's a matter of imagination. He was a romantic person who had dreamed of swords and run away to sea; and found himself in a service where he wasn't even allowed to wear a sword except about once in three years. He thought he was quite alone on the sands where he played as a boy. If you don't understand what he did, I can only say, like Stevenson, "you will never be a pirate." Also you will never be a poet; and you have never been a boy.'*

'I never have,' answered Olive gravely, 'and yet I think I understand.'

'Almost every man,' continued the priest musing, 'will play with anything shaped like a sword or dagger, even if it is a paper-knife. That is why I thought it so odd when the lawyer didn't.'

'What do you mean?' asked Burns, 'didn't what?'

'Why, didn't you notice,' answered Brown, 'at that first meeting in the office, the lawyer played with a pen and not with a paper-knife; though he had a beautiful bright steel paper-knife in the pattern of a stiletto? The pens were dusty and splashed with ink; but the knife had just been cleaned. But he did not play with it. There are limits to the irony of assassins.'

After a silence the Inspector said, like one waking from a dream: 'Look here . . . I don't know whether I'm on my head or my heels; I don't know whether you think you've got to the end; but I haven't got to the beginning. Where do you get all this lawyer stuff from? What started you out on that trail?'

Father Brown laughed curtly and without mirth.

'The murderer made a slip at the start,' he said, 'and I can't think why nobody else noticed it. When you brought the first news of the death to the solicitor's office, nobody was supposed to know anything there, except that the Admiral was expected home. When you said he was drowned, I asked when it happened and Mr Dyke asked where the corpse was found.'

He paused a moment to knock out his pipe and resumed reflectively:

'Now when you are simply told of a seaman, returning from the sea, that he has been drowned, it is natural to assume that he has been drowned at sea. At any rate, to allow that he may have been drowned at sea. If he had been washed overboard, or gone down with his ship, or had his body "committed to the deep," there would be no reason to expect his body to be found at all. The moment that man asked where it was found, I was sure he knew where it was found. Because he had put it there. Nobody but the murderer need have thought of anything so unlikely as a seaman being drowned in a land-locked pool a few hundred yards from the sea. That is why I suddenly felt sick and turned green, I dare say; as green as the Green Man. I never *can* get used to finding myself suddenly sitting beside a murderer. So I had to turn it off by talking in parables; but the parable meant something, after all. I said that the body was covered with green scum, but it might just as well have been seaweed.'

It is fortunate that tragedy can never kill comedy and that the two can run side by side; and that while the only acting partner of the business of Messrs. Willis, Hardman and Dyke blew his brains out when the Inspector entered the house to arrest him, Olive and Roger were calling to each other across the sands at evening, as they did when they were children together.

THE CRIME OF THE COMMUNIST

THREE men came out from under the low-browed Tudor arch in the mellow façade of Mandeville College,* into the strong evening sunlight of a summer day which seemed as if it would never end; and in that sunlight they saw something that blasted like lightning; well-fitted to be the shock of their lives.

Even before they had realized anything in the way of a catastrophe, they were conscious of a contrast. They themselves, in a curious quiet way, were quite harmonious with their surroundings. Though the Tudor arches that ran like a cloister round the College gardens had been built four hundred years ago, at that moment when the Gothic fell from heaven and bowed, or almost crouched, over the cosier chambers of Humanism and the Revival of Learning—though they themselves were in modern clothes (that is in clothes whose ugliness would have amazed any of the four centuries) yet something in the spirit of the place made them all at one. The gardens had been tended so carefully as to achieve the final triumph of looking careless; the very flowers seemed beautiful by accident, like elegant weeds; and the modern costumes had at least any picturesqueness that can be produced by being untidy. The first of the three, a tall, bald, bearded maypole of a man, was a familiar figure in the Quad in cap and gown; the gown slipped off one of his sloping shoulders. The second was very square-shouldered, short and compact, with a rather jolly grin, commonly clad in a jacket, with his gown over his arm. The third was even shorter and much shabbier, in black clerical clothes. But they all seemed suitable to Mandeville College; and the indescribable atmosphere of the two ancient and unique Universities of England. They fitted into it and they faded into it; which is there regarded as most fitting.

The two men seated on garden chairs by a little table were a sort of brilliant blot on this grey-green landscape. They were clad mostly in black and yet they glittered from head to heel, from their burnished top-hats to their perfectly polished boots. It was dimly felt as an outrage that anybody should be so well-dressed in the well-bred freedom of Mandeville College. The only excuse was that they were foreigners. One was an American, a millionaire named Hake, dressed in the spotlessly and sparklingly gentlemanly manner known only to the rich of New York. The other, who added to all these things the outrage of an astrakhan overcoat (to say nothing of a pair of florid whiskers), was a German Count of great wealth, the shortest part of whose name was Von Zimmern. The mystery of this story, however, is not the mystery of why they were there. They were there for the reason that commonly explains the meeting of incongruous things; they proposed to give the College some money. They had come in support of a plan supported by several financiers and magnates of many countries, for founding a new Chair of Economics at Mandeville College. They had inspected the College with that tireless conscientious sightseeing of which no sons of Eve are capable except the American and the German. And now they were resting from their labours and looking solemnly at the College gardens. So far so good.

The three other men, who had already met them, passed with a vague salutation; but one of them stopped; the smallest of the three, in the black clerical clothes.

'I say,' he said, with rather the air of a frightened rabbit, 'I don't like the look of those men.'

'Good God! Who could?' ejaculated the tall man, who happened to be the Master* of Mandeville. 'At least we have some rich men who don't go about dressed up like tailors' dummies.'

'Yes,' hissed the little cleric, 'that's what I mean. Like tailors' dummies.'

'Why, what do you mean?' asked the shorter of the other men, sharply.

'I mean they're like horrible waxworks,' said the cleric in a faint voice. 'I mean they don't move. Why don't they move?'

Suddenly starting out of his dim retirement, he darted across the garden and touched the German Baron on the elbow. The German Baron fell over, chair and all, and the trousered legs that stuck up in the air were as stiff as the legs of the chair.

Mr Gideon P. Hake continued to gaze at the College gardens with glassy eyes; but the parallel of a waxwork confirmed the impression that they were like eyes made of glass. Somehow the rich sunlight and the coloured garden increased the creepy impression of a stiffly dressed doll; a marionette on an Italian stage. The small man in black, who was a priest named Brown, tentatively touched the millionaire on the shoulder, and the millionaire fell sideways, but horribly all of a piece, like something carved in wood.

'Rigor mortis,'* said Father Brown, 'and so soon. But it does vary a good deal.'

The reason the first three men had joined the other two men so late (not to say too late) will best be understood by noting what had happened just inside the building, behind the Tudor archway, but a short time before they came out. They had all dined together in Hall,* at the High Table;* but the two foreign philanthropists, slaves of duty in the matter of seeing everything, had solemnly gone back to the chapel, of which one cloister and a staircase remained unexamined; promising to rejoin the rest in the garden, to examine as earnestly the College cigars. The rest, in a more reverent and right-minded spirit, had adjourned as usual to the long narrow oak table, round which the after-dinner wine had circulated, for all anybody knew, ever since the College had been founded in the Middle Ages by Sir John Mandeville,* for the encouragement of telling stories. The Master, with the big fair beard and the bald brow, took the head of the table, and the squat man in the square jacket sat on his left; for he was the Bursar or business man of the College. Next to him, on that side of the table, sat a queer-looking man with what could only be called a crooked face; for its dark tufts of moustache and eyebrow, slanting at contrary angles, made a sort of zig-zag, as if half his face were puckered or paralysed. His name was Byles;* he was the lecturer in Roman History, and his political opinions were founded on those of Coriolanus,* not to mention Tarquinius Superbus.* This tart Toryism, and rabidly reactionary view of all current problems, was not altogether unknown among the more old-fashioned sort of dons; but in the case of Byles there was a suggestion that it was a result rather than a cause of his acerbity. More than one sharp observer had received the impression that there was something really wrong with Byles; that some secret or some great misfortune had embittered him; as if that half-withered face had really been blasted like a storm-stricken tree. Beyond him again sat Father Brown and at the end of the table a Professor of Chemistry, large and blond and bland, with eyes that were sleepy and perhaps a little sly. It was well known that this natural philosopher regarded the other philosophers, of a more classical tradition, very much as old fogies. On the other side of the table, opposite Father Brown, was a very swarthy and silent young man, with a black pointed beard, introduced because somebody had insisted on having a Chair of Persian; opposite the sinister Byles was a very mild-looking little Chaplain, with a head like an egg. Opposite the Bursar, and at the right hand of the Master, was an empty chair; and there were many there who were glad to see it empty.

'I don't know whether Craken* is coming,' said the Master, not without a nervous glance at the chair, which contrasted with the usual languid freedom of his demeanour. 'I believe in giving people a lot of rope myself; but I confess I've reached the point of being glad when he is here, merely because he isn't anywhere else.'

'Never know what he'll be up to next,' said the Bursar cheerfully, 'especially when he's instructing the young.'

'A brilliant fellow, but fiery of course,' said the Master, with a rather abrupt relapse into reserve.

'Fireworks are fiery, and also brilliant,' growled old Byles, 'but I don't want to be burned in my bed so that Craken can figure as a real Guy Fawkes.'*

'Do you really *think* he would join a physical force revolution, if there were one,' asked the Bursar smiling.

'Well, *he* thinks he would,' said Byles sharply. 'Told a whole hall full of undergraduates the other day that nothing now could avert the Class War turning into a real war, with killing in the streets of the town; and it didn't matter, so long as it ended in Communism and the victory of the working-class.'

'The Class War,' mused the Master, with a sort of distaste mellowed by distance; for he had known William Morris* long ago and been familiar enough with the more artistic and leisurely Socialists. 'I never can understand all this about the Class War. When I was young, Socialism was supposed to mean saying that there are no classes.'

' 'Nother way of saying that Socialists are no class,' said Byles with sour relish.

'Of course, you'd be more against them than I should,' said the Master thoughtfully, 'but I suppose my Socialism is almost as old-fashioned as your Toryism. Wonder what our young friends really think. What do you think, Baker?' he said abruptly to the Bursar on his left.

'Oh, I *don't* think, as the vulgar saying is,' said the Bursar laughing. 'You must remember I'm a very vulgar person. I'm not a thinker. I'm only a business man; and as a business man I think it's all bosh. You can't make men equal and it's damned bad business to pay them equal; especially a lot of them not worth paying for at all. Whatever it is, you've got to take the practical way out, because it's the only way out. It's not our fault if nature made everything a scramble.'

'I agree with you there,' said the Professor of Chemistry, speaking with a lisp that seemed childish in so large a man. 'Communism pretends to be oh so modern; but it is not. Throw-back to the superstitions of monks and primitive tribes. A scientific government, with a really ethical responsibility to posterity, would be always looking for the line of promise and progress; not levelling and flattening it all back into the mud again. Socialism is sentimentalism; and more dangerous than a pestilence, for in that at least the fittest would survive.'

The Master smiled a little sadly. 'You know you and I will never feel quite the same about differences of opinion. Didn't somebody say up here, about walking with a friend by the river, "Not differing much, except in opinion." Isn't that the motto of a university? To have hundreds of opinions and not be opinionated. If people fall here, it's by what they are, not what they think. Perhaps I'm a relic of the eighteenth century; but I incline to the old sentimental heresy, "For forms of faith let graceless zealots fight; he can't be wrong whose life is in the right."* What do you think about that, Father Brown?'

He glanced a little mischievously across at the priest and was mildly startled. For he had always found the priest very cheerful and amiable and easy to get on with; and his round face was mostly solid with good humour. But for some reason the priest's face at this moment was knotted with a frown much more sombre than any the company had ever seen on it; so that for an instant that commonplace countenance actually looked darker and more ominous than the haggard face of Byles. An instant later the cloud seemed to have passed; but Father Brown still spoke with a certain sobriety and firmness.

'I don't believe in that, anyhow,' he said shortly. 'How can his life be in the right, if his whole view of life is wrong? That's a modern muddle that arose because people didn't know how much views of life can differ. Baptists and Methodists knew they didn't differ very much in morality; but then they didn't differ very much in religion or philosophy. It's quite different when you pass from the Baptists* to the Anabaptists;* or from the Theosophists* to the Thugs.* Heresy always does affect morality, if it's heretical enough. I suppose a man may honestly believe that thieving isn't wrong. But what's the good of saying that he honestly believes in dishonesty?'

'Damned good,' said Byles with a ferocious contortion of feature, believed by many to be meant for a friendly smile. 'And that's why I object to having a Chair of Theoretical Thieving in this College.'

'Well, you're all very down on Communism, of course,' said the Master, with a sigh. 'But do you really think there's so much of it to be down on? Are any of your heresies really big enough to be dangerous?'

'I think they have grown so big,' said Father Brown gravely, 'that in some circles they are already taken for granted. They are actually unconscious. That is, without conscience.'

'And the end of it,' said Byles, 'will be the ruin of this country.'

'The end will be something worse,' said Father Brown.

A shadow shot or slid rapidly along the panelled wall opposite, as swiftly followed by the figure that had flung it; a tall but stooping figure with a vague outline like a bird of prey; accentuated by the fact that its sudden appearance and swift passage were like those of a bird startled and flying from a bush. It was only the figure of a long-limbed, high-shouldered man with long drooping moustaches, in fact, familiar enough to them all; but something in the twilight and candlelight and the flying and streaking shadow connected it strangely with the priest's unconscious words of omen; for all the world, as if those words had indeed been an augury, in the old Roman sense; and the sign of it the flight of a bird. Perhaps Mr Byles might have given a lecture on such Roman augury; and especially on that bird of ill-omen.

The tall man shot along the wall like his own shadow until he sank into the empty chair on the Master's right, and looked across at the Bursar and the rest with hollow and cavernous eyes. His hanging hair and moustache were quite fair, but his eyes were so deep-set that they might have been black. Everyone knew, or could guess, who the newcomer was; but an incident instantly followed that sufficiently illuminated the situation. The Professor of Roman History rose stiffly to his feet and stalked out of the room, indicating with little *finesse* his feelings about sitting at the same table with the Professor of Theoretical Thieving, otherwise the Communist, Mr Craken.

The Master of Mandeville covered the awkward situation with nervous grace. 'I was defending you, or some aspects of you, my dear Craken,' he said smiling, 'though I am sure you would find me quite indefensible. After all, I can't forget that the old Socialist friends of my youth had a very fine ideal of fraternity and comradeship. William Morris put it all in a sentence, "Fellowship is heaven; and lack of fellowship is hell."'

'Dons as Democrats; see headline,' said Mr Craken rather disagreeably. 'And is Hard-Case Hake going to dedicate the new Commercial Chair to the memory of William Morris?'

'Well,' said the Master, still maintaining a desperate geniality, 'I hope we may say, in a sense, that all our Chairs are Chairs of good-fellowship.'

'Yes; that's the academic version of the Morris maxim,' growled Craken. ' "A Fellowship is heaven; and lack of a Fellowship is hell." '

'Don't be so cross, Craken,' interposed the Bursar briskly. 'Take some port. Tenby, pass the port to Mr Craken.'

'Oh well, I'll have a glass,' said the Communist Professor a little less ungraciously. 'I really came down here to have a smoke in the garden. Then I looked out of the window and saw your two precious millionaires were actually blooming in the garden; fresh, innocent buds. After all, it might be worth while to give them a bit of my mind.'

The Master had risen under cover of his last conventional cordiality, and was only too glad to leave the Bursar to do his best with the Wild Man. Others had risen, and the groups at the table had begun to break up; and the Bursar and Mr Craken were left more or less alone at the end of the long table. Only Father Brown continued to sit staring into vacancy with a rather cloudy expression.

'Oh, as to that,' said the Bursar. 'I'm pretty tired of them myself, to tell the truth; I've been with them the best part of a day going into facts and figures and all the business of this new Professorship. But look here, Craken," and he leaned across the table and spoke with a sort of soft emphasis, 'you really needn't cut up so rough about this new Professorship. It doesn't really interfere with your subject. You're the only Professor of Political Economy at Mandeville and, though I don't pretend to agree with your notions, everybody knows you've got a European reputation. This is a special subject they call Applied Economics. Well, even to-day, as I told you, I've had a hell of a lot of Applied Economics. In other words, I've had to talk business with two business men. Would you particularly want to do that? Would you envy it? Would you stand it? Isn't that evidence enough that there is a separate subject and may well be a separate Chair?'

'Good God,' cried Craken with the intense invocation of the atheist. 'Do you think I don't want to apply Economics? Only, when we apply it, you call it red ruin and anarchy; and when you apply it, I take the liberty of calling it exploitation. If only you fellows would apply Economics, it's just possible that people might get something to eat. We are the practical people; and that's why you're afraid of us. That's why you have to get two greasy Capitalists to start another Lecture-ship; just because I've let the cat out of the bag.'

'Rather a wild cat, wasn't it,' said the Bursar smiling, 'that you let out of the bag?'

'And rather a gold-bag, wasn't it,' said Craken, 'that you are tying the cat up in again?'

'Well, I don't suppose we shall ever agree about all that,' said the other. 'But those fellows have come out of their chapel into the garden; and if you want to have your smoke there, you'd better come.' He watched with some amusement his companion fumbling in all his pockets till he produced a pipe, and then, gazing at it with an abstracted air, Craken rose to his feet, but even in doing so, seemed to be feeling all over himself again. Mr Baker the Bursar ended the controversy with a happy laugh of reconciliation. 'You are the practical people, and you will blow up the town with dynamite. Only you'll probably forget the dynamite, as I bet you've forgotten the tobacco. Never mind, take a fill of mine. Matches?' He threw a tobacco-pouch and its accessories across the table; to be caught by Mr Craken with that dexterity never forgotten by a cricketer, even when he adopts opinions generally regarded as not cricket. The two men rose together; but Baker could not forbear remarking, 'Are you really the only practical people? Isn't there anything to be said for the Applied Economics, that remembers to carry a tobacco-pouch as well as a pipe?'

Craken looked at him with smouldering eyes; and said at last, after slowly draining the last of his wine:

'Let's say there's another sort of practicality. I dare say I do forget details and so on. What I want you to understand is this'—he automatically returned the pouch; but his eyes were far away and jet-burning, almost terrible—'because the inside of our intellect has changed, because we really have a new idea of right, we shall do things you think really wrong. And they will be very practical.'

'Yes,' said Father Brown, suddenly coming out of his trance. 'That's exactly what I said.'

He looked across at Craken with a glassy and rather ghastly smile, saying: 'Mr Craken and I are in complete agreement.'

'Well,' said Baker, 'Craken is going out to smoke a pipe with the plutocrats; but I doubt whether it will be a pipe of peace.'

He turned rather abruptly and called to an aged attendant in the background. Mandeville was one of the last of the very old-fashioned Colleges; and even Craken was one of the first of the Communists; before the Bolshevism of to-day. 'That reminds me,' the Bursar was saying, 'as you won't hand round your peace pipe, we must send out the cigars to our distin-guished guests. If they're smokers they must be longing for a smoke; for they've been nosing about in the chapel since feeding-time.'

Craken exploded with a savage and jarring laugh. 'Oh, I'll take them their cigars,' he said. 'I'm only a proletarian.'

Baker and Brown and the attendant were all witnesses to the fact that the Communist strode furiously into the garden to confront the millionaires; but nothing more was seen or heard of them until, as is already recorded, Father Brown found them dead in their chairs.

It was agreed that the Master and the priest should remain to guard the scene of tragedy, while the Bursar, younger and more rapid in his movements, ran off to fetch doctors and policemen. Father Brown approached the table on which one of the cigars had burned itself away all but an inch or two; the other had dropped from the hand and been dashed out into dying sparks on the crazy-pavement. The Master of Mandeville sat down rather shakily on a sufficiently distant seat and buried his bald brow in his hands. Then he looked up at first rather wearily; and then he looked very startled indeed and broke the stillness of the garden with a word like a small explosion of horror.

There was a certain quality about Father Brown which might sometimes be called blood-curdling. He always thought about what he was doing and never about whether it was done; he would do the most ugly or horrible or undignified or dirty things as calmly as a surgeon. There was a certain blank, in his simple mind, of all those things commonly associated with being superstitious or sentimental. He sat down on the chair from which the corpse had fallen, picked up the cigar the corpse had partially smoked, carefully detached the ash, examined the butt-end and then stuck it in his mouth and lit it. It looked like some obscene and grotesque antic in derision of the dead; and it seemed to him to be the most ordinary common sense. A cloud floated upwards like the smoke of some savage sacrifice and idolatry; but to Father Brown it appeared a perfectly self-evident fact that the only way to find out what a cigar is like is to smoke it. Nor did it lessen the horror for his old friend, the Master of Mandeville, to have a dim but shrewd guess that Father Brown was, upon the possibilities of the case, risking his own life.

'No; I think that's all right,' said the priest, putting the stump down again. 'Jolly good cigars. Your cigars. Not American or German. I don't think there's anything odd about the cigar itself; but they'd better take care of the ashes. These men were poisoned somehow with the sort of stuff that stiffens the body quickly... By the way, there goes somebody who knows more about it than we do.'

The Master sat up with a curiously uncomfortable jolt; for indeed the large shadow which had fallen across the pathway preceded a figure which, however heavy, was almost as soft-footed as a shadow. Professor Wadham,* eminent occupant of the Chair of Chemistry, always moved very quietly in spite of his size, and there was nothing odd about his strolling in the garden; yet there seemed something unnaturally neat in his appearing at the exact moment when chemistry was mentioned.

Professor Wadham prided himself on his quietude; some would say his insensibility. He did not turn a hair on his flattened flaxen head, but stood looking down at the dead men with a shade of something like indifference on his large froglike face. Only when he looked at the cigar-ash, which the priest had preserved, he touched it with one finger; then he seemed to stand even stiller than before; but in the shadow of his face his eyes for an instant seemed to shoot out telescopically like one of his own microscopes. He had certainly realized or recognized something; but he said nothing.

'I don't know where anyone is to begin in this business,' said the Master.

'I should begin,' said Father Brown, 'by asking where these unfortunate men had been most of the time to-day.'

'They were messing about in my laboratory for a good time,' said Wadham, speaking for the first time. 'Baker often comes up to have a chat, and this time he brought his two patrons to inspect my department. But I think they went everywhere; real tourists. I know they went to the chapel and even into the tunnel under the crypt, where you have to light candles; instead of digesting their food like sane men. Baker seems to have taken them everywhere.'

'Were they interested in anything particular in your department?' asked the priest. 'What were you doing there just then?'

The Professor of Chemistry murmured a chemical formula beginning with 'sulphate,' and ending with something that sounded like 'silenium'; unintelligible to both his hearers. He then wandered wearily away and sat on a remote bench in the sun, closing his eyes, but turning up his large face with heavy forbearance.

At this point, by a sharp contrast, the lawns were crossed by a brisk figure travelling as rapidly and as straight as a bullet; and Father Brown recognized the neat black clothes and shrewd doglike face of a police-surgeon whom he had met in the poorer parts of the town. He was the first to arrive of the official contingent.

'Look here,' said the Master to the priest, before the doctor was within earshot, 'I must know something. Did you mean what you said about Communism being a real danger and leading to crime?'

'Yes,' said Father Brown smiling rather grimly, 'I have really noticed the spread of some Communist ways and influences; and, in one sense, this is a Communist crime.'

'Thank you,' said the Master. 'Then I must go off and see to something at once. Tell the authorities I'll be back in ten minutes.'

The Master had vanished into one of the Tudor archways at just about the moment when the police-doctor had reached the table and cheerfully recognized Father Brown. On the latter's suggestion that they should sit down at the tragic table, Dr Blake threw one sharp and doubtful glance at the big, bland and seemingly somnolent chemist, who occupied a more remote seat. He was duly informed of the Professor's identity, and what had so far been gathered of the Professor's evidence; and listened to it silently while conducting a preliminary examination of the dead bodies. Naturally, he seemed more concentrated on the actual corpses than on the hearsay evidence, until one detail suddenly distracted him entirely from the science of anatomy.

'What did the Professor say he was working at?' he inquired.

Father Brown patiently repeated the chemical formula he did not understand.

'*What?*' snapped Dr Blake, like a pistol-shot. 'Gosh! This is pretty frightful!'

'Because it's poison?' inquired Father Brown.

'Because it's piffle,' replied Dr Blake. 'It's simply nonsense. The Professor is quite a famous chemist. Why is a famous chemist deliberately talking nonsense?'

'Well, I think I know that one,' answered Father Brown mildly. 'He is talking nonsense, because he is telling lies. He is concealing something; and he wanted specially to conceal it from these two men and their representatives.'

The doctor lifted his eyes from the two men and looked across at the almost unnaturally immobile figure of the great chemist. He might almost have been asleep; a garden butterfly had settled upon him and seemed to turn his stillness into that of a stone idol. The large folds of his froglike face reminded the doctor of the hanging skins of a rhinoceros.

'Yes,' said Father Brown, in a very low voice. 'He is a wicked man.'

'God damn it all!' cried the doctor, suddenly moved to his very depths. 'Do you mean that a great scientific man like that deals in murder?'

'Fastidious critics would have complained of his dealing in murder,' said the priest dispassionately. 'I don't say I'm very fond of people dealing in murder in that way myself. But what's much more to the point—I'm sure that *these* poor fellows were among his fastidious critics.'

'You mean they found his secret and he silenced them?' said Blake frowning. 'But what in hell was his secret? How could a man murder on a large scale in a place like this?'

'I have told you his secret,' said the priest. 'It is a secret of the soul. He is a bad man. For heaven's sake don't fancy I say that because he and I are of opposite schools or traditions. I have a crowd of scientific friends; and most of them are heroically disinterested. Even of the most sceptical, I would only say they are rather irrationally disinterested. But now and then you do get a man who is a materialist, in the sense of a beast. I repeat he's a bad man. Much worse than——' And Father Brown seemed to hesitate for a word.

'You mean much worse than the Communist?' suggested the other.

'No; I mean much worse than the murderer,' said Father Brown.

He got to his feet in an abstracted manner; and hardly realized that his companion was staring at him.

'But didn't you mean,' asked Blake at last, 'that this Wadham is the murderer?'

'Oh, no,' said Father Brown more cheerfully. 'The murderer is a much more sympathetic and understandable person. He at least was desperate; and had the excuses of sudden rage and despair.'

'Why,' cried the doctor, 'do you mean it was the Communist after all?'

It was at this very moment, appropriately enough, that the police officials appeared with an announcement that seemed to conclude the case in a most decisive and satisfactory manner. They had been somewhat delayed in reaching the scene of the crime, by the simple fact that they had already captured the criminal. Indeed, they had captured him almost at the gates of their own official residence. They had already had reason to suspect the activities of Craken the Communist during various disorders in the town; when they heard of the outrage they felt it safe to arrest him; and found the arrest thoroughly justified. For, as Inspector Cook radiantly explained to dons and doctors on the lawn of Mandeville garden, no sooner was the notorious Communist searched, than it was found that he was actually carrying a box of poisoned matches.

The moment Father Brown heard the word 'matches,' he jumped from his seat as if a match had been lighted under him.

'Ah,' he cried, with a sort of universal radiance, 'and now it's all clear.'

'What do you mean by all clear?' demanded the Master of Mandeville, who had returned in all the pomp of his own officialism to match the pomp of the police officials now occupying the College like a victorious army. 'Do you mean you are convinced now that the case against Craken is clear?'

'I mean that Craken is cleared,' said Father Brown firmly, 'and the case against Craken is cleared away. Do you really believe Craken is the kind of man who would go about poisoning people with matches?'

'That's all very well,' replied the Master, with the troubled expression he had never lost since the first sensation occurred. 'But it was you yourself who said that fanatics with false principles may do wicked things. For that matter, it was you yourself who said that Communism is cropping up everywhere and Communistic habits spreading.'

Father Brown laughed in a rather shamefaced manner.

'As to the last point,' he said, 'I suppose I owe you all an apology. I seem to be always making a mess of things with my silly little jokes.'

'Jokes!' repeated the Master, staring rather indignantly.

'Well,' explained the priest, rubbing his head. 'When I talked about a Communist habit spreading, I only meant a habit I happen to have noticed about two or three times even to-day. It is a Communist habit by no means confined to Communists. It is the extraordinary habit of so many men, especially Englishmen, of putting other people's match-boxes in their pockets without remembering to return them. Of course, it seems an awfully silly little trifle to talk about. But it does happen to be the way the crime was committed.'

'It sounds to me quite crazy,' said the doctor.

'Well, if almost any man may forget to return matches, you can bet your boots that Craken would forget to return them. So the poisoner who had prepared the matches got rid of them on to Craken, by the simple process of lending them and not getting them back. A really admirable way of shedding responsibility; because Craken himself would be perfectly unable to imagine where he had got them from. But when he used them quite innocently to light the cigars he offered to our two visitors, he was caught in an obvious trap; one of those too obvious traps. He was the bold bad Revolutionist murdering two millionaires.'

'Well, who else would want to murder them?' growled the doctor.

'Ah, who indeed?' replied the priest; and his voice changed to much greater gravity. 'There we come to the other thing I told you; and that, let me tell you, was not a joke. I told you that heresies and false doctrines had become common and conversational; that everybody was used to them; that nobody really noticed them. Did you think I meant *Communism* when I said that? Why, it was just the other way. You were all as nervous as cats about Communism; and you watched Craken like a wolf. Of course, Communism is a heresy; but it isn't a heresy that you people take for granted. It is Capitalism you take for granted; or rather the vices of Capitalism disguised as a dead Darwinism. Do you recall what you were all saying in the Common Room, about life being only a scramble, and nature demanding the survival of the fittest, and how it doesn't matter whether the poor are paid justly or not? Why, *that* is the heresy that you have grown accustomed to, my friends; and it's every bit as much a heresy as Communism. That's the anti-Christian morality or immorality that you take quite naturally. And that's the immorality that has made a man a murderer to-day.'

'What man?' cried the Master, and his voice cracked with a sudden weakness.

'Let me approach it another way,' said the priest placidly. 'You all talk as if Craken ran away; but he didn't. When the two men toppled over, he ran down the street, summoned the doctor merely by shouting through the window, and shortly afterwards was trying to summon the police. That was how he was arrested. But doesn't it strike you, now one comes to think of it, that Mr Baker the Bursar is rather a long time looking for the police?'

'What is he doing then?' asked the Master sharply.

'I fancy he's destroying papers; or perhaps ransacking these men's rooms to see they haven't left us a letter. Or it may have something to do with our friend Wadham. Where does he come in? That is really very simple and a sort of joke too. Mr Wadham is experimenting in poisons for the next war; and has something of which a whiff of flame will stiffen a man dead. Of course, he had nothing to do with killing these men; but he did conceal his chemical secret for a very simple reason. One of them was a Puritan Yankee and the other a cosmopolitan Jew; and those two types are often fanatical Pacifists. They would have called it planning murder and probably refused to help the College. But Baker was a friend of Wadham and it was easy for him to dip matches in the new material.'

Another peculiarity of the little priest was that his mind was all of a piece, and he was unconscious of many incongruities; he would change the note of his talk from something quite public to something quite private, without any particular embarrassment. On this occasion, he made most of the company stare with mystification, by beginning to talk to one person when he had just been talking to ten; quite indifferent to the fact that only the one could have any notion of what he was talking about.

'I'm sorry if I misled you, doctor, by that maundering metaphysical digression on the man of sin,'* he said apologetically. 'Of course it had nothing to do with the murder; but the truth is I'd forgotten all about the murder for the moment. I'd forgotten everything, you see, but a sort of vision of that fellow, with his vast unhuman face, squatting among the flowers like some blind monster of the Stone Age. And I was thinking that some men are pretty monstrous, like men of stone; but it was all irrelevant. Being bad inside has very little to do with committing crimes outside. The worst criminals have committed no crimes. The practical point is why did the practical criminal commit this crime. Why did Baker the Bursar want to kill these men? That's all that concerns us now. The answer is the answer to the question I've asked twice. Where were these men most of the time, apart from nosing in chapels or laboratories? By the Bursar's own account, they were talking business with the Bursar.

'Now, with all respect to the dead, I do not exactly grovel before the intellect of these two financiers. Their views on economics and ethics were heathen and heartless. Their views on Peace were tosh. Their views on Port were even more deplorable. But one thing they did understand; and that was business. And it took them a remarkably short time to discover that the business man in charge of the funds of this College was a swindler. Or shall I say, a true follower of the doctrine of the unlimited struggle for life and the survival of the fittest.'

'You mean they were going to expose him and he killed them before they could speak,' said the doctor frowning. 'There are a lot of details I don't understand.'

'There are some details I'm not sure of myself,' said the priest frankly. 'I suspect all that business of candles underground had something to do with abstracting the millionaires' own matches, or perhaps making sure they had no matches. But I'm sure of the main gesture, the gay and careless gesture of Baker tossing his matches to the careless Craken. That gesture was the murderous blow.'

'There's one thing I don't understand,' said the Inspector. 'How did Baker know that Craken wouldn't light up himself then and there at the table and become an unwanted corpse?'

The face of Father Brown became almost heavy with reproach; and his voice had a sort of mournful yet generous warmth in it.

'Well, hang it all,' he said, 'he was only an atheist.'

'I'm afraid I don't know what you mean,' said the Inspector, politely.

'He only wanted to abolish God,' explained Father Brown in a temperate and reasonable tone. 'He only wanted to destroy the Ten Commandments and root up all the religion and civilization that had made him, and wash out all the common sense of ownership and honesty; and let his culture and his country be flattened out by savages from the ends of the earth. That's all he wanted. You have no right to accuse him of anything beyond that. Hang it all, everybody draws the line somewhere! And you come here and calmly suggest that a Mandeville Man of the old generation (for Craken was of the old generation, whatever his views) would have begun to smoke, or even strike a match, while he was still drinking the College Port, of the vintage of '08—no, no; men are not so utterly without laws and limits as all that! I was there; I saw him; he had not finished his wine, and you ask me why he did not *smoke*! No such anarchic question has ever shaken the arches of Mandeville College. . . . Funny place, Mandeville College. Funny place, Oxford. Funny place, England.'

'But you haven't anything particular to do with Oxford?' asked the doctor curiously.

'I have to do with England,' said Father Brown. 'I come from there. And the funniest thing of all is that even if you love it and belong to it, you still can't make head or tail of it.'

THE POINT OF A PIN

FATHER BROWN always declared that he solved this problem in his sleep. And this was true, though in rather an odd fashion; because it occurred at a time when his sleep was rather disturbed. It was disturbed very early in the morning by the hammering that began in the huge building, or half-building, that was in process of erection opposite to his rooms; a colossal pile of flats still mostly covered with scaffolding and with boards announcing Messrs. Swindon & Sand as the builders and owners. The hammering was renewed at regular intervals and was easily recognizable: because Messrs. Swindon & Sand specialized in some new American system of cement flooring which, in spite of its subsequent smoothness, solidity, impenetrability and permanent comfort (as described in the advertisements), had to be clamped down at certain points with heavy tools. Father Brown endeavoured, however, to extract exiguous comfort from it; saying that it always woke him up in time for the very earliest Mass, and was therefore something almost in the nature of a carillon.* After all, he said, it was almost as poetic that Christians should be awakened by hammers* as by bells. As a fact, however, the building operations were a little on his nerves, for another reason. For there was hanging like a cloud over the half-built skyscraper the possibility of a Labour crisis, which the newspapers doggedly insisted on describing as a Strike. As a matter of fact, if ever it happened, it would be a Lock-out. But he worried a good deal about whether it would happen. And it might be questioned whether hammering is more of a strain on the attention because it may go on for ever, or because it may stop at any minute.

'As a mere matter of taste and fancy,' said Father Brown, staring up at the edifice with his owlish spectacles, 'I rather wish it would stop. I wish all houses would stop while they still have the scaffolding up. It seems almost a pity that houses are ever finished. They look so fresh and hopeful with all that fairy filigree of white wood, all light and bright in the sun; and a man so often only finishes a house by turning it into a tomb.'

As he turned away from the object of his scrutiny, he nearly ran into a man who had just darted across the road towards him. It was a man whom he knew slightly, but sufficiently to regard him (in the circumstances) as something of a bird of ill-omen. Mr Mastyk was a squat man with a square head that looked hardly European, dressed with a heavy dandyism that seemed rather too consciously Europeanized. But Brown had seen him lately talking to young Sand of the building firm; and he did not like it. This man Mastyk was the head of an organization rather new in English industrial politics; produced by extremes at both ends; a definite army of non-Union and largely alien labour hired out in gangs to various firms; and he was obviously hovering about in the hope of hiring it out to this one. In short, he might negotiate some way of out-manœuvring the Trade Union and flooding the works with blacklegs. Father Brown had been drawn into some of the debates, being in some sense called in on both sides. And as the Capitalists all reported that, to their positive knowledge, he was a Bolshevist; and as the Bolshevists all testified that he was a reactionary rigidly attached to *bourgeois* ideologies, it may be inferred that he talked a certain amount of sense without any appreciable effect on anybody. The news brought by Mr Mastyk, however, was calculated to jerk everybody out of the ordinary rut of the dispute.

'They want you to go over there at once,' said Mr Mastyk, in awkwardly accented English. 'There is a threat to murder.'

Father Brown followed his guide in silence up several stair-ways and ladders to a platform of the unfinished building, on which were grouped the more or less familiar figures of the heads of the building business. They included even what had once been the head of it; though the head had been for some time rather a head in the clouds. It was at least a head in a coronet, that hid it from human sight like a cloud. Lord Stanes, in other words, had not only retired from the business but been caught up into the House of Lords and disappeared. His rare reappearances were languid and somewhat dreary; but this one, in conjunction with that of Mastyk, seemed none the less menacing. Lord Stanes was a lean, long-headed, hol-low-eyed man with very faint fair hair fading into baldness; and he was the most evasive person the priest had ever met. He was unrivalled in the true Oxford talent of saying, 'No doubt you're right,' so as to sound like, 'No doubt you think you're right,' or of merely remarking, 'You think so?' so as to imply the acid addition, 'You would.' But Father Brown fan-cied that the man was not merely bored but faintly embittered, though whether at being called down from Olympus to con-trol such trade squabbles, or merely at not being really any longer in control of them, it was difficult to guess.

On the whole, Father Brown rather preferred the more *bourgeois* group of partners, Sir Hubert Sand and his nephew

Henry; though he doubted privately whether they really had very many ideologies. True, Sir Hubert Sand had obtained considerable celebrity in the newspapers; both as a patron of sport and as a patriot in many crises during and after the Great War. He had won notable distinction in France, for a man of his years, and had afterwards been featured as a triumphant captain of industry overcoming difficulties among the munition-workers. He had been called a Strong Man; but that was not his fault. He was in fact a heavy, hearty Englishman; a great swimmer; a good squire; an admirable amateur colonel. Indeed, something that can only be called a military make-up pervaded his appearance. He was growing stout, but he kept his shoulders set back; his curly hair and moustache were still brown while the colours of his face were already somewhat withered and faded. His nephew was a burly youth of the pushing, or rather shouldering, sort with a relatively small head thrust out on a thick neck, as if he went at things with his head down; a gesture somehow rendered rather quaint and boyish by the pince-nez that were balanced on his pugnacious pug-nose.

Father Brown had looked at all these things before; and at that moment everybody was looking at something entirely new. In the centre of the wood-work there was nailed up a large loose flapping piece of paper on which something was scrawled in crude and almost crazy capital letters, as if the writer were either almost illiterate or were affecting or parodying illiteracy. The words actually ran: 'The Council of the Workers warns Hubert Sand that he will lower wages and lock out workmen at his peril. If the notices go out to-morrow, he will be dead by the justice of the people.'

Lord Stanes was just stepping back from his examination of the paper, and, looking across at his partner, he said with rather a curious intonation:

'Well, it's you they want to murder. Evidently I'm not considered worth murdering.'

One of those still electric shocks of fancy that sometimes thrilled Father Brown's mind in an almost meaningless way shot through him at that particular instant. He had a queer notion that the man who was speaking could not now be murdered, because he was already dead. It was, he cheerfully admitted, a perfectly senseless idea. But there was something that always gave him the creeps about the cold disenchanted detachment of the noble senior partner; about his cadaverous colour and inhospitable eyes. 'The fellow,' he thought in the same perverse mood, 'has green eyes and looks as if he had green blood.'

Anyhow, it was certain that Sir Hubert Sand had not got green blood. His blood, which was red enough in every sense, was creeping up into his withered or weather-beaten cheeks with all the warm fullness of life that belongs to the natural and innocent indignation of the good-natured.

'In all my life,' he said, in a strong voice and yet shakily, 'I have never had such a thing said or done about me. I may have differed——'

'We can none of us differ about this,' struck in his nephew impetuously. 'I've tried to get on with them, but this is a bit too thick.'

'You don't really think,' began Father Brown, 'that your workmen——'

'I say we may have differed,' said old Sand, still a little tremulously, 'God knows I never liked the idea of threatening English workmen with cheaper labour——'

'We none of us liked it,' said the young man, 'but if I know you, uncle, this has about settled it.'

Then after a pause he added, 'I suppose, as you say, we did disagree about details; but as to real policy——'

'My dear fellow,' said his uncle, comfortably. 'I hoped there would never be any real disagreement.' From which anybody who understands the English nation may rightly infer that there had been very considerable disagreement. Indeed the uncle and nephew differed almost as much as an Englishman and an American. The uncle had the English ideal of getting outside the business, and setting up a sort of an alibi as a country gentleman. The nephew had the American ideal of getting inside the business; of getting inside the very mech-anism like a mechanic. And, indeed, he had worked with most of the mechanics and was familiar with most of the processes and tricks of the trade. And he was American again, in the fact that he did this partly as an employer to keep his men up to the mark, but in some vague way also as an equal, or at least with a pride in showing himself also as a worker. For this reason he had often appeared almost as a representative of the workers, on technical points which were a hundred miles away from his uncle's popular eminence in politics or sport. The memory of those many occasions, when young Henry had practically come out of the workshop in his shirt-sleeves, to demand some concession about the conditions of the work, lent a peculiar force and even violence to his present reaction the other way.

'Well, they've damned-well locked themselves out this time,' he cried. 'After a threat like that there's simply nothing left but to defy them. There's nothing left but to sack them all now; instanter; on the spot. Otherwise we'll be the laughing-stock of the world.'

Old Sand frowned with equal indignation, but began slowly: 'I shall be very much criticized——'

'Criticized!' cried the young man shrilly. 'Criticized if you defy a threat of murder! Have you any notion how you'll be criticized if you don't defy it? Won't you enjoy the headlines? "Great Capitalist Terrorized"—"Employer Yields to Murder Threat."'

'Particularly,' said Lord Stanes, with something faintly unpleasant in his tone. 'Particularly when he has been in so many headlines already as "The Strong Man of Steel-Building."'

Sand had gone very red again and his voice came thickly from under his thick moustache. 'Of course you're right there. If these brutes think I'm afraid——'

At this point there was an interruption in the conversation of the group; and a slim young man came towards them swiftly. The first notable thing about him was that he was one of those whom men, and women too, think are just a little too nice-looking to look nice. He had beautiful dark curly hair and a silken moustache and he spoke like a gentleman, but with almost too refined and exactly modulated an accent. Father Brown knew him at once as Rupert Rae, the secretary of Sir Hubert, whom he had often seen pottering about in Sir

Hubert's house; but never with such impatience in his movements or such a wrinkle on his brow.

'I'm sorry, sir,' he said to his employer, 'but there's a man been hanging about over there. I've done my best to get rid of him. He's only got a letter, but he swears he must give it to you personally.'

'You mean he went first to my house?' said Sand, glancing swiftly at his secretary. 'I suppose you've been there all the morning.'

'Yes, sir,' said Mr Rupert Rae.

There was a short silence; and then Sir Hubert Sand curtly intimated that the man had better be brought along; and the man duly appeared.

Nobody, not even the least fastidious lady, would have said that the newcomer was too nice-looking. He had very large ears and a face like a frog, and he stared before him with an almost ghastly fixity, which Father Brown attributed to his having a glass eye. In fact, his fancy was tempted to equip the man with two glass eyes; with so glassy a stare did he contemplate the company. But the priest's experience, as distinct from his fancy, was able to suggest several natural causes for that unnatural waxwork glare; one of them being an abuse of the divine gift of fermented liquor. The man was short and shabby and carried a large bowler hat in one hand and a large sealed letter in the other.

Sir Hubert Sand looked at him; and then said quietly enough, but in a voice that somehow seemed curiously small, coming out of the fullness of his bodily presence: 'Oh—it's you.'

He held out his hand for the letter; and then looked around apologetically, with poised finger, before ripping it open and reading it. When he had read it, he stuffed it into his inside pocket and said hastily and a little harshly:

'Well, I suppose all this business is over, as you say. No more negotiations possible now; we couldn't pay the wages they want anyhow. But I shall want to see you again, Henry, about—about winding things up generally.'

'All right,' said Henry, a little sulkily perhaps, as if he would have preferred to wind them up by himself. 'I shall be up in number 188 after lunch; got to know how far they've got up there.'

The man with the glass eye, if it was a glass eye, stumped stiffly away; and the eye of Father Brown (which was by no means a glass eye) followed him thoughtfully as he threaded his way through the ladders and disappeared into the street.

It was on the following morning that Father Brown had the unusual experience of over-sleeping himself; or at least of starting from sleep with a subjective conviction that he must be late. This was partly due to his remembering, as a man may remember a dream, the fact of having been half-awakened at a more regular hour and fallen asleep again; a common enough occurrence with most of us, but a very uncommon occurrence with Father Brown. And he was afterwards oddly convinced, with that mystic side of him which was normally turned away from the world, that in that detached dark islet of dreamland, between the two wakings, there lay like buried treasure the truth of this tale.

As it was, he jumped up with great promptitude, plunged into his clothes, seized his big knobby umbrella and bustled out into the street, where the bleak white morning was breaking like splintered ice about the huge black building facing him. He was surprised to find that the streets shone almost empty in the cold crystalline light; the very look of it told him it could hardly be so late as he had feared. Then suddenly the stillness was cloven by the arrowlike swiftness of a long grey car which halted before the big deserted flats. Lord Stanes unfolded himself from within and approached the door, carrying (rather languidly) two large suitcases. At the same moment the door opened, and somebody seemed to step back instead of stepping out into the street. Stanes called twice to the man within, before that person seemed to complete his original gesture by coming out on to the doorstep; then the two held a brief colloquy, ending in the nobleman carrying his suitcases upstairs, and the other coming out into full daylight and revealing the heavy shoulders and peering head of young Henry Sand.

Father Brown made no more of this rather odd meeting, until two days later the young man drove up in his own car, and implored the priest to enter it. 'Something awful has happened,' he said, 'and I'd rather talk to you than Stanes. You know Stanes arrived the other day with some mad idea of camping in one of the flats that's just finished. That's why I had to go there early and open the door to him. But all that will keep. I want you to come up to my uncle's place at once.'

'Is he ill?' inquired the priest quickly.

'I think he's dead,' answered the nephew.

'What do you mean by saying you think he's dead?' asked Father Brown a little briskly. 'Have you got a doctor?'

'No,' answered the other. 'I haven't got a doctor or a patient either. . . . It's no good calling in doctors to examine the body; because the body has run away. But I'm afraid I know where it has run to . . . the truth is—we kept it dark for two days; but he's disappeared.'

'Wouldn't it be better,' said Father Brown mildly, 'if you told me what has really happened from the beginning?'

'I know,' answered Henry Sand; 'it's an infernal shame to talk flippantly like this about the poor old boy; but people get like that when they're rattled. I'm not much good at hiding things; the long and the short of it is—well, I won't tell you the long of it now. It's what some people would call rather a long shot; shooting suspicions at random and so on. But the short of it is that my unfortunate uncle has committed suicide.'

They were by this time skimming along in the car through the last fringes of the town and the first fringes of the forest and park beyond it; the lodge gates of Sir Hubert Sand's small estate were about half a mile farther on amid the thickening throng of the beeches. The estate consisted chiefly of a small park and a large ornamental garden, which descended in terraces of a certain classical pomp to the very edge of the chief river of the district. As soon as they arrived at the house, Henry took the priest somewhat hastily through the old Georgian rooms and out upon the other side; where they silently descended the slope, a rather steep slope embanked with flowers, from which they could see the pale river spread out before them almost as flat as in a bird's-eye view. They were just turning the corner of the path under an enormous classical urn crowned with a somewhat incongruous garland of geraniums, when Father Brown saw a movement in the bushes and thin trees just below him, that seemed as swift as a movement of startled birds.

In the tangle of thin trees by the river two figures seemed to divide or scatter; one of them glided swiftly into the shadows and the other came forward to face them; bringing them to a halt and an abrupt and rather unaccountable silence. Then Henry Sand said in his heavy way: 'I think you know Father Brown . . . Lady Sand.'

Father Brown did know her; but at that moment he might almost have said that he did not know her. The pallor and constriction of her face was like a mask of tragedy; she was much younger than her husband, but at that moment she looked somehow older than everything in that old house and garden. And the priest remembered, with a subconscious thrill, that she was indeed older in type and lineage and was the true possessor of the place. For her own family had owned it as impoverished aristocrats, before she had restored its fortunes by marrying a successful business man. As she stood there, she might have been a family picture, or even a family ghost. Her pale face was of that pointed yet oval type seen in some old pictures of Mary Queen of Scots; and its expression seemed almost to go beyond the natural unnaturalness of a situation, in which her husband had vanished under suspicion of suicide. Father Brown, with the same subconscious movement of the mind, wondered who it was with whom she had been talking among the trees.

'I suppose you know all this dreadful news,' she said, with a comfortless composure. 'Poor Hubert must have broken down under all this revolutionary persecution, and been just maddened into taking his own life. I don't know whether you can do anything; or whether these horrible Bolsheviks can be made responsible for hounding him to death.'

'I am terribly distressed, Lady Sand,' said Father Brown. 'And still, I must own, a little bewildered. You speak of persecution; do you think that anybody could hound him to death merely by pinning up that paper on the wall?'

'I fancy,' answered the lady, with a darkening brow, 'that there were other persecutions besides the paper.'

'It shows what mistakes one may make,' said the priest sadly. 'I never should have thought he would be so illogical as to die in order to avoid death.'

'I know,' she answered, gazing at him gravely. 'I should never have believed it, if it hadn't been written with his own hand.'

'What?' cried Father Brown, with a little jump like a rabbit that has been shot at.

'Yes,' said Lady Sand calmly. 'He left a confession of suicide; so I fear there is no doubt about it.' And she passed on up the slope alone, with all the inviolable isolation of the family ghost.

The spectacles of Father Brown were turned in mute inquiry to the eyeglasses of Mr Henry Sand. And the latter gentleman, after an instant's hesitation, spoke again in his rather blind and plunging fashion: 'Yes, you see, it seems pretty clear now what he did. He was always a great swimmer and used to come down in his dressing-gown every morning for a dip in the river. Well, he came down as usual, and left his dressing-gown on the bank; it's lying there still. But he also left a message saying he was going for his last swim and then death, or something like that.'

'Where did he leave the message?' asked Father Brown.

'He scrawled it on that tree there, overhanging the water, I suppose the last thing he took hold of; just below where the dressing-gown's lying. Come and see for yourself.'

Father Brown ran down the last short slope to the shore and peered under the hanging tree, whose plumes were almost dipping in the stream. Sure enough, he saw on the smooth bark the words scratched conspicuously and unmistakably: 'One more swim and then drowning. Good-bye. Hubert Sand.' Father Brown's gaze travelled slowly up the bank till it rested on a gorgeous rag of raiment, all red and yellow with gilded tassels. It was the dressing-gown and the priest picked it up and began to turn it over. Almost as he did so he was conscious that a figure had flashed across his field of vision; a tall dark figure that slipped from one clump of trees to another, as if following the trail of the vanishing lady. He had little doubt that it was the companion from whom she had lately parted. He had still less doubt that it was the dead man's secretary, Mr Rupert Rae.

'Of course, it might be a final after-thought to leave the message,' said Father Brown, without looking up, his eye riveted on the red and gold garment. 'We've all heard of love-messages written on trees; and I suppose there might be death-messages written on trees too.'

'Well, he wouldn't have anything in the pockets of his dressing-gown, I suppose,' said young Sand. 'And a man might naturally scratch his message on a tree if he had no pens, ink or paper.'

'Sounds like French exercises,' said the priest dismally. 'But I wasn't thinking of that.' Then, after a silence, he said in a rather altered voice:

'To tell the truth, I was thinking whether a man might not naturally scratch his message on a tree, even if he had stacks of pens, and quarts of ink, and reams of paper.'

Henry was looking at him with a rather startled air, his eyeglasses crooked on his pug nose. 'And what do you mean by that?' he asked sharply.

'Well,' said Father Brown slowly, 'I don't exactly mean that postmen will carry letters in the form of logs, or that you will ever drop a line to a friend by putting a postage stamp on a pinetree. It would have to be a particular sort of position—in fact, it would have to be a particular sort of person, who really preferred this sort of arboreal correspondence. But, given the position and the person, I repeat what I said. He would still write on a tree, as the song says, if all the world were paper and all the sea were ink; if that river flowed with everlasting ink or all these woods were a forest of quills and fountain-pens.'

It was evident that Sand felt something creepy about the priest's fanciful imagery; whether because he found it incomprehensible or because he was beginning to comprehend.

'You see,' said Father Brown, turning the dressing-gown over slowly as he spoke, 'a man isn't expected to write his very best handwriting when he chips it on a tree. And if the man were not the man, if I make myself clear——Hullo!'

He was looking down at the red dressing-gown, and it seemed for the moment as if some of the red had come off on his finger; but both the faces turned towards it were already a shade paler.

'Blood!' said Father Brown; and for the instant there was a deadly stillness save for the melodious noises of the river.

Henry Sand cleared his throat and nose with noises that were by no means melodious. Then he said rather hoarsely: 'Whose blood?'

'Oh, mine,' said Father Brown; but he did not smile.

A moment after he said: 'There was a pin in this thing and I pricked myself. But I don't think you quite appreciate the point . . . the point of the pin, I do'; and he sucked his finger like a child.

'You see,' he said after another silence, 'the gown was folded up and pinned together; nobody could have unfolded it—at least without scratching himself. In plain words, Hubert Sand never *wore* this dressing-gown. Any more than Hubert Sand ever wrote on that tree. Or drowned himself in that river.'

The pince-nez tilted on Henry's inquiring nose fell off with a click; but he was otherwise motionless, as if rigid with surprise.

'Which brings us back,' went on Father Brown cheerfully, 'to somebody's taste for writing his private correspondence on trees, like Hiawatha* and his picture-writing. Sand had all the time there was, before drowning himself. Why didn't he leave a note for his wife like a sane man? Or, shall we say. . . . Why didn't the Other Man leave a note for the wife like a sane man? Because he would have had to forge the husband's handwriting; always a tricky thing now that experts are so nosey about it. But nobody can be expected to imitate even his own handwriting, let alone somebody else's, when he carves capital letters in the bark of a tree. This is not a suicide, Mr Sand. If it's anything at all, it's a murder.'

The bracken and bushes of the undergrowth snapped and crackled as the big young man rose out of them like a leviathan,* and stood lowering, with his thick neck thrust forward.

'I'm no good at hiding things,' he said, 'and I half-suspected something like this—expected it, you might say, for a long time. To tell the truth, I could hardly be civil to the fellow—to either of them, for that matter.'

'What exactly do you mean?' asked the priest, looking him gravely full in the face.

'I mean,' said Henry Sand, 'that you have shown me the murder and I think I could show you the murderers.'

Father Brown was silent and the other went on rather jerkily.

'You said people sometimes wrote love-messages on trees. Well, as a fact, there are some of them on that tree; there are two sort of monograms twisted together up there under the leaves—I suppose you know that Lady Sand was the heiress of this place long before she married; and she knew that damned dandy of a secretary even in those days. I guess they used to meet here and write their vows upon the trysting-tree. They seem to have used the trysting-tree for another purpose later on. Sentiment, no doubt, or economy.'

'They must be very horrible people,' said Father Brown.

'Haven't there been any horrible people in history or the police-news?' demanded Sand with some excitement. 'Haven't there been lovers who made love seem more horrible than hate? Don't you know about Bothwell* and all the bloody legends of such lovers?'

'I know the legend of Bothwell,' answered the priest. 'I also know it to be quite legendary. But of course it's true that husbands have been sometimes put away like that. By the way, where was he put away? I mean, where did they hide the body?'

'I suppose they drowned him, or threw him in the water when he was dead,' snorted the young man impatiently.

Father Brown blinked thoughtfully and then said: 'A river is a good place to hide an imaginary body. It's a rotten bad place to hide a real one. I mean, it's easy to *say* you've thrown it in, because it *might* be washed away to sea. But if you really did throw it in, it's about a hundred to one it wouldn't; the chances of it going ashore somewhere are enormous. I think they must have had a better scheme for hiding the body than that—or the body would have been found by now. And if there were any marks of violence——'

'Oh, bother hiding the body,' said Henry, with some irritation; 'haven't we witness enough in the writing on their own devilish tree?'

'The body is the chief witness in every murder,' answered the other. 'The hiding of the body, nine times out of ten, is the practical problem to be solved.'

There was a silence; and Father Brown continued to turn over the red dressing-gown and spread it out on the shining grass of the sunny shore; he did not look up. But, for some time past he had been conscious that the whole landscape had been changed for him by the presence of a third party; standing as still as a statue in the garden.

'By the way,' he said, lowering his voice, 'how do you explain that little guy with the glass eye, who brought your poor uncle a letter yesterday? It seemed to me he was entirely altered by reading it; that's why I wasn't surprised at the suicide, when I thought it was a suicide. That chap was a rather low-down private detective, or I'm much mistaken.'

'Why,' said Henry in a hesitating manner, 'why, he might have been—husbands do sometimes put on detectives in domestic tragedies like this, don't they? I suppose he'd got the proofs of their intrigue; and so they——'

'I shouldn't talk too loud,' said Father Brown, 'because your detective is detecting us at this moment, from about a yard beyond those bushes.'

They looked up, and sure enough the goblin with the glass eye was fixing them with that disagreeable optic, looking all the more grotesque for standing among the white and waxen blooms of the classical garden.

Henry Sand scrambled to his feet again with a rapidity that seemed breathless for one of his bulk, and asked the man very angrily and abruptly what he was doing, at the same time telling him to clear out at once.

'Lord Stanes,' said the goblin of the garden, 'would be much obliged if Father Brown would come up to the house and speak to him.'

Henry Sand turned away furiously; but the priest put down his fury to the dislike that was known to exist between him and the nobleman in question. As they mounted the slope, Father Brown paused a moment as if tracing patterns on the smooth tree-trunk, glanced upwards once at the darker and more hidden hieroglyph said to be a record of romance; and then stared at the wider and more sprawling letters of the confession, or supposed confession of suicide.

'Do those letters remind you of anything?' he asked. And when his sulky companion shook his head, he added:

'They remind me of the writing on that placard that threatened him with the vengeance of the strikers.'

'This is the hardest riddle and the queerest tale I have ever tackled,' said Father Brown, a month later, as he sat opposite Lord Stanes in the recently furnished apartment of No. 188, the end flat which was the last to be finished before the interregnum of the industrial dispute and the transfer of work from the Trade Union. It was comfortably furnished; and Lord Stanes was presiding over grog and cigars, when the priest made his confession with a grimace. Lord Stanes had become rather surprisingly friendly, in a cool and casual way.

'I know that is saying a good deal, with your record,' said Stanes, 'but certainly the detectives, including our seductive friend with the glass eye, don't seem at all able to see the solution.'

Father Brown laid down his cigar and said carefully:

'It isn't that they can't see the solution. It is that they can't see the problem.'

'Indeed,' said the other, 'perhaps I can't see the problem either.'

'The problem is unlike all other problems, for this reason,' said Father Brown. 'It seems as if the criminal deliberately did two different things, either of which might have been successful; but which, when done together, could only defeat each other. I am assuming, what I firmly believe, that the same murderer pinned up the proclamation threatening a sort of Bolshevik murder, and also wrote on the tree confessing to an ordinary suicide. Now you may say it is after all possible that the proclamation was a proletarian proclamation; that some extremist workmen wanted to kill their employer, and killed him. Even if that were true, it would still stick at the mystery of why they left, or why anybody left, a contrary trail of private self-destruction. But it certainly isn't true. None of these workmen, however bitter, would have done a thing like that. I know them pretty well; I know their leaders quite well. To suppose that people like Tom Bruce or Hogan would assassinate somebody they could go for in the newspapers, and damage in all sorts of different ways, is the sort of psychology that sensible people call lunacy. No; there was somebody, who was not an indignant workman, who first played the part of an indignant workman, and then played the part of a suicidal employer. But, in the name of wonder, why? If he thought he could pass it off smoothly as a suicide, why did he first spoil it all by publishing a threat of murder? You might say it was an after-thought to fix up the suicide story, as less provocative than the murder story. But it wasn't less provocative *after* the murder story. He must have known he had already turned our thoughts towards murder, when it should have been his whole object to keep our thoughts away from it. If it was an after-thought, it was the after-thought of a very thoughtless person. And I have a notion that this assassin is a very thoughtful person. Can you make anything of it?'

'No; but I see what you mean,' said Stanes, 'by saying that I didn't even see the problem. It isn't merely who killed Sand; it's why anybody should accuse somebody else of killing Sand and then accuse Sand of killing himself.'

Father Brown's face was knotted and the cigar was clenched in his teeth; the end of it glowed and darkened rhythmically like the signal of some burning pulse of the brain. Then he spoke as if to himself:

'We've got to follow very closely and very clearly. It's like separating threads of thought from each other; something like this. Because the murder charge really rather spoilt the suicide charge, he wouldn't normally have made the murder charge. But he did make it; so he had some other reason for making it. It was so strong a reason that perhaps it reconciled him even to weakening his other line of defence: that it was a suicide. In other words, the murder charge wasn't really a murder charge. I mean he wasn't using it as a murder charge; he wasn't doing it so as to shift to somebody else the guilt of murder; he was doing it for some other extraordinary reason of his own. His plan had to contain a proclamation that Sand would be murdered; whether it threw suspicion on other people or not. Somehow or other the mere proclamation itself was necessary. But why?'

He smoked and smouldered away with the same volcanic concentration for five minutes before he spoke again.

'What could a murderous proclamation do, besides suggesting that the strikers were the murderers? What *did* it do? One thing is obvious; it inevitably did the opposite of what it said. It told Sand not to lock out his men; and it was perhaps the only thing in the world that would really have made him do it. You've got to think of the sort of man and the sort of reputation. When a man has been called a Strong Man in our silly sensational newspapers, when he is fondly regarded as a Sportsman by all the most distinguished asses in England, he simply can't back down because he is threatened with a pistol. It would be like walking about at Ascot* with a white feather* stuck in his absurd white hat. It would break that inner idol or ideal of oneself, which every man not a downright dastard does really prefer to life. And Sand wasn't a dastard; he was courageous; he was also impulsive. It acted instantly like a charm; his nephew, who had been more or less mixed up with the workmen, cried out instantly that the threat must be absolutely and instantly defied.'

'Yes,' said Lord Stanes, 'I noticed that.' They looked at each other for an instant, and then Stanes added carelessly: 'So you think the thing the criminal really wanted was——'

'The Lock-out!' cried the priest energetically. 'The Strike or whatever you call it; the cessation of work, anyhow. He wanted the work to stop at once; perhaps the black-legs to come in at once; certainly the Trade Unionists to go out at once. That is what he really wanted; God knows why. And he brought that off, I think, really without bothering much about its other implication of the existence of Bolshevist assassins. But then . . . then I think something went wrong. I'm only guessing and groping very slowly here; but the only explanation I can think of is that something began to draw attention to the real seat of the trouble; to the reason, whatever it was, of his wanting to bring the building to a halt. And then belatedly, desperately, and rather inconsistently, he tried to lay the other trail that led to the river, simply and solely because it led away from the flats.'

He looked up through his moonlike spectacles, absorbing all the quality of the background and furniture; the restrained luxury of a quiet man of the world; and contrasting it with the two suitcases with which its occupant had arrived so recently in a newly-finished and quite unfurnished flat. Then he said rather abruptly:

'In short, the murderer was frightened of something or somebody in the flats. By the way, why did *you* come to live in the flats? . . . Also by the way, young Henry told me you made an early appointment with him when you moved in. Is that true?'

'Not in the least,' said Stanes, 'I got the key from his uncle the night before. I've no notion why Henry came here that morning.'

'Ah,' said Father Brown, 'then I think I have some notion of why he came. . . . I *thought* you startled him by coming in just when he was coming out.'

'And yet,' said Stanes, looking across with a glitter in his grey-green eyes, 'you do rather think that I also am a mystery.'

'I think you are two mysteries,' said Father Brown. 'The first is why you originally retired from Sand's business. The second is why you have since come back to live in Sand's buildings.'

Stanes smoked reflectively, knocked out his ash, and rang a bell on the table before him. 'If you'll excuse me,' he said, 'I will summon two more to the council. Jackson, the little detective you know of, will answer the bell; and I've asked Henry Sand to come in a little later.'

Father Brown rose from his seat, walked across the room and looked down frowning into the fire-place.

'Meanwhile,' continued Stanes, 'I don't mind answering both your questions. I left the Sand business because I was sure there was some hanky-panky in it and somebody was pinching all the money. I came back to it, and took this flat, because I wanted to watch for the real truth about old Sand's death—on the spot.'

Father Brown faced round as the detective entered the room; he stood staring at the hearthrug and repeated: 'On the spot.'

'Mr Jackson will tell you,' said Stanes, 'that Sir Hubert commissioned him to find out who was the thief robbing the firm; and he brought a note of his discoveries the day before old Hubert disappeared.'

'Yes,' said Father Brown, 'and I know now where he disappeared to. I know where the body is.'

'Do you mean——?' began his host hastily.

'It is here,' said Father Brown, and stamped on the hearthrug. 'Here, under the elegant Persian rug in this cosy and comfortable room.'

'Where in the world did you find that?'

'I've just remembered,' said Father Brown, 'that I found it in my sleep.'

He closed his eyes as if trying to picture a dream, and went on dreamily:

'This is a murder story turning on the problem of How to Hide the Body; and I found it in my sleep. I was always woken up every morning by hammering from this building. On that morning I half-woke up, went to sleep again and woke once more, expecting to find it late; but it wasn't. Why? Because there *had* been hammering that morning, though all the usual work had stopped; short, hurried hammering in the small hours before dawn. Automatically a man sleeping stirs at such a familiar sound. But he goes to sleep again, because the usual sound is not at the usual hour. Now why did a certain secret criminal want all the work to cease suddenly; and only new workers come in? Because, if the old workers had come in next day, they would have found a new piece of work done in the night. The old workers would have known where they left off; and they would have found the whole flooring of this room already nailed down. Nailed down by a man who knew how to do it; having mixed a good deal with the workmen and learned their ways.'

As he spoke, the door was pushed open and a head poked in with a thrusting motion; a small head at the end of a thick neck and a face that blinked at them through glasses.

'Henry Sand said,' observed Father Brown, staring at the ceiling, 'that he was no good at hiding things. But I think he did himself an injustice.'

Henry Sand turned and moved swiftly away down the corridor.

'He not only hid his thefts from the firm quite successfully for years,' went on the priest with an air of abstraction, 'but when his uncle discovered them, he hid his uncle's corpse in an entirely new and original manner.'

At the same instant Stanes again rang a bell, with a long strident steady ringing; and the little man with the glass eye was propelled or shot along the corridor after the fugitive, with something of the rotatory motion of a mechanical figure in a zoetrope.* At the same moment, Father Brown looked out of the window, leaning over a small balcony, and saw five or six men start from behind bushes and railings in the street below and spread out equally mechanically like a fan or net; opening out after the fugitive who had shot like a bullet out of the front door. Father Brown saw only the pattern of the story; which had never strayed from that room; where Henry had strangled Hubert and hid his body under impenetrable flooring, stopping the whole work on the building to do it. A pin-prick had started his own suspicions; but only to tell him he had been led down the long loop of a lie. The point of the pin was that it was pointless.

He fancied he understood Stanes at last, and he liked to collect queer people who were difficult to understand. He realized that this tired gentleman, whom he had once accused of having green blood, had indeed a sort of cold green flame of conscientiousness or conventional honour, that had made him first shift out of a shady business, and then feel ashamed of having shifted it on to others; and come back as a bored laborious detective; pitching his camp on the very spot where the corpse had been buried; so that the murderer, finding him sniffing so near the corpse, had wildly staged the alternative drama of the dressing-gown and the drowned man. All that was plain enough, but, before he withdrew his head from the night air and the stars, Father Brown threw one glance upwards at the vast black bulk of the cyclopean building heaved far up into the night, and remembered Egypt and Babylon, and all that is at once eternal and ephemeral in the work of man.

'I was right in what I said first of all,' he said. 'It reminds one of Coppée's* poem about the Pharaoh and the Pyramid. This house is supposed to be a hundred houses; and yet the whole mountain of building is only one man's tomb.'

THE INSOLUBLE PROBLEM

THIS queer incident, in some ways perhaps the queerest of the many that came his way, happened to Father Brown at the time when his French friend Flambeau had retired from the profession of crime and had entered with great energy and success on the profession of crime investigator. It happened that both as a thief and a thief-taker, Flambeau had rather specialized in the matter of jewel thefts, on which he was admitted to be an expert, both in the matter of identifying jewels and the equally practical matter of identifying jewel-thieves. And it was in connection with his special knowledge of this subject, and a special commission which it had won for him, that he rang up his friend the priest on the particular morning on which this story begins.

Father Brown was delighted to hear the voice of his old friend, even on the telephone; but in a general way, and especially at that particular moment, Father Brown was not very fond of the telephone. He was one who preferred to watch people's faces and feel social atmospheres, and he knew well that without these things, verbal messages are apt to be very misleading, especially from total strangers. And it seemed as if, on that particular morning, a swarm of total strangers had been buzzing in his ear with more or less unenlightening verbal messages; the telephone seemed to be possessed of a demon of triviality. Perhaps the most distinctive voice was one which asked him whether he did not issue regular permits for murder and theft upon the payment of a regular tariff hung up in his church; and as the stranger, on being informed that this was not the case, concluded the colloquy with a hollow laugh, it may be presumed that he remained unconvinced. Then an agitated, rather inconsequent female voice rang up requesting him to come round at once to a certain hotel he had heard of some forty-five miles on the road to a neighbouring cathedral town; the request being immediately followed by a contradiction in the same voice, more agitated and yet more inconsequent, telling him that it did not matter and that he was not wanted after all. Then came an interlude of a Press agency asking him if he had anything to say on what a Film Actress had said about Moustaches for Men; and finally yet a third return of the agitated and inconsequent lady at the hotel, saying that he was wanted, after all. He vaguely supposed that this marked some of the hesitations and panics not unknown among those who are vaguely veering in the direction of Instruction, but he confessed to a considerable relief when the voice of Flambeau wound up the series with a hearty threat of immediately turning up to breakfast.

Father Brown very much preferred to talk to a friend sitting comfortably over a pipe, but it soon appeared that his visitor was on the warpath and full of energy, having every intention of carrying off the little priest captive on some important expedition of his own. It was true that there was a special circumstance involved which might be supposed to claim the priest's attention. Flambeau had figured several times of late as successfully thwarting a theft of famous precious stones; he had torn the tiara of the Duchess of Dulwich out of the very hand of the bandit as he bolted through the garden. He laid so ingenious a trap for the criminal who planned to carry off the celebrated Sapphire Necklace, that the artist in question, actually carried off the copy which he had himself planned to leave as a substitute.

Such were doubtless the reasons that had led to his being specially summoned to guard the delivery of a rather different sort of treasure; perhaps even more valuable in its mere materials, but possessing also another sort of value. A world-

famous reliquary, supposed to contain a relic of St Dorothy*
the martyr, was to be delivered at the Catholic monastery in a
cathedral town; and one of the most famous of international
jewel-thieves was supposed to have an eye on it; or rather
presumably on the gold and rubies of its setting, rather than
its purely hagiological importance. Perhaps there was something in this association of ideas which made Flambeau feel
that the priest would be a particularly appropriate companion
in his adventure; but anyhow, he descended on him, breathing
fire and ambition and very voluble about his plans for preventing the theft.

Flambeau indeed bestrode the priest's hearth gigantically
and in the old swaggering musketeer attitude, twirling his
great moustaches.

'You can't,' he cried, referring to the sixty-mile road to
Casterbury. 'You can't allow a profane robbery like that to
happen under your very nose.'

The relic was not to reach the monastery till the evening;
and there was no need for its defenders to arrive earlier; for
indeed a motor-journey would take them the greater part of
the day. Moreover, Father Brown casually remarked that there
was an inn on the road, at which he would prefer to lunch, as
he had been already asked to look in there as soon as was
convenient.

As they drove along through a densely wooded but sparsely
inhabited landscape, in which inns and all other buildings
seemed to grow rarer and rarer, the daylight began to take on
the character of a stormy twilight even in the heat of noon;
and dark purple clouds gathered over the dark grey forests. As
is common under the lurid quietude of that kind of light, what
colour there was in the landscape gained a sort of secretive
glow which is not found in objects under the full sunlight; and
ragged red leaves or golden or orange fungi seemed to burn
with a dark fire of their own. Under such a half-light they
came to a break in the woods like a great rent in a grey wall,
and saw beyond, standing above the gap, the tall and rather
outlandish-looking inn that bore the name of the Green
Dragon.

The two old companions had often arrived together at inns and other human habitations, and found a somewhat singular state of things there; but the signs of singularity had seldom manifested themselves so early. For while their car was still some hundreds of yards from the dark green door, which matched the dark green shutters of the high and narrow building, the door was thrown open with violence and a woman with a wild mop of red hair rushed to meet them, as if she were ready to board the car in full career. Flambeau brought the car to a standstill, but almost before he had done so, she thrust her white and tragic face into the window, crying:

'Are you Father Brown?' and then almost in the same breath; 'who is this man?'

'This gentleman's name is Flambeau,' said Father Brown in a tranquil manner, 'and what can I do for you?'

'Come into the inn,' she said, with extraordinary abruptness even under the circumstances. 'There's been a murder done.'

They got out of the car in silence and followed her to the dark green door which opened inwards on a sort of dark green alley, formed of stakes and wooden pillars, wreathed with vine and ivy, showing square leaves of black and red and many sombre colours. This again led through an inner door into a sort of large parlour hung with rusty trophies of Cavalier arms, of which the furniture seemed to be antiquated and also in great confusion, like the inside of a lumber-room. They were quite startled for the moment; for it seemed as if one large piece of lumber rose and moved towards them; so dusty and shabby and ungainly was the man who thus abandoned what seemed like a state of permanent immobility.

Strangely enough, the man seemed to have a certain agility of politeness, when once he did move; even if it suggested the wooden joints of a courtly step-ladder or an obsequious towel-horse. Both Flambeau and Father Brown felt that they had hardly ever clapped eyes on a man who was so difficult to place. He was not what is called a gentleman; yet he had something of the dusty refinement of a scholar; there was something faintly disreputable or *declassé* about him; and yet the smell of him was rather bookish than Bohemian. He was thin and pale, with a pointed nose and a dark pointed beard; his brow was bald, but his hair behind long and lank and stringy; and the expression of his eyes was almost entirely masked by a pair of blue spectacles. Father Brown felt that he had met something of the sort somewhere, and a long time ago; but he could no longer put a name to it. The lumber he sat among was largely literary lumber; especially bundles of seventeenth-century pamphlets.

'Do I understand the lady to say,' asked Flambeau gravely, 'that there is a murder here?'

The lady nodded her red ragged head rather impatiently; except for those flaming elf-locks she had lost some of her look of wildness; her dark dress was of a certain dignity and neatness; her features were strong and handsome; and there was something about her suggesting that double strength of body and mind which makes women powerful, particularly in contrast with men like the man in blue spectacles. Nevertheless, it was he who gave the only articulate answer, intervening with a certain antic* gallantry.

'It is true that my unfortunate sister-in-law,' he explained, 'has almost this moment suffered a most appalling shock which we should all have desired to spare her. I only wish that I myself had made the discovery and suffered only the further distress of bringing the terrible news. Unfortunately it was Mrs Flood herself who found her aged grandfather, long sick and bedridden in this hotel, actually dead in the garden; in circumstances which point only too plainly to violence and assault. Curious circumstances, I may say, very curious circumstances indeed.' And he coughed slightly, as if apologizing for them.

Flambeau bowed to the lady and expressed his sincere sympathies; then he said to the man: 'I think you said, sir, that you are Mrs Flood's brother-in-law.'

'I am Dr Oscar Flood,' replied the other. 'My brother, this lady's husband, is at present away on the Continent on business, and she is running the hotel. Her grandfather was partially paralysed and very far advanced in years. He was never known to leave his bedroom; so that really these extraordinary circumstances . . .'

'Have you sent for a doctor or the police?' asked Flambeau.

'Yes,' replied Dr Flood, 'we rang up after making the dreadful discovery; but they can hardly be here for some hours. This roadhouse stands so very remote. It is only used by people going to Casterbury or even beyond. So we thought we might ask for your valuable assistance until——'

'If we are to be of any assistance,' said Father Brown, interrupting in too abstracted a manner to seem uncivil, 'I should say we had better go and look at the circumstances at once.'

He stepped almost mechanically towards the door; and almost ran into a man who was shouldering his way in; a big, heavy young man with dark hair unbrushed and untidy, who would nevertheless have been rather handsome save for a slight disfigurement of one eye, which gave him rather a sinister appearance.

'What the devil are you doing?' he blurted out, 'telling every Tom, Dick and Harry—at least you ought to wait for the police.'

'I will be answerable to the police,' said Flambeau with a certain magnificence, and a sudden air of having taken command of everything. He advanced to the doorway, and as he was much bigger than the big young man, and his moustaches were as formidable as the horns of a Spanish bull, the big young man backed before him and had an inconsequent air of being thrown out and left behind, as the group swept out into the garden and up the flagged path towards the mulberry plantation. Only Flambeau heard the little priest say to the doctor: 'He doesn't seem to love us really, does he? By the way, who is he?'

'His name is Dunn,' said the doctor, with a certain restraint of manner. 'My sister-in-law gave him the job of managing the garden, because he lost an eye in the War.'

As they went through the mulberry bushes, the landscape of the garden presented that rich yet ominous effect which is found when the land is actually brighter than the sky. In the broken sunlight from behind, the tree-tops in front of them stood up like pale green flames against a sky steadily blackening with storm, through every shade of purple and violet. The same light struck strips of the lawn and garden beds; and whatever it illuminated seemed more mysteriously sombre and secret for the light. The garden bed was dotted with tulips that looked like drops of dark blood, and some of which one might have sworn were truly black; and the line ended appropriately with a tulip tree; which Father Brown was disposed, if partly by some confused memory, to identify with what is commonly called the Judas tree. What assisted the association was the fact that there was hanging from one of the branches, like a dried fruit, the dry, thin body of an old man, with a long beard that wagged grotesquely in the wind.

There lay on it something more than the horror of darkness, the horror of sunlight; for the fitful sun painted tree and man in gay colours like a stage property; the tree was in flower and the corpse was hung with a faded peacock-green dressing-gown, and wore on its wagging head a scarlet smoking-cap. Also it had red bedroom-slippers, one of which had fallen off and lay on the grass like a blot of blood.

But neither Flambeau or Father Brown was looking at these things as yet. They were both staring at a strange object that seemed to stick out of the middle of the dead man's shrunken figure; and which they gradually perceived to be the black but rather rusty iron hilt of a seventeenth-century sword, which had completely transfixed the body. They both remained almost motionless as they gazed at it; until the restless Dr Flood seemed to grow quite impatient with their stolidity.

'What puzzles *me* most,' he said, nervously snapping his fingers, 'is the actual state of the body. And yet it has given me an idea already.'

Flambeau had stepped up to the tree and was studying the sword-hilt through an eye-glass. But for some odd reason, it was at that very instant that the priest in sheer perversity spun round like a teetotum, turned his back on the corpse, and looked peeringly in the very opposite direction. He was just in time to see the red head of Mrs Flood at the remote end of the garden, turned towards a dark young man, too dim with distance to be identified, who was at that moment mounting a motor-bicycle; who vanished, leaving behind him only the dying din of that vehicle. Then the woman turned and began to walk towards them across the garden, just as Father Brown turned also and began a careful inspection of the sword-hilt and the hanging corpse.

'I understand you only found him about half an hour ago.' said Flambeau, 'Was there anybody about here just before that? I mean anybody in his bedroom, or that part of the house, or this part of the garden—say for an hour beforehand?'

'No,' said the doctor with precision. 'That is the very tragic accident. My sister-in-law was in the pantry, which is a sort of out-house on the other side; this man Dunn was in the kitchen-garden, which is also in that direction; and I myself was poking about among the books, in a room just behind the one you found me in. There are two female servants, but one had gone to the post and the other was in the attic.'

'And were any of these people,' asked Flambeau, very quietly, 'I say *any* of these people, at all on bad terms with the poor old gentleman?'

'He was the object of almost universal affection,' replied the doctor solemnly. 'If there were any misunderstandings, they were mild and of a sort common in modern times. The old man was attached to the old religious habits; and perhaps his daughter and son-in-law had rather wider views. All that can have had nothing to do with a ghastly and fantastic assassination like this.'

'It depends on how wide the modern views were,' said Father Brown, 'or how narrow.'

At this moment they heard Mrs Flood hallooing across the garden as she came, and calling her brother-in-law to her with a certain impatience. He hurried towards her and was soon out of earshot; but as he went he waved his hand apologetically and then pointed with a long finger to the ground.

'You will find the footprints very intriguing,' he said; with the same strange air, as of a funereal showman.

The two amateur detectives looked across at each other. 'I find several other things intriguing,' said Flambeau.

'Oh, yes,' said the priest, staring rather foolishly at the grass.

'I was wondering,' said Flambeau, 'why they should hang a man by the neck till he was dead, and then take the trouble to stick him with a sword.'

'And I was wondering,' said Father Brown, 'why they should kill a man with a sword thrust through his heart, and then take the trouble to hang him by the neck.'

'Oh, you are simply being contrary,' protested his friend. 'I can see at a glance that they didn't stab him alive. The body would have bled more and the wound wouldn't have closed like that.'

'And I could see at a glance,' said Father Brown, peering up very awkwardly, with his short stature and short sight, 'that they didn't hang him alive. If you'll look at the knot in the noose, you will see it's tied so clumsily that a twist of rope holds it away from the neck, so that it couldn't throttle a man at all. He was dead before they put the rope on him; and he was dead before they put the sword in him. And how was he really killed?'

'I think,' remarked the other, 'that we'd better go back to the house and have a look at his bedroom—and other things.'

'So we will,' said Father Brown. 'But among other things perhaps we had better have a look at these footprints. Better begin at the other end, I think, by his window. Well, there are no footprints on the paved path, as there might be; but then again there mightn't be. Well, here is the lawn just under his bedroom window. And here are his footprints plain enough.'

He blinked ominously at the footprints; and then began carefully retracing his path towards the tree, every now and then ducking in an undignified manner to look at something on the ground. Eventually he returned to Flambeau and said in a chatty manner:

'Well, do you know the story that is written there very plainly? Though it's not exactly a plain story.'

'I wouldn't be content to call it plain,' said Flambeau. 'I should call it quite ugly.'

'Well,' said Father Brown. 'the story that is stamped quite plainly on the earth, with exact moulds of the old man's slippers, is this. The aged paralytic leapt from the window and ran down the beds parallel to the path, quite eager for all the fun of being strangled and stabbed; so eager that he hopped on one leg out of sheer lightheartedness; and even occasionally turned cart-wheels——'

'Stop!' cried Flambeau, angrily, 'What the hell is all this hellish pantomime?'

Father Brown merely raised his eyebrows and gestured mildly towards the hieroglyphs in the dust. 'About half the way there's only the mark of one slipper; and in some places the mark of a hand planted all by itself.'

'Couldn't he have limped and then fallen?' asked Flambeau.

Father Brown shook his head. 'At least he'd have tried to use his hands and feet, or knees and elbows, in getting up. There are no other marks there of any kind. Of course the flagged path is quite near, and there are no marks on that; though there might be on the soil between the cracks: it's a crazy pavement.'

'By God, it's a crazy pavement; and a crazy garden; and a crazy story!' And Flambeau looked gloomily across the gloomy and storm-stricken garden, across which the crooked patchwork paths did indeed give a queer aptness to the quaint old English adjective.

'And now,' said Father Brown, 'let us go up and look at his room.' They went in by a door not far from the bedroom window; and the priest paused a moment to look at an ordinary garden broomstick, for sweeping up leaves, that was leaning against the wall. 'Do you see that?'

'It's a broomstick,' said Flambeau, with solid irony.

'It's a blunder,' said Father Brown; 'the first blunder that I've seen in this curious plot.'

They mounted the stairs and entered the old man's bedroom; and a glance at it made fairly clear the main facts, both about the foundation and disunion of the family. Father Brown had felt from the first that he was in what was, or had been, a Catholic household; but was, at least partly, inhabited by lapsed or very loose Catholics. The pictures and images in the grandfather's room made it clear that what positive piety remained had been practically confined to him; and that his kindred had, for some reason or other, gone Pagan. But he agreed that this was a hopelessly inadequate explanation even of an ordinary murder; let alone such a very extraordinary murder as this. 'Hang it all,' he muttered, 'the murder is really the least extraordinary part of it.' And even as he used the chance phrase, a slow light began to dawn upon his face.

Flambeau had seated himself on a chair by the little table which stood beside the dead man's bed. He was frowning thoughtfully at three or four white pills or pellets that lay in a small tray beside a bottle of water.

'The murderer or murderess,' said Flambeau, 'had some incomprehensible reason or other for wanting us to think the dead man was strangled or stabbed or both. He was not strangled or stabbed or anything of the kind. Why did they want to suggest it? The most logical explanation is that he died in some particular way which would, in itself, suggest a connection with some particular person. Suppose, for instance, he was poisoned. And suppose somebody is involved who would naturally look more like a poisoner than anybody else.'

'After all,' said Father Brown softly, 'our friend in the blue spectacles is a doctor.'

'I'm going to examine these pills pretty carefully,' went on Flambeau. 'I don't want to lose them, though. They look as if they were soluble in water.'

'It may take you some time to do anything scientific with them,' said the priest, 'and the police doctor may be here before that. So I should certainly advise you not to lose them. That is, if you are going to wait for the police doctor.'

'I am going to stay here till I have solved this problem,' said Flambeau.

'Then you will stay here for ever,' said Father Brown, looking calmly out of the window. 'I don't think I shall stay in this room, anyhow.'

'Do you mean that I shan't solve the problem?' asked his friend. 'Why shouldn't I solve the problem?'

'Because it isn't soluble in water. No, nor in blood,' said the priest; and he went down the dark stairs into the darkening garden. There he saw again what he had already seen from the window.

The heat and weight and obscurity of the thunderous sky seemed to be pressing yet more closely on the landscape; the clouds had conquered the sun which, above, in a narrowing clearance, stood up paler than the moon. There was a thrill of thunder in the air, but now no more stirring of wind or breeze; and even the colours of the garden seemed only like richer shades of darkness. But one colour still glowed with a certain dusky vividness; and that was the red hair of the woman of that house, who was standing with a sort of rigidity, staring, with her hands thrust up into her hair. That scene of eclipse, with something deeper in his own doubts about its significance, brought to the surface the memory of haunting and mystical lines; and he found himself murmuring: 'A secret spot, as savage and enchanted as e'er beneath a waning moon was haunted by woman wailing for her demon lover.'* His muttering became more agitated. 'Holy Mary, Mother of God,* pray for us sinners . . . that's what it is; that's terribly like what it is; *woman wailing for her demon lover.*'

He was hesitant and almost shaky as he approached the woman; but he spoke with his common composure. He was gazing at her very steadily, as he told her earnestly that she must not be morbid because of the mere accidental accessories of the tragedy, with all their mad ugliness. 'The pictures in your grandfather's room were truer to him than that ugly picture that we saw,' he said gravely. 'Something tells me he was a good man; and it does not matter what his murderers did with his body.'

'Oh, I am sick of his holy pictures and statues!' she said, turning her head away. 'Why don't they defend themselves, if they are what you say they are? But rioters* can knock off the Blessed Virgin's head and nothing happens to them. Oh, what's the good? You can't blame us, you daren't blame us, if we've found out that Man is stronger than God.'

'Surely,' said Father Brown very gently, 'it is not generous to make even God's patience with us a point against Him.'

'God may be patient and Man impatient,' she answered, 'and suppose we like the impatience better. You call it sacrilege; but you can't stop it.'

Father Brown gave a curious little jump. 'Sacrilege!' he said; and suddenly turned back to the doorway with a new brisk air of decision. At the same moment Flambeau appeared in the doorway, pale with excitement, with a screw of paper in his hands. Father Brown had already opened his mouth to speak, but his impetuous friend spoke before him.

'I'm on the track at last!' cried Flambeau. 'These pills look the same, but they're really different. And do you know that, at the very moment I spotted them, that one-eyed brute of a gardener thrust his white face into the room; and he was carrying a horse-pistol. I knocked it out of his hand and threw him down the stairs, but I begin to understand everything. If I stay here another hour or two, I shall finish my job.'

'Then you will not finish it,' said the priest, with a ring in his voice very rare in him indeed. 'We shall not stay here another hour. We shall not stay here another minute. We must leave this place at once!'

'What!' cried the astounded Flambeau. 'Just when we are getting near the truth! Why, you can tell that we're getting near the truth because they are afraid of us.'

Father Brown looked at him with a stony and inscrutable face, and said:

'They are not afraid of us when we are here. They will only be afraid of us when we are not here.'

They had both become conscious that the rather fidgety figure of Dr Flood was hovering in the lurid haze; now it precipitated itself forward with the wildest gestures.

'Stop! Listen!' cried the agitated doctor. 'I have discovered the truth!'

'Then you can explain it to your own police,' said Father Brown, briefly. 'They ought to be coming soon. But we must be going.'

The doctor seemed thrown into a whirlpool of emotions, eventually rising to the surface again with a despairing cry. He spread out his arms like a cross, barring their way.

'Be it so!' he cried. 'I will not deceive you now, by saying I have discovered the truth. I will only confess the truth.'

'Then you can confess it to your own priest,' said Father Brown, and strode towards the garden gate, followed by his staring friend. Before he reached the gate, another figure had rushed athwart him like the wind; and Dunn the gardener was shouting at him some unintelligible derision at detectives who were running away from their job. Then the priest ducked just in time to dodge a blow from the horse-pistol, wielded like a club. But Dunn was just not in time to dodge a blow from the fist of Flambeau, which was like the club of Hercules. The two left Mr Dunn spread flat behind them on the path, and, passing out of the gate, went out and got into their car in silence. Flambeau only asked one brief question and Father Brown only answered: 'Casterbury.'

At last, after a long silence, the priest observed: 'I could almost believe the storm belonged only to that garden, and came out of a storm in the soul.'

'My friend,' said Flambeau, 'I have known you a long time, and when you show certain signs of certainty, I follow your lead. But I hope you are not going to tell me that you took me away from that fascinating job, because you did not like the atmosphere.'

'Well, it was certainly a terrible atmosphere,' replied Father Brown, calmly. 'Dreadful and passionate and oppressive. And the most dreadful thing about it was this—that there was no hate in it at all.'

'Somebody,' suggested Flambeau, 'seems to have had a slight dislike of grandpapa.'

'Nobody had any dislike of anybody,' said Father Brown with a groan. 'That was the dreadful thing in that darkness. It was love.'

'Curious way of expressing love—to strangle somebody and stick him with a sword,' observed the other.

'It was love,' repeated the priest, 'and it filled the house with terror.'

'Don't tell me,' protested Flambeau, 'that that beautiful woman is in love with that spider in spectacles.'

'No,' said Father Brown and groaned again. 'She is in love with her husband. It is ghastly.'

'It is a state of things that I have often heard you recommend,' replied Flambeau. 'You cannot call that lawless love.'

'Not lawless in that sense,' answered Father Brown; then he turned sharply on his elbow and spoke with a new warmth:

'Do you think I don't know that the love of a man and a woman was the first command of God and is glorious for ever? Are you one of those idiots who think we don't admire love and marriage? Do I need to be told of the Garden of Eden or the wine of Cana?* It is just because the strength in the thing was the strength of God, that it rages with that awful energy even when it breaks loose from God. When the Garden becomes a jungle, but still a glorious jungle; when the second fermentation turns the wine of Cana into the vinegar of Calvary. Do you think I don't know all that?'

'I'm sure you do,' said Flambeau, 'but I don't yet know much about my problem of the murder.'

'The murder cannot be solved,' said Father Brown.

'And why not?' demanded his friend.

'Because there is no murder to solve,' said Father Brown.

Flambeau was silent with sheer surprise; and it was his friend who resumed in a quiet tone:

'I'll tell you a curious thing. I talked with that woman when she was wild with grief; but she never said anything about the murder. She never mentioned murder, or even alluded to murder. What she did mention repeatedly was sacrilege.'

Then, with another jerk of verbal disconnection, he added: 'Have you ever heard of Tiger Tyrone?'

'Haven't I!' cried Flambeau. 'Why, that's the very man who's supposed to be after the reliquary, and whom I've been commissioned specially to circumvent. He's the most violent and daring gangster who ever visited this country; Irish, of course, but the sort that goes quite crazily anti-clerical. Perhaps he's dabbled in a little diabolism in these secret societies; anyhow, he has a macabre taste for playing all sorts of wild tricks that look wickeder than they are. Otherwise he's not the wickedest; he seldom kills, and never for cruelty; but he loves doing anything to shock people, especially his own people; robbing churches or digging up skeletons or what not.'

'Yes,' said Father Brown, 'it all fits in. I ought to have seen it all long before.'

'I don't see how we could have seen anything, after only an hour's investigation,' said the detective defensively.

'I ought to have seen it before there was anything to investigate,' said the priest. 'I ought to have known it before you arrived this morning.'

'What on earth do you mean?'

'It only shows how wrong voices sound on the telephone,' said Father Brown reflectively. 'I heard all three stages of the thing this morning; and I thought they were trifles. First, a woman rang me up and asked me to go to that inn as soon as possible. What did that mean? Of course it meant that the old grandfather was dying. Then she rang up to say that I needn't go, after all. What did that mean? Of course it meant that the old grandfather was dead. He had died quite peaceably in his bed; probably heart failure from sheer old age. And then she rang up a third time and said I was to go, after all. What did that mean? Ah, that is rather more interesting!'

He went on after a moment's pause: 'Tiger Tyrone, whose wife worships him, took hold of one of his mad ideas, and yet it was a crafty idea, too. He had just heard that you were tracking him down, that you knew him and his methods and were coming to save the reliquary; he may have heard that I have sometimes been of some assistance. He wanted to stop us on the road; and his trick for doing it was to stage a murder. It was a pretty horrible thing to do; but it wasn't a murder. Probably he bullied his wife with an air of brutal common sense, saying he could only escape penal servitude by using a dead body that couldn't suffer anything from such use. Anyhow, his wife would do anything for him; but she felt all the unnatural hideousness of that hanging masquerade; and that's why she talked about sacrilege. She was thinking of the desecration of the relic; but also of the desecration of the deathbed. The brother's one of those shoddy "scientific" rebels who tinker with dud bombs; an idealist run to seed. But he's devoted to Tiger; and so is the gardener. Perhaps it's a point in his favour that so many people seem devoted to him.

'There was one little point that set me guessing very early. Among the old books the doctor was turning over, was a bundle of seventeenth-century pamphlets; and I caught one title: *True Declaration of the Trial and Execution of My Lord Stafford*. Now Stafford was executed in the Popish Plot* business, which began with one of history's detective stories; the death of Sir Edmund Berry Godfrey.* Godfrey was found dead in a ditch, and part of the mystery was that he had marks of strangulation, but was also transfixed with his own sword. I thought at once that somebody in the house might have got the idea from here. But he couldn't have wanted it as a way of committing a murder. He can only have wanted it as a way of creating a mystery. Then I saw that this applied to all the other outrageous details. They were devilish enough; but it wasn't mere devilry; there was a rag of excuse; because they had to make the mystery as contradictory and complicated as possible, to make sure that we should be a long time solving it— or rather seeing through it. So they dragged the poor old man off his deathbed and made the corpse hop and turn cartwheels and do everything that it *couldn't* have done. They had to give us an Insoluble Problem. They swept their own tracks off the path, leaving the broom. Fortunately we did see through it in time.'

'You saw through it in time,' said Flambeau. 'I might have lingered a little longer over the second trail they left, sprinkled with assorted pills.'

'Well, anyhow, we got away,' said Father Brown, comfortably.

'And that, I presume,' said Flambeau, 'is the reason I am driving at this rate along the road to Casterbury.'*

That night in the monastery and church at Casterbury there were events calculated to stagger monastic seclusion. The reliquary of St Dorothy, in a casket gorgeous with gold and rubies, was temporarily placed in a side room near the chapel of the monastery, to be brought in with a procession for a special service at the end of Benediction.* It was guarded for the moment by one monk, who watched it in a tense and vigilant manner; for he and his brethren knew all about the shadow of peril from the prowling of Tiger Tyrone. Thus it was that the monk was on his feet in a flash, when he saw one of the low-latticed windows beginning to open and a dark object crawling like a black serpent through the crack. Rushing across, he gripped it and found it was the arm and sleeve of a man, terminating with a handsome cuff and a smart dark-grey glove. Laying hold of it, he shouted for help, and even as he did so, a man darted into the room through the door behind his back and snatched the casket he had left behind him on the table. Almost at the same instant, the arm wedged in the window came away in his hand, and he stood holding the stuffed limb of a dummy.

Tiger Tyrone had played that trick before, but to the monk it was a novelty. Fortunately, there was at least one person to whom the Tiger's tricks were not a novelty; and that person appeared with militant moustaches, gigantically framed in the doorway, at the very moment when the Tiger turned to escape by it. Flambeau and Tiger Tyrone looked at each other with steady eyes and exchanged something that was almost like a military salute.

Meanwhile Father Brown had slipped into the chapel, to say a prayer for several persons involved in these unseemly events. But he was rather smiling than otherwise, and, to tell the truth, he was not by any means hopeless about Mr Tyrone and his deplorable family; but rather more hopeful than he was for many more respectable people. Then his thoughts widened with the grander perspectives of the place and the occasion. Against black and green marbles at the end of the rather rococo* chapel, the dark-red vestments of the festival of a martyr were in their turn a background for a fierier red; a red like red-hot coals: the rubies of the reliquary; the roses of St Dorothy. And he had again a thought to throw back to the strange events of that day, and the woman who had shuddered at the sacrilege she had helped. After all, he thought, St Dorothy also had a Pagan lover; but he had not dominated her or destroyed her faith. She had died free and for the truth; and then had sent him roses from Paradise. . . .

He raised his eyes and saw through the veil of incense smoke and of twinkling lights that Benediction was drawing to its end while the procession waited. The sense of accumulated riches of time and tradition pressed past him like a crowd moving in rank after rank, through unending centuries; and high above them all, like a garland of unfading flames,

like the sun of our mortal midnight, the great monstrance*
blazed against the darkness of the vaulted shadows, as it
blazed against the black enigma of the universe. For some are
convinced that this enigma also is an Insoluble Problem. And
others have equal certitude that it has but one solution.

APPENDIX 1

THE ORIGINS OF FATHER BROWN

The *Saturday Evening Post*, a Philadelphia weekly founded in 1728, published the first Father Brown story before its first English appearance in print. When one takes into account the delays dictated by transatlantic steamer mail, this seems to confirm that the series began as an American commission. The first stories bore different names in the *Saturday Evening Post*, all of the initial six having the title 'The Innocence of Father Brown' with subtitles markedly differing from the British versions for the first four: 'Valentin Follows a Curious Trail' was what Britain read as 'The Blue Cross'; 'The Secret of the Sealed Garden' as 'the Secret Garden'; 'Why the True Fishermen Always Wear Green Evening Coats' as 'The Queer Feet'; 'The Bolt from the Blue' as 'The Hammer of God'. After that the names were the same on either side of the Atlantic, but the ninth story bore the title 'The Strange Justice' in magazine printings to become 'The Honour of Israel Gow' between book covers (the *Saturday Evening Post* abandoned the use of 'The Innocence of Father Brown' as its main title and simply used the case-titles to head the stories when the second six started). These discrepancies suggest that initially Chesterton did not find satisfactory story-names until revisal, or that he was having difficulty in making them snappy. The stories, therefore, would seem to have been organic creations, thrown off in two fairly quick successions of six; with appropriately Chestertonian paradox, it was the titles that came slowly.

Nevertheless, the stories may not have burst into being simply at the news of a series being sought by the *Saturday Evening Post*. Lucian Oldershaw recalled Chesterton staying with him at Maidenhead 'and searching in vain for a new detective story. Unable to find anything, he decided to write one himself and read it aloud to Lucian' (Maisie Ward, *Return to Chesterton* (1952), 110). Oldershaw dated this from the time when Chesterton and his wife Frances were moving from London to Beaconsfield, in October 1909, ending his thirty-five years of London residence. If this gave him a draft of 'Valentin Follows a Curious Trail' alias 'The Blue Cross', it accounts for his alacrity in volunteering when he heard of the *Post*'s need for a detective series. In the same passage Maisie Ward quotes Mildred Ware (who as Mildred d'Avigdor was a recipient of *The Innocence of Father Brown*'s book dedication in tandem with her husband Waldo) staying with the Chestertons in their first Beaconsfield residence when Gilbert said, 'I want you and Frances to bring some rugs and a bag of gooseberries, and we will go into the field. I want to read you something,' which proved to be one of the Father Brown stories. This could hardly have been much later than October, so perhaps it indicates another story had been written on impulse (if it was not simply a rereading of the first). If Father Brown did begin as the outlet of a writer frustrated in his reading, he was not left waiting in the wings long, there being at most six months between conception and commission.

The *Saturday Evening Post* apparently wanted an English detective story series as occasional foreign fictional diet: and it showed little sign of excitement at what it received. The first story was simply followed by the 'Editor's Note' declaring that 'This is the first of a series of six tales of Father Brown by Mr. Chesterton' and that the second would appear in an 'early' subsequent number (which proved to be six weeks later). Detective appetites among *Post* readers in summer 1910 were receiving considerable sustenance from standard contributors, among them the finest American mystery writer of the day (as Wallace Robson maintained), Melville Davisson Post (1871–1930), author of the rural Virginia 'Uncle Abner' stories and the cases of the devious New York lawyer Randolph Mason. Factual muck-raking of a strongly detective-fiction structure was plentiful here as in other American magazines of these years: the first Father Brown story shared the same covers as 'The Money Side of the Ministry', in which the Reform journalist and political theorist Walter E. Weyl uncovered the financial squalor and spiritual compromises of many American pastors. The *Post* since 1899 had flourished under the vigorous editorship of George Horace Lorimer (1867–1937), author of the famous *Letters of a Self-Made Merchant to his Son* preaching a gospel of orthodox ethics, sound methods, and due rewards: one can see why he might find Father Brown acceptable without unduly enthusing about either his Catholicism or his paradoxes. But he was no fool: Catholics bought magazines, and wit sold ethics.

If Father Brown's birth in Philadelphia on 23 July 1910 was gentle, his first London appearance was a baptism of fire. Cassell's published Chesterton's *What's Wrong with the World* in June 1910, and saw it go into eight editions before the year was out. The future Sir Arthur Spurgeon (1861–1938) was manager of the firm from 1905 to 1922, founded a pulp-paper monthly the *Story-Teller* in 1907 to cater to a somewhat lower status of reader than its prestigious *Cassell's Magazine*, and, while utilizing his new recruit and future owner of the firm, Walter Newman Flower (1879–1964), must have been the prime mover of the address of welcome heralding Father Brown in its pages. The *Story-Teller* in 1910 was featuring such stars as Edgar Wallace (for his *Angel Esquire* series), Jacques Futrelle, E. Phillips Oppenheim, and Arthur Morrison; and no subordinate would have dared eclipse them so dramatically as did the manifesto for August 1910, whose very existence constituted a most unusual editorial proceeding for the paper:

Important Notice to My Readers

The next issue of THE STORY-TELLER will be the most important in its history. And the principal reason why this will be so is that it will contain the first of a new series of *detective* stories written especially for this magazine by

G. K. CHESTERTON

These stories differ entirely from any work this famous writer has yet produced. They are long detective stories, the plots of which are so amazing and so cleverly worked out that I believe they will prove to be the best detective stories of our time. The first story, which appears in our next issue, is entitled:—

The Innocence of Father Brown

and this will be followed month by month by the following:—

The Secret Garden	The Hammer of God
The Queer Feet	The Wrong Shape
The Sign of the Broken Sword	

THE STORY-TELLER is recognized everywhere as the premier all-fiction magazine, and it was the knowledge of this fact that led me to secure these stories by Mr Chesterton at enormous cost—a cost which far exceeds the price ever paid for any short stories by THE STORY-TELLER.

Each story is entirely complete in itself, and is easily the most dramatic work I have ever published. I urge every reader, therefore, to take particular care not to miss the next issue, which

Will be published on JULY 29th.

Other advance information was then given, to conclude in italics:

Remember that this grand number will be published on July 29th, and will be the same price as usual, 4½d. net. Give your newsagent an order for it now, as although thousands of extra copies are being printed the demand will be phenomenal.

DO NOT MISS THE NEXT STORY-TELLER

THE EDITOR

Despite its claims of stories 'written specially' for itself, the notice made it clear that the 'enormous cost' had resulted from inspection of work completed. The extraordinary decision to bring the actual date of publication forward into the second month preceding the nominal September supports the assumption that Spurgeon, seeking more money-spinners from his new best-selling author, was shown copies of the six Father Brown stories already sent to the *Post*, that he bid a sum tempting enough to prevent any thought of alternative British publication elsewhere, and that he implemented the record contract at top speed, taking an option on a second six for *Cassell's Magazine*. The existing episodic series running in the *Story-Teller*—Grenville Hammerton's 'The League of the Watching Eye'—was suddenly cut off after five instalments in place of the usual six. The September number itself prefaced what it now headed 'No. 1—The Blue Cross' in the series 'The Innocence of Father Brown' by an editorial note:

These stories are undoubtedly the most extraordinary work Mr Chesterton has yet penned, and show this clever writer in quite a new vein. Father Brown is a character destined to be long remembered in fiction.

An advertisement in the same issue announced the fourth edition of *What's Wrong with the World*; and the conclusion of 'The Blue Cross' was followed by the words:

Next month Mr Chesterton will tell the story of 'The Secret Garden' which I claim it [*sic*] the finest detective story I have ever published.

Chesterton seems to have agreed with Spurgeon's high estimate to the extent of making that story his choice of his own writing in making his selections for his anthology *A Century of Detective Stories* twenty years after. And Spurgeon, a patriotic East Anglian, may also have been moved by Father Brown's topographical origins as indicated in 'The Blue Cross'. He was so anxious to maintain the series that when moving the second six to the more up-market (and profusely illustrated) *Cassell's Magazine* he printed the first of the new series in the number for February 1911, the same month in which the last of the first six was appearing in the *Story-Teller*. We may nevertheless be safe in dating the composition of 'The Invisible Man' as later than that of 'The Sign of the Broken Sword', all the more as it appeared in the *Saturday Evening Post* at the end of January 1911, where the 'Sign' had preceded it on the 7th of that month; and this chronology shows that Chesterton carried on with the second series with small delay. He was at this time also producing weekly essays both for the

Daily News and for the *Illustrated London News*, and was working on his poems from 'The Ballad of St Barbara' to his most lyrical and satirical ballades. The publication of the Father Brown stories in the magazines under Cassell's imprint inaugurated a long association between author and publisher for Chesterton's fiction: the firm would publish three (consistently expanding) Father Brown omnibus books, all five volumes of collected Father Brown stories, and also *The Man Who Knew Too Much*, *Tales of the Long Bow*, *The Poet and the Lunatics*, and *Four Faultless Felons*.

AHO

APPENDIX 2
TEXTUAL VARIANTS

from *The Innocence of Father Brown*

THE BLUE CROSS

3 l.6 *gravity*: 'gayety' (*Post*), printer's error.

l.11 *idler*: 'idea' (*Post*), printer's error.

4 l.9 *Tyrolean*: 'Anglo-Swiss' (*Post*).

5 l.7 *Norfolk*: 'Sussex' (*Post*), printer's error for 'Suffolk', which C evidently thought of as Father Brown's county (see Introduction above). Spurgeon of the *Story-Teller* was a Norfolk man.

l.19 *with*: 'water-' (*Post*), printer's error.

l.22 *arrived (somehow) at Stratford*: 'got out (somehow) at Tottenham' (*Post*).

6 l.37 *without*: 'with' (*Post*), printer's error.

l.38 *Here he had no strong first principles*: sentence not in *Post*.

9 l.8 *soup*: 'beef essence' (*Post*), both times. See also p. 520 below.

l.35 *two a penny*: '2d. each' (*Post*).

l.37 *4d. a lb.*: '2d. a lb.' (*Post*). Presumably C (or his English editors) adjusted the figures to British realities in proof.

10 l.34 *urgent*: 'very urgent' (*Post*).

12 l.29 *Good God*: absent from *Post*, probably for house editorial taboo.

l.36 *informative to them*: 'informing' (*Post*).

13 l.24 *three*: 'the' in omnibus printings, British and American, printer's error.

16 l.18 *wallpaper*: 'wall-papers' (*Post*).

17 l.15 *its*: missing from omnibus printings, British and American, printer's error.

19 l.16 *The Private Secretary*: *Post* here simply reads 'with timid eagerness', the play being presumably unknown in Philadelphia.

21 l.18 *curiosity*: the paragraph in the *Post* simply ran: 'Flambeau was stunned with the utmost curiosity.'

22 l.14 *our*: 'your' (*Post*). 'our' looks like a significant revision by C.

THE SECRET GARDEN

22 l.18 *Police*: 'The Chief of the Paris Police, Aristide Valentin' (*Post*).

24 l.1 *these*: 'those' in omnibus printings, British and American, printer's error.

25 l.27 *He lost his way . . . general laughter*: 'As he went towards it he could hear along passages the high-pitched, didactic voice of the doctor, and then the dull voice of the priest, followed by violent laughter.' (*Story-Teller*.)

26 l.10 *storm-wrack*: 'storm-wreck' (*Post*).

l.33 *bloody*: 'blood-stained' in English editions, presumably from Cassell's house editorial taboo. The contrast with the American proscription of 'Good God!' (see above) seems a significant one.

27 l.30 *though he was used to anatomical abortions*: absent from *Post*, presumably from motives of squeamishness.

30 l.36 *stood*: 'stood up' in pre-omnibus texts, but not in GKC anthologies.

31 l.9 *in pure Irish*: absent from *Post*, whose editors presumably knew Irish to be a Celtic language and not, as C chose to presume here, an English dialect. All first printings and GKC anthologies have 'bhoy' for 'boy', absurdly but traditionally for English-made stage Irishry.

l.34 *bloody*: 'cavalry' in English editions, but C clearly meant the English Ambassador to say 'bloody' even if Cassell's would not.

32 l.12 *paramours*: 'favourites' (*Post*).

33 l.3 *and rose for the first time*: 'rising' (*Post*).

36 l.15 *To O'Brien . . . saint*: the entire sentence not present in English editions, having been presumably deleted from *Story-Teller* for reasons of space and not noticed by C in any preparation for book publication.

38 l.2 *with whom we had a great deal to do*: 'whom we had a great deal to do with' (English texts), but the speaker is

Francophone if not actually speaking French whence the *Post* version seems the more probable and the English transposition an editorial error.

l.8 *up the clue*: not in *Post*.

39 l.9 *whatnot*: 'what not' in late editions.

l.31 *exclaimed*: 'said' (*Post*).

40 l.23 *Frenchified*: absent from *Post*.

41 l.2 *in his plain black clothes ... drawing-room*: omitted from *Story-Teller* and hence later English printings, initially (it would seem) for reasons of space.

l.34 *that failing*: 'When that failed' (*Post*).

l.37 *Ivan of the Scar sprang up ... scruff of the neck*: 'Ivan of the Scar sprang up. "You lunatic", he yelled; "you'll go to my master now, if I take you by——"' (English printings, apparently substituted for *Post* text printed here in order to enable *Story-Teller* text to end flush with end of page).

42 l.8 *If he does, it is not so very bad, you know, after all*: omitted from *Story-Teller* and subsequent English printings, presumably for reasons of space.

l.11 *human*: deleted in English printings.

l.12 *towards the back part of the house and tumbled somehow*: deleted in English printings, presumably to enable story to finish flush with end of page in *Story-Teller*.

THE QUEER FEET

52 l.33 *assuredly*: 'Your Grace' (*Post*). A duke would commonly be addressed as 'Duke' by an acquaintance or colleague when dining out. For Audley to call Chester 'Your Grace' when they were president and vice-president of the same small dining-club would be excessively formal.

53 l.12 *if the inanimate world disobeyed*: not in *Post*.

54 l.22 *Empire*: lower-case in English texts, but obviously incorrectly. (Ditto, p. 51, l.33.)

l.28 *fish service*: not in *Post*.

55 l.18 *the Jew*: 'Lever' (*Post*).

l.29 *The twenty-four pearls*: followed by 'of the club' in first printings, but not in GKC anthology or omnibus.

THE FLYING STARS

63 l.15   *where he might very well have broken his legs*: not in
Post.

70 l.29   *dropped it*: in the magazines the second line of the old
play-rhyme was also included here, namely: 'and some of you
have picked it up and put it in your pocket' ('some' probably a
printer's error for the correct form 'one'). In children's games
this would be followed by: 'not you, not you, not you, not you,
not you, but *you*', as one person is unexpectedly caught. This
would symbolize the fate of the jewels, and the surprising discovery of the thief's identity, but since the piano tunes are
otherwise directly in allusion to the policeman and chosen by the
clown or Socialist, C presumably decided against mixing the
clown's symbolisms and the crime's.

74 l.31   *stamped into slime*: 'stamped with slime' (omnibus).

75 l.16   *die*: 'come to die' (*Post*).

THE INVISIBLE MAN

The story was subtitled 'The Mystery of Himylaya Mansions' in
magazine printing, and the spelling following throughout. In book
publication the subtitle was dropped and the spelling regularized to
'Himalaya'.

78 l.12   *Ludbury*: 'Sudbury' (a real Suffolk town) in *Cassell's*.

82 l.2   *rivalry*: followed in *Cassell's* by 'and goes down to the
roots of the soul'.

83 l.14   *wheel*: 'handles' in magazines and early editions.

THE HONOUR OF ISRAEL GOW

97 l.34   *little*: omitted in omnibus.

104 l.31   *There's nothing*: 'There's something', erroneously, in
Omnibus texts.

105 l.10   *Lord*: omitted twice in *Post*, probably by house editorial
taboo.

l.27   *He . . . gravity*: 'Father Brown spun round once, then
faced them with gravity.' (*Post*).

106 l.10   *The garden . . . friend went on*: not in *Post*.

l.20   *Archibald*: 'Archbishop' in British and American
omnibus editions. A fairly Freudian slip, given the Calvinism of

Ogilvie and the Catholicism of Brown, not to speak of the Anglo-Catholicism (until 1923) of C.

107 l.3 *mad*: 'wild' in British book texts.

l.19 *right word . . . laughter of the fairies*: (*Post*); rendered simply as 'word' in *Cassell's* (and thereafter), apparently to bring last line of story flush with end of magazine page.

THE WRONG SHAPE

108 l.11 *pugarees*: 'pugrees' (*Post*); 'puggarees' (*Story-Teller*).

l.21 *small church*: 'Community' (*Post*), which suggests C had a sense of Father Brown possibly as in a religious order: if this were so it may be that to the obvious antecedent of O'Connor we must add his other great friend in the Roman Catholic priesthood, the Dominican Vincent McNabb (1868–1943). There are some points in common between McNabb and Brown. Religious orders do sometimes get assigned to run parishes with one member designated parish priest, but the still non-Roman Catholic C may not have realized this, and hence decided the identity of Brown as parish priest was incompatible with making him a Community or Order priest ('Community' in any case is found chiefly in Anglo-Catholic religious orders). But the substitution of 'small church' should not obliterate the important evidence in this. In 'The Mirror of the Magistrate' Brown, like McNabb, is attached to a London Church called St Dominic's, serving a similar residential neighbourhood.

111 l.3 *capability*: 'capacity' (*Post* and *Story-Teller*).

116 l.26 *little*: not in *Post*.

119 l.3 *Quite so*: 'Quick, side' (*Post*), printer's error.

120 l.21 *Hindoo*: 'Hindu' (*Post*).

l.36 *in the world*: not in *Post*, which seems to make better sense (i.e. 'my only friend in this house'). 'World' could be taken to mean 'world bound by this case'. It is difficult to believe C meant so hardworking a spiritual adviser as Brown to be friendless: indeed he speaks of 'a friend of mine' in 'The Blue Cross' with similar expressions in many other cases.

121 l.30 *track of a man*: 'back [presumably a misprint] of a man— or of a woman' (*Post*). A significant change, indicating that C on reflection wished to eliminate Mrs Quinton from ultimate suspicion of complicity, although keeping her degree of knowledge of the crime and its perpetrator in ambiguity. WWR noted that C

followed his master Conan Doyle in this presentation of a silent, ambiguous woman, often of great significance within the story but preserving her outward silence almost as a weapon against the reader's confidence. (For another example, although not a potential penitent in confession with Father Brown, see Joan Stacey in 'The Eye of Apollo'.)

122 l.35 *Flambeau laid his cigar down...he said*: simply 'Flambeau said' in *Post*, in place of 'he' without first five words.

123 l.18 *said the priest...shooting star*: not in *Post*.

l.28 *Good-night*: not in *Post*. It seems an important revision to have made Harris's last oral statement to Father Brown a good wish.

124 l.5 *I am really getting morbid*: not in *Post*.

125 l.15 *operator*: 'anatomist' (*Story-Teller*).

THE HAMMER OF GOD

126 l.26 *clarity*: 'charity' in omnibus texts.

132 l.31 *brained*: not in *Post*.

134 l.31 *Wilfred*: 'William' at this point in omnibus texts.

136 l.25 *Those popish priests are deucedly sly*: '"That priest is deucedly sly."' (*Post*), possibly an in-house emendation in fear of appearing anti-Catholic!

139 l.21 *Bohun followed him...smashed fly*: not in magazine versions.

l.25 *Immediately beneath...cloud-burst*: this superb paragraph, epitomizing the essence of Gothic architecture, was not in the original magazine version: it was added to the first English edition of the *Innocence*. See p. 529.

140 l.34 *Wilfred's face...the parapet of stone*: not in magazine versions.

THE EYE OF APOLLO

142 l.16 *That singular smoky sparkle...said his friend*: these eleven paragraphs replace the ensuing four which began the story in *Post* and *Cassell's*:

'When Flambeau applied his talents to the capturing of spoilers instead of the capturing of spoil, it was not remarkable that he should meet with considerable success. He was even in the habit of lightly asserting that the trades of thief and detective were so like each other that he hardly knew the difference. In truth, however, from having been a highly unscrupulous bandit, he became a particularly scrupulous inquirer, and would touch no business except what was worthy of an old family solicitor. Hence his cases, though quaint, and sometimes serious, were seldom squalid, and sometimes brought him into intellectual atmospheres, too, seldom associated with the police.

One of the strangest of such occurrences was that accident or violence, or whatever it was, that left (as some think) a faint fleck upon the splendour of the new religion now so fashionable in London and New York; I mean the religion founded by that remarkable man Kalon, who called himself the New Priest of Apollo. With the tenets and subsequent history of this gospel of Greek ideality we are not much concerned. It was one of the many new religions of the twentieth century that taught a superior innocence of sin and pain; and seemed devised not so much to lighten the troubles of the unfortunate, as to complete the satisfaction of the lucky. Its principal symbols were the Sun and the Open Eye; its priests professed (as a type of their strength and knowledge) that they could gaze unblinking at the sun at noon. It was, they said, a morbid human superstition that such fires are not to be endured; the fountain of light cannot blind us. Kalon, the founder, is now a pope of whole prairies full of villages in Central [i.e. probably mid-Western United States of] America, with a church of many million souls. But these incidents occurred earlier in his career, when he was not so successful, though, perhaps, equally conspicuous.

After his first successes in Hampstead, Flambeau had moved into ampler offices in Westminster. The building was a new pile of flats within sight of the Abbey; the official machinery of the mansions was in the swiftest and most American style, but not fully completed; the service was still understaffed, and only three tenants, including Flambeau, had managed to move into the flats. Outside, save for the remains of a scaffolding, the one conspicuous object was an enormous effigy of the human eye, surrounded by rays of gold, erected over the balcony and office of the Priest of the New Apollo.

Immediately under this modern and official Delphi were Flambeau's chambers, modestly marked as those of an inquiry agent; immediately under that was the office of two lady type-writers. The ground floor and the rest of the house were empty.'

143 l.36 *little*: not in magazine texts.

144 l.1 *humanity*: 'human nature' (magazine texts).

l.19 *castles and gardens*: 'castles and grounds and gardens' (magazine texts).

l.20 *peculiar to*: 'invented by' (magazine texts).

l.23 *masterful utilitarianism*: 'masterful and prosaic utilitarianism' (magazine texts).

l.29 *this slightly prosaic idealism*: 'these positive plans and ideals' (magazine texts).

146 l.6 *But why among the stars . . . whenever I choose*: 'But I am above the sun, I am immortal: and I will open my eyes and stare at it whenever I choose' (magazine texts.)

l.15 *heard of his special notion about sun-gazing*: 'heard that its great type of the real impotence of evil was this strength of the eye to meet the sun'.

l.25 *genuine*: 'actual' (magazine texts).

147 l.10 *Apollo*: omits next sentence of magazine texts: 'He had crossed Westminster Bridge with Flambeau, coming from the south London slum in which he was now officiating, in order to see his friend's new business apartments.'

l.33 *white flames and white flowers and white peaks*: 'white clouds and white flowers and white birds' (magazine texts).

l.38 *Five . . . three*: 'Six . . . four' (magazine texts).

148 l.2 *half the street*: 'the whole street' (magazine texts).

l.9 *little*: not in magazine texts.

l.23 *that beautiful woman who denied the existence of tragedy*: 'the most beautiful woman in Westminster' (magazine texts).

l.33 *secret vividness which is all the bitterness of death*: 'secret realisation which is all the dreadfulness of death' (magazine texts).

149 l.10 *said the other*: 'said the little priest faintly' (magazine texts).

l.11 *We have half an hour before the police will move*: not in magazine texts.

l.21 *let us*: 'let us all' (first British printings).

150 l.14 *more or less crowded with sophistries*: 'more or less clouded with theories' (magazine texts).

l.17 *very quietly*: omits ensuing 'after a long pause' (magazine texts).

151 l.3 *you can convict me or no*: 'you can tie this to my name or no' (magazine texts).

l.23 *Penal servitude*: 'Going to penal servitude' (magazine texts).

l.24 *The gallows*: 'Being hanged' (magazine texts).

l.27 *amazed admiration*: 'surprised admiration' (magazine texts).

l.30 *leaned easily against the mantelpiece and resumed*: 'resumed with an arresting gesture' (magazine texts).

152 l.12 *all you want to know*: 'the whole truth that you want to know' (magazine texts).

l.20 *in our occult wisdom*: 'in our creed' (magazine texts).

l.36 *vanquished*: 'apparently vanquished' (magazine texts).

153 l.29 *priest of the sun*: 'priest of Apollo' (magazine texts).

l.37 *Yankee shrillness*: 'harsh shrillness' (*Post*, evidently in its own emendation).

154 l.3 *it was like*: 'as of' (magazine texts).

l.5 *in broad American*: not in *Post*, evidently in its own emendation.

l.12 *ugly*: 'great' (magazine texts).

l.17 *will say*: 'will tell you' (magazine and first edition texts).

l.20 *suicide*: omits ensuing 'No, nor levitation either' (magazine texts).

155 l.19 *and peer?*: 'and peer and find things out?' (magazine texts).

l.21 *thrown the door wide open*: 'thrown open the door' (magazine texts).

156 l.16 *huge*: not in magazine texts.

l.18 *Pauline*: 'this poor woman' (magazine texts).

l.27 *naked*: not in magazine texts.

l.27 *has*: 'must have' (magazine texts).

l.28 *can blast and blind*: 'could blast and blind' (magazine texts).

l.32 *through her blindness*: 'by using her blindness' (magazine texts).

157 l.17 *legal forms*: omits ensuing 'Joan had managed this somehow' (magazine texts).

l.25 *carefully*: 'regularly' (magazine texts).

l.31 *Flambeau . . . in ten minutes*: 'Flambeau was leaning back in his chair and looking at his friend with a queer and wondering expression. "You must have followed everything that has happened here devilish closely", he said, "to have traced the crime to Kalon at all."' (magazine texts.)

THE SIGN OF THE BROKEN SWORD

163 l.23 *to it*: not in omnibus volumes.

164 l.24 *'A horrid story', he said*: accidentally omitted from later omnibus collections.

165 l.1 *the priest*: thus in *Post*. 'Paul' (*Story-Teller* and first British edition), misprinted from misreading. Altered in later English printings to 'the other'.

There seems to be little post-magazine rewriting or textual emendation for the ensuing stories from *The Wisdom of Father Brown*, probably because Chesterton felt confident about his finished products in the Father Brown saga; nor do the subsequent stories from the mid-1920s and mid-1930s show evidence of emendation, apart from an additional section added to 'The Curse of the Golden Cross' which (as WWR remarked) did nothing to clear up the obscurity of that story, and the two frame-pieces 'The Secret of Father Brown' and 'The Secret of Flambeau' in *The Secret of Father Brown*. A few minor variations have been noted.

THE DUEL OF DR HIRSCH

177 l.16 *Simon*: 'he' (*Cassell's*).

178 l.34 *the black moustache*: 'the big black moustache' (*Pall Mall Magazine*).

THE GOD OF THE GONGS

210 l.21 *snows*: 'snow' in omnibus editions, 'snows' (next line) in all editions.

215 l.27 *Gaza*: English printings incorrectly have 'Gath', which was actually the birthplace of the giant Goliath.

220 l.26 *nor, for the matter of that, that I can't prove it*: 'or that I can't prove it' (*Cassell's*).

THE ORACLE OF THE DOG

273 l.5 *four words: "He was made Man"*: 'three words: *Homo factus est*' (*Nash's–Pall Mall*). The Latin version is that used in the Nicene Creed recited in the Mass (then).

THE DAGGER WITH WINGS

275 l.22 *'It seems rather odd, . . . You are the compromise.'*: Not in *Nash's–Pall Mall*.

276 l.30 *Through a low ornamental . . . accidentally left ajar, and he*: Not in *Nash's–Pall Mall*, which reads 'Though the house was compact and comparatively small like a villa, it seemed to lie open in an informal fashion to be found in some old classical houses. He could not decide where the regular entrance was supposed to be, so he entered by some glass doors standing open, and'.

280 l.25 *'I am sure . . . certainly strike'*: Not in *Nash's–Pall Mall*.

291 l.7 *'Then there dawned . . . practical man'*: Not in *Nash's–Pall Mall*.

293 l.39 *'Why,' said Boyne, . . . As he shuffled*: Not in *Nash's–Pall Mall*, which reads: 'But as the priest picked up his shovel hat and went shuffling'.

THE CHIEF MOURNER OF MARNE

389 l.6 *squalid treason*: 'squalid reason' in omnibus edition.

AHO

EXPLANATORY NOTES

Sir Newman Flower (see Appendix I) was on the staff of Cassell's throughout Father Brown's lifetime of publication, and, while confusing the firm's publication of all the books with its magazines' publication of the stories later forming the *Innocence*, the *Secret*, and the *Scandal*, nevertheless gave noteworthy evidence on the series in his optimistically entitled *Just as it Happened* (1950): 'G. K. Chesterton published all his "Father Brown" romances through the *Story-Teller*. Here was a fresh detective; here a new figure in an unknown manner of criminal fiction.

'The behaviour of this gentle parson enthralled so many readers that we were cursed by people inquiring about him. Some said they had met "Father Brown". An inhabitant of Scotland told us that he actually entertained him in his house for a night. "Father Brown" went on quietly, a new story now and again, as brilliant, as clever in deduction as the last had been. We were still bothered with letters about him. Was he a Catholic? Someone suggested that he was what might be called a "discarded" Buddhist! "Father Brown" said nothing' (p. 30). AHO

from *The Innocence of Father Brown* (1911; New York 1911)

THE BLUE CROSS

First published *Saturday Evening Post* (Philadelphia) (23 July 1910) (Curtis Publishing Co.); *Story-Teller* (London) (Sept. 1910) (Cassell & Co.).

For the influence of 'The Blue Cross' on the Latin American writer Jorge Luis Borges see an article in *Hispanic Review*, 49 (Autumn 1981).

3 *Harwich*: seaport on the coast of Essex, in south-east England.

Flambeau: French word for 'torch'. It was not Flambeau's real name (see 'The Queer Feet'). In the prologue to the collection entitled *The Secret of Father Brown* his family name is revealed as Duroc. In depicting Flambeau C may have had in mind the Parisian master criminal François Eugène Vidocq (1775–1857), who after a life of crime offered his services to Napoleon and became the first chief of the police department. A similar metamorphosis of criminal into detective is illustrated in fiction by

3 Arsène Lupin 'the Gentleman-Burglar', invented by the French writer Maurice Leblanc (1845–1941).

the Hook of Holland: Hoek van Holland; a small port on the west coast of the Netherlands.

Eucharistic Congress: a celebratory assembly of Roman Catholic clergy and laity. The one mentioned in 'The Blue Cross' was held in London from 9 to 13 Sept. 1908. The Congress held in Dublin in 1932 was discussed by C in a book of essays entitled *Christendom in Dublin* (1932). C's interest in the 1908 Congress is noteworthy, since he did not himself become a Roman Catholic till 1922.

Roland: Hruodland, prefect of the Breton march, was killed by a Basque ambush in the Pyrenees in 778 while covering the rearguard of Charlemagne's retreat from Spain, supposedly at Roncevaux, an event which later legend transformed into a massacre by the Moors to end with Roland sounding his horn for aid only when all but 60 were slain, and sounding it once again, alone, before death as the last survivor. From the *Chanson de Roland*, the famous chivalric epic, to the *Orlando furioso* of Ariosto (1516), the heroic life and death of Roland inspired medieval poetry (and modern neo-medievalists such as C), and their use in the context of Flambeau asserts his favoured status however reprehensibly criminal. AHO

4 *juge d'instruction*: French for 'examining magistrate': in the French legal system, an official investigator of crime.

his singular height: cf. Conan Doyle's Sherlock Holmes story 'The Empty House', included in *The Return of Sherlock Holmes* (1903); '"I am glad to stretch myself", said [Holmes]. "It is no joke when a tall man has to take a foot off his stature for several hours on end."' For an original variation on the theme of the criminal's height see the detective novel *The Crooked Hinge* (1938) by John Dickson Carr (1906–77), in which the epigraph is this sentence from 'The Blue Cross'. For a discussion of C's influence on Carr see an article in the *Chesterton Review*, X (1984). One of Carr's detective protagonists, Dr Gideon Fell, is modelled on C himself.

5 *Liverpool Street*: railway terminus in east central London.

Scotland Yard: the best-known name for the (London) Metropolitan Police headquarters.

6 *Soho*: a district of central London then famous for its foreign restaurants and resident writers and artists.

victory: C's readers knew Nelson died on the victory. AHO

elfin coincidence: for Williams and Williamson (the Ratcliffe Highway murders) see P. D. James and T. A. Critchley, *The Maul and the Pear Tree* (1971). In the essay 'Five Hundred and Fifty-Five' in *Alarms and Discursions* (1910) C says: 'A journalist of my acquaintance [himself] did move quite unconsciously from a place called Overstrand to a place called Overroads. When he had made this escape he was very properly pursued by a voting card from Battersea, in which a political agent named Burn asked him to vote for a political candidate named Burns.'

the paradox of Poe: Edgar Allan Poe (1809–49), US poet, critic, and journalist, was the creator of the modern detective story in his tales about the Chevalier Auguste Dupin. C was a great admirer of his work, ranking him above Conan Doyle. Poe occasionally discusses the topic of paradox, e.g. in *The Mystery of Marie Rogêt* (1842). (Cf. Hugh Kenner, *Paradox in Chesterton* (1948).) Most critics of C's style agree that he himself made excessive use of this figure of speech; but it was also much used by contemporaries such as Wilde and Shaw. Cf. his posthumous collection *The Paradoxes of Mr Pond* (1937).

'a thinking machine': a reference to the then popular mystery stories *The Thinking Machine* (1907) and *The Thinking Machine on the Case* (1908) by the American Jacques Futrelle (1875–1912), who died in the sinking of the *Titanic* in 1912. His logician detective was called Professor Augustus F. X. van Dusen. For criticism by C of the notion of 'artificial intelligence' see the later Father Brown story 'The Mistake of the Machine' (1913), included in *The Wisdom of Father Brown* (1914).

7 *Wimbledon Common*: the recreational grounds of Wimbledon, a residential suburb south-east of London, now best known as the home of international lawn tennis matches.

9 *soup*: Martin Gardner has noted that in the *Story-Teller* what Father Brown threw at the wall is called 'bovril'. Bovril is the trade name for an instant beef soup, still marketed; the name appears to be derived from a combination of Latin *bos* (ox) and *vril*, an imaginary form of energy in the novel *The Coming Race* (1871), by Bulwer-Lytton (1803–73).

4d.: '*d.*' (derived from *denarius*) was the denotation for a penny (twelve of which equalled the modern 5p), although its purchasing power in 1910 equalled about twenty times that sum in today's prices.

10 *shovel hat*: at this time many clergymen in England wore a style of black hat that projected front and back like a shovel.

11 *Hampstead*: a London suburb on a hill north of Camden Town.

12 *Tufnell Park*: in C's time a region of villas in north London.

   Camden Town: an area of London north-east of Regent's Park.

14 *Hampstead Heath*: a vast, undulating open space of heathland north of Hampstead.

   bull's-eye lantern: a lantern with a convex lens which creates a beam of light. One of them figures in the Sherlock Holmes long story *The Sign of the Four* (1890).

15 *the Vale of Health*: originally a swamp, it was given this name when it was drained in 1800.

19 '*The Private Secretary*': three-act farce, first produced in 1884, written by the English comedy actor Sir Charles Henry Hawtrey (1858–1923). It features a comically innocent clergyman.

20 *the spiked bracelet*: a term perhaps invented by C. Martin Gardner in *The Annotated Innocence of Father Brown* (1987) suggests that it refers to a mechanism for switching playing-cards in the course of a game. The cardsharper Sparrow McCoy had one in A. Conan Doyle *The Man with the Watches*, a non-Holmes story (*Strand*, July 1898).

   Hartlepool: an eastern seaport in the county of Durham.

21 *the Donkey's Whistle . . . the Spots*: probably terms invented by C to suggest criminal tricks.

THE SECRET GARDEN

First published *Saturday Evening Post* (3 Sept. 1910); *Story-Teller* (Oct. 1910).

The title of the story is the same as that of a novel by Frances Hodgson Burnett (1849–1924), author of the Victorian children's classic *Little Lord Fauntleroy* (1886). Her *The Secret Garden* is about Mary, a spoilt and disagreeable orphan who finds an abandoned garden.

Frances Hodgson Burnett had left the story to be serialized in the *American Magazine* under the title 'Mistress Mary Quite Contrary' and sailed for Britain in Apr. 1910. Ann Thwaite observes, 'there is no record of how it came to have the familiar title' (*Waiting for the Party: The Life of Frances Hodgson Burnett 1849–1924* (1974), 222). Serialization began as *The Secret Garden* in Nov. 1910; the inference would seem to be that Burnett saw the Father Brown story in its English magazine printing, liked the title, and adopted it. She would just have had time to send to the USA her instructions to have it substituted for the existing title. AHO

A secret garden also figures prominently in the section called 'The Honest Quack' in C's *Four Faultless Felons* (1930).

The nonchalance with which heads are rolled about in C's story makes it improbable that he remembered the story *Herodias* by Gustave Flaubert (1821–80), in which it is said of the men taking away John the Baptist's severed head that 'Comme elle était très lourde ils la portaient alternativement.' ('As it was very heavy they took turns in carrying it.')

23 *Cobhole*: WWR remarked that 'Cob' means a seashore and 'Cobhole' presumably inspired the opening of 'The God of the Gongs'. AHO

24 *Julius K. Brayne*: O. D. Edwards has suggested that in his description of Brayne C may have had in mind such opinionated American millionaires as Andrew Carnegie or William Randolph Hearst. There is an obvious pun on his name when it is said that Brayne's 'crazy millions . . . had been scattered' and shortly afterwards that 'like so many scatter-brained sceptics' he was drifting towards Roman Catholicism.

Walt Whitman: the great US poet (1819–92), much admired by C (see e.g. his poem 'Dedication' of *The Man who was Thursday* in which C says: 'I feel the hour that flings | Far out of fish-shaped Paumanok'). 'Paumanok' was Long Island, NY, where Whitman came from. Whitman was at this time at the height of his British popularity.

'progressive': Edwards notes a probable play on words here between the contemporary meaning of this word in British English (theological) and in the USA (political).

25 *logomachy*: battle of words.

26 *Watteau*: Jean Antoine Watteau (1684–1721), delicate and fantastic Parisian painter.

29 *at assize*: presiding at a court session.

35 *The Guillotine*: in 'The Secret Garden' C's attitude to extreme French Catholic Nationalism seems more disapproving than in 'The Duel of Dr Hirsch'.

38 *Aquinas*: St Thomas Aquinas (1255–74), greatest of the medieval Scholastic philosophers. C was to publish a book on him in 1933.

However, in 1910 C was evidently as yet unacquainted with the gigantic extent of St Thomas's writings. AHO

42 *Cato*: Marcus Porcius Cato (85–46 BC), Roman Stoic and statesman, who killed himself after a military defeat by Julius Caesar
rather than yield to him.

THE QUEER FEET

First published *Saturday Evening Post* (1 Oct. 1910); *Story-Teller*
(Nov. 1910).

WWR described this story as a 'parable, with a keen edge of social
satire . . . It is the "outsiders", first of all Death . . . then the crook
Flambeau, and finally the shabby Father Brown, who point the satire
on the Twelve True Fishermen. Chesterton, like Kipling, vividly describes the ritualism of English upper-class life; but he sees it more
ironically than Kipling. The members of the select club The Twelve
True Fishermen parody the twelve apostles, who were fishermen, and
fishers of men like Father Brown, who can bring the reformed criminal back from the ends of the earth with "a twitch upon the thread".
Light and amusing as the story is, it is an exposure not only of social
class, but of plutocracy employing the traditions of social class, to
eliminate brotherhood. Yet all the Fishermen are very likeable, and
the story ends with an amusing touch' ('Father Brown and Others',
68–9). AHO

43 *Belgravia*: a residential district of London adjacent to Hyde
Park, associated with high society.

44 *pale horse*: 'And I looked, and behold, a pale horse: and his
name that sat on him was Death' (Rev. 6: 8).

49 *whosoever . . . save it*: 'For whosoever will save his life shall lose
it: and whosoever will lose his life for my sake shall find it'
(Matt. 16: 25). AHO

51 *Gladstone collars*: the British statesman William Ewart
Gladstone (1809–98) was famous for his high stiff collars.

the Albany: a block of residential chambers in London between
Burlington Gardens and Piccadilly, where only bachelors resided
(Lord Macaulay, A. J. Raffles, Sir Edward Heath).

57 *a fisher of men*: when Jesus saw the brothers Simon and Andrew
casting a net into the Sea of Galilee he said, 'Come after me, and
I will make you to become fishers of men' (Mark 1: 17).

a twitch upon the thread: see the use made of this passage in the
second book of Evelyn Waugh's novel *Brideshead Revisited*
(1945).

58 *dance of death*: a series of allegorical pictures representing the universal power of death.

> *St Peter's*: 'He saith unto them, But whom say ye that I am?
>
> And Simon Peter answered and said, Thou art the Christ, the Son of the Living God.
>
> And Jesus answered and said unto him, Blessed art thou, Simon Bar-Jona: for flesh and blood hath not revealed it unto thee, but my Father which is in heaven.
>
> And I say also unto thee, That thou art Peter, and upon this rock shall I build my church; and the gates of hell shall not prevail against it.
>
> And I will give unto thee the keys of the kingdom of heaven: and whatsoever thou shalt bind on earth shall be bound in heaven: and whatsoever thou shalt loose on earth shall be loosed in heaven' (Matt. 16: 15–19).

C, not to become a Roman Catholic for another dozen years, gives a quotation favoured by Roman Catholic clergy, who cite it as proof of the establishment of the Papacy and of clerical absolution. AHO

THE FLYING STARS

First published *Saturday Evening Post* (20 May 1911); *Cassell's Magazine* (June 1911).

In *The Defendant* (1901), in an essay called 'A Defence of Farce', C discusses pantomime characters.

62 *Millet*: Jean-François Millet (1814–75), French artist most famous for his painting of *The Angelus*.

Putney: a London suburb on the south side of the Thames, the residence in his later years of Algernon Charles Swinburne (1837–1909), a poet much admired by C.

monkey tree: usually called monkey-puzzle tree; an evergreen (*Araucaria araucana*) from Chile, introduced into Britain in the eighteenth century. Cf. Kipling's near-contemporary story 'The Puzzler' in *Actions and Reactions* (1909), which features such a tree.

Boxing Day: the day after Christmas Day.

64 *The Clarion*: radical paper started in 1891, part-edited by the socialist Robert Blatchford (1851–1943), a friend and controversial antagonist of C.

64 *The New Age*: periodical edited (1907–22) by Alfred Richard Orage (1875–1934), assisted initially by Holbrook Jackson (1874–1948). Originally a Fabian socialist, Orage became an advocate of Social Credit. After leaving the *New Age* he came under the influence of the esoteric teacher G. I. Gurdjieff (d. 1949).

Sirdars or Pashas: military and political leaders in India and Egypt respectively.

67 *a proper old English pantomime*: the harlequinade is a traditional pantomime comedy inherited from Italy. It influenced much in C's fiction: see William J. Scheik's essay, 'The Twilight Harlequinade of Chesterton's Father Brown Stories', in *Chesterton Review* (Fall–Winter 1977–8). In 'The Flying Stars' C alludes to traditional characters of harlequinade: Harlequin the hero, who wears a black cat-face mask, Columbine his lady-love, who is a dancer with roses in her hair, Pantaloon the foolish old father in spectacles and slippers, and the Clown, Pantaloon's comic servant, who constantly plays tricks on him. A leading character (as in 'The Flying Stars') is the Policeman, who is sometimes turned into a string of sausages. C's great friend and fellow-writer Maurice Baring (1874–1945) included a skit on the harlequinade in his *Diminutive Dramas* (1911). See also 'Pond the Pantaloon' in *The Paradoxes of Mr Pond*, where the policeman proves villain rather than victim.

Blue Birds: a reference to the then fashionable Belgian poet-dramatist Maurice Maeterlinck (1862–1949), whose *L'Oiseau Bleu* (1908: translated into English as *The Blue Bird*, 1909) enjoyed great contemporary popularity. C, like Baring, did not care for the sentimentality and whimsicality of Maeterlinck.

Blue Beard: significantly, a French legend, from Charles Perrault (1628–1703), in which Barbe Bleue is discovered by his latest wife to have murdered her predecessors and be intending to murder her, but she is rescued and saved despite his pursuit. In the Italian *commedia dell'arte* in some versions Harlequin elopes with Columbine, eluding the pursuit by her father, the pantaloon. Presumably C does not intend the threat of paternal incest implied in this conflation. AHO

towel-horses: wooden frames on which to hang towels.

70 *the Pirates of Penzance*: comic opera (1880) with libretto by Sir William Schwenck Gilbert (1836–1911) and music by Sir Arthur Sullivan (1842–1900). It includes a chorus of policemen, singing

two famous numbers, 'A Policeman's Lot is Not a Happy One' and 'When the foeman bares his steel, Tarantara-tarantara, we uncomfortable feel, Tarantara...'

75 *'narks'*: police informers.

held ... leash: probably a deliberate echo of Father Brown's metaphor in 'The Queer Feet' on Flambeau (p. 57): 'I caught him, with an unseen hook and an invisible line'. AHO

THE INVISIBLE MAN

First published *Saturday Evening Post* (28 Jan. 1911); *Cassell's Magazine* (Feb. 1911).

In calling this story 'The Invisible Man' C would have had in mind the science-fiction novel with the same title (1897) by his friend H. G. Wells (1866–1946).

WWR also cited Ralph Ellison, *Invisible Man* (1952), the famous novel graphically realizing how US white culture in the first half of the twentieth century reduced blacks to invisibility. 'Seeing the invisible in Chesterton's story means what Ellison means: discovering human brotherhood. Some of the incidental themes in this story are interesting, especially considering its date. We note that the victim Isidore Smythe is a characteristically modern man, who not only has a fast car, but more remarkably, a complete staff of robots to wait on him' ('Father Brown and Others', 68). AHO

76 *John Turnbull Angus*: he shares a name with James Turnbull, the Scottish atheist in C's fantasy *The Ball and the Cross* (1910).

78 *Ludbury*: imaginary. See p. 512.

Christian air: 'Jesus Christ, son of God, Saviour' in Greek has 'fish' as its acronym and a fish-sign became a code for Christian allegiance. Angus means that a pub would be more Christian than a confectioner's, but the double meaning symbolizes C's identification of alcohol and Christianity. AHO

80 *hoardings*: a board fence on which advertisements etc. are displayed after payment.

82 *stamp paper*: the blank marginal paper on sheets of postage stamps.

dado: a skirting of wood (or wallpaper or painting etc.) along the lower part of the walls of a room.

86 *harquebuses*: German sixteenth-century guns.

88 *serried*: usually describes ranks of soldiers.

89 *killed their master*: Martin Gardner notes a possible allusion to the story 'Moxon's Master', published in *Can Such Things Be?* (1893) by the US writer Ambrose Bierce (1842–1914?), in which an infuriated chess machine kills its inventor after losing a game. Cf. also a story by Jerome K. Jerome (1859–1927) called 'The Dancing Partner' (1893), included in Dorothy L. Sayers's anthology *Detection Mystery Horror* (1928).

THE HONOUR OF ISRAEL GOW

First published *Saturday Evening Post* (25 Mar. 1911); *Cassell's Magazine* (Apr. 1911). Originally entitled 'The Strange Justice'.

94 *chimney-pot hat*: a top hat.

Scotland Yard: Scotland was in fact outside Scotland Yard's jurisdiction. AHO

97 *Wilkie Collins's*: (William) Wilkie Collins (1824–89) was the author of the famous novel *The Woman in White*, discussed in a later Father Brown story 'The Pursuit of Mr Blue' (1934); (in *The Scandal of Father Brown*).

Louis XVI: king of France 1765–93, husband of Marie Antoinette; guillotined in 1793. He was particularly fond of repairing locks. (Is 'locksmith' an error for 'clocksmith'?)

Diamond Necklace: Marie Antoinette (1755–93), Queen of France to Louis XVI (both to be guillotined in the French Revolution), was unjustly presumed to have betrayed her husband by persuading Cardinal de Rohan-Guémênée (1734–1803) to stand guarantor so she could acquire a diamond necklace; the affair was ultimately revealed as a fraud by Jeanne de Valois, Comtesse de La Motte (1756–91), the Cardinal's mistress, subsequently imprisoned and branded. Alexandre Dumas *père* cast the story as a novel in *Le Collier de la reine* (1849). AHO

101 *we survived even that piece of paper*: a reference (in the book a forward reference) to the story called 'The Wrong Shape', published in the *Story-Teller* (Jan. 1911).

105 *on the nail*: 'on the spot, at once, without the least delay' (*Oxford English Dictionary*). O. D. Edwards explains the origin of the phrase in undertakers' habits of protecting their dues from a bankrupt corpse's estate by ensuring that they received payment when the job was concluded, i.e. when the final nail in the coffin was hammered down.

THE WRONG SHAPE

First published *Saturday Evening Post* (10 Dec. 1910); *Story-Teller* (Jan. 1911).

WWR elsewhere noted that 'some readers remember most in the Father Brown stories . . . Chesterton's powers of description. His liking for . . . backcloths [with] a decor which links Chesterton to Swinburne and the Decadents. His moral and religious outlook could not be more different from theirs; but his imagination has been formed on their work. Lurid, or fanciful, or grotesque decoration dominates stories like "The Wrong Shape"' ('Father Brown and Others', 69). AHO

108 *pugarees*: light scarves of silk or muslin worn in India.

    St Mungo: a sixth-century bishop who founded the see of Glasgow.

109 *Mr Quinton*: he suggests Samuel Taylor Coleridge (1772–1834) (cf. his relations with his wife). But like many poets in C's fiction he has a flavour of Swinburne, especially in his exoticism.

    Bond Street: London Street well known for its fashionable shops and art galleries.

110 *Virgil*: the great Roman poet Publius Vergilius Maro (70–19 BC), who was Dante's guide through the *Inferno*.

118 *the night in Coleridge*: this refers to the line 'At one stride comes the dark' from 'The Ancient Mariner' (*Lyrical Ballads*, 1798) by Samuel Taylor Coleridge.

    sermon paper: writing paper of foolscap size.

119 *Roi des Apaches*: French for king of the apaches. Apaches was a name given to Parisian thieves and ruffians, in the belief that American Apache Indians were unusually savage and warlike. The Irish mass-leader Daniel O'Connell (1775–1847) was known as 'the King of the Beggars'.

123 *Vicisti, Galilæe*: Latin for 'Thou hast conquered, Galilean', a saying attributed to the pagan Roman Emperor Julian the Apostate (reigned AD 361–3) when dying in battle, in acknowledgement of the triumph of Christianity. Swinburne versified the saying as 'Thou hast conquered, O pale Galilean; the world has grown grey from thy breath' ('Hymn to Proserpine', 1866).

125 *quire*: one-twentieth of a ream (500) of sheets of paper.

THE HAMMER OF GOD

First published *Saturday Evening Post* (5 Nov. 1910); *Story-Teller* (Dec. 1910).

'I think the unforgettable descriptions of gardens, houses, land-scapes, and the effects of *light* in these stories are not mainly there for camouflage, or merely for scene painting. I think they have something to do with the meaning of the stories; and this in turn has something to do with the attraction of the detective story, as a genre, both to Chesterton himself and to his readers. But first of all let us note that, even at the level of the plot, the descriptions are highly relevant. This passage ["Immediately beneath and about them . . . mid-air."] read in its context, contains the explanation of the mystery. . . . This is the sort of passage that we feel is "too good" for a detective story. Yet it is surely an artistic virtue, if only a minor one, that the height of the church and the way the landscape below it looks like "a map of the world" should, for the attentive, explain both the crime's motive, and the method of its commission.

'. . . phrases about "monstrous foreshortening and disproportion", "dizzy perspectives", "glimpses of great things small and small things great" . . . are clues to Chesterton's imagination. First of all, it was intensely visual. He began as a painter, and we can find the painter's eye in all his descriptions. But—more important—it was child-like' (WWR in 'Father Brown and Others', 69–70). AHO

125 *Bohun Beacon*: imaginary.

126 *Mohocks*: aristocratic ruffians who infested the streets of London in the early eighteenth century.

Mashers: late Victorian dandies.

127 *Greenford*: a suburb some miles to the west of London.

131 *the Nelson Column*: a statue of the British naval hero Admiral Lord Nelson (1758–1805) in Trafalgar Square, London.

137 *Sennacherib*: an Assyrian king whose palace was at Nineveh. After his failure to take Jerusalem he was murdered in 681 BC by his sons (2 Chr. 32: 21). C may have had in mind Byron's poem 'The Destruction of Sennacherib'.

THE EYE OF APOLLO

First published *Saturday Evening Post* (25 Feb. 1911); *Cassell's Magazine* (Mar. 1911).

142 *M. Hercule Flambeau*: this is the first time that we learn Flambeau's first name. Did it suggest M. Belloc Lowndes's 'Hercule Popeau' and in turn Agatha Christie's 'Hercule Poirot'?

Cf. 'the fist of Flambeau, which was like the club of Hercules', in 'The Insoluble Problem' (1935).

Camberwell: a poor suburb in south London.

143 *Christian Science*: a religion founded in the USA in 1866 by Mary Baker Eddy. C makes adverse comments on it in, for example, essays included in *The Uses of Diversity* (1920) and *All is Grist* (1931). In this story Pauline's sun-staring may allude to it. Cf. Aldous Huxley's (mistaken) defence of the ophthalmologist W. H. Bates in *The Art of Seeing*.

Kalon: neuter form of the ancient Greek adjective *kalos*, meaning 'beautiful'.

lady typewriters: obsolete term for female typists.

146 *dazzle the sun*: cf. the poem 'The Sunne Rising', by John Donne (1572–1631), in which, addressing the sun, Donne says of his mistress, 'If her eyes have not blinded thine'.

Nietzsche: 'Auf dem Grunde aller dieser vornehmen Rassen ist das Raubtier, die prachtvolle nach Beute und Sieg lüstern schweifende blonde Bestie nicht zu verkennen' [At the base of all these aristocratic races the predator is not to be mistaken, the splendorous blond beast, avidly rampant for plunder and victory] (Friedrich Nietzsche 1844–1900), *Zur Genealogie der Moral*, i. 11.

Nietzsche's doctrine of the Superman was expounded in English by C's friend George Bernard Shaw (1856–1950) in his *Man and Superman* (1903) and attacked by C in his *George Bernard Shaw* (1909, 1935) as well as in his satirical essay 'How I Found the Superman'. C would probably have liked the parody of the above by the Scots poet Norman MacCaig: 'if you climb a Scottish aristocratic family tree, however high you climb, you will discover at the top a grinning and rapacious ape.' AHO

147 *the shock of noon*: Cf. Alfred, Lord Tennyson's poem 'Godiva' (1842): 'with twelve great shocks of sound, the shameless noon | Was clash'd and hammer'd from a hundred towers.'

149 *Joan Stacey*: the very unusual (for C) portrayal of this character suggests the influence of Maupassant.

Doré's Christ: (Louis Auguste) Gustave Doré (1832–83) was a French artist well known for his illustrations of the Bible (1866).

149 *Pretorium*: in the time of Christ the Praetorium was the head-quarters of the Roman procurator in Jerusalem.

150 *Salisbury Plain*: a great chalk plateau in Wiltshire: home of Stonehenge.

Hellas: the ancient name for Greece.

Caiaphas: the high priest who condemned Jesus, demanding his death of Pontius Pilate.

THE SIGN OF THE BROKEN SWORD

First published *Saturday Evening Post* (7 Jan. 1911); *Story-Teller* (Feb. 1911).

This story throws an interesting light on C's view of history and historical method. For a historian's discussion of it see Melvin Cherno, 'Father Brown and the Historians', *Chesterton Review* (May 1984). C's other 'historical' detective story, 'The Fairy Tale of Father Brown', was included in *The Wisdom of Father Brown* (1914).

O. D. Edwards has suggested as possible sources for C's story (1) C's personal memories of the Boer War period, with the wild public hostility in Britain to military enemies who were, from their own point of view, patriots. [There may be particular inspiration from the Jameson Raid, which preceded the Boer War in 1896. AHO] (2) Thomas Babington Macaulay's portrait of the first duke of Marlborough in his *History of England* (1848–55), in which it is alleged that Marlborough deliberately sacrificed the lives of British troops in order to save himself from the consequences of his own treason. This allegation was vehemently contested in *Marlborough* (1933–8) by his descendant Sir Winston Churchill (1874–1965). (3) The Charge of the Light Brigade (1854), with the part played in it by the feud (probably no secret) of Lords Cardigan and Lucan.

158 *Colonel Newcome*: a simple and lovable British army officer in *The Newcomes* (1853), a novel by William Makepeace Thackeray (1811–63).

159 *wagonettes*: small four-wheel carriages, serving as horse-drawn omnibuses. Cf. W. B. Yeats's poem 'Why should not Old Men be Mad?' (in *Last Poems*, 1936–9) in which he says he has seen 'A Helen of social welfare dream, | Climb on a wagonette to scream'.

sham ones: evidently an allusion to the as yet unpublished 'The Flying Stars', suggesting that C had commenced work on it soon after completing 'The Queer Feet', but had set it aside for a time. AHO.

...

160 *the Embankment*: an arrangement of stone walls, paved roads, and paths on each side of the river Thames in London.

161 *Brazil*: M. Gardner notes that 'in about 1900 a bitter boundary dispute broke out between Britain and Brazil over the northern border of British Guiana ... it was settled in 1904'.

    Olivier: O. D. Edwards suggests that Olivier may have been based on the Boer leader Louis Botha (1862–1919).

    Achilles was timid and Hector was treacherous: for the converse cf. Shakespeare, *Troilus and Cressida*, v. viii: 'HECTOR: I am unarmed; forgo this vantage, Greek. ACHILLES: Strike, fellows, strike; this is the man I seek. [HECTOR *falls*]'

    the Mutiny: a reference to the Indian Mutiny (1857), also known as the Sepoy Rebellion.

166 *the Lincolnshire Fens*: a marshy area whence many rivers empty into the Wash, a great bay of the North Sea.

168 *'read their Bibles'*: the 'Bible-thumping' generals C may have had in mind include Charles Gordon (1833–85), John Nicholson (1821–57), and Sir Henry Havelock (1795–1857).

172 *Park Lane*: a street bordering the eastern edge of Hyde Park, well known for its fashionable residences.

from *The Wisdom of Father Brown* (1914; New York 1915)

THE DUEL OF DR HIRSCH

First published *Pall Mall Magazine* (Aug. 1914).

    C's hostility to Jews had been intensified by the 'Marconi case', in the course of which his brother Cecil Chesterton (1879–1918) was successfully prosecuted for a criminal libel on the Jewish financier Godfrey Isaacs.

    In 'The Duel of Dr Hirsch' C had in mind the case of Alfred Dreyfus (1859–1935), a Jewish officer in the French army who was convicted in 1894 of betraying military secrets to Germany. 'The Affair', as it came to be called, split French society, with military and clerical forces affirming the guilt of Dreyfus while radicals and socialists proclaimed his innocence.

    Father Brown's suggestion that the Dreyfus case was 'got up' by the Jews for nefarious purposes may have been derived from C's friend Hilaire Belloc (1870–1953).

176 *'Aux grèves, citoyens'*: French for 'To strikes, citizens': parody of the 'Marseillaise' ('To arms, citizens').

176 *the Élysée*: the residence, then and now, of the French president.

177 *forked radish*: from Shakespeare, *2 Henry IV*, III. ii. 305.

Chauvinist: one who exhibits excessive and irrational patriotism. The word derives from the name of Nicolas Chauvin, a French soldier of the First Republic and First Empire who was passionately devoted to Napoleon. (The modern feminist sense, as in 'male chauvinist', was not then current.)

Dreyfus case: see notes on this story above.

178 *Camille Desmoulins*: born 1760, guillotined 1794, he was a French journalist and pamphleteer of the French Revolutionary period. C refers here to the part he played in exhorting a Parisian crowd to take up arms in 1789.

180 *Clemenceau*: Georges Clemenceau (1841–1929), French politician and journalist: beginning as a Radical, he became a patriotic war leader in the Third Republic, in which he was prime minister (1917–20).

Déroulède: Paul Déroulède (1846–1914) was a French nationalist politician and poet admired by C.

183 *Cenci or Borgia*: proverbial examples of heinous criminality whose Mediterranean origins made them less likely to come instinctively to the tongue of a Roman Catholic than of a Protestant English clergyman (C still non-RC). Francesco Cenci (1549–98), bastard son of a priest, was a dissolute wealthy Roman murdered by his wife and children (with whom he probably did not have incestuous relations, contrary to legend). Shelley's tragedy *The Cenci* (1819) fictionalizes the story, minimizing the children's depravity and exaggerating the father's. Cesare (1476–1507) and Lucrezia Borgia (1480–1519) were the children of Cardinal Rodrigo Borgia (originally 'Borja') (1431–1503), who became Pope Alexander VI in 1492, and made Cesare Cardinal in 1493. The legendary charges of their incest are again probably baseless, but the men were certainly murderers, simoniacs, predators, libertines, and traitors to God and man. Cesare's career furnished many useful examples for the treatise on statecraft *The Prince* by his admirer Niccolò Machiavelli (1469–1527). AHO.

186 *sur le terrain*: French for 'on the spot'.

187 *gamin*: French for 'urchin'.

189 *a queer psychological story*: a reference to *The Way It Came* (1896), by Henry James (1843–1916). The title was changed to *The Friends of the Friends* in the New York edition.

190 *the face of Judas laughing horribly*: this vision, which must have made an indelible impression on many readers, all too aptly concludes the most anti-Semitic of the Father Brown stories.

THE MAN IN THE PASSAGE

First published *Pall Mall Magazine* (Sept. 1913).

190 *the Adelphi*: once an area south of the Strand, built 1769–71 by the four Adam brothers, it now consists of blocks of flats.

192 *Velazquez*: Diego Rodríguez de Silva y Velázquez (1599–1660), the glorious court painter of the Spanish Habsburgs, was enjoying great popularity in England at this time (cf. Wilde's 'The Birthday of the Infanta'), but not particularly for his admirals. C surely means Don John of Austria (1547–78), bastard Spanish son of the Emperor Charles V, whose portrait Velázquez painted in 1632–3 (now in the Prado museum in Madrid), and whom C had just celebrated in heroic strains in his poem 'Lepanto' on Don John's naval victory over the Turks in 1571: the painting influenced the poem. C probably also refers to Velázquez's much more famous 'Las Lanzas' (Prado), depicting the surrender of the Dutch fortress of Breda in the Thirty Years War (1625, painted 1635). The Spanish commander was Ambrose Spinola (1569–1630), actually a general, the family sailor being his brother Frederick, killed in action against the Dutch in 1603. Spinola's beard is as serviceable for Seymour as Don John's. AHO

Chaucer said of the Miller's: in general the Miller anticipated Captain Cutler:

> The MILLERE was a stout carl for the nones;
> Ful byg he was of brawn, and eek of bones.
> That proved wel, for over al ther he cam,
> At wrastlynge he wolde have alwey the ram.
> He was short-sholdred, brood, a thikke knarre;
> Ther was no dore that he nolde heve of harre,
> Or breke it at a rennyng with his heed.
> His berd as any sowe or fox was reed,
> And therto brood, as though it were a spade.
> Upon the cop right of his nose he hade
> A werte, and theron stood a toft of herys,
> Reed as the brustles of a sowes erys;
> His nosethirles blake were and wyde.
> A swerd and bokeler bar he by his syde.

(*The Canterbury Tales*, General Prologue, i (a). 545–58)

192 *Mr Max Beerbohm*: styled 'the incomparable Max' by Bernard Shaw, Sir Henry Maximilian Beerbohm (1872–1956), essayist, dramatic critic, parodist, and caricaturist, is today most remembered for his Oxford fantasy *Zuleika Dobson* (1911). He and C admired each other and were great friends.

195 *wooden Noah*: Noah (Gen. 6–9) inspired a popular nursery model Ark housing figures of Noah, Mrs Noah, three sons and wives, and two of the more obvious kinds of animal: additional model beasts and birds could be acquired and the set built up. It was a popular Christmas present for middle-class children in the late Victorian and Edwardian periods, satisfactorily combining science and religion. C always liked miniature theatres, and unlike most families would have known the toy Noah set descended from the medieval Noah play. AHO

197 *mirrors*: see the discussion of C's interest in mirrors in Hugh Kenner's *Paradox in Chesterton* (1948), and cf. the later Father Brown story 'The Mirror of the Magistrate'.

201 *humorous judges*: cf. the sympathetically portrayed judge who denounces the mean-souled Premier in C's story 'The Tremendous Adventure of Major Brown' in *The Club of Queer Trades* (1905).

Patrick Butler, KC: KC stands for 'King's Counsel' (the monarch at the time being a king, George V). Patrick Butler was later adopted as a detective protagonist by John Dickson Carr.

flâneur: an idler, lounger, stroller, usually flirting or preening on boulevards or promenades. But C seems to mean an empty exhibitionist in general. AHO

THE GOD OF THE GONGS

First published *Pall Mall Magazine* (Sept. 1914).

This story is marred by a contradiction not infrequent in C's work as a whole: he attacks vulgar distortion of Catholicism while seemingly unaware of the beam in his own eye, his European racialism.

WWR, having written these paragraphs and subjoined notes, came to the conclusion that this story, if read from the standpoint of Nigger Ned, is a brilliant revelation of the lynch-mob attitudes to blacks in pre-war England. C intended no such reading, he observed, but his creative imagination had subverted his intentions. Nigger Ned's alliterative identity suggests an origin in the Texas-born Jack Johnson (1878–1946), who became the world heavyweight boxing champion by defeating the Canadian Tommy Burns at Sydney in 1908, and retained the title against the attempted come-back of 'the Great White Hope', former champion James Jackson Jeffries, in 1910. Johnson aroused bitter racial hostility, was banned from the English Sporting Club, and had his proposed fight against the Australian challenger Bombardier Billy Wells prohibited by the English legal authorities in 1911, after a stop-the-fight campaign led by the Baptist minister of Regent's Park Chapel, Revd Frederick Brotherton Meyer (1847–1929), from whose anti-pugilism Father Brown implicitly distances himself in the story. Johnson was defeated in a controversial 26th-round knock-out by Jess Willard in 1915. AHO

210 *St John the Baptist's head*: see Mark 6: 21–8.

214 *the Cake-Walk*: a prancing movement (later developed into a dance) performed by American blacks in competition for a cake.

215 *Gaza*: Judg. 16: 1–3.

   Anchises: he was carried out of burning Troy by his son Aeneas in Virgil's *Aeneid*, Book II.

219 *Voodoo*: religious beliefs and sorceries of African origin found among blacks of the West Indies and the southern United States. Cf. the fearsome voodooist cook in the Sherlock Holmes story 'Wisteria Lodge', collected in *His Last Bow* (1917), but originally published in the *Strand* (Sept.–Oct. 1908), and thus known to C when writing.

222 *a basilisk*: a fabulous monster, with fiery death-dealing eyes and breath (so named, according to Pliny, because of its crown-like crest—*basileus* is ancient Greek for 'king').

   the Black Man: old Scottish name for the Devil.

THE STRANGE CRIME OF JOHN BOULNOIS

First published *Pall Mall Magazine* (July 1913).

   Like many Roman Catholic spokesmen at the time, C was deeply interested in current controversies over Darwin's theory of evolution by natural selection. This may be seen in the polemics between Hilaire Belloc and H. G. Wells (cf. C's *The Everlasting Man*). Their controversy was by no means one-sided: thus even the anti-Catholic *New Statesman* (27 Nov. 1926) found for Belloc on this issue. And Boulnois's 'Catastrophism', or something like it, has been put forward in recent times by the (Marxist) Harvard thinker Stephen Jay Gould in his *Ever since Darwin* (1977), in which he writes of 'punctual equilibrium', the idea that 'evolution proceeds . . . in relatively short bursts interspersed by long periods of relative equilibrium'. For futher comment on this see A. G. N. Flew, *Darwinian Evolution* (1984).

Two further points: (1) It is perhaps a fault in this story that Boulnois's ideas have nothing to do with its central motif, the incredible wickedness of Sir Claude Champion, who (although a Catholic) commits suicide in the course of trying to get an innocent man hanged. (2) It has the best punch line of all the stories.

223 *hustling*: like most fellow English popular writers, C used the word as a signature-tune for his fictional American creations, taking it to mean 'vigorously to pursue business enterprise'. But 20th-century Americans actually employed the word, as a rule, to mean 'to solicit for purposes of sexual prostitution', or 'to pressure for custom illicitly', as in the film *The Hustler*.

William James: 1842–1910; American psychologist and philosopher, most famous for his *Varieties of Religious Experience* (1902). He was celebrated as a popularizer of the American philosophy he called 'Pragmatism', though this was really the creation of Charles Sanders Peirce (1839–1914), then little known but today universally agreed to be by far the greatest of all American philosophers. (Peirce himself called his own philosophy 'Pragmaticism' to dissociate it from William James.) James was a son of Henry James, Sen., the Swedenborgian and Fourierite, and brother of Henry James, Jun., the famous novelist. Both brothers were on the friendliest terms with C. The mention of William James's name adds to the distinctly American, and highly philosophical, flavour of this story.

228 *Scott's great tragedy*: *The Bride of Lammermoor* (1819), a romance by Sir Walter Scott (1771–1832) in which the tragic hero is the Master of Ravenswood.

He was a man with more literary . . . strangely unreal: 'Such things show the literary critic in Chesterton, the power of verbal analysis which we associate with a critic of our own day like William Empson, and which Empson himself has praised in Chesterton' (WWR in 'Father Brown and Others', 66).

235 *Haroun Alraschid*: Harun ar Rashid (763–809), Abbasid caliph of Baghdad, who appears in many tales of the ancient Arabic story-sequence *The Thousand and One Nights*. To English-speaking readers he would be most familiar for his spectacular

appearance to the poet Tennyson at the end of the latter's
'Recollections of the Arabian Nights' (1830).

Mordecai the Jew: see the book of Esther in the Old Testament.
Mordecai, like John Boulnois, was deliberately framed and
nearly hanged. A symbol of Jewish piety, he and his enemy
Haman, who was hanged instead of him, are commemorated by
the Jewish festival of Purim on Adar 14 (Jewish calendar), when
the book of Esther is read in the synagogue at the evening and
morning services.

 The way in which Father Brown speaks of Mordecai makes it
improbable that C was inherently anti-Semitic. No one hostile to
Judaism could have said what C said, though perhaps he (and
Belloc, and Cecil Chesterton) sometimes forgot that the Old
Testament is Scripture for Christians as well as Jews.

236 *large letters*: US sensational journalism is frequently ridiculed by
C elsewhere, e.g. in the title story of *The Scandal of Father
Brown* (1935).

THE FAIRY TALE OF FATHER BROWN

No previous magazine publication. It was announced in the *Pall Mall
Magazine* for Sept. 1914 as part of the contents of its October
number, but the pressure of unexpected wartime economics and
improvident expansion a month or so previously had forced a merger
with *Nash's Magazine*, whose regular features took the lead; wartime
features and propaganda also prohibited the publication. It is also
possible that in the heat of chauvinism on the outbreak of war the
story was editorially deemed too kindly or too romantic in its treat-
ment of Germans: it certainly captures some of the charm of
Germany. AHO

238 *Heiligwaldenstein*: imaginary. The name means literally 'holy
wood stone'.

 fifty years before: presumably during the Prussian conflict
against Denmark in 1864 (Flambeau speaks shortly afterwards
of 'the time of Bismarck's very earliest schemes of consolidation') when the Prussian statesman Otto von Bismarck (1815–
98) inaugurated his strategy for the unification of Germany (to
culminate in 1871) by conquest of the disputed duchies of
Schleswig and Holstein.

 wild justice: a definition of revenge by Francis Bacon (1561–
1626).

238 *Potsdam*: palace near Berlin, associated with Frederick the Great and Prussian militarism.

239 *Munich*: i.e. Munich beer.

240 '*Wolves with the hair of the ermine*': pastiche of Swinburne's declamatory manner.

241 *Grimm*: this name is probably an intentional reminder of the *Household Tales* collected 1812–15—or, as J. M. Ellis thinks, fabricated—by the German brothers Jacob Ludwig Carl Grimm (1785–1863) and Wilhelm Carl Grimm (1786–1859).

245 *Sadowa*: or Königgrätz. Place of the Prussian victory over the Austrians in 1866.

Gravelotte: place of the Prussian victory over the French in 1870.

247 *They trust . . . Lord of Hosts*: 'Some trust in chariots, and some in horses: but we will remember the name of the Lord our God.' (Psalm 20: 7).

249 *the Epistle of St James*: the complete quotation reads: 'Even so the tongue is a little member, and boasteth great things' (Jas. 3: 5.).

from *The Incredulity of Father Brown* (1926; New York 1926)

The Incredulity of Father Brown was opened in its book publication by the following 'NOTE' from C: 'I do not know if it is necessary to say, of stories so slight, that the archaeology and history are largely assumed for the sake of the story. Problems of a very similar sort do exist; but I have deliberately avoided reproducing any real one.'

THE ORACLE OF THE DOG

First published *Nash's—Pall Mall Magazine* (sometimes—justifiably—catalogued or bound as *Nash's and Pall Mall Magazine* and sometimes—incorrectly—as *Nash's Pall Mall Magazine*) (Dec. 1923).

251 *Yes . . . spelt backwards*: One of a set of examples previously chosen by WWR (others including the last two paragraphs of 'The Man in the Passage' and the exchange on the limits of charity in 'The Chief Mourner of Marne') to show that while 'Father Brown is . . . not a thaumaturge . . . he has exceptional moral insight. . . . Chesterton's aim is not really a psychological study of such a man. Almost at once Father Brown becomes largely a mouthpiece for Chesterton's own wit and wisdom.

[These] examples ... could all have been starting-points for Chestertonian essays. The artistic reason for Father Brown's powers of repartee, and his wittiness in general, is that we look straight at him as we do not look at Sherlock Holmes, who is reflected in the—sometimes exasperated—admiration of Dr Watson. Chesterton has dispensed with a Dr Watson; and so Father Brown has to seem brilliant to *us*. And the only way this can be done is by making him brilliant' ('Father Brown and Others', 63–4). AHO

252 *right ... left hand did*: 'But when thou doest alms, let not thy left hand know what thy right hand doeth' (Matt. 6: 3). This is one of the instructions of Jesus in the Sermon on the Mount, not strictly a parable, which is a story used as metaphor for instruction. But it is a metaphor without a story. AHO

255 *Nox*: Latin for 'night'.

260 *a frightful wax*: a bad temper.

262 *the Encyclical Rerum Novarum*: the Latin title means 'of new things'. Issued in 1891 by Pope Leo XIII (1810–1903), it was partly designed to further the reconciliation of the French Church with the Third Republic. In the title story of *The Secret of Father Brown* Father Brown says Leo XIII was 'always rather a hero of mine'.

264 *Citizen Riquetti*: a reference to the use of his family name Riqueti (*sic*) by the French Revolutionary statesman the Comte de Mirabeau (1749–91). C is thinking of a passage in *The French Revolution* (1837) by Thomas Carlyle (1795–1881) (World's Classics edn. 1989), i. 356: 'With your *Riquetti* you have set Europe at cross-purposes for three days.' Possibly C had just been reading Belloc's edition of Carlyle's book.

270 *the Yellow Room*: a reference to the French detective story *Le Mystère de la chambre jaune* (1907), by Gaston Leroux (1868–1928), translated into English as *The Mystery of the Yellow Room* (1908).

273 *Anubis*: the best-known dog-god of the ancient Egyptians, god of the dead, and of embalming, supervising the balance when the soul is weighed before Osiris. Magicians 'compelled' him to fetch and feed the gods in the second century AD. At different times he was held to be the son of Osiris, and of the sun-god Ra. The comparative points with Jesus as the Son of God in Christianity account for Father Brown's loathing, and emphasis on the distinction between Dog and God. AHO

273   *great green-eyed Pasht*: more correctly 'Pakht', a lioness-headed
      goddess, believed to guard the living and dead in Ancient Egypt,
      known as 'she who scratches', or 'the tearer'; she is associated
      with functions comparable to those of the Greek Artemis (Latin
      Diana), the huntress goddess of the moon and of virginity,
      dangerous to male intruders. The woman Pharaoh Hatshepsut
      set up a shrine to her in Beni Hasan between 1473 and 1458 BC.
      (Our deepest thanks are due to the Egyptologist Dr Sarah Cullis
      of Edinburgh for this note.) AHO

      Bulls of Bashan: 'Many bulls have compassed me; strong bulls
      of Bashan have beset me round.
          'They gaped upon me with their mouths, as a ravening and a
      roaring lion.' (Ps. 22: 12–13).
          The passage has caused difficulty. Cf: 'It's the unknown that is
      to be dreaded,' said Sir Nicholas. 'If Skatterly took it into his
      head to represent a Bull of Bashan, well, I'd rather not be here.'
          'Of course we shan't allow any Bible characters. Besides, I
      don't know what the Bulls of Bashan really did that was so
      dreadful; they just came round and gaped, as far as I remember.'
          'My dear, you don't know what Skatterly's Hungarian imagi-
      nation mightn't read into the part; it would be small satisfaction
      to say to him afterwards: "You behaved as no Bull of Bashan
      would have behaved".' (Saki [Hector Hugh Munro] (1870–
      1916), 'A Touch of Realism', *Beasts and Super-Beasts* (1914))
          C had known Munro and shortly before writing this story had
      introduced his posthumous collection *The Toys of Peace*. AHO

      St Francis: the great Italian saint, Francis of Assisi (Giovanni
      Francesco Bernardone) (1181–1226). C wrote a book on him
      published in 1923. On this occasion C is referring to the story of
      the wolf of Gubbio in the *Little Flowers of St Francis* (Italian,
      fourteenth century), translated into English by H. E. Manning in
      1864.

THE DAGGER WITH WINGS

First published *Nash's—Pall Mall Magazine* (Feb. 1924).
    'Lurid, or fanciful, or grotesque decoration dominates stories
like . . . "The Dagger with Wings". Of course this decoration is there
in part to distract us. A classical detective story exists to fool the
reader; and Chesterton likes to avert our attention from the "simple
centre" to the "rococo excrescences". These are Chesterton's own
expressions . . . in "The Queer Feet". . . .
    'This child-like quality in Chesterton attracts some readers and

repels others. Those whom it repels dislike the association he makes between childish fantasies about winged daggers and flying vampires, and serious themes of good and evil. They feel that the former degrade the latter. This sort of criticism has been levelled against a later writer, Charles Williams, who also attempted to use thriller material as a means of saying something serious. I cannot answer this objection, except by saying that Chesterton himself seems to have been aware of it, and tries to answer it in his story "The Dagger with Wings". Here the real mystery of nature is contrasted with the spurious mystery, the 'white magic', which the criminal mystagogue exploits. Father Brown, as usual, appears as the agnostic: "I do believe some things, of course, and therefore, of course, I don't believe other things." ... Crime and insanity in this story are associated with changing colours, pantheistic unities, mixed-upness; goodness and innocence with the whiteness of snow, the dualism of black and white, truth and error, artifice and nature. The villain Strake has the wilfullness, the perversity, the distortions, of a naughty child. It is the normal imagination of the child that shows him up' (WWR, 'Father Brown and Others', 69, 71). The exceptional number and intricacy of C's revisions (see Appendix 2) confirms WWR on the story's centrality to C's view of the Father Brown cycle. AHO

273 *Dr Boyne*: his name is a reminder of the Battle of the Boyne (1690), the name of the river in Ireland which signalized the defeat of the Catholic King James II by the Protestant King William III.

274 *Commissioners in Lunacy*: in earlier times they were officially appointed to safeguard the legal interests of the mentally deranged.

277 *caryatides*: a caryatid is a female figure in architecture used instead of a column.

280 *cabalistic*: usually spelt 'cabbalistic'. Originally used to describe esoteric mystical interpretations of the Jewish Scriptures: from the Hebrew *qabbalah* (tradition).

281 *Simon Magus*: see Acts 8: 9–24. He tried to buy the apostles' thaumaturgical powers.

Antichrist: the chief enemy of Christ at the end of time. See the letters of St John (1 John 2: 18, 22, and 2 John 7). There are allusions to Simon Magus and Antichrist in the story 'Lost Hearts' (1895) included in *Ghost Stories of an Antiquary* (1904) by Montague Rhodes James (1862–1926).

283 *the Covenanters*: supporters of the Covenant (1638), a bond of
     association uniting the Scottish religious opponents of King
     Charles I. Claverhouse (1648–89), later Viscount Dundee,
     crushed their heirs in rebellion against Charles II and his brother
     James (*c.f.* Walter Scolt, *Old Mortality*).

284 *Dalrymple of Stair*: the then Scottish Secretary of State, Sir John
     Dalrymple (1648–1707), created earl of Stair in 1703. See the
     very dark picture of him and his family history painted in
     Macaulay's *History of England*.

     the Massacre of Glencoe: in 1692 Dalrymple persuaded the
     Protestant King William III to agree to the suppression of
     the MacDonalds of Glencoe in Scotland who had supported
     the Catholic King James II. This was carried out in the vale of
     Glencoe in circumstances of peculiar treachery and atrocity.

292 *Arabian Nights*: *The Book of the Thousand and One Nights*,
     originating in translations into Persian from Indian languages as
     early as the ninth century, many Iraqi and Egyptian tales were
     added and about the thirteenth century the present form existed,
     namely, that a king, having discovered his wife's adultery, killed
     her and took a succession of wives, killing each after the bridal
     night. Shahrazad married him and kept him enthralled by a
     succession of stories for 1,001 nights whence he lived with her
     happily ever after. (One popular version had her breaking off
     each story before the end and resuming the next night, thus
     deferring her execution.) C is, rightly, more hostile to the homi-
     cidal husband than is the original narration. AHO

293 *the dust shall they eat*: from the Lord God's curse on the serpent
     (Gen. 3: 14).

294 *a Wesleyan Methodist*: a follower of the eighteenth-century
     Christian leader John Wesley (1703–91).

     Sandemanian: the Sandemanians were a Christian sect founded
     *c.*1730 in Scotland; Robert Sandeman (1718–71) became their
     leader.

295 *the star of Bethlehem*: see Matt. 2: 2–10.

THE GHOST OF GIDEON WISE

First published *Cassell's Magazine* (Apr. 1926).

296 *wasted its sweetness*: a reference to Thomas Gray's 'Elegy Writ-
     ten in a Country Church-Yard' (1751): 'Full many a flower is
     born to blush unseen, | And waste its sweetness on the desert air.'

hickory: North American genus of the walnut family, renowned for its strong tenacious wood. The demagogic frontier hero President Andrew Jackson (1767–1845) was familiarly known as 'Old Hickory'.

the Manchester School: name given to the political group led by Richard Cobden (1804–65) and John Bright (1811–89), which stood for Free Trade.

298 *Jefferson*: Thomas Jefferson (1743–1826), 3rd president of the USA (1801–9), principal author of the Declaration of Independence.

301 *Cyclops*: in classical mythology thunderbolts were manufactured for Zeus or Jupiter by Hephaistos or Vulcan with the assistance of Cyclopes or Cyclops: Velázquez, for instance, paints Vulcan and his attendant Cyclops as a master-smith and his workers. A single Cyclops is usually synonymous with Polyphemus (who is in fact a shepherd), one-eyed devourer of Odysseus's sailors until his sole eye is put out by Odysseus with red-hot iron. Hesiod (*Theogony*) champions the first or smith interpretation, Homer (*Odyssey*) the second or cannibal pastoral. The conflict between these identities remains unresolved and C seems to be conflating both. In either case a Cyclops is a giant. AHO

308 *the brand of Cain*: cf. Gen. 4: 15: 'And the Lord set a mark upon Cain, lest any finding him should kill him.'

312 *Barabbas*: 'Now Barabbas was a robber' (John 18: 40).

Idumean: Idumaea or Edom was supposedly between Moab and the Gulf of Akaba, i.e. SE of the Dead Sea, under the first kings of Israel a dependency ruled by a viceroy. Later Idumaeans migrated to western Palestine, settling between Beit Jibrin and red-rocked Petra, and by Ptolemy's time trans-Jordanic Idumaea was absorbed into Arabia so that Idumaea now entailed residence west of Jordan, whence Julius Caesar chose Antipater as procurator of Judaea, Samaria, and Galilee for services against Pompeius Magnus (Herod the Great being son to Antipater). Herod was thus a foreigner in Jewish eyes. Since he died in 4 BC he was not the murderer of the Holy Innocents, if 0 is the year of Jesus's birth. But he seems to have killed at least three of his own sons: the Emperor Augustus is said to have remarked that it was better to be Herod's swine than his son. Two surviving sons were Herod Antipas, who succeeded him as tetrarch of Galilee and Peraea (and killed John the Baptist) and Herod

Philip, tetrarch of Itruraea. Herod Agrippa, who ousted Antipas, was the brother of his wife Herodias. AHO

from *The Secret of Father Brown* (1927; New York 1927)

The stories collected under this title are framed between two sections entitled respectively 'The Secret of Father Brown' and 'The Secret of Flambeau'. In the former Father Brown explains his method of detection by imaginatively identifying himself with the criminal; in the latter Flambeau (now known by his real name of Duroc) confesses his quite non-figurative criminal past.

THE MIRROR OF THE MAGISTRATE

First published *Cassell's Magazine* (Apr. 1925) (there titled 'The Mirror of Death').

314 *The Mirror of the Magistrate*: an allusion to *The Mirror for Magistrates*, a collection of cautionary tales, mostly in verse, which first appeared in 1559. The best edition is by Lily B. Campbell (1938).

317 *Aladdin*: a reference to the oriental tale 'Aladdin and the Wonderful Lamp', often assumed (incorrectly) to be part of the *Thousand and One Nights*. Turned into a broad farce, it became the basis of a popular English pantomime.

319 *arabesque*: originally a fantastic painted or sculptured ornament among the Spanish Moors.

320 *Dance of Death*: see note to p. 58.

323 *Mr Orm*: Osric Orm's small stature, eccentricity, and spectacular head of hair all suggest Swinburne. (No doubt coincidentally there was an actual English poet called Orm, who wrote in the east Midlands in the late twelfth century.)

327 *De Quincey*: Thomas de Quincey (1785–1859), autobiographer and prose poet, wrote about various murderers in an essay entitled 'Murder Considered as One of the Fine Arts'. See also p. 520, l.1.

troglodyte's: 'troglodyte' means 'cave-dweller'.

THE ACTOR AND THE ALIBI

First published *Cassell's Magazine* (Mar. 1926).

This story is remarkable for almost the only unsympathetic woman character in the whole of C's work.

334 *Peter Pan*: Sir James Matthew Barrie (1860–1937) created the immortal boy who will not grow up and lives in the Never-Land, in his eponymous play (1904). C argues that pantomime enables us to return to our lost youth: *Peter Pan* is in fact the greatest modern pantomime. AHO

335 *Neronian*: resembling the Roman Emperor Nero (reigned AD 54–68).

337 *weltschmerz*: German *Weltschmerz* (in English 'world-sorrow') was associated with the German Romantic movement.

338 *The School for Scandal*: comedy by Richard Brinsley Sheridan (1751–1816), first performed in 1777. The role-descriptions by Father Brown are absolutely accurate.

344 *nil nisi bonum*: from the Latin saying 'De mortuis nil nisi bonum' (nothing but good about the dead).

345 *jeune premier*: French for 'male juvenile lead'.

THE WORST CRIME IN THE WORLD

First published *Cassell's Magazine* (Nov. 1925).

WWR wrote elsewhere: 'Chesterton's stories, though often fantastic, are not fantasies. Again and again it is emphasized that Father Brown is himself an ordinary man: an extraordinarily ordinary man.

'But Father Brown's ordinariness is ordinariness *à la* Chesterton. He shares his creator's aesthetic sense. . . . It is an aesthetic sense that sometimes provides Father Brown with an essential clue; as in "The Worst Crime in the World", where his perception of the balanced arrangement of a hall enables him to spot that one suit of armour, out of what must have been a pair, is missing' ('Father Brown and Others', 65).

The story was evidently influenced by Conan Doyle's *The Valley of Fear* to the level of homage: the missing armour echoes the missing dumb-bell, with other echoes in the solutions, in the moats, even in the citation of *Marmion* in the context of Douglas in his hall (which last shows that C had read the clue of Conan Doyle's use of the name 'Douglas': see the note on that name in *The Valley of Fear*, Oxford Sherlock Holmes (1993) p. 177). AHO

352 *a young relative*: this is the only story to mention Father Brown's family.

353 *post obit*: a document taking effect after someone's death.

354 *is the old man friendly?* 'Fred . . . is the old min [*sic*] friendly?' asks Dick Swiveller in ch. 2 of *The Old Curiosity Shop* (1841) by Charles Dickens (1812–70).

357 *the West Riding*: one of the three former divisions of Yorkshire.

the Grampians: mountains in the Highlands of Scotland.

358 *"Mysteries of Udolpho"*: *The Mysteries of Udolpho* (1794), sensational novel by Mrs Ann Radcliffe (1764–1823).

361 *Marmion, his guest*: see Sir Walter Scott's narrative poem *Marmion* (1808), canto VI, verse 13.

THE CHIEF MOURNER OF MARNE

First published *Cassell's Magazine* (July 1925).

369 *Sir John Cockspur*: the Canadian newspaper proprietor in this story has various points in common with the real-life first Lord Beaverbrook (1879–1964). See A. J. P. Taylor, *Beaverbrook* (1972), which however makes little of Beaverbrook's anti-Catholic newspaper crusades.

371 *'In Memoriam'*: the great elegy (1850) by Alfred Tennyson (1809–92) for his friend Arthur Hallam (1811–33). AHO

David and Jonathan:
> 'How are the mighty fallen in the midst of the battle!
> O Jonathan, thou wast slain in thine high places.
> I am distressed for thee, my brother Jonathan: very
> pleasant has thou been unto me: thy love to me was
> wonderful, passing the love of women.' (2 Sam. 1:
> 25–6)

374 *a Toronto Orangeman*: named after William of Orange (William III, king of England), an Orangeman strictly speaking means a member of the Orange Order, but it often simply means an Ulster Protestant. The Orange Order is a quasi-Masonic institution, hostile to Catholics, founded in 1795, and prominent in Ontario politics in the nineteenth century.

382 *Aceldama*: explained as 'the field of blood' (Acts 2: 19), purchased with the money Judas Iscariot was paid for betraying Jesus.

388 *St Peter when the cock crew*: a reference to the story of Peter's denial of Jesus (Mark 14: 30, 72).

from *The Scandal of Father Brown* (1935; New York 1935)

THE QUICK ONE

First published *Story-Teller* (Feb. 1934).
   The flippancy or insensitiveness about Islam is a flaw in this otherwise excellent story.

389 *Band of Hope*: an association (founded *c*.1847) of young people pledged to lifelong abstention from alcoholic drink.

390 *scimitars*: short, single-ended, curved swords, in use among the Turks and Persians.

   tulwars: Indian sabres.

   yataghans: long Turkish daggers, usually curved.

395 *Mahomet*: archaic form of the name of Muhammad (*c*.570–632), the great Prophet of Arabia. Called 'Mahound' in C's poem 'Lepanto': this form of the name is also used by S. Rushdie in *The Satanic Verses*.

399 *Wordsworth's Cloud*:

> the sky seem'd not a sky
> Of earth, and with what motion mov'd the clouds!
> The mind of Man is fram'd even like the breath
> And harmony of music. There is a dark
> Invisible workmanship that reconciles
> Discordant elements, and makes them move
> In one society.

   (Wordsworth, *The Prelude*, i. 338–43)

401 *Inverness cape*: a cloak or overcoat named after a town in Scotland.

402 *Dean Swift*: Jonathan Swift (1667–1745), Anglo-Irish writer who became dean of St. Patrick's, Dublin: famous for his *Gulliver's Travels* (1926).

   Dr Johnson: Samuel Johnson (1709–84), English scholar and writer, most famous for his *Dictionary* (1755) and the *Life* of him (1791) by James Boswell (1740–95).

   William Cobbett: William Cobbett (1763–1835) was originally an anti-Radical journalist who later leaned towards Radicalism. His best-known book is *Rural Rides* (1830). See C's *William Cobbett* (1926).

405 *making fun of Welshmen*: an example is Captain Fluellen in *Henry V*.

407 *'Something has happened'*: a reminiscence of a dialogue between Father Brown and the detective James Bagshaw in 'The Mirror of the Magistrate'.

408 *a Glengarry bonnet*: a Highlander's thick woollen cap, with ribbons hanging down behind: named after a parish in Inverness-shire.

THE BLAST OF THE BOOK

First published *Story-Teller* (Oct. 1933) (original title 'The Five Fugitives').

413 *Titania . . . Oberon*: the fairy queen and king in Shakespeare's *A Midsummer Night's Dream*.

Kilmeny: young girl who was stolen by fairies in a poem by James Hogg (1770–1835).

Thomas the Rhymer: poet (*c.*1220–97) stolen by the queen of the fairies in a Border Ballad.

414 *Montaigne*: Michel Eyquem de Montaigne (1533–92), French moralist and essayist, famous for his philosophical scepticism.

418 *Babbage*: Charles Babbage (1792–1871), English inventor of a pioneering mechanical computer.

421 *MD, MRCS*: these letters stand respectively for Doctor of Medicine ('Medicinae Doctor' in Latin) and Member of the Royal College of Surgeons.

423 *Macbeth*: *First Witch*. All hail, Macbeth! hail to thee, thane of Glamis!
Second Witch. All hail, Macbeth! hail to thee, thane of Cawdor!
Third Witch. All hail, Macbeth, that shalt be king hereafter!

(Shakespeare, *Macbeth*, I. iii. 48-50)

Macbeth knows he has inherited Glamis, he is about to learn of his award of Cawdor in place of its doomed treacherous incumbent, and, although on hearing this he has hopes 'If chance will have me king, why, chance may crown me, | Without my stir' (I. iii. 143-4), he is quickly disabused when in the next scene Duncan settles the royal succession on Malcolm. AHO

THE GREEN MAN

First published in *Ladies' Home Journal* (Nov. 1930).

'One adverse critic saw in Father Brown's ability to divine the truth, where plodding mundane detectives fail, a typical dishonest trick of the Catholic apologist. But it is made quite clear that Father Brown owes his success not to supernatural insight but to the usual five senses. He is simply more observant, less clouded by conventional anticipations and prejudices, than the average man. The kind of clue he notices is not cigar ash or footprints, but something like this:

"I am sorry to say we are the bearers of bad news. Admiral Craven was drowned before reaching home...."
"When did this happen?" asked the priest.
"Where was he found?" asked the lawyer.

Most of the clues in the stories are of this kind. It is true that at the end of this story ... Father Brown does show some knowledge which, in terms of the story, he could not have acquired by natural means; he knows [the motive of] the murder ... This is a fault in the story. But the same sort of fault can be found in greater writers when they are winding up the plot. Shakespeare makes Iago confess that he dropped Desdemona's handkerchief in Cassio's chamber. Surely a man like Iago would never have confessed anything. The essential discovery that Father Brown makes in this story is the identity of the murderer, not his motive' (WWR, 'Father Brown and Others', 62–3).

427 *Pinafore*: HMS. *Pinafore* (1878), comic opera by W. S. Gilbert and Arthur Sullivan.

428 *sea-holly*: otherwise known as 'eryngo' (*Chambers English Dictionary*).

430 *the Green Man*: this name probably originated as a reference to 'Jack-in-the-Green', a May Day dancer wrapped in a framework of green shrubs.

438 *Mercury*: Mercury was the Roman equivalent of Hermes, famous for his speed of movement (the metal mercury is sometimes known as quicksilver).

443 *never been a boy*: conflation of 'To the Hesitating Purchasor' prefacing *Treasure Island*, and 'A Humble Remonstrance' (*Longman's Magazine* (December 1884)), RLS's defence of the story in answer to Henry James's '*I have been a child, but I have never been on a quest for buried treasure*':

Here is, indeed, a wilful paradox; for if he has never been on a quest for buried treasure, it can be demonstrated that he has never been a child. There never was a child (unless Master James) but has hunted gold, and been a pirate, and a military commander, and a bandit of the mountains; but has fought, and suffered shipwreck and prison, and imbrued its little hands in gore, and gallantly retrieved the lost battle, and triumphantly protected innocence and beauty.

(Reprinted, *Memories and Portraits* (1887): we must thank Jenni Calder and Ernest Mehew for running down this source for us. AHO)

THE CRIME OF THE COMMUNIST

First published *Story-Teller* (Sept. 1934).

The writer of this Note, having lived in Oxford for a great part of his life, can testify that, although C (like Father Brown) has nothing particular to do with Oxford, he conveys the 'feeling' of Oxford better than any other writer—with the exception of G. M. Hopkins in his line 'Towery city and branchy between towers'.

445 *Mandeville College*: imaginary.

446 *Master*: title of some heads of Oxford (and Cambridge) colleges.

447 *Rigor mortis*: Latin: the stiffness of joints and muscular rigidity of a dead body.

Hall: the dining-room for all the members of a college.

the High Table: the dining-table reserved to Fellows of the college and other senior members and their guests.

Sir John Mandeville: the probably fictitious author of a probably fictitious travel book and European best seller which first appeared in Anglo-Norman in 1356–7.

Byles: the suggestion of 'bile' seems relevant.

448 *Coriolanus*: the hero of a tragedy by Shakespeare first printed in the First Folio (1623), based on Sir Thomas North's version of Plutarch's *Life of Caius Marcius Coriolanus* (1579). Coriolanus shows an arrogant contempt for the common people of Rome.

Tarquinius Superbus: the last of the legendary kings of ancient Rome, whose name became a byword for tyranny.

Craken: Craken may be in part a satirical sketch of G. D. H. Cole (George Douglas Howard Cole, 1889–1959), Oxford economist and the chief exponent of Guild Socialism. He was said to have been converted to socialism by reading William Morris's *News from Nowhere* (1891). Like C he wrote detective stories (in collaboration with his wife Margaret, née Postgate). He resembled Craken in being both a holder of radical political views and a connoisseur of wine.

Guy Fawkes: seventeenth-century Catholic conspirator in the reign of James I, burnt in effigy in Great Britain every 5 November, when his and his co-conspirators' attempt to blow up the Houses of Parliament in 1605 is commemorated by fireworks and bonfires.

449 *William Morris*: 1834–96: Victorian poet and socialist.

450 *'For forms of faith . . . right'*: slightly misquoted from the *Essay on Man* (1733–4), by Alexander Pope (1688–1744), lines 305–6: 'For Modes of Faith let graceless zealots fight; | He can't be wrong whose life is in the right.'

the Baptists: name applied to various Christian sects which affirm the necessity of baptism (usually of adults and by total immersion).

the Anabaptists: members of various sixteenth-century Protestant sects who rejected infant baptism. What C has in mind here is that some of them favoured a kind of Christian communism, to be imposed if necessary by violence.

the Theosophists: those sharing the beliefs of the Theosophical Society (founded 1875), supposedly based on the sacred scriptures of Brahmanism and Buddhism.

the Thugs: originally members of a gang of robbers and murderers in India who strangled their victims; more widely applied to brutal and violent criminals in general.

455 *Professor Wadham*: Wadham is the name of an Oxford college.

461 *the man of sin*: probably refers to the Antichrist (in the New Testament).

THE POINT OF A PIN

First published *Story-Teller* (Oct. 1932).

464 *carillon*: a tune played on a special set of bells: here, a summons to church worship.

hammers: an allusion to the nailing of Jesus to the cross.

475 *Hiawatha*: hero of *The Song of Hiawatha* (1855), a series of narrative poems in trochaic tetrameters based on American Indian stories by the US poet Henry Wadsworth Longfellow (1807–82).

leviathan: a huge sea-monster (Hebrew).

476 *Bothwell*: third husband of Mary Queen of Scots (1542–87), accused of complicity with her in the murder of her second husband Lord Darnley.

480 *Ascot*: sometimes called Royal Ascot: a socially prestigious English horse-race meeting held annually at Ascot in Berkshire.

a white feather: a symbol of cowardice: cf. the novel *The Four Feathers* (1902) by A. E. W. Mason (1865–1948).

483 *zoetrope*: an early process of colour cinematography.

484 *Coppée's*: François Coppée (1842–1908), a French poet.

THE INSOLUBLE PROBLEM

First published *Story-Teller* (Mar. 1935).
It is interesting to note the large number of distinctively Roman Catholic motifs in this Father Brown story, in contrast to the earlier ones.

486 *St Dorothy*: or Dorothea. A Christian martyr who suffered in the persecution under the Roman Emperor Diocletian in AD 303.

488 *antic*: grotesque.

495 *'A secret spot . . . lover'*: slightly misquoted from Coleridge's 'Kubla Khan' (first published 1816): 'A savage place! As holy and enchanted. | As e'er beneath a waning moon was haunted | By woman wailing for her demon lover!'

495 *Holy Mary, Mother of God*: Roman Catholic prayer appended to the 'Hail Mary' ('Ave Maria').

rioters: possibly alludes to the growing anti-Catholic violence in Spain in the years preceding the Spanish Civil War (1936–9).

498 *the wine of Cana*: at Cana in Galilee, according to the Gospel of John, Jesus performed his first miracle by changing water into wine at a wedding feast (John 2: 1–11).

499 *Popish Plot*: fictitious Catholic conspiracy fabricated in 1678 by Titus Oates (1649–1705), the 'Corah' of John Dryden's *Absalom and Achitophel* (1681).

500 *Sir Edmund Berry Godfrey*: see John Dickson Carr, *The Murder of Sir Edmund Godfrey* (1936). A more recent study of this famous seventeenth-century mystery is to be found in *The Killing of Justice Godfrey* (1984) by Stephen Knight.

Casterbury: imaginary: the name is perhaps a conflation of 'Canterbury' and 'Glastonbury'.

Benediction: short Roman Catholic service in which the congregation is blessed with the Host.

501 *rococo*: a style of architecture, decoration, etc. prevalent during the reign of Louis XV of France, marked by frequent multiplication of ornamental details.

502 *monstrance*: ornate receptacle in which the consecrated Host is displayed for adoration in Roman Catholic churches.

